Acclaim for Gene

THE

"Certain to take its place on the top shelf of books about the civil rights movement. . . . Indispensable to a full understanding of the movement, simply because the book makes such a compelling case that media coverage was the sine qua non of success in the civil rights movement."
—*The Baltimore Sun*

"Every gracefully written page of *The Race Beat* prompts big thoughts about the nature of America. . . . Reverberates with large lessons in democracy and peace." —*Columbia Journalism Review*

"A heartening and illuminating book about a time when some journalists got the story right and did so to the enormous benefit of this country."
—*Lexington Herald-Leader*

"Powerful, absorbing. . . . Recounts in graphic detail and from rare perspective the struggles that awakened the nation's conscience to the evils of racial segregation." —*The St. Louis Post-Dispatch*

"One of those remarkable works of history that make you see your own times more clearly." —*The Nation*

"Thorough [and] intimate. . . . Reminds us of the heroism of civil rights demonstrators and strategists and introduces us to the bravery of the storytellers." —*The State* (Columbia, SC)

"A masterly history and assessment of the press's performance during the major campaigns of the civil rights movement. . . . The authors have earned a place alongside other prizewinning chroniclers of that time like Taylor Branch, Garry Wills and David Halberstam." —*America*

"Marvelously detailed. . . . An outstanding contribution to the discussion of civil rights." —*Blue Ridge Business Journal*

"Vivid and intense. . . . In no other story did the press distinguish itself so admirably and effectively. The stories of these men . . . are essential to the history of the civil rights movement." —*The Washington Post Book World*

GENE ROBERTS *and* HANK KLIBANOFF

The Race Beat

Gene Roberts is a journalism professor at the University of Maryland, College Park. He was a reporter with the *Goldsboro News-Argus* and *The Virginian-Pilot,* and a reporter and editor with *The News & Observer* and the *Detroit Free Press* before joining *The New York Times* in 1965, where until 1972 he served as chief southern and civil rights correspondent, chief war correspondent in South Vietnam, and national editor. During his eighteen years as executive editor of *The Philadelphia Inquirer,* his staff won seventeen Pulitzer Prizes. He later became the managing editor of *The New York Times.*

A native of Alabama, Hank Klibanoff is the managing editor for news at *The Atlanta Journal-Constitution.* He is a former metro reporter, national correspondent based in Chicago, business editor, and deputy managing editor of *The Philadelphia Inquirer,* where he worked for twenty years. He was also a reporter for three years at *The Boston Globe* and six years in Mississippi for *The Daily Herald,* the *South Mississippi Sun* (now the *Sun Herald*), and the *Delta Democrat-Times.*

THE RACE BEAT

*The Press, the Civil Rights Struggle,
and the Awakening of a Nation*

GENE ROBERTS
AND HANK KLIBANOFF

VINTAGE BOOKS
A DIVISION OF RANDOM HOUSE, INC.
NEW YORK

FIRST VINTAGE BOOKS EDITION, SEPTEMBER 2007

The Library of Congress has cataloged the Knopf edition as follows:
Roberts, Gene.
The race beat : the press, the civil rights struggle, and the awakening of a nation /
Gene Roberts and Hank Klibanoff.—1st ed.
p. cm.
1. Race relations—Press coverage—United States.   2. African Americans—Press coverage—
History—20th century.   3. African Americans—Civil rights—History—
20th century.   I. Klibanoff, Hank.   II. Title.
PN4888.R3R63 2006
070.44'93058—dc22
200645251

Vintage ISBN: 978-0-679-73565-6

Gene Roberts photograph © University of Maryland
Hank Klibanoff photograph © The Atlanta Journal-Constitution
Book design by Iris Weinstein

www.vintagebooks.com

Printed in the United States of America
10 9 8 7 6 5 4 3 2 1

We dedicate this book to our late parents,
Eugene L. "Pop" and Margaret Roberts,
and Morris and Roslyn Klibanoff,
who continue to inspire us.

Contents

THE RACE BEAT

CHAPTER 1

AN AMERICAN DILEMMA:

"AN ASTONISHING IGNORANCE . . ."

The winter of 1940 was a cruel one for Gunnar Myrdal, and spring was shaping up even worse. He was in the United States, finishing the research on the most comprehensive study yet of race relations and the condition of Negroes in America. But he was having trouble reaching conclusions, and he struggled to outline and conceptualize the writing. "The whole plan is now in danger of breaking down," he wrote the Carnegie Foundation, which was underwriting his project.

What's more, the gathering crisis in Europe had thrown him into a depression; he feared for the very existence of his native Sweden. In April, Nazi Germany had invaded Denmark and Norway. Myrdal believed Sweden would be next. He put aside more than two years of work by 125 researchers and began arranging passage home for himself, his wife, Alva, and their three children. He and Alva wanted to fight alongside their countrymen if the worst should come. The boat he found, the *Mathilda Thorden,* a Finnish freighter, was laden with explosives, and the captain tried to dissuade the Myrdals from boarding the dangerous ship. When this failed, the captain jokingly urged Myrdal to look on the bright side. He would not have to worry about his family freezing to death in icy waters. If German U-boats attacked, the resulting explosion would almost certainly kill everyone instantly.

The U-boats did not attack, and the Myrdals arrived in Sweden only to be appalled by what was happening there. Rather than preparing for war with Germany, the Swedish government was seeking an accommodation with the Nazis.

Knowing that Germany was monitoring the Swedish press for anti-

German sentiment, the government first confiscated copies of anti-Nazi newspapers; then, emboldened, it interfered with the distribution of one of the nation's most important dailies, *Göteborgs Handelstidning*. This, Myrdal believed, could not happen in America. He was outraged. "The press is strangled," he wrote to a Swedish friend in the United States. "Nothing gets written about Germany. News is suppressed."[1]

There and then, Myrdal's understanding of America and its race relations became crystallized. In a book that quickly took precedence over his Carnegie project, then became its seed, Gunnar and Alva Myrdal wrote *Kontakt med Amerika* (*Contact with America*), which was crafted largely to rally Swedish resistance against Hitler. In *Kontakt,* published in 1941, the Myrdals argued that Swedes had much to learn from America about democracy, dialogue, and self-criticism. "The secret," they wrote, "is that America, ahead of every other country in the whole Western world, large or small, has a living system of expressed ideals for human cooperation which is unified, stable and clearly formulated."[2] The Carnegie project, they added, was evidence of America's willingness to sanction a sweeping examination and discussion of a national problem.

Almost all of America's citizens, the Myrdals said, believed in free speech and a free press. Americans respected other viewpoints even when they strongly disagreed. As a result, diverse ethnic groups were living with one another in peace while Europe was tearing itself apart.

Before writing *Kontakt,* Myrdal didn't have the insight or context he needed for his weightier book on race in America. Nor did he have the words he felt would serve as the road map to change. Three years earlier, in 1938, he had reached the South, the dark side of the moon. There, he had found an enigmatic, sometimes exotic, always deeply divided and repressive society whose behavior was known to, but overlooked by, the world beyond. In pursuit of an understanding and insight that was still beyond his grasp, his immersion had been total, the details of his discoveries had been staggering, and he had come to a point where he was no longer horrified by the pathology of racism or stunned by the cruelty and pervasiveness of discrimination. He had found himself fascinated by the way an entire social order had been built, and rationalized, around race.

By early 1940, Myrdal frequently found himself feeling oddly optimistic about attitudes he found despicable, and he was moving, somewhat unwittingly, toward the conclusion that would become the core definition of his landmark work, *An American Dilemma:* that Americans, for all their differences, for all their warring and rivalries, were bound by a distinct "American creed," a common set of values that embodied such concepts as fair play and an equal chance for everyone. He was coming to that view in the unlikeliest of settings. He had been able to sit with the rapaciously racist U.S. senator from Mississippi Theodore Bilbo, listen to his proposal for shipping Negroes back to Africa, ask why he hadn't proposed instead that they be sterilized, and come away uplifted by Bilbo's answer. "American opinion would never allow it," Bilbo had told him. "It goes against all our ideals and the sentiments of the people."[3]

But for all his excitement, information, and knowledge, Myrdal remained mystified. How had the South's certifiable, pathological inhumanity toward Negroes been allowed to exist for so long into the twentieth century? Why didn't anyone outside the South know? If they did know, why didn't they do something about it? Who could do something about it? Who would? Where would the leadership for change come from?

Myrdal returned to the United States and his racial study in 1941, brimming with the insights he would need for *An American Dilemma* to have an impact on the country.[4] Seeing his homeland's willingness to trade freedoms for security of another kind, Myrdal came to appreciate the vital role the American press could play in challenging the status quo of race relations.

In Sweden, newspapers wanted to report the news but were blocked by the government. In America, the First Amendment kept the government in check, but the press, other than black newspapers and a handful of liberal southern editors, simply didn't recognize racism in America as a story. The segregation of the Negro in America, by law in the South and by neighborhood and social and economic stratification in the North, had engulfed the press as well as America's citizens. The mainstream American press wrote about whites but seldom about Negro Americans or discrimination against them; that was left to the Negro press.

Myrdal had a clear understanding of the Negro press's role in fostering positive discontent. He saw the essential leadership role that southern moderate and liberal white editors were playing by speaking out against institutionalized race discrimination, yet he was aware of the anguish they felt as the pressure to conform intensified. There was also the segregationist press in the South that dehumanized Negroes in print and suppressed the biggest story in their midst. And he came to see the northern press—and the national press, such as it was—as the best hope for force-feeding the rest of the nation a diet so loaded with stories about the cruelty of racism that it would have to rise up in protest.

"The Northerner does not have his social conscience and all his political thinking permeated with the Negro problem as the Southerner does," Myrdal wrote in the second chapter of *An American Dilemma*. "Rather, he succeeds in forgetting about it most of the time. The Northern newspapers help him by minimizing all Negro news, except crime news. The Northerners want to hear as little as possible about the Negroes, both in the South and in the North, and they have, of course, good reasons for that.

"The result is an astonishing ignorance about the Negro on the part of the white public in the North. White Southerners, too, are ignorant of many phases of the Negro's life, but their ignorance has not such a simple and unemotional character as that in the North. There are many educated Northerners who are well informed about foreign problems but almost absolutely ignorant about Negro conditions both in their own city and in the nation as a whole."[5]

Left to their own devices, white people in America would want to keep it that way, Myrdal wrote. They'd prefer to be able to accept the stereotype that Negroes "are criminal and of disgustingly, but somewhat enticingly, loose sexual morals; that they are religious and have a gift for dancing and singing; and that they are the happy-go-lucky children of nature who get a kick out of life which white people are too civilized to get."[6]

Myrdal concluded that there was one barrier between the white northerner's ignorance and his sense of outrage that the creed was being poisoned. That barrier was knowledge, incontrovertible information that was strong enough, graphic enough, and constant enough to overcome "the opportunistic desire of the whites for ignorance."

"A great many Northerners, perhaps the majority, get shocked and shaken in their conscience when they learn the facts," Myrdal wrote. "The average Northerner does not understand the reality and the effects of such discriminations as those in which he himself is taking part in his routine of life."

Then, underscoring his point in italics, Myrdal reached the conclusion that would prove to be uncannily prescient. Even before he got to the fiftieth page of his tome, he wrote, "*To get publicity is of the highest strategic importance to the Negro people.*"

He added, "There is no doubt, in the writer's opinion, that a great majority of white people in America would be prepared to give the Negro a substantially better deal if they knew the facts."[7]

The future of race relations, Myrdal believed, rested largely in the hands of the American press.

An American Dilemma was both a portrait of segregation and a mirror in which an emerging generation of southerners would measure themselves. In a few short years, the book would have a personal impact on a core group of journalists, judges, lawyers, and academicians, who, in turn, would exercise influence on race relations in the South over the next two decades. The book would become a cornerstone of the Supreme Court's landmark verdict against school segregation a full decade later, and it would become a touchstone by which progressive journalists, both southern and northern, would measure how far the South had come, how far it had to go, and the extent of their roles and responsibilities.

The Myrdal investigation was so incisive and comprehensive—monumental, even—that it would for many years remain a mandatory starting point for anyone seriously studying race in the United States. Its timing was perfect. Most of its fieldwork occurred in the three years before the United States entered World War II, a period in which segregation in the South was as rigid as it ever got. The book ran 1,483 pages long yet was a distillation of a raw product that included 44 monographs totaling 15,000 pages.[8]

More remarkable than the study's impact was its foresight. The coming years would prove, time and again, the extraordinary connection between news coverage of race discrimination—publicity, as Myrdal called it—and the emerging protest against discrimination—the civil rights movement, as it became known. That movement grew to be the most dynamic American news story of the last half of the twentieth century.

At no other time in U.S. history were the news media—another phrase that did not exist at the time—more influential than they were in the 1950s and 1960s, sometimes for better, sometimes for worse. From the news coverage came significant and enduring changes not only in the civil rights movement but also in the way the print and television media did their jobs. There is little in American society that was not altered by the civil rights movement. There is little in the civil rights movement that was not changed by the news coverage of it. And there is little in the way the news media operate that was not influenced by their coverage of the movement.

An American Dilemma began with a decision by the Carnegie Corporation to conduct a comprehensive study of race in America, and especially of segregation and white supremacy in the South. Recalling the contribution of Alexis de Tocqueville, a Frenchman, in his book *Democracy in America,* the foundation decided its racial study should be headed by a non-American scholar from a country with no history of colonialism or racial domination.

In the beginning, Myrdal declined the Carnegie offer. He was, after all, a member of the House of the Swedish Parliament, the rough equivalent of the U.S. Senate. He was also a director of the national bank at a moment when Sweden was hobbled by economic depression. He would have to resign both positions and take leave from a prestigious chair in economics at the University of Stockholm, where he was considered one of the nation's most brilliant academics. What's more, the Myrdals had recently found an ideological home and leadership positions in the reform policies of the Social Democratic Party, which favored social engineering and economic planning.

He was fluent in English and no stranger to the United States. He and Alva, a psychologist, had been fellows in the Rockefeller Foundation's social science program in 1929–30. He had refused the Rockefeller Foundation traveling fellowship for himself until the foundation agreed to make Alva a fellow as well.[9] No one at the foundation had reason to regret the deal. Indeed, officials of the Rockefeller Foundation regarded Gunnar Myrdal as one of the program's great successes and recommended him with enthusiasm to Frederick P. Keppel, president of the Carnegie Corporation.

After saying no, Myrdal changed his mind, but only on the condition that he have complete control over planning the study. The foundation agreed. Myrdal became enthusiastic. "I shall work on the Negro—I will do nothing else," he wrote. "I shall think and dream of the Negro 24 hours a day. . . ."[10]

He began work in September 1938, almost immediately on his arrival, and plunged into it with confidence; he viewed himself as "born abnormally curious" and specially suited to the investigation of a complicated social problem.[11]

On his first field trip, Myrdal was accompanied by his primary researcher and writer, Ralph Bunche, a UCLA- and Harvard-educated Negro whose urbane presence was more jarring than Myrdal's in some parts of the South. Myrdal was stunned by what he saw. Though prepared for the worst, the Swedish economist had not anticipated anything like this. "I didn't realize," he promptly wrote his sponsor, Keppel, "what a terrible problem you have put me into. I mean we are horrified."[12]

To get an understanding of segregation, the talkative Myrdal and his team moved through the southern states, absorbing experiences, data, impressions, previous studies, and viewpoints.[13] The South they discovered was but a single lifetime, fifty-six years, removed from the end of Reconstruction.

As an economist, he was staggered by the material plight of Negroes. It was so grindingly desperate that only one word seemed to describe it: pathological. For southern Negroes, poverty had become a disease of epidemic proportions. "Except for a small minority enjoying upper or middle class status, the masses of American Negroes, in the rural south and in the segregated slum quarters in southern cities, are destitute," Myrdal wrote. "They own little property; even their household goods are mostly inadequate and dilapidated. Their incomes are not only low but irregular. They thus live day to day and have scant security for the future."[14]

Under slavery, whites had used Negroes as domestic servants and field hands, but also as artisans and craftsmen. On the typical plantation, slaves had erected houses and barns, shod the horses and mules, and repaired whatever needed repairing. After Reconstruction, the folklore developed among whites that Negroes were not mechanically inclined, and they were excluded in industry from all but janitorial, laboring, and other menial jobs. Although new industries were created and old ones expanded in the boom years of the 1920s, Negroes didn't benefit significantly. "Gas and electrical companies have never used Negroes to any appreciable degree," Myrdal wrote. "Negroes don't operate streetcars and buses. Telegraph and telephone companies exclude them almost altogether. Furniture factories depend in the main on white labor. The vast expansion in wholesale and retail trade, banking, insurance, and brokerage benefited the Negroes only so far as they could be used as delivery men, porters, janitors, charwomen and so on."[15]

As bad as the economic conditions were, Myrdal found that the treatment of Negroes in the courts was worse. Whites tended to respect the justice system. Negroes were terrified of it. Whites were the judges, the jurors, the bailiffs, the court clerks, the stenographers, the arresting officers, and the jailers. Only the instruments of execution—the electric chair and the gas chamber—were desegregated, used for whites and Negroes alike. In this case, desegregation didn't mean fairness. Negroes were far more likely than whites to be put to death. Though they made up one third of the population across the South, Negroes received twice as many death sentences as whites.[16]

Neither a Negro's person nor his property was safe in the courts, Myrdal concluded. Whites could cheat and steal from Negroes, knowing that when it was white testimony against Negro, white almost always prevailed. Grand juries were notorious for seldom indicting a white man if his accuser was Negro. Myrdal couldn't find a single case in which a grand jury had indicted a white man for participating in a lynch mob, although some lynchers were named, even caught by newspaper photographers, as they stood smiling a few yards from the dangling feet of lifeless bodies.[17]

Discrimination against Negroes was also widespread in the voting process. "Most of the time the Negro is not allowed to register or to vote, and he might risk anything up to his life in attempting to do it," Myrdal wrote. "But sometimes he is allowed: because he is a 'good nigger,' because 'he has the right,' because his voting 'proves' there is no discrimination, or for no particular reason at all, or just for the fun of doing the opposite of what is expected."[18]

Myrdal found no weakening in the resolve of southern whites to deprive Negroes of equal educational opportunities. They said they were prepared to support the U.S. Supreme Court's 1896 *Plessy v. Ferguson* ruling that separation was permissible so long as Negroes were provided with substantially equal facilities. But their eloquence in defense of Plessy was but a thin disguise for their contempt for—and fear of—Negro education. While politicians often said Negroes' illiteracy and ignorance were reasons for denying them the vote, government spending almost everywhere in the South was significantly less for Negro education than for white schooling. In segregated states as a whole in 1933–34, Negro elementary teachers struggled with 26 percent more pupils in their classrooms than white teachers and with considerably less pay for doing so. Negro teachers' pay was $510 a year, whites received $833.[19]

Despite the obstacles, a Negro middle class had emerged, and from it came the teachers that white people counted on for the segregated schools, the ministers for the churches, the undertakers to handle funeral arrangements and corpse preparation—and, especially significant to Myrdal, the blacks who ran their own newspapers.

Myrdal, the foreigner, saw clearly what even the most astute Americans saw only dimly, if at all: that the black press was at the center of a developing Negro protest in the United States. But if the protest were to succeed, the mainstream press—the white press—would have to discover racial discrimination and write about it so candidly and so repeatedly that white Americans outside the South could no longer look the other way. Then they would see segregation, white supremacy, and black disenfranchisement as being at odds with the American conscience (or creed, as Myrdal called it) and demand change.

Given the dearth of national coverage, it is remarkable that Myrdal came to believe that the best hope for Negroes was to attract national attention—"publicity." No major publication had a news bureau in the South. Even so thorough a paper as *The New York Times* wrote about antisegregationist leaders and organizations almost entirely on the inside pages, when it reported on them at all. Only once between 1935 and 1940, in a story involving A. Philip Randolph, the Negro labor leader, did the *Times* run a front-page story mentioning the name of any of the country's leading Negro racial reformists. Neither Walter White, executive secretary of the National Association for the Advancement of Colored People, nor William E. Burghardt Du Bois, the brilliant sociologist and editor of the NAACP's *The Crisis* magazine, made it onto the *Times'* front page during that five-year period.[20]

What Myrdal missed was how protracted the struggle within the press would be, how strongly the northern publications would be loathed by most southern newspapers, and how a small band of liberal white southern editors would become their region's conscience. He did not anticipate how the northern press would overcome a predisposition to local news in order to play up the southern racial story. He did not anticipate how all of this would occur while many southern journalists, and virtually all of the region's politicians, decried the northern press for hiding its own racial problems while laying bare the South's.

What would it take for the northern press to see that race in America was an ongoing story of massive importance? When would a turning point come? Would the change in the press be evolutionary? What would precipitate it? Would it come at all?

CHAPTER 2

"A Fighting Press"

I f Myrdal's research had relied upon Frank Luther Mott's biblically revered 1941 textbook on the profession, *American Journalism,* he might have missed altogether the only newspapers that were covering race in any meaningful way. Mott devoted a mere half sentence to the Negro press—a passing reference to Frederick Douglass.[1]

Before World War II, Negro newspapers drew such little notice from their white counterparts that even when they clearly had the inside track on a story of national importance, the white press tended to ignore it. When A. Philip Randolph warned in 1941 that "a wave of bitter resentment, disillusionment and desperation was sweeping over the Negro masses" and that it might erupt into "blind, reckless and undisciplined outbursts of emotional indignation," accounts of his statements in the Negro newspapers were largely ignored by the white press. When Randolph a year later decried the lack of Negro employment in defense industries and insisted that 10,000 Negroes—later upped to 100,000—would march on Washington in a protest guided by a Gandhian commitment to nonviolence, he got little coverage in the white press.[2]

But all the warnings, all the harbingers, all the reports exploded onto the pages of Negro newspapers. Across the South, almost without limitation, Negroes had access to black weeklies that ridiculed white hypocrisy, spoke out bitterly against racial injustice, reinterpreted the mainstream press, and covered Negro social and religious organizations in detail. "It is," Myrdal said, "a fighting press,"[3] and he was in awe of the fact that Negro newspapers enjoyed—strangely—the kind of freedom of expression that might have meant death to the lone Negro who dared to make such utterances in some parts of the South.

Myrdal understood that white newspapers were written for whites and

Negro papers for Negroes. He could see that Negroes were most likely to appear in white newspapers only if they committed a crime against whites and that Negro institutions and organizations were seldom covered, except in a smattering of southern dailies with "black star" editions that were distributed only in Negro neighborhoods.

But how could the Negro press attack white power with such impunity? Myrdal theorized that whites simply didn't read Negro newspapers and were unaware of their militancy, even of their existence. Perhaps, he mused, the Negro press was tolerated because of something more fundamental in the American outlook, a "certain abstract feeling among all Americans for the freedom of the press which, even in the South, covers the Negro newspapers."[4]

Whatever the reasons, the Negro press clearly understood that its audience wanted racial inequities in America examined and denounced. This had been the case since March 16, 1827, when the country's first Negro newspaper, *Freedom's Journal,* had gone on New York streets to oppose slavery and push for full rights for Negro Americans. "We want to plead our own case," said its publishers, John B. Russwurm and the Reverend Samuel E. Cornish, in the first issue. "Too long have others spoken for us."[5]

In its short life—three years—it set two enduring standards: henceforth, most Negro newspapers in the United States would live hard and die young. By 1951, there had been 2,700 Negro papers, fewer than 175 of which were still around. On average, they died after nine years of publication.[6]

But the more important standard was the legacy of protest. The earliest newspapers, both Negro and white, were primarily advocates and special pleaders. But long after white papers had turned to coverage of general-interest news, their Negro counterparts remained loud, clear instruments of protest, by turns educative and provocative. And for virtually all of their history into the 1950s, they had the race story all to themselves.

That so many Negro newspapers were coming and going for 120 years on the mass of land between the Atlantic and Pacific Oceans, Mexico, and Canada is itself remarkable. More extraordinary is that white people did not know about it.

By the late 1800s and early 1900s, interest was growing among Negroes in newspapers that would reflect their lives, tell their stories, and give them political insight and social guidance. Literacy was up, and so, in a small way, was the income available to purchase newspapers. Churches and religious organizations became involved in publishing and found support from various northern welfare and missionary groups working in the South. As more Negroes became eligible to vote, newspapers fed a new hunger for political coverage.[7]

Very quickly, papers that would become the most insistent and most effective advocates of civil rights were created. In Baltimore in 1907, a Sunday school superintendent, John H. Murphy, Sr., whose full-time job was as a whitewasher, created the *Baltimore Afro-American.* He vowed on the paper's masthead to "stay out of politics except to expose corruption and condemn injustice, race prejudice and the cowardice of compromise."

In Chicago, Robert S. Abbott, a Georgia-born lawyer whose tar-black skin caused him to be ridiculed and rejected by other Negroes, pumped a little money and a lot of gumption into creating the *Chicago Defender* in 1905[8]—which a decade later claimed a stunning 230,000 circulation.[9]

The Norfolk *Journal and Guide,* which would come to have a circulation and influence far beyond its home base, began as a fraternal publication. Taken over in 1909 by P. B. Young, Sr., the *Journal and Guide* espoused a conservatism that reflected Young's close association with the gradualist Booker T. Washington; the paper, like Young himself, became more progressive in the years following the latter's death. And in 1910, the presses started rolling at *The Pittsburgh Courier.*

Those and other Negro newspapers began publishing at a time, unlike any other, when four of the most dynamic, strong-willed, and persuasive black leaders in the nation's history shared a common stage, even as they divided Negro thought. Each came with his own journalistic base and retinue, each had his own devoted following, and each helped crystallize the debate that Negro editors would wrestle with for the next seventy-five years.

Booker T. Washington's accommodationist views were evident in his own newspaper, the *New York Age,* and other ostensibly independent papers that he infused with thousands of dollars to spread his gospel.[10] W. E. B. Du Bois, as much as anyone, led the break from Washington and toward a more confrontational strategy. The Massachusetts-born sociologist's crisp, aggressive editorial attacks against discrimination were the hallmark of *The Crisis,* the NAACP's monthly magazine. It began in 1910 with a circulation of 1,000; within three years, 30,000 copies were being circulated; and by 1920, it was selling 95,000 copies each month.[11]

The most relentless advocate for mass action was A. Philip Randolph, coauthor of the monthly *Messenger.* The socialist pitch of this self-described "magazine of scientific radicalism" may not have had widespread appeal among the Negro masses, but its strident criticism of black leaders who weakened in the face of white persuasion was popular well beyond the Negro trade unions that viewed it as their official mouthpiece.[12] And the angry separatist push of Marcus Garvey, who had been a printer before he became an advocate, was touted in his own newspapers, most prominently *The Negro World,* which routinely lacerated other notable blacks.

Though operating at odds that frequently became intensely personal, these four men pushed the outer limits of the debate and defined the journalistic tone for the more mainstream press. The *Defender,* the *Afro-American,* the *Journal and Guide,* and the *Courier* survived without conforming to the white press's notions about separating objective news from subjective editorials.

Readers of Negro newspapers, in the North and South, got a heavy dose of news, opinion, and polemic, sometimes blended together. In presenting a constant flow of reports about the brutality, mayhem, and deprivation caused by race discrimination, the Negro press sought not to take its readers' minds off their troubles, as one analyst pointedly put it, but precisely to keep their minds on them.[13]

World War I presented a dilemma for Negro editors. They wanted to support the war effort, and did, but they were troubled that the need to "make the world safe for democracy" was undercutting the push to make the United States a battleground in the fight for equal opportunity. The pressure on Negro editors to support the war effort without reservation came not merely from the cresting wave of national patriotism; the war was generating thousands of jobs for Negroes, many of them in the backyards of the most important Negro newspapers of the North.

Sacks full of letters flowed into the newsrooms of northern Negro papers, many of them barely literate scrawlings from southern readers seeking subscriptions and more information about jobs, housing, bus schedules, and all the golden opportunities ballyhooed in each week's editions. At the same time, readers' demand increased for more coverage of Negro soldiers at war. Circulation rose, largely and ironically because of a war the Negro press felt reluctant to support unconditionally.

There was one exception to the latitude white leaders gave the Negro press: when the newspapers criticized the government for taking the nation to war abroad when it hadn't resolved problems at home, they paid a price. In World War I, Negro newspapers were not spared by the freshly adopted federal antisedition laws. After the editor of a paper in San Antonio criticized the army for hanging thirteen Negro soldiers and sentencing forty-one others to life imprisonment following a 1917 Houston uprising that had killed seventeen white people, the editor was convicted of disloyalty and sent to Leavenworth for two years.[14] In the summer of 1918, Randolph and Chandler Owen, co-editors of the *Messenger,* spent two days in jail on charges of treason; copies of their magazine were confiscated, and they lost their second-class mailing privileges because of their antiwar speeches and articles.[15]

Bridling at any suggestion that criticism of race discrimination in the United States might hurt the war effort,[16] Negro editors kept their spotlight aimed on unequal treatment, particularly against Negro troops at home and abroad. They treated aberrant, disloyal, or mutinous behavior by black soldiers as the natural consequence of race discrimination.[17]

All the newspapers found a common result from their coverage: readers wanted more—from the front lines, the sidelines, and in between the lines. Negro papers, with few limits on the infusion of drama and parochialism, filled their pages with personal and effusive stories about the essential importance, valor, and loyalty of Negro soldiers. The war was a marketing bonanza.

The black press came out of World War I reasserting its role as crusader, muscling its way into the white political domain, and still encouraging one of the greatest mass movements in the nation's history: the migration of southern Negroes to the North. Circulation grew prodigiously, to more than a million copies each week.[18]

By the early 1920s, northern Negro papers, sent by mail, bus, and train, had reached deep into the South. The *Chicago Defender,* with a circulation of more than 150,000, was selling more than two thirds of its copies outside Chicago.[19] Over the next several decades, the major Negro newspapers developed networks of bureaus, zoned editions, and national editions, making it possible to pick up the *Defender* just as readily in Alabama or Mississippi. The *Afro-American* fought for dominance in Maryland, North Carolina, South Carolina, and Virginia, often competing head to head with Norfolk's *Journal and Guide,* the largest of the southern weeklies. *The Pittsburgh Courier* sold widely across the South and was easily the largest of all the Negro papers.

Negroes in the southern and border states had no shortage of indigenous race newspapers as well; indeed, most Negro newspapers were published in the South. The southern press sometimes tiptoed around local issues and customs, but on national and regional matters, they were no less militant than their northern counterparts.

The existing papers were achieving higher circulations, and newer ones were reaching the streets every day.[20] The close of the war also produced several national Negro news services, the largest and most enduring of which was the Associated Negro Press. A cooperative whose members provided news to the service and shared its expenses, the ANP could never truly call itself a wire service: the items it gathered from correspondents across the nation were distributed to its clients by mail.

With growth came influence and, for the newspaper publishers, a measure of prosperity. An examination of the social and economic trends in the South in the early 1920s concluded that the Negro press had become "the greatest single power in the Negro race."[21]

Its explosive gains in circulation had explanations that went beyond race-angled political crusades and campaigns for self-improvement. The papers, however inconsistently, were full of voices; Negro papers gave more of their space to columnists than did the white press.

Thomas Sancton, a white New Orleans writer who later became managing editor of *The New Republic,* was impressed by the Negro newspapers. "In some of their columns, fierceness is apparent in every sentence. In others, it lies beneath a calm and subtle prose, and sometimes dullness," he observed in 1943.

"The white reader will not find dullness very often. Almost everything in the Negro press will be new to him, or if not new, written in a strange new key. Sometimes these columnists are inaccurate with facts and careless in their attitudes. But the white reader must be careful about what he allows to anger him, for there is a vast amount of raw, solid fact which they handle well within the bounds of accuracy, and which the white reader simply has got to gulp down and let it educate him. . . . There are a lot of white columnists and reporters who are drawing pay today on writing they did in the 1920s, and their weariness is inescapable. The white reader doesn't find this weariness in the Negro columnists. They live and write at the beginning of a new era for their people, and they are swept along by it."[22]

The bread and butter of Negro newspapers were stories touting some new achievement by Negroes in business, literature, the arts, or something much less momentous. The reports, which fairly screamed at readers, tended to be skimpy on facts and heavy on hyperbole. "The appointments of Negroes to minor positions in the federal and state governments are reported as great achievements," the black sociologist E. Franklin Frazier complained. "In the Negro press, police magistrates become judges. As the result of the exaggeration of the achievements of Negroes, myths grow up about the accomplishments of Negroes. Myths grow up concerning the importance of books written by Negroes. A Negro student who makes a good record in a northern university may be reported to be a genius. The awarding of a doctorate to a Negro by a northern university is still reported as if it had great significance."[23]

For all their interest in bettering the opportunities for their race, Negro publishers found, as did their white counterparts, that stratospheric circulation and the influence that went with it could more easily be theirs in exchange for muckraking, for stories of sensational crimes (especially race crimes and race-sex crimes), and for coverage of lynchings and riots—all captured in bold, uppercase, jugular-squeezing, groin-grabbing headlines.[24] There was ongoing concern among Negro leaders that the Negro weeklies, stricken by a sensationalist fever, had succumbed to the same maladies of carelessness, inadequate corroboration, distortion, and flamboyance as the white Hearst dailies had.[25]

The *Chicago Defender* frequently went overboard in its early years, particularly when providing southern Negroes one-sided and alluring portraits of Chicago and the North as the Promised Land. When it was competitive on race stories with the white dailies, the *Defender* was not reluctant to stretch the truth in some stories and just plain fabricate others—in ways that Abbott's otherwise admiring biographer, Roi Ottley, concluded were not harmless. During racial confrontations, the *Defender* would design, for the front page, box scores showing how many Negroes had been injured and killed versus how many whites; it was a technique some segregationist southern newspapers would adopt during racial battles nearly fifty years later. "It produced a feeling that the score must be kept even—that is, on an eye-for-an-eye basis," Ottley later wrote.[26]

In the era between the world wars, the black press broadened its coverage areas, but never to the point of neglecting lynchings and other sensational atrocities against Negroes. In one view, the coverage of lynchings was good copy to throw at a readership that tended to be lower class. In another, the coverage was partly responsible for the reduction in the violence.[27]

Typically, lynch stories were assigned not to local correspondents but to staff reporters operating out of Chicago, Cleveland, Kansas City, Baltimore, New York, and other cities. Spending long hours on buses and trains, the reporters moved across the South, working their way into backwater towns where white dominance frequently slipped into tyranny.

One of those journalists was Vincent Tubbs, a *Baltimore Afro-American* reporter whose career climb to correspondent in the South Pacific in World War II began in Dallas when he was six and stood on a box to feed the printing press that was the source of his father's livelihood. By the time Tubbs was twenty-six, he had graduated from Morehouse College and worked for four Negro newspapers, each bigger and better than the previous one.

Tubbs got an early taste of the competitive nature of the Negro papers along the eastern seaboard. While he was serving as bureau chief of the Richmond edition of the Norfolk *Journal and Guide* for $25 a week, the publisher of the paper, P. B. Young, heard that Tubbs had been seen with the Richmond bureau chief of the *Afro-American*. Tubbs had consorted with the enemy. "You're fired," the Norfolk publisher told him. The *Afro-American* quickly hired him and gave him a $5-a-week pay increase. "I was moving up," Tubbs said later. Part of moving up meant taking on the challenging assignment, in 1941, of "lynch reporter."

At his desk in Baltimore, the call might come from Sikeston, Missouri, from Texarkana, Arkansas, or from any number of remote spots he knew nothing about. There had been a lynching, he would be told, and off he'd go, always unsure whether he'd be able to find lodging, a ride, or anything resembling a friendly reception. The reporter would not be heard from again until he got the story—or didn't. "When I got on the train, I was on my own until I got back," Tubbs recalled years later. "I mean, there was no communication with anybody."

White journalists could drive themselves into town and not draw suspicion. Not Negro reporters. Tubbs would have to get off the bus one town earlier than his destination, stash his city duds, throw on some local garb, muss himself up to blend with the local scenery, and hitchhike, Old Black Joe–like, to where the lynching had taken place. He'd hope to get in a couple of days of reporting, then slip out of town and hightail it either to a telephone where he could dictate his story or, if his deadline permitted, to the home office, where he'd write it.

It didn't always work. In the early 1940s, in Texarkana, Arkansas, Tubbs was caught in the act of reporting. The sheriff ordered him into his patrol car, quizzed him, then delivered him to the chief of police, deeper into the Dante's Hell of southern law enforcement. After another series of questions disclosed Tubbs's mission, the chief put it plainly.

"Do you see that street?" He pointed out the window. "That is the borderline between Texas and Arkansas. Texas that side, and Arkansas over here."

Sometimes a voice of authority is so clear that shouting would only diminish its power. Quietly, firmly, the chief concluded: "I'll give you five minutes, and I want you to be in Texas."

"Of course," Tubbs said in recalling that incident, "there was no dispute. In four minutes, I was in Texas."[28]

Motivated by the discrimination that had stunted his own opportunities for a pro baseball career, Wendell Smith, sports editor of *The Pittsburgh Courier,* made integration of baseball his mission. He had some influence. Pittsburgh was home to two highly regarded Negro baseball teams, and the *Courier* was the largest Negro newspaper in the nation. It was Smith who first mentioned a young player named Jackie Robinson to Branch Rickey, Sr., the president of the Brooklyn Dodgers.

Sam Lacy, a sportswriter for the *Chicago Defender* and later sports editor of the *Baltimore Afro-American,* combined vivid, persuasive writing with a strategic mind as he made personal appeals to the owners. Joe Bostic of the *People's Voice,* the Harlem newspaper founded by the pastor, and later congressman, Adam Clayton Powell, Jr., was the most aggressive of the group. His seething about discrimination was frequently reduced to mere angry cynicism.[29]

Though integration had the backing of some key white sportswriters, the Negro reporters pretty much operated alone. Typical of the opposition was this from *Sporting News,* the weekly statistical and informational bible of baseball: "There is not a single Negro player with major league possibilities."[30] Such arguments, it was plain, were smokescreens. Ultimately, as advocates of integration knew, the decision would rest with the baseball owners, who would look to their commissioner for guidance. There were no laws, rules, or regulations banning mixing on the diamond.

The *Courier*'s campaign was built on reporting stories of inequality, not on editorial harangues. Wendell Smith started out with his own poll of racial attitudes in the National League. He found that 80 percent of the league's players and managers had no objections to integration. Plenty of major leaguers, including southerners, hit the barnstorming road every off-season, playing in competitive games with Negroes.[31]

In 1942 and 1943, an owner here and there scheduled halfhearted tryouts for Negroes, including Jackie Robinson.[32] But in 1943, Sam Lacy, writing for the *Chicago Defender,* got the baseball owners to hear a personal appeal from him. Lacy was accustomed to setbacks, but he was not prepared for what happened next. His own paper, the *Defender,* picked him off clean. It decided to send the actor and former all-American football player Paul Robeson, instead of Lacy, to meet with the owners.

Fine actor and a credit to the race, Lacy thought, but Robeson had too many Communist ties at a time when Lacy and Wendell Smith had decided the Communist Party's efforts to integrate baseball were backfiring. The team owners listened to Robeson, then did nothing. Lacy quit the *Defender* and joined the *Baltimore Afro-American.*[33] Soon after the 1944 season, Lacy suggested to the owners that they establish a committee to examine the possibilities of integrating baseball. "It will be a step in the right direction," he wrote, adding that a step, when he really wanted to leap, was "a sort of compromise for me as a colored man in that it embraces the element of 'appeasement.' "[34]

The owners agreed to let Lacy address their group. He set forth his proposal, and the owners formed a Major League Committee on Baseball Integration, naming Lacy to it. But the committee foundered when Larry MacPhail, president of the New York Yankees, managed to prevent every scheduled meeting from taking place. One day Rickey went to the despondent Lacy. "Well, Sam, maybe we'll forget about Mr. MacPhail," Rickey said. "Maybe we'll just give up on him and let nature take its course.' "[35]

It was inconceivable at the time that there was a hidden meaning behind Rickey's words. But there was. From the front office of his baseball organization, Rickey had seen the tide starting to turn. Months before the end of the war, he had quietly begun making preparations. Looking for studies that might make the desegregation of his team easier, he had read widely in sociology, history, and race relations, including *An American Dilemma.* The crusade by the Negro press was providing the precise dynamic that Myrdal felt most essential for improvement of the blacks' lives: creating publicity. The Negro press was making Rickey's secret plan more plausible.

. . .

In the first months after the Japanese bombed Pearl Harbor, the mainstream press in the United States was focused on one overriding story: the mobilization of American armed forces and its factories into a war machine. But the nation's Negro papers were in a quandary. Should they support the war? Or sit on their hands? They had been in this position twenty-three years earlier. The betrayal that many Negro editors had felt after World War I, when they had given their support and gotten nothing in return, survived during World War II.

The pressure to withhold their advocacy of the war machinery, and to keep hammering away against discrimination on the home front, came from subscribers and the general Negro population. "It would surprise and startle the majority of white Americans if they knew what the so-called mass of Negroes is thinking," the editor of *The Philadelphia Tribune,* E. Washington Rhodes, said during the war. "The mass of Negroes is more radical than [Norfolk editor] P. B. Young and those of us who publish Negro newspapers. Anyone would tell you that a lot of Negroes are saying that they should not participate in this war."[36]

"We are on the spot," the Norfolk *Journal and Guide* wrote in the spring of 1942. "Our people cry out in anguish: This is no time to stick to a middle of the road policy; help us get some of the blessings of Democracy here at home first before you jump on the free-the-other-peoples bandwagon."[37]

Two weeks after Pearl Harbor, the *Chicago Defender* stated its case—and its dilemma: "The Negro press will not blemish its magnificent record of sound patriotism by indulging in subversive advocacy to the impairment of the national will. However, unless and until constitutional guarantees are suspended, the Negro press will continue to use its moral force against the mob in its criminal orgy, against such ultra violences as lynching, burning at [the] stake and judicial murder."[38]

That might not qualify as disloyalty, the Roosevelt administration felt, but it resembled its evil twin, divided loyalty. Paramount to Roosevelt was his "Double V" campaign, pursuing victory at war and victory in his 1944 reelection bid. The Negro press was important to both wings of that campaign. The combined circulation of the papers was rising, in part because of the war coverage, from 1,265,000 in 1940 to 1,613,255 million in 1943, to 1,809,000 in 1945.[39] Roosevelt understood that trying to run a war with the bitter opposition of a press that spoke to, and probably for, 13 million people, or 10 percent of the population, would be suicidal. Even more problematic was the issue of morale among Negro troops, who represented an even larger share, 16 percent, of the enlistments.[40]

From the Roosevelt administration, there was equal and opposite pressure on Negro newspapers to give their wholehearted support to the war effort and to back off their coverage of discrimination. The antisedition laws were still there, and so was the threat they would be used. The government had agencies, including the J. Edgar Hoover–led FBI, that had the power to intimidate the Negro press, and seemed prepared to use it.

In the end, the Negro press's path was chosen for it by a cafeteria worker in Wichita, who wrote *The Pittsburgh Courier* an impassioned letter that evoked all the emotional conflicts and contradictions facing many Negro Americans. Bearing the title "Should I Sacrifice to Live Half American?" James G. Thompson's letter suggested that "we colored Americans adopt the double VV for a double victory. The first V for victory over our enemies from without, the second V for victory over our enemies from within. For surely those who perpetuate these ugly prejudices here are seeking to destroy our democratic form of government just as surely as the Axis forces."[41]

Readers' reaction was immediate, and the *Courier* swung into action. Its issue the week after Thompson's letter presented four Double V drawings; a week later, the paper announced a full-scale campaign. By the end of the first month, in each issue, the paper was running more than 340 column inches—roughly three full pages—of stories, photographs, and graphics.[42] And 200,000 people each week were buying it.

The counter–Double V campaign became a national cause for the Negro press—as well as a poke in the eye of the Roosevelt administration and a jab in the ribs to other federal authorities, such as Hoover. During the course of the war, Hoover launched investigations into the content of news stories in the Negro press, tried to interest Justice Department prosecutors in bringing sedition charges against some, and routinely sent his men to quiz editors about their criticisms of race discrimination, or of Hoover himself.[43]

Negro papers said they suffered inexplicable cutbacks and limits in newsprint supplies, as well as investigations by the Justice Department and the FBI, the Post Office, the Office of Facts and Figures, the Office of War Information, and the Office of Censorship.[44]

The enthusiasm of Negro columnists and editorial writers for the Double V campaign led them to become even bolder as the war progressed, pushing for an end to all segregation when peace came, if not sooner. Even the most liberal of white southern editors were shocked by the Negro press's expectations. After all, liberal editors became pariahs among many segregationists not by advocating racial integration but by opposing demagogic politicians, calling for better Negro schools, and campaigning against lynching and the poll tax. Sometimes they went a bit further, but they always stopped short of advocating an end to segregation. That, they believed, could invite racial cataclysm.

Virginius Dabney, the editor of the *Richmond Times-Dispatch,* who had himself argued editorially for equal pay for Negro teachers and an end to separate seating on wartime buses, couldn't believe what he was reading in the Negro press and decided to write national magazine articles calling for moderation. "Liberal minded whites concede that many grievances of the Negroes should be corrected, and they concede, further, that the Negro's disabilities are often the fault of whites," he wrote in *Saturday Review of Literature.* "But they cannot view with other than apprehension the speed with which Negro leadership, as exemplified in the Negro press, is pushing matters to a climax. Many Southerners who have long been conspicuous champions of Negro rights, and some Northerners as well, are saying that much can be done hereafter by evolutionary processes in providing better levels of living and more valid opportunities for the Negroes, but that the current effort to effect a drastic revolution overnight can only result in violence and bitterness, with the Negro suffering heavily, in the end."[45]

His fears were shared by Mark Ethridge, the Mississippi-born publisher of the Louisville *Courier-Journal,* who was widely recognized as the dean of the handful of liberal editors in segregated states. "Those Negro newspaper editors who demand 'all or nothing' are playing into the hands of the white demagogues," he said in a speech. "There is no power in the world— not even all the mechanized armies of the earth, Allied and Axis—which could now force the Southern white people to the abandonment of the principle of social segregation."[46]

Jonathan Daniels of the Raleigh *News & Observer* and Ralph McGill of *The Atlanta Constitution* muted their criticism of the Negro editors but said publicly that Negro progress could be made without ending segregation. McGill wrote in 1942 that the "Negro problem" was "economic almost entirely and not at all a 'social equality' problem." He added, "Anyone with an ounce of common sense must see . . . that separation of the two races must be maintained in the South."[47] Daniels wrote, also in 1942 as the war intensified, that "sometimes it is easier to ask people to give their lives than to give up their prejudices."[48]

Negro editors were dismayed by the reaction of the white liberal editors they regarded as their allies, but not enough to dampen their enthusiasm for full equality in the coming years. What the white editors did not see was that the Negro editors, perhaps without knowing it, were preparing new generations of their race for what would ultimately become the civil rights movement. The Negro press was ready for the future; it sensed it was on the cusp of one of the great stories in American history.

How long would it take the white press to share the vision?

CHAPTER 3

SOUTHERN EDITORS IN A TIME OF FERMENT

I n September 1945, just weeks after the Japanese government surrendered to end World War II, Harry Ashmore and his wife, Barbara, drove their 1940 Ford convertible out of metropolitan Washington with a heady sense of relief. The former lieutenant colonel had just been honorably discharged after nearly four years of army duty. He had seen heavy fighting near Bastogne and in the Saar as assistant operations officer for the 95th Infantry Division. He received the Bronze Star with two oak-leaf clusters. He had spent his last three months of Army service in the Pentagon, where he had discovered that lieutenant colonels were as common as messengers and perhaps less useful. Now he was twenty-nine, a civilian at last, and on his way to a job with the *Charlotte News,* where he would become one of the rarest of southern journalists: a liberal newspaper editor.

For more than a dozen years, Ashmore would be at the forefront of that small group of white southern editors who would fight to open the southern mainstream to Negroes and to bring the South into the national mainstream. These were editors who, influenced by Mark Ethridge, Virginius Dabney, and Jonathan Daniels, underwent their own personal evolution on racial matters as they began assuming positions of importance in communities throughout the South.

There was Ashmore in Charlotte and later in Little Rock; Ralph McGill in Atlanta; Hodding Carter, Jr., in Greenville, Mississippi; Buford Boone in Tuscaloosa, Alabama; Lenoir Chambers in Norfolk, Virginia; Bill Baggs in Miami; and Hazel Brannon Smith in Lexington, Mississippi, among others. While most of their colleagues would address the paramount issues of the day in calls for resistance, in faint whispers of support for civil rights, or in silence, these editors would write and speak with the proselytic power and majesty of the newly converted. While each had local issues to tackle editorially, they could be relied on to push for national unity, obeying federal law, and rising above regionalism.

Ashmore did not expect it to be easy. While he was in Europe, he had received a letter from J. E. Dowd, the publisher of the *Charlotte News,* offering him a job after the war.

"Some day when the weariness has passed," Ashmore had responded, trying to keep the door ajar, "I will want to get back into the old fight, of which this war is a military phase. I've come to believe that the important things, the essential freedoms, the democratic processes are luxuries, not inalienable rights, and the price we must pay for them is high. Sometimes we fight to preserve them with guns, sometimes with typewriters, but always we must stand ready to fight." Rereading this paragraph many years later, Ashmore would be amused and add, "Whatever else may be said of it, this was a sentiment that would serve to winnow prospective employers."[1]

It did not winnow Dowd, who seems not to have quailed at all. This appealed to Ashmore. So did the *News's* location, just across the state line from South Carolina, where he had spent all but six months of his life before entering the Army. He had grown up in Greenville, then a cotton mill town and shopping center where Negroes made up more than a quarter of the population. His father's mercantile business had gone into bankruptcy soon after the economic collapse of the late 1920s, and his mother had kept the family going by opening a boardinghouse. To help out, Harry had taken a paper route that veered into the poorest Negro neighborhood in town. Every morning, riding on dirt roads and past a fetid creek, he had seen the gaunt faces, distended bellies, and scabs that revealed tuberculosis, rickets, and pellagra. He had become aware of a standard of living beneath even that of the sharecropper: Negro residents had been systematically shut out of employment in the town's mills and retail businesses.[2] "I can't claim that these sights and sounds suffused me with moral indignation," he reflected later. "I had been conditioned to accept inequality as the natural order and I did not then equate it with injustice."[3]

Starting in 1937 as a cub reporter on the afternoon paper, the *Piedmont,* in Greenville, he performed well covering the police beat, the courthouse, and city government. He wrote fluidly and with flair. After little more than a year, his city editor suggested that he might want to go north on his vacation and, with expenses paid by the paper, "defend the honor" of Greenville and, indeed, the South. President Roosevelt had declared the South the nation's number one economic problem, prompting northern reporters to document the low wages and sweatshop conditions in the South's stridently nonunion cotton mills. This offended the mill owners, nowhere more than in Greenville, which considered itself to be the textile center of the South. Clearly the time had come to write about the North's problems. And when the *Piedmont* asked other southern papers whether they might be interested in such a series, twenty-two signed up before a word had been written.

The young reporter found problems aplenty north of the Mason-Dixon Line, where he was on his first protracted visit. "In six snappy articles," sniffed *Time* magazine, "the purposeful vacationist concluded that the North was as bad as the South."[4] The southern response was considerably more enthusiastic. As favorable mail began to appear on his desk from around the South, Ashmore started to reflect on his series and, by now feeling more contrition than pride, concluded that he had just provided fellow southerners with an excuse for not solving their own problems. He resolved that the series would be his only venture into the "you're another one" school of journalism.

He was soon elevated to the bigger paper in Greenville, the morning *News,* and was shortly thereafter packed off to Columbia, the state capital, to cover the South Carolina legislature, government, and politics. He took so well to political coverage that his friends thought he might have been a successful politician himself had his ambitions carried him in that direction. He had a gift for making friends, a keen eye for the ironic, and an anecdotist's sense of humor that he turned on himself more than on others. In Columbia, he had a front row center seat at the state legislature, where, he wrote later, he developed "a genuine fondness for the assorted jackleg lawyers, farmers, undertakers, hardware merchants and the like who stream in from the hills and plains to serve their interests while transacting the public's business."[5]

In 1938, as Gunnar Myrdal was making his first swing into the South, Harry Ashmore was keeping a close watch on Ellison Durant Smith, a demagogue known by all as Cotton Ed, who was seeking reelection to the U.S. Senate from South Carolina. Cotton Ed made much of Roosevelt's interference in South Carolina politics and even more of his own record as a white supremacist. Wearing a Panama hat and a black string tie that accented his white linen suit, Cotton Ed charmed rural audiences, who gathered under chinaberry trees to hear him tell "The Phillydelphy Story." This was Cotton Ed's account of how he had walked out of the Democratic National Convention in Philadelphia in 1936 as the opening prayer was being delivered by a Negro minister—in Cotton Ed's words, a "slew-footed, blue-gummed, kinky-headed Senegambian."[6]

In 1941, while Hitler's armies tightened their hold on the countries they were occupying in Europe, and as Myrdal was returning to America to continue his race study, Ashmore was selected for a Nieman Fellowship, a program established to elevate the standards of journalism by annually financing a dozen reporters and editors to attend a year at Harvard University.

Ashmore's adjustment to Harvard was not totally comfortable. Barbara, his new wife, was from Massachusetts and liked it, but Ashmore thought he was being patronized. Several times he was welcomed by students and faculty who patted him on the shoulder as if he were in need of sympathy. He was not. "I was determined to go back South," he said years later. "I wanted to see how the story came out."[7] True, he didn't agree with all its customs and practices, but what he didn't like, he would help change.

Just as he was beginning to feel comfortable at Harvard, the Japanese bombed Pearl Harbor and the nation was at war. By early February 1942, halfway through the academic year, he was on his way to Fort Benning, Georgia, his second lieutenant's commission having been activated. He was assigned to the 95th Division at Camp Swift, Texas, and would stay with it until the European phase of the war was over. All thirteen thousand men in the division were white, and Ashmore found himself, for the first time in his life, completely isolated from blacks. He would have only two brief encounters with Negroes during the next three years.[8]

Within three weeks of the victory in Europe, Ashmore was flown to the Pentagon, where it was suggested that he take some leave until an assignment could be arranged for him. He and Barbara thought this would be the perfect time—May 1945, a month ahead of the tourist season—to go to Nantucket for a second honeymoon. Ashmore thought he would also catch up on his reading. There was a new book, a hefty two-volume affair a year or so off the presses. He took it along. It was Myrdal's *An American Dilemma.*

The book impressed Ashmore, although Myrdal's writing did not overwhelm him. The book was tedious in places and repetitive, but full of insights and meticulous in its research and reporting. Myrdal sensed that World War II had set forces into motion that would ultimately force reform in the South, a belief that Ashmore shared. After all, the nation had just fought and won battles against racial bigotry and injustice in Europe; how could it condone them in America? This was one reason Ashmore wanted to return home; it might prove to be the most exciting part of the country in which to be a newspaperman.

With the war winding down, he easily found time to go to Charlotte and explore the job offer at the *News.* The proposal was that Ashmore be the paper's editorial voice, with the title of associate editor. The paper was notorious for its low pay and heavy workload, even in a region with unimpressive newsroom salaries. But it was famous in Carolina circles for attracting talent and giving it enough freedom to pursue good local stories, with special emphasis on the word "local." It would not, the word was, have sent a reporter to see the Statue of Liberty piss.

On the other hand, it was almost certainly the most readable paper in the two Carolinas. One of the best-selling books in the opening months of World

War II, *See Here, Private Hargrove,* had grown out of columns sent back to the paper by a former reporter, Marion Hargrove, as he suffered through basic training and other army attempts to indoctrinate him into military life. The editorial chair being offered to Ashmore had distinguished lineage. From 1937 to 1941, it had been held by W. J. Cash, author of *The Mind of the South,* which in time would be recognized as one of the most original and readable studies ever of the psyche of the southern white. With rhetoric that rolled from the page like thunder from a southern sky, the ever-fretting, ever-moody Cash examined the southerner's propensity toward violence, impulsiveness, and racial intolerance past the point of cruelty.[9]

Ashmore took the job and within a year had established himself as one of the South's freshest voices. He campaigned on his editorial page for better schools and better pay for teachers. He was for a two-party South. He especially wanted greater involvement of Negroes in the South's political and judicial systems: They should sit on juries, he felt, and no obstacles should be placed in their path to the voting booth. Although these stands were considerably more liberal fare than that being served up by the editorial page of *The Charlotte Observer,* the *News*'s gray and conservative competitor, Ashmore was quick to note that they did not cause any great consternation in Charlotte. North Carolina was not Georgia or Mississippi. And nothing Ashmore was advocating constituted a breach in the social separation of the races. You can't be accused of advocating social equality when you say that Negroes have every right to vote. After all, Ashmore figured, "Intercourse of any sort was forbidden by law within a hundred feet of the polling place."[10]

Meanwhile, the more established editors liked what they saw on the editorial pages of the *News* and reached out to young Ashmore. At the time, there were about a dozen liberal newspapers in the South, and their editors formed a tight-knit fraternity that was always on the lookout for kindred spirits. At his first meeting of the American Society of Newspaper Editors in the spring of 1946, Ashmore got to know Virginius Dabney and established an immediate kinship that they quickly reinforced with correspondence that would continue for years. Another close relationship, with Mark Ethridge, also developed from an editors' meeting. Skillful raconteurs, they charmed each other with stories from the South's political wars. The old lions of progressive thought in journalism delighted in knowing that their lineage would remain strong with Ashmore.

Later that year, when Georgia was faced with a dicey political problem— a winning incumbent governor who had died before he could be inaugurated for another term, and three men claiming to be the rightful heirs—Ashmore went to Atlanta to write on-the-scene editorials. While there, he contacted another member of the fraternity and initiated one of the closest friendships of his life—with Ralph McGill, the editor of *The Atlanta Constitution.*

. . .

Ralph Emerson McGill, whose name suggested a destiny that his upbringing did not, was a fellow southerner, born in Igou's Ferry in east Tennessee. The location fell between the towns of Soddy and Daisy, a tough little region that obstinately resisted the two purposes to which it was put: farming and coal mining. In ill health throughout his youth, the shy McGill had a hungry, open mind, an appealing modesty, and a lasting interest in virtually every enlightening influence that came his way: history, fiction, poetry, theater, and writing of all sorts. As a student at Vanderbilt University in the early 1920s, he was exposed to the Fugitives—the poets and faculty members John Crowe Ransom, Robert Penn Warren, Allen Tate, and Donald Davidson—who advocated the preservation of southern culture against the onslaught of modern industrialism, but who sought to shed old-fashioned artistic conventions. The group, which a decade later evolved into the Agrarian movement, was widely credited with launching the Southern Literary Renaissance.

As a cub reporter at the *Nashville Banner,* McGill was game for all sorts of assignments, ebullient in his attitude, a bit caught up in the romantic naughtiness of his newfound profession, and possessed by a muse whose ability to reach, touch, and grab readers seemed limitless. In Atlanta, McGill made his reputation as a sportswriter on the *Constitution,* but he had greater ambitions. He applied for a Rosenwald Fellowship, set up by the philanthropist and former Sears, Roebuck & Co. president Julius Rosenwald, to study farming innovations and rural education in Scandinavia.

When McGill's application came before the Rosenwald selection committee, one of its members took special note. Ethridge, then editor of *The Telegraph* in Macon, Georgia, said the committee felt McGill "was far too intelligent and too socially conscious to be a mere sports editor. If the cycle of sports writing could be broken, Ralph would come into his own."[11] McGill won the fellowship. One generation of progressive editors had given a lift to the next.

On his 193-day tour, McGill met Myrdal in Sweden even before the economist had started his race project, and watched as Hitler consolidated his power and stirred the masses with three-hour anti-Jewish harangues. "Here was an evil evangelist with something in his voice which thrilled men," he wrote. "Even one hostile to him could feel the power of it, and see its effect on the men who listened."[12]

While in Europe, McGill wrote more than two hundred columns and stories. Within ten days after his return to Atlanta in 1938, he was named executive editor of the *Constitution,* in charge of the paper's news, sports, and society departments. Still shaken by the racism he had encountered in Germany and having drawn parallels in his mind with the treatment of Negroes in the South, his first directive to department heads was that henceforth the *Constitution* would capitalize the word "Negro" whenever it was used. He may have been the first editor in the South to abandon the common practice among journalists in the region of writing the word with a lowercase *n*.

McGill had hoped that by the time of the governor's race in 1946, the experiences of Georgians at war against Hitler and fascism would have loosened their political attitudes and that they would reject old-fashioned race baiting. But such hopes were quickly stanched that year after the Supreme Court outlawed the all-white Democratic primary. Using the Supreme Court as his punching bag, Gene Talmadge, a gallous-snapping white supremacist, unleashed the most racist campaign the South had seen since the 1930s. He assailed the high court and accused McGill and James Carmichael, the candidate McGill was supporting, of plotting to integrate the races. McGill and Talmadge had a history of highly public, rawboned political warfare, and Talmadge aimed his most pointed and most popular stump barbs at "Rosenwald Ralph."

McGill, by serving briefly and unwisely on the state payroll as state athletic director years earlier, had provided Talmadge the ammunition he needed. As part of his traveling campaign theater, Talmadge the impresario would be trailed by a scraggly backwoods equivalent of a Greek chorus, the doltish "Tree-Climbing Haggards," who would hoist themselves into trees at his campaign appearances and blurt, on cue, "Tell 'em about ole Ralph McGill, Gene." Talmadge would nod and yell back, "I'm a-comin' to that!" Then, to a rousing reception, he'd pull out the state checks that had been paid to McGill.[13]

Although McGill's candidate, Carmichael, led the balloting in popular votes, the state's well-established anti-Atlanta method of electoral mathematics, known as the county unit system, gave more weight to votes from rural counties, where racial fears ran highest. Talmadge swept those counties and won the primary. But he was physically weakened by the intensity of the campaign and known to be dying, so his strategists devised a plan to place his son, Herman Talmadge, on the general election ballot as a write-in candidate in case the father didn't make it to election day.

He did make it and was elected governor on his deathbed. His son's write-in campaign attracted only 775 votes, but it was more than Carmichael's 669 write-ins. Gene Talmadge died before his inauguration, and Herman claimed the governor's chair. So did the lieutenant governor–elect, M. E. Thompson. And the outgoing governor, Ellis Arnall, a longtime Talmadge adversary and McGill ally, refused to relinquish the office until the courts could decide the matter. Ultimately, the courts ruled for Thompson, though the Talmadge machine was hardly put out of commission.[14]

Unable to resist witnessing such political combustion, Ashmore hunkered down in Atlanta for a while. Over drinks, he came to know McGill and liked what he saw. McGill was combative and took on racist politicians head-on in his front-page column. More than that, it was clear that McGill was a humanist. They held similar hopes about the South and its promise, and they had similar worries about the way southern newspapers were tackling, or avoiding, the region's problems. As they spoke, McGill and Ashmore kindled a friendship that would endure and gain strength in the years ahead.

Within months after Ashmore returned to Charlotte, the ownership of the *Charlotte News* changed hands. The new proprietor elevated Ashmore's title from associate editor to editor but did not give him a pay raise. "He carried on all the old traditions," Ashmore later recalled, "including parsimony."[15] Having just become a father, Ashmore decided to look around quietly for another job.

In Richmond, Virginius Dabney knew that Douglas Southall Freeman, the biographer of Robert E. Lee, would soon be retiring as editor of his company's afternoon paper, the *Richmond News Leader.* Dabney invited Ashmore to lunch with his publishing executives. Ashmore met with D. Tennant Bryan, publisher of the *News Leader* and the *Times-Dispatch,* and with John Dana Wise, the company's general manager. At the time, Dabney and Wise were in the midst of an ongoing quarrel. While Negroes and white liberals may have worried about Dabney's attacks on the Negro press, Wise accused Dabney of being intolerant of conservative views.[16] As Ashmore talked with Wise and Bryan, he kept wondering how Dabney managed to survive there. Even before lunch was over, Ashmore knew that Richmond was not for him.[17]

As he looked for opportunities, he saw fewer, not more, venues for an independent-minded journalist. The overall circulation of daily newspapers was steadily growing and was so strong that the average household received more than one paper. But the overall number of newspapers had been diminishing from the prewar years. In 1947, there were 1,769 dailies, down from 1,983 a decade earlier; 80 percent were delivered in the afternoon.

What's more, in the postwar boom, the kind of people who owned and ran newspapers was changing. Increasingly, the men who were ascending to the level of publisher were links in corporate chains, with few ties to the community. They had little or no journalism background. They were much friendlier to the business interests in town. They gave more scrutiny to the bottom line. They wanted editors who felt, or could be induced into feeling, the same way. "He is a rich man seeking power and prestige," William Allen White wrote in characterizing publishers in the late 1940s. "He has the country club complex. The business manager of this absentee owner quickly is afflicted with the country club point of view. Soon the managing editor's wife nags him into it. And they all get the unconscious arrogance of conscious wealth. Therefore it is hard to get an American newspaper to go the distance to print all the news about many topics."[18]

For Ashmore, the challenge was to find the exception to that sad rule. Word reached Atlanta that he was shopping around. *The Atlanta Constitution* had no vacancies in the higher levels of the newsroom, but its competitor, *The Atlanta Journal,* invited him in for interviews. It was McGill's *Constitution* that Ashmore admired, but he agreed to hear out George C. Biggers, an advertising salesman who had become the *Journal's* president. He could find no meeting of the minds.

He was next invited to Little Rock to talk to executives at the *Arkansas Gazette.* The atmosphere there was far different. John Netherland Heiskell, who was then seventy-five years old, had been the editor of the paper for forty-five years—since 1902. His father, a Confederate colonel who after the Civil War had become a prosperous Memphis lawyer and judge, had purchased a majority interest in the *Gazette* for his children. It was the perfect legacy for Heiskell, who was already an accomplished newsman.

Heiskell, known in the newsroom as "Mr. J.N.," could be amazingly resolute for a man so seemingly mild-mannered. Nothing sidetracked his mildness nor summoned up his resoluteness more than mob violence. In 1927, when a white mob lynched a Negro man, burned his body, then dragged the charred remains through Little Rock's streets, Heiskell's *Gazette* cried out against the mob, and against the police for failing to contain it. The *Gazette* accused the police in a front-page headline: WITH OFFICERS MAKING NO ATTEMPT AT RESTRAINT, MOB BURNS NEGRO'S BODY AND CREATES REIGN OF TERROR.[19]

Lest some reader miss the point, Mr. J.N. declared in a front-page editorial: "The City of Little Rock suffered last night the shame of being delivered over to anarchy. Little Rock and Pulaski County must demand an accounting from the officers who have failed us."[20]

It was clear during Ashmore's weekend in Little Rock that Mr. J.N. was looking not simply for an editor to relieve him of some of the workload but for a successor who would carry on the traditions established by his family. Mr. J.N.'s daughter had married Hugh Patterson, a Mississippian and former air corps major who was being groomed to become publisher and, as such, the paper's ranking businessman. Now, Mr. J.N. felt, he could delay no longer in arranging the editorial succession.

Ashmore had spoken a few weeks before at the spring meeting of the American Society of Newspaper Editors, and Mr. J.N. had been intrigued. He called one of his favorite editors, Ethridge, who had moved from Macon to the Louisville *Courier-Journal,* and asked about Ashmore. Ethridge, who had helped boost McGill's career, now did so for Ashmore. He said that Ashmore would be perfect for the job. During the weekend in Little Rock, Mr. J.N. interviewed Ashmore at length in his office, then entertained him at the country club and his stately mansion. The Heiskell home was memorable. Ashmore saw a Negro butler, a long banquet-sized dining table, and bookshelves lined with Mr. J.N.'s prized collections of antiquarian books about Arkansas and the South. Mr. J.N. listened quietly but intently to see if Ashmore and Patterson were compatible; he seemed to be reflecting upon Ashmore's every opinion. Ashmore was making his own assessment and becoming impressed.

Later Ashmore would draw an analogy between Mr. J.N.'s racial views and those of Harry Truman. Both men favored the separation of the races in social matters but thought in terms of fair play and justice for all. He called Ethridge to get his advice, not knowing that Ethridge had recommended him for the job. Ethridge urged him to take it and pledged to find him a spot on the *Courier-Journal* if it didn't work out. Ashmore thought it the best insurance policy he'd ever had.[21]

Back home in Charlotte, Barbara's first reaction was "Little Rock? Little Rock? Why, it's not even on the way to anywhere." But she was game. The Ashmore family drove to their new home by way of Atlanta. Ashmore stopped by to see McGill and was whisked off to what appeared to be a luncheon party at a downtown businessmen's club. "You may wonder why I'm tendering you this honor," McGill said with a grin as he passed around drinks and pointed to fellow executives from the *Constitution*. "Well, you sonofabitch, you're being honored because you didn't take the job on the *Journal*."[22]

As Ashmore was leaving Charlotte and heading toward Little Rock in 1947, the social, political, and journalistic landscape was changing all across the South—at the same time that the ferment of the race movement was intensifying and the federal judiciary was creating cracks in the South's protective armor. It was clear, too, that the nation was feeling more uncomfortable with racial discrimination at home in the wake of a world war that had highlighted the Nazis' mistreatment of Jews.

Many key developments that year didn't seem so important at the time. Only in retrospect is it possible to see the quickening of activity that comes with the formation of something that seems too big, too persistent, to be accidental. That year, an eighteen-year-old junior at Morehouse College in Atlanta, Martin Luther King, Jr., who had planned to pursue a career in law or medicine—anything but the ministry—changed history by changing his mind. He decided that he wanted to be a minister. At the Ebenezer Baptist

Church, where his father was pastor, he delivered a trial sermon, was immediately licensed by the church to preach, then was named associate pastor even before pursuing theological studies.[23]

Northern newspapers were still eight years and more away from fulfilling Myrdal's dream of seeing intensive coverage of the plight of Negro Americans. But by 1947, when Jackie Robinson broke the color barrier in Major League Baseball, he had become the first running race story that the white press joined the black press in covering. Blacks saw Robinson's performance as a major opportunity to show they could compete with whites if given a level, desegregated playing field. Robinson did not disappoint them. He gave the Brooklyn Dodgers a stunning Rookie of the Year season as they churned their way to the National League championship and came within a game of winning the World Series.

The press itself also broke a color barrier that year, in congressional coverage. Harry McAlpin had become the first Negro reporter to win entry into White House press conferences in 1944 through the efforts of Jonathan Daniels, the liberal Raleigh editor, who had taken a leave to be a special assistant to President Roosevelt. But every attempt by Negro journalists to gain access to the House and Senate press galleries to see legislative action had been rejected—by the white journalists who formed the Standing Committee of Correspondents on Capitol Hill. When Congress met in 1947 and began addressing the top item on its agenda—whether to seat Mississippi's Theodore Bilbo as a senator—the Negro reporter whose stories had the greatest reach, Louis Lautier of the National Negro Publishers Association, had to queue up for admission to the public galleries. Later that year, after Republicans took control of the House and Senate and evicted southern Democrats from critical committee chairmanships, the Senate Rules Committee overrode the Standing Committee and voted to admit Lautier to the Senate press gallery. The Standing Committee was sufficiently chastened to admit Lautier to the House press gallery.[24]

There was one other—seemingly small—development that had outsized consequences in 1947: a short, dapper, cheery gentleman with a lilting Tidewater accent, John N. Popham, arrived in Chattanooga to set up a regional reporting bureau for *The New York Times*. Among national news organizations other than wire services, only *Time* magazine and its sister, *Life,* had planted a flag in the South. The *Times'* Virginia-born managing editor, Edwin L. James, and its Mississippi-born assistant managing editor, Turner Catledge, sensed that the return of white and Negro soldiers who had triumphed over fascism would have special impact in the South, where the concept of freedom ran aground in daily realities.

What the *Times* wanted was thoughtful stories, sensible, high-minded coverage, with little expectation that the job would entail daily reports of breaking news. The bureau would be placed not in Atlanta or Birmingham but in Chattanooga, the home of the family that owned the *Times,* the Ochses. In sending Popham to serve as its first full-time correspondent in the South, *The New York Times* picked a reporter who was likely to encounter only the rarest Southerner who could claim a longer lineage, a greater number of friends in the region, or a sharper memory for every dot that connected to his life.

Popham's family had come to Virginia in 1680, virtually at the founding of the country, he liked to say, and he seemed to know every turn in his family's saga since then. He knew the men with whom his grandfather had served as a Senate page and who had appointed him. He knew how his great-grandfather, who had published a Reconstruction weekly newspaper in Richmond, had become close friends with William Jennings Bryan and with General George Washington Goethals, the engineer who had directed construction of the Panama Canal. Connections meant a lot to Popham. He had gotten his first newspaper job, at the Brooklyn *Standard-Union,* because the managing editor had been his father's sergeant in the Marine Corps in World War I. Even at the *Times,* Popham had his connections: James, the managing editor, had lived just a few miles from where Popham had been raised in Virginia.[25]

Popham proved himself worthy. Joining the *Times* in 1934, when there were seventeen newspapers and hundreds of reporters crawling across the city all day and night, Popham got in on some lively stories, the juicy crime and grime tales that were the trademark of newspapers engaged in circulation wars.

But it was his southern roots that brought him into consideration when James and Catledge decided to open a bureau in the South. In those early years, Popham's ability to make friends seemed as important to the *Times* as it did to Popham. While the newspaper wasn't looking to win friends in the South, and certainly not subscribers, its top editors nonetheless seemed to have been pleased that Popham was both a reporter and a goodwill ambassador to the region, and they did nothing to discourage him from devoting considerable time to diplomacy.

Popham had a distinctive accent and an easygoing style that instantly marked him as southern. He had exhibited the uncanny ability to talk himself, quite relentlessly, into or out of any problem. His byline was John N. Popham, but no such formality came between him and those he met. As a grown man, he remained Johnny, or Pop.

There was one thing Popham would not do. He would not fly in an airplane. He intended to drive anywhere he went. Popham's pace seemed perfectly matched with the mandate from the *Times,* and he proceeded to cover the South in a manner he considered fitting. "This region is strictly a grassroots region and must be covered and reported as such; it can't be done from railroad depots and airports; you just don't get the flavor that way," he explained to Catledge.[26] So in company-owned Dodges and Buicks, Popham rolled across the Dixie landscape at a rate of 30,000 to 40,000 miles a year for the next eleven years.[27] His method seemed to be a mix of strategy and rationalization. "You can't walk in and ask a few questions and get away," he wrote Catledge on another occasion. "You have to give the Southern tale spinner his chance to act it out."[28]

Catledge did little to discourage Popham's approach. "Take your time, take your time, take your time," he implored Popham once when he was tackling a story about Memphis.[29] Popham always felt that Catledge, because he was a compatriot, supported him and his methods, but he knew that not everyone at the *Times* did.[30]

As long as the South moved at a slow pace, Popham and the *Times* were fine. But the pace would quicken as the struggle for racial equality intensified, and the *Times* would just about be shoved to the side of the road. To gain control over the story, it would be forced to veer sharply from the course it had set.

A foretaste of how divisive the future might be for southerners also came in 1947 in South Carolina when two civil rights cases landed in the lap of J. Waties Waring, a federal judge and eighth-generation member of one of Charleston's most influential families. At the urging of John H. McCray, the energetic new editor of the Negro newspaper in Charleston, *The Lighthouse and Informer,* the NAACP Legal Defense Fund sued South Carolina for trying to bypass a 1944 Supreme Court decision outlawing all-white political primaries. The fund also sued to integrate the law school at the University of South Carolina.[31]

There was no reason to doubt that Judge Waring would follow tradition by upholding the state and wait to be overturned on appeal. But Waring had had the moss and magnolias lifted from his eyes, as he would later say.[32] He had recently read Myrdal's *An American Dilemma* and Cash's *Mind of the South.* He had heard arguments in both cases. And he was not going to play by the script. He stunned the state by trumping every effort of the whites, every subterfuge, to keep Negroes out of their law school and voting booths. He ruled in July 1947 that Negroes were entitled to attend a state-provided law school and to participate in the Democratic Party primary. The U.S. Supreme Court agreed with him.

Adding an all-too-southern layer of family strife to the episode, the Charleston *News and Courier* led the charge against the judge, urging the Democratic Party to continue seeking ways to circumvent the rulings.

The managing editor of the newspaper, the man who would soon become the editor and one of the South's leading resisters of the civil rights movement over the next two decades, was the judge's nephew Thomas R. Waring, Jr.

Tom Waring was the son of Waties Waring's favorite brother, who, until his death in 1935, had been the editor of Charleston's afternoon newspaper, *The Evening Post*. After graduating from the University of the South at Sewanee and reporting for two years on the *New York Herald Tribune*, Young Tom returned to Charleston in 1931 to become city editor of the other newspaper in town, the morning paper, *The Charleston News and Courier*. In going to work for the morning newspaper that was the rival of his father's afternoon paper, Tom was not abandoning any family enterprise. The morning paper's top editor, William Watts Ball, was young Tom Waring's uncle on his mother's side. The Waring family had covered all its bases. Tom, with two uncles as influential totems that represented two vastly different ideologies, fell under the sway of the one with whom he worked every day.[33]

William Watts Ball was as conservative as they came. He was described at one point by *The Atlanta Constitution* as the "only completely honest reactionary since 1865."[34] Ball's attitudes on blacks, then young Tom's, were those of Charleston's aristocracy and had less to do, in the beginning, with race than with class. The thinking had developed generations earlier, when the social ascent of Negroes in Charleston was not even an issue and when the threat to patrician rule in the South came from untutored, mud-spattered whites whose presence as a political force tarnished the high polish on the halls of governance. The aristocracy didn't like the idea of lowlifes horning in on their deal, and they especially didn't like it when they saw that the next wave of people banging on the door was not even white. They defended segregation because it represented the best way to hold on to what they had. Segregation was the essence of life in the South. It was the rock. It would not be moved, no matter what Uncle Waties thought or did. When Ball's voice on those issues faded with age, Tom Waring, Jr., became as forceful a spokesman for segregation as there was in the South.

Following Judge Waring's two decisions, the Waring family would never be put back together again. The judge had already infuriated some Charlestonians by divorcing his well-bred, longtime wife, a Charlestonian, and marrying a Yankee divorcee who was quite public with her liberalism. They were soon to be found socializing with Negro people, and he continued to order changes in social customs to accommodate Negroes in federal courtrooms, jury rooms, and lunchrooms. Judge Waring found that the rest of his family wanted little to do with him. The relatives he heard from "waited until two thirty one morning to call and say hello and tell me that they didn't think it wise to see me any more."[35]

But the Warings—Judge Waties and young Tom—were not done with each other. In the same month that Judge Waring handed down his rulings, a simple two-page letter was being written in rural, time-forgotten Clarendon County. The letter would have an impact of atomic proportions. It was written by an attorney on behalf of a Negro farmer, Levi Pearson, and his three school-age children. Addressed to the county superintendent of education, it asked that Negro children attending the Negro public schools in the county be provided the same free transportation that was available to white children attending white public schools.[36]

Pearson was not asking that the benefits of the majority be applied to the minority. Quite the contrary: The school district's 2,375 white schoolchildren rode to and from twelve consolidated schools aboard thirty buses; the district's 6,531 Negro schoolchildren had not a single bus for the sixty-one tumbledown one- and two-room buildings that served as schools for the county's majority race.[37] The 1947 letter, and the lawsuit that would emanate from it, would land on Judge Waring's docket, put the two Warings on another collision course, and, seven years later, result in the Supreme Court's landmark ruling *Brown v. Board of Education.*

The outcry provoked by Judge Waring was soon overtaken by an even louder explosion in October 1947, when a civil rights committee appointed by President Harry Truman recommended, after ten months of study, that the federal government adopt a sweeping program. The 178-page report, "To Secure These Rights," called for "a broad and immediate program" to eliminate all forms of legally sanctioned segregation and discrimination. It advocated a detailed agenda to bring this about: laws requiring states to end discrimination in education, and mandating a ban against discrimination in the armed services; laws to guarantee fair employment practices for blacks; federal prohibition of lynching; repeal of poll taxes and other discriminatory voting restrictions; denial of federal grants when discrimination was in evidence; an expanded civil rights division of the Justice Department; the creation of permanent civil rights commissions at the federal and state levels; a specific federal ban on police brutality; and enforcement of a Supreme Court decision against restrictive real estate covenants.[38]

The concept of "separate but equal," it said, had been tried and "stands convicted" of contravening "the equalitarian spirit of the American heritage," perpetuating inequality, and institutionalizing social disharmony.[39] Truman praised the document but did not immediately embrace its every component. Opposition formed quickly, certainly more rapidly than support for it did.

At the *News and Courier,* Ball and Tom Waring evoked the second-most-effective argument that demagogic politicians typically used to alienate poor whites from Negroes—second only to the imagery that played on sexual fears: they picked at the scab of economic insecurity in the South.

The "campaign of Truman and his harlemites" to establish a Fair Employment Practices Commission, it said, would "open the cotton mills to Negroes . . . probably double the supply of mill labor and reduce textile wages."[40] The cotton mill historically had become precisely the kind of segregated workplace where poor, unskilled whites could get jobs and not fear an invasion by blacks; it was the poor white man's opportunity, probably his only chance in life, to stay above the Negro man.[41]

In Greenville, Mississippi, the editor of the *Delta Democrat-Times,* Hodding Carter, Jr., was troubled by the report. Though he had recently won the Pulitzer Prize for editorials that attacked bigotry across racial, economic, and religious lines, Carter opposed federal intervention against lynching, poll taxes, and discrimination in hiring. He felt that lynching's evilness would become so self-evident that it would disappear, and he thought the poll tax and job discrimination were not the federal government's business.[42] By 1947, he had warmed to the idea of extending full voting rights to Negroes "whenever the education standard of the Negro approaches [that] of the white people."[43]

The committee report provided a gauge by which the definition of a southern liberal could be measured. The editor of the *Morning News* in Florence, South Carolina, James A. Rogers, had developed a reputation as courageous by believing that "separate but equal" should be more than window dressing, more than a ruse.

Rogers had long felt that elevating the economic, educational, political, and social standing of Negroes was essential if the South were to move forward. But ending segregation? "This newspaper is liberal in its view of the racial issue . . . but we reject completely that a correction of the evils can be found in breaking down the principle of racial segregation, a principle which is just as cardinal and traditional to Southern society as is the principle of freedom in democratic America. The South's basic problems are to be found in dilapidated Negro shanties, totally inadequate and discriminative educational opportunities, political injustice, economic discriminations, poor churches, and, to a less extent, injustice in the court."[44]

McGill had taken a similar position, writing that "separation of the races [is] the best and only workable system." But the South was, after all, part of the nation and could move into the national mainstream if it granted equality to Negroes short of social integration. "There may be separation of the races," McGill added, "and still equal justice before the law; equal opportunity to use one's skills and still not have to mix with other workers; equal opportunity for education, without mixing in schools."[45]

In February 1948, Truman slimmed down the committee's recommendations to a handful and submitted them to Congress. He said he would support federal laws against lynching and poll taxes, and he called for permanent commissions and offices within the government to study and enforce civil rights and fair employment practices.

A few days later, McGill, who had consistently opposed federal laws against lynching and the poll tax as usurpations of state responsibilities, conceded that it was hard to hold that line so long as the South refused to enforce its own laws or abide by the equal half of the separate-but-equal doctrine. "The plain truth is that national public opinion is against us," he wrote in a column, "They Simply Do Not Trust Us," that branded him as an emerging liberal. ". . . We have allowed enough evil to make the rest of the nation look upon us without sympathy. We have plenty of laws against violence, such as lynching. We have not enforced them well in Georgia. We have allowed local pride to cover up the most ghastly crimes."[46]

Many southern politicians felt betrayed by Truman. He had become vice president, after all, when they had pressured President Roosevelt to ditch the more liberal Henry Wallace in 1944. They were gagging on the notion that anyone would seek to institutionalize in the law any concept of equality for a race they felt was clearly inferior. James Eastland, the Mississippi senator and Bilbo neophyte, said he could only conclude that "organized mongrel minorities control the government. I am going to fight it to the last ditch. They are not going to Harlemize the country."[47] One by one, then by the dozens, southern politicians followed Eastland's lead and called for an alternative to Truman.

For young newspaper editors in the South, who were forming the political understandings that would guide them in the years to come, the 1948 election was catalytic.

The Republicans held their convention first that summer, in Philadelphia. With no discord, they unanimously nominated for president New York Governor Tom Dewey, who was viewed by segregationists as perhaps even more liberal on race than Truman. When the Democrats met three weeks later, also in Philadelphia, party leaders were in no mood to hear the southern plea. When states' rights advocates demanded that the party dilute or reject its civil rights plank, northern leaders made it even more aggressive, pledging "full and equal protection" for all racial and religious minorities in access to voting, public accommodations, and work. Upon the adoption of that language, thirty-three Southern delegates walked out of the convention.

The newly formed Progressive Party nominated Henry Wallace, whose presence threatened to drain significant liberal Democratic votes from Truman. A groundswell of southern Democrats looked to the States' Rights Jeffersonian Democratic Party, whose name would be shortened in the newspapers to Dixiecrats. They demanded that the Democrats reject the Truman civil rights legislation and platform. But by the time the Dixiecrats gathered in July in Birmingham, many early pontificators had quietly slipped back into the Democratic fold. The convention lacked many big-name stalwarts it had hoped to attract[48] and drew mostly from the two states with the highest proportion of Negroes of voting age,[49] South Carolina and Mississippi. It would nominate the governors of those states, Strom Thurmond and Fielding Wright, as their presidential and vice presidential candidates.

The electorate was harder to read than usual. From the tobacco roads to the statehouses to the Potomac, there was much posturing. The southern states were sharply divided. Liberals, too, were split, and not just between Truman and Wallace. Some, such as Hodding Carter, were backing Dewey. Negro voters had shown a tendency in the Roosevelt years to break their long-standing fidelity to the party of Lincoln, but the editors and publishers of Negro newspapers were not so quick to jump. Virtually every major Negro newspaper, except the *Chicago Defender,* endorsed Dewey.[50]

For the South's handful of liberal editors, the 1948 political campaign, and the underlying civil rights debate, was waged in the national, political context they preferred. By supporting a progressive candidate, they were almost certain to have allies. If they simply advocated racial reform, they risked fighting alone. Liberal editors such as Ashmore and Daniels, as well as many moderates, took a simple position: They were for party loyalty. The Democratic Party, with the New Deal programs of Franklin Roosevelt, had been loyal to the economically troubled South, and the South, in return, should be loyal to the party.

McGill was angered but also distressed by the Dixiecrats' headstrong determination to stay on a course that would splinter the South. "I figure I am as Southern as cornbread, having lived, worked, studied and thought nowhere else," McGill wrote two weeks after the Democratic convention. "My immediate Confederate ancestors, and my Welsh ancestry, which causes me to weep over sad pictures, books and lost causes, are so much a part of me that when I sat down to write the story of the Southern demonstration at the Philadelphia Convention, I was so emotionally upset I had trouble writing it fast enough."[51] He said the Dixiecrats were "supported by fear, not principles, and motivated by forces and money which for years have supported every reactionary trend in the South. . . . They do not represent the South. They are a minority's minority. But they do represent many Southern fears."[52]

Going into election day, Truman was still being hammered from three sides. The Republicans and mutinous Democrats, flying under the colors of Dixiecrats as well as the Progressives, appeared to have succeeded in shanghaiing the president. There seemed to be little he could do to avoid being thrown overboard. All that was left was to analyze the obvious irony in which Truman's own party had robbed him of the White House and handed it to Tom Dewey and the Republicans.

In the end, fate intervened. But it was not merely that Truman won a stunning, storybook upset. Nor was it that the Dixiecrats, who were on the ballot in fifteen states, polled barely over a million votes, and just 12,000 more than Wallace and the Progressive Party, whose own efforts collapsed in the final month. The southern upstarts carried Alabama, South Carolina, Louisiana, and Mississippi, while Truman easily won the other seven states of the former Confederacy.

The unexpected turn was not that two thirds of the Negro voters who cast ballots in 1948 disregarded the editorial importuning of the Negro publishers and voted overwhelmingly, and in critically decisive places, for Truman. The election of Truman turned out to be one of the most fateful, consequential moments in civil rights history because voters, by denying Dewey the presidency, also denied his running mate, the governor of California, the vice presidency. American voters, by rejecting the Dewey ticket, had set into motion a series of events that led to Dewey's running mate landing a job that would bring him much greater and more enduring influence, notoriety, and acclaim than anything he ever could have accomplished as vice president.

Earl Warren would emerge five years later, in 1953, as chief justice of the U.S. Supreme Court. Within two months, he would come face to face with the legal juggernaut that farmer Levi Pearson had started in Clarendon County, in the low country of South Carolina, in 1947, when he had sought the same county-funded school transportation for his children as was provided white schoolchildren. Warren would find himself mulling over the same contentious issues that Judge Waties Waring had boldly confronted. And within seven months, Earl Warren, who likely would never have been on the Supreme Court if the motley mix of Dixiecrats, Negro editors, southern conservative editors, and progressives had had their way, would render the single most important judicial decision in modern civil rights history, relying in no small measure on Myrdal's study of race relations.

CHAPTER 4

ASHMORE VIEWS THE SOUTH

H arry Ashmore saw in the 1948 election results a vindication of his South, the decent South, the South he hoped would prevail in the years ahead. Given the opportunity to punch Truman in the nose, make him pay the ultimate political penalty, and shove states' rights to the top of the national agenda, the South had backed down. As far as Ashmore could tell, Strom Thurmond and all his Dixiecrat disciples in politics and newspapers were incapable of forging any lasting regional bulwark against the incoming tide of civil rights.

He read the results to mean that the South, if left to its own devices during a time of enlightened national leadership, would make the right choices more often than not. The notion that the federal government, through a raft of federal edicts and legislation, could come down and dismantle all the parts of the segregated society and rebuild it into something else struck Ashmore as not only ludicrous but now unnecessary.

In the next state over, in the Mississippi Delta, Hodding Carter, Jr., felt much the same way, only more fiercely. Carter did not believe that the South, under any circumstance, would accept forced integration—or any of Truman's federal solutions to the South's problems. To Carter, all the early signs of artillery lining up on the hill were not helpful. Nor was he happy to see the South being tweaked by outsiders. That was for him to do from the inside.

By so positioning themselves, Ashmore and Carter, both of whom were endlessly chatty and charming, soon found themselves frequently invited onto the national stage not as liberal dissenters in the South but as moderate defenders of the South, willing to go forth in the North and tell everybody to lay off. When northern organizations and publications, particularly northern liberal organizations and publications, wanted the southern point of view, particularly the southern conservative point of view, they frequently turned to southern editors, particularly southern liberal editors such as Ashmore and Carter—and put them into a position where they felt compelled to defend the southern way of life.

This ritual was a living example of Myrdal's conclusion that the North didn't want to face the cold, hard facts of race discrimination in the South. The North didn't want to hear from editors who were at heart white supremacists or implacable segregationists because they only proved how wide the gap was, how intractable the problem was, between Negro and white in the South. When they were called on to face northern audiences, the hard-core segregationist editors, at least several of the prominent ones, bullyragged northerners about their own ghetto cesspools, their own arrogance, their own hypocrisy, their own racism. The zeal of the segregationist editors, the fear that giving them a national platform might only encourage and provoke the rowdier elements of the resistant South, and the conviction that they were simply wrong and misguided led many national organizations and publications to shut them out, pulling what segregationist editors called a "paper curtain" between them and the North.

Northern audiences wanted a warmer, simpler view of life in that complicated land and sought to achieve it by inviting progressive southern editors to explain, justify, protect, and defend it. In speeches, panels, seminars, and magazine articles, Ashmore, Carter, Jonathan Daniels, Mark Ethridge, and Ralph McGill frequently found themselves counterpoised to people even more publicly liberal than they were, a situation that so challenged their southern honor that they had no choice but to defend the South in their own genteel, good-humored way.

In late 1948, Ashmore and Carter were cast as the conservatives in a radio debate broadcast nationally from Town Hall in New York. They were pitted against Walter White, the NAACP's influential executive secretary, and Ray Sprigle, an old-style white reporter for the *Pittsburgh Post-Gazette.*

Sprigle, whose Dutch ancestry was evident in his fair complexion, had won the Pulitzer Prize for his revelation that Supreme Court Justice Hugo Black had once been a member of the Ku Klux Klan. And he had more recently posed as a Negro man in the South for four weeks and written a twenty-one-part series, "In the Land of Jim Crow," that described in raw detail the daily degradation of being Negro in the South.[1]

Sprigle's series, syndicated nationally by the *New York Herald Tribune,* had provided jolting examples of the horrors that awaited many Negroes, especially those trying to make something of their lives. Sprigle, who was sixty-one years old when he toured the South, had experienced firsthand what it was like to be hungry and not be allowed into a restaurant, to be shooed out of a state park, to be demeaned in every shop and at every step. He had heard stories of hapless sharecroppers working themselves to the bone for little pay, only to be stiffed of that small amount by greedy land-lords. He had heard eyewitness accounts of Negroes who had been lynched for voting, or killed randomly, just because a white man got his dander up.

In town after town, the easiest story to do in the South was the one show-ing the disparity between the preaching and the practice of "separate but equal." A few courageous southern white papers eventually did that story, but Sprigle's came early and got widespread attention. "Separate but equal," he concluded, was a trick used by whites to "justify all phases of segregation with its inevitable train of discrimination, oppression, brutality and petty chicanery."[2]

When the northern press went seeking reaction to Sprigle's drubbing of the South, they didn't ask Fred Sullens in Jackson, William Watts Ball or Tom Waring, Jr., in Charleston, or any of a number of certified reactionaries; They went to Hodding Carter. At the request of *The Providence Journal,* Carter wrote a six-part response, which the *New York Herald Tribune* syndi-cated. His response found a ready market in southern newspapers that had declined to run the Sprigle series. Carter was defensive, sarcastic, and prickly, taking issue with Sprigle's characterizations, word selection, and descriptions—everything but his findings. In a xenophobic voice that became more common in later years from far more segregationist editors, Carter essentially said that outside journalists had no business singling out the South for a focus on race relations. Sprigle's tour had been "a good stunt," he wrote, flawed by the limited time given the project and its affilia-tion with the NAACP. In any case, he added, "The white South is as united as 30 million people can be in its insistence on segregation. Federal action can-not change them."[3]

Now, as they prepared for their radio debate against White and Sprigle in New York, Carter and Ashmore came face to face with one of those house-of-mirrors distortions that lend both startling clarity and warped confusion to the issue at hand. Carter, whose ancestry entitled him to all the rights and privileges of a free and empowered American, was darker-skinned than the blue-eyed, blond-haired White, whose Negro ancestry was a constant limita-tion on his exercise of similar rights and privileges. Before the show began, the makeup man was told to lighten Carter's face—and to darken White's.[4]

On the air, White quickly identified the core of the national debate and defined the line that divided northern liberals and southern liberals: "sepa-rate but equal" is impossible, he said, adding, "There can never be any equality within the framework of segregation."[5]

Neither Ashmore nor Carter, whose own convictions were evolving every day, would try to argue with White. Instead, they offered the final defense typically mounted by white southerners of virtually all political shades: even if segregation was the root of the social evils, it was impossible to dismantle it totally and immediately. There was evidence of progress. There was a pace to the progress. Gentle pressure was producing tangible results.

Ashmore then pulled out his analysis of the 1948 election. The results, he said, made it clear that southerners had "declared race a dead issue in the great majority of Southern states. Seven hundred thousand Negroes were qualified to vote in the South last Tuesday, and so far as I know, most of them did vote. . . . In 80 years, only a moment in the sweep of history, the Negro has moved within sight of his traditional goal of proper civil rights. Tolerance, it has always seemed to me, is a considerable virtue, and I suggest to you that the Southern white man, who also finds himself in a political minority, has earned a full measure of it."[6]

Walter White was disturbed that Ashmore, whom he had believed was enlightened, was wearing blinders. Following the debate, White worked on Ashmore: Why was he so unwilling to understand the impatience of Negroes and so ready to give the white South another excuse for doing nothing? "You know segregation is morally indefensible and has to go," White said to Ashmore. "There you are, six feet tall, blond, blue-eyed, a certified Confederate WASP. You've been a colonel in the Army, you've been in combat. What are you afraid of?"[7]

Ashmore, chastened, would have many more opportunities than he could then imagine to show he was not afraid. More important, he would have a unique opportunity to prove once and for all—to the nation's satisfaction, not merely his own—the absolute truth of White's argument, the link between segregation and discrimination, the failure and inherent flaws in the concept of "separate but equal," and the fundamental incompatibility of segregation and democracy.

Levi Pearson's initial lawsuit in Clarendon County had been thrown out on a technicality: he was declared to have no legal standing since his farm was a few feet outside the school district where his children attended school. Pearson had suffered greatly when his local lenders had cut off his credit, and all of his crops had rotted in the field. His punishment only emboldened the NAACP and the chief lawyer for the Legal and Educational Defense Fund, Thurgood Marshall. They began looking for a bigger, better case in Clarendon County, and they found it: a large group of plaintiffs whose complaints went well beyond Pearson's plea for transportation to school. In their lawsuit, now called *Briggs v. Elliott,* they cited inadequacies in teachers' pay, the number of teachers, materials, physical plants, the whole shooting match.

On the day the three-judge panel was to hear arguments in the *Briggs* case a few blocks away from his office at *The News and Courier,* Tom Waring's view was defiant in tone and low-country in dialect: "Law or no law, no matter what decisions federal courts shall hand down, in South Carolina will not be 'integration' of the white and Negro races in schools."[8]

Waring, in fact, seemed willing to welsh on the commitments implicit in *Plessy,* saying that even providing equal schools was too great a burden for white southerners. It was patently unfair, Waring said, that white residents of Pickens County, who vastly outnumbered Negroes, should pay taxes for public education in Clarendon County, where Negro students outnumbered whites by more than two to one.

Between the close of the hearing and the panel's decision, as tension mounted throughout the Palmetto State, Waring's editorials became ever more strident: "The Southern Negroes have been generously treated since they were brought to North America out of savagery—and SLAVERY—in Africa. . . . That which *The News and Courier* resents, that which sickens it, is that many a Southern politician, some of them white ignoramuses, are in servile, suppliant and obsequious manner, confirming filthy accusations incessantly droned and shrieked by the Northern city 'Liberals,' white and colored, against the white South."[9]

The three federal judges who heard the *Briggs* case ruled, 2–1, that separate but equal was essentially a fine doctrine that had been poorly executed, and they ordered school officials to increase their commitment to Negro schools to reach parity with white schools. There was the one dissenter, Judge Waties Waring. "Segregation in education can never produce equality and . . . is an evil that must be eradicated," he wrote ". . . *Segregation is per se inequality.*"

The *Briggs* finding that the states had defaulted on their commitment to Negro schools was, in a twisted way, cause for celebration among southern white leaders. Never have states been so happy with an order to spend money they didn't have. Anything was better than the collapse of the separate but equal doctrine. Tom Waring was not cheered by the prospect of white people shelling out more money to improve Negro education. But he called *Briggs* a "victory for human rights" and a "wise ruling" not likely to be overturned on appeal. As for his uncle's dissent, Tom Waring was in a state of great agitation but seemed mostly relieved that the other two judges had managed to wrestle the heinous monster to the ground. Judge Waring's views, his nephew wrote, would lead to "the exterminat[ion] of the White race."[10]

The *Briggs* case was not over. Its next stop was the U.S. Supreme Court, where it joined four similar cases that would become known together as *Brown v. Board of Education of Topeka.*

. . .

Walter White's challenging words were still echoing in Harry Ashmore's head in June 1953 when he got a telephone call from the Fund for the Advancement of Education, a Ford Foundation spin-off created to disburse millions of dollars for educational programs.

The fund's board of directors wanted to know, once and for all, whether the segregated system of educating children in the South was working. There had been no comprehensive analysis of the subject, and information was sparse and unreliable. The fund felt a special urgency. It was clear that the *Briggs* challenge to school segregation had more than passing merit, that the nation's high court would probably rule on it in late 1953 or in 1954. The fund was willing to foot the cost of a large research team to make an independent review of segregation's impact and write up the findings. It wanted Ashmore to direct that project.[11]

This was the kind of extracurricular involvement that appealed to Ashmore. As progressive and forward-looking as he was, Ashmore seemed to have a near-genealogical connection to the days when editors were not satisfied limiting their influence to the editorial page and occasional speeches to the Exchange Club. Ashmore, an outgoing raconteur who would always have plenty of admirers, even among his enemies, wanted to be a player and was frequently invited to be one.

This time, he was being asked to work with a team of experts who would ferret out data on enrollment, numbers of teachers and library books, education and pay levels of teachers, classroom sizes, lengths of school year, and capital expenditures for every county and every state in the South—virtually all of it information that the school districts and states did not want anyone from the outside to have. The reason was simple: "separate but equal" had been a failure and a myth. The white schools might have their problems, but they were spectacular compared to the Negro schools, many of which had no plumbing and relied on outdoor privies.

Much of the South was in denial about what the Supreme Court might do. Ashmore and Ralph McGill were not. In an April 1953 column titled "One Day It Will Be Monday," McGill wrote:

> Days come and go, and Monday is among them, and one of these Mondays the Supreme Court of the United States is going to hand down a ruling which may, although it is considered by some unlikely, outlaw the South's dual school system, wholly or in part.
>
> It is a subject which, because of its emotional content, usually is put aside with the remark, "Let's don't talk about it. If people wouldn't talk about these things, they would solve themselves."

It is an old reaction, best illustrated by Gone With The Wind's Miss Scarlett O'Hara who, when confronted with a distasteful decision, pushed it away with the remark, "We'll talk about that tomorrow."

But "tomorrow" has an ugly habit of coming around. . . . So, somebody, especially those who have a duty so to do, ought to be talking about it calmly, and informatively.[12]

McGill explained the case and the options facing the court, and the South. He concluded, "The vital point is—there is no reason for violence, whatever the decision. Leadership everywhere in the South must talk about this and make it clear. Anger and violence solve nothing."

Ashmore could see that the Supreme Court, while never knocking over the china cabinet that held the fragile *Plessy* ruling, seemed to be shaking the floor all around. On a single day in June 1950, the court had issued three rulings aimed at halting the various tricks that were being used to sneak around the "equal" half of the "separate but equal" concept. In *Sweatt v. Painter,* the court had said that the University of Texas Law School—which had set up a separate school for Negro students, then loaned it a handful of professors from the white law school, some library books, and other trappings of a law school—hadn't come close to offering a legal education equal to that offered white students. Herman Sweatt, the court said, must be admitted to the law school. The case marked the first time the court directed that a white school must accept a Negro student because the school's separate facility failed to provide equal educational opportunity.

In *McLaurin v. Oklahoma Board of Regents,* the University of Oklahoma had admitted George W. McLaurin to study education in its regular graduate school, then assigned him separate and remote places to sit outside his main classrooms, in the library, and in the cafeteria. This was unacceptable, the court had said, because it limited his educational opportunities. The high court carried that same mind-set into its third ruling that day. It declared in *Henderson v. United States* that Southern Railway's standard practice of using curtains, partitions, signs, and separate tables to divide Negroes from whites in its dining cars did not pass constitutional muster. All three decisions were unanimous.[13]

Ashmore was being asked to jump into the middle of the biggest news action around, and he wanted in on it. The ethics and journalistic propriety of the offer were not in question; there was a well-established tradition of editors taking leave from their editing chairs to run into and out of prestigious government and foundation positions with no expectation that, upon returning to their editing posts, they would recuse themselves from commenting on matters relevant to their nonediting roles. But there was one major concern: whoever took the assignment, no matter how it came out, was virtually certain to face a blizzard of criticism. The South's refusal to meet the "equal" half of "separate but equal" was its dirty little secret, and anyone who pulled back the curtain on the condition of Negro schools would face regionwide reprobation.

Ashmore took the fund's offer to Heiskell and Patterson at the *Arkansas Gazette.* "It would be an act of fiscal imprudence if we didn't insist that Ashmore accept," Patterson said. "When that Supreme Court decision comes down, every newspaper in the South is going to have to deal with the consequences, and we'll have the best-informed editor available—at Ford Foundation expense."

Ashmore accepted. "Son," said one veteran Arkansas politician when he heard about it, "it sounds to me like you have got yourself in the position of a man running for sonofabitch without opposition."[14]

Few could overcome that characterization the way Ashmore did. He and his team accomplished it by putting together the most thorough statistical examination of the impact of biracial education in the United States. Ostensibly a national examination—more states required segregation than banned it—the project was focused especially on the South.

While Ashmore was preparing for a future court decision that might end segregation in public elementary and high schools, the editor of the most important black newspaper in Alabama, the *Birmingham World,* was busily trying to take advantage of earlier court decisions against discrimination in higher education to desegregate the University of Alabama. The two tacks, while different, would ultimately put both editors in the eye of howling racial storms and attract the attention of journalists across the nation and around the world.

Emory Overton Jackson was born for battle. Since becoming the top editor of the *Birmingham World* in 1942 when he was thirty-four, he had taken on J. Edgar Hoover of the FBI, police commissioner Theophilus Eugene "Bull" Connor of Birmingham, the owners of his newspaper, and a bevy of Jim Crow practices such as the poll tax, police brutality, and the all-white primary election.

But Jackson was a rare editor indeed. It was one thing to be *The Pittsburgh Courier* or *Chicago Defender* or *Baltimore Afro-American* and hammer the Deep South week after week for its obstinacy; it was another to be the *Birmingham World* dishing it out in the heart of Dixie.

Jackson saw black journalism and the struggle for racial equality as intertwined. He had been born deep in Klan country, in the west central Georgia town of Buena Vista. At Morehouse College, where he had studied education, he had become a zealous reader of Negro history, literature, and social criticism. As he made the transition from educator to editor, he took his social activism with him. In Birmingham, he became secretary of the local branch of the National Association of Colored People and a leader in various groups fighting for fairer zoning, equal schools, and Negro voter registration.

He was a bachelor whose life was focused on the twin values of righteousness and hard work. He didn't own the paper he worked for, didn't enrich himself financially, didn't care about being fashionable in his dress, and wasn't interested in the emoluments that frequently took the eyes of Negro newspaper publishers off the prize. Birmingham's most activist black pastor, Reverend Fred Shuttlesworth, met with Jackson hundreds of times but could not recall a single instance when Jackson's tie fit right or when his clothes, while clean, didn't look as if he'd slept in them.

The newspaper was owned by the politically conservative, gradualist Scott Newspaper Syndicate of Atlanta, whose major holding was the only Negro daily in the United States, the *Atlanta Daily World.* The Scott family was Negro and solidly Republican. Emory Jackson had leaned toward the party of Lincoln early on, supporting Dwight D. Eisenhower's election in 1952. But Eisenhower's uncertainty and timidity on civil rights upset Jackson, who then became a Democrat, putting him at sharp political odds with his newspaper's owners.

Jackson complained about every element of the way the Scotts ran their newspapers. The twice-a-week *Birmingham World* was supposed to contain as much local material as the Birmingham staff could produce, with the rest coming from wire services and Scott newspapers in Atlanta and Memphis. Jackson would send his local material to Atlanta, where the paper was reedited, composed, formatted and printed, then shipped back to Birmingham for distribution. This setup meant that the final decision on story selection, story play, copyediting, and headlines were in the hands of the Scotts.[15]

By mangling stories and inserting errors, Atlanta's editors "make us look ridiculous over here," Jackson complained to the editor and general manager of the syndicate. "I challenge you to try to read the *Birmingham World.* If so, you'll throw your hands up in horror." Jackson resigned from the *World* frequently—without ever actually leaving. "I am not able nor willing to work any longer under the present conditions," he wrote in 1945. Eight years later, he was saying the same thing: "I cannot any longer do the work of three persons and I see no chance of either relief or progress on the newspaper. . . . So I have decided to move out of the way."[16]

During World War II, Jackson took on Hoover's FBI by running a column by an *Atlanta Daily World* editor attacking the agency for not hiring a significant number of Negroes in law enforcement positions and for holding a "Nazi-like racial philosophy." When the Dixiecrats held their convention in

Birmingham, Jackson attempted to cover it from the balcony until Bull Connor's police took him to the street and ordered him to run. Jackson ambled away, believing that running might give police an excuse to shoot him in the back.[17]

In the summer and fall of 1952, Jackson became even more directly involved. Inside his newsroom, Pollie Anne Myers, a recent graduate of Miles College who divided her time between jobs at the *World* and the NAACP, hatched a plan to desegregate the University of Alabama. Myers had ambitions to work for *Ebony* magazine in Chicago and thought that taking journalism courses at the university would help get her there. Jackson threw his considerable energies behind the decisions by Myers and her best friend, Autherine Juanita Lucy, a quiet library science student, to apply to the university. They did so, without indicating their race, on September 4, 1952. The university accepted Myers and Lucy, and Jackson ran a front-page story announcing their acceptance. Once aware of the hopeful students' race, the university began backpedaling. Myers and Lucy missed the next term, and the next and several thereafter.

But Myers, Lucy, and Jackson were determined. Jackson not only editorialized on behalf of the two women, he raised money for their tuition, worked closely with the NAACP as it pushed the desegregation case through the courts, and stood ready to escort the two to the university when, and if, they were admitted. True to his past, Jackson was not about to give up.

During 1953 and early 1954, as the U.S. Supreme Court pondered the *Briggs* case from South Carolina and four other desegregation cases that had been consolidated into *Brown v. Board of Education,* Harry Ashmore and his staff of forty-two dove into the research that would be the backbone of their book *The Negro and the Schools.*

They found some surprises: the states of the South, though lowest ranking in per capita income, were outspending the rest of the nation, proportionally, in public school education; school attendance in the South was rising while it was flat elsewhere; southern states had indeed increased their spending on education of Negro schoolchildren.

But virtually every measurement showed not so much how far the South had come but how staggeringly far behind it had been. The southern states weren't spending money out of any sense of nobility. They were frantically ripping open their purses and pouring money into Negro education—schools, teachers, bands, football teams—to try to prove that the separate-but-equal doctrine was working. In 1940, the southern states had spent only 43 percent as much on public education of Negro children as on white children; by 1952, they were spending 70 percent as much.

The same pattern held true for capital expenditures: They were substantially up for Negro schools from 1940, but the Negro schools, which were in far worse condition historically and needed much more aid than white schools to reach equality, still were receiving in 1952 only about eight dollars for every ten dollars that white schools received.[18]

The Ashmore project also showed that Negro teachers had nearly as much training as white teachers and, in four of the twelve states that reported data, actually had more training. The salary gap between white and Negro teachers also showed signs of closing. In the twelve southern states in 1940, Negro teachers had received salaries that were 54 percent of the salaries of white teachers. In 1952, they made 87 percent of the average salary of white teachers; in three states—North Carolina, Virginia, and Tennessee—Negro teachers, on average, made more than white teachers because they had more training. Overall, across the South, libraries in white schools in 1952 had 4.7 books for every student, while libraries in Negro schools had 1.8 books for every student.

Ashmore's statistical analysis of the South and its attitudes was eye-opening to nonsoutherners who viewed the South as a monolith. While merely raising the subject of inequality was considered treasonous in parts of the South, Ashmore positioned the 228-page book as a relatively bias-free documentary. He saved his strongest point for the last paragraph. Its upbeat tone was a strong reverberation of Myrdal:

> In the long sweep of history the abandonment of *Plessy* by the Supreme Court may be written down as the point at which the South cleared the last turning in the road to reunion—the point at which finally, and under protest, the region gave up its peculiar institutions and accepted the prevailing standards of the nation at large as the legal basis for its relationship with its minority race. This will not in itself bring any great shift in Southern attitudes, nor even any far-reaching immediate changes in the pattern of bi-racial education. But it clearly re-defines the goal the Southern people, white and Negro, are committed to seek in the way of democracy.[19]

. . .

After Ashmore and his team of experts had finished *The Negro and the Schools* and were waiting for it to be printed, he was struck by a chilling realization: it was the spring of 1954, and the number of Mondays available for the Supreme Court to act on *Brown* was dwindling. Ashmore realized that if the Supreme Court imposed consequential changes in racial customs, traditions, and infrastructure, an explosive test of wills would be ignited in the South. He was convinced that southern editors were not ready for what was about to happen. No matter what the Supreme Court said, a whole new phase would open up. The legal battles over schools, voting rights, property rights, all civil rights, would be sideshows to the war waged over public opinion. Newspaper editors, the presumptive thought leaders in the community, would come under terrific pressure to conform to the wishes of the loudest, most strident, most powerful voices, no matter how irrational.

Ashmore was worried about where the South and its people would get the information they needed to reach rational judgments. He knew they would rely on the single most important source of information at the time, their local newspaper, but that didn't give him any great comfort. Where would all those southern newspapers, day in and day out, get *their* information? How would they judge, interpret, and analyze it? How would they decide what to use, how much to use, and where to display it? Were they up to the task of covering the race story?

Ashmore saw little help coming from the outside. The large, national news operations had the potential for grasping the problem, but who in the South would be guided by them? *Time* magazine was roundly despised for its snootiness toward the South; *Newsweek* had little cachet; and the only newsmagazine that had any appeal was David Lawrence's *U.S. News & World Report,* which, ideologically, sounded as if it had come rolling off the Citizens' Council's own press.

Seven years after becoming the first national news operation, other than wire services, to establish a southern bureau, *The New York Times* remained the only national newspaper providing regular coverage of the race story in the South. But nobody in the South was reading it. The new technology of television was taking hold in middle-class homes at a lightning pace, having reached 58 percent of the homes in the nation in 1954, up from just 7 percent four years earlier.[20] But not many people in the South were looking to television for their news and information. While television sets had proliferated since 1948, when two thirds of the 102,000 sets in the nation were located in New York City, the reach was not as deep in the South as across the rest of the nation.[21] Southerners represented fewer than 5 percent of the national television audience.[22]

There was no question that television network news departments were producing some distinguished programs and documentaries in those early years, presentations that showed a fearlessness that newspapers might have done well to emulate. While many southern white newspapers showed only disregard for Negro news subjects, television—both news and entertainment—seemed to be having a humanizing effect on white's perception of Negro people. It was the CBS newsman Edward R. Murrow who, in 1953, took viewers inside the home of the Negro baseball player Roy Campanella, and, in Korea, put Negro American soldiers on television.[23]

But as strong as those programs were, they frequently were aired on Sunday afternoon, which Murrow called the "intellectual ghetto,"[24] and Ashmore saw little indication that they had much general viewership. What viewers saw when they watched the fifteen-minute national news segment was quick-hit stuff that failed to lend perspective or wisdom to complicated stories.[25]

But what kind of wisdom and perspective could Ashmore count on from southern newspapers? He had concerns, of course, about what Waring, James Jackson Kilpatrick, and other ardent segregationist newspaper editors would put on their editorial pages, and how far they would go in stirring up opposition. But there were also hundreds of other daily and weekly newspaper editors across the South who were desperate for reliable information upon which they could build their editorial position. More important, he saw the significant distinction between what editors put on their editorial and opinion pages—which most readers understood as personal commentary—and what they put on their news pages. Ashmore had serious concerns about the cast and content of the front page and the news pages, about the ingredients that went into the daily feeding of the public curiosity. For the most part, they treated Negro communities as a creepy corner of the world not worthy of their readers' time.

Many newspapers didn't carry any news at all about Negroes; some printed only social snippets under such headlines as "Activities of Colored People." And some devoted a full page to Negro news, in editions circulated only in Negro neighborhoods; to make space for the page, editors would cut the financial news page that appeared in the editions that went to white readers.[26] The papers didn't carry Negro wedding announcements or obituaries. Journalistic orthodoxy still demanded that the newspapers unfailingly refer to white women as "Miss" or "Mrs." but drop the title when referring to Negro women, no matter what their station in life. The practice, which had its origins in slavery and had changed little in the years since the Civil War, was not limited to newspapers, which both reflected and perpetuated the custom. One dutiful rookie Mississippi reporter recalled asking a detective in the 1950s whether a particular crime victim was a Miss or Mrs. "It ain't either one," the detective blurted out. "It's a damn nigger."[27] A Negro woman, on second reference, traditionally would be referred to by her last name, as in "the Jones woman." When Constance Baker Motley was traveling tirelessly through the South as an attorney for the NAACP Legal Defense and Educational Fund, some newspapers delighted in referring to her as "the Motley woman."[28]

There was the ongoing debate among some newspapers in the late 1940s and early 1950s over whether they should print the word "Negro" with an uppercase *N*, a convention that Negro newspapers, at the instigation of *The Crisis* magazine, had been advocating since World War I.[29] Many white southern newspapers had given up the fight on that one, but many had not.

The New York Times changed its policies on racial tagging in 1946 and announced the fact in an editorial, which prompted coverage by *Time* magazine. "This may seem like a small thing," the *Times* said. "The Negroes don't think so." Under the new policy, race would not be mentioned without a legitimate purpose, such as providing a way to identify a crime suspect who was being sought or to explain a racial confrontation. "The press, we believe, has a special and heavy responsibility, not merely editorially . . . but in its treatment of news," the *Times* declared.[30]

When Ashmore arrived in Little Rock in 1947, he decided to take up the question of courtesy titles for Negroes with Mr. J.N. The paper's policy not only created resentment among Negroes, he told Heiskell, but was "illogical and awkward." The policy made it impossible to convey a Negro woman's marital status, which sometimes was relevant; using "the Jones woman" or some such on second reference sounded terrible and was disrespectful. Ashmore proposed that "Mr." be dropped altogether, except in the case of the president, the governor, the clergy, and the deceased. Heiskell quickly agreed—not, Ashmore felt, to correct any injustice, "but because he was a meticulous grammarian who could see that the style forced clumsy convolutions in the use of his beloved English language."[31]

Ashmore, in trying to figure out how to arm southern editors and educators with the knowledge they needed, had seen with his own eyes the unfortunate ease with which misinformation could seize an uninformed public in the South. He had seen, from Cotton Ed Smith to Joe McCarthy, the difficult path that straight news faced in reaching the public, especially when it had to steer around roadblocks of twisted truths. Add to all that the combustible issue of race in the emotional South. Editors and educators were in danger of being overtaken by events or, worse, by the excitations of Chicken Littles stirring the barnyard into frenzy.

It was these concerns that prompted Ashmore and the Fund for the Advancement of Education to call together a group of southern editors during a meeting of the American Society of Newspaper Editors in Washington in April 1954. Ashmore had sent the editors galleys of *The Negro and the Schools,* hoping to find out if he had succeeded in positioning the book in the journalistic straight and narrow or if his own proclivities were showing.

It would be a fine reference, progressive and segregationist editors told Ashmore, and their copies probably would be well thumbed and dog-eared soon after the Supreme Court ruled. But the book would be static. Who could supply them with that kind of data in the future? They wanted to know what was happening on the issue of school desegregation in other parts of the South, and they didn't want their information twisted by adjectives or poisoned by opinion or analysis. They also wanted news accounts that were better informed than the wire service stories they received.

The wires—chiefly Associated Press, United Press and International News Service—were a magic pill for newspapers, giving them a little coverage on many subjects, keeping them in the ebb and flow of the world at large, making every editor seem a little bit smarter and more aware than everyone else. That was usually sufficient. But the wires served a lot of masters who had vastly different tastes and who demanded to be fed at different times. The requirement to churn out as many news stories as possible, as quickly as possible, and as often as possible made thorough, detailed, and comprehensive coverage of any single subject impossible. The datelines that spewed forth from the teletypes made the wire services appear more ubiquitous than they really were. The wires actually had small staffs in each state and depended on dispatches from an inconsistent pool of piecework correspondents and reporters for local papers, whose dispatches would be written, or rewritten, in the ever-chaotic wire service bureaus across the country.

The editors who joined Ashmore shared his concerns. Their conversation marked the beginning of a unique experiment in the history of American journalism: the Southern Education Reporting Service (SERS).

As the editors conceived it, the chief purpose of the SERS would be to publish *Southern School News,* a monthly, regionwide newspaper that would be a reliable source of fair, objective, in-depth, statistically supported information about the way school districts in the South were responding to desegregation orders. There were three target audiences: educators, editors, and government leaders, all of whom had no other reliable way to learn how their colleagues in other states, or sometimes even within their own state, were handling the issue.

Southern School News hired nineteen of the top newspaper reporters and editors in the South to write from seventeen southern and border states and the District of Columbia. In that group were editorial writers and education reporters, an assistant city editor and statehouse political reporters, a top editor and general assignment reporters; there were Nieman Fellows, a Rhodes Scholar, and reporters with master's degrees from top-flight journalism schools. There were women, but no Negroes. The project would pay them very well—$100 a month—while they retained full-time jobs that did not. They would be encouraged to provide details of every desegregation agreement that worked, every arrangement that fell apart.[32]

The editors realized they couldn't change, and wouldn't try to change, the gut thinking of southern editors on the race question. They could never impose any uniformity on newspaper editors. Indeed, warned a couple of the original organizers, they dare not try. But *Southern School News* could supply them all with the same basic play-by-play of desegregation in the South. By providing stories that were combed free of loaded adjectives and bias, and with headlines and display shorn of emotion, they might add some depth and breadth to the race story, might debunk wild rumors, might clarify fuzzy understandings, might find the truth in widely varying reports. They hoped the stories would be suitable for newspapers across the South to simply clip, set in type, and publish, or as fodder for editorial commentary on the subject. No one needed to say it, but Ashmore couldn't help but think it: if newspaper editors were so willing to be spoon-fed, they might as well get a strong dose of straight, unadorned truth.[33]

By virtually every definition, *Southern School News* was to perform precisely the same function that southern newspapers should have been performing. Weren't newspapers supposed to report accurately and factually? Objectively? Comprehensively? Yes, of course, and the inability of many mainstream editors to achieve such basics in the charged atmosphere of hardening racial attitudes was not something about which journalists could be proud. But it was a fact of life, and Ashmore could see the futility of missionary chiropractic work aimed at stiffening the spines of even half the editors in the South. The creation of SERS and *Southern School News* in 1954 was a reflection not of how farsighted southern editors were, but of how needy.

The most critical early problem would be winning credibility across the South—no easy task since the Fund for the Advancement of Education was an arm of the Ford Foundation, frequently viewed in the South as integrationist. Ashmore could see that the SERS needed a director who would keep *Southern School News* free of bias and a board of directors composed of whites and Negroes, editors and educators.

The board would also have to cross ideological lines; segregationists would have to be included. Ashmore decided to seek out a man he had known for years, a friend and fellow South Carolinian whose political views rarely meshed with his own: Tom Waring. He personally liked Waring. He could sit down and drink quite comfortably with him, but he also knew that Waring could be an inoculation against criticism that the SERS was just another sinister satellite orbiting in the Communist galaxy.

Waring had as many concerns as Ashmore about how southern editors would respond to breaches in the wall of segregation—but from the other side. "There are too many weak sisters in the Southern press willing to give this fort and surrender that hill," he wrote Kilpatrick. "I say make the enemy fight for every inch, and somewhere along the line we may take a prisoner or two ourselves."[34]

In discussing the offer with Waring, Ashmore appealed to their common values as newsmen, as southerners, and as South Carolinians. The Charleston editor was insistent that the reporting service had to stay on the straight and narrow, be nothing more than a fact-gathering agency, and never allow itself to be suspected as propagandist. Ashmore was comfortable with that commitment and had something else to offer as well: should he agree to join the board, Waring would become vice chairman of the organization under chairman Virginius Dabney of the *Richmond Times-Dispatch.* Waring signed on.

The other board members covered fairly wide ideological ground that cut off the extremes. The Negroes included Charles S. Johnson, the urbane, low-key president of Fisk University in Nashville, a sociologist whose pedigree in southern liberal causes was impeccable.[35] Another Negro member, considerably less definable, was P. B. Young, editor of the Norfolk *Journal and Guide,* who had swung from Lincoln Republican to New Deal Democrat but never stayed politically put. He embraced school desegregation only lightly, worrying that neither Negroes nor whites were ready for integration, that integration might lead to closing Negro schools and firing Negro teachers, and that white families would abandon public schools.[36]

The top editors of both Nashville dailies were named to the board: Coleman A. Harwell of *The Tennessean,* who had been a New Deal advocate, a backer of Adlai Stevenson, and a supporter of the Tennessee Valley Authority; and Charles Moss of the *Banner,* who supported William Howard Taft and opposed TVA as socialist. They were merely the latest embodiments of a five-decade economic and editorial rivalry between the newspapers, and desegregation was merely the latest source of division. "We have never supported the same person at any level, from magistrate up to the President," Moss once observed. Both were put on the reporting service board because life inside journalism's fraternity house would have been impossible if one had been named and the other had not.[37] Another editor on the board, Frank Ahlgren of the Memphis *Commercial Appeal,* believed, somewhat queasily, that downplaying racial news was a responsible course of action; he would later do just that when school desegregation came to Memphis.[38]

Other members of the board were academics: Chancellor Harvie Branscomb of Vanderbilt University; President Henry Hill of George Peabody College for Teachers, which provided office space for the reporting service; Dr. Gordon Blackwell, director of the Institute for Research in Social Science at the University of North Carolina; and Dr. Henry Willett, superintendent of schools in Richmond, Virginia.

Even before the first edition of *Southern School News* came out, it was clear that these men would oversee something very different from most southern newspapers. The press release that announced the creation of the reporting service listed the names, occupations, and titles of all the board members but did not mention their races. The newspaper would break many of the old-fashioned customs and style rules that southern newspapers had historically employed when dealing with Negroes.

Enlisting SERS board members was easier than keeping them. They joined based on a theoretical game plan, and the members remained somewhat uncertain of the direction they would be asked to take because they didn't know who the director would be—or where he would fall on the race-ideology spectrum. But within days after the board was put together, even that concern was overtaken by something much larger.

CHAPTER 5

THE *BROWN* DECISIONS HARDEN THE SOUTH

On Sunday, May 16, *The Negro and the Schools* was released, weeks after advance copies had been sent to the U.S. Supreme Court. The next day, a quiet Monday, editors and other reviewers in newsrooms throughout the nation began publishing their stories about the book and reviews of it. As they went to press, even up until nearly noon central time, the *Plessy* "separate but equal" doctrine was still the law of the land.

In an instant, all that changed, and the editors went scrambling. Less than twenty-four hours after Ashmore's book came out, the Supreme Court handed down its decision in *Brown v. Board of Education*. The Ashmore book hardly made a ripple before the newest judge on the high court, Chief Justice Earl Warren, began reading the decision. In keeping with Warren's goal of producing an opinion that would be "short, readable by the lay public, non-rhetorical, unemotional and, above all, non-accusatory," the decision was neither long nor notably eloquent.[1] It had no rousing passages that could be put to stirring John Philip Sousa oompahs. It provided no remedy, and it delayed until the following fall arguments about fashioning a timetable for the only obvious remedy: desegregation. But the decision shattered *Plessy*.

"We come then to the question presented: Does segregation of children in public schools solely on the basis of race, even though the physical facilities and other 'tangible' factors may be equal, deprive the children of the minority group of equal educational opportunities? We believe that it does," the court said. Later in the ruling it added, "To separate them from others of similar age and qualifications solely because of their race generates a feeling of inferiority as to their status in the community that may affect their hearts and minds in a way unlikely ever to be undone."

Warren had won unanimity among the justices of the Supreme Court, including those from Alabama, Texas, and Kentucky, largely by showing a willingness to delay the actual dismantling of segregation and by allowing the states of the South an opportunity to influence the timetable for implementation. To Warren, the greater achievement would be not in mandating integration on demand but in slaying *Plessy* and ending the charade. The Court, therefore, had not ordered integration; it had ordered an end to discrimination in the enrollment and assignment of pupils.

Senator Harry Byrd of Virginia said it was "the most serious blow that has yet been struck against the rights of the states . . ." Mississippi Governor Hugh White called the decision "the most unfortunate thing that ever happened." U.S. Senator James Eastland of Mississippi, who almost invariably sounded the most strident chords, went a significant leap beyond: the South, he said, "will not abide by or obey this legislative decision by a political court." Eastland's message carried enormous weight. The Democratic Party, in an effort to lure him back after he had run with the Dixiecrats in 1948, had given him the chairmanship of the Senate Judiciary Committee's subcommittee on civil rights. That made Eastland, in the eyes of resisters to *Brown,* the most important legal authority on civil rights in the nation, an interpretation he did nothing to diminish. If they resisted, they could say he told them they could.

When word of the *Brown* decision arrived on the ticker in the United Press bureau in London, it was accompanied by a message that the *Atlanta Constitution* editor, Ralph McGill, was somewhere in London and that a reporter should get his reaction. McGill had seen this day coming; a full year before *Brown,* McGill had written a column, "One Day It Will Be Monday," urging the South to prepare for its treasured way of life to be upended.[2] The assignment to find McGill went to a fellow Georgian, Eugene C. Patterson. Working the phone, Patterson tracked McGill down at a second-class hotel, introduced himself, and asked if he had heard about the Supreme Court ruling. McGill had not, so Patterson explained.

"And what was the vote?" McGill asked. Patterson told him, then awaited McGill's response. A minute passed as McGill gathered his thoughts. His progressive attitudes on race issues had evolved. And that evolution had been accelerating as he watched the white South abandon all sense of justice and fair play in dealing with Negroes. But even so towering an editor as McGill had not always been free to say so. The president of the *Constitution* as well as the *Journal,* George Biggers, had been clamping down on McGill so much that one reader had complained to McGill that he had gone from contradicting himself to "contradicting your contradictions." The conservative columnist Westbrook Pegler had poked fun at McGill as "the editor dimly seen."[3]

As McGill sat in his London hotel room and pondered what to say to the reporter at the other end of the phone, he was mindful how his reaction would play back home—not merely in the South, but in Biggers's office. He concluded that nothing he might say could match in eloquence, clarity, or force the 9–0 vote by the Supreme Court.

"Well, all I can say is I'm surprised it was unanimous," he finally answered.

"Anything else?" Patterson asked.

"No, that's all."[4]

Southern segregationist editors were remarkably calm on the first day. Perhaps Ashmore's book had had the restraining effect he had sought. Or perhaps the editors, in denial, were simply stupefied.

"We receive the decision with distaste and apprehension," Waring wrote in a front-page editorial the day after the decision. Saying that neither secession nor civil war would be practical, he called for "common sense and goodwill on all sides," then added, "Patience will be necessary on the part of both whites and Negroes."[5]

By the third day after the decision, Waring had a plan. He urged that South Carolina refuse to comply as a way of provoking the NAACP to sue, providing the state an opportunity to tie the case up even longer. "Are we suggesting a delaying action?" he asked. "Well, yes."[6]

In private letters, he expressed less restraint. "We are only sniping editorially at this time," he wrote his colleague Virginius Dabney, "but if the going really gets rough we may be talking about civil disobedience, underground activity and bootleg segregation. I know this sounds fantastic to enlightened people . . ."[7]

Most southern newspapers seemed to develop a quiver in their voice as they faced up to the high court's decision. There was no defiance from the *Montgomery Advertiser*. Its editor, Grover C. Hall, Jr., who was keeping the paper in the progressive mold created by his father, had months earlier declared the *Plessy* doctrine ineffectual; by the time *Brown* came down, Hall was advocating that Negro police officers be hired as a solution to crime in Negro neighborhoods.[8]

James J. Kilpatrick, the editor of the *Richmond News Leader*, also sounded conciliatory. At age thirty-three, the transplanted Oklahoman was one of the nation's youngest editors. He had quickly proved himself intellectually a worthy successor to Douglas Southall Freeman, a distinguished editor and oft-published historian of the South. Kilpatrick's range seemed just as wide, and his drive seemed just as strong. But he had grit, a sense of mission, and a bulldog attitude that set him apart. A year earlier, in 1953, Kilpatrick had been placed in the Richmond *Afro-American* newspaper's Honor Roll for his successful three-year effort to win freedom for a Negro man whom Kilpatrick felt had been unjustly convicted of killing a police officer.[9] Kilpatrick's first words in reaction to *Brown* might have given the *Afro-American* reason to applaud itself for having honored him.

"We accept the Supreme Court's ruling," Kilpatrick wrote. "We do not accept it willingly, or cheerfully or philosophically. We accept it because we have to, and we accept it in the profound and prayerful hope that the Court, when it comes to a final decree, many months from now, will exercise vision and forbearance in drafting a mandate that will preserve good race relations, and recognize that the States and localities should be left a wide area for local responsibility consistent with the Court's opinion."[10]

A small number of influential newspapers quickly urged full compliance. As the story came spewing from the wire machine inside the *Delta Democrat-Times* in Greenville, Mississippi, Hodding Carter, Jr., told his staff, "It's about time," then sat down to write his editorial.

"If ever a region asked for such a decree, the South did through its shocking, calculated, cynical disobedience to its own state constitutions, which specify that separate school systems must be equal," he wrote. "For 75 years, we sent Negro kids to school in hovels and pig pens . . ." The South must, he said, "replace trickery and subterfuge in our educational structure with an honest realization that every American child has the right to an equal education."[11]

In Little Rock on the day after the decision, Harry Ashmore was in his office, reading newspapers, taking a measure of the reaction in the South, and typing out his thoughts for distribution to those who had worked on his book project. He had, by a mere one day, gotten his book out to the public before the Supreme Court's tidal wave threatened to sink it from view. But reading editorial reaction throughout the South, he could retain some hope—well founded, it turned out—that the book would quickly pop to the surface and maintain its ballast.

"Looking out over the debris this morning . . . I'm right proud of the South. Herman Talmadge exploded on schedule, but virtually every other politician of standing took to the high ground. And the Southern press, as I have had a chance to check it so far, seems to have acted with complete responsibility. Put this down to immodesty if you will, but I am convinced that the project had a lot to do with it. The book was in the hands of key editors and most of the politicians by the time the blow fell, and it can only have had a soothing influence . . ."

He had talked with dozens of people in Arkansas, he wrote. A few were distressed, but all seemed calm. "I think I can see the beginning of that time I have always dreamed of—when you can conduct a conversation in the South without having it degenerate into an argument over where a man should sit in a street car," he wrote.

He signed off as Dred Scott Ashmore.[12]

For all his insights, Ashmore misread a couple of things. Hearing no thunder from the editorial pages of southern newspapers—coupled with the widespread endorsements his book received from editors—Ashmore may have been misled into thinking the forecast was for sunny days and blue skies. "We of the South were living then in a sort of postoperative shock; nobody was very mad about anything," Kilpatrick would later explain, after he had become one of the major catalysts for resistance. "It wasn't until the following summer that the anesthesia wore off."[13]

In Washington, D.C., Eastland's calls for disobedience got lost in the cacophony that followed the *Brown* decision. But back home, in the Mississippi Delta, they would sink into the soil a few miles from the Eastland plantation, fertilize, and spring forth in less than two months in the form of the most potent segregationist organization to emerge during the modern civil rights movement, the Citizens' Council. There was no countervailing force, particularly among moderate whites, to stand in its way. Most southern newspapers encouraged the movement or stood on the sidelines.

Within two months after the *Brown* decision, a Mississippi Delta plantation manager named Robert B. Patterson brought together fourteen fear-stricken men who had not been calmed by the counsel of wait-and-see. Patterson, known to his friends as Tut, was thirty-one years old, a World War II army paratroop major, and a former Mississippi State football star who'd played in an Orange Bowl. In the winter before the *Brown* decision, Patterson had become alarmed when he had attended a meeting at his two daughters' school in Indianola where a state legislator had told the audience that cases pending before the Supreme Court, by striking down segregated schools, might essentially end life as they knew it. Most of the parents had just nodded, Patterson later recalled, until one older man finally asked, "You mean I have to send my grandchildren to school with niggers after we built that good nigger high school?" Patterson said he, like the other parents, had just sat there, "like a bump on a log. But I couldn't sleep that night. I got up out of bed and went to the bathroom and turned on the light and started writing a letter to the editor. Then I wrote to everybody I could think of."[14]

"A lot of people are resigning themselves to seeing their children crammed into schools and churches with children of other races and being taught the Communist theme of all races and mongrelization," he wrote in one letter he distributed. He vowed to stop it.

He was not interested in appeals for calm and reason: "You say this is not a time for hotheads and flag-waving, but for clear, cold thinking. We need those hotheads, just as we always have when our liberty has been threatened.

Let's let the hotheads be the forge, and the clear thinkers be the armorer to reforge and retemper the bright shield of segregation which is our heritage."[15]

By July 11, 1954, Patterson had attracted the core group that founded the Citizens' Council. They met in a private home in Indianola, the seat of government in Sunflower County, where Negroes made up 68 percent of the 56,000 residents but a mere .03 percent of the registered voters.[16] The fourteen men were, deliberately, not the riffraff of the region but its middle-class exemplars: a mayor, a dentist, a druggist, a banker, a farmer, a sheriff, a lawyer, a farm implement dealer, a ginner, a hardware store owner, two auto dealers, a planter.

The council, and a couple of similar organizations in other states, spread slowly but methodically. Early on, the council did not want or seek publicity, and the first reports on it were vague. The bureau chief for United Press in Jackson, Mississippi, John Herbers, had perhaps the earliest story. Herbers wrote in early September 1954 that cells of vigilantes were quietly forming in the Mississippi Delta to oppose school desegregation. A few days later, the *Delta Democrat-Times* of Greenville, whose owner-editor, Hodding Carter, Jr., would become the Council's greatest nemesis, followed up with the organization's name, a sense of its scope, and comments from Patterson about its mission.[17]

By October, when the Supreme Court hearings into the implementation of *Brown* were postponed until the spring, there were about thirty Citizens' Councils in Mississippi, enough to justify creation of a statewide association of Citizens' Councils. In marked contrast to the Ku Klux Klan, members of the Citizens' Councils wore their affiliation proudly. The councils, in an effort to allay fears about their mission, were quick to contrast their membership and tactics to those of the Klan; indeed, they said, they were the nonviolent alternative willing to work within the system to maintain segregation. The organizers made their appeals to the finest white people in town. Mayors, legislators, police chiefs, bankers, school superintendents, and other white-collar power brokers and major employers in town after town fell into line with the Citizens' Councils. So did some newspaper editors.

Even before the organizational meeting of the first Mississippi Citizens' Council in Indianola, a group of Virginians was making similar plans. One of the five federal lawsuits consolidated into *Brown* had come out of Prince Edward County, Virginia, in the heart of a region known as Southside Virginia. Southside held the highest proportion of Negroes in Virginia, a number almost equal to the number of whites, and had never quite forgotten the impact of Nat Turner's slave uprising 120 years earlier.

The inspiration for grassroots resistance in Southside came largely from the owner and publisher of the twice-weekly newspaper in Farmville, J. Barrye Wall, a stout, cigar-smoking businessman who used his *Farmville Herald* to advance the cause of school segregation. Wall, whose interest in the newspaper was only faintly journalistic, was known about town as a lively storyteller and orator who turned deadly serious when the subject turned to segregation. His newspaper exhibited a pure devotion to state sovereignty. And when Wall concluded that his newspaper was a limited outlet for his crusade, he helped found an organization to amplify the message. With a name his son had seen on the base of a Confederate monument in front of a Farmville church[18]—"Defenders of State Sovereignty"—the elder Wall drafted a nine-paragraph statement of beliefs for the organization; nowhere is segregation or race mentioned. The Defenders' arguments were simultaneously intellectual and bare-knuckled. So fixated were the Defenders on the states' rights argument that they would quickly jettison the white supremacist materials that floated into Virginia from the Citizens Councils.[19] The Defenders' goal was simple: keep the public schools segregated until you can't anymore, then shut them down.

The fallout from the *Brown* decision caused Tom Waring to reassess his involvement with the SERS almost as soon as it began. As a newsman, he saw the purpose and the rationale for *Southern School News*. As a committed segregationist, he saw that one of the secrets of the success of segregation had been the way newspapers had neglected it. And there was a tempting corollary: more attention might lead to less segregation. For his personal standing in Charleston and elsewhere in the segregationist South, Waring could not allow himself to be linked with any group that seemed soft on segregation. He could affiliate with a neutral party, but only if he were absolutely certain that it would remain neutral. In a letter to Virginius Dabney, the board's chairman, a troubled Waring wrote, "As you of course understand, I cannot afford to be identified at any time with a group that is trying to 'sell' an idea which I am devoting most of my efforts to unselling in the *News and Courier*."[20] Waring had further concerns as attention turned to the selection of the first director of the reporting service.

In casting his net, Ashmore had called an old friend of his, Colbert Augustus "Pete" McKnight, and sought names of potential directors. McKnight, who was editor of the Charlotte *News,* was one of the brightest and most versatile young journalists in the South. His career in newspapers had come to him quite by accident. Having lost an eye at age thirteen, he had imagined for himself the sedentary life of a Spanish professor until he visited his brother, an Associated Press correspondent, in Cuba in 1934. A political revolt and a hurricane had thrown Pete McKnight, then eighteen, into action helping his brother and given him a taste for journalism that changed his life.[21] In a few short years, he would make his way to the Charlotte *News,* where he not only worked for Ashmore but joined him frequently after work for beer and poker sessions.

McKnight's youthful exposure to Ashmore, his early studies and travels, and his well-known talent as a jazz pianist earned him a reputation as a man of great versatility, energy, and good humor. By age thirty-three, he had become editor of the Charlotte *News,* the kind of successor Ashmore would call for advice as he sought names of potential directors for the SERS. The more Ashmore talked with McKnight about the venture, the more McKnight himself became interested. He was looking for something fresh to do. From all appearances, the reporting service seemed stable, beginning with the Fund for the Advancement of Education's plan to pump about $100,000 into it the first year. The director would make $20,000, which was good money in a time when a family of four could get by on about $60 a week.[22] Well into his conversation with Ashmore, after several names had been bandied about, McKnight finally asked, "Well, why don't you ask me?"[23] Ashmore quickly anointed him.

When Tom Waring wondered what kind of director McKnight would be and what his views on the race question were, he called Ashmore. "I've known old Pete, had a few drinks with him, but what's his political position on this issue?" Waring asked. Ashmore responded in his trademark fashion: "I think you can assume it's to the left of yours, because there ain't no room on the right."[24] Waring, nonetheless, wrote Ashmore that he would give McKnight the benefit of the doubt. ". . . if he puts out a factual sheet of good journalism I'll be satisfied," Waring wrote. "If we can just keep the roughnecks on both sides of this issue from rioting, we may squeak through without serious trouble."[25]

McKnight had hardly started setting up the reporting service's headquarters in Nashville when a hot wind from Augusta, Georgia, hit the agency. The heat came from the pen of Roy V. Harris, a lawyer-politician-publisher who had become obsessed with the subjects—which he linked together—of integration and communism. Harris had a vivid imagination, a view of the world in which conspiracies sprouted like corn, and a remarkable ability to make people pay attention to him—in his letters, his speeches, or his screeching weekly newspaper, *The Augusta Courier.* Harris was extreme, he was nutty, and he somehow managed to get under the skin of anyone who showed the slightest faintheartedness about segregation. He had political cachet: he had been Speaker of the House of the Georgia legislature. And he used his newspaper to bully people.

Harris concluded that the SERS's connection to the Ford Foundation gave it a blood relationship to a separate, openly prointegration group based in

Atlanta, the Southern Regional Council. Harris wrote that the reporting service was secretly designed to advocate integration. Dabney, he added, "has also been affiliated in an active capacity with Communist-front groups."[26]

Several editors associated with the reporting service were stunned by Harris's allegations and went through a period of self-doubt. But most got firm purchase and came out even stronger advocates than they had been. Waring took umbrage at Harris's slippery allegations, the shrill pitch of his defiance, and his oversized effort to discredit coverage of the school desegregation issue. "We are outnumbered in the country as a whole," he reminded Harris. "We should not let fly with the rebel yell every time somebody plays 'Yankee Doodle' on a piccolo."[27]

Harris, it seems, inadvertently helped Waring resolve his own internal dispute about whether he was a newsman first and segregation advocate second, or vice versa. Waring decided that he disagreed with Harris's opinion that newspapers ought to stay away from the subject of race. "Being in the newspaper business, I believe in shedding light on everything, including the things we don't like. People put floodlights in their yards so they can aim better at prowlers. We have to be able to see our enemies. If the SERS turns up communities that accept mixing of schools, who are you and I to hide it? . . . If SERS discovers that the South accepts an end of segregation meekly, that will be the story to print."[28]

McKnight set about getting out the first issue of *Southern School News.* His primary interest was in journalism, not the race question, and he worked to overcome the early suspicions that the newspaper would be a propaganda sheet. The first rule: Throw out all adjectives and adverbs. In *Southern School News,* McKnight liked to say, nobody would be "vigorously" saying anything.[29] He had a secondary goal—more of a wild dream, really—that he didn't ballyhoo much beyond the board members' circle: in the early years, he would prepare and submit *Southern School News* stories for major journalism prizes, for he very much wanted *Southern School News* to come out of nowhere and win a Pulitzer Prize.[30]

The premier issue of the newspaper, a sixteen-page tabloid, came out in September 1954, carrying a banner headline that signaled the straightforward nature of the publication: REPORTING SERVICE TO TELL SCHOOL STORY. The newspaper published a state-by-state review, in alphabetical order, of everything that had happened in school desegregation in the seventeen southern and border states and the District of Columbia since the May 17 *Brown* decision; the headline for the report from each state was merely the state's name, nothing more. Photographs were nonexistent in the first issue and rare throughout the life of the newspaper. The stories ranged in length from about 1,000 words to as many as 3,000, and the paper carried the full text of the *Brown* decision as well as some charts and graphics from *The Negro and the Schools*. While the reporters' excessive language may have been trimmed, they did not have to eliminate all characterizations. They were considered expert observers, and their assessments were not merely allowed but considered a valuable part of the newspaper. From the earliest issues, readers got a clear sense of which states might ease into desegregated schools and which might throw up the barricades.

But the paper built its reputation by providing details. If a school system set up a three-stage process for desegregation, *Southern School News* wanted to know when those stages were, how many students were involved in each stage, and how many schools and buses would be affected. If a school board established a process for transferring students and announced four criteria for obtaining an exemption from transfer, *Southern School News* wanted to know the four criteria.

The first issue, distributed free in September 1954, was a huge success, if for no other reason than it proved that the newspaper had appeal across ideological lines. Commendations and letters requesting more copies flowed from the widest possible range of people. The Florence, South Carolina, chapter of the Association for the Advancement of White People sent in names of fifty people who wanted copies. The librarian of the U.S. Supreme Court asked for twelve additional copies. Requests for the newspaper came from all the southern and border states and twenty-eight northern and western states, and from the political extremes: one day's mail produced subscription forms from U.S. Senator Herman Talmadge of Georgia and the writer Lillian Smith, whose novel *Strange Fruit* and monthly periodical, *South Today,* established the metes and bounds of extreme liberal thought in the South in the mid-1940s.

By the close of the *Southern School News*'s first year, many newspapers had come to depend on it—some because they vitally wanted the information the newspaper dug up, others because they wanted to be able to publish the articles, yet claim some distance from them. Editorial pages across the South sang great praise for the little newspaper and urged its continuation. In separate editorials, the Nashville papers showed they had found something else they agreed on: the importance of extending the life of SERS and the newspaper.

The Fund for the Advancement of Education was pleased and renewed the SERS for two more years, but put a $2 price tag on a year's newspaper subscription. Satisfied with the work he'd done in launching the paper, Pete McKnight returned to Charlotte as editor of his old newspaper's rival, *The Charlotte Observer.* His successor was Don Shoemaker, editor of the *Asheville Citizen* in North Carolina; he would serve for three years and compile a book about desegregation, using contributions from the *Southern School News*'s correspondents.

The newspaper's mailing list shrank, as expected, when the subscription price was added, settling in at a steady 11,000 by the end of the second year. But the paper's commitment did not diminish. Issue after issue, it covered the same story over and over again, always with a sense that the story was fresh and that what mattered most, as the great infrastructure of segregation was being dismantled, were the nuts and bolts.

In the year since the first *Brown* decision, the Citizens' Councils, the Defenders, and a raft of similar segregationist organizations across the South had solidified their hold on local school boards, governments, businesses, and no small number of newspapers. In Mississippi alone, the Citizens' Councils claimed to have organizations in 110 towns, representing more than 25,000 people,[31] a claim that would grow to 253 councils and 60,000 members three months later.[32]

On May 31, 1955, the high court rendered its decision implementing *Brown*—again unanimous, again short. In a mere seven paragraphs, the Court restated the "fundamental principle that racial discrimination in public education is unconstitutional."

The Court then gave the South the kind of latitude, flexibility, and opportunity for delay that it was seeking. "Full implementation of these constitutional principles may require solution of varied local school problems," the Court said. "School authorities have the primary responsibility for elucidating, assessing, and solving these problems; courts will have to consider whether the action of school authorities constitutes good faith implementation."

The Supreme Court ordered the lower courts in the five cases that made up *Brown* "to require that the defendants make a prompt and reasonable start toward full compliance." At the same time, the Court said, it understood a whole host of reasons why the states might need more time to implement desegregation: the condition of the physical plants, the assignment of personnel, changes in transportation, and altering lines within school districts, to name a few.

Fuzzy language abounded. The Court ordered or urged, insisted or recommended, demanded or suggested. Scholars have been perplexed ever since by the ambiguity of the most memorable expression in the decision: that the lower courts act "with all deliberate speed" to admit the Negro plaintiffs to previously all-white public schools.

By virtually every measure, the southern states had won the day. Reed Sarratt, editorial director of the *Winston-Salem Journal* in North Carolina and a moderate, was pleased with the outcome. "The long-awaited Supreme Court order . . . is about as lenient as it possibly could be," he wrote.[33]

But the South was too far down the road of opposition to see the decision for what it really was. And among those who were blindest to that fact were editors who only a year before had been far more restrained in their reactions. Waring was angered by the decision in a way that made it seem as if he actually had expected the Supreme Court to reverse *Brown*.

The extent to which positions had hardened between May 1954 and May 1955 was evident in Kilpatrick's editorials as well. Though the court had fundamentally granted all three wishes that Kilpatrick had expressed after *Brown,* he had moved too far to even acknowledge it. His response to *Brown* II deftly avoided any mention of the previous standards he had set and announced seven new ones. "Is all this to advocate that Virginia attempt, by lawful means, to get around the law? That is exactly what we advocate," he wrote. His tenor was much different this time, showing a mean-spiritedness that had been absent a year earlier. "In May 1954, that inept fraternity of politicians and professors known as the United States Supreme Court chose to throw away the established law. These nine men repudiated the Constitution, spit upon the tenth amendment, and rewrote the fundamental law of this land to suit their own gauzy concepts of sociology. If it be said now that the South is flouting the law, let it be said to the high court: *You taught us how.*"

He urged the South to fight back. "Litigate? Let us pledge ourselves to litigate this thing for 50 years. If one remedial law is ruled invalid, let us try another; and if the second is ruled invalid, then let us enact a third. . . . When the court proposes that its social revolution be imposed upon the South 'as soon as practicable,' there are those of us who would respond that 'as soon as practicable' means never at all."[34]

Kilpatrick in later years would seek to portray himself as having kept his end of the school desegregation debate on an intellectual plane that rose above the racist vernacular employed by backwoods segregationists. Most of his public writings support that image. But some of his earliest writings, public and private, do not. In his first letter to Waring, a week after *Brown* II, Kilpatrick wrote, "My impression here in Virginia is that the court's opinion of May 31, far from quieting opposition to integration, served to increase our determination to resist mongrelization of our society. We are going to keep fighting."

Southern newspapers were most strident in states that had the greatest proliferation of segregationist organizations, in particular Mississippi, Virginia, and South Carolina. Make a prompt and reasonable start toward full compliance? "It won't happen in Mississippi," wrote the *Jackson Daily News.* "We are slow starters, and this is one time that we won't start at all.

Any attempt toward a start in this state is going to be met with stern resistance right at the beginning."

The Citizens' Council frequently denied that it was using economic pressure against Negroes as a tactic to terrorize or intimidate those who signed petitions seeking desegregated schools; if individual council members were firing Negro employees, or withholding credit, or calling in notes, Robert Patterson would say, well, there wasn't much the Citizens' Councils could do about it. But the evidence of such pressure was abundant. On July 26, 1955, Negroes in Natchez filed their formal petition for admission to the white public schools for the coming fall. Whites in Natchez hastily called the Citizens' Council's Patterson and its executive director, William J. Simmons, for guidance on how to resist. On August 4, the Citizens' Council staged a mass rally and formed a Natchez branch of the council. Six days later, the daily *Natchez Democrat* stopped the petition cold by publishing the names of those who signed the petition to desegregate and by asking readers to "check" the names.[35] Later that month, the *Yazoo City Herald* sold a full page of advertising to the Citizens' Council so that it could list the names and addresses of fifty-three local Negroes who had petitioned the school board there to desegregate. All but two were bullied into withdrawing their names—and still they lost their jobs, their credit, their interest in staying in Mississippi.[36]

Soon after *Brown* II, Waring visited Patterson, Simmons, and other Citizens' Council leaders in Mississippi and became both a quick convert to its mission and an early victim of its conceits. Waring declined to join, but he did all he could in his newspaper and personal letters to encourage the development and growth of Citizens' Councils in South Carolina. When the Association of Citizens' Councils in Mississippi began publishing a newspaper in the fall of 1955, it ran a three-part series on how the councils had been formed, what their mission was, how they operated, and who the leaders were. The series was purely a public relations production, the kind a trade association might run in its newsletter to celebrate its cause—only in this case, the three articles were provided by Waring. The first paragraph of the first article in the first issue declared that the Citizens' Councils were "mobilizing Mississippi to guard both whites and Negroes." The article added that the councils "are dedicated to protect the rank and file of Negroes from the wrath of ruffian white people who may resort to violence."

Few other journalists became so deeply persuaded of the nobility of the Citizens' Councils. Even fewer editors had the nerve to attack them. One who did was Hodding Carter Jr. in Greenville. It was Carter who wrote the first major article on the Citizens' Councils—at a time and in a place that the Councils hated most: on a national stage, in a national magazine, *Look,* in March 1955, even before the councils had been able to fully promulgate the benign image that Waring projected. Headlined "A Wave of Terror Threatens the South," the magazine piece sent the growing ranks of council members into fits of anger. Carter's article swept through the Mississippi legislature, which commenced immediately to attacking it. No description of Carter was too vile, too scatological, too inappropriate for the debate. The magazine article, said state Representative Eck Windham, was "a willful lie a nigger-loving editor made about the people of Mississippi." The House then incorporated all of the day's invective into a resolution defending the state and accusing Carter of spreading lies.

His response, toned down on the advice of friends, became a classic. Under the headline "Liar by Legislation," the four-paragraph editorial said, in part, "By a vote of 89 to 19, the Mississippi House of Representatives has resolved the editor of this newspaper into a liar because of an article I wrote about the Citizens' Councils for *Look* magazine. If this charge were true, it would make me well qualified to serve with that body. It is not true. So to even things up, I herewith resolve by a vote of 1 to 0 that there are 89 liars in the State Legislature, starting with Speaker Sillers and working way down to Rep. Eck Windham of Prentiss, a political loon whose name is fittingly made up of the words 'wind' and 'ham.' "

Carter concluded, "I am hopeful that this fever like the Ku Kluxism which rose from the same kind of infection, will run its course before too long a time. Meanwhile, those 89 character mobbers can go to hell collectively or singly and wait there until I back down. They needn't plan on returning."[37]

Carter had some newspaper allies. Ralph McGill attacked the Councils early, as did Buford Boone, editor of *The Tuscaloosa News* in Alabama. Another Alabama editor, Grover C. Hall, Jr., in Montgomery, also took on the Citizens' Councils—at least for a while. "The manicured Kluxism of these White Citizens' Councils is rash, indecent and vicious. . . . The nightriding and lash of the 1920s have become an abomination in the eyes of public decorum," Hall wrote. "So the bigots have resorted to a more decorous, tidy and less conspicuous method—economic thuggery."[38]

But the councils and their like had found solid footing across the South—due in part to newspapers and local television stations that threw their full editorial weight behind them, but due in greater part to a larger number of quiescent editors who failed to take a stand against them.

The councils would ride the crest of white anger that would break over Alabama, Mississippi, and Arkansas in the next two years and ultimately propel Harry Ashmore into the eye of a raging hurricane.

CHAPTER 6

INTO MISSISSIPPI

Simeon Booker was serving as Washington bureau chief for the most prominent Negro publications in the nation, *Ebony* and *Jet* magazines, when word reached him that two Negro grocers in the Mississippi Delta were operating an upstart voter registration drive that was showing success. Booker liked reporting because it gave him the opportunity to do things he'd never done. Now, in the spring of 1955, with a Nieman fellowship and a pioneering stint as a *Washington Post* reporter behind him, one of those opportunities was at his doorstep.

Booker had been born in Youngstown, Ohio, and attended college in Virginia. But until this trip to Mississippi in the spring of 1955, he had never ventured into the Deep South. His second trip would come two weeks later, accompanying tragedy. His third, fourth, and fifth trips to the Deep South followed close behind; soon the number of trips became incalculable, and not just for Booker. He frequently found himself in the company of a cadre of Negro reporters who, for the next couple of years, traveled from one story in the South to the next.

The string of race stories seemed endless, the appetite for them in the Negro press was insatiable, and the pace for reporters was exhausting. The datelines on stories jumped from Mound Bayou, Mississippi, to Tuscaloosa, Alabama, to Hoxie, Arkansas, to Money, Mississippi, to Mayflower, Texas, to Montgomery and other towns throughout the southern and border states. From the Negro press, and only the Negro press, came the commitment to cover all the stories, and to cover them with a mix of hard news, profiles, features, photographs, columns, and editorials.

A few of the white papers shared a sense of journalistic fraternity with the Negro reporters, but only a few; most were openly hostile to any dismemberment of the body of segregation, as well as to any effort by the outside press to portray local civil rights activities to the world at large. Still, the Negro press remained in 1955 and 1956 much as Gunnar Myrdal had found it fifteen years earlier: able to operate relatively freely and unmolested. Consequently, it had the front-row seat during the early dramas, while the white press sat in the balcony, if it came to the performance at all.

From town to town, the same reporters kept running into one another, sharing rooms in private homes while working competitively on stories. In addition to *Ebony* and *Jet,* the *Chicago Defender* would be there, and *The Pittsburgh Courier.* The *Norfolk Journal and Guide,* the *Afro-American* newspapers, and the *Amsterdam News* were also devoted to full coverage of the race story, as were a handful of U.S. socialist and Communist newspapers. The Negro press of the Deep South—the *Birmingham World,* the *Tri-State Defender* of Memphis, the *Arkansas State Press* in Little Rock, and *The Lighthouse and Informer* in Columbia, among others—covered the regional story as best they could with their limited resources.[1]

Even before it was clear that all the datelines, taken together, constituted a civil rights movement, it had become clear in the Negro press that the race story had developed into something constant and enduring. It had become the race beat, and the Negro press was seriously staffing it. When, if ever, would the northern press join in?

Booker's first trip took him to Humphreys County, fewer than twenty-five flat, somnolent miles from the birthplace of the Citizens' Councils, where he met the grocers Gus Courts and Reverend George W. Lee and saw the daunting task they faced. In 1955, Mississippi had the highest percentage of Negroes in the nation and the lowest percentage registered to vote. It had not always been that way: in 1868, one year after freed slaves were allowed to register under the military rule of Reconstruction, the 86,973 registered Negro voters represented 56 percent of the Mississippi electorate. A state constitutional convention in 1890 took care of that: by 1892, there were only 8,922 Negroes registered to vote, representing 11 percent of the electorate. By 1955, when Lee and Courts began their work, 41 percent of Mississippi's voting age population was Negro, and the number of Negroes registered to vote had plummeted to less than 5 percent.[2]

To Courts and Lee, who was pastor at four churches, the promise of *Brown* and school desegregation meant nothing if Negroes remained politically powerless. Besides, the math made sense. In many pockets across the South, including the Mississippi Delta, Negroes outnumbered whites, in some places substantially; in Humphreys County, 70 percent of the population was Negro.[3] But their goals seemed many mountains away. To those who paid their poll taxes and subjected themselves to threats and indignities as they registered, Lee and Courts could offer little more than the platitudes of democracy's virtues. They certainly couldn't promise would-be voters that there would not be an additional price to pay for their insouciance.

Courts, on three occasions, was pressured to leave his store to attend "committee meetings" of the local Citizens' Council. There, inside a bank, he would face two prominent planters and the bank president. Be aware, they told him, that colored people of Humphreys County were not going to be permitted to vote, the NAACP was not going to be permitted to operate, and his own ability to stay in business was at risk.[4]

The Citizens' Council saw even small gains by Lee and Courts as a threat. Of 16,000 Negroes eligible to register in Humphreys County, Lee and Courts persuaded 400 to pay their poll taxes. They got 94 of those to continue through registration; that involved repeated visits to the registrar's office, which frequently claimed to be too busy.[5] The 94 obviously were not enough to turn an election. But each represented a hard-won victory, a cause for celebration, a profile in courage.[6]

Ebony and Simeon Booker were attracted to the story of Lee and Courts because they were making inroads against overwhelming political domination. When Booker arrived in Mississippi, Lee mesmerized him at a rally that drew thousands of people. "Pray not for your mom and pop," Lee told the crowd. "They've gone to heaven. Pray you can make it through this hell." Lee saw voter registration as a mandatory act of racial self-definition, and he urged congregants to envision the day when their mathematical dominance would add up to a Negro congressman elected from the Mississippi Delta.[7] Booker left Mississippi convinced that he had just witnessed the future, that the electrifying leadership of people such as Lee and Courts would usher in that day.

Two weeks later, Booker returned—not to praise Lee, but to bury him.

Simeon Booker had had an inauspicious start in journalism. He had been fired from his first job, at the Cleveland *Call and Post,* a Negro weekly, for trying to organize a local chapter of the Newspaper Guild. Unable to land another position, he worked at a gas station while trying to figure out his next move. He would apply, he decided, for a position he'd been rejected for several times already: a Nieman fellowship at Harvard. This time, he was invited for an interview, which set off a new round of panic. Booker had never flown in an airplane. He was vastly relieved to learn that the interview would take place in Chicago, easily accessible by bus. He also had never slept in a hotel.[8] Booker won the fellowship for the 1950–51 academic year and joined a group of men who would later become enormously influential in journalism, politics, and literature.

Booker's experience as a Nieman gave him not only the confidence that he was a solid journalist[9] but the rare opportunity to jump from the limitations of the Negro press and into the greater exposure of the mainstream white press. He became *The Washington Post*'s first full-time Negro reporter, one of the first at any major newspaper. But he couldn't do what he wanted to do. Assigned stories on the police beat, he found himself being treated more like a criminal than a reporter. At various federal agencies, he was essentially stranded on a moving island, unable even to get lunch anywhere.[10] The mainstream white press, with all its rules and regimens, with all its pretensions of objectivity, had limitations of its own and lacked any kind of social mission. He decided to return to the Negro press, but not to newspapers.

Negro newspapers were undergoing a difficult time between the postwar disappointment with racial progress in the late 1940s and the crystallization of the civil rights story in the mid-1950s. In 1954, the year of *Brown,* the newspapers were hit by a recession and by a marked change in the kind of news their readers wanted. By canceling subscriptions in massive numbers, readers seemed to be revolting against sensationalism and the front-page trifecta of race, sex, and violence. *The Pittsburgh Courier,* which had hit a circulation high of 358,000 in 1948, was holding on to a little more than half that many in 1955. The *Chicago Defender*'s national edition, circulated to 75,000 in 1952, was down to 37,000 three years later; in Chicago, which had 700,000 Negro residents, the *Defender* had lost nearly 20 percent of its readers since 1952 and was reaching only 49,000. The newspapers, once so proud of their reach into faraway areas, began retrenching. The *Afro-American,* which was published weekly in thirteen local and regional editions, and twice a week in Washington, D.C., and Baltimore, began cutting back when its circulation dropped from 230,000 immediately after the war to 188,000.[11]

The Negro newspapers also had stronger competition from within their own ranks: magazines, which were inherently more national in their scope. In Chicago, the Negro businessman John H. Johnson was trying several magazine formulas and succeeding. Though Johnson in 1942 had to buy up thousands of copies of his first publication, *Negro Digest,* so that newsstands and advertisers would believe it was instantly popular, he did not have to pull such stunts for long.[12] The publication was modeled after *Reader's Digest,* so much so that the *Reader's Digest* feature "Most Embarrassing Moments" became "My Most Humiliating Jim Crow Experience" in *Negro Digest.* The new monthly was largely a compendium of all race-related news from other publications, but it also featured original pieces by outstanding Negro and white writers, including Langston Hughes, Carl Sandburg, Quentin Reynolds, and Marquis Childs. A popular series was "If I Were a Negro," whose contributors included Eleanor Roosevelt, Edward G. Robinson, Marshall Field, and Norman Thomas. More important, *Negro Digest* abandoned a 128-year tradition in the Negro press of special pleading: it carried no editorials, protests, or harangues. Some issues sold an extraordinary 150,000 copies.[13]

Johnson's success led to his creation of *Ebony,* with the promise that it would present "the happier side of Negro life." Its first issues in 1945 were poorly organized, editorially emaciated, and visually bland.[14] They offered a positive, upbeat, but pabulum view of life in Negro America. Before long, Johnson tried a new formula that sent *Ebony*'s circulation soaring: sensationalism. Month after month, Johnson watched as sales rose with every story on interracial marriage, on sex, on Negroes passing themselves off as white, and on bizarre people more commonly found in P. T. Barnum freak shows. Stories about well-known Negroes marrying whites were a surefire circulation booster.[15]

Politically, *Ebony* landed with a feathery thud—and admitted it. "There are some who have accused *Ebony* of fence sitting," the magazine wrote of itself in its fifth-anniversary issue in 1950. "If being a middle-of-the-roader who refuses to carry either a chip on the shoulder or a hat in hand is fence sitting, we plead guilty. Frankly, we are big believers in carrying both a big stick and soft glove when approaching white folks on the race question." That philosophy, Johnson's philosophy, was actually written by a white man, Ben Burns, who spent his entire career as an editor with Negro newspapers and magazines in Chicago.[16] Such a confession did not, however, pull the stingers from *Ebony*'s most vigorous critics in the Negro journalism community. "*Ebony* was never in the vanguard of the 'Negro revolution,'" Chuck Stone, once the editor of the *Chicago Defender,* would write a few years later. "An apostle of *ex post facto* militancy, it rode in the caboose as a frightened passenger, praying that white businessmen would continue to love it."[17]

Many people did love it. In the early 1950s, *Ebony*'s circulation had climbed to 500,000, almost all of it newsstand sales in urban areas outside the South. In 1954, the numbers dropped precipitously due to the recession and the apparent incongruity between the magazine's fare and the suddenly serious tenor of the news affecting Negro lives. As *Ebony* was celebrating its tenth anniversary—and as Booker was traveling to Mississippi to cover the voter registration drive—the magazine was making a radical, lifesaving changeover. To win back the 100,000 readers he had lost, Johnson threw out cheesecake photographs, gossip, and froth and began providing a more thoughtful and sober portrayal of life, while putting more emphasis on success stories.

. . .

While driving in Belzoni from a tailor shop where he had picked up his pressed preaching pants for Sunday services, Reverend George Lee had been shot to death by someone in a passing car. The gunshots had ripped away much of his face and pierced his vocal chords. His car had crashed into an occupied shanty. The sheriff had examined Lee's body but missed the lead pellets embedded in his face; he declared that death had resulted from a concussion Lee had received when the car crashed into the shanty. When the presence of lead pellets became undeniable, the sheriff said they were probably tooth fillings.[18]

In the Negro press, George Lee died a hero, of an unsolved murder. In the southern white press, Lee's death was just freakish and inexplicable. The Jackson *Clarion-Ledger* accepted the sheriff's explanation, as it usually did in such matters. Its headline said: NEGRO LEADER DIES IN ODD ACCIDENT.[19]

Booker, who had been so taken by Lee's magnetism, returned to attend his funeral. Booker was an urban dandy of sorts, but this time he was not interested in casting an image of big-city prowess or journalistic detachment. He dressed in old clothes and dirt-dulled shoes so he could sit with farmers and read the message behind their tears. He saw in their faces exactly what the segregationists wanted: a belief in their own inferiority, reconciliation to their own destiny of defeat. And he heard them declare that Lee, in stupidly challenging the white man, had gotten what he asked for.[20]

The names of registered Negro voters in Humphreys County began falling from the rolls at a fast clip. It was an election year, a lot was at stake, and many Negroes were not able to withstand the pressure. In August 1955, the state secretary of the NAACP, Medgar Evers, told a reporter that the number of registered Negroes in Humphreys County had dropped even below what he considered the "hard core" and amounted to about thirty- five.[21]

By primary election day, pressure from the Citizens' Council had reduced the number of registered Negro voters to only 22 out of the 16,000 who were eligible. Even that was too many for some whites. Gus Courts was warned that if any of the 22 walked onto the courthouse lawn to vote, they would be killed. They gathered in his store that morning and made a decision: they had not resisted the pressure that long only to crumble on election day. They walked to the courthouse, where each was handed a sheet of paper containing ten questions. "Do you want your children to go to school with white children?" was one. "Are you a member of or do you support the NAACP?" was another. County officials would not permit them to vote.[22]

Lamar Smith, a successful Negro farmer and World War II veteran, faced similar threats in Lincoln County, Mississippi. Smith spent the weeks leading up to the 1955 state elections registering voters and training them to cast absentee ballots. He also urged Negro voters to oust a particular county supervisor on primary election day. The results of the Democratic primary showed how effective Smith had been: when the countywide results were tabulated, white officials were perturbed to see that the number of votes cast by absentee ballot had jumped from the typical 600 to about 1,100.[23] With the deciding runoffs in races from justice of the peace to governor just ten days away, several white men decided they had better have a talk with Lamar Smith.

They found him in the center of downtown Brookhaven on a busy Saturday in broad daylight as he crossed the lawn of the Lincoln County courthouse square. They surrounded him and argued with him briefly before one of them yanked out a .38-caliber pistol and shot Smith under his right arm, killing him.

There were witnesses, who provided descriptions of one of the fleeing, blood-splotched assailants; eight days later, three men were arrested. But the witnesses wouldn't talk, and the sheriff was focused not on who had killed Smith but on whether Smith's absentee ballot operation had been legal. The grand jury expressed frustration that because "people standing within 20 or 30 feet claim to know nothing about it," someone had just gotten away with murder. "Most assuredly," the grand jury concluded, "somebody has done a good job of trying to cover up the evidence in this case."[24]

Newspaper coverage was of little value in ferreting out what had happened or why. Indeed, the sheriff and other officials who might have been interested in shoving the case to a dead file were able to do so without much concern that newspapers might ask an untoward question or pursue any line other than the official one. The dominant Jackson newspapers, *The Clarion-Ledger* and *Daily News,* sent a reporter to Brookhaven who filed a report that ran as the main story in the next day's combined Sunday edition. The story—with the four-column headline "Links Shooting of Negro with Vote Irregularities"—shifted the blame for Smith's death to Smith himself, saying he had been "linked to voting irregularities" in urging Negroes to cast absentee ballots.

The newspapers were able to ascertain quickly that Smith had once been convicted of bootlegging but never managed to report why Smith had urged Negroes to vote by absentee ballot. That and subsequent stories never explained what the law on absentee voting was or whether Smith was within his legal rights. No effort was made to interview anyone other than the district attorney, the sheriff, the chief of police, and the shooter. Friends and associates of Smith were not interviewed, so that even as he went to his grave recognized in the Negro community as a fearless political organizer, he appeared in the white press as a cipher, a schemer, and an aging boot-legger.

The newspapers even got his nickname, Ditney, wrong three times before they got it right. Nowhere in their stories was there a quote, a reaction, or even a passing suggestion that murderous vigilantism was not an appropriate political response.

A week after the 1955 statewide elections—Lee had been dead nearly four months, Smith two weeks—the *Jackson Daily News* reported a story that paid unintended tribute to the two dead political organizers. The all-white executive committee of the state Democratic Party had analyzed the election returns and had become alarmed by what it saw. "I'm concerned about Negroes registering to vote," said Tom Tubb, the party chairman. "They perhaps played too large a part in the last election." The party then set into motion a series of recommendations intended to undo everything Lee, Smith, and Courts had done. The party did not merely want to stop any future voter registrations among Negroes; it vowed to reduce the number already registered.[25]

Two months later, in Humphreys County, only one Negro person remained registered to vote: Gus Courts. That, too, ended. In November, soon after the general election in which the Democrats were routinely elected, Courts was gunned down inside his own grocery store, the fulfill-ment of many threats against him for refusing to remove his name from the rolls. Courts lived but moved to Chicago, "an American refugee from Mis-sissippi terror."[26] As in the Lee and Smith cases, no one was ever prosecuted.

The dismissive daily newspaper coverage of the attacks on Lee, Smith, and Courts was fairly standard. In some southern cities, Negroes were better served by no coverage from dailies than by what they got. That was fre-quently the case with coverage by *The Clarion-Ledger* and the *Jackson Daily News,* the newspapers owned by the Hederman family in Jackson. They were journalistically the worst major-city newspapers in the South, not because the owners, top editors, and columnists were fervently segregation-ist—which they were—but because they allowed their zealotry to dictate the scope, depth, tone, and tilt of their coverage. The newspapers were vindic-tive, poorly written, and error-ridden. Their management of the news helped explain why Mississippi remained the most reactionary state in the South. Nowhere in the region was there a clearer example of why Harry Ashmore feared that many southern white newspapers had neither the will nor the spine to cover racial news professionally.

Mississippi's segregationist and Confederate traditions were a comfort-able fit for the Hederman publishing family, which dated its ownership of

The Clarion-Ledger to 1871, the zenith of the Reconstruction it vociferously opposed. In 1920, brothers Robert and Tom Hederman, after working for their cousin at the paper for years, put together enough money to buy it.

Together, the Hederman brothers became intrinsically part of all that was white Jackson. They were deacons and officers at the church, trustees of banks and thrifts, Shriners, masons, members of numerous corporate boards, and civic committees, and had long-standing, ironclad political loyalties and friendships they did not squander. One of their schoolmates was Woods Eastland, who would become a district attorney and father of U.S. Senator James Eastland. Their teacher was a man named Johnson, whose son and grandson, Paul B. Johnson, Sr., and Paul B. Johnson, Jr., would become governors of the state. When U.S. Senator Pat Harrison died in office in 1941, Governor Paul Johnson, Sr., offered the job to Tom Hederman. When he declined, the governor offered it to Bob Hederman, who also passed on it. The Hedermans then suggested Woods Eastland, who then recommended his son Jim, who was in only his first term in the state House of Representatives.[27] The younger Eastland took it.

The five sons of Robert Hederman and Tom Hederman led the generation that took the family empire and *The Clarion-Ledger* into the racially torn second half of the twentieth century. Robert had Robert Jr., Zach, and Henry. Tom had Tom Jr. and Arnold. All were born into opportunity, and none walked away from it. They all left the nest at some point, for jobs and schooling as far away as New York and Pittsburgh. But they all returned, and their greatest success came when they operated as a unit, as a team.

That, too, was no accident. The elder Hedermans had frequently used a walk in the woods to impress upon the five boys the importance of family unity and conformity. One of the senior Hedermans would gather up five twigs and hand them in a bundle to each of the boys to try to snap. None of them could do it, they realized, as long as they held the twigs together.[28]

When the printing shop and newspaper were passed to the next generation, the political loyalties of the elder Hedermans went with them. The Hedermans were taught to treat those friendships as part of the family birthright, as "perennial plantings," the younger Bob Hederman would remark, "not the mere annual sproutings that wither and die after the fall elections."[29]

The Hedermans had not possessed the afternoon *Daily News* very long. Major Frederick Sullens, a bombastic, piss-and-vinegar rival of the Hedermans, had owned and edited it until 1954, when the Hedermans managed to buy enough stock from Sullens's estranged daughter to force Sullens to sell them the newspaper even as he maintained editorial control.

Sullens represented the tail end of an entire genre of editors: the personal journalist who loved to mix it up with the political power, fight tooth and nail, and always get the last word. Sullens, born in 1877, the same year as

Theodore Bilbo, delighted in being the last of the personal journalists roaming the land. He was not a kindly curmudgeon just entertaining himself. He could be deeply antagonistic. His column, "The Lowdown on the Higher Ups," could be fun and infuriating, though he would have been offended that some found it fun. He once suggested that Bilbo be confined "to a small room with a dozen polecats until they stink each other to death."

His animus for the senior Paul B. Johnson, a Hederman favorite, was so great that Sullens once ordered that mule ears be drawn atop Johnson's head in a photograph and that the accompanying story report not that Johnson would be speaking at a local park but that a jackass would be braying there. Johnson once sued Sullens for libel and won, which provoked an altercation at the elevator of a Jackson hotel. By most accounts, Johnson began banging Sullens with a cane. Sullens, more experienced as a fistfighter, struck back. As Sullens told the story, "I knocked him down, took the walking cane away and sat astride him and beat my $25,000 worth out of him."[30]

By taking control of the *Daily News* and owning one of the three television stations in the city, a radio station, and one of the largest printing companies, the Hederman sons moved the family more deeply into the vascular system of Jackson commerce. Their business and real estate holdings were massive, and they used their newspaper as a corporate cudgel that went well beyond their expressed editorial opinions. Led by the junior Tom and Robert Hederman, the brothers were aggressive in putting themselves at the centers of influence: the boards of the politically powerful electric company, banks, thrifts, institutions of higher learning, and public schools. They held sway at the largest Baptist church, the largest Baptist hospital, and the largest Baptist college in the state.

They worked quietly and tried to not draw attention to themselves. They were temperate, if not teetotalers. They were not ostentatious country clubbers, and they projected a public image of being serious civic boosters. Tom Hederman, Jr., who spoke with a stutter, did not voice his views from podiums; he did it in *The Clarion-Ledger,* rarely with any intellectual depth, lucidity, eloquence, or wit. Though none of the Hedermans got into politics, they managed to work their way into the offices of governors, mayors, and other political leaders. As their corporate interests grew, it was difficult to separate their editorial support for downtown and regional development—better roads, better recreational facilities, a better airport, a better stadium, a new reservoir they wanted to name for a governor—from their own economic advancement. Even among corporate leaders who respected power, the Hedermans were considered much too clannishly committed to their own causes.[31]

In reaction to the Hedermans' commercial hegemony, a group of business leaders, including major advertisers, had begun organizing in 1954 to launch a rival newspaper, the Jackson *State Times*. Racial coverage in the Hederman papers was not a major motivating force, but for a while it was the beneficiary.

With nearly one million dollars, more than six hundred owner-stockholders, and enough advertising commitments from its own founders to sustain it, the rival *State Times* constructed a new plant, purchased new presses, and began hiring. On the news side, it attracted an editor, Norman Bradley, who believed the *Brown* decision had been just and fair and who was given a written contract promising him complete editorial freedom. The news department was built with a staff committed to producing an honest voice of moderation on racial issues.

The *State Times* published for the first time on February 28, 1955, and ran smack into a buzz saw of emotional, line-in-the-sand news: the second *Brown* decision, the Belzoni voter registration drive, and the rapid growth of the manipulative Citizens' Council, which was quite satisfied with the Hedermans' thinking. At the beginning, the *State Times* took editorial positions decidedly different from those of the Hedermans. In the fury of the times, it was quite bold to write, as it did, that Mississippians should not defend themselves by pointing to brutality outside the South. The newspaper's moderate position did not seem to hurt it. The goal was to sell enough advertising in the first six to nine months to project one million dollars in advertising sales for the following year. It reached that point in three months.[32]

The one place the *State Times*' modulated viewpoint had no impact was at the Hederman newspapers. Whenever the flames of bigotry began to flicker, Sullens would pull out his fan, as if journalistic detachment were cowardice. When *Brown* came down, he put a black border around his front-page editorial entitled "Blood on the White Marble Steps." Shortly before *Brown* II came down in the spring of 1955, Sullens tried to shift responsibility for any untoward consequences that might result from defiance. "Mississippi will not obey the decision," he told the American Society of Newspaper Editors in Washington. "If an effort is made to send Negroes to school with white children, there will be bloodshed. The stains of that bloodshed will be on the Supreme Court steps."[33]

It was a battle cry that seemed to justify virtually any act taken to maintain segregation, and it helped make Mississippi the most precarious place in which to be a Negro.

Nothing underscored that point more emphatically than another murder in the Mississippi Delta later that same year: the abduction, beating, torture, and killing of a fourteen-year-old boy, Emmett Till. But this time the press reaction would be radically different. If students of journalism and race were looking for signs that the mainstream press was about to take the southern racial story more seriously, the Till case would generate not one or two straws in the wind but an entire boxful.

CHAPTER 7

THE TILL TRIAL

The murder of Emmett Till had nothing directly to do with school desegregation, voting rights, or the use of public accommodations. It was not even seen initially as having an impact on any organized or disorganized push for civil rights. It was just another in a long history of racial murders in the Mississippi Delta. But no single event intensified the interest of the Negro press more than the story of the Chicago kid visiting his mother's uncle in the late summer of 1955 and the trial of the two white men accused of beating him, shooting him in the head, and ditching him in a river with a seventy-pound cotton gin fan tethered to his neck with barbed wire.

Individually and as a group, the Negro reporters had never felt such a sense of journalistic agreement that all the disparate, disconnected events leading up to that moment suddenly were linked and were being propelled toward some goal. It wasn't choreography, but it was movement, and the Negro press was not only moving with it but sometimes leading it.[1]

The Till trial would represent another significant journalistic milestone. In his death, Emmett Till not only brought Negro reporters into the heart of the white man's kingdom—the courtroom—but he brought white reporters into the Deep South in unprecedented numbers to cover a racial story. It was the first massive move by the northern press, and it had exactly the impact that Myrdal had predicted more than a decade before. Northerners were shocked and shaken by what they read.

White and Negro reporters worked in the same room covering the same story with virtually the same amount of access and opportunity. These were not Negro and white sportswriters in the same ballpark watching Jackie Robinson. These were some of the best hard news reporters sitting within a few feet of each other in a hall of justice, covering a dynamic story of mutual journalistic and racial interest. They conducted the same interviews, exchanged notes, filled in one another's quotes, and took turns getting photographs inside the courtroom. Even more remarkably, some Negro and white reporters would find themselves traveling secretly in the same car on dark and dusty delta roads in search of witnesses who had disappeared.

On August 24, 1955, inside Bryant's Grocery and Meat in Money, Mississippi, Till either whistled at Carolyn Bryant and boasted that he had been with white women before or was hit by a longtime stuttering problem and inadvertently let out a sound that resembled a wolf whistle.[2]

Three nights later, Carolyn Bryant's husband, Roy, and his half brother, J. W. Milam, drove to the home of Till's great-uncle, Mose Wright, woke up Till, and took him away. The abduction of Till, even before his body was found or his death was confirmed, quickly became news, partly because the sheriff of Leflore County acted swiftly to take Roy Bryant into custody as a suspect. When the first Associated Press story broke on August 29, it pretty much outlined the entire story in ten sentences. Not until the final sentence, at least as it appeared in the *Jackson Daily News,* did readers learn that Till was still missing and that Bryant had told officers that Till "had been released." Only by such indirection did astute readers figure out that Bryant had acknowledged abducting Till that night.[3]

By the second news day, Till had not been found, Milam had joined Bryant in custody and in acknowledging they had taken Till, and the *Daily News* was putting the wire story inside the newspaper. The sheriff was saying there might have been foul play, relatives might be hiding Till, or he might have returned to Chicago. The paper's headline conveyed skepticism, oddly putting quotation marks around the one allegation to which Bryant and Milam had essentially confessed: " 'Kidnaped' Negro Boy Still Missing; Fear Foul Play," it said.[4]

On August 31, three days after Till was reported abducted, his tortured, bloated, and decomposed body floated partially to the surface of the Tallahatchie River. It was a ghastly sight, made all the more horrible because Till's neck was wrapped in barbed wire attached at the other end to a cotton gin fan that weighed twice its seventy pounds because of the mud on it. The left side of the boy's head was beaten in and "cut up pretty badly, like an axe was used," the sheriff said. One eyeball was dangling from its socket; his tongue extended from his mouth, swollen to eight times its normal size. Behind his left ear was a bullet hole. Around one of his fingers was an oversized ring that his mother had finally agreed he could wear with a little tape to help it fit. The ring was engraved "LT," the initials of his dead father, Louis Till.[5]

Bryant and Milam were charged with murder, and Emmett Till was launched as one of the most shocking and enduring stories of the twentieth century. As the story unfolded, with Bryant and Milam so quickly under arrest, the news was unavoidably a big story across Mississippi, less so elsewhere. Many of the articles, particularly in the Hederman newspapers, treated the charges with doubt and the Negro subjects with carelessness: Emmett became "Emmitt," sometimes "Emmet," and there was inconsistency between the spellings in the stories and in the headlines. He was a Negro boy, and he was a "Nego" boy. His mother, Mamie Bradley, was "Mamie Brandley."

In Mississippi, there was editorial outrage, but most of it blamed not the unrestrained impulses of white people but the extremist if not Communist political agenda of the South-hating NAACP. Roy Wilkins issued a strong response: "It would appear that the state of Mississippi has decided to maintain white supremacy by murdering children." He added a wiser, more thoughtful observation: "The killers of the boy felt free to lynch him because there is in the entire state no restraining influence, not in the state capital, among the daily newspapers, the clergy nor any segment of the so-called better citizens."[6]

The strongest reaction was yet to come. After Till's mother finally persuaded Mississippi officials not to bury her son in Mississippi as they had planned, the young boy's body was sent to Chicago. At the Illinois Central station, accompanied by Simeon Booker, other reporters and photographers for the Negro press, and scores of mourners, Mrs. Mamie Bradley waited for the pine box to arrive. Booker later wrote that when the box was handed down and opened for her to see, some of the young boy's skull fell off and some of his brains fell out.[7] Mrs. Bradley fell limp in a wheelchair and screamed a prayer to the heavens. She decided that she would never be able to describe the condition of her son's body to anyone who had not seen it, so she insisted that the casket remain open for all to witness.[8]

For those who were not among the tens of thousands who lined up to see the body in Chicago, *Jet* magazine carried a close-up photograph of Till's wildly disfigured and indiscernible face in mid-September. When that issue sold out, the magazine, for the first time, printed more. Then it published the photo again the next week. Few whites saw the photo, and Negroes had to buy *Jet* to see it. Johnson Publications held and exercised exclusive rights to the photograph, taken by one of its staffers, David Jackson, thus keeping it out of the hands of white newspapers, television, and all but a few Negro papers that disregarded the restrictions and ran grainy reprints of the *Jet* photograph.[9]

Mrs. Bradley's decision was widely seen in the South, even by otherwise progressive editors, as unconscionable propaganda. Hodding Carter, Jr., went so far as to suggest that the NAACP was trying to poison the atmosphere and win acquittals for Milam and Bryant so that the organization would have "another excuse to apply the torch of world-wide scorn to Mississippi." He found the "macabre exhibitionism, the wild statements, and the hysterical overtones" of the funeral "too well-staged not to have been planned to inflame the hatred and to set off a reverse reaction in Mississippi."[10]

Whether it was staged or not (Mrs. Bradley insisted it was not), the northern press responded quickly and with outrage at the brutal hand of Jim Crow. This was an easy one without a lot of complicating factors. There were an innocent victim and his loving mother against two murderous bullies who seemed to have the backing, maybe the sanction, of an entire racist region behind them. In a court of law, yes, they deserved a fair trial; they deserved to be presumed innocent. But as a news story, were there really two sides to it? The press responded sympathetically to Mrs. Bradley's sorrow, in effect linking arms with her in portraying the evils of race discrimination in the South. The coverage in turn linked her with an empathetic nation. With all the reporters and photographers around her, Mamie Bradley, a heretofore anonymous face in America, had the overwhelming feeling that much of the nation was standing beside her, crying with her. Much of the nation felt the same way.[11]

Bryant and Milam were in custody within two days of Till's abduction. Indictments came quickly, and the trial began fourteen days later. The testimony spanned four and a half days. The jury deliberations took one hour and seven minutes. From the moment Emmett Till had the encounter that led to his abduction to the moment the jury returned its not guilty verdict against his accused killers, a mere thirty days passed.

For the 550 people of Sumner, little good could come from hosting the Emmett Till trial. It was a distraction from the more important business at hand: harvesting one of the best cotton crops in many years. Besides, there was no evidence that Till had been killed in Tallahatchie County—one of many missing pieces as the case went to trial; the trial was carried out there because the river that had disgorged his body flowed through it. Nonetheless, reporters took note of Sumner's slogan and portrayed it as cruelly ironic under the circumstances: "A Good Place to Raise a Boy."

As they walked the streets of downtown Sumner, the reporters assigned to cover the trial were quite a sight. There were so many—at least fifty reporters and photographers when the trial began, more than anyone could recall gathering in a single place in north Mississippi and the most to cover any trial since Dr. Sam Sheppard had been tried the year before in Cleveland, Ohio, for the murder of his wife. Western Union, through which most reporters filed their stories, beefed up its staff and equipment.

Most of the reporters were white, stayed in a boardinghouse in Sumner, and used workspace in the courthouse lobby or across the street at the weekly *Sumner Sentinel*. A dozen were Negro reporters, writing mostly for weekly or monthly publications, staying in private homes in Clarksdale, twenty miles away, and working where they could. They did have one advantage: the only café in town was for a Negro clientele.

James Kilgallen of International News Service drew a lot of attention— not because he was the oldest or most experienced criminal trial reporter, having covered the trial of "Machine Gun" Kelly in Oklahoma City and the execution of Bruno Hauptmann. The septuagenarian correspondent was recognized because his daughter, Dorothy Kilgallen, the syndicated columnist, was a regular on the television game show *What's My Line?*[12]

Every glimpse of the reporter Rob Hall was accompanied by whispers and expressions of disbelief: the forty-nine-year-old newsman, who spoke and drew on his pipe slowly, had all the attributes of a true-blue southerner. The silver-haired father of three was a native Mississippian. His mother had been one of Theodore Bilbo's teachers, his grandfather had been a prominent Baptist preacher, and his father was a banker and weekly newspaper owner. But Rob Hall was covering the trial for the New York *Daily Worker,* the official newspaper of the Communist Party in America.[13] Feature articles about Hall noted that the stories he was sending to New York were pretty straight and showed no obvious bias. How did reporters in Sumner have any idea about the tone of Hall's stories? Curiosity about the Communist reporter was so great that Western Union employees were peeking at the stories he was filing and telling other reporters how surprisingly un-Communist they were.[14]

Life magazine, which was intensely competitive on the emerging race story with *Look* and *The Saturday Evening Post,* sent three people down, the Associated Press sent four, and International News Service had three. United Press, ever parsimonious, sent only one reporter, but he was John Herbers, who, as bureau chief in Jackson, had been breaking new ground in his coverage of civil rights activities. Merely covering Negro leaders and their activities—as Herbers had done as far back as 1952—constituted groundbreaking reporting in those years; Herbers and the United Press bureau under him were presenting a mix of profiles and features about the Negro leaders, giving them names, faces, and a humanity that they did not get from the Associated Press in Mississippi.[15]

Three major New York newspapers were on hand: Popham drove over from *The New York Times'* bureau in Chattanooga; Jim Desmond came down for the New York *Daily News,* and columnist Murray Kempton covered for the *New York Post.* In one regard, Popham and Kempton represented two extremes. While Popham was the only person in the sweltering courtroom who kept his tie knotted and his coat on, Kempton drew curious looks by wearing Bermuda shorts to dinner one night—until Popham gave him a tutorial on southern manners.[16]

In his eighth year covering the South, the forty-five-year-old Popham remained the only correspondent assigned to the region for a national newspaper. His feeling about reporters dipping into and out of the race story fell somewhere between amusement and irritation. "I think I know what commands a Southerner's respect, and so many people never do," he wrote the *Times'* managing editor, Turner Catledge, in mid-1955. "Still the boys, very talented ones, come down this way and pour a few drinks and search out the story, but they never understand the technique of getting a box of candy and going to the home and paying your respects to the wives and children."[17]

Popham had purposely spent his time in the South seeking out and writing about "voices of sanity," the progressives who saw hope for the South to avert its own self-destruction. Popham's coverage shed light on a region that had been ignored in news reports. Popham's South was multidimensional, of freely differing minds. It was also sanguine in the extreme. In 1949, Popham gave a speech in New York that was so hopeful about race relations in the South that the *Times'* headline on a story about the talk said, CIVIL RIGHTS FIGHT FOUND BEING WON. Now, six years later, he was saying the same thing. His soundings before the Till trial led him to report that "overridingly, the white community of Mississippi reacted to Till's slaying with sincere and vehement expressions of outrage. From one end of the state to the other, newspaper editorials denounced the killing, demanded swift retributive justice and warned that Mississippians could defend their theories of separation of the races only if the law enforcement machinery was geared to equal justice for both races." He added, "Perhaps to a depth hitherto unknown in Mississippi race-relations annals, Negroes working in white homes and in downtown stores and in restaurants heard on every side a strong and vigorous condemnation by white people, friend and stranger alike, of brutality in race relations."[18]

In Atlanta, the *Constitution* editor, Ralph McGill, read Popham's preview of the trial and concluded that Popham and the *Times* had done a "national service" by showing a South not often seen in the North. In the days that followed, his close reading of trial coverage in newspapers and magazines convinced him that Popham, both in his writing and in his "extracurricular job" of interpreting "the several 'Souths' " to other reporters, had set the tone for everyone else's coverage.[19]

The southern vision that Popham described, and his own delightful personality, served to deflate a lot of antipathy for the *Times*. Other reporters were often amazed at Popham's reach. When Robert E. Lee Baker of *The Washington Post* did a long tour of the South around that time, he decided to veer from the beaten path and drive deep into the Mississippi Delta. When the road turned to dirt, he kept going, looking for the spirit of a South untainted by modernity, by technology, by news. At a dusty crossroads, he spied a little general store and saw the prototypical white, Old South porch sitter idling away the afternoon. Baker got out of his car and walked up to the man. "I'm Bob Baker of *The Washington Post,*" he began.

"That a newspaper?" the man asked.

"Yeah," Baker replied.

"Oh. You know Johnny Popham of *The New York Times*?"[20]

In the highest government and academic circles in the various states of the South, Popham's coverage helped solidify his position as a dominant figure in southern journalism. As the Till trial neared, it was Popham who landed a lunch with the trial judge before jury selection; and it was Popham, at the judge's request, who found himself serving as unofficial liaison between a judge who truly intended to run a fair trial and a visiting press corps that was rolling into town like lava.[21]

The trial coverage was immensely competitive for the dailies in Till's hometown, so the *Chicago Tribune, Chicago Sun-Times,* and *Chicago Daily News* all sent reporters to Sumner. The *St. Louis Post-Dispatch* staffed the story every day, and *The Detroit News* was there because one of the nation's few Negro congressmen, Charles Diggs of Detroit, was attending the trial. Reporters representing newspapers in London and Toronto came to town.

Word circulated quickly that William Faulkner, who had begun to make conflicting and contentious statements about race, had come down from Oxford. But it was just Clark Porteous, a reporter for the *Memphis Press-Scimitar* and former Nieman fellow, whose full hair, mustache, pipe, and Faulknerian mien frequently led to such confusion in north Mississippi.[22] Porteous might have been just another run-of-the-mill southern reporter with standard southern prejudices except for one reporting experience: in 1935, in Slayden, Mississippi, he had stood a short distance from a mob of fifty white men as they drove a Model T Ford into a schoolyard, propped an abducted, hymn-singing Negro man, A. B. Young, on the back of the auto, fitted his neck snugly with a noose that was tied tightly at the other end to a limb of an oak tree, then drove the car away.[23] Porteous had traveled frequently with the NAACP executive secretary, Walter White, to investigate such lynchings in the South, and had won the respect of Negro leaders and activists in north Mississippi.

Porteous would prove tireless and resourceful in his coverage. Writing for an afternoon paper, he would spend his morning running into and out of the courtroom filing updates to rewrite men and taking photographs with a heavy 4×5 Speed Graphic camera, the kind where you slam a film pack into the back, pull a tab, and shoot, blinding your subject with the flash. To get the film to the *Press-Scimitar,* Porteous would race out to the highway and flag down Memphis-bound truckers until he found one willing, for five dollars, to carry his film to a Memphis hotel, where a copyboy would pick it up.[24]

Porteous's chief rival, the largest-circulation newspaper in north Mississippi, *The Commercial Appeal* of Memphis, sent down four newsmen. The largest-circulation paper in south Mississippi, the New Orleans *Times-Picayune,* sent Wilson F. "Bill" Minor, who, after seven years as the newspaper's bureau chief in Jackson was about to encounter a story as engaging as his first assignment in the state, the funeral of Theodore Bilbo. Hodding Carter, Jr., sent a reporter to cover the trial for his *Delta Democrat-Times* in nearby Greenville. But most of the Mississippi press skipped it and relied on the wire services.

The *Jackson Daily News* sent two reporters, neither of whom was nearly as pure a segregationist as their editor, Sullens. Jim Featherston, who the previous year had been a member of the tiny *Sunday Post-Herald* of Vicksburg, which had won a Pulitzer Prize for coverage of a devastating tornado, was assigned to write the main story, hitting three deadlines a day for the afternoon paper. W. C. "Dub" Shoemaker, who at age twenty-four had already been working for the *Jackson Daily News* for five years, was assigned sidebars and photo coverage.

Remarkably, their estranged sister paper, the Jackson *Clarion-Ledger,* the biggest Mississippi-published daily, decided to rely on the Associated Press for its main coverage and sent one reporter to write sidebars. The upstart *State Times* sent two reporters.

Local television and radio reporters came down from Memphis and up from New Orleans and Jackson. The three television networks—NBC, CBS, and ABC—arranged to turn a field in nearby Tutwiler into a landing strip for private planes that picked up film and flew it to editing rooms and broadcast studios in New York.[25]

Even more startling to residents of Sumner was the presence of Negro reporters and photographers. The Negro residents, especially, observed the visiting black journalists with awe: these people were decidedly different in appearance and behavior. On this assignment, these reporters did not throw on rumpled work clothes as they sometimes had to do when reporting alone in the South; they wore their Sunday best, every day. They seemed to be able to have professional relationships, even something resembling eye-to-eye friendships, with their white colleagues.[26]

Simeon Booker, wearing a bow tie and suit, arrived from Washington for *Ebony* and *Jet* and was met by the photographer David Jackson and the reporter Cloyte Murdock, sent from Chicago by Johnson Publications.

James Hicks, who would later be executive editor of the *Amsterdam News* of New York, came for the *Afro-American* newspapers, which blanketed much of the mid-Atlantic seaboard. The president of the company that owned *The St. Louis Argus,* Nannie Mitchell-Turner, dispatched herself and two others to cover the trial. *The Pittsburgh Courier* sent its national editor, Robert Ratcliffe, who was Negro, and a reporter, James Boyack, who was white.

Because Till was from Chicago, the *Chicago Defender* had already taken a special, almost personal interest in the story. Nine of the ten stories on the front page of its September 10 issue were about Till; the next week, all but four paragraphs on page one concerned the case. The coverage sometimes went overboard; its caption with a photograph of Carolyn Bryant said, "The Cause of It All." Its stories frequently overlapped and repeated one another. It clearly was sympathetic to Till, his mother, Uncle Mose Wright, and the plight of southern Negroes. Yet the newspaper did not simply abandon all journalistic balance. In a way that was inconceivable in most of the white southern press, the *Defender* engaged in crossover journalism, reporting the story in both the white and Negro communities. While the southern white press did not send a reporter to Chicago to learn more about Till, to interview his family and witnesses to the abduction who had fled to Chicago, or to cover the funeral, the *Defender* did much of its reporting in the white community and asked some tough questions in the Negro community. It got Mississippi Governor Hugh White on the phone for an interview, and when doubts were raised about whether the body was truly Till's, it asked Mrs. Bradley a series of challenging questions. It also exposed some Negroes who were profiteering from the Till death by setting up a collection that falsely claimed to have NAACP sanction.

Because of a bold, strategic move by the *Defender* four years earlier, the newspaper was poised to beat all others on the story. In 1951, the Sengstacke family, which published the *Chicago Defender,* had set into motion a difficult and enduring battle with the other major Negro newspaper family, the Scotts of Atlanta. In that year, the Sengstackes had launched the *Tri-State Defender* in Memphis as a direct challenge to the *Memphis World,* published by the much more conservative Scott family, which also owned the *Atlanta Daily World* and the *Birmingham World.* While the *Memphis World* was reserved, reluctant, and Republican, the *Tri-State Defender* was aggressive, gregarious, and Democrat.

To raise the flag over their new paper and to send the message that it was ready to compete, the Sengstackes sent one of their most trusted reporters and editors, L. Alex Wilson, to serve as general manager in Memphis. Wilson moved quickly to establish the *Tri-State Defender* as essential reading for anyone interested in politics in Memphis, where Negroes were allowed to assert more influence than in just about any other Deep South city.[27]

Wilson's colleagues marveled at his ability to work his way inside fortresses of white power and come out with something without seeming to compromise anything. He was forthright and persuasive, and saw through smoke screens. Many credited Wilson's editorial endorsement with swinging enough Negro votes that a challenger was able to oust the incumbent in the 1955 Memphis mayor's race. Under Wilson's guidance, the *Tri-State Defender* was steadfast in its pursuit of equal opportunity and maintained a healthy sense of outrage. When Ralph Bunche was hauled before Congress and asked if he were a Communist, Wilson's *Defender* warned, "The Statue of Liberty will be next."[28]

The Sengstackes got more than a good Memphis paper out of the deal. They got a newspaper perfectly positioned in time and geography to cover the dawn of the civil rights activities in the region, "as if cued to appear by some divine plan," Alex Wilson's wife, herself a newspaperwoman, would write later.[29] When the Till case broke, the Sengstackes decided that no one knew the Mississippi Delta as well as their own Memphis staff, which had been covering voting and civil rights activities in north Mississippi.

To join him in reporting the Till trial, Wilson tapped his most experienced man, Moses J. Newson, a twenty-eight-year-old graduate of the same journalism school Wilson had attended, Lincoln University in Missouri. More personally binding, however, was that both Wilson and Newson were from nearby towns in central Florida, where racial discrimination was only slightly less virulent than in southern Alabama. In the same way that Emmett Till would become the most defining event in the childhood lives of Negro children in Mississippi, the terrifying story of Claude Neal had made an indelible impression on the lives of Negro residents in north and central Florida. Newson had been seven years old in 1934 when Claude Neal was tortured and lynched in Marianna, a north Florida town not far from Alabama and Georgia. Neal, who was accused of having killed a white woman, was scalded repeatedly with a hot iron, castrated, and dragged through the streets before being stretched and displayed in a tree. This had not been an impulse lynching; newspaper and radio stories had given advance notice of it. As Neal was being hauled by a mob from an Alabama jail to Marianna, a crowd estimated at about four thousand had time to get to the scene. By some accounts, he was forced to eat his own genitals, and his finger and toes were put on display in the town.[30] It was a story that haunted the Negroes of north and central Florida for decades.

In his third year with the *Tri-State Defender,* Newson had been covering voting rights and related stories in north Mississippi, working many of those stories with Ernest Withers, a Memphis freelance photographer whom the

Defender newspapers hired to cover the Till trial. In Withers, Newson felt he had more than a photographer; he had a man with good antennae and a sharp sense of danger. Before becoming a professional photographer, Withers had achieved a completely unrelated distinction in Memphis history: in 1948, he had been in the first group of nine Negro men selected as police officers in Memphis, which entitled them to do all the things that white police officers did, except one: arrest white people. Withers had stayed with the police force three years, then turned his sideline of photography into his occupation, which provided him steady work covering the civil rights activities in north Mississippi.[31]

The courthouse where the trial was to be held sat in the town square and was a three-story Gothic-style gray-brick building with an adjoining clock tower. On the courthouse lawn stood a statue of a Confederate soldier whose stance confounded visitors. Was he saluting with his left hand or shading his eyes to sharpen his view of the invading Yankees?

Bryant and Milam would be tried on the second floor of the fifty-three-year-old courthouse in a room that had space for 156 spectators, not including those who lined the green plaster walls or sat on the deep sills of the tall windows. The trial would be held beneath bare lightbulbs that hung from the ceiling and two wooden-blade fans that moved too slowly to clear the fog of cigarette and cigar smoke. The courtroom had a wood railing that separated the judge, jury, defendants, lawyers, and press from the general spectators. The benches and chairs were all wood, and most of the chairs had cane backs and seats. With temperatures reaching 95 degrees outside, the judge urged men to shed their coats.

As the trial opened, Sheriff H. C. Strider, who fit the stereotype of the swaggering, side-talking, potbellied, autocratic sheriff, declared that Negro reporters would not be permitted to cover the trial from inside the court-room. That was not a surprise. More than 63 percent of Tallahatchie County's population was Negro, but not a single Negro person was registered to vote; therefore, none was allowed to sit on a jury. (Women were not permitted on state juries, either.)

Negro reporters and a handful of white journalists made polite appeals to the presiding circuit court judge, Curtis Swango. The judge said Negro reporters should be given access to the trial but had a disagreement with the sheriff over who would control such courtroom details.[32] Strider was a man who liked control, and he used it all over town. He had a 1,500-acre cotton farm, tended with the help of thirty-five Negro families who lived as tenants on his property and purchased their food and supplies at his store. On the roofs of the seven tenant homes that stretched along the driveway to his house, he had painted letters, one letter per roof, to spell out S-T-R-I-D-E-R. A better vantage of the roofs came from the three crop-dusting airplanes he owned.

Under pressure from Judge Swango, the sheriff begrudgingly changed his mind and permitted the Negro reporters in. "We haven't mixed the races so far in Mississippi," he told reporters, "and we don't intend to." The Negro reporters, as well as Till's mother and the visiting Negro congressman, Charles Diggs, would be required to sit at a long table set up in the spectator section, not inside the railing, where the testimony could be more easily heard.

Judge Swango allowed the Negro newspeople the same latitude to enter and leave the courtroom as the white journalists had. Negro photographers were given the same opportunity to take pictures before and between court sessions as white photographers. There would be no such warmth from Sheriff Strider. In an atmosphere *The New York Times* described as "controlled hostility," his morning greeting set the tone for the day. As he walked into the crowded courtroom, his 270 pounds cleaving groups of spectators, Strider turned to the white reporters and said, "Mawning, ladies and gentlemen." Half nodding to the Negro reporters, he said, "Mawning, nigguhs."[33]

The prosecutor, District Attorney Gerald Chatham, didn't have much to go on. He had no witnesses and no murder weapon. Investigators had made none of the obvious ownership links with the fan or barbed wire, and nobody had any idea where Till had been killed or even if the trial was being held in the proper county.

The most intense spotlight of the pretrial stories therefore turned on Mose Wright, a quiet, work-worn sixty-four-year-old cotton picker known around town as "Preacher" because he served as pastor of a little church. It was Wright who lived with the memory of watching Bryant and Milam haul his great-nephew away that night; it was Wright who had pleaded with them to understand that the youngster hadn't known what he was saying and was just exhibiting some youthful exuberance. Soon after Till was abducted, Wright's wife had sought safety in Chicago, but Wright had stayed on. He sharecropped twenty-five acres of land with a German-American man who always gave him his fair share of the proceeds and was willing to keep Wright working through all the commotion.[34]

Reporters, Negro and white, flocked to Wright's unpainted, four-room home, which was mounted on cinder blocks. They were awed by the calm of this slight man, who didn't show the fear and superstitions he said he held. Interviewing him on his porch, Negro and northern white reporters would feel a chill as they saw suspicious cars pull toward Wright's house, then move slowly past. Wright would detect their nervousness. "Don't worry," he said to one jittery reporter. "It is all right here."[35]

When it became clear that Wright was the state's best witness and that the case would ride on whether or not this small, leathery field hand would violate southern tradition and publicly accuse two white men of abducting and killing a Negro teenager, there arose a tension in the town and a dread in the courtroom that something terrible could go wrong. Even with the latitude that the judge permitted—smoking allowed, colas passed around, deputies coming in and out with pitchers of ice water, the Bryant and Milam children romping playfully in the aisles—the strict regimen that guided race relations in the South tensed the courtroom. At one point, a glass bottle fell from a spectator's hand, sounding like a gunshot as it shattered on the wood floor. In a single motion, everyone ducked.[36]

At another point, the implausibility of Sheriff Strider's own testimony drove Cloyte Murdock to bolt from the reporters' table during a break and approach Judge Swango. Strider had maintained that the body found in the river was not Till's, that someone working on behalf of the NAACP had planted the ring of Till's late father on the finger of another corpse and thrown it into the river. Strider testified that Till was probably living in Detroit, that the decomposed body had been in the river considerably longer than Till was alleged to have been dead, and that the body was so decomposed that he couldn't tell if it was that of a Negro man or a white one. Incensed, Murdock rushed to the bench and asked Judge Swango: If Strider didn't know whether the body was Negro or white, why had he called a Negro undertaker to handle the remains?[37]

The prosecutor, Chatham, would go a step further. When the physician who had examined the body for the county testified that he could not tell if the corpse was that of a white man or a Negro man, Chatham prompted a silent cheer at the Negro press table when he scoffed and said, "We're wasting an awful lot of money in our schools educating people who can't tell a white man from a Negro. I don't want anybody filling prescriptions who can't tell black from white."

On both sides—law enforcement and the Negro press—there was fear of vigilantism in the courtroom. The Negro reporters decided among themselves that if Wright's identification of Bryant and Milam sparked any violent reaction, Jimmy Hicks of the *Amsterdam News* was to grab a gun from the bailiff seated near the Negro press table, while another was to help Murdock escape out the window. Then they would pick up chairs and force their way out of the courtroom.[38]

When Mose Wright took the stand, he was a slight figure in yellow-and-brown suspenders, a bright white shirt, and a thin black tie. The pictures that newspapers had published of him had typically been shot from below, looking up, portraying Wright as tall, almost giant. But when the district attorney asked Wright to identify the men who had come onto his porch that night, the man who rose from the cane-seated witness chair in the hushed court-room barely topped five feet, six inches. Against the six-foot-two, 235-pound man he was asked to accuse, J. W. Milam, Wright was "a black pigmy standing up to a white ox," Murray Kempton wrote down.[39]

Mose Wright, his chin up, stood slightly on his toes, extended his arm toward the defendants, pointed his finger at Milam's cold, stoic face, and said, "There he is; that's the man." For Roy Bryant, he had a similar designation.[40] Wright's identification of Milam and Bryant only corroborated their own acknowledgment that they had come to Wright's porch and taken Till. But the *Jackson Daily News* wasn't conceding anything. A headline writer went deep into testimony about the lighting conditions that morning and crafted this headline to run six columns across the front page: DIM LIGHT CASTS SOME DOUBT ON IDENTITY OF TILL'S ABDUCTORS.

If the reporters were a bit less interested in Wright's testimony by the time he took the stand, it was not merely because they had heard it before. It was also because several of them, Negro and white, had been receiving some stunning information that the prosecution itself did not have. On the night of the first day of the trial, Simeon Booker, L. Alex Wilson, Jimmy Hicks, and Clark Porteous had gotten phone calls from the most respected Negro physician and surgeon in the Delta, Dr. T. R. M. Howard of Mound Bayou. Howard, who was active in the NAACP and head of a state organization of Negro leaders, urged the reporters to come to his office as soon as they could. Cloyte Murdock was also there, as well as Jim Featherston and Dub Shoemaker of the *Jackson Daily News*.[41] There, Howard revealed that a Negro field hand had come to him earlier in the day with information that there were Negro witnesses—five, probably—who had seen Till in a truck with Milam, Bryant, two other white men, and two other Negro men long after the defendants said they had released him. Now, Howard told the shocked reporters, the field hand had disappeared.

There was more, Howard said. The witnesses had heard Till being smacked, then screaming, inside a closed barn. They had heard him fall deathly silent. Later, the witnesses had seen a tractor removed from the barn. A truck had moved in. The truck had then come rolling out with a tarpaulin spread over its back. Among the witnesses were Negro men who had been inside the barn. These witnesses, Howard reported, had also vanished.[42]

Howard wanted the Negro reporters to find the witnesses—were they hiding, or had they been taken somewhere against their will?—and persuade them to assist the prosecution. That would not be easy, and not simply because the witnesses were afraid to testify against white men. There was another, larger matter that the witnesses would have to confront within themselves: Howard's tipster revealed that one or two of them were Negro field hands who had been forced by Milam and Bryant to clean the blood from the killing floor of the barn and to help haul the body away.

Howard wanted the white reporters to discreetly tell law enforcement and the prosecutors that other witnesses had been identified and would be turned over. All the reporters agreed to withhold publication of any information about the existence of the witnesses, at least for a day or so.

The search began, but not as planned. While white reporters did contact law enforcement officers and the district attorney, they also joined Negro reporters in the all-night pursuit of the witnesses. Law enforcement, not surprisingly, found out what was going on and soon began searching as well. Sheriffs from Leflore and Sunflower counties made Negro reporters part of their search efforts, putting them in their cars to travel the back roads of the Delta. The Negro reporters' role was to persuade the witnesses to help. There would be no force and no warrants. The sheriffs would provide them a guarantee of protection.

For one night and much of the next day, in what Simeon Booker saw as "an incredible interracial manhunt,"[43] cars of white deputy sheriffs and white and Negro reporters kicked up dust and gravel as they rolled through the high cotton and onto plantations, knocked on doors, and asked questions. Three witnesses were found; two were not. The next day, based on information conveyed to him by Porteous, the district attorney asked the judge for a continuance so the new witnesses could be interviewed. When the three took the stand, they were able to testify that, from a distance, they had seen Till in a truck with three white men and two Negro men long after Bryant and Milam said they had released Till. They testified that they had heard loud and repeated "hollering" and the sound of a beating from inside the barn of a farm managed by Milam's brother. One witness said he had seen Milam, wearing a pistol, emerge from the shed, get a drink of water, then return to the barn. Two witnesses who were not located until after the trial were the two who purportedly had been on the truck with Till, been inside the barn, seen the evidence of the killing, and helped clean up the mess.

In the end, the reporters handed the prosecutors witnesses and a case they didn't have, slightly raising hope that the jury might find the defendants guilty. In his closing, the prosecutor, Chatham, said that Bryant and Milam had had every right to discipline young Till. "As a Southerner born and bred, I know the worst possible punishment for this boy was to take a razor strap, turn him over a barrel and give him a little whipping." But to kill the boy, Chatham said, was unconscionable. The defense attorneys, who had not put either defendant on the stand, made a direct appeal to the racial heritage of the men on the jury. One attorney called the jurors "custodians of American civilization," and said, "your forefathers would turn over in their graves" if the jury brought guilty verdicts.[44]

As the jury began deliberations, the Negro reporters could take some solace that they had survived the week in Sumner unscathed. Jimmy Hicks had had a run-in with law enforcement when he had tried to pass a school bus in his car. He said at the time that he had been treated courteously by a deputy sheriff and released. Two of his white colleagues later told a somewhat different account. Popham said he had had to intervene with the judge to win Hicks's release.[45] Featherston said he had inadvertently entered a room where a deputy sheriff was waving a gun at Hicks and yelling about his traffic transgression. The deputy was jittery and blurting out that he didn't know what to do. Featherston had calmly told the deputy to put the gun away, and he did.[46]

The jury of ten farmers, an insurance man, and a dragline operator took sixty-seven minutes to return its verdict of not guilty. "If we hadn't stopped to drink pop," said one juror, "it wouldn't have taken that long."[47] Popping flashbulbs caught the smiling faces and embraces of the Bryants and Milams.

The press corps that had covered the Till trial was hardly out of town before one of the more unusual journalists of the time, William Bradford Huie, was working his way into an extraordinary, secret meeting with Roy and Carolyn Bryant and J. W. Milam. To most everyone else, the Till story was over and done. To Huie, it was just beginning. "I'm in the truth business," Huie liked to say. He had come to town to get it, and he was willing to pay for it.

Huie was a tenth-generation north Alabamian who had sold 40 million books, hosted one of the first national television interview programs, edited one of the most prestigious national magazines, and broken some of the biggest national news stories. A product of the Alabama public school system and a Phi Beta Kappa at the University of Alabama, Huie had jumped into the newspaper business in Birmingham in 1931 and lasted five years before breaking free of the sure paycheck and risking it all on his own entrepreneurial skills. He had started and folded magazines and newspapers, written his first novel, *Mud on the Stars,* then jumped to the big leagues, joining H. L. Mencken and *American Mercury* magazine as a writer, then associate editor. In World War II, he had been a Seabee, taking part in the D-day invasion at Omaha Beach; when he got out, he had headed to the Pacific theater as a war correspondent. The military and the war had provided him fodder that he recycled into both fiction and nonfiction books for years to come.

He tried his hand in television, hosting the *Chronoscope,* forerunner of *Meet the Press,* from 1951 to 1953. At the same time, he was finishing his first well-known novel, *The Revolt of Mamie Stover,* and succeeding Mencken as editor of *American Mercury.* Next came *The Execution of Private Slovik,* about the soldier who during World War II became the only American since the Civil War executed for deserting the military. When he had first read something about Slovik, he scratched out a note to himself: "The *one* man in such a situation always deserves to be known," he wrote. "Someday I must dig him up."[48]

Huie spent his professional life digging, writing, and marketing. He saw stories in everything, and the only decision was whether to play it straight and write a nonfiction account or develop a fictionalized version. Critics who had no problem with the influence of real-world events on his novels sometimes questioned whether fiction was influencing some of his nonfiction. No one ever questioned his tenacity. He faithfully followed advice he said had been given to him by W. Somerset Maugham: Never let a day go by without writing something.[49] And when the writing was done, he was a dogged pursuer of deals. He always had deals going for this book or that screenplay, this magazine piece or that movie. He had deals moving forward, deals being delayed, deals awaiting tax rulings, and deals simply falling apart.[50]

Huie slipped into Sumner a week after Bryant and Milam lighted their victory cigars, then talked his way into the law office of J. J. Breland and John Whitten, the lead defense attorneys. Huie didn't leave until five hours later. He felt camaraderie with them, felt like he was a member of the lodge, as he put it, a part of the network of good ole boys who worried almost as much about keeping the rednecks and peckerwoods in line as they did about keeping a foot on the neck of the niggers. Huie had graduated from the University of Alabama, their sheepskins came from the University of Mississippi; Breland was sixty-five, Whitten thirty-five, Huie between them at forty-five. They could match one another's bourbon intake and not lose track of the story. When Huie was ready to get straight to the issue and talk from the heart, so were they.

Huie saw that the defendants meant nothing to the lawyers. Breland called Roy Bryant just a "scrappin' pine-knot with nuthin'." Milam, he said, was a bootlegger and scofflaw whom his own law firm had had to sue on occasion. "He comes from a big, mean, overbearing family," Breland told Huie. "Got a chip on his shoulder. That's how he got that battlefield promotion in Europe: He likes to kill folks. But hell, we've got to have our Milams to fight our wars and keep the niggahs in line."[51]

Therein was the lawyers' interest in having Milam and Bryant explain how they had killed Till. The lawyers had not heard the story, had never asked Bryant and Milam if they had done it, but didn't harbor much doubt. Breland wanted their story to scare the living hell out of any Negro people who might be thinking of coming into Tallahatchie County. He wouldn't mind seeing a mass exodus among those who were already there. With mechanization in the cotton fields, the white man didn't need so many anymore. "If any more pressure is put on us," Breland told Huie, "the Tallahatchie River won't hold all the niggers that'll be thrown into it."[52]

Huie told them that he wanted to write a "step by step, hour by hour" account of the kidnapping, torture, execution and disposal of Emmett Till. He intended to write a story about "a community-approved murder," in which the trial became the mechanism not for seeking justice but for celebrating the white man's dominion.[53]

In exchange for "every last line of the truth" from Bryant and Milam and for complete releases to use their information, he told the lawyers, he would pay the defendants cash and a percentage of whatever he grossed from the story. He would keep their cooperation secret. He would not testify against them. He would write the story in a way that it could not be used as a confession.[54] He would, he decided, "leave the defendants in a position in their own community where they could deny having talked with me."[55]

What Huie did not have was a publisher or financial backer willing to fork over the several thousand dollars he planned to pay the defendants. Huie may well have believed that no publisher would get involved in paying Bryant and Milam because his first appeal for money, strangely, went to Roy Wilkins at the NAACP. And he must have thought that such an arrangement would forever remain more secret than the Manhattan Project, because nothing would have exploded the deal quicker than for Milam, Bryant, and their lawyers to find out that the money had come from that group.

In the end, that didn't matter because *Look* magazine was interested. The magazine's editorial director, Daniel D. Mich, wanted his own representative on hand when the defendants signed their releases and took the money. Huie was concerned that *Look* would send down some loud-mouthed New York pinstripe who would sweep into Sumner, show offense at the rednecks, and wreck the deal. He sent Mich basic pointers: "I hope you'll cast your emissary with some care. If he doesn't speak the language, he should at least be an Anglo who can drink bourbon straight out of the bottle without making a face, and who can *enjoy* maybe a meal and an hour's 'good fellowship' with me and Bryant and Milam and Breland."

Two pages later, he was again expressing worry about the New York companion who would be thrust upon him: "Warn your man that I am not a 'liberal'; that I only write about the human race. I don't try to reform it; that my sympathies encompass the Bryants and the Milams; and that I am capable of drinking out of the same jug with Milam and letting him drink first."[56]

Huie got the interviews with Bryant, Milam, and Carolyn Bryant. He came away rattled by their description. Milam and Bryant had not killed Till simply because he had insulted Carolyn Bryant or humiliated Roy Bryant in the eyes of his Negro customers who knew of the incident; they had killed him because, in their threatened minds, Till stood for the much larger, more complicated insult to white people. Huie could see that even their younger attorney, Whitten, found their story shattering.[57] For a total payment of $3,150 to the Bryants and Milam, and $1,260 to the law firm, he got signed releases. The agreement gave Huie extremely wide latitude: "This includes the right to report any and all of the details of my private life and that of my family, and to describe me, my character and actions in such manner as Mr. Huie, in his sole judgment, believes to be accurate. This includes the right to portray me as one of those persons who was in some manner connected with the abduction and killing of the negro, Emmett Till."[58]

The story was published in January 1956 under the headline THE SHOCK-ING STORY OF APPROVED KILLING IN MISSISSIPPI. It was extraordinary by any standard, for several reasons: it was a detailed, narrative reenactment showing how Bryant and Milam had beaten, tortured, killed, and submerged Till. Neither the author nor the magazine ever stepped outside the narrative to say, with any journalistic detachment, that Bryant and Milam had been interviewed for the story, that they had confessed to the murders, or that the series of events reported in the story had come from them—even though at a couple of key places they were quoted, seemingly out of thin air, explaining their reactions during the ordeal.

The account varied in some key respects from the testimony of the prosecution witnesses, and from statements Bryant and Milam had made before the trial about the abduction of Till.[59] In any case, Milam and Bryant were portrayed in the story as intending only to "whip" Till with Milam's Colt .45 automatic pistol and to "scare some sense into him." Till, they told Huie, even after being smashed and beaten, had remained mouthy and wouldn't retreat from his claim that he had "had" white women.

"Well, what else could we do?" Milam asked. "He was hopeless. I'm no bully; I never hurt a nigger in my life. I like niggers—in their place—I know how to work 'em. But I just decided it was time a few people got put on notice. As long as I live and can do anything about it, niggers are gonna stay in their place. Niggers ain't gonna vote where I live. If they did, they'd control the government. They ain't gonna go to school with my kids. And when a nigger even gets close to mentioning sex with a white woman, he's tired o' living. I'm likely to kill him. Me and my folks fought for this country, and we've got some rights. I stood there in that shed and listened to that nigger throw that poison at me, and I just made up my mind. 'Chicago boy,' I said, 'I'm tired of 'em sending your kind down here to stir up trouble. Goddam you, I'm going to make an example of you—just so everybody can know how me and my folks stand.' "

Milam and Bryant had gone to a ginning company looking for a metal fan, three feet high, that Milam had seen discarded. It was daylight, so Milam got worried that someone might see them and accuse them—not of brutalizing Till, but of stealing the fan. Till was ordered to load the fan into the truck. They drove to the steep bank of the Tallahatchie River and ordered Till to take off all his clothes.

"You still as good as I am?" Milam asked.

"Yeah," said Till.

"You've still 'had' white women?"

"Yeah."

The bullet from Milam's .45 tore through Till's head at the right ear. They wrapped the barbed wire around the fan, then around his neck. They rolled him into the river and went home.

When the magazine hit the stands, the denials, as expected, as *planned,* came swiftly from Milam and Bryant. No, they hadn't said those things, hadn't spent any time with Huie, certainly hadn't commited the murders or confessed to them, they told reporters. Yes, they added, they would definitely be talking with their lawyers about what they could do. It was all part of the charade.[60]

The syndicated columnist John Temple Graves wrote that his fellow Alabamian was a "notorious author" who had been allowed "to tell the murder story as he imagines it—and he is a masterly and dastardly imaginist." Among the newspapers that ran Graves's column was the Charleston *News and Courier,* whose editor, Waring, had already written that Huie's article was "a wretched piece of journalism" that "appears to be no more than Mr. Huie's imagination."

Huie was outraged. The attacks were wrong, and they were wrong in a dozen or more newspapers in the South that regularly ran Graves's column. Graves, born in Georgia but educated at Horace Mann School in New York, then at Princeton University, had been a 1930s liberal and opponent of the Klan who had swung emphatically to the segregationist side when he became offended that Negro leaders and editors pressed for domestic racial equality in the midst of World War II. Now, in his sixties and syndicated from the *Birmingham Post-Herald,* Graves had become a specialist in defending "The Southern Way of Life." Huie demanded that Graves retract his statement: "Back up, admit that you have gone off half-cocked, and apologize. If not, I'll see you in court."[61]

After several weeks of angry correspondence and legal threats, Huie, through a lawyer, was able to show Graves that he had had access to Bryant and Milam. Graves issued a correction for all the newspapers to run.[62] Waring later wrote Huie privately to acknowledge something he did not write in public: that the *Look* story had caused him to "readjust" his thinking on the Till case. "At first I was shocked and maybe angry at the stark and unattributed story you told," he wrote Huie. After thinking about it, "I am coming to the conclusion that you did, as you say, render a service in puncturing the mystery. I am a believer in telling the truth, no matter where it may lead."[63]

There were incalculably important lessons to be learned from Huie's story. Huie showed the value of aggressive, gumshoe reporting on the race story. He showed that reporting could and should operate independently of law enforcement in trying to find the truth behind racial killings. He showed that men like Reverend George W. Lee and Lamar Smith should not go to their graves without some journalistic effort to ferret out the truth behind their murders.

Huie, who would spend all but a dozen of his seventy-six years in his little hometown of Hartselle and other North Alabama towns, also showed that there was a significant role for the white press, even southern white reporters. His innate familiarity with the race subject and the southern people had permitted him to establish relationships with sources that in effect proved how valuable beat coverage could be to the race story. He showed that the lazy practice of starting and ending coverage at the trial was not good enough. He showed what every newspaper editor and reporter knew instinctively: that there was a story behind the story, and that the hidden story was accessible.

For John Popham, the Till trial was a low point. He was pleased that his coverage, painting a South of variegated beliefs, had been well received. He came away feeling that the judge and the prosecutor, white men with deep southern roots, had been fair and responsible. But Popham also felt discouraged because the story of the South had become so focused on race and the pressure to take sides had become so intense. The lines were being drawn with stark clarity, eliminating from the public debate a large swath of intellectual leaders whose sensible, moderate-to-progressive ideas and understandings about the future of the South formed the essence of Popham's thinking. He feared that people of goodwill would be barked back into the corners and would find it easier to be quiet and fade away, making it more difficult for him and other reporters to represent their enlightened views in the paper.

"I rather think our handling of the Till case may be the last time anyone is going to be able to get out and get decent respect for balanced coverage," he lamented in a letter to Turner Catledge. "It just isn't going to be possible again, sad to report. I am convinced there is no reporter who again for some time will honestly be able to do justice to all that is erupting there. You can't search it out anymore, it is too complicated now and you will have to let the passions run high for the time it takes to find reason again."[64]

More disturbing to him was the fear that the *Times* would change the course and pace he had set and direct him to churn out more stories about racial antagonism. Popham wanted to keep covering the high-minded stories on regional education projects, the transition from an agricultural to an industrial economy, nuclear energy development, scientific discoveries, academic trends, and the postwar cultural evolution in the South. Race, of course, would be the inevitable subplot to his stories, he wrote, because he would treat academic breakthroughs at Fisk College no differently from agricultural discoveries at Mississippi State. And he would write about events and situations, many in academic settings, where Negroes and whites came together, not where they fell apart.

Popham alerted Catledge that he might soon see a rash of race stories from other newspapers and magazines and intimated that he hoped Catledge would not overreact and change the *Times'* direction. *The Reporter* magazine had been encamped in the Mississippi Delta for a few weeks, he wrote, and the New York *Daily News* was roaming the region to write a Citizens' Council story. Popham was troubled by the hit-and-run stories they would produce. "Of course, they have no intention of doing anything else in the South from day to day and month to month, just one hot, juicy case (and it is a nasty thing) and they will look good to all the northern groups, so fearless and public-like." He suggested that someone from the New York staff be sent down to help on race stories.[65]

Catledge received the letter just after a visit to the South, where he had met with newspaper editors. He was disturbed by what he had heard and seemed for the moment uncertain how his newspaper should proceed. "I came away from the place not only depressed but frightened," he wrote Popham. "I am really afraid. The thing has deteriorated so rapidly since I was last there that it is impossible to measure the extent of it. Emotion has taken place of all reason, and you know what sensitive people are liable to do when they get emotionally stirred up."

Catledge said he would not be surprised to see a number of lynchings in the next year or so. "These damn citizen's councils are also applying economic pressure where it really hurts and people with any sense of decency and justice are running for cover," he wrote.

For Catledge, the emergence of the councils only crystallized the urgency of the race story. His instincts told him his newspaper should be all over the emerging situation, including an examination of the Citizens' Councils. But Popham made a good case for not being swallowed up by it. Catledge acceded to Popham's definition of the beat, but tentatively. "I think your idea of coverage from our standpoint is the right one for the time being,"

CHAPTER 8

WHERE MASSIVE AND PASSIVE

RESISTANCE MEET

Massive and passive resistance were born ten days apart in the same incubator of the South.

Massive resistance emerged on the editorial pages of the *Richmond News Leader* on November 21, 1955. In the weeks that followed, the idea was welcomed with great excitement as it rolled across the South.

Passive resistance was ushered into the world quietly on December 1, 1955, greeted the next day by a five-paragraph news story at the bottom of page nine of the *Montgomery Advertiser* beneath the headline "Negro Jailed Here for 'Overlooking' Bus Segregation."[1]

Massive resistance was delivered by James Jackson Kilpatrick, the young, brash Richmond newspaper editor who christened it "interposition," after a 157-year old doctrine. Interposition was presented on that day—and for the next six weeks—in the form of lengthy, pedantic and passionate editorials that declared the right and obligation of the individual states to stand between the people and their federal government in order to take back powers seized unconstitutionally from the states.

Passive resistance was midwifed by a Negro seamstress and NAACP activist, Rosa Parks, who violated city ordinance and Alabama state law by refusing to give up her seat on a municipal bus to a white man. Her decision to challenge the laws inspired Montgomery's 48,000 Negro residents to launch a bus boycott that was immediately 90 percent effective and that continued for an extraordinary 381 days, constituting the first large-scale and enduring modern protest for Negro rights.

Both massive and passive resistance were conceived from the same seed: Supreme Court verdicts that upheld desegregation. Massive resisters sought to nullify such verdicts; passive resisters sought to expand them. Neither attracted much national attention. They differed in the attention they received in the South. As the tactic of interposition stormed through every southern state capital, the press covered it as if a supernatural force had been discovered to save a troubled region; but the birth of passive resistance received little notice.

Most newspapers and the emerging journalism on television showed their propensity to cover the hot and simple story, not the complex one; they were drawn to the raging fire, not to the slow burn, so the successful boycott on the Negro side of the racial line went on for weeks with little notice. Similarly, white newspapers both inside and outside the South took little note of the fact that more southern states had integrated institutions of higher learning than had not, and that peace and tranquillity prevailed at the colleges and universities that had admitted Negroes in Louisiana, Tennessee, Kentucky, Virginia, and other states. "Most newspapers seem to have forgotten that there is another side to the story," Ralph McGill complained in early 1956, "that Texas is going ahead with integration, that Arkansas is quiet, that North Carolina is quiet, that Tennessee is quiet, that southern Missouri, which is very Southern in attitude, is going with integration."[2]

One exception, but to a fault, was *The New York Times.* Following Turner Catledge's disturbing visit to the South in late 1955, the *Times* sent ten reporters into the seventeen southern states and the District of Columbia to take a measure of the region's willingness to accept desegregation. John Popham brought to the project a belief that his native land was educable and filled with progressive, creative people who were open to new ideas.

Popham spent a month with the five reporters who were assigned to the most critical areas and coordinated the tours of the others. Early on, he developed habits and reflexes that became a virtual rulebook, a set of commandments, on how to cover the South at public confrontational events: Stay back from the crowd while taking notes, don't let them see you do it. Hide your notebook when you're not using it. Dress casually, not as a dandy. Report in teams, never alone. Cover the segregationists, take their insults, and don't argue with them or provoke them. Keep your thoughts and emotions to yourself, no matter how ugly things get.[3]

During their tour of the South, Popham, with calls placed to the right people, made sure things were "red carpeted," as he put it, for the correspondents.[4] In Mississippi, he spent four days accompanying the *Times'* Los Angeles correspondent, Gladwin Hill, and introduced him to plantation owners and the Greenville editor Hodding Carter, Jr., before taking him to Starkville to meet the president of Mississippi State University, who had been Catledge's classmate there. They went to Tupelo, where they sat with another moderate newspaper editor, George McLean. Popham then spent four days in Georgia and South Carolina with *Times* reporter Russell Porter and two days in Florida with reporter Peter Kihss, and accompanied other reporters in North Carolina and Tennessee. The reporters met governors, federal judges, scholars. While not all the people interviewed were moderate, those who were staunchly segregationist were nonetheless mainstream civic leaders a few steps removed from ground zero of the resistance.[5]

The *Times'* eight-page, 50,000-word "Report on the South," a pull-out section, was published on March 13, 1956.[6] A front-page box promoting the report carried the headline "*Times* Study in South Finds Some Integration Progress." The story's introduction, written by Popham, was a detached, academic bit of fuzzy word craftsmanship that made it unclear how things were going and essentially failed to note that the region was about to explode. The rigidity and popular appeal of the hard-core segregationist movement and the determination of an increasingly emboldened Negro population were dismissed amid a lot of sociological camouflage. "This matter of coming to terms largely explains why many leaders in the South, including some who are directing resistance movements, believe that some form of racial integration is inevitable," Popham wrote.

Popham added that the South, while fundamentally segregationist, was defined by "the quiet, thoughtful and nonspectacular years of work invested in better race relations by thousands of Southerners and Northerners whose names have never made headlines and never will."[7]

The *Times'* report failed to measure the depth of the segregationist feeling. It did not see that the overwhelming success of the two-month-old Montgomery bus boycott—which it had covered almost entirely with small wire stories—was indicative of a civil rights movement that had no intention of quitting. By misreading the sentiment of the South at its extremes, it also failed to see that the extremes would soon be in control. It missed the resoluteness of the passive and massive resistance movements to do battle, if necessary.

Perhaps the most important influence of the *Times* report was on the *Times* itself. In evaluating how best to cover the unfolding race story, the newspaper's own conclusions misguided the editors and led them to some ill-advised decisions in their coverage of the South over the next two years.

The *Times'* failure did not distinguish it from the pack. The newsrooms of the southern newspapers where the stories of massive and passive resistance were playing out never got hold of the whole story in front of them. They had no sense of the depth of feeling on either side of the racial divide, had no idea who the leaders of the civil rights protests were, frequently misjudged the commitment and motives of the leaders on both sides, played fast and loose with the names and titles of anyone outside the white power circle, and sometimes served as adjunct investigative bodies for law enforcement in trying to squeeze out whodunit information about the leadership of the civil rights protests.

At the time the race story began developing strength in the white press, the top editors of most daily newspapers ran and wrote their newspaper's editorial pages and had little if anything to do with routine news coverage. The editors did not attend the daily news meetings at which decisions were made about what stories to cover, did not make assignments, and did not participate in discussions about where to play the stories; that frequently fell to the managing editor. As the demands of the race story grew and the pace quickened, the top editors would more frequently find themselves involved in news decisions—in urging that certain stories be played up or down, in insisting that wire services be jangled for more aggressive coverage, and in demanding conformity to certain style rules created solely for race stories.

But for the most part, in key parts of the South in the 1950s—Richmond, Montgomery, Raleigh, Charleston, Jackson, Atlanta, and a raft of smaller towns such as Greenville, Anniston, and Norfolk—newspapers were better known for their editorial pages than for their news coverage. Their editors spoke with loud and authoritative voices. The editors were men, and infrequently women, whose great minds, big thoughts, deep sense of history, hardheaded convictions, and informed wittiness made their editorial pages and public appearances lively and engaging.

Each of them felt a crushing pressure to conform, to fall into line with prevailing sentiment, even to lead it. Some did, some didn't.

While many of his colleagues at other southern newspapers were artfully dodging editorial commentary on race, Jack Kilpatrick could not. A two-fisted writer of enormous intellect and energy, Kilpatrick, editor of the *Richmond News Leader*, wanted to be in on the race issue even though—or perhaps because—he could not claim to have had a Dixie childhood forged in the fires of racial discontent. Kilpatrick had grown up in Oklahoma City seeing practically no Negro people and having no strong feelings about race, other than paternalistic ones. The only Negroes he had known as a child, he later recalled, were his "beloved mammy, name of Lizzie, and old Nash who came on Mondays to do the laundry."[8]

But Kilpatrick, with a neophyte newsman's knack, had found himself situated at an important place, and at an important time, in the nation's race history. At sixteen years of age, he had begun attending the University of Missouri journalism school in 1936, the same year a Negro man named Lloyd Gaines applied for admission to the University of Missouri law school. Kilpatrick had been appalled. The University of Missouri was not big enough for both of them, he wrote his mother, and if Gaines got in, he would quit.[9]

Gaines won a major victory two years later. The Supreme Court ruled that since the state did not offer a comparable education at a Negro institution, the university had to admit Gaines to the white law school. By then, very mysteriously, Gaines had disappeared. Some rumors had him a victim of foul play; others said the stress had driven him to flee the country. And while his name went on the record books as the winner of a significant civil rights case, he never claimed it—and was never found. Kilpatrick did not have to drop out of school.

Fresh out of college, Kilpatrick began seeking newspaper jobs. Years later, the story would be told that he included in his job-seeking letters the statement that he "knew the streets of Paris as well as he knew the streets of Philadelphia." That was true. He'd never been to either city.[10] The best nibble Kilpatrick got was from the *Richmond News Leader*. The managing editor, Charles H. Hamilton, responded to Kilpatrick's application with a question of his own: Would Kilpatrick accept $37 a week? It was just a feeler, not an offer. Kilpatrick fired back a telegram, "Will arrive Monday," and showed up for work before anyone could do anything but marvel at his temerity.[11]

Kilpatrick was an aggressive reporter with a deft writing style. He also had a serious asthma problem and a military deferment, which made him exactly the kind of staffer the newspaper needed when World War II broke out and the newsroom was depleted.[12] He was twenty-nine when he became associate editor of the paper and fell heavily under the influence of the paper's editor, Douglas Southall Freeman, whom Kilpatrick called "the first genius I ever met."

Freeman was notable as a prolific historian, less well known as a man so efficient in his use of time that he had quit smoking when he calculated that the dramaturgy of smoking cigarettes—tapping them, firing them up, stubbing them out—was costing him thirty-seven minutes each day.[13] The way to write and keep writing, Freeman told Kilpatrick, was simple: "Keep your belly against the typewriter, boy."[14]

Kilpatrick did. Working for the afternoon newspaper in town, he arrived by 7:30 every morning and worked almost without break until 4:30 in the afternoon. His responsibilities were the editorial and op-ed pages, as well as the book reviews, written mostly by a librarian at the University of Virginia. Kilpatrick wrote editorials, articles for national magazines, and dozens of letters each day—eighty-four letters on one day alone—setting aside as much time for research as he could.[15] Sometimes he would write solely from his gut and wind up sounding mean and offensive. At other times, he kept his gut on a leash, listened only to his head, and produced editorials that were academic and obtuse. Mostly, he wrote his words beautifully and powerfully with a poet's sense of meaning, a dancer's sense of rhythm, and a boxer's sense of impact.

He loved and raised camellias and was active in the local camellia society.

Had he made grand-scale references to his love for the camellia in speeches and writings, it might have been seen as an Oklahoman's southern affectation. But he kept it pretty private. Not that he was without affectations as a proper Virginia countryman. At home, Kilpatrick favored an old blue corduroy smoking jacket with fading maroon silk lapels and facings. His garden wall was built from bricks salvaged from the collapsing mansion of Spencer Roane, who had been chief judge of Virginia's Supreme Court in Thomas Jefferson's day, Patrick Henry's son-in-law, and a states' righter.[16]

In public appearances, Kilpatrick was quite full of himself. He would open some speeches with anecdotes that had Latin punch lines.[17] If the speech was political—on the subject of interposition, for example—he'd get past the thank-yous and the opening jokes, then signify that he was prepared to make his case by coming to a pause and holding it melodramatically. Then, as if unfurling the closing argument before the Final Judgment, he would say in a low, tightly coiled voice, "Ladies and gentlemen, and may it please the court . . ."[18]

Mixing Latin phrases with backwoods southernisms, he would suggest to the members of his audience that they really could not begin to comprehend Keynesian economics unless they read Gibbon on the fall of Rome, could not fully understand the WPA without knowing Pericles, and would be lost in any discussion about pork barrel in Congress without going back to Hammurabi and the spoils of Babylon. The key to grasping the Korean War? Thucydides.[19]

At his office, some colleagues found Kilpatrick to be prickly and irascible. But he had more than bureaucratic support from the publisher and general manager; he had their love. In the general manager, John Dana Wise, Kilpatrick found an intellectual mentor, a man who knew Burke, Rousseau, and Locke and who was not reluctant to push their writings in front of his young and hungry associate editor.[20] Most general managers at newspapers ran the business for the publisher and left the oddballs down in news and editorial alone. Not Wise. He was in the business to have a political and ideological impact, and his publisher, Tennant Bryan, found no displeasure in that.

Wise, who ran both the *News Leader* and the *Richmond Times-Dispatch* for Bryan, had had only limited success with the other editor in the building, Virginius Dabney, who had steered the *Times-Dispatch* on a moderate course when Bryan's father had run the paper. Now Dabney was drifting quite emphatically back to the middle, but never fast or far enough for Bryan's more conservative son, Tennant, or for Wise. Dabney bridled at Wise's efforts to mess with the editorial pitch of the paper and very nearly left because of it. Wise was the man Harry Ashmore had found so disagreeable over lunch in 1947 that Ashmore had decided he could never work for him. Chances are, the feeling had been mutual.

By the time the interposition fight arrived, Jack Kilpatrick had shown several different editorial faces, and there would be more to come. In the early 1950s, Kilpatrick almost single-handedly won the release of a Negro man named Silas Rogers, a twenty-one-year-old handyman who was serving a life sentence for killing a police officer. Kilpatrick, troubled by inconsistencies in the evidence and testimony, made a fresh investigation. He became certain that Rogers had been falsely charged and that the two primary witnesses against him, two white AWOL soldiers, had lied to save their own skins.

Two years after Kilpatrick's first article doubting the verdict, the governor granted Rogers a pardon and Kilpatrick won induction into the *Afro-American* newspapers' Honor Roll "for a work of simple justice and human decency."[21]

But Kilpatrick was appalled a year later when Rogers was charged with rape in New Jersey. When a colleague at a Tampa newspaper wrote that he was considering pursuing a similar case of injustice, Kilpatrick counseled him not to waste his time: "All of my crusading instincts in cases of this sort have vanished altogether. . . . Sometimes you have to learn lessons the hard way."[22]

This Jack Kilpatrick felt there was a profound genetic, behavioral, and cultural gulf between white and Negro people that could not be closed. This Jack Kilpatrick used social science when it fit the racial and cultural stereotypes he wanted to believe and discounted social science as irrelevant when it didn't. In addressing the white segregationist southerner's concerns about school integration, this Jack Kilpatrick grabbed everything he could and threw it into the mix so that a sober treatise on the problems of interracial education would veer into the subjects of illegitimate births, syphilis, and gonorrhea.[23]

In November 1955, Kilpatrick, Bryan, Wise, and other editors at the *News Leader* convened a meeting to explore the possibility of editorially advocating complete defiance of the Supreme Court. It was an attractive position to Kilpatrick, but he knew that anyone who pushed an absolute position must be prepared to take the next step: to advocate secession from the Union. So the Richmond editors, largely as an academic exercise, considered a scenario that ended in secession. When they worked through their feelings, they realized they were not prepared to go that far. They left their conference unsure exactly how to proceed.[24]

In scholarly circles and a few journalistic covens through the region, segregationists who understood the futility of secession or another civil war were seeking a way to detour around, escape, or undermine federal authority, particularly *Brown.* It seemed as though everyone was panning and sifting through American legal history, hoping to find the gold nugget that would allow the South to bargain its way out of the Supreme Court noose. The pan glinted with John C. Calhoun's speeches imploring South Carolina to nullify federal tariffs in 1828 and 1832. From U.S. Senator Herman Talmadge's office came research into Georgia's successful nullification of an 1832 federal court ruling concerning the Cherokee Nation. Down in Alabama, the *Montgomery Advertiser* editor, Grover Hall, was impressed by information that President Franklin Roosevelt had once developed a bold plan to defy a Supreme Court order that was anticipated on the gold standard but that had never come to pass.[25]

Then, from the office of a country lawyer in Virginia, William Old, came a self-published pamphlet that resurrected the theory of interposition from Virginia's past and insisted that it could be legitimately applied in 1955.[26] The pamphlet made its way into the hands of Jack Kilpatrick.

The theme and theology of interposition hit Kilpatrick "like a bolt of lightning" in mid-November, he wrote one colleague,[27] and he began his own relentless research into the related issues of sovereignty, states' rights, and nullification. Kilpatrick concluded that interposition provided him an elevated platform from which to attack desegregation intelligently. It was a platform that would also enable him to both rise above, and rail against, the white riffraff whose small minds and stupidity led them to resort to mob violence.

Kilpatrick began feverishly writing his series and launched the first installment a week later. Working inside his small, unremarkable office at the *News Leader,* he became a single-minded crusader. "I was on a horse," he would write later, "and the pen was a lance."[28] His sleeves rolled up, his necktie loosened, his forehead wrinkled with scowling intensity over a burning cigarette, the short, balding Kilpatrick would work quickly and prodigiously behind a desk stacked high with books, some opened to the point that their spines ached, some closed and marked in a dozen places by slivers of torn paper.[29] Day after day, week after week, Kilpatrick committed his editorial page not only to his long-winded explanations of the viability and legitimacy of interposition but also to arcane and frequently impenetrable archival documents.

From November 21 until February 1 of the next year, readers of Kilpatrick's editorial pages were fed the Virginia Resolution of 1798, the First Kentucky Resolution of 1798, and the Second Kentucky Resolution of 1799, in which both states interposed themselves in opposition to the federal Alien and Sedition Acts. Readers were introduced to John Calhoun's 1831 speech at Fort Hill, South Carolina, in which he had defined interposition in its purest form. They got a steady diet of old speeches, new speeches, treatises, and ruminations on the topic, then reactions to those speeches, treatises, and ruminations. Kilpatrick's ideology even altered the newspaper's grammar. If the U.S. Constitution could become the basis of our governance without ever using the word "nation" or "national," he asserted, then the United States should never be treated by the *Richmond News Leader* as anything more than a collection of individual, sovereign states. Consequently, Kilpatrick frequently noted, readers would never see the term "United States" take the singular in his editorials. Awkward as it was stylistically, the United States was not mentioned in his editorials. But the United States were.

Though a stickler on such things, Kilpatrick was not a prude about editorial humor or detours into lighter topics. His paeans to the seasons, his salutes to the rolling hills of Virginia, and his odes to a Richmond fountain were highly popular but writing challenges for him. Colleagues in his office would see him breeze through construction of an interposition editorial, then struggle through a softer essay, ripping and abandoning one piece of copy paper after another until he was ankle deep in confetti.[30]

Kilpatrick would not put editorial cartoons on the editorial page. It was a place for reflective thought and reasonable discussion, he felt, and cartoons were inherently reflexive and unreasonable.[31] He would run photographs of Virginia scenes and pictures of fine art, but his interposition pages were usually a sea of gray, broken up only mildly by large portraits of Calhoun, Madison, Jefferson, and others.

Fifty thousand words after Kilpatrick began his case for interposition, most Virginia newspapers had leapt aboard the train and the General Assembly had voted to throw itself between its people and federal authority.

Not all Virginia newspapers fell into line behind Kilpatrick. Phil Scruggs, editor of the *Lynchburg News,* let the interposition train leave the station without him. He didn't like it. The strongest editorial opposition came from the largest city in the state, Norfolk, where *The Virginian-Pilot* banged steadily against massive resistance. Lenoir Chambers, the editor, had previously supported *Brown* II as a "superb appeal to the wisdom, intelligence and leadership of the Southern states" and urged his state to "rise to leadership in the probably long and difficult task."[32]

At the *Times-Dispatch,* separated by a wall from the *News Leader,* the juggernaut of interposition was causing a great deal of consternation. Dabney, on both sides of his family, was the true-blue Virginian that Kilpatrick would never be. Kilpatrick could write eloquently about Thomas Jefferson; Dabney could trace his bloodlines to him.[33] What's more, Dabney was a regional historian of significance. He looked upon the arguments for and against interposition as some fine historical reading. But it was a theory that essentially had flopped when applied in the real world and was certain to prove itself bunk when tried again. He worried that impulsive people acting in the name of interposition could do some terrible harm to Virginia's education system.

Dabney sought the analysis of friends in legal and judicial circles. They told him that interposition was a mighty porous bucket to be carrying so much water. Lewis F. Powell, Jr., who would become an associate justice of the same U.S. Supreme Court that interposition was trying to circumvent, told him it was simply unconstitutional.

But even for a man of his stature, with the Pulitzer Prize on the wall and books and magazine articles he had authored on the shelf, it was not easy for Dabney to proclaim his thoughts editorially or even to express them to his publisher or general manager. Dabney felt that Bryan and Wise—and Wise's equally conservative successor, Alan S. Donnahoe—had become hypnotized by Harry F. Byrd, the Virginia political kingpin in his fourth term as U.S. senator, and dazzled by Jack Kilpatrick. If Byrd said the road to the Promised Land led through interposition, then it did.

Outside Virginia, the campaign awakened the sleeping giants of southern liberalism. In Raleigh, the editor Jonathan Daniels called interposition "a silly dream."[34] In Louisville, the *Courier-Journal* publisher, Mark Ethridge, said of Virginia's interposition leaders, "They're riding off like a bunch of headless horsemen."[35]

Kilpatrick, meanwhile, was bundling up all his editorial pages, reprinting them in a booklet, and bombarding the region with them, hoping they'd serve as kindling. An associate justice of the North Carolina Supreme Court opened his mail one day and found six copies and a note from Kilpatrick asking him to distribute them among his judicial brethren.[36]

Legislators and editorial writers took up the call. They railed against the overreach of the Supreme Court and the federal government and quibbled endlessly about the differences between interposition and nullification.[37] When all was said and done, most of the states of the South had enacted prointerposition laws and resolutions, some more enthusiastically than others. By the end of 1956, eleven southern states had enacted 106 pro-segregation laws.[38] Among them were laws that abolished mandatory school attendance; allowed public school property to be leased to private, all-white academies; let private school teachers retain state-funded benefits; forced teachers to report organizations they belonged to; banned members of the NAACP from government employment; and provided for the payment of legal fees for officials sued for enforcing segregation.[39] North Carolina and Florida showed more reluctance to join the cause, frustrating segregationist forces by adopting fewer and less draconian measures.[40]

In the end, while prosegregation laws had dramatic impact across the South, the various legislative performances on interposition had no bearing on the law, no standing, and no impact on the balance of power between the states and the federal government. Still, the concept of interposition, with its scholarly masquerade, had a profound impact. Kilpatrick, by propagating a whole vernacular to serve the culture of massive resistance—interposition, nullification, states' rights, state sovereignty—provided an intellectual shield for nearly every racist action and reaction in the coming years.

It took only two days for the story that spurred passive resistance—the arrest of Rosa Parks and the call for a bus boycott—to leap from page nine to page one of the *Montgomery Advertiser*. While it ran below a story that said Georgia's governor was trying to prevent Georgia Tech from playing in the Sugar Bowl because its opponent, the University of Pittsburgh, had a Negro player, the story was timely and appropriately played, given what was known at the time.

That front-page story, written by the city editor, Joe Azbell, said that Montgomery Negroes had called a "top secret" meeting to plan a one-day bus boycott. The third paragraph said, "Negro sections were flooded with thousands of copies of mimeographed or typed letters asking the Negroes to refrain from riding city busses Monday." The letters invited everyone to a mass meeting. That the *Advertiser* felt a notice so freely distributed among Negroes was "top secret" was a measure of how detached the paper and its white readers were from that community.[41]

Azbell's story said that the action was being "initiated by unidentified Negro leaders." But he knew who was behind it. His source for the story was a key boycott planner, E. D. Nixon, a founder of the Montgomery branch of the NAACP and a leader of the Brotherhood of the Sleeping Car Porters. Nixon had planted the story with Azbell to rally support for the boycott.[42]

Sloppiness infected the coverage. The leaflet calling for the boycott meeting referred to an incident nine months earlier in which Claudette Colvin, a fifteen-year-old Negro girl, had been booted from a Montgomery bus because she would not give up her seat. The flyer mistakenly called the girl Claudette Colbert, the name of an actress. The *Advertiser* didn't catch the error, then repeated it over the next few days. The newspaper tended to accept on faith statements from City Hall. It printed a claim by the police commissioner, who was a fervent member of the Citizens' Council, that "Negro 'goon squads' " had been organized to bully Negroes into staying off the buses, though no evidence of them would ever emerge.[43]

At a mass meeting attended by thousands of people, years of neglecting the news of the Negro community came back to haunt the white press. None of the evening's speakers was introduced by name, to provide them some protection beyond the walls of Holt Street Baptist Church. As one after another took the podium and gave a stirring, thundering speech, the four local reporters and photographers were at a complete loss: they didn't know the names of the speakers. But everyone else seemed to. Azbell's story was able to identify and quote one local pastor, a Reverend M. L. King, but failed to mention that boycott organizers had formed the Montgomery Improvement Association and elected King their leader earlier that day.[44]

What's more, King's most ringing statement of the night was not attributed to him and was misquoted in a way that made the speaker appear anti-American if not an anarchist. "If we are wrong," King had said, "then the Supreme Court of this nation is wrong. If we are wrong, the Constitution of the United States is wrong. If we are wrong, God Almighty is wrong." But Azbell had the quote this way: "If we are wrong, the Constitution is wrong, the Supreme Court is wrong and our whole foundation of government is wrong."[45]

Advertiser readers had to search deep into Azbell's story to learn how effective the one-day boycott had been. In the twentieth paragraph out of 47, readers learned that 90 percent of the Negro riders had refused to ride. Nowhere was it noted that Negroes normally made up 75 percent of the riders and accounted for 20,000 to 30,000 fares each day. The *Advertiser* reported only that "several thousand Negroes use the buses on a normal day."[46]

Azbell, who had left Alabama in the early 1950s for a stint as an investigative reporter for the *New York Herald Tribune,* had returned to become an editor and reporter. He was dogged and loved the influence he and his stories could wield. He was plugged in to white political leaders and frequently let their segregationist sentiments light up his stories with ungrounded hype. But he came away from the first boycott meeting impressed. "It proved beyond any doubt that there was a discipline among Negroes that many whites had doubted," he wrote. "It was almost a military discipline combined with emotion."[47]

Still, anyone wanting any details from within the boycott had to read the *Birmingham World,* which published twice a week. Over the weeks and months, no other newspaper would be more committed to covering the story, and no other newspaper would have the *World*'s unique view from inside the Montgomery Improvement Association. Its editor, Emory Jackson, who had met and given good coverage to King a year before,[48] managed to work his way into the organization's strategy sessions. From there, he racked up some early scoops and published some important early impressions that the white press would not see or report for months.

It was Jackson who brought early attention to King's strategy of passive resistance and his appreciation for Mohandas K. Gandhi's nonviolent liberation campaign in India. It was Jackson who reported, when the boycott was barely three weeks old, that King was trying "to find a suitable adaptation of the Gandhi philosophy and method and apply it to the Montgomery problem." It was Jackson who first reported that the boycott's leaders were preparing to make it a yearlong campaign. When white leaders who were negotiating with the association tried to drive a wedge into the opposition by spreading word that King was blocking an agreement, Jackson quickly wrote that the other boycott leaders had "built a solid phalanx around this leader and told the upper-hand [city] leadership that he would never be deserted or shelved."[49]

From his first editorial about the boycott, Jackson expressed great admiration for Rosa Parks and criticized Montgomery officials harshly. But he did not leap to provide editorial support for the boycott. In the coming weeks, even as he praised King and the courage of the boycotters and kept firing away at Montgomery's city leaders, he was reluctant to make such a declaration.

Meanwhile, the *Advertiser* was showing why it was the kind of newspaper Harry Ashmore worried about. The paper, even if excused for not understanding the historic nature of the story unfolding in front of it, proved itself not up to the basic journalistic task of covering it. It had done nothing to show readers the seeds of discontent, white or Negro. When the boycott took root and spread, its reporters had no idea what to do, where to go, or who to see.

The *Advertiser* was put out by a mismatched collection of hard-drinking has-beens and inexperienced wannabes. The executive editor checked out around three every afternoon and headed for the country club. The managing editor's drinking had long since undermined his decision-making capacities. A third top editor dealt with his boredom by sending the freshest recruit on the staff to the only place where a pint of whiskey could be transacted on a Sunday, the VFW hall. One top reporter held a strong segregationist bias that he would later display in an oddball penny press publication of his own.[50]

Azbell consequently had a lot of latitude. The police reporter to whom many of the assignments would go was Stephan Lesher, a Jewish kid out of Brooklyn who had married a Montgomery woman and was living in her father's home. Lesher had not yet finished college and, at the time of the boycott, had an accumulated lifetime career experience of seven months; at $50 or $55 a week, he made little more than his wife, who was a nurse. The whole collection of editors and reporters operated under R. H. Hudson, Sr., who had steadily climbed from a lowly position in circulation to the top ownership position of publisher.[51]

In its 127 years, the *Advertiser* had periodically taken some progressive, even liberal stands. It had stood forthrightly against secession in 1861 but after the Civil War had become devoted to the cause of white supremacy. It was adamant in its opposition to national prohibition, favoring local option, and dismissed creationism while successfully opposing efforts to ban the teaching of evolution.

In 1928, in Grover Cleveland Hall, Sr.'s, second year as editor, the paper won a Pulitzer Prize for his attacks on the Ku Klux Klan, whom he described as the "drill sergeants of hatred, the go-getters of intolerance, the high powered salesmen of bigotry, aided and abetted by the Machiavellis of politics."[52] In the 1930s, Hall had taken up the cause of the Scottsboro Boys, nine Negroes whom he felt had been falsely accused of raping two white women.[53] Inside the fraternity of editors, Hall's friendships were with the liberals, especially Virginius Dabney.

But Hall died unexpectedly in 1941, two days before his fifty-third birthday, leaving such a painful void in Montgomery and southern journalism that the newspaper's publisher chose not to fill the editor's job for six years. When the publisher did finally name an editor in 1947, he chose the person closest to Hall, the late editor's son and thirty-two-year-old namesake, Grover C. Hall, Jr.

The succession seemed certain to continue the Hall editorial style and philosophy. The younger Hall described himself as "an ardent, unflinching and unapologetic Rooseveltian."[54] Like his father, he was acerbic, grumpy, confrontational, personal, literate, and influential. Ashmore soon came to think of Hall as "perhaps the most eloquent editorial writer" in the region.[55]

Hall wanted to be known not as merely an editor but as a "writing editor." To him, they were altogether different breeds. He was certain that newspaper readers had a near-biological "craving" for editorial comment. And it was pretty damned hypocritical, he felt, for him and the other medicine men of journalism to produce vacuous editorial pages that left readers anemic and gasping for fresh air.[56]

A well-groomed, perpetually tan lifelong bachelor and bon vivant who seemed quite thrilled by his reputation as a brilliant swashbuckler, Hall injected vivacity into his editorial page. He seemed to enjoy hearing and reading himself argue, which some observers believed masked his insecurity for never having attended college. He spoke and wrote with a flair that matched his natty attire: Hall wore colored dress shirts long before they were fashionable. He favored suspenders and added some spice with a porkpie hat and a carnation in his lapel. He would indicate a coming moment of newsroom informality by carefully rolling up his starched sleeves twice on each forearm, each fold defined by a perfect crease.[57] Such moments were rare.[58]

Hall was a man of conviction, certainly, but what he thought about things was not nearly so important to him as how well he expressed what he thought. On an impulse, he could crack open some extraordinarily rare and expensive bottles of verbiage.

One of the men he loved to target was Jim Folsom, Alabama's colorful, populist, racially progressive, and occasionally sober governor. He and Folsom had once been pals, had run around together as bachelors. He admired some things about the six-foot-eight politician, who styled himself as "the little man's big friend." He liked the fact that Folsom never took a cheap shot at the Negro race.[59] He shared with Folsom the view that an Alabama legislative resolution declaring Supreme Court desegregation rulings "null and void" was "like a hound dog baying at the moon. It doesn't mean a thing."[60]

But he gave Folsom no reprieve. "The anthropoid antics of Folsom attained a state of advanced depravity yesterday at Jasper," Hall reported in the *Advertiser* at one point. "He there belched an orangutan slander that the Alabama constitution was written by 'carpetbaggers.' This untaught Knave, who lacked the grace and prudence to keep zippered his flapping mandible to conceal his void, doesn't know that the 1901 Convention was called to undo the work of carpetbaggers."[61]

The more Hall watched the boycotters, the more impressed he was by their unbending determination. Every weekday, some 15,000 to 25,000 Negro residents of his hometown, many of whom lived all the way across town from where they worked, somehow managed to get to and from work without the bus transportation they had always used. The car pool system alone, involving more than two hundred cars and forty regular pickup points, was an organizational wonder. Hall, like so many others, had figured that the first light shower would send all the maids, babysitters, and cleaning ladies scurrying back onto the bus. But the boycott went on and on and on, each and every day, hot or cold, rain or shine.[62]

The Montgomery Improvement Association made three demands: One, more courteous treatment by bus drivers of Negro passengers. Two, a seating arrangement in which Negro patrons would enter the back of the bus and white patrons would enter the front; Negro customers would sit in the back so long as seats were available there but would be permitted to take seats progressively closer to the front as the back filled up. Nobody would be asked to give up a seat for anyone else. Three, the hiring of Negro bus drivers on predominantly Negro routes.

Hall was impressed by the moderation of the seating demand. "If the grievance is confined to that," the *Advertiser* said in its first editorial on the subject, "then attention should be given to it promptly. Any other grievance should be fairly heard." Regular readers of the *Advertiser* could see no inconsistency in this position and Hall's general editorial attitude over the eight years he had been editor.

By all indications, the boycotters seemed to have an admirer, perhaps a friend, and at least not an enemy, in Grover Hall. He was even on the national board of the American Civil Liberties Union. More than most editors, Hall opened his letters to the editor column—"Tell It to Old Grandma"—to moderate and liberal opinions. His editorials, while full of savage condescension toward high-profile targets, stopped short of injecting haughtiness toward Negroes as a race, as Kilpatrick and Waring frequently did.

Hall felt that as odious as the bus boycott was, segregationist whites had started it and had gotten what they had asked for. Negroes, he said, were foolish to think they could disarm white political or economic dominance. But the segregationists were not using their heads, either. Having deployed such extreme measures to cut off the employment, credit, and supplies of Negroes who participated in civil rights activities, the Citizens' Councils could hardly complain about retaliatory boycotts. "It's a dangerous weapon, like a missile that returns to its launching ground," he wrote.[63]

But Hall would soon face political strains beyond anything his father had faced against the Klan. As the stakes in Alabama got higher, the pressure on the newspaper to aid and advance the strategy of the white segregationist leadership and the incessant demands on Hall to stick with his own class, his own breed, his own race, would become difficult to resist. Growing fears among businessmen in Montgomery, and in Tuscaloosa, where the NAACP was winning court battles that seemed certain to put Autherine Lucy inside the University of Alabama, pushed more of Hall's peers into the Citizens' Council, the same group he'd attacked for "manicured Kluxism" and "economic thuggery" against Negroes.[64]

Hall's publisher was acutely prosegregation. Hall himself was filled with conflict. Six weeks into the boycott, he expressed his feelings to another Alabamian, a man who had known his father well, Supreme Court Justice Hugo Black.

In a letter to Black, he noted the moderate demands of the boycotters, then added, "It could have been handled in the beginning, but poor leadership let the concrete get set. The white community is afraid to 'lose face' lest it open the dike. . . . Never in my nine years as editor have I seen Montgomery so inflamed as now. Trying to be moderate, I have taken quite a mauling. Facts and reason are nothing to [white segregationist leaders]; you are either for white folks or against 'em."[65]

Hall's understanding of southern history presented him with a persuasive parallel between the 1950s and the 1850s; he felt that a century earlier, southern white moderates had been prepared to eliminate slavery gradually but had been undercut by the aggressiveness of northern abolitionists. He feared the South had now come to the same crossroads.

"Despite my contempt for the feeble-minded emotionalism of the mass mind," he wrote Black, "I must say in candor that I'm uneasy over letting the ignorant, easily-led Negroes prevail in this bus boycott. The white mass, with all its centuries of experience and training, readily becomes an incompetent mob. The Negroes are even more primitive and can be led about as easily now as they were when the carpetbaggers sold them the 'painted sticks.' Several years ago I wrote, without challenge, that no longer could an Alabama politician be elected by bawling 'nigger.' I was right—then. It is otherwise now. Not for a long time to come is any politician going to be elected who fails to make himself clear."[66]

One who did make himself clear was Senator James Eastland, who came into Montgomery for a Citizens' Council rally. A week earlier, Eastland had addressed the first statewide gathering of Citizens' Councils in South Carolina. His speech, in which he said the NAACP was backed by groups "of all shades of red . . . the blood red of the Communist party," was interrupted by applause eighty-seven times.[67]

The turnout was even greater in Montgomery: 15,000 people jammed into the Cow Coliseum; they stood in long lines to reach the membership tables and the donation barrels. Everywhere Grover Hall looked, he saw people he respected. He would later tell colleagues that his appreciation of the enormity of the support for segregation had crystallized in those weeks and that his own personal endorsement of it had solidified on that night.[68] Hall would still take his shots at the city's white leadership, which he felt was bungling its management of the crisis. And he couldn't stand any association with the rougher elements among the segregationist forces. When six white men jumped onto a Birmingham stage to assault Nat King Cole, a native Alabamian, as he sang to 3,500 white people, Hall expressed shame. He wrote an editorial, "It Makes Us Flinch," that described his violence-prone segregationist allies as "so utterly odious, so abjectly stupid, so hell-bent on bringing disrepute upon the 'cause' they are allegedly championing. . . . It is no wonder that respectable Southerners, fighting for legitimate rights of the South, should sometimes feel like chucking it all and letting the Yankees and the NAACP work their will."

When segregationists threw a metal chain around a television transformer to short-circuit the local broadcast of a widely advertised, nationally televised Sunday morning interview with Martin Luther King, Jr., in the midst of the boycott, Hall questioned whether the perpetrators ought to be walking around outside cages. All they had done, he said, was double the audience when a taped version was rebroadcast. "Brilliant Press Agentry," Hall wrote. "Thousands who wouldn't have listened in the first place will now glue themselves to their sets. . . . Dr. King has had nothing but the ablest promotion service from whites."[69]

But Hall's own newspaper would soon find itself responsible for an even clumsier segregationist strategy that would backfire.

CHAPTER 9

ALABAMA

Where Simeon Booker had seen fear and cowardice among Mississippi Negroes earlier that year, Carl Rowan saw self-confidence when he visited bus boycotters in Alabama. Rowan, a *Minneapolis Tribune* reporter who was one of the few black journalists employed by a white newspaper, had been visiting the South since at least 1951. Over the years, he had come to rely on Emory Jackson for guidance, and the two of them gained access to the movement's brain trust that no white reporter had.

In late 1955, when Rowan and white *Tribune* reporter Richard Kleeman arrived in Montgomery while traveling together to write a series, "Dixie Divided," Rowan was welcomed into the inner circle of the boycott's organizers. He met King at the home of JoAnn Robinson, the Negro college English instructor who had produced the thousands of flyers announcing the initial one-day boycott. Rowan, who had grown up in McMinnville, Tennessee, where Negro preachers were teetotalers or secretive about drinking, watched as King approached the bar and poured himself a glass of Jack Daniel's. King's sidekick, another Montgomery pastor, Ralph David Abernathy, did the same thing. Rowan was impressed. Maybe there *was* a New South. He walked over to the two men to introduce himself. "Man," he said to them warmly, "these are some modern preachers."[1]

King told Rowan that the energy and inspiration for the boycott and the "coming of integration" would come from the Negro church. Rowan sensed that King understood intuitively the various strategies of delay, subterfuge, and trickery that white segregationists would use to stymie the Negro movement and knew innately the power of his own words and voice to counter them.

But neither of them could have imagined that the segregationists' strategy to end the boycott would include a nefarious little hoax that would take advantage of the *Montgomery Advertiser*'s complicity, indifference, or laziness.

Upon their return to Minneapolis, Rowan and Kleeman wrote their series, which was set to begin on Sunday, January 22, 1956. The night before, as the presses were running with the Sunday editions, an editor at the *Minneapolis Tribune* saw a story with a Montgomery dateline coming over the wires. The story said the forty-nine-day-old bus boycott had ended after the city commission and three Negro ministers had reached agreement. The editor on duty tracked down Rowan, told him about the settlement, and asked if he wanted to kill the first story or rewrite it to conform to the development.

The report didn't sound right. Rowan began working the phone, finally tracking down King in Montgomery at about 9 p.m. King was stunned by the report. No one in the Montgomery Improvement Association had been authorized to reach an agreement, and he couldn't imagine that there were any defectors who might have cut their own deal. Any "agreement" was a fraud, he was certain, and the report on it was a trap. King could see that when all of Montgomery opened the next morning's newspaper and read there had been a settlement, the boycotters would be splintered in their reaction and the boycott would be over simply because the *Advertiser* had said it was.

King asked Rowan to call Police Commissioner Clyde Sellers to get the names of the three ministers. Sellers refused but named the denominations they represented. When Rowan told King that one minister represented the "Holiness" church, King knew he was being scammed. There was no "Holiness" church of importance. Before midnight, King had identified the three ministers and had spoken with them. They said they had been called to the mayor's office to discuss an unrelated subject, had been given copies of a settlement they had not signed or endorsed, then had departed without any idea what would transpire.

That night, all night, King and other boycott leaders worked with the only form of communication available—word of mouth—to reverse the impact that a huge headline on a Sunday front page would have. Pastors called colleagues and asked them to set aside sermon time the next morning to disavow the *Advertiser* story; others, such as King, went out in the night to juke joints and speakeasies, spreading the word that people shouldn't believe anything they read in the Sunday-morning paper.[2]

The hoax was exposed. The intended effect of the *Advertiser* story was undermined. And the boycott continued as if that day's newspaper had never come off the press. Mayor Gayle, in high dudgeon over the ridicule he was facing, insisted that there had been a legitimate agreement. But the mayor knew that the three "prominent ministers" cited in the *Advertiser* story had never been involved in negotiations, had no affiliation with the boycotters' organization, and could never speak for King and other boycott leaders.

More important, Gayle and Sellers could assume with near certainty that the newspaper would not question their authority or their word and would not double-check their claim. It was a pretty good bet that the newspaper, which was still treating the boycott primarily as a police story, wasn't going to try to call one of the preachers or a leader of the boycott for a comment or reaction. In fact, one reporter on the staff at the time said years later that he was quite certain that no one in the newsroom, seven weeks into the boycott, had King's telephone number.[3]

Up to the end of January, when the boycotters stiffened their demands and bombs started going off in Montgomery, none of the nation's more influential newspapers and magazines had made a substantial commitment to the boycott story. Only one major publication with a predominantly white audience had sent a reporter to Montgomery to cover the story. *Time* magazine ran its first story on January 16, six weeks after the boycott began. *Newsweek* would not show up until the thirteenth week of the boycott.

The New York Times and *The Washington Post* relied exclusively on wire services and stringers from the beginning. In both papers, all the stories ran inside. Most were only a few paragraphs long and devoid of context. Neither newspaper would send its own staff writer down until twelve weeks after the boycott began.

That is not to say that all those publications were ignoring racial confrontation in Alabama. All of them, and many, many more, had recently parachuted into the state, but they had all headed to Tuscaloosa, where the Goliath of Jim Crow was about to square off against a quiet, fearful, but determined Negro woman who had just won complete clearance to enroll at the University of Alabama.

Autherine Lucy had been trying to enroll for 1,243 days when she received word on January 29, 1956, that the school had agreed to let her in. She got the clearance ten days after the Alabama legislature ruled, by its own authority, that the U.S. Supreme Court had no standing to force the desegregation of schools or anything else run by the states. As a document of defiance, the legislature's act of nullification was merely a piece of paper. But the confluence of events turned it into something much greater: a call for massive resistance—a call that the Ku Klux Klan, the Citizens' Councils, and other segregationists answered with a show of force soon after Lucy arrived on campus.

On the day Lucy was told she would be admitted to the school, the *Birmingham World* employee who had roped her into applying in the first place, Pollie Anne Myers Hudson, was told she would not be allowed to enroll. Though Hudson had married the father of her child back in 1952, two months after she applied for admission, the university's trustees acted indignant that she had married after becoming pregnant. In an atmosphere in which King could be arrested for driving five miles over the speed limit, the trustees felt they were sitting in high cotton with such scandalous evidence of Hudson's moral turpitude.

Lucy was twenty-six years old. In the three and a half years it had taken to gain entrance, the world around her had changed considerably. The core issue of her application—race—had moved from the background in 1952 to the forefront of the American agenda. Older and wiser, she was nonetheless still a very reticent woman, the last person in the world likely to take on the giants of white supremacy. Indeed, in rejecting Hudson and admitting Lucy, the university was playing a strategic card.

Jackson, the *Birmingham World* editor, had not been discreet about telling white people that it was Hudson who had the gumption to challenge Jim Crow and that the more reticent Lucy was more of a follower. When word came down that Lucy was in and Hudson was out, Jackson figured that the university's antennae had picked up his observations and that it had rejected Hudson in an attempt to scare Lucy from going it alone. Outwardly, Lucy seemed as determined as ever. "I regret that I won't have her with me," Lucy said. "We are good friends. But I won't let that keep me from going. I'm proud to know that I am now able to embark upon the steps of the University. I shall go with a great desire to make a splendid showing academically."[4]

But Jackson, the NAACP's Ruby Hurley, and others were concerned that Lucy might not persevere. She had been living under enormous pressure for a long time, and it would only get worse. Lucy knew what the press would later find out: her parents, who farmed in a tiny south Alabama community named Shiloh, were totally opposed to their daughter, the youngest of ten children, injecting herself into so dangerous a thicket as integration. She had already heard the same questions her father, Milton Lucy, would later ask in the presence of reporters: "Why, I keep asking myself, out of all the colored folks in Alabama, did this have to fall to my baby daughter's lot?" Her father, who split and whittled white ash to make chairs, baskets, and ax handles, had urged her to come back home "or else go to some school that's all right for colored folks." What the stories never said, but what she firmly believed, was that, despite her father's comments, he and her mother were deeply proud of her.[5]

The story of Lucy's determination to attend the university is also the story of Emory Jackson's determination to live a life worthy of his journalistic ancestors, the men he so admired because they had made the Negro press the fighting press.

It was Jackson who had backed the girls from the beginning, gotten them jobs, and arranged for financial assistance. Knowing that Lucy would need money for tuition, room and board, and other expenses, Jackson took charge of fund-raising. He landed scholarship money from a New York foundation, only to be blocked from accepting it by the university. He was also responsible for finding students on campus who would befriend Lucy; he contacted a Catholic priest he knew and made those arrangements.[6]

It was Jackson who carried Lucy's tuition money for her the day she registered, sat with her during a contentious meeting at which the university told her she could not live on campus, and drove her to campus on her first day of classes. It was Jackson whose advice to Thurgood Marshall and other NAACP Legal Defense Fund lawyers might have led to a more satisfying outcome if they had heeded it.[7]

By the time Lucy walked onto campus on February 3, there were more reporters than protesters. She went largely unnoticed by the other students; one fellow made a demonstration of walking out of her first class, but several students in her second class sat in the same row with her.[8] Reporters were everywhere. Before the week ended, the university would hand out 260 press passes,[9] virtually all of them to reporters from outside Alabama. By one account at the time, the Birmingham and Tuscaloosa newspapers were the only Alabama dailies to send staffers to cover Lucy's enrollment; all the others relied on wire service coverage.[10]

No single racial clash in the South had attracted so many reporters. The bus boycott was droning on down in Montgomery with extraordinary cult-like precision. But the press found the more compelling story to be about the shy, quiet woman who smiled as she walked into the lair of the segregationist lion.

At the end of the first day, Lucy told reporters she was pleased. Some students had spoken with her, and some had even wished her well. Nightfall, however, brought trouble. Drunken fraternity boys gathered on a lawn and fashioned some old socks into a cross they tried to set afire. When a university policeman stopped them, they persuaded the officer to allow them to move the cross off campus and into the middle of a road. The officer then provided the matches needed to light the cross.[11] The Tuscaloosa News described the ensuing rally, which included a march to the university president's home, as congenial, run-of-the-mill, semester-christening festiveness. The Associated Press sensed it was about "resentment" over Lucy's admission and noted that some students were clamoring, "Keep Bama white," and "To Hell with Autherine."[12]

Lucy attended class the next day, a Saturday, again without problems. Then Saturday night turned wild and raucous both on the campus and in Tuscaloosa. This was not teenage testosterone out for a misguided evening; in even greater numbers than the students, hostile townspeople, including a sizable number of Klansmen who came out of organized labor, torched a cross, smashed and trashed cars driven by Negroes, and rocked a Greyhound bus. They threw gravel and firecrackers at the balcony where the university president tried to speak, poured and ignited gasoline at a labor building, and listened as one student active in the Citizens' Council climbed a flagpole and reminded the crowd where and when Lucy's first class would be held on Monday morning. The university and the city did little to break up the night's demonstrations or to send a message that violence, destruction, and threats would not be tolerated.

On the Sunday before Lucy was to attend her third day of classes, Emory Jackson became concerned about the demonstrations and their portent. He tried to call the governor and the university president. Neither could be reached, but the president's wife comforted Jackson by saying that Lucy's safety was paramount.

By 8:30 on Monday morning, even before Lucy arrived on campus, the university had lost control of the situation. Local workers and students who opposed Lucy had begun amassing in numbers far beyond the university's ability to contain. During her first class, a core group of fifty unionized workers from a rubber plant and a foundry grew to a mob of five hundred belligerents. There were not enough law enforcement officers assigned, and some were dispatched too late to be effective.

To leave her first class, Lucy had to be spirited into a waiting car by a university vice president and the dean of women. Detected by spotters who had staked out the exits, the three were the targets of rocks, eggs, and foul mouths. Only by accelerating his car as it whipped past the crowd, straddling a ditch, and racing the length of two football fields, was the vice president able to break free of danger. He and the dean of women delivered Lucy to her second class.

By the time that ended, the crowd had grown larger, to about 1,000; it would, by several estimates, reach as many as 3,000 as curious students stopped to look. The mob grew more frenzied. "Hey! Hey! Ho! Ho! Autherine has got to go!" rang out across the campus, while others urged that she be killed. Even when the university vice president walked out of the building alone and drove away, he was attacked; he jumped into the car, gunned the accelerator, and lurched away, but not before a brick crashed through his rear window.

Too little and too late, university officials and pastors deployed diversionary tactics to take the demonstrators' eyes off Lucy as she tried to escape from her second class. A strategy to start arguments with the demonstrators met minimal success. The angry crowd turned on H. N. Guinn, an older Negro man who had arrived on campus to drive Lucy home. He was hit by a truck but not seriously injured, though that seemed very likely as the crowd gathered around him.

To his rescue came an Episcopal priest and Peter Kihss, a *New York Times* reporter, both of whom were splattered with eggs, who joined a police officer in moving Guinn from the scrum. In doing so, Kihss hit several of the demonstrators with a forearm, others with a straight-arm. Then he abandoned the Popham rules of journalistic decorum completely. "If anybody wants to start something, let's go," Kihss told the crowd. "I'm a reporter for *The New York Times* and I have gotten a wonderful impression of the University of Alabama. Now I'll be glad to take on the whole student body, two at a time."[13] No one challenged him. Newspapers the next day would suggest that Guinn might have been a "daring decoy" and that Kihss might have been part of the plan to divert attention.[14] Both would deny this. Kihss was one of the first of many visiting reporters to be accused of working to help the civil rights cause.

To get Lucy out of her second classroom, a highway patrol car was sent to the back of the building. Lucy, frightened and reluctant to leave the building, was whisked into the backseat of the patrol car and told to lie on the floor. She got off the campus and went to the office of the Negro newspaper in town, the *Tuscaloosa Citizen.*

Over a four-day span, she had attended two and a half days of classes before she was run off campus. The school's board of trustees, unable or unwilling to guarantee her safety, then voted to suspend Lucy "until further notice."[15]

While the mob may have been distracted from Lucy enough for her to escape, the reporters covering her were not. Murray Kempton, the *New York Post* columnist who was one of the few white journalists to turn the early civil rights struggles into a beat, watched in awe as Lucy "went into the bearpit." He watched her intently. She seemed so guileless, so lacking in affectation, so innately without a glimmer of flamboyance. And her quiet strength provoked him to write one of the loveliest sentences penned during the coverage of the entire civil rights movement: "What is this extraordinary resource of this otherwise unhappy country that it breeds such dignity in its victims?"[16]

From his nearby office at *The Tuscaloosa News,* the publisher, Buford Boone, viewed the events of that Monday with alarm. Boone was deeply offended that a mob had been allowed to rule the campus in his town. Every report told him Lucy had only narrowly escaped alive. It became clear to him that if the mob prevailed, it would mean that the highest authority in the land, the Supreme Court, had been not merely demeaned but defeated. Suddenly, Lucy and the sweeping issues of race and racism were of small moment compared to the much larger question of whether the government—

and democracy—would be able to withstand the determination of a group of people to disregard it. How could the Supreme Court continue to function if thugs could thwart its rulings? And if the Supreme Court couldn't function, what could?

Boone was no liberal, not even an integrationist. He was not looking to enter the fight over segregation if he could avoid it, and he was planning to hold off any commentary as long as he could. Racial ferment was everywhere, and he saw no reason to propound on every issue that came down the pike. Two days after Lucy was chased from the campus, the University of North Carolina accepted three Negro undergraduates with hardly any notice, thirty-three Negro children in Little Rock filed suit to integrate schools there, the Georgia House of Representatives voted 179 to 1 in favor of nullifying *Brown,* and the Philadelphia schools got their first Negro high school principal. Boone was certainly not interested in commenting on all those developments.[17] Had the defiance of a Supreme Court order been anywhere other than Tuscaloosa, he realized, he probably would never have commented editorially on the subject.

But the action *was* in Tuscaloosa, and something had to be done. The way he saw it, the university had no choice but to accept Lucy. Well, Boone would concede on further thought, there was one other choice. The people of Alabama—the white people, the university administrators, and the students—had another option. They would have to let her in, Boone would say, or they would have to kill her.[18]

When they almost killed her, Boone would be provoked to do several things he had never done before. Though he was the publisher, he took over the editorial writing from the editor, a native of New Jersey, whose views, Boone felt, would be suspect for that reason alone. Boone also, for the only time in his otherwise ethically upright career, planted a letter to the editor in his own paper in order to make a point more credibly than he otherwise might have. And he walked straight into an angry Citizens' Council meeting to explain to a seething audience why it was essential that the Supreme Court ruling be obeyed and that Negroes be admitted peacefully to the university.

Boone had long been under the influence of open-minded and courageous people in his family and in his newspaper career. He had been born in 1909 in Newnan, Georgia, about thirty miles southwest of Atlanta, into a family that had Confederate credentials on both sides. His great-grandfather had been killed at Bull Run, and his grandfather on the other side had been injured in the war. But he had seen even his grandfather, who lived into his nineties, put aside old racial prejudices. After years as a soldier, a farmer, and legislative leader, Boone's grandfather had concluded that Negro people must be treated as human beings. He had not only felt it, he had said it. When Boone's grandfather had run for the Georgia legislature the last time,

his own brothers had been so disturbed by his conversion that they had campaigned against him.[19]

Boone had gotten his degree in journalism from Mercer University in
Macon, a Southern Baptist–affiliated institution of higher learning, then
signed on with the *Macon Telegraph and News*. There he fell under the influence of another man whose experience and courage inspired him, the newspaper's editor, Mark Ethridge. Under Ethridge, Boone came to the view that
the subjugation of Negro people, aside from being inhumane, was economic
suicide for the South. He wanted his fellow southerners to define themselves
not by their skin color but by the overall contribution they could make to the
economy and culture of the region.[20]

Like Ethridge, Boone left the newspaper business for a period of time to
join the government. In 1942, he joined the Federal Bureau of Investigation
and became a speechwriter for the director, J. Edgar Hoover, a man he
deeply admired. In 1946, he returned to Macon as editor of the paper, and a
year later he moved to Tuscaloosa to become publisher and part owner of
The Tuscaloosa News. He understood the complexity and explosiveness of
the racial issue in the South. He had a good sense for how swiftly the change
might come and the need for southern newspapers to prepare the region for
it. Without such preparation, he believed, there was no hope that the South
would swallow sweeping change overnight. "If you are pouring water into a
gallon jug through a funnel," he would say, "you can't pour it any faster than
the neck of the funnel would take."[21]

Boone watched as the storm gathered over Tuscaloosa but offered little
editorial comment. He knew what he felt and was waiting for the right
opportunity to say it. "There comes a time when people ought to stand for
what our country stands for, other than on Mount Suribachi," Boone would
say. Timing was key. To say the right thing at the wrong time was pointless.
To have impact, you had to know, almost instinctively, when your readers
were going to turn to your page for whatever clarity and wisdom you could
offer.

In the days leading up to her admission, his only editorial had concerned
Lucy's complaint that the school had refused to assign her a dorm room.
Boone's response was that the university, by litigating every last inch of
ground since 1952, had pushed the issue beyond the most extreme bound-
aries of common sense but that Lucy was now pressing "too hard, too fast
and too much." In an editorial entitled "This Pushing, Pushing Is No Good,"
he urged Lucy, for now, to be satisfied with winning admission and to focus
on getting onto campus and into classes. She had every right to demand a
room assignment on campus, he said, "but we do think it foolish, and fraught
with grave danger."[22]

Even such moderate thoughts from a white man were viewed as extreme in Alabama in 1956. To accept the Supreme Court's authority was heresy, and Boone had gone well past that. In the segregationist mind, he did not seem to be scolding Lucy so much as coaching her, as if they were on the same team. And when he referred to southern Negroes as "our friends and fellow citizens" who "deserve fair treatment, equal opportunities," he made himself a lightning rod.

During the weekend when the night demonstrations took place, Boone became concerned by reliable reports that ammunition was being sold around town. He became alarmed that firepower in jittery hands would lead to a tragedy. The university seemed to be doing shockingly little to curb the nighttime gatherings or to protect Lucy. The day after she was hounded off the campus, when it was still unclear whether she would try to return, Boone turned out an editorial that he decided had to break from its traditional position inside the newspaper. He put "What a Price for Peace" on page one.

"When mobs start imposing their frenzied will on universities," Boone opened, "we have a bad situation." Compared to the richness and acuity of Grover Hall's writing style, Boone's was somewhat pedestrian. But in his unwillingness to let the smoke from the sideshows of boycotts and interposition arguments fog his vision, he moved out of the range of Hall's long shadow. "The target was Autherine Lucy," he wrote. "Her 'crimes'? She was born Negro, and she was moving against Southern custom and tradition—but with the law, right on up to the United States Supreme Court, on her side.

"What does it mean today at the University of Alabama, and here in Tuscaloosa, to have the law on your side?

"The answer has to be: Nothing—that is, if a mob disagrees with you and the courts."

Whereas the university and its trustees should have used "whatever force is necessary to restrain and subdue" lawbreakers, he wrote, they instead had "knuckled under to the pressures and desires of a mob." The result had been "an abject surrender to what is expedient rather than a courageous stand for what is right."[23]

Boone's editorial received widespread attention and reprinting. He was also subjected to intense local condemnation, subscription cancellations, and threats. In subsequent days, when Lucy's future remained unclear, Boone's critics would not let him sleep. In the middle of the night, the phone would start ringing. The calls came every twenty minutes, just as Boone, his wife, and children were falling back asleep. He finally put in a second telephone line and kept it unlisted, then at night took the listed phone off the hook. On other occasions, windows in his house were broken, or his wife was called when Boone was away and was told he was in grave trouble.[24]

The mob—"mad dogs," Boone called them—was relentless. People who wrote letters to the editor of his paper to express sentiments in any way favorable to Lucy's admission found themselves harassed. Boone knew of one case when a faculty member on the staff of Stillman College, a Negro institution in town, was so intimidated night after night that his wife had to be admitted to a mental institution.[25]

Boone was determined to run all the letters he received but had no interest in handing the Citizens' Councils and other segregationists the map to the homes of his letter writers. So he took the extraordinary step of publishing letters without the names of the letter writers.[26]

Much of the time, he found little support for his position about town, or around the state. Just about the only editor who consistently agreed with him was Neil O. Davis of the *Lee County Bulletin* in Auburn. Davis had been in the fourth Nieman class, in 1941–42, with fellow southern journalists Harry Ashmore and Thomas Sancton. Davis's weekly was brave but small. The student newspaper at the university, *The Crimson-White,* was also showing notable courage, as would several student papers in the South over the critical years. The student newspaper, since 1950, had said editorially that desegregation was inevitable, was nothing to panic about, and should be adopted gradually. The editor at the time of Lucy's enrollment, Nelson Cole, urged support for the university's president, who, though largely ineffectual in keeping the campus secure, was committed to enrolling Lucy in accordance with the Supreme Court mandate. Students caught in indecision, he wrote, ought to stack the university's efforts "against those of the howling few."

Other than that, Boone didn't see many editors lined up on his side of a fence that was itself sagging under the weight of uncertain editors. Even the sound coming out of Atlanta, from the office of the editor Ralph McGill, was silence. Boone, while comfortable in his beliefs, nonetheless felt very lonely.[27]

The Tuscaloosa rumor mill seemed to be working when everyone else was asleep, spitting out one falsehood after another. The national news media didn't always help the situation, either, and in some ways just fanned the flames. When NBC's John Cameron Swayze went on the *Camel News Caravan* with the evening report of the mob that had confronted Lucy, the film that accompanied the report showed an ambulance with a dome light stopping for a victim. The film sent Tuscaloosa citizens into a rage: no ambulance had been called to campus, and Tuscaloosa's ambulances were not even equipped with dome lights.[28] In correcting the report the next night, Swayze said the film had come from a Montgomery television station and showed a Montgomery ambulance picking up an injured person there.[29]

In that atmosphere, when the rumor mill ran out of fabrications about Lucy, it turned on people like Boone. One persistent rumor was that the *News* was secretly owned by a group of New York Negroes and that Boone was their pawn. Boone was not quite sure how to refute the rumor without giving it more prominence. In frustration one day, he blurted out, in the presence of a reporter, that he wished someone would write him a letter to the editor asking about the ownership of the paper, so that he could respond.

"I can get you a dozen," the reporter responded instantly.

"I don't need but one," Boone said, thinking that was the end of it.

That afternoon, the reporter arranged for a friend of his to act as an intermediary provocateur and to engage an unsuspecting *News* reader in a discussion about the newspaper's editorial position. The reader took the bait. He said he sure wished he knew the truth behind all the rumors about the paper's ownership.

"Why don't you write a letter?" asked the intermediary.

"I can't write a letter," the reader said.

"Well," said the intermediary, "I'll help you write one."

The next day, the reporter came in with an authentic letter signed by an authentic reader who was genuinely curious about the ownership of the paper. "Okay," said the reporter, handing it to Boone, "here it is."

Boone took the opportunity to inform his readers that he owned 80 percent of the newspaper's stock and that another Tuscaloosa resident, a white man, owned the other 20 percent. They and the employees, alone, decided the editorial position, he wrote. "No other person, organization or corporation has any voice in such decisions whatsoever." Boone then listed all his southern credentials, including his family's ties to the Confederacy, and quietly put the rumors to rest.[30]

The question facing Emory Jackson and Lucy's attorneys and allies was whether they could go into the U.S. District Court, presided over by Judge Hobart Grooms, and accuse the university of conspiring with the thugs to keep her away. Jackson argued strongly against it. Running between his editing responsibilities in Birmingham, his seat at the table of the Montgomery Improvement Association, and his meetings with Lucy and her lawyers, Jackson nonetheless maintained sharp instincts about where the land mines were located. He warned that there was little more than atmospheric evidence of a conspiracy and that the tactic would blow up in their face. Jackson, whose contacts on campus told him that the university's suspension was genuinely intended to be only temporary until her safety could be ensured, wanted Lucy's attorneys to keep their request for judicial relief simple. She remained an enrolled student, he insisted, and her attorneys needed only to request that the university readmit her.[31]

But Lucy's legal team rejected Jackson's warning. Over Thurgood Marshall's signature, Constance Baker Motley of the Legal Defense Fund and the Birmingham attorney Arthur Shores filed papers accusing the university of conspiring with four men who had been arrested for disorderly conduct "to assimilate the air of riot and disorder and rebellion on the campus . . . as a subterfuge" to block Lucy.[32]

Not only was there no evidence of a conspiracy—which Marshall later conceded by trying to withdraw the claim—but the strategy offended the university administrators, who had shown goodwill by trying to protect and guide Lucy and who were dismayed at the thought of sharing the role of defendant with Klansmen.[33]

Following a hearing, Judge Grooms scolded the university and lifted its suspension of Lucy. But that only opened the door for the administration to bring a more serious charge. Almost immediately, the board members put together a resolution accusing Lucy of falsely defaming the university. They then voted to expel her permanently, an act it had not taken against any student in a decade.

Boone, who had urged Lucy's peaceful admission, was left on a lonely limb. Lucy, he declared editorially, had every right to press a legal claim for readmission. But she would do everyone a favor to pull back. In an editorial entitled "Could We Have a Gift of Peace?" Boone said the city, the university, the state, and all the forces amassed on both sides needed a pause in the action. "Autherine Lucy does have a great gift within her power. It could be a gift of time—time for us to think, time to adjust to the changes that have been decreed as a result of her efforts, and time for us to re-establish an equilibrium."[34]

The day after she was expelled, Lucy left the state. The NAACP would terminate its lawsuit. Though Negroes had won the legal right to enroll at the University of Alabama, another seven years would pass before any Negro students would be admitted.

In his editorials, Jackson was remarkably sanguine about the developments. "These two friends," he wrote of Autherine Lucy and Pollie Anne Myers Hudson, "opened doors that will never be closed. In more sober days when sanity has been restored, the University of Alabama's board of trustees is likely to try to make peace with history and square itself with the conscience of humanity."[35]

As the bus boycott approached the end of its second month, a state grand jury meeting in Montgomery returned indictments against King on the charge of illegally conspiring to hinder a lawful business by boycotting the bus service. The grand jury didn't stop with King. By the time the grand jury got through all the charges, it had indicted 115 people, including two dozen Negro pastors and many other prominent Negro leaders.

Grover Hall was stunned. Such a sweeping attack by state and county officials was ham-handed and self-defeating and would serve only to pull the curtain back on southern stupidity for the entire world to see. "The dumbest act that has ever been done in Montgomery" was how he described it.[36]

From the moment the indictments came down on February 21, the Montgomery bus boycott grew to a national news story, and King became the journalistic touchstone for what suddenly was being recognized as a civil rights movement. Montgomery had not been such an important dateline since Jefferson Davis had been inaugurated as president of the Confederacy ninety-five years earlier.

The New York Times put Associated Press accounts of the indictments on the front page for two days and immediately sent a reporter to Montgomery who kept the story on the front page with the angle that Emory Jackson had developed weeks before: the movement's roots in Gandhian principles of passive resistance. The Washington Post, for the first time, flew a reporter into Montgomery and began playing the boycott on the front page. Newsweek, already several beats behind Time magazine, threw together an extensive story, then joined the Times in staking out the story for the next several weeks.

Law enforcement officials kept stepping into their own traps. When they decided to put King on trial first—and alone—they might as well have sent out engraved invitations to his coronation as emperor of the movement. Reporters, photographers, and courtroom artists flowed into Montgomery from Chicago, Boston, and New York, then from London, Paris, and New Delhi.

The Negro newspapers intensified their coverage, sending in waves of reporters and photographers, including the civil rights beat correspondents who had covered the Till trial and the Lucy enrollment.

Those closest to King were amazed and delighted by the impact the swarm of reporters and their coverage were having on the spirit of the protesters. "It was a cosmopolitan lot: friendly, forward, warm, generous, incessantly smoking and talking," King's associate and first biographer, L. D. Reddick, later recalled. "It gave the slow-moving town a fillip. The sympathies of the working newsmen were definitely with the boycotters. Their personal views were much stronger than they could afford to show in their news stories and radio-TV comments."[37] The protesters became instant news consumers, turning on their televisions and radios, sharing copies of The New York Times, and seeing themselves, for the first time, in the heroic image that the world was beginning to witness.[38]

The Hartford Courant showed remarkable prescience. In an editorial entitled "Martin Luther King, Negro Leader," the Courant noted the "growing leadership" of King, then added, "By virtue of his intelligence and piety, Mr. King has gradually become the spokesman for passive resistance. It is well to remember his name. For if this movement is successful, as it appears likely, the Reverend Dr. King will become not only a national hero among his race, but the continuing spearhead in the fight against segregation."[39]

The New York Times wrote the first detailed biography of King, a "Man in

the News" story headlined "Battle Against Tradition." The article characterized King as "a rather soft-spoken man with a learning and maturity far
beyond his twenty-seven years." His speaking style caught the reporter's
attention: ". . . he can build to his climax with a crescendo of impassioned
pulpit-pounding that overwhelms the listener with the depth of his convictions." The story carried a photograph of King appearing trim, fashionable,
and serious.[40]

The charge against King was a misdemeanor. Still, the nonjury trial lasted
four days. King's lawyers were able during that time to put the bus company's behavior on trial. They presented a series of witnesses whose stories
made wrenching front-page reading across the nation. In the end, King was
convicted—and martyred. The news made page one in most major newspapers, and the newsmagazines carried the kind of contextual color and irony
that served to chisel King's heroic stature into the national consciousness.

Jet magazine dubbed King "Alabama's Modern Moses." The *Norfolk
Journal and Guide*'s editor, P. B. Young, Jr., traveled to Montgomery and
wrote a firsthand, two-part series that spanned several pages and was loaded
with photographs. "Dixie Black Moses Says Boycott Fight to Finish,"
declared the first story. A headline in *The Pittsburgh Courier* declared, REV.
M. L. KING — "GANDHI" IN ALABAMA.[41]

Ebony weighed in with the most extensive and meaningful piece, "The
King Plan for Freedom," which carried King's eight-point road map to integration and presented him, in words and pictures, as the determined but personally modest "leader Negroes have been seeking for a quarter of a
century."[42] By the end of the summer of 1956, the King story, well on the
path to legend, was reaching into an altogether different and potent market.
Redbook carried a piece on King, "Our Weapon Is Love," in August 1956.[43]

Not all the visiting reporters were transfixed by King. One notable journalist found King, and the press's embrace of him, unappealing. Writing for
The Manchester Guardian, its U.S. correspondent, Alistair Cooke, displayed
sympathy for the bus company, whose buses remained idled while King
arranged car transportation for the city's Negro residents.

"Understandably, Montgomery is made to feel like a culprit city, for again
the Northern reporter's instinct is to ignore the bus company except to count
the long lines of buses gleaming idly in the hot sun, and to be welcomed as a
brother-in-arms by the Rev. Martin Luther King, jun., the young Negro
organiser of the boycott who flies in and out of the airport a couple of times
a week buying station wagons from 'neutral' outlanders as the Arabs go
scouting for Soviet planes."

Cooke described King as "a young, bland man with solemn good looks"
who, among Negroes, stood behind only Abraham Lincoln in the pantheon
of emancipators. Whites, Cooke said, found King to be "a very smooth arti-

cle and as willing to be the cat's paw of the NAACP as the stubborn woman who started it all was to become the Paul Revere of the boycott."[44] The *Montgomery Advertiser* reprinted Cooke's observations.

Other than Cooke and some minor examples, the national coverage of King and the movement was overwhelmingly favorable, sometimes fawning. Part of his enduring heroic stature, eventually, would derive from his ability to manage his coverage, to manipulate reporters, and to calculate outcomes. Still, the Montgomery movement was a spontaneous and serendipitous convergence of events and circumstances. The pervasive belief, inside the movement, that the legitimacy of the boycott—and the illegitimacy of bus segregation—would be judicially supported was real, fresh, honest, and appealing to reporters, who, for the first time in their lives, were covering a story that had no grays.

If King and his followers had any hope that national exposure of the civil rights movement would help defang the snake of official segregation in Alabama, they quickly learned otherwise. Even as the state was swarming with reporters—and perhaps because of it—the state of Alabama proved willing to take whatever action it felt was necessary to undercut the juggernaut of integration.

In the spring of 1956, the state attorney general, John Patterson, demanded that the state NAACP provide him a copy of its membership list, so he could sift it for Communists. The organization refused. On June 1, Patterson obtained a state court order barring virtually all of the NAACP's activities in the state and fining it $100,000. Patterson accused the organization of helping to organize and finance the bus boycott and paying for Lucy's entry to the University of Alabama.[45]

The NAACP had to shut down its state and regional offices in Birmingham, shift its operation to Atlanta, and leave leaders such as Emory Jackson without their most effective political base. It would take seven years and four trips to the U.S. Supreme Court for the NAACP to win its lawsuit challenging the state actions and to get back into business. By then, Negro leaders in the state were disorganized, and they weren't getting anymore encouraging visits from people such as Marshall and Motley. Fearing they would be subpoenaed, harassed, and hit by a monetary assessment if they crossed into Alabama, both stayed away, for seven years.[46]

Four days after the NAACP was banned, and six months to the day after the bus protest started, the boycott won its first major legal victory. A panel of federal judges, each born and raised in Alabama, ruled 2–1 that local bus segregation in Montgomery was unconstitutional. Five months later, in November, the U.S. Supreme Court upheld that decision. And it took another month for the Supreme Court to refuse to reconsider its decision and for the city of Montgomery to accept defeat.

As King called together a mass meeting to end the boycott, reporters again flocked to the capital. The Negro press, which had been there first a year earlier, had a special sense of excitement. For L. Alex Wilson and Ernest Withers of the *Tri-State Defender* in Memphis, the Supreme Court decision represented a joyous vindication. Virtually every civil rights story they'd covered in the previous two years had ended with a funeral or without satisfactory resolution. They had seen the brutal impact of massive resistance on George W. Lee, Gus Courts, Lamar Smith, and Emmett Till. Montgomery and the power of passive resistance were at last providing the validation and victory they so desperately wanted.

Following the decision to end the boycott, King made plans to rise early the next morning and formally become the first to break the boycott by boarding a bus with a white pastor. That, in fact, is what was widely reported the next day and for years to come. But someone else may have been first. In his hotel room after the meeting, Alex Wilson was feeling too inspired and exhilarated to let the story pass by him routinely. He came up with a plan of his own. At four in the morning, he woke Withers up and told him to get dressed, Withers would later say. The two of them went out onto Montgomery's dark streets and waited for a bus. When the first one arrived, Withers began shooting pictures of Wilson boarding the bus, then took some more shots of Wilson sitting in the front of the bus. The driver, Withers recalled, was hiding his face.[47]

CHAPTER 10

TOWARD LITTLE ROCK

S oon after completing *The Negro and the Schools* and setting up the SERS, Harry Ashmore had returned to the quiet of Little Rock to become the newspaper editor he really wanted to be. It was a position that would allow him to watch politics at all levels and to witness the race story as it unfolded across the region.

But merely watching and witnessing were not Ashmore's way. Within a very short time, the race story would be not unfolding but exploding, not across the region but in his own front yard. Ashmore would find himself involved in a story that was cataclysmic as an episode in the history of civil rights and crucial as a turning point in how the gathering racial storm was presented to the American people and the world.

It would be in Little Rock that news organizations would change, in just about every respect, the way they covered what would become known as the civil rights movement.

Upon his return to full-time newspapering, Ashmore had almost immediately jumped into the political fray, on behalf of a candidate who seemed to be moving from an outpost of political acceptability to the center. As the 1954 governor's race took shape, Ashmore was attracted not to Francis Cherry, the smooth, mannerly, silver-haired incumbent, whose reform record Ashmore applauded, but to Orval Eugene Faubus, a lesser-known former schoolteacher, postmaster, highway commissioner, and weekly newspaper owner who had come out of the Ozarks with a populist agenda and a lot of moxie.

Faubus was willing to say, privately at least, that if he had been on the Supreme Court, he would not have parted from the unanimous verdict on *Brown*.[1] He seemed less likely to be swayed by the rising wind of racial emotion, less likely to alter Arkansas's course of racial moderation. The state had developed a reputation for going its own way, for more closely resembling a border state, or a southwestern state, on matters of race. The University of Arkansas had been the first public institution of higher learning in the South to integrate, doing so peacefully in 1948. Following the *Brown* decision, Fayetteville had been the first town in the former Confederacy to agree to integrate its public schools; its school board approved an integration plan a mere four days after the Warren Court had spoken.[2] Another Arkansas town, Charleston, had been the first actually to do so, in August 1954.

Little Rock, Ashmore felt confident, would fall into that progressive line. The leadership was in place at the school board, in the mayor's office, in the business community, and at the newspaper to move forward with strategic, phased-in desegregation. All a governor had to do was to leave it alone and let it happen. To Ashmore, Faubus seemed the more likely candidate to resist the opportunities for derailing the process. Put another way, Faubus seemed more likely to listen to Ashmore. When Ashmore editorially upbraided Faubus early in the campaign for declaring desegregation the most important issue, Faubus dropped the subject from his stump speech.[3]

And when, in the closing days of the Democratic primary, Faubus's past jumped from a closet and nearly killed him politically, it was Ashmore who saved him.

Ashmore had known Faubus enough to know he bore an unusual political legacy. Faubus's father, Sam Faubus, had been a disputatious leafleter against organized religion and for socialism. He so worshiped the Socialist leader Eugene V. Debs that he had named his son Orval Eugene after him.

Orval had attended tiny Commonwealth College in western Arkansas, an unusual institution that was distinct because of the socialist tilt to its founding, mission, curriculum, and funding. For Cherry, who could feel Faubus gaining on him at the close of the 1954 Democratic primary, Faubus's connection to Commonwealth was delicious.

His advisers first tried to place an ad in the *Gazette* to initiate the attack, but the newspaper refused to accept it and put the campaign on notice that any effort to use the issue would be met by editorial rebuke.[4] In the final eight days of the campaign, in a flurry of speeches, Cherry unleashed the Commonwealth issue, suggesting that Faubus had subversive ties.

Faubus's early explanations were stumbling. He falsely denied having attended the school, then contradicted himself. His campaign started to falter.

Ashmore watched with dismay. He was deeply offended that Cherry would stoop to such tactics. This was precisely the kind of demagoguery that Ashmore had feared would ruin any hope for progress in the South. It was this type of preying on ignorance that had led him to write *The Negro and the Schools* and help create the SERS and its *Southern School News*. When Faubus's aides came seeking help, Ashmore agreed to draft a speech that could save Faubus.

A week before the primary, Ashmore met with two Faubus aides and began crafting a speech that Faubus would deliver that night in a statewide radio broadcast from a Pine Bluff ballpark. As Ashmore finished each page, he handed it to a runner who took it to Faubus, who made revisions and gave it to another runner, who gave it to a typist. The speech was finished just in time for the broadcast. In Ashmore's words, Faubus explained how his poverty and his desire for an inexpensive college education had led him to the subsidized education available at Commonwealth. Faubus took special delight in delivering one particular phrase crafted by Ashmore: "When I went out from the green valley of my youth . . ." Faubus said he had stayed at the school only briefly and had left when he saw what he'd gotten into. In high dudgeon, he sharply rebuked the personal smear campaign unfurled against him. As he uttered Ashmore's words, the audience in front of him began weeping and cheering. The speech was the turning point.[5]

Faubus won the Democratic nomination. "I know the obligation that a politician has," he told Ashmore one day. "You have a blank check on me that you can cash anytime."[6] It never occurred to Ashmore then that he might consider the possibility only three years later.

In the general election, Faubus faced the mayor of Little Rock, a Republican, whose certainty of losing was underscored by the fact that he drew an endorsement from the Negro newspaper, the *Arkansas State Press*. L. C. and Daisy Bates had run the *State Press* since 1941, and they could be neither pushed nor purchased into an easy rationalization for segregation. The Bateses concluded that Faubus was unmistakably a segregationist and not the more benign populist Ashmore saw. In endorsing the Republican, they declared, "If we are to be hanged, we'll be damned if we'll furnish the rope."[7] Their endorsement was futile.

Faubus served as a progressive model for much of his first two years and through his next election. When the *New York Herald Tribune* sent Homer Bigart, one of its toughest correspondents, into the South in the fall of 1955 to survey the political crop against the racial backdrop, he came away convinced that only two "good men" occupied governors' offices in the South: Faubus and Florida's LeRoy Collins.[8]

In the fall of 1955, Ashmore decided to take a leave from his job to serve as a personal assistant to Adlai Stevenson during the campaign for the Democratic nomination for president. One of the first notes of congratulations Ashmore received came from Turner Catledge at *The New York Times*. Ashmore quickly responded, then added a handwritten postscript: "Would the *Times'* policy bend far enough to spare John Popham for a year? He's my—and Stevenson's—first choice as a press secretary for the campaign." The answer from Catledge was no, the policy was not flexible; Popham said he was not interested anyway.[9]

During the time Ashmore was with the campaign, 101 of the 128 members of Congress from the Confederate states signed a "Declaration of Constitutional Principles," which became known as the Southern Manifesto.[10] It declared war on *Brown* and sent the message that acts of defiance in furtherance of the declaration were acts of virtue.

By huge margins, Arkansans voted in late 1956 for prosegregation and interposition resolutions. The next year opened with fresh laws allowing parents to refuse to send their children to integrated schools, requiring the NAACP to reveal financial and membership information, permitting school districts to use public funds to fight integration, and creating a Sovereignty Commission to investigate integration activities in the state.

Ashmore and other civic leaders felt they had a legal obligation to comply with the Supreme Court and an opportunity to make integration work. It was mostly a matter of methodically working things out ahead of time, appealing to the better instincts of the better people, giving them the clearest information available, and creating a groundswell that gave comfort to the queasy and left the objectors standing alone. It looked like an obvious strategy, but not an easy one.

As the southern states began responding to the complicated issues of school desegregation, it became clear to Ashmore that the old divisions and habits would remain. The border states of Kentucky, Maryland, Missouri, Delaware, West Virginia, and Oklahoma would probably continue to proceed smoothly with school integration. For the most part, those states had progressive political, educational, and religious leadership, as well as vigorous sanction from their leading newspapers. Atlanta, where Negro voters had contributed to the election of Mayor William Hartsfield and where the business community had an enlightened approach to racial problems, responded much the same way.

Ashmore had good reason to be hopeful about desegregation efforts in three North Carolina cities in the summer of 1957: Charlotte, Greensboro, and Winston-Salem. Pete McKnight had left the *Southern School News* to become editor of *The Charlotte Observer* after it was purchased by Knight Newspapers; he wanted Charlotte to desegregate peacefully and was in regular touch with Ashmore and the editors in Greensboro and Winston-Salem. In the end, the North Carolina editors and their school boards decided upon tight coordination among the three cities and months of secret planning—a departure from the openness opted for by the Little Rock school board and by Ashmore and the *Gazette*.

The North Carolina editors believed that any advance coverage might give segregation extremists more time to organize disturbances, so they kept their own reporters in the dark. Out of view and off the record, the school boards had been meeting in hotels and restaurants. They brought in speakers from border states that had desegregated, developed plans to assign a limited number of pupils to schools, and tried to achieve desegregation without the pressure of a court mandate. It was essential, the three school boards agreed, to dilute the opposition.[11]

The school boards could not stay underground for long. Each board had to meet openly to decide how many applications from Negro students to accept to the white schools for the fall of 1957. As planned in secret, the three boards scheduled their meetings for the same night in late July. They left nothing to chance. The board in Winston-Salem, for example, had gathered extensive educational and personal records about Negro students who might qualify as the first enrollees. The editors were equally controlling, scripting coverage to the extent that Larry Jinks, the education writer for *The Charlotte Observer,* who was uncomfortable with all the secrecy, had already written his main story and two sidebars before he even got there. All that planning led to the decisions to select twelve students: six in Greensboro, five in Charlotte, and one in Winston-Salem.[12]

What Ashmore saw as hope in North Carolina, Jack Kilpatrick saw as a problem in Virginia. Charlottesville, Norfolk, Newport News, and Arlington County were under orders to admit Negro students in September, and the opposition had run out of delaying tactics. "Things are moving toward a showdown here in Virginia, and between us girls, I am rather gloomy about what is likely to happen," Kilpatrick wrote Bill Simmons, director of the Citizens' Councils in Jackson, in July 1957. "If the will of the people were stronger," he wrote, "everybody would simply say 'no' and wait for the marshals to show up with writs of contempt."

He concluded, "We have our backs to the wall in this fight now, but maybe that's not so bad a place to fight from. At least, they can't goose us from the rear."[13]

A week later, faced with the news that Charlotte, Greensboro, and Winston-Salem had approved desegregation, Kilpatrick was despairing. "That means that eight States no longer are standing firm," he wrote Simmons. "We are only seven now, and I doubt that Florida will hold out much longer. With North Carolina cracked, the pressure will turn harder than ever on Virginia, and unhappily, I doubt that our people have guts enough to stand up against it."[14]

A month later, in August 1957, Kilpatrick and other segregationist editors were even grumpier. A civil rights bill they vigorously opposed, the first such bill to get up a head of steam in Washington since 1875, was headed for certain congressional approval. Kilpatrick was turning bitter. "As one old friend to another," he wrote Don Shoemaker, editor of the *Southern School News,* "I confess I am so sick of the whole business of school segregation I try most of the time not to read about it, think about it or even to write about it. Most of the Southside Virginia counties, I expect, will abandon their school systems before they will integrate. Over the rest of the State, the people probably will accept mongrelization, a little at first, then a lot. I expect the word offends you. It used to offend me. The longer we fight, though, the more intransigent each side becomes, and the more bitter becomes the emotional involvement. I'll never yield. I have no idea that the Afro-American will either. Where does that leave us?"[15]

In the end, only one U.S. senator was still trying to defeat the 1957 civil rights bill: Strom Thurmond of South Carolina, the 1948 Dixiecrat candidate, waged a one-man filibuster that lasted twenty-three hours and twelve minutes and failed. On August 29, diluted to win approval, the civil rights bill was steered by Majority Leader Lyndon B. Johnson to final passage by a 60–15 vote in the Senate. The new law authorized the Justice Department to enjoin election officials who interfered with a citizen's right to register or vote. It created a Commission on Civil Rights to investigate violations and created a Civil Rights Division within the Justice Department to prosecute violations of the law.

Ashmore drew little solace from knowing that few southern senators had rushed to support Thurmond's filibuster. He saw stiff-necked trouble all across Dixie. He saw segregationists whose violent trespasses would be forgiven, if not encouraged, by law enforcement. Now, more than three years after he'd pulled together southern editors at the American Society of Newspaper Editors meeting and joined them in launching the SERS, he still saw white community leaders, including newspaper publishers and editors, who were certain to fall prey to popular, often hysterical, sentiment. Many of the mainstream white editors would be paralyzed by indecision, hoping the pressure for change would just go away and they could get back to writing about the benefits of industrial parks or weighing whether their women's page should announce the wedding engagements of women who had previously been married.[16]

As his mind clicked through the cities of the South, Ashmore was not confident about the coming months. Birmingham would be bloody tough. The blue-collar unionists in that steel town had been persuaded that Negroes posed a greater threat to their livelihoods than their management. Industrialists weren't about to intervene and turn the wrath their own way. The newspapers there, the *Birmingham Post-Herald* and *The Birmingham News,* while different in many respects, wanted little more than to protect business interests and promote the image of a city moving forward in harmony, even if it meant downplaying the huge racial fault line looming in the road ahead.

In Mississippi, Ashmore concluded, civic and government leaders would be more genteel in their approach, but no less resistant. The Delta-born Citizens' Councils were spreading their influence across government, business, religion, and journalism with the subtlety and thoroughness of a soaking acid rain. The calls for resistance were most strident from the state's dominant U.S. senator, James Eastland, and its Hederman-owned newspapers, the Jackson *Clarion-Ledger* and the *Jackson Daily News.*

Virginia was virtually hopeless for early or easy integration. Even if Virginius Dabney at the *Richmond Times-Dispatch* was free to reassert his ever-fading brand of moderation, Kilpatrick at the *Richmond News Leader* was creating so much noise that Dabney could hardly be heard. Ashmore took Kilpatrick seriously but found his arguments so preposterous that his response typically was to poke fun at him. Ashmore liked to say that Kilpatrick believed that "nothing of significance has happened since Calhoun and Webster concluded their last debate."[17]

South Carolina was unpromising, Ashmore believed. His Charleston friend Tom Waring, whom he had put on the board of the SERS, was making sure of that. Ashmore believed that Waring saw racial problems as a subset of class problems that had developed with the demise of southern aristocracy. "The *News and Courier* feels that what's wrong with this country is democracy," Ashmore liked to say.[18]

Tennessee was perplexing. The two major cities, Nashville and Memphis, were torn, forever unsure if they were Deep South and inward-looking, or Mid-South and outward-looking. In Nashville, the rivalries between the *Banner* and *The Tennessean* went back to the early 1900s, when the publishers couldn't stand each other. The disagreements had survived through the generations. The *Banner* had backed the Dixiecrats in 1948; *The Tennessean* never veered from the Democrats. While the *Banner* was the first paper in the South to hire (and then pigeonhole) a Negro reporter to a full-time staff position, the paper invoked all the states' rights arguments in opposing civil rights. *The Tennessean* had fought the poll tax and established itself as more liberal and more aggressive in writing about the race story. But it could not guarantee the peace.[19]

Memphis was divided much the same way. The two newspapers, by virtue of mergers that had led to the Scripps-Howard empire, were owned by the same chain. But they differed on most race questions. *The Commercial Appeal,* which had the largest circulation in the state, had long taken the implausible position that educational opportunity for Negroes should be expanded, as long as it could be achieved without disturbing the status quo for whites. Led by an editor, Frank Ahlgren, who gave credence and news space to the writings of white supremacists who touted "scientific evidence" that Negroes were genetically inferior, *The Commercial Appeal* had resisted every desegregation court ruling of the early 1950s. But when the *Brown* decision had come down, the paper stepped back and counseled "calmness, reason and a genuine spirit of cooperation" to abide by the law of the land.[20]

Under its editor, Edward J. Meeman, the *Press-Scimitar* had been consistently more liberal for nearly a quarter of a century when *Brown* came down. The *Press-Scimitar* had begun covering the Negro community long before most other white newspapers and had started using honorifics and proper courtesy titles such as "Mr." and "Mrs." for Negroes earlier than most other southern papers.[21] But it was the smaller and less influential of the two newspapers.

So where, Ashmore wondered, would the leadership for change come from? There was the Negro press, of course, as determined as ever to help usher in an era of racial equality. Negro reporters still went places white reporters wouldn't go, in search of stories white reporters didn't even know about. Many Negro papers and their newsrooms displayed the Negro Press Creed: "The Negro press believes that America can best lead the world away from racial and national antagonisms when it accords every man, regardless of race, color, or creed, his human and equal rights. Hating no man, fearing no man, the Negro press strives to help every man in the firm belief that all are hurt as long as anyone is held back."[22]

Negro newspapers still were not of the same mind when the pace of integration was under discussion. But most editors and reporters working in the Negro press were like L. C. and Daisy Bates of the *Arkansas State Press* in Little Rock. The Bateses were vigorous supporters of civil rights and did not leave confusion about where they stood. In their first week of publication in May 1941, the Bateses had set an editorial tone that positioned them in the advocacy tradition of the Negro press. They had urged a federal ban on job discrimination against Negroes in defense industries. Winning the war was paramount, the Bateses had written, and the nation weakened itself by not putting Negro labor to work in factories, shipyards, and airplane works. "This is no time to quibble with stupid race prejudice," they had written.[23]

In 1950, when *Ebony* magazine had asked a dozen Negro publishers to write the headline they would most like to see in their newspapers, *The Pittsburgh Courier* had wanted Ralph Bunche to be named secretary of state. *The Philadelphia Tribune* had hoped to see all Southern colleges open to Negroes. The *Norfolk Journal and Guide* had imagined Negroes being admitted to all labor unions, and other papers had played with the idea that federal courts or Congress might demand an end to segregation. L. C. Bates had had a grander vision: "South Abolishes All Jim Crow."[24]

L. C. and Daisy Bates had come to operate in Little Rock much the same way Emory Jackson operated in Alabama: They ran the newspaper by day and the state NAACP by night. L. C. Bates, who was the paper's voice, had gotten his start on the Kansas City *Call,* the same paper that had made Roy Wilkins a newspaperman before he had become head of the NAACP. L.C. had been a friend of Daisy's father and was considerably older than Daisy when they married. They were prospering with the newspaper, well enough to have a housekeeper and to host popular parties where Daisy was known for her charm and poise, L.C. for being quiet and wry and offering good Scotch. To go beyond her high school education, Daisy Bates had taken accounting, speaking, and public relations courses and was sought after by a growing number of organizations that saw she was an effective leader.

By the middle of 1957, Daisy Bates, who served as the paper's manager, editor, and writer, was devoting an increasing amount of time to her duties as head of the state NAACP. In that job, she fought in federal court for an accelerated desegregation plan. Having lost, she was thankful there was any such plan at all and saw no evidence that anything would stop it. She began working with parents and educators to select the students who would cross the line.

From town to town, the question in Arkansas was rarely whether they would integrate, but when and how. In Fort Smith, Ozark, and Van Buren, plans for integrating in the fall of 1957 were moving forward. Would the others start with the high school or the elementary school? With five students or fifty? With the more academically advanced Negro pupils or with any willing student?

In Little Rock, the school board had been talking for two and a half years. It was ready even before the Supreme Court issued the implementation order in May 1955. The phased-in integration plan for Little Rock would begin at Central High School in 1957 and take six years to reach the first grade.

The school year was to open on a Tuesday, September 3, the day after Labor Day. As the day neared, the mayor, the school board, the superintendent, the NAACP, the leading businessmen, Ashmore, his publisher, J. N. Heiskell, and the *Arkansas State Press* were all on board, more or less, to place 15 Negro students among the 2,000 whites at Central High. The NAACP had sued to force integration sooner, and two segregationist groups had made a final effort to halt the plan altogether, but they had all lost in federal court.

Two ardent segregationists from Georgia, Governor Marvin Griffin and former House Speaker Roy V. Harris, came to Little Rock, spoke to the Capital Citizens' Council, then met with Orval Faubus at the Governor's Mansion. Their goal was to stiffen Faubus's spine. Their rip-snorting speeches were greeted by wild cheering and rebel yells. Faubus had sent mixed signals all along, and he was known to suffer from fits of uncertainty and be vulnerable to uncertainty's friend, persuasion. "Faubus will fall for any story, however fantastic, if it is told with sufficient conviction," George Douthit, an *Arkansas Democrat* political reporter and close ally of Faubus, wrote as the events were unfolding.[25]

Ashmore hoped, on the Sunday before the Tuesday opening, to have that last word with Faubus; he tried in a front-page editorial, "A Time of Testing." Urging that Central High be desegregated peacefully, Ashmore wrote, "There are those who have suggested that this cannot be done without inciting the populace of this city to violence. They have, we believe, too little faith in the respect of our people for law and order."[26]

Faubus heard the same from other powerful voices, including Winthrop Rockefeller, the wealthiest person in the state and the governor's own head of industrial development. But Ashmore and Rockefeller were competing against segregationists who, outside the public eye, were urging Faubus to focus on getting elected to a third term.[27] They pushed on the governor the idea that carloads of armed white marauders were preparing to roll into Little Rock and that knife and gun stores were being depleted of their stocks as competing camps armed themselves.

Yet even as Faubus uttered that concern in court a week before school was to open, he made no public declaration to indicate that desegregation would not go forward as planned. As the days to the school opening became hours, the only deviation from the plan was the number of Negro students who would enroll; it had dropped to nine.

Then, on Sunday, September 1, two days before school was to open, Faubus reached a decision. He tried to find his attorney. He located him on a golf course and called him to the Governor's Mansion. Faubus said he wanted the lawyer to draw up an official proclamation announcing a plan he would reveal the next evening. Hearing the plan, the lawyer protested that Faubus's action would be viewed as hasty and provocative.[28]

It was a plan no one else heard that day. *Arkansas Gazette* readers picked up their newspapers on Labor Day, September 2, to find a comforting assessment of how the next day would go: "Little Rock Quiet on Eve of Opening Integrated Schools," said the headline on the newspaper's lead story. But the story was laced with ominous hints. "Mr. Faubus said that reports that he was considering declaring martial law to prevent the School Board from obeying the federal court order were 'strictly rumors,'" the *Gazette* reported. "He said he was watching the situation but had no plans to announce at this time."[29]

The *Gazette* was barely on doorsteps Monday morning when Ashmore was called to a meeting of his newspaper's principal owner, J. N. Heiskell, and Heiskell's son-in-law, the publisher Hugh Patterson. It was time to talk about what the paper's position would be if all the carefully laid plans were detonated and the city became a battleground. The decision would be Heiskell's.

Ashmore loved Heiskell. The old man had never let him down; his fifty-five years as a newspaper owner had not dulled his instincts as a newsman.

Heiskell remained so much the newshound that he had pushed away corporate executive titles in favor of the only title he wanted: editor. He liked to spend money on stories. He liked to give space over to news. He had once told Patterson to quit being so stingy, so profit-oriented, and to spend whatever it took to produce a high-quality newspaper.[30]

Downtown Little Rock was holiday quiet as they gathered at the *Gazette* building in Heiskell's second-floor office. Heiskell's political antennae, at eighty-four years of age, still picked up clear signals. His soundings of the business community were portentous, he said. If Faubus went completely to the other side, as Heiskell had heard, he would take many people with him. The *Gazette,* if it insisted on riding the desegregation wave, would ride alone, probably at great cost. This was precisely the situation Ashmore had long worried that other editors in the South would face; he had never expected that the problem would be Little Rock's, or his.

Ashmore and his newsroom were ready to fight their way out, but the paper was not his to lose. He wasn't sure that Heiskell was interested in losing the paper at this stage of his career. Heiskell looked out the window to the deserted streets. "I'm an old man," he said, "and I've lived too long to let people like that take over my city."[31] To Patterson, there was no question about what the newspaper should do. It could not abandon its principles. "That's not a difficult kind of decision to make if you're basically honest," he said. "There's no other way to go."[32]

The nine Negro Little Rock students spent the final day of summer vacation, and the final day of their own personal anonymity, trying to relax and enjoy the outdoors with family and friends. One, Jefferson Thomas, dropped by the Bateses' home. Their house, frequently with a television or radio dishing out news, had become the general headquarters for the teenagers and their parents; Daisy and L.C. had no children together, so she called the nine students "my children." Their spare bedroom had become lodgings for visiting members of the Negro press, and their living room and kitchen table had become the chief staging areas for the integration plan.[33]

As Jeff Thomas went into the Bateses' kitchen and began pulling a snack from the refrigerator, the radio issued a jolting news bulletin: Governor Faubus was seeking television time later that night, at 10:15, to address the citizens of Arkansas.[34] The governor, it seemed, had a plan after all.

In early August, as schools in the South prepared to reopen amid the most earnest integration attempts so far, news organizations began making their coverage plans. In Little Rock, the Associated Press bureau chief, Keith Fuller, was so confident of a smooth process that he scribbled on his calendar a reminder that he would need to write a September story on "the peaceful integration of LRHS." His bureau had gone so far as to write a tentative top of a story noting that Little Rock would be "the first capital of a Confederate state to integrate a public school."[35]

The New York Times was also bullish. Even with a correspondent based in the South, and even after sending ten reporters across the region for five weeks, the *Times* was not picking up strong signals of problems ahead. John Popham, having spent his ten years in the South seeking out intellectuals, humanitarians, optimists, and "voices of sanity," had found them. Through them, his stories frequently portrayed a moderate South that, while sometimes besieged, was rational.

The *Times'* national editors thus anticipated little violence in the fall school openings, certainly none in Little Rock. They decided to send Popham to Clinton, Tennessee, where integration had been accompanied by violence a year earlier. He was more familiar with the history there, and it was closer to his Chattanooga base, allowing him to drive to the assignment. The national desk then decided that Little Rock was an education story more than an integration resistance story. They sent the paper's longtime education reporter, Dr. Benjamin Fine.

Fine, who had carried the title of education editor for seventeen of his twenty years at the *Times,* had spent two days covering the orderly Louisville desegregation a year earlier. He believed that 1957 would be no different. As the school year was set to begin, 740 of the South's 2,300 school districts had begun or achieved desegregation, most in the border states from Delaware to Oklahoma and mostly without incident. Of the 27 school districts slated to begin desegregation, 20 were doing so voluntarily because of local school board decisions that had not been challenged in court. Overall, the *Times* editors concluded, the outlook was very positive for a quick and relatively painless transition.

Fine went first to Nashville. The shrill and angry opposition surprised him, but since peaceful integration appeared likely, he headed to Little Rock. He visited with Harry Ashmore, then spent several days confirming his notion, and Ashmore's, that Little Rock would go as smoothly as Louisville had a year earlier. Fine's Sunday story in the *Times* reflected that sentiment. "School integration begins here Tuesday morning," his story opened. The next day, Labor Day, September 2, Fine, like everyone else, was unaware that Faubus had developed a plan. "On the eve of school opening, everything is peaceful and quiet here in Little Rock," Fine wrote for the next day's *Times,* the day school was to open. "Integration is going to proceed along the Louisville pattern."[36]

After editing the story, the national editor sent Fine a telegram: "All right, everything looks quiet, why don't you go to a movie and take it easy before coming home?" Then he added: "Unless the town breaks open."[37]

· · ·

John Chancellor knew when he went to the NBC office in Chicago on Labor Day that he would soon be hitting the road to cover the school desegregation story in the South. He didn't know when, or where. His boss, Reuven Frank, who was producer of the fifteen-minute nightly news program featuring Chet Huntley and David Brinkley, was in his office in New York that same afternoon, trying to make that decision.

The commitment to cover the race story had come down the chain of command as an imperative. Frank's boss, NBC's news and public affairs vice president, Davidson Taylor, was a southerner whose native instincts told him what Frank's journalistic senses indicated: that school desegregation was a huge story and a serious test for television.[38] "This," Frank told his correspondents, "is going to change the whole country."[39] NBC, though its news staff was not as large as CBS's, decided it would lead the way.

Frank looked at his staff roster and knew he would have to make a little go a long way. A former newspaper reporter and editor, he had worked his way up from writer for NBC's pioneer news program, *Camel News Caravan* with John Cameron Swayze, to producer of the fledgling *Huntley-Brinkley Report*. Every day, trying to fill a twelve-minute news program, Frank found himself relying on a small band of committed reporters bound by their potentially suicidal decision to jump from the ocean liner of newspaper journalism into the flimsy dinghy of television.

Frank had four reporters to work with: Chancellor, Herbert Kaplow, Merrill Muller, and Frank McGee. All but Chancellor had been assigned to various school openings and were on their way. Nashville and Little Rock remained. While Frank was pondering a map of the South late in the afternoon, Chancellor called. The thirty-year old reporter, who had been NBC's Midwest correspondent for four years, held the phone in one hand and an airline guide in the other.[40]

Chancellor had started at the *Chicago Sun-Times* as a copyboy in 1948 and left as a feature writer two years later to join NBC. He had covered the Korean War and the national elections of 1952 and 1956, and had gotten a heavy dose of the fallout from *Brown*. He could remember all too sharply a scary encounter he'd had the day Emmett Till's trial had ended.

Already in Mississippi when the verdict came down, Chancellor had been sent to the Delta to get reactions for NBC. With a tape recorder the size of a shoebox slung over his shoulder and a microphone as small as a postage stamp in his hand, he began interviewing. As he talked with a Negro woman, he saw fear flash across her face. She turned and ran. He saw a flying wedge of white toughs coming at him. Chancellor squared off against them and held up the only object he could find to defend himself, an object whose power he had not, until that moment, truly fathomed. Thrusting the tiny microphone toward the men, Chancellor blurted out, "I don't care what you're going to do to me, but the whole world is going to know it." The men stopped.

Seeing the men immobilized by what he later called "the technological equivalent of a crucifix," Chancellor ran for his car. He had no idea whether the men thought he was holding a camera or some direct line to an omnipresent radio wave prepared to broadcast their every move instantly. All he knew was that the mystical and confusing power of the microphone had given him the vital step-and-a-half jump he needed to get away from the men.[41]

Now, two years later, the power of broadcast was becoming even more evident. Both Chancellor and Frank had gambled their careers in 1950. Had they switched to the obvious alternative, radio news, maybe nobody would have been shocked. More than 95 percent of the homes in the United States owned radios in 1950. But television? Only 5 percent owned them, and there were only ninety-six television stations nationwide. But by 1957, Chancellor and Frank could look back and marvel at their own wisdom: now more than eight out of ten homes owned televisions, and the number of stations had surpassed five hundred.[42]

The nation had reached an even more important milestone that year. In January, the number of homes in the United States with television sets had equaled, for the first time, the number of homes receiving a daily newspaper. By June, the number of homes with television sets, 41 million, exceeded the 39 million getting a daily newspaper. Newspaper circulation was growing, but not as fast as the number of families with TVs.[43]

Chancellor and Frank believed that television news coverage had put to rest early criticisms that it would be little more than glorified newsreels; they were determined to show that it was serious, legitimate journalism. Frank loved television pictures but was adamant that he wanted television news to tell stories and wanted the stories to be content-driven and word-perfect. Chancellor could still hear Frank's assessment of a simple ninety-second story he had done about agriculture. Frank had called to congratulate him on the piece's "Mozartian quality."[44]

As they spoke on that Labor Day afternoon, they agreed that Nashville would be the livelier story. The likely appearance of John Kasper held some appeal. The twenty-six-year-old Kasper had bolted onto the segregationist scene out of nowhere. Chancellor had seen Kasper in action a year earlier in Clinton, Tennessee, where he had stirred up so much trouble that the governor had had to send in tanks, armored personnel carriers, and more than six hundred National Guardsmen to accompany integration efforts.[45] Kasper, a native of Camden, New Jersey, had spent much of 1956 and 1957 winning and losing various trials and showing up uninvited at segregationist activities across the South, almost always espousing violence.

What made Kasper more interesting was this: In early 1957, the *New York Herald Tribune* had revealed that Kasper, while operating an avant-garde bookstore in Greenwich Village, had led a devil-may-care interracial lifestyle until a few months before he showed up in the South. In his bookstore, far from being a racist zealot, he had close Negro friends and associates. Friends described him as an affable fellow who frequently partied and danced with Negro women.[46]

With all that as fodder, Chancellor told Frank, he thought Kasper was good reason to head for Nashville. As he spoke, a copyboy rushed up to Frank's desk and handed him an urgent message from the Associated Press. Frank read the one-sentence message to Chancellor. It was the same report that Jefferson Thomas and Daisy Bates were hearing on the radio in Little Rock: the governor of Arkansas had asked for time to speak on statewide television at 10:15 that night, Little Rock time.

"That's pretty interesting," Frank said. It didn't seem like the act of a man who wanted to downplay the next morning's carefully planned admission of nine Negro students. "We got nobody in Little Rock. Maybe you better go to Little Rock."

"Really?" Chancellor said

Little Rock was suddenly the more unsettled story. "Yeah, you better go," he told Chancellor. A few minutes later, Chancellor called back to say that the next plane to Little Rock was departing in a half hour. "If I'm to go to Little Rock, I gotta go right now. I can't go home and pack."

"You better go," Frank said.

Early that evening, a reporter knocked on the Bateses' front door seeking a reaction to the latest development: Scores of National Guardsmen were taking up positions around Central High. Stunned, L. C. Bates got his shotgun, gave it to a friend with orders that he guard the house, then hustled with his wife to their car. At Central High, they saw stern-faced Arkansas National Guardsmen, armed and in full gear, silently fanning out across the lawn, taking up positions around the school's perimeter.[47]

The school superintendent of education, Virgil Blossom, also heard about the National Guard deployment from a reporter.[48] Faubus had not confided in him, nor in anyone else directly involved in the next day's planned opening. Blossom could do nothing but race home, answer a flood of calls, and join the rest of Arkansas in watching Faubus on television.

Ben Fine hadn't taken his editor's advice: he hadn't gone to see a movie. He headed for the *Gazette* newsroom. He joined reporters and editors as they gathered anxiously in front of a television set flickering in black and white.

As Faubus began speaking, Fine could see that his tidy education story had suddenly become a constitutional calamity, rendering it incorrect with little time to fix it.

Faubus reviewed all he had done to uphold a tradition of racial progressiveness in the state. Left to its own devices, the state was handling race relations quite well, he said, but there was pent-up anger and the possibility of violence because federal courts were ignoring the public's wishes and usurping the state's authority.

A telephone campaign "of massive proportions" was under way to recruit prosegregation protesters for the opening, he said. Caravans of people (for or against segregation, he didn't say) would arrive in the city by 6 a.m. the next day, he warned, and gun and knife stores in the area were reporting an uncharacteristically large number of weapons sales. "It is my opinion—yes, even a conviction—that it will not be possible to restore or to maintain order and protect the lives and property of the citizens if forcible integration is carried out tomorrow in the schools of this community," Faubus said.

Negro students would not be allowed into Central High the next day, he declared. The National Guard was being sent in "not as segregationists or integrationists but as soldiers" to maintain order. As Faubus was wrapping up his speech, and as Fine was rewriting his entire story, Chancellor arrived in the *Gazette* newsroom from the Little Rock airport.

Looking around, Chancellor could think of only one word to describe what he saw: pandemonium.[49]

CHAPTER 11

LITTLE ROCK SHOWDOWN

Rumor by rumor, store by store, reporters at the *Arkansas Gazette* spent the first day of school checking Faubus's claims that "caravans" of troublemakers were descending on Little Rock and that stores were experiencing a run on knives and guns. None of it checked out, which the newspaper reported prominently on the front page, alongside an Ashmore editorial, "The Crisis Mr. Faubus Made."

U.S. District Judge Ronald N. Davies ordered that Central High be opened to the Negro students. The governor insisted that it not be. The collision heightened anxiety on the second day of school, the morning of September 4. The schools superintendent had urged that the nine Negro students arrive at Central High without their parents.

Daisy Bates and several ministers decided that white and Negro ministers should accompany the students. Well after midnight on September 3, Bates had phoned the parents to establish a meeting time and place. But she hadn't reached the family of Elizabeth Eckford because they didn't have a telephone; by daybreak, in the hectic efforts to get everyone prepared for school, Bates forgot to send anyone to tell the Eckfords.

Before the eight students arrived at the school together, Elizabeth Eckford arrived alone, aboard a municipal bus. Departing the bus, clutching her books to her chest, her eyes shielded by sunglasses and her expression fixed, the fifteen-year-old began making the block-long walk to a barrier of National Guardsmen.

"They're here! The niggers are coming!" someone in the growing crowd of more than two hundred people shouted. Fine, Chancellor, CBS News television and radio reporter Robert Schakne, and several local reporters and photographers watched as Eckford approached the Guardsmen. To Fine, the young girl looked sweet and in a state of shock. As the Guard turned her away, he saw she was trembling. She crossed the street and kept walking, then turned around and headed back to the Guardsmen. "Don't let her in our school—that nigger," one person shouted. "Go back where you came from," yelled a woman who lunged at her.[1]

Television news cameras raced for position, then focused on Eckford and the hostile crowd around her. But the CBS cameraman had gotten into place too late to catch on film the contorted faces and the yelling and the Confederate flag waving and the "Nigger Go Home" signs. When Schakne realized he didn't have the footage, he did something that revealed the raw immaturity of this relatively new medium of newsgathering: he ordered up an artificial retake. He urged the crowd, which had fallen quieter, to demonstrate its anger again, this time for the cameras. "Yell again!" Schakne implored as his cameraman started filming.[2]

The television reporter had carried journalism across a sacrosanct line. It wasn't the first time a line had been crossed. Photojournalists and photo editors had all sorts of tricks at their disposal, if they wanted them, to change reality; typically, they happened in the darkroom or with touch-up devices, using methods more sophisticated than sending a crowd into a photogenic tizzy. But here, in Little Rock, where a domestic confrontation of unsurpassable importance was unfolding, where journalistic propriety and lack of it were being put on public display, reporters who were inches from the drama found themselves making up rules as they went along and doing it in front of everyone in a volatile situation with a hot, erratic new technology.

Suddenly, the lawn at Central High had become the set, the television reporter had become the director, and the demonstrators had become his actors. It wasn't as bad as creating news, or making it up; but it was re-creating the news, with the possibility, even probability, that the re-creation would beget a whole new round of demonstration and gesticulation, which another cameraman might miss, leading to a new re-creation, which would beget even more flamboyant exhibitions of protest until it was no longer clear what was real and spontaneous, what was engineered and manipulated.

If the impact of what was happening, and of the ethical breach, wasn't clear right there at the scene, it would become powerfully clear that night when the images of Eckford, walking the line, approaching the National Guard, were broadcast. A riveted nation could not help but react with awe at the bravery of this teenage girl; anger at the mob jostling to stop her, even if it was take two; and despair at the visual suggestion that even the National Guard could not, or would not, protect or comfort her.

For a second time, Eckford was turned away. Stuck and unable to leave the scene until the next bus arrived, she sat on a bench at the bus stop, her head tilted downward. For minutes that seemed eternal, she absorbed the jeers, epithets, and threats of an angry crowd that seemed to be bouncing out of control all around her. Eckford sat alone, motionless, her arms folded over her lap.

Schakne's cameraman struggled to move his heavy, cumbersome sound camera, tripod, and lens into place to catch the crowd's hostile mood. Schakne leaned in toward her, extended a microphone close to her face, and asked, "Can you tell me your name, please?" Eckford remained statue-like, her face unresponsive. "Are you going to go to school here at Central High?" Eckford didn't move a muscle. The sights and sounds of the young girl, frozen in fear and under assault by a boisterous, noisy mob, were sucked into the television camera without filter. Schakne's simple questions came off as a cruel inquisition of an innocent victim. Seeing that she was petrified, Schakne seemed to look for a way out. "You don't care to say anything, is that right?" he asked, turning then to the camera to describe the scene.[3]

Fine saw tears streaming down her cheeks behind her sunglasses and began thinking about his own fifteen-year-old daughter. His emotions carried him beyond the traditional journalistic role of detached observer. He moved toward Eckford and sat beside her. He put his arm around her, gently lifted her chin, and said, "Don't let them see you cry."

A white woman, Grace Lorch, whose husband was a teacher at a local Negro college, joined Fine and Eckford. "What are you doing, you nigger lover?" one protester yelled at Lorch. "You stay away from that girl."

"She's scared," the white woman replied. "She's just a little girl." Then she walked away with Eckford in search of a taxi. "Six months from now," she told another member of the mob, "you'll be ashamed at what you are doing." She and Eckford made their way to a public bus and left together.[4]

Fine's act in giving Eckford comfort that day was seen by many around him as humane but completely inappropriate and probably provocative. Schakne's attempt to interview Eckford at least fell within the bounds of journalistic propriety. Fine, on the other hand, had inserted himself into a live story—only to remove himself from it when he wrote about the day's events a few hours later for the *Times*.[5]

Segregationists exploited the behavior of reporters. Schakne's re-creation of the mob's display may have been competitive impulse, and Fine's sheltering of Eckford may have been paternalism, but the segregationists were not discerning. The two were blended as acts of provocation. Even the segregationists, as happy as they may have been to provide a second opportunity for their hostility to be shown on national television, understood that an important line had been crossed. The governor, facing a large number of out-of-state reporters, administered a lecture: "We want you to get the story in its fullest detail as it develops, but don't try to make stories."[6]

Other journalists were also concerned. The news editor of the *Gazette*, Bob

Douglas, would laugh while observing how Fine had given his critics the ammunition they needed to allege that he was the center of an anti-South conspiracy: he was from New York, he was Jewish, and he talked too damn much.[7]

Before classes opened on the third day, some sixty reporters were milling around in front of the school, mingling among the five hundred white men and women who came to witness desegregation stopped in its tracks. Fine, his notebook open, tried to interview teenagers. His questions, his manner, or their visceral reaction to any questions posed by outside reporters, provoked them as they gathered in a clot around him. "Let us ask *you* some questions," they insisted.[8]

"Go ahead and ask me," Fine responded.

Why did he seem more interested in the NAACP's point of view than in theirs? Why didn't he talk to local Negroes about their reaction? The crowd around him was no longer just teenagers, and the questions turned to threats. "You better get out unless you want your head broken," one person said.

"Just leave us alone. We'll solve the problem ourselves," said another as Fine tried to interview a teenager. A middle-aged woman, seething at Fine, blurted, "Have you been to Moscow lately?"

A National Guard major stepped into the crowd and waved a club. Then a lieutenant colonel approached Fine. "Come along," the colonel said to Fine. "I don't want you to talk to these people." If Fine wanted to stay there, he said, "act like the rest of us."

"All right, sir," Fine responded as newsmen quickly gathered around him and the colonel. Fine decided to qualify the limits he was willing to accept. "I intend to do my job as I see it for *The New York Times,*" he said. "All I've been doing is trying to interview students and get a sampling of their feeling. I have been doing nothing else. I am going to continue to interview the people as a reporter and try not to draw a crowd."

But there was already a crowd around Fine—other newsmen. Some thought he was asking questions, some thought he was merely asking insistent questions, and some thought he was arguing.[9] Gathered around that crowd was another horde, whites who jeered and taunted the newsmen as they were herded toward Major General Sherman Clinger, the governor's appointee as adjutant general in charge of the Guard.

"Gentlemen, this is not a press conference," Clinger said, resting his right foot on a stump. "I will not answer questions. But I do have something to say." By seeking to interview people, he said, reporters were inciting protesters to riot. "Any member of the press will be barred and arrested if it seems in the judgment of the troop commander or myself that he is inciting to violence," Clinger said.

The reporters fired questions back. "Are you referring to the incident that Mr. Fine had this morning?" one reporter asked.

"Yes, I am," he said. "Any repetition will bar him from the grounds and get him arrested."

Military or civil arrest? He didn't know. Would the reporter have the right to habeas corpus? Clinger didn't like the implications of the question. "Does that mean," Clinger asked testily, "that if you had that right, you would be ready to incite to violence? I am not going to answer that question."

Fine was escorted to a private half-hour meeting with Clinger, where he was told his limits: No interviews if a crowd gathered. Interviews with single students were permitted, but only inside the school with the principal's clearance. Clinger told Fine that he was on probation, then added, "Any repetition of the incident of this morning and you will be kept out of here. You would likely be arrested, too."

Who would determine the bounds? Fine asked. "We will determine that," Clinger said. Clinger had a final comment that took some of the edge off his tough talk. In a tone that Fine found almost fatherly, Clinger added, "I would advise you to be careful."

Fine had become so much a part of the story that the *Times* had to allow him to do something that was rare indeed for the newspaper in the 1950s. His front-page news story about all the events of the day, written under his byline, included a passing reference to the warning given to "this reporter." On the inside, also under his byline, was Fine's first-person account of his confrontation with protesters and Clinger.[10]

Overnight, an education story had become a civil rights story and Little Rock had become an international symbol of racial discord. Even the words "Little Rock," when uttered by the character Nellie Forbush in the popular Broadway musical *South Pacific* began drawing boos and jeers from a Long Island audience.[11]

Though most national and regional media relied on the wire services for the first few days, editors understood the significance of Little Rock. The story took the lead position in major newspapers, television newscasts, and newsmagazines from the beginning and grew from there. In *The Washington Post* and *The New York Times,* one-column lead stories became two columns, then three. As the confrontation developed over the next month, both papers were stripping their Little Rock headlines across all eight columns at the top of the front page.

The play of the Little Rock story showed no geographic bias. A week after school opened, 67 percent of the newspapers in the North and 68 percent of the newspapers in the South were giving the events in Little Rock front-page headlines of five or more columns, and virtually all were running two or three related sidebars on the front page each day. Many were carrying two photographs on the front, and some devoted an entire page to photos.

For two months, Little Rock would have a firm grip on page one.[12] In *The New York Times,* Little Rock was the lead story on twenty-three of the first twenty-eight days of the crisis; on nine of those days, the *Times* would publish more than fifteen stories about desegregation in Little Rock and other school systems in the South and devote considerable attention to photographs, profiles, and editorials.[13]

There were other school desegregation stories popping up across the South, and news organizations scrambled to get there. In Birmingham, when the prominent Negro pastor Reverend Fred Shuttlesworth was beaten up by fifteen to twenty white men outside a white high school, AP called a reporter off vacation and sent in three staffers with experience in covering Autherine Lucy and the Montgomery bus boycott. One of the AP reporters who went into the high school with police following a bomb scare was quickly recruited to answer phone calls from worried parents. That night in Nashville, hours after a six-year-old girl had integrated a new elementary school, a bomb demolished one of the school's wings.[14]

Some editors and reporters were shocked by the ferocity of the opposition and found it difficult to keep their feelings out of the story. If the segregationists had hoped to win over the mainstream southern out of the story, their tactics backfired. "The unusual aspect of this story was its emotional impact upon the newsman," *The Tennessean*'s editor, Coleman A. Harwell, wrote soon after the bombing. "I recall no instance when everyone felt so deeply about an occurrence. . . . There is something so very personal about a school. It involves our children, their happiness, their safety, their dreams, and our dreams for them."[15]

Little Rock was everyone's big story. *Time* and *Newsweek* sent in teams of reporters whose coverage led their national reports. *Time* had a six-year jump on *Newsweek* in establishing a bureau in the South but had used those years not so much to get ahead of the story as to make a point of trying to straighten out this backward, troglodyte region. *Time* devoted two covers to Little Rock in the first five weeks. *Newsweek* signaled that it intended to be competitive: while it made the choice to send its bureau chief to Nashville, it also dispatched a reporter to Little Rock before the school opening. *Life* magazine assigned a team of reporters and photographers, including two of its most prominent shooters, Grey Villet and Francis Miller, whose work would gain a cover and ten inside pages in early October.

The number of reporters grew every day. *The New York Times* moved in four to help Fine, and the *New York Post* and New York *Daily News* sent in some. The Associated Press put sixteen different staffers there in that first month, International News Service had thirteen, and United Press placed nine. *The Washington Post* and its competitor, *The Washington Star,* sent in top-flight writers, as did *The Wall Street Journal* and papers in Chicago,

Denver, Detroit, Saint Louis, Toronto, and Boston. Three separate London papers were represented. At any given time, the number ranged from forty to a hundred reporters on the scene.[16]

Many journalists landed at Adams Field with little preparation for the story and only three names in their notebooks: Harry Ashmore, Daisy Bates, and Sam Peck, which was the name of the hotel where most stayed. For many white reporters, the *Gazette* newsroom became a workplace, and Ashmore's office served as the classroom for tutorials on the South and coverage of race relations. Day after day, visiting journalists would troop into his office, make his acquaintance, absorb his informed and witty take on the story, then secure an invitation for later that evening to Ashmore's house or the Little Rock press club, where the libations and talk flowed freely. Many came to share his sensibilities about the unfolding story, some without even being there.

"Last night I talked twenty minutes on the telephone to Melbourne, Australia," a weary Ashmore told a visiting newsman as the crisis slogged through its first month. "This fellow wasn't sure where Arkansas was—or what it was, a state or a city. I started out telling him it was a thousand miles south of Chicago. Finally, he said, 'I want you to know that the press of Australia is with you.' " Ashmore laughed at the reach of this story in front of him, then added, "Thank God for that. I may have to fall back there."[17]

The Little Rock story also drew the most talented Negro journalists. These reporters and photographers had seen just about every big civil rights story. But this had the markings of becoming the most dramatic of them all. This, it seemed, was when all those years of hiding in the shadows to cover backwater indignities and quiet brutalities would finally pay off for the Negro reporters. This was a direct challenge to a federal court's enforcement of a Supreme Court mandate—and it would be played out in the open, for the entire world to see.

As the black reporters arrived in Little Rock, most skirted past Ashmore and sought a separate indoctrination, and sometimes a room and a bed, at the home of L. C. and Daisy Bates. They gathered at their kitchen table or in their living room, where the picture window that had been cracked by a rock was crisscrossed with masking tape. They gave and received information and became part of the strategic planning.[18] Two of those wrote for mainstream big city papers: Ted Poston of the *New York Post* and Carl Rowan of the *Minneapolis Tribune*.

Ernest Withers, the photographer who had been at the Till trial, the Montgomery boycott, and other stops for the *Tri-State Defender* in Memphis, was part of the retinue, as was commercial photographer Earl Davy, who frequently shot photos for Bates's *Arkansas State Press*.

Moses Newson was on his first assignment for the *Baltimore Afro-*

American, which had just hired him from the *Tri-State Defender.* He, too, had covered the Till trial and other big stories in the South, including a school desegregation battle in the northeast Arkansas town of Hoxie two years earlier.

James L. Hicks, editor of the New York *Amsterdam News,* was there. Hicks was tough—on other Negro leaders. Earlier in the summer, he had pronounced Reverend Martin Luther King, Jr., "the number one leader of sixteen million Negroes in the United States," then accused Roy Wilkins and the NAACP of "dragging their feet" in organizing a Prayer Pilgrimage in Washington in March 1957. Wilkins had fired back, saying that Hicks's article was "an effort to destroy unity by planting suspicion, jealousy and rivalry." Hicks arrived in Little Rock having responded by printing a series of stories criticizing Negro leaders on a new litany of issues.[19]

The most striking of them all was L. Alex Wilson, age forty-nine, editor of the *Tri-State Defender,* which was also covering for its influential parent, *Chicago Defender.* Wilson was a dark-skinned, lanky, towering figure at six feet, four inches. He was serious and fearless, or made himself appear so. His clipped, professorial speech and his stern demeanor provoked uprightness and formality in others, so much that his colleagues, even in their most casual, shorthand conversations, would frequently refer to him not as "Alex" or "Wilson" but as "L. Alex Wilson." He could be so dour that his friends joked about it; they said he didn't smile much because it hurt when he did so.[20]

Wilson had known as a child in Florida that he wanted to be a newspaperman. Most afternoons, he would come home from school and disappear into his bedroom, where his mother would find him writing, writing, writing.[21] He had gotten his bachelor's degree at Florida A&M, studied in the journalism program at Lincoln University in Missouri, and done graduate work at the University of Wisconsin and Roosevelt College in Chicago. He had served as a Marine in World War II and been a high school principal in Florida. Not long after he fulfilled his longtime ambition and got a job on a newspaper, he had made a name for himself. For his first newspaper, the *Norfolk Journal and Guide,* he had covered the Korean War and had won Negro journalism's highest honor, the Wendell Willkie Award, for feature writing.[22]

John Chancellor had a major problem on his hands. As if getting a meaningful story on film were not difficult enough (and doing so in the same clothes day after day, since he had left Chicago without packing), Chancellor faced a mountain of challenges trying to get the film on the air. NBC's affiliate in Little Rock, KARK, did not have the loops, lines, and other technology available to broadcast anything to New York.

The only way Chancellor could get his stories on the air was to fly to Oklahoma City each day at 3 p.m. to have the film edited and transmitted to New York. In an effort to squeeze in an additional hour of reporting time, Chancellor and Reuven Frank arranged for Chancellor's film to fly by chartered plane to Oklahoma City at 3 p.m., and he'd leave on another plane an hour later to review the processed film and write his scripts before turning around and flying back to Little Rock.

But Frank didn't want to spend the money to bring the Little Rock station into the loop without knowing that the story would last more than four days. AT&T wasn't inclined to install lines for free just to make NBC happy. But after a couple of weeks of Chancellor ping-ponging back and forth to Oklahoma City, running up airplane bills, Frank wrote a few words for Chet Huntley to say on the evening newscast. They were basically a shot across the bow of AT&T: "You may be wondering why John Chancellor is always signing off his Little Rock story from Oklahoma City instead of Little Rock. The reason is, we can't. AT&T hasn't installed the lines making a newscast possible from Little Rock." A few days later, Chancellor was able to broadcast his reports directly from Little Rock.[23]

At the end of the first week, NBC reinforced Chancellor with Frank McGee, whose spectacular reporting on the bus boycott for the network's Montgomery affiliate a year earlier had been his ticket to the big leagues.

McGee was becoming a master of the one-hour, two-hour, sometimes four-hour specials and documentaries that were so much a part of early television journalism. The race specials were unique in one regard: advertising sponsors were much harder to come by and would sometimes find themselves either offered by the networks at unpopular hours or held by local stations for airing at odder hours, if they were aired at all.[24]

McGee's assignment in Little Rock was to focus on how the white students were handling the upheaval. McGee headed first to the *Gazette* newsroom, where Ashmore gave him a desk near the clanging boxes that were spitting out stories from the Associated Press, United Press, and International News Service.

A few desks away sat Ira Lipman, a dutiful high school student who worked Friday and Saturday nights taking high school sports scores from across the state. Lipman had been a student at Central High until this, his senior year, when a new school had opened. Lipman was active in the school newspaper and the yearbook, as well as the national Jewish service organization for young people, the B'nai B'rith Youth Organization. But nothing charged him up like working for the *Gazette*.

Lipman would sit at a metal desk with a Royal typewriter and a phone and compose short stories from shards of information that were phoned in by youthful stringers from noisy stadiums across the state. "The Hot Springs Trojans defeated the Pine Bluff Zebras by a score of 7–6 at Trojan Stadium last night . . ." For a kid who had a keen interest in journalism, being inside the *Arkansas Gazette* was big stuff. It got even bigger when McGee finally spoke to him.

"Kid, where's a good place to get something to eat?" McGee asked. Lipman told him how to get to the Marion Hotel and what to order. McGee returned later with another question: "Kid, where's a good place in town to stay?" Lipman directed him to the Sam Peck Hotel. McGee then popped the big question: Could Lipman round up some kids to participate in a live network show on Sunday? Two days later, for a Sunday-afternoon telecast from the grounds of Central High and the studio of the local NBC affiliate, Lipman and a friend had brought together fifteen teenagers.

The lights went on and they were on the air, speaking their minds to a national audience. Lipman said he felt the law was clear: the Negro students should be allowed into school. Would he mind attending school with Negroes? Absolutely not, he said without hesitation. Less than an hour after the show concluded, Lipman's mother received three phone calls threatening her son's life. The next day, Lipman wrote a letter to Jewish youth leaders across the nation, seeking their support for forcing Faubus to comply with the law. "Integration is coming," he confidently wrote his young colleagues, "regardless of the mouthings of rabid segregationists." He urged them to stand up and play a role, whatever it might be, in bringing change.[25]

As McGee was leaving town, he did something perfunctory that, unexpectedly, would help establish television news as legitimate, respectable journalism: he passed Lipman's name to Chancellor as someone who could help.[26]

Over the next three weeks, Little Rock was locked in a standoff. The federal court wouldn't modify its order to enroll the Negro students, President Eisenhower would not intervene, the governor wouldn't pull out the National Guard or allow the Negro students in, the Negro students wouldn't withdraw their intention to enroll, and the white protesters wouldn't leave the lawn of Central High.

Reporters were unsparing in their portrayals of the hundreds of sign-toting, chanting white opponents of integration who gathered in front of the school every morning. Many who showed up in protest had no ties to the school system at all. In *Newsweek,* protesters were "shabby" and "ragged," "trash," and "unshaven men and frowsy women." They were "the riffraff," *Newsweek* said, defining them as "truculent street-corner drunks, the viragos of the back-alley tenements, the squatters on near forgotten Tobacco Roads." It was not just in Little Rock that writers took such liberties.[27]

Time magazine was as demeaning in writing about the Arkansas governor. Describing a reporter's private meeting with Faubus, it portrayed the governor as a backwater slob. It showed him greeting a visitor perfunctorily, collapsing into a contour chair, groaning from eating too much sweet corn and sweet potatoes the night before, and snapping rudely at his wife when she served him stewed chicken and rice. He ordered her to pour milk into the rice, then "wolfed it down, milk dribbling down his chin." He then turned to his guest and "belched gustily."[28]

As crowds gathered outside Central High every morning, reporters routinely came under harassment, finding themselves elbowed, jostled, stepped on, heckled, and, especially in the case of Negro reporters, escorted from the scene by National Guardsmen. Fine, William Hines, a *Washington Star* reporter who asked Faubus tough questions during the ABC television interview, and just about any Negro reporter drew the crowd's wrath as soon as they showed up.

"That's the man who made Faubus look like a fool last night," one man shouted toward Hines, who was then booed. Unable to get any interviews, Hines left, and some in the crowd of five hundred turned their attention to Fine.[29]

A waitress from a Little Rock tavern aimed a steady stream of invective at Fine, asking sharp questions he would not acknowledge. "You got a nigger wife?" she bellowed at one point. Fine gave no response. She kept at it. "Are you a Jew?" she asked. This time, Fine answered, "Yes."

Negro reporters faced a more frightening challenge as they tried to get close to the action. "Let him come over here and we'll take care of him," a white protester shouted at Alvin Nall, a young reporter for the New York *Amsterdam News,* when Nall was spotted in front of the school. National Guard leaders and state troopers fell into line next to Nall, but the taunting continued. "Send that New York nigger home," said one demonstrator.[30] As the jeering continued, Nall was stymied. Another reporter asked if he planned to interview people. He looked at the crowd around him, responded, "Not in this area," and left, escorted by Guardsmen.[31]

The limitation on the Negro press's ability to cover the story, and the humiliation that went with it, were evident the next day when Moses Newson arrived for the *Baltimore Afro-American.* Newson, a camera around his neck, reached the barricades at Central High, where a National Guard colonel told him that no Negroes, including journalists, were being allowed at the scene.

Seeing a white colleague from *The Commercial Appeal,* Newson went to speak with him—not because he had anything to say but because he didn't want to leave the scene and didn't want to be pushed or escorted away. He wanted to show the Guard, the crowd, and whoever else was looking that he was a known and familiar figure to *somebody* there. So Newson made up a conversation about wanting the white reporter's help in getting a photograph from the scene for the *Afro-American*. Then, to the tune of heckles and insults from two white men who walked along with him, he was escorted away by the Guard.[32] Newson would return to the school two weeks later with other Negro reporters—only to face trouble of a more brutal kind.

Day and night for weeks, reporters and editors for the *Arkansas Gazette* and its afternoon competitor, the *Arkansas Democrat,* buzzed around the city with a sense of high purpose and the adrenaline rush of a hot story that was drawing a national audience. Both the *Gazette* and the *Democrat,* which in those days could still find room on the front page for stories about $57 robberies, devoted massive space to their desegregation coverage.

Each paper churned out a dozen or more stories in the first days, most of them staff-written, for the next day's editions. Virtually every day, stories and photos about the school dominated the eight-column front of the *Gazette,* the front of the first section, and the general local news pages. On many days, at great cost, both papers would add pages, for which no advertising was purchased, to devote the equivalent of two to three full pages to the story. The daily mix included news from the White House, the governor, the mayor, and the streets. Small sidebars noted historical milestones or quirks. The papers gave summaries of editorial opinions from around the state and the world, as well as full texts of rulings by judges and speeches and press conferences by the president, the governor, and the mayor. The papers also carried a half-dozen race-related and school desegregation wire stories from elsewhere in the South.

Both newspapers' editorial pages were consumed by the issue. The *Gazette,* which added space for letters and printed as many as twenty-five on some days, explained to its readers that the tilt of its published letters was against Faubus because that was the tilt of the letters it received. The *Democrat* published mostly pro-Faubus letters because that was the overall bias in its mailbox.[33]

Both had supported the *Brown* decision in 1954. Leading up to the opening day of school, both supported the compromise desegregation plan; the *Democrat* called it "exceptionally favorable." But the *Gazette* and *Democrat* were quickly perceived as representing two separate and opposing camps.

Ashmore's editorials remained steadfast throughout. They did not dwell on whether integration was good or bad—though *The Negro and the Schools* was the benchmark study in showing the failure of the dual education system. Ashmore instead focused the issue almost solely on the Supreme Court's interpretation of the law, the importance of obeying the court, and the utter futility of defying the federal government and courts.

Ashmore portrayed Faubus, in his "naked defiance," as the politically motivated captive of a "small and militant minority of whites."[34] He outlined repeatedly how Faubus's words and actions contradicted his own prior commitments and how they attempted to rearrange the facts of recent history to fit his actions. When Faubus complained that the federal court was trying to force desegregation "overnight," Ashmore's editorial, "Mr. Faubus Also Needs a Dictionary," noted that the Little Rock plan had been in the works for three years; the plan was designed "to accomplish the minimum integration over the longest period of time permissible," it was the subject of about two hundred speeches around town by the superintendent of education, and it fit Faubus's earlier call for voluntary, locally controlled desegregation as perfectly as any plan could.[35]

When Faubus claimed that Ashmore and the *Gazette* "had misrepresented, slanted, distorted and colored the news in reference to me and Little Rock," Ashmore was able to examine his newspaper's own reporting and point out that the *Gazette* had published a verbatim transcript of every speech and news conference and public comment made by Faubus, and virtually every word he had uttered at any time other than in his sleep. "Indeed, the chances are that if the governor himself wants to find out what he actually said on some of those occasions, he will have to consult the files of the *Gazette,* which is the only complete source of record in existence."[36]

A single Faubus speech could give Ashmore fodder for days, and the editor frequently offered two editorials on the subject each day. He hit Faubus head-on, not from behind, refusing time and again to poke fun at the governor, though opportunities to do so abounded. Faubus's thinking became increasingly murky and paranoid as the days went by, and he frequently made statements that contradicted either themselves or the truth, or both. He expressed concern, for example, that the White House had tapped his phones and that the feds were going to come into the Governor's Mansion and arrest him.

In the beginning, Ashmore resisted the easy shots, choosing instead to examine the marrow of Faubus's position. There was no evidence whatsoever, Ashmore wrote, that the city, when Faubus called out the National Guard, had been about to erupt in violence—and he cited the long list of people who had testified to that in federal court, including the mayor, police chief, school superintendent, school principal, and chairman of the school board. It was Faubus, Ashmore wrote, who had "invited violence and disorder."[37] Faubus, in response, frequently attacked Ashmore as an "an ardent integrationist" whose reporters were "agents of an integrationist newspaper."[38]

Faubus deeply resented the fact that Ashmore was the first person many visiting journalists met and that Ashmore seemed to influence them so easily. It grated the governor that Ashmore and his colleagues would file their stories or editorials, then gather for long evenings of drinks and banter at the private Little Rock Club, where Negro waiters served them. The journalists joked that they were "the battle and bottle scarred" heroes of Little Rock. To Faubus, it was not a joke. He accused Ashmore and Hugh Patterson of luring the newsmen into their web "to indoctrinate them with a biased and prejudiced viewpoint toward me."[39]

Ashmore, in response, was having increasing difficulty not holding Faubus up as a ludicrous but dangerous figure. When Faubus claimed to have discovered a plot by the *Gazette*'s publisher to place a psychiatrist at one of Faubus's press conferences and report his findings to the *Gazette*'s readers, Ashmore wrote that Faubus had again come up with a pinch of fabricated spice that "he delights in dropping into the political pot when it shows signs of simmering."

"Although a few of our readers have suggested that Mr. Faubus may be suffering from some aberrations," Ashmore added, "this newspaper has never been that charitable in its own view. We believe Mr. Faubus knows exactly what he is doing—and we suspect we have earned his wrath because through accurately reporting his devious course step by step, we have shown precisely where he is taking the people of his state in the furtherance of his political ambitions, and the terrible price all of us are going to have to pay as a result."[40]

What's more, Ashmore said, it was unthinkable that the nation would let a governor invent an excuse to mobilize the National Guard, then use it to block a court order. This was the road to anarchy. Where was President Eisenhower in all of this? Ashmore wanted to know. He was keenly aware that Eisenhower had not liked the *Brown* decision, but the Supreme Court had ruled. Would it be obeyed? "The issue is no longer segregation vs. integration," the editor wrote. "The question now has become the supremacy of the government of the United States in all matters of law. And clearly the government cannot let this issue remain unresolved, no matter what the cost is to the community."[41] Other liberal southern editors, such as Ralph McGill in Atlanta and Jonathan Daniels in Raleigh, shared many of Ashmore's concerns and expressed them in print. It would make it easier for the White House, when finally it acted, that southern editors had joined their northern colleagues in wanting the law upheld.

Ashmore contrasted Faubus's actions with those of Governor Luther Hodges of North Carolina, who had taken no stand either way as schools desegregated in Charlotte, Greensboro, and Winston-Salem on the same day Negro students were blocked in Little Rock. "The North Carolina governor simply said that 'North Carolinians do not like lawlessness' and made it quite clear that anybody who had other ideas would promptly be dealt with," Ashmore wrote. He pointed out that hecklers and a white boy who threw a stick at a Negro girl in Charlotte had quickly been "taken in hand" by local authorities and that the second day of school desegregation had been peaceful. "That," the editor wrote, "is how it could have been in Little Rock."[42]

The *Arkansas Democrat* went the other way. From the moment Faubus thwarted the desegregation plan, the *Democrat* modified its earlier thinking. While the paper found opportunity to criticize Faubus, it drifted, after a period of sounding lost at sea, into the camp of states' rights. In its news pages, the *Democrat* was more inclined to publish rumors of hysteria, violence, and the potential for them both, stories sometimes planted by Faubus's forces to justify placement of the Guard. But the *Democrat* didn't duck the story. It, too, turned over acres of newsprint to produce a prodigious number of articles. And the *Democrat* had one thing the *Gazette* didn't have.

Through the paper's longtime political writer, George Douthit, the *Democrat* had access to Faubus. As the crisis opened, Douthit wrote a story portraying Faubus as a heroic figure working under enormous stress. On the first Sunday after school opened, the *Democrat* published the first of three exclusive interviews with Faubus. Another exclusive in the *Democrat* during the first week showed Faubus inside the Governor's Mansion running the government calmly and with great self-assurance. The *Democrat* also wrote a feature about a young Dutch girl who was attending school in Arkansas and who wanted to meet Faubus. She had heard many negative things about him in the European press, the article said, and she wanted to see for herself if he was as bad as portrayed. The story then provided a notable little detail: the Dutch girl was staying in the home of a Little Rock family: *Democrat* political writer George Douthit's.[43]

Ashmore felt the *Democrat* was pandering to the governor and to popular opinion, taking advantage of the *Gazette*'s decision to take the unpopular route, and getting fat on the *Gazette*'s blood. The *Gazette* and Ashmore paid a price for their aggressive coverage and editorials. They became as much a target as the nine Negro students, and certainly a more accessible one. In 1957, the *Gazette* held a strong lead in circulation over the *Democrat,* owning 53 percent of the daily market and 55 percent of the Sunday subscribers. A year later, it had lost nearly 14 percent of its circulation daily and Sunday, as well as its lead over the *Democrat.* The *Gazette*'s weekday advertising revenues dropped by nearly 13 percent from 1956 to 1958, and Sunday's fell by more than 8 percent. The paper lost more than $2 million. The *Democrat*'s weekday ad revenues increased by 3 percent from 1956 to 1959, while its Sunday revenues jumped by nearly 10 percent.[44]

Though Heiskell, Ashmore, and Patterson stood up to the pressure, they felt compelled at times to clarify—or perhaps muddle—their position. When the newspaper saw a copy of a letter that urged a boycott of businesses still advertising with the *Gazette,* Ashmore went so far as to write, "The *Gazette* has never advocated integration. The *Gazette* has never called for the breaking down of our segregation laws. The *Gazette* has consistently supported every legal effort to maintain the social patterns of segregation, and will continue to do so."[45]

Personal threats became quite common for Ashmore. His home phone would ring constantly with warnings that snipers were trailing him, and his mail was filled with vile threats. He and Hugh Patterson would find some relief in telling the story of the subscriber who had written that she was so distraught by the *Gazette*'s editorials that she had lost seven pounds. She urged the paper to keep it up for three more pounds.[46]

While both the *Gazette* and *Democrat* provided better ongoing coverage of the Negro community than many southern dailies during ordinary times, neither newspaper broke through the protective cocoon that Bates, the NAACP, and the students' parents wove around the students. The cocoon allowed the Negro press inside, where it assumed its customary front-row seat at events the mainstream press never saw. Notably absent from the *Gazette* and *Democrat* were authoritative, consistent reports explaining what the students might do or how they, their parents, or the Bateses were reacting to developments. When the papers carried a response from Daisy Bates, rarely were more than two paragraphs printed. Both papers misspelled the names of the students early in the coverage, and neither devoted any time or space in the first days to providing profiles of the courageous students or an explanation of what they and their families were experiencing. When the newspapers did finally carry profiles, the Associated Press typically provided them, and they were short, shallow, and not prominently played.[47]

What Moses Newson, Alvin Nall, and other Negro reporters couldn't get from the high school scene, they more than made up for with their access to the Negro community. They were part of the regular gatherings of the nine students, their parents, and Negro leaders and lawyers. Anyone wanting to know more about the Negro students and how they felt could turn to the stories written by Negro journalists. Encamping at the Bateses' home, the reporters got the story of the fear, travail, and determination that marked the lives of the students and their families. The *New York Post*'s Ted Poston immediately began churning out a series of profiles, "Nine Kids Who Dared." Only through reading this series would one know, for example, that Gloria Ray wanted to be an atomic scientist.[48]

As the situation drew more attention, Faubus's refusal to budge inspired stronger national censure. But the person who had to break the standoff was neither Faubus nor the federal judge handling the case. The break had to come from President Eisenhower, whose own conflicted views about racial integration made him slow to express outrage that a governor was thumbing his nose at federal authority. Eisenhower, against the advice of Vice President Richard Nixon and Attorney General Herbert Brownell, accepted an Arkansas congressman's proposal to invite Faubus to Newport, Rhode Island, where the president was vacationing.[49]

As the president and the governor spoke, Faubus was quite persuasive that all would work out if only the federal government would give the state a couple more weeks. Eisenhower was warm to the idea. Brownell and Eisenhower's chief of staff, Sherman Adams, were not.[50]

In the end, Faubus agreed to issue a statement declaring that *Brown* was "the law of the land and must be obeyed." He then returned to Little Rock and took the opposite position in court. "Just because I said it doesn't make it so," Faubus explained.[51]

Six days later, Judge Davies ordered Faubus to remove the National Guard from the school. By nightfall, the Guard was gone. The question that lingered over the weekend was whether the Negro students would try to enroll the following Monday, September 23, and whether the city police force stood a chance of holding back a mob. This time, Daisy Bates was the one keeping plans under wraps. The students would enroll, she told reporters, but she wouldn't say when.

With the Guard gone, Little Rock lapsed into an uncertain fear over what would happen when the Negro students arrived. News organizations began implementing their coverage plans. The Associated Press had supplemented its already sizable Little Rock bureau with reporters and photographers from Chicago, Dallas, Kansas City, New Orleans, and Memphis.

AP signaled the importance of the story by sending in Relman "Pat" Morin, one of its most respected and tested reporters. Morin, who would spend his fiftieth birthday covering Little Rock, had been collecting far-flung datelines since 1930, when he had covered the meat-cleaver murder and decapitation of ten people in the French Concession of Shanghai. He still recalled his first editor insisting that the story would be strongest if Morin didn't get fancy and just wrote what he saw: the blood running so deep a cop slipped in it and fell. Over the next several years, he went to Tokyo, China, Korea, Manchuria, Mongolia, Indonesia, Malaya, Thailand, and Indochina.[52]

It seemed as though nothing could keep the lanky correspondent from the hottest stories in Asia—until he found himself on temporary assignment in Saigon the day the Japanese attacked Pearl Harbor. An abrupt knock at his door produced four Japanese men, three in military garb. For the next nine months, Pat Morin was a prisoner, confined mostly to his room. He was offered the chance to leave, in exchange for broadcasting propaganda. He refused, then kept his wits by writing a novel. When his release finally came and he was aboard a ship, he opened a porthole and pitched it into the ocean, grateful, he liked to say, that fish can't read.

Postings to London, Africa, Italy, Paris, and Washington followed before he was sent to cover the conflict in Korea. Nothing he saw in war had as much impact on him as something he witnessed in June 1953: the executions of Julius and Ethel Rosenberg. He relieved the tension leading up to the execution the way he had learned to handle stress in war: by furious note taking. Almost mindlessly, he scribbled in his notebook as much as he could, as fast as he could, leaving nothing out, making himself a mechanical device and detaching himself from the emotional scene before him. It was a strategy that would rescue him again in Little Rock.

AP planned to have two or three reporters, sometimes more, at Central High at all times, with one stationed at each end of the high school building. Since the AP reporters would have to dictate most of their stories live, they took note of the three phone booths the telephone company had installed on the perimeter of the school, then made additional arrangements with one of the teachers who lived near the school to use her home phone if necessary.

Bob Ford, sent in from Dallas, would write the leads for the morning papers; Pat Morin would handle them for the afternoon papers. Bureau chief Keith Fuller would take their dictation, help craft their stories, and send them out.

AP assumed, correctly, that Daisy Bates and the NAACP would try to enroll the students at the first opportunity, the following Monday, September 23. On that morning, in his hotel room, Pat Morin's telephone rang with a wake-up call, as it had every morning for weeks. "Seven o'clock," the hotel operator said enthusiastically. "Mustn't be late for school today."[53]

Across town, the Bateses' home was the staging area for the day's drama. Well before eight o'clock, it was crowded with the nine students, their parents, friends, advisers, and reporters. After the white reporters left her house, Daisy Bates told the Negro reporters and photographers that they, too, would have to go to the school on their own, and they'd have to go a different way. She let them know which entrance the students planned to use. Alex Wilson, whose experience and bearing led others to view him as the leader among the Negro editors and reporters, took a last look at the nine students and marveled at how stouthearted they were. Then he jumped into his car with Jimmy Hicks, Moses Newson, and Earl Davy and headed toward ground zero of the confrontation.

When Pat Morin arrived at the school, the two to three hundred people gathered in front struck him as curious, not menacing. As Morin was surveying the scene, taking note of the greens and golds of a lovely fall day, Alex Wilson was parking two blocks away. This was not the first time they had covered the same story: both had reported from the Korean War; Morin's articles had won a Pulitzer Prize.

Morin stepped into one of the glass-encased phone booths to update the AP office. To one side, he could see the front of the high school; to the other, he could view the street running along the school's south side. At the AP office, Keith Fuller answered. "Do you want to dictate?" he asked Morin.

"Such as it is . . . not much to report," Morin said.

"I'll take it myself," Fuller said. "The boys are busy."

Down the street, the four Negro newsmen were drawing a small and hostile crowd as they started walking apprehensively toward the school. Wilson and Newson walked in front; Hicks and Davy, who had a Graflex camera dangling from his neck, in back. Wilson, so tall and noticeable above the crowd, impeccable with his suit coat fastened at the middle button and wearing a wide-brimmed tan hat, saw that the mass of white people in front of them seemed to be metastasizing as they walked toward it. Behind them, two white men quickly jumped into their traces and trailed them.[54]

"Get out of here!" one segregationist yelled at them. "Go home, you son of a bitch nigger!" bellowed another.

Two other men jumped in front of the newsmen and spread out their arms as if to block them. "You'll not pass," one of them said.

"We are newspapermen," Wilson responded.

"We only want to do our jobs," said Hicks.

"You'll not pass."

Blocked in, Wilson turned the only way he could and headed toward a police officer. "What is your business here?" the officer asked. Wilson showed his press card. The officer reviewed it, slowly. "You better leave," he finally said. "Go on across the sidewalk." As Wilson and the others crossed the street, they could see that the officer had let the whites trailing them keep pace and close in on them.

"Anyone got a rope?" one white man shouted. "We'll hang 'em. I can get one awful quick."

As Morin was finishing dictating what little he had, a shout from the outside penetrated the booth. "The niggers are coming!" Morin could see everyone turn away from the school and start moving in the other direction. "Hang on!" Morin yelled into the phone, "Hang on! There's a helluva fight starting."

"Roll it," Fuller told Morin calmly. Turning to another editor at the office, Fuller said, "Get ready for a bulletin."

Suddenly, two men, one wearing a crash helmet, assaulted Davy and chased after him, terror written all over Davy's face as he looked back. They caught him, muscled him toward some high grass, then slugged and kicked him while others smashed his Graflex onto a concrete sidewalk, destroying his film. Another group of white men sputtered curses as they kicked and hit Newson and Hicks until they could break free and run away.

Morin, with a front-row view inside the phone booth, held his position, opening the door to hear the commotion better and breathlessly dictating everything he saw and heard. Using his war-reporting technique, he didn't feel he was fashioning stories so much as mechanically sucking up the entire scene with his eyes and funneling it into the phone with his voice.[55] At one point, a magical moment for Morin, he took his eyes away from the confrontation to look at the panorama afforded by the booth's glass walls. To his amazement, he saw a station wagon ease up to the south entrance of the school, and he watched—one of the few newsmen who did—as the nine Negro students and two adults emerged. Morin saw that they were not running and not even walking fast. He was able to jot down what they were wearing, how they were carrying their books, and the way they examined the crowd with curiosity but little interest.

Closer to Morin, other white reporters were drawn to the attack on the four Negro newsmen, but they could do nothing to stop it, and policemen did not intervene. Wilson, taunted, pushed, and slapped as he kept walking, was suddenly rushed from behind by a man who planted one foot and swung the other as hard as he could, landing it solidly just below Wilson's back. Another man surged forward with a kick that landed so hard that Wilson's lanky frame looked as though it was folding as he went lurching forward. His hat fell to the ground, so Wilson stopped, then paused to pick it up. In that moment, he had a chance to run. The idea crossed his mind long enough to reject it. Elizabeth Eckford had not run, he told himself. And all that time spent training as a Marine in World War II, then working as a reporter in Korea, then covering the gruesome, demeaning Emmett Till case made him want to stand up and hold his ground. So did an incident years earlier down in Florida, one he had told few people about.

Long before he became a journalist, Wilson had been a teacher in Leesburg, Florida. Just to intimidate local Negro residents, the Ku Klux Klan liked to parade through town every now and then. Wilson had a long, sharp memory of a time when they had rolled through, sending Negro residents, including himself, scattering in fear. Wilson never forgot it and never forgave himself for it, and he vowed never to run away again.[56] Now, as the members of the mob darted in and out at him, throwing fists and feet, Wilson picked up his hat, stood erect, and took some time to run his hand along the crease. But they wouldn't let him go. Wilson's refusal to show fear was provoking the mob. "Run, damn you, run," one man said as others started cuffing Wilson around inside a moving scrum.

One man jumped onto Wilson's back and wrapped his left arm around Wilson's neck, locking him in a stranglehold. Two feet away, a burly, muscular man gripping a brick stared at the immobilized Wilson, ready to start swinging. But he couldn't. A man standing beside him had a tight grip on his arm, not allowing him to throw punches with the brick. As the man on Wilson's back drove him to the ground, the man with the brick got close enough to crack Wilson's skull but again was pulled back by the man beside him. Finally, the man with the brick settled for a hard kick into the center of Wilson's chest.

Wilson, still holding his hat even as he fell to the ground, got up, recreased it, and kept walking, taking one last powerful blow to the head before being pushed away by the crowd just as it realized that the nine Negro students had quietly slipped into the high school.[57] As the mob went crazy over the latest information, Wilson walked to his car. He still had not unfastened the middle button of his suit coat.

Amid the hysteria, Morin suddenly felt his phone booth rocking back and forth. Looking out, he saw a boy trying to topple it, with him inside, by bouncing on the cable that connected the booth to the telephone pole. The booth tipped but never fell, and Morin was able to continue as a one-man wire service telling the Little Rock story to the world.[58]

Protesters yelled to their children inside the school, demanding that they come out. They cheered those who did, as well as the police officer who turned in his badge. Chaos reigned, and every rumor caught a tailwind. When protesters surmised that the Negro newspapermen had conspired to be part of a ruse to draw attention from the students, they grew angrier.[59] Benjamin Fine, feeling like a marked man every time he showed up, came in for some bony elbows in the ribs. A reporter for the Pine Bluff newspaper, mistaken for an out-of-stater, was slugged under the chin and knocked down. A United Press photographer from Dallas was manhandled, and a New Orleans television reporter and cameraman were assaulted when they filmed a white girl leaving the school.

When *Life* magazine's three-person team—the photographers Grey Villet and Francis Miller and reporter Paul Welch—tried to take pictures of a white girl who had walked out of the school in protest, whites retaliated. One attacker punched Miller in the mouth and drew blood. Police threw Miller into a police wagon—along with his assailant. Villet and Welch were cornered by toughs and not allowed to move. They were pushed, shoved, and hit in the face, neck, and ribs. *Life* later agreed to help the FBI bring the agitators to heel. It supplied names, photographs, and whatever help agents needed from *Life*'s files.[60]

Almost all of the day's violence had been directed at journalists, but it was sufficient to make school officials worry that they could not contain the crowd and protect students at dismissal time. Three hours and thirteen minutes after the Negro students had entered the building, even as mobs were beating reporters, the students were removed without the demonstrators' even knowing it. The only way they became convinced that the Negro students had departed for the day was to have two members of the mob enter the school and search for them.

The attack on the reporters prompted a new surge of interest among newspapers. *Washington Post* publisher Philip Graham's interest was less in how his paper covered the exploding story than in getting the Eisenhower administration to respond with force. Graham got Ashmore on the phone, then abruptly transferred him to the deputy attorney general, William Rogers. Ashmore told Rogers that the police could no longer control the situation. "I'll give it to you in one sentence. The police have been routed, the mob is in the streets and we're close to a reign of terror." It was a call that Ashmore would spend years explaining, for it appeared he had stepped beyond his role of editor to urge that federal troops be sent in. No, Ashmore would later say, he had not. He had told Rogers only what the *Gazette* would report the next day.[61]

As that newspaper was heading for the presses, President Eisenhower went on national television and told an audience of 100 million people—62 percent of the nation's television sets were tuned to him—that he had decided to intervene. Within hours, 1,000 soldiers from the racially integrated 101st Airborne Division were flooding into town.[62] Nearly 10,000 members of the Arkansas National Guard were federalized, and some were told to return to the school, working this time for the president under orders to protect the students, not block them, as they entered.

On the 101st Airborne's first full day in Little Rock, news directors for the three networks got clearance to break into daytime programming virtually at will. CBS broke in eleven times, NBC eight times. ABC joined later in the day. Far away, in the Pentagon, Army Secretary Wilber M. Brucker was handed an update on the troops in Little Rock. "But what's happening there right now?" he snapped.

"Why not turn on the television set?" an officer suggested. A television was brought into the room, plugged in, and turned on, and images of soldiers at stiff parade rest emerged on the screen.

"They look good, sharp," said Chief of Staff Maxwell D. Taylor, who had previously commanded the 101st. Then he blurted out, "Why, there's one man whose belt is undone!" Looking closer, he concluded that the man was off duty and resting.[63]

That an army secretary and his chief of staff were able to examine their soldiers in action from nine hundred miles away, live, was a powerful sensation, one the American public would share in the coming years.

In the days after the nine students started attending classes, John Chancellor began reporting information that other reporters weren't getting. He seemed to have details from inside the school on how the white students were responding to the Negro students and vice versa, how the teachers were treating the new arrivals, what questions they asked the Negro students, and how the students answered. There was a reason.

Days before, Chancellor had called Ira Lipman, the high schooler Frank McGee had befriended in the *Gazette* newsroom. "I understand you're our contact," the newsman said. From that point, and for weeks to come, Lipman became a critical conduit of valuable information to Chancellor. Though Lipman had transferred to the new high school that year, he made regular visits to Central in his capacity as business manager of the school newspaper, and he knew students throughout the building.

Calling sometimes from a phone inside Central, Lipman would reach Chancellor at the Sam Peck Hotel, the *Gazette,* or KARK or one of the temporary phone booths that the telephone company had installed outside the high school. Speaking in a whisper, he provided Chancellor with interior scenes, action, and insights from the corridors of Central High. The information was pure gold because school officials and the 101st Airborne weren't giving any hint at all about what was going on inside the school.

Lipman himself had a fortuitous link to the Negro students. His parents were members of a Jewish country club outside Little Rock. While swimming there, he had come to know a locker room attendant, a Negro kid his own age. Lipman would sometimes drive the fellow back to his home in Little Rock. The attendant was Ernest Green, the only senior among the Negro students trying to get into Central High.

On the day Faubus was ordered to pull back the National Guard and let the students enter, Lipman placed a call to Green. Would he tell Lipman which entrance the students would be using on Monday? Would he pause on his way in to give John Chancellor an exclusive interview? The next morning, Chancellor and his cameraman, Maurice Levy, were positioned in the right place at the right time to watch the students walk by, then to have a few moments with Green.

In such ways, Chancellor set a standard for television reporting that lifted it, even in the eyes of its cynical competitors on the print side. Night after night, Chancellor's reports from Little Rock, enhanced by dramatic images, became a fixture in the American household. The evening news show ran fifteen minutes, of which twelve minutes and forty seconds were news. Race stories dominated, none so much as those from Little Rock, presented to viewers by the midwestern man with the nice voice, pleasant disposition, and owlish face.

CBS did some serious reporting with Schakne and Bob Allison. Because ABC came in late and gave the story less attention, Faubus provided that network with his first national interview. Watching that live program, *New York Times* television critic Jack Gould was impressed by television's immediacy. Now when Faubus chose not to respond to questions, he did so under the critical eyes of an entire nation. "Whatever may be the individual set owner's reaction . . . it still is TV as its best," Gould wrote. But television news owed its viewers a "comprehensive and searching study of the Little Rock story," Gould added. "Television registered a beat in putting the governor on the air, but it has an obligation to dig more deeply into the other side of the story."[64]

The television coverage was provocative and in some ways confusing. There were reporters and commentators, and the line between them wasn't always clear. Night after night, words, phrasings, tones, and inflections became a concern to some television critics and certainly to the segregationists. The networks had pledged earlier in the year to keep opinion out of newscasts. The pledge seemed to dissipate at Little Rock, *The Atlanta Constitution*'s television critic wrote, where "all of the newscasters have become 'analysts' and 'commentators' with a free rein to speak their own minds about what is right and what is wrong in the integration dispute."[65]

On the eastern seaboard, the segregationist editors Tom Waring and Jack Kilpatrick watched the television coverage with disgust. Waring suggested in a letter to Kilpatrick that some sort of media monitoring committee be set up to examine race reporting by news outlets they considered anti-South. Kilpatrick wasn't ready to support any kind of watchdog but shared Waring's reaction. "These past two weeks have seen Faubus absolutely crucified by the television and radio people," Kilpatrick wrote, "and some gesture ought to be made of resistance to the incredible influence on public opinion exerted by these radio and TV people."[66]

Nonetheless, in ways even Gunnar Myrdal could never have anticipated in pretelevision days, the daily visual broadcasts of news as it happened had a profound impact on the nation's understanding of the race drama in the South.

On the print side, the *Arkansas Gazette* was proving to be exactly the kind of newspaper that Ashmore had hoped for when his concerns about the shortcomings of southern papers had led to the creation of *Southern School News*. The *Gazette* demonstrated that local newspapers in the South could provide vigorous, hard-nosed, in-depth and fair coverage of their own communities in the midst of a racial crisis.

The *Gazette* showed that by swarming the story; by becoming the paper of record and carrying the transcripts of every important court ruling, speech, press conference, and interview; by challenging official versions of events and relying on more than official sources; by routinely publishing the editorial views of other newspapers; and by foreseeing the long-term impact of the daily events, it could comprehensively and for a sustained period cover the difficult, breaking, explosive story. It also found it could stay in business in the face of circulation boycotts and advertising cancellations.

Ashmore's courageous editorials and civic leadership, backed by a fearless owner, would show his southern brethren that they could challenge racial and political orthodoxy, survive, and get national praise and prizes. In 1958, the *Gazette* won two Pulitzers, the paper for its news coverage and Ashmore for his editorials.

The lesson at the *Arkansas State Press* would be harder. The *Gazette,* though hurt by the advertising boycott, could endure more pain than L. C. and Daisy Bates could. National advertisers, feeling the heat of wholesale distributors in the state, dropped their advertising in the *State Press,* costing the Negro weekly almost its entire national base. Having aimed editorial wrath at Negro leaders it considered complacent, the newspaper found that the combination of slashed advertising and rapidly diminishing circulation put it on an irreversible death spiral.[67] Its epitaph, said a scholar of the Negro press, should have read: "A survivor of terror, but a victim of boycott."[68]

But the more immediate problem for the Negro press was evident on the streets, where the day's events, the violence, made it impossible for the reporters to do their jobs. The impact was devastating. On the power side of the barricade, the white side, Negro reporters could never go unnoticed and untargeted. Negro journalists, to protect themselves, could pull all the little tricks that white reporters deployed to hide their notebooks, dress low-key, avoid arguments—and still they would be unmistakable in a mob scene. As the civil rights movement reached across the South, and as confrontations at other notorious datelines made Little Rock look like a beginner course in racial violence, the Negro press lost its front-row seat.

Chapter 12

New Eyes on the Old South

At *The New York Times,* editors were hit by the wrenching realization that they had blown the coverage of Little Rock. They were able to pull Ben Fine back to New York, return Popham to Chattanooga, and send in Homer Bigart, the two-time Pulitzer Prize winner they had hired from the *New York Herald Tribune,* to accompany the 101st Airborne into Little Rock.

But what about the longer haul in front of them? *Times* editors had watched in dismay as their education story had erupted into a race war that turned into a constitutional crisis that was shown on national television in the form of an occupying force in a militarized zone. They had misread not just Little Rock and the South but the entire civil rights story unfolding in front of them. They had accumulated the datelines of Tuscaloosa and Montgomery, Belzoni and Brookhaven, Clinton, Charlotte, and Clarendon County, but they had failed to tap the depth of the anger and resistance rising across the land.

The Popham notion of driving everywhere from Chattanooga, then writing around the edges of the race matter, was taking the paper in the wrong direction. Far more than other newspapers, the *Times* was willing to flood the South with reporters in reaction to events and become the national paper of record on civil rights coverage. But what good was it to send ten reporters into the South to take its temperature if they missed the fever? Arriving days or weeks after an event occurred and running texts of speeches and court rulings was not sufficient. The truest journalism came from coverage that kept pace with the events, even got ahead of them.

In 1955, Popham had encouraged Catledge to send someone else to tackle the distasteful race story full-time, but the paper had done so only on breaking stories. Since then, Popham, while advancing his optimistic view of the

South's progress, had sent even stronger signals that he was probably not the best man to cover race. But his signals had been couched inside long, long letters, some as many as twelve pages and typed to the edges, that were filled with ingratiating praise for Catledge and other editors, rambling salutes to the worthiness of the *Times'* unique mission in American journalism, a little chest thumping at the value of his public relations efforts, and overly detailed explanations of why he needed more expense money, a new car, or more time to write thank-you letters.[1]

Now, after Little Rock, Popham became more explicit in explaining to Catledge his emotional difficulties with race stories. The South was his family, he wrote, and he didn't want to be in the middle of its fight. He had too many friends on both sides who, he could see, were going to end up in a direct confrontation. He was uncomfortable with the role he would have to play as the chronicler of their ugly showdown. What troubled him even more was that while he saw himself as relatively liberal on race issues and was personally close to a large number of intellectual Negro leaders, he understood how the intransigent whites of the Old South felt.

"As I've said before, you and I understand the cousinships, the conversational techniques of the old south, and it is fast disappearing," he wrote Catledge. "But perhaps that is why, although I know a better south is needed and is sure to come, I can never be angry about the last-ditch fights of some of these people, because I understand what made them, I knew their type and often their families, they inundated the Marine Corps in my youth, and I never find it in my heart to be angry with them although I do wish at times they would make more wonderful contributions to the dialogue and the charting of the future because many of them are damned bright and often they have great virtues and strengths all this country could benefit from."[2]

If Catledge's patience had not quite run out, Ernest von Hartz's had. Von Hartz was one of the *Times'* top news editors, a key player in what was known as "the bullpen," the bank of senior editors who for many years pretty much decided which stories would be published in the paper, where, and at what length. What influence that powerful job didn't give him, he got from his longtime friendship with Catledge, with whom he had worked in Chicago. Von Hartz had leveled with Popham that he was not happy with the reporter's coverage, reporting style, or focus.[3]

In the spring of 1958, the *Times* got an opportunity to replace Popham in a respectable manner. Popham was offered the job of managing editor of *The Chattanooga Times,* which Adolph Ochs had purchased and turned into a worthy newspaper long before he did the same with *The New York Times.* The editor there had retired, and Ben Golden, publisher of *The Chattanooga Times* and Arthur Hays Sulzberger's son-in-law, asked for permission to hire him. Sulzberger asked Catledge, who responded, "This is a free world, including a free market. If Ben wants to offer Johnny a job and Johnny wants to take it, more power to both of them."[4]

Catledge immediately began looking for Popham's replacement. The civil rights story needed a reporter who knew the region well, had the right accent, abided by all the rules, wouldn't get emotionally involved, wouldn't argue with anyone, wouldn't *become* the news, who would just write what he saw, wouldn't get beat, wouldn't get snookered, and was willing to give up his family, perhaps his life, for the story. Catledge knew you could no longer cover the South by driving to stories in hopes of finding pleasantness. Civil rights had become a galloping hard news story that required quick reaction, speed, ubiquity, and a healthy appreciation for what the evil men were willing to do to hold on to what they were afraid of losing.

As Catledge looked around the *Times* newsroom, he didn't see such a person on his reporting staff. But he wasn't alarmed. Six months earlier, the newspaper had hired a thirty-two-year-old, Georgia-born reporter, Claude Sitton, whom Catledge had immediately seen as a strong possibility to go south for the *Times*.[5] But Sitton hadn't been given a reporting position at the *Times*. He had been put on the copydesk, where headlines were written, inconsistencies caught, bad punctuation and spellings fixed, every man's name got a "Mr." thrown in front of it, and adverbial life was squeezed out of stories as they were molded to meet the strictures of *Times* style in the late 1950s.

It was rare for anyone to jump from a copydesk to a reporting assignment at the *Times,* but Catledge was ready to consider it. He dispatched his top assistant to check some references on Sitton and to invite Sitton in for a talk.

Claude Fox Sitton was a bona fide son of the South. His genetic lines linked him with the region's historic fidelity to the military, the church, railroads, farming, segregated education, bluegrass music, and assorted lost causes— all useful attributes for a card-carrying member of *The New York Times* staff. But what was he like? Did he have the right sensibilities and toughness under pressure and under fire? Would he try to cover the South or change it? Would he write from his notebook or from a soapbox? Was he really a reporter after all? His résumé showed he had been a solid wire service reporter for years in several southern cities, but then he'd quit journalism to go to Ghana as press attaché for the U.S. Information Agency. What good would that do him in Bogalusa? Could he move swiftly in the South without startling anyone? Could he find a permanent parking space, maybe even a burial bayou, for Popham's Buick and avail himself of the modern convenience and speed of air travel? Could he work sources, file daily stories, bang out 1,200 words for "The Week in Review" section, and develop an off-speed pitch that would enable him to write effectively in longer form for the Sunday magazine, all at the same time? Was he serious about his work? Was he fearless?

The genealogy was fine. Claude Sitton's father's family had come from the far northwest reaches of South Carolina, where Sitton's great-grandfather had served the Confederacy by being a tax collector. He owned some slaves, made buggies, speculated in land, and served as mayor of the town of Pendleton. Sitton's grandfather ran a flour mill and farmed about a thousand acres. The religion came from his mother's side; her father had been a minister in the North Georgia Conference, the Methodist Church, one of the last of the circuit-riding ministers in the Appalachian foothills of north Georgia.[6]

Sitton's father was a railroad man. He'd risen to the position of conductor with the Southern Railway, known simply as "The Southern," only to have the Depression reduce him to being a brakeman on a local freight run. The demotion had severe consequences: while moving a load of skins to a shoe factory in Beaufort, he snagged a sleeve on a twenty-penny nail and was flipped over, landing hard and breaking his back. The Southern tried to deny him benefits and might have gotten away with it if Sitton's father hadn't been so determined to fight back. He hired a leading claims lawyer who won a settlement that allowed the Sittons to take up farming—cotton, beef cattle, broilers—in Loganville, then Conyers, in north Georgia. Like so many white boys of his generation, young Claude worked side by side on the farm with Negro sharecroppers and came to feel strongly that they had meaningful lives, and meaning in his life.

Sitton's mother taught high school and was one of those teachers loved by all. Books became a part of Sitton's life early because his mother's sister, also a teacher, belonged to the Book-of-the-Month Club. The books—by Joseph Conrad, Marjorie Kinnan Rawlings, just about every author whose work was chosen for the club—became his daily dose of the world beyond Rockdale County.

In Georgia, families divided into two camps: for and against Gene Talmadge, the theatrical demagogue whose trademark red suspenders and fiery oratory enthralled the state across three decades. The Sitton family was decidedly anti-Talmadge, partly because one of Claude's aunts had gone to school with Talmadge long before and just hadn't thought he was upstanding. The Sittons were also decidedly against race baiting. Sitton had never heard either of his parents utter the word "nigger."

Sitton had grown up reading *The Atlanta Journal,* which introduced him to the unusual parade of characters leading the South into the middle of the twentieth century. The stories made him curious about the political oddballs who were running the show, so much that he had begun skipping school in the ninth grade and hitchhiking to Atlanta to watch the Georgia legislature in session. Sitton played varsity sports, showed some leadership, and decided that when graduation rolled around in 1943, he wouldn't be sticking around to farm. He had his mind set on being a merchant captain until near-sightedness stopped him. He enlisted in the U.S. Maritime Service, a Coast Guard–run operation that trained merchant seamen, and began a peripatetic life that would become his trademark. After two years at Sheepshead Bay in New York and Swansea, South Wales, Australia, Sitton volunteered for the navy, which took him to the South Pacific. In and out of Shanghai, he helped haul Chinese troops and Japanese repatriates. In the spring of 1946, he returned to Georgia knowing only that he wanted to go to college.

He went to the closest one, a two-year school, Oxford College, which was affiliated with Emory University, then moved to Atlanta to attend Emory itself. His journalism career began in the spring of 1948, when a classmate who was a stringer for *The Atlanta Constitution* became ill and couldn't make his assignment to cover a graduation speech by Alben Barkley, President Truman's running mate in that year's presidential campaign. Sitton called in some notes to the *Constitution,* caught the newspaper fever, and enlisted in the school's journalism department.

At Emory, Sitton fell under some critical influences. Floyd Baskett, who headed the journalism department and who had written *the* book on copy-editing, made journalism seem like a mission, a calling. To underscore his point, he brought in fellow disciples, such as Ralph McGill and Hodding Carter, Jr., to talk to the class. Sitton was also impressed by the passion of a political science professor, Cullen Gosnell, whose efforts to break down segregation had included introducing his classes to probably the most edu-cated Negro man any of them had ever seen, Dr. Benjamin Mays, president of Morehouse College.

Catledge needed only to examine the portion of Sitton's résumé listing his first three years in the business, 1949–52, to know he could move quickly, learn fast, and overcome obstacles. The young reporter had worked in five cities in three years for two different wire services.

Sitton's first job was working the four-to-midnight shift in the Atlanta bureau of the International News Service. A veteran night manager, a tele-type operator, and Sitton the rookie were the gatekeepers for all news flow-ing into and out of the Southeast on the INS wire each night. During Sitton's first week, the night manager left early, saying he had to go see a fellow about a dog. He came back an hour and a half later, drunk. The next night, the manager left early again, stayed out two hours, and came back drunk. By the second week, the manager was leaving early and not returning at all, leaving the entire region in the hands of a rookie and a teletype operator.

Sitton encountered terrific stories in his three months there. He got to interview the boxer Joe Louis, who had just retired but was continuing to fight against Jim Crow. He covered the tragic death of Margaret Mitchell, the star-crossed author of *Gone With the Wind,* who had been run over by a taxi cab on Peachtree Street. She had lingered for five days—each of them requiring round-the-clock press attention—before dying. He covered the murder of John Garris, the Metropolitan Opera tenor, found dead on railroad tracks in Atlanta.

Sitton got to work with a photographer, too. George the photographer had a handicap: he was blind. Years of lighting scenes with exploding powder in the old days had taken their toll on George's eyes. One night Sitton and George were sent to Stone Mountain to cover a Ku Klux Klan rally. At the scene, Sitton positioned himself right behind George, who held up his SpeedGraphic camera. When Sitton saw something worth shooting, he'd grab George's shoulders, turn him, aim him, and say, "Fire!" George would have his photos.

Miami, a party town in 1949–50, followed, then Birmingham. He jumped to INS's rival, United Press, which sent him to Nashville, then to Atlanta, then, in 1952, to the biggest opportunity of them all in journalism, New York, where he fell in with one of the unlikeliest collections of humanity the city had to offer: the Beats.

At United Press, the twenty-seven-year-old Sitton became close friends with several of his colleagues. But his most fascinating friendship was with the wire editor, Lucien Carr, whose career path into journalism had been singularly unconventional. In a realm far removed from writing radio splits and staccato leads on breaking news stories, Carr had a much larger and more eccentric life. Before coming to United Press, he had been a magnet for the powerful influences who came to define the Beat Generation. As a student at Columbia University, Carr had met floor mate Allen Ginsberg and had introduced him to the Bohemia of Greenwich Village. Separately, Carr had befriended Jack Kerouac and had introduced him to Ginsberg. Carr had then brought Ginsberg and Kerouac together with William S. Burroughs, forming the core of the offbeat, intellectual milieu of the Beats.

Carr and Sitton shared the night trick, the 7-p.m.-to-3-a.m. shift, and formed a friendship around their common interests in journalism and music. Carr, who lived in Greenwich Village, brought Sitton into his ever-growing avant-garde circle. Carr married Francesca "Cesa" von Hartz, a talented guitar player who had previously dated the folksinger Pete Seeger and who shared with Sitton a love of bluegrass music. Sitton became a regular after-hours visitor at the Carrs' apartment, spending time with Ginsberg, seeing Kerouac now and then, and meeting Gregory Corso in passing. And Sitton made another more important acquaintance during that time: Cesa's father, Ernest von Hartz, news editor at *The New York Times.*[7]

Sitton took easily to New York. He was married in 1953, and he and his wife, Eva, rented an apartment in Greenwich Village. They spent summer vacations on Long Island with Lucien and Cesa Carr and others from United Press. Sitton really wanted to work overseas, and newspapers were not leaping to hire him for an overseas post, so he joined the U.S. Information Agency as an information officer and press attaché. His assignment was to a newsworthy place at a momentous time: the Gold Coast of Africa as Ghana became the first African state south of the Sahara to win its independence.

His next USIA stop was to be Tehran, with an intermediate visit to New York. Sitton arrived in New York in August 1957 and hooked up with old United Press friends who had joined the *Times.* They knew of an opening on the copydesk and pushed Sitton to go for it. He met with von Hartz and the legendary *Times* style master, Ted Bernstein, who loaded him down with the *Times* stylebook and urged him to study it and return for a tryout.

Sitton passed the test, took the job, and was assigned to be a copy editor on the city desk; he felt a million miles from the big action on the national desk. He spent the fall of 1957 watching the events from Little Rock dominating the front page, with coverage from the South dominating the national news inside the front section. He knew the datelines, had covered stories at many of them, knew people involved (could just *hear* their voices), and wanted more than anything to be down there. He had no idea what was coming.

In the spring of 1958, one of Sitton's fellow copy editors sat down next to him. "So, did you hear about Popham?" he asked Sitton.

"No, what happened?" Sitton asked.

"He's leaving the *Times,* moving over to *The Chattanooga Times* as general managing editor."

"Gee, I'd give my right arm for that job," Sitton said.

In so short a time that it seemed eerie, Catledge's assistant for personnel, Richard D. Burritt, materialized at Sitton's desk to sample his interest in the job. A man of medium height, Sitton was not imposing to look at. He was built for the long haul—halfback solid, well proportioned, with a horseman's hands—but his was not the kind of presence that quieted a room or parted a crowd when he walked through. His hair had begun thinning, which gave him an avuncular appearance at an early age. He was not a sphinx, but his facial expressions ran a limited range, from mildly amused to mildly worried to mildly intense; his friends knew he was intense, as intense as they come, but he was not visibly high strung. His brow never furrowed. His eyes never darted. But he could move quickly, like a shot, if he had to get somewhere in a hurry. One second he'd be there, the next second he'd be gone.

Burritt's background check had produced glowing reports. His former boss at United Press in New York had described Sitton as "accurate and tenacious; he comes back with what he went after." As a writer, he was "considerably better than average and fast."[8] Sitton's bosses on the *Times'* city desk said his performance there had been "of the highest caliber."[9]

Sitton's enthusiastic interest in the job was immediately evident, Burritt reported to Catledge, and he was even "willing to undertake the job for a time with the understanding that he would be brought back to New York if he proved not to be up to our expectations."[10]

Catledge calculated that Sitton would see through the fog of the South, read all the signs, know what was ahead, and get there. He offered the job. Sitton accepted and, in a single instinct, Catledge was about to right the past wrongs in the *Times'* coverage of civil rights. He was about to set into motion a level of reporting that would establish the national standard for two decades. The man he would choose was unknown then and would remain unknown to the world at large for the six years he reported from the South for the *Times.* Third-string television reporters would have higher name recognition than this *Times*man, but nobody in the news business would have as much impact as he would—on the reporting of the civil rights movement, on the federal government's response, or on the movement itself. Sitton's byline would be atop the stories that landed on the desks of three presidents. His phone number would be carried protectively in the wallets of civil rights workers who saw him, and the power of his byline, as their best hope for survival.

The South that Sitton returned to in 1958 was vastly different from the one he had left in 1952. Much of the region had become angry, hostile, mean, and obsessed with race. Among segregationists, Little Rock had become a rallying cry, like the Alamo; the Citizens' Councils stationery depicted a soldier pushing two girl students with a bayonet. Encircling them were the words: REMEMBER LITTLE ROCK.

In the three years since the decision implementing *Brown,* not a single school district had desegregated in Alabama, Florida, Georgia, Louisiana, Mississippi, South Carolina, or Virginia. North Carolina had only three districts integrated, out of 172 with biracial populations, and Tennessee had only three out of 141. Of 2,889 districts with Negroes and whites in them, 764, or 26 percent, were integrated, most of them in the perimeter states.

Sitton flew to Nashville, where Popham was covering a trial, and began a Popham-style introduction to the South: they took a leisurely drive in the Green Hornet to Kentucky Lake, where the Southern Education Reporting Service was meeting. SERS, with its biracial, cross-ideological board, was Popham's kind of organization, and he wanted Sitton to see it as a resource and adopt its ever-hopeful belief that truthful reporting would lead to Southern enlightenment.

The SERS they found had survived some critical tests. Two years earlier, P. B. Young, Sr., editor of the Negro newspaper in Norfolk, had become so upset by fellow board member Tom Waring's advocacy of the Citizens' Councils that he had quit the board, with some fanfare. While praising "the objectivity which characterizes the *Southern School News*," Young said in a telegram that the "spirit of moderation" had left the board and a majority of the members were "nullificationists and discriminationalists."[11] Word spread quickly in the Negro press that little honor would accrue to anyone who might affiliate with the SERS. "Dominating its board are some of the most rabid, inflammatory and bitter end racists of Southern journalism," the *Baltimore Afro-American* said in urging that no Negro accept an invitation to replace Young. ". . . No self-respecting and decent person would want to sit on the board or associate with them."[12]

The only other Negro on the board, Dr. Charles Johnson, was browbeaten by critics who wanted him to bolt with Young,[13] but he saw more virtues than liabilities in the reporting service and stayed. As the board tried and failed to enlist a Negro replacement, Waring grew testy. He did not want the board groveling before Negro people to seek their participation. "Maybe SERS will just have to worry along with white people in charge," he wrote a colleague. "I could think of a worse fate."[14]

By the time Sitton arrived at the SERS meeting, the board had added the name of Dr. Luther H. Foster, president of the Tuskegee Institute, and the *Southern School News* had kept its footing and continued to stand apart from the crowd in its race coverage. Over three days at the SERS gathering, Sitton met some of the top newspaper reporters in the South who bridged the ideological spectrum. He listened to their reports and absorbed their knowledge. The monthly publication cycle of *Southern School News* was well suited to Popham's pace, but it would not be as helpful to Sitton.[15]

Sitton and Popham then drove to Chattanooga, spent three or four days there, then headed out again. Popham had a lot he wanted to impart to Sitton, and Sitton was a willing and receptive audience. In his captivating Tidewater accent, where "about" becomes "aboot," Popham began talking about the South as they pulled out of Chattanooga. He continued chatting as they crossed Tennessee, north Alabama, and north Mississippi, didn't pause even as they spent two nights on the road, and was still talking—and Sitton was still listening—when they reached Little Rock a few days later.[16]

Little Rock was closing out one historic school year and warily facing another. Federal authority had eked out a victory over state sovereignty. The nine Little Rock students had gotten inside the school, the school year had proceeded with only minor eruptions, and the senior among the nine, Ernest Green, was headed toward graduation. But nothing was settled.

Little Rock, nervously awaiting Faubus's next move, was jittery, divided, and headed for more trouble. Pat Morin, the Associated Press reporter whose 1957 coverage had won a Pulitzer Prize, returned to find sentiments hardened. "A year ago, you found many shades of opinion in Little Rock . . . People who believe in segregation but opposed violence or defiance of law . . . People who believe in desegregation but not the use of force to achieve it," Morin wrote. "Now, 12 months later, the feeling looks solid, a monolithic slab of resistance against desegregation."[17]

The second time around, Little Rock would be watched by different eyes. NBC's John Chancellor called Ashmore to say he had been given a foreign posting and also was being replaced. When Ashmore asked the name of his replacement, Chancellor knew the name would mean nothing to Ashmore, so he heaped praise on his successor, telling Ashmore the fellow was a terrific former United Press and *New York Times* reporter. His name was Sander Vanocur.

Ashmore pondered the news and the discordant sound of the name, then put Chancellor at ease with the same sense of humor that endeared him to so many reporters. "That's not a name," he said. "That's a typographical error."[18]

Just as Popham was bringing Sitton to Little Rock for introductions, Chancellor was bringing Vanocur to town. Among them all, and Ashmore, there was a spirit of kinship. Vanocur had known and revered Popham: when Vanocur had been a green reporter on the *Times* city desk a few years earlier, Popham had befriended him during one of his return visits from the South. Vanocur would never forget how Popham had taken enough interest in him to invite him out of the office for coffee in the cafeteria of the Dixie Hotel in Manhattan.

There was another important changing of the guard taking place in Little Rock that spring: Negro reporters who had pioneered the civil rights coverage found themselves pushed to the sidelines at one of the most momentous events of the story, Ernest Green's graduation. As Central High graduates and their families, including Green and two dozen other Negroes, flowed into the Central High stadium, veteran Negro journalists who had covered some of the seminal civil rights milestones—including writer Simeon Booker and photographer Ernest Withers, covering for *Ebony* magazine—were turned away from the baccalaureate and commencement, as well as from a school board news conference.[19] The Negro press was losing not merely its eyewitness position on the story; it was losing the story.

Sitton, meanwhile, was going through a near ritual in finalizing the transition from the Popham years. His handshake tour of the South over, he and Popham drove back to Chattanooga. Sitton took the keys to the Green Hornet, put Popham's sparse files into it, and headed to the new location of the *Times'* southern bureau, Atlanta, where he settled in. The next time Sitton got into the Green Hornet to reach an assignment as the new southern correspondent for *The New York Times,* he took it only as far as the Atlanta airport, where he left it in order to fly to Little Rock. He would not return to Atlanta, his wife, his three children, or the Green Hornet for six weeks.

From the end of July, when he covered Faubus's easy reelection to a third term, until deep into October, when it was clear that Faubus had succeeded in taking the most extreme action of all—shutting down all Little Rock high schools for the year—Sitton put his stamp on the Little Rock coverage by producing a story in the *Times* just about every day.

The news bounced quickly and without predictability from the governor's mansion to the school board, from the federal courts to the legislature, from the White House to the Supreme Court, then back again. Sitton's days were filled with coverage of legal stays and delays, of declarations of defiance, of grand plans that had no chance of succeeding, and of great confusion. "The emotions of the majority of white Arkansans in the school integration crisis," Sitton wrote in late August, "might well be compared to those of a drowning man who has taken refuge on a log that is being swept along toward a waterfall."[20]

A special session of the legislature handed Faubus extraordinary powers to shut schools, transferred state funds to private segregated schools, made it easier to oust school board members, and gave the attorney general power to seize the NAACP's membership and financial records. Days later, Chief Justice Earl Warren called a rare extraordinary session of the Supreme Court— the first since the case of Julius and Ethel Rosenberg—to reject the Little Rock school board's appeal for a delay in integration.

The issues were fraught with cloudiness, but Sitton brought clarity to them as he banged away at the first of four portable Olivetti typewriters he would wear down over the next six years. He wrote the procedural and the personal, and he packed massive amounts of information into taut word pictures. He described respectable school board members, all unpaid for their work, who were struggling with harassing midnight phone calls, who were being accused of having Communist affiliations and Negro paramours, who were finding their employers boycotted, and who were choosing to avoid social gatherings rather than face ostracism.[21]

Vanocur decided that Ashmore was the wise man to listen to and that Sitton was the reporter to keep an eye on. He saw that if he followed Ashmore's advice or simply followed Sitton, he wouldn't be awakened in the morning darkness with a call from his desk in New York wondering why he didn't have something *The New York Times* was reporting or that AP had plucked from the *Arkansas Gazette.* He tried to talk with each of them at least once a day.

Vanocur became one of many reporters who attended a sort of Gunnar Myrdal School of Southern Racial Behavior, as interpreted and taught by

Harry Ashmore; required reading was *An American Dilemma* and *The Mind of the South,* and recommended reading was works by William Faulkner and Robert Penn Warren. The class was portable, held in Ashmore's office, at the Little Rock Club, at the all-night coffee shops of the Sam Peck and Marion Hotels, or, less soberly and more popularly, at the press club or Ashmore's home. Vanocur thought Ashmore was one of the most delightful companions he'd ever met and constantly marveled at his own good fortune to be in the midst of any conversation in which Ashmore had a part. He loved the way Ashmore defined the difference between the South and North: in the South, whites would say to Negroes, "Come close, but don't go too high." In the North, whites would say, "Go high, but don't come too close."[22]

Vanocur also became devoted to Claude Sitton and freely traded information with him. Sitton helped Vanocur peel back southern nuances and interpret southern culture. Vanocur couldn't imagine how Sitton knew so much. The day the Arkansas legislature finished its special session giving Faubus all the segregationist tools he wanted, Vanocur and Sitton left the Sam Peck Hotel, rounded a corner, and were walking past a bank that featured a clock that played music. "You know what they're playing?" Sitton asked.

Vanocur didn't have the foggiest idea. "What?"

" 'Where He Leads Me, I Will Follow,' " Sitton said.

CBS News's Harry Reasoner, who, like Sitton, had had a previous life with the U.S. Information Agency, never let Sitton stray too far either, for fear of losing the story.[23] Bill Emerson, *Newsweek*'s bureau chief in Atlanta, settled into Little Rock for the duration, joined by a colleague, Joe Cumming; the magazine went to some lengths to tell its readers that Emerson was from North Carolina, Cumming from Georgia. They, too, ran with Sitton, who also established working relationships with correspondents for *Time* magazine.

It was a fresh but keenly professional group of reporters, for the most part. They wore coats and ties every day; criticism of Fine, Schakne, and others in their ranks a year earlier had helped reestablish proper frontline behavior. Vanocur felt as though he were at the center of the world's attention. Reasoner thought that no future story could give him the satisfaction he got from covering Little Rock. Among the reporters was a foreign contingent that lent some spice to the lives of the reporters and a sense of heft to the story. Because of the shortage of hotel rooms, Joe Cumming was forced to share lodgings with Neville Maxwell of *The Times* of London. One day as Cumming was leaving the room, Maxwell was at the typewriter struggling to describe the attitude exhibited by the governor at a press conference. He finally hit on the proper literary analogy but couldn't remember the precise words. He turned to Cumming and asked, "If you're going downtown, would you be good enough to pop into the bookstore and check a quote from *Henry V* when, before the Battle of Agincourt, Henry saw where the French had slaughtered the boys and he made a speech to the effect, 'Not since I left

England was I angry ere this morning'? " Cumming felt certain no American reporter would have asked such a favor.[24]

Some reporters, particularly those to whom the South was unknown, found the leading characters, even the villains, curious, enigmatic, and occasionally endearing. At one of Faubus's many press conferences, Reasoner pressed the governor with a line of questioning that agitated him. The governor struck back with some barbs. When the conference was over and the camera lights were off, Faubus sidled over to Reasoner, threw his arm over the newsman's shoulders, and said, "Sorry as hell to have to do that to you, Harry, but you know how it is."[25]

Little Rock never did open its white high schools in 1958, but the race story didn't disappear. Instead, it atomized. From Little Rock, the army of reporters and photographers dispersed, following Sitton across the South. Most of them southern and operating in familiar territory with familiar people, they moved into Virginia, Georgia, Mississippi, Alabama, Louisiana, Florida, and Tennessee, picking off race stories as they emerged, seeking out stories that were hard to find, and seeing ordinary stories through a new racial prism. In a gothic region where pervasive inhumanity had become a perverse condition and custom, the reporters and photographers were becoming the witnesses, transmitters, and agents of change that Myrdal had foreseen. At a pace that became day after day after day, they showed the essential importance of being there and of seeing, hearing, and reporting the stories firsthand. While operating in an environment that was hostile and increasingly dangerous to them, the reporters and photographers found an audience hungry for more and more information. Letters, calls, and telegrams encouraged the reporters and their editors to keep turning over rocks, to expose the situation in all its ugliness.

As vigorously as the South resisted any change in the order of things, it could not hide its customs and frequently was brash in parading them for outsiders. The eyewitness accounts were shocking and provocative, and they had an impact that only encouraged the reporters to seek out more. They didn't call them civil rights stories because the events they described still didn't seem to fit into any kind of pattern that could be called a movement. Some were just articles about the cruel and crushing fate of Negro people trapped in a Jim Crow society, articles that amplified and vivified the prosaic sociology of Myrdal. They called them race stories. The newsmen dispatched to cover race stories called themselves race reporters. They called their assignment the race beat.

Following Little Rock, one of the new race reporters to hit the South from the mainstream national press was a man whose byline was especially memorable on any southern story: Robert E. Lee Baker. Bob Baker took a bite of the race beat every chance he got. He toured the South in the mid-1950s, jumping into breaking news now and then, reviewing South- and race-related books for the paper. *Washington Post* publisher Phil Graham had been obsessed with getting Eisenhower to send federal help to Little Rock, but his newspaper was noticeably absent in its coverage of the confrontations there. Through nearly all of the 1957 incidents, then again in 1958, the *Post* newsroom's involvement in the Little Rock story was minimal. Then the capital's number two paper behind *The Washington Star,* the *Post* relied almost entirely on wire services for race stories outside its region, sending its own reporters only when the story moved to the Supreme Court or Capitol Hill, or when Virginia joined Arkansas in closing schools in the fall of 1958.[26]

In June 1958, Baker mined one of the earliest high-impact stories when he followed some research findings down to Dawson in Terrell County, Georgia. There he found a town where white authorities were brutalizing and terrorizing the Negro residents and systematically pulling trapdoors every time they came close to registering to vote. They were also quite willing to talk themselves right onto the front pages of *The Washington Post* and speak in a vernacular that was so offensive that it seemed like a caricature.

Baker learned that police had severely beaten one young Negro man who had asked them to stop hitting his father. The young man, who had been clubbed with a blackjack, slapped across the face with a gun, kicked in the groin, and slammed on the feet by a car door, was "senseless, unable to speak or support himself" when he appeared in court, Baker reported. Five days later, he was dead from a skull fracture caused by a blow from a blunt instrument.

Other Negro residents of Terrell County told how police, with little provocation, had opened fire on another Negro man in his backyard, how they handled juke joint drunkenness by shooting at Negroes, how they attacked Negroes for being out past an unofficial "curfew," and how a policeman had slapped a Negro woman who had gone to visit her son in jail. Baker provided a clear view of how the voting registrars operated. He listed the questions Negroes had to answer in order to register ("What does the Constitution of Georgia provide regarding the suspension of the privilege of habeas corpus?" "What are the names of the federal district judges in Georgia?"). He told of the Negro teacher with a bachelor of science degree who had been rejected because he slurred the word "original." It was the third time he had tried to register, so he clearly had not gotten the message. He was soon fired from his teaching job.

If there had been any uncertainty about the veracity of the accounts, the sheriff, Z. T. "Zeke" Mathews, and the Dawson police chief, Howard L. Lee, pretty much squelched them when they opened their mouths and Baker opened his notebook. "You know Cap', there's nothing like fear to keep the niggers in line," Mathews said. "I'm talking about outlaw niggers. And we always tell them there are four roads leading out of Dawson in all directions and they are free to go any time they don't like it here."

Chief Lee said that police had smashed a blackjack over the head of the young man who had tried to help his father because he "bucked up and put up a scuffle." Even white residents had complained about the beating. Of the man killed in his backyard, Lee said, "I remarked on the way to the hospital how quick he died. I had to shoot one in the stomach a few years ago and he lived five or six days. The doctor opened [him] up and he had bled all over inside. You could smell the moonshine in his blood."

The FBI had been in town checking on the accounts, Baker reported. Chief Lee couldn't believe it. "It aggravates me worse than anything because the FBI starts talking to niggers and then the niggers get to thinking they're important and it stirs them up."

As for Negro residents voting, Sheriff Mathews saw it this way: "Well, Cap', I believe we ought to be strict about who votes. There isn't a nigger in Georgia who wouldn't take over if he could. They want all the power." Mathews expressed disgruntlement that the current administration had ended the curfew. "But we need it, the way things are going. A man who knows the nigger can tell when dissatisfaction is brewing. Niggers up late at night are suspicious."

Baker described the sheriff as "a pleasant-appearing man whose only symbol of authority is a tiny badge clipped to his shirt pocket. A veteran of 27 years supervising a chain gang, he is now watching his waistline and drinks only one Coke a day."

Chief Lee gave his wisdom: "Everything that has happened is due to drinking, mixing wine and beer and 'shine,' and, hell, you can't wait to find out what a crazy nigger is going to do. We're just as good to niggers as they'll let us be."

In his closing comments, which he insisted that Baker write in his note-book, Lee said, "The nigger resents everything the white man has, all you've got, all I've got. I've noticed things have gotten worse since television. They all got television sets up there and hear all the news over NBC and CBS, telling what the Supreme Court has done and what the Federal Courts say and all about civil rights, and they been thinking. We've had trouble. We're going to have a lot more of it."

The Justice Department three months later brought charges of voting discrimination against Terrell County and, in a case argued before the U.S. Supreme Court by Attorney General William Rogers himself, won a 9–0 verdict that led to a ban on giving Negroes and whites different tests. Chief Lee would prove right on one count: there would be more trouble.[27]

Baker could always return to Washington, and Sitton could always return to Atlanta. But local newsmen chasing the stories stirred up by the national reporters, or digging up their own stories that segregationists wanted ignored, faced a special set of challenges. The pressure to accede to segregationist ideology—that is, to ignore the story—was enormous for frontline reporters and editors. In four years' time, the Citizens' Councils, the sovereignty commissions, and the newspaper and broadcast editors propounding Old South conformity had worked their ideology and their ideas of governance so deeply into the civic, social, and political grain of the Deep South that few dared challenge it openly, even when horrible things were done in its name.

Probably no small collection of reporters faced up to the political and social pressures and challenges as professionally as the United Press bureau in Jackson, Mississippi. There, the bureau chief, John Herbers, applied a simple standard—newsworthiness—in deciding what stories to assign. Race was never a reason not to cover a story. That simple declaration set him apart and caused him a lot of trouble. Soon after the *Brown* decision, Herbers got word that Aaron Henry, a Clarksdale pharmacist, was going to hold a Sunday rally and planning session for local Negro leaders to decide how to seek changes under the law.

So Herbers piled his wife and three blond-haired, blue-eyed daughters into his car on that Sunday morning and drove toward the Mississippi Delta to see what all those Negro people were up to. When he got there, he saw a human side of the emerging race story that wasn't obvious when he was sitting back at the United Press office. He and his family were greeted warmly, but what he witnessed behind the eyes of the people around him was an animated spirit of strength, courage, and absolute resolve. He wrote a story not about harangues and postures from the podium but about people; not just what they said but who they were and the situation they were in.

Covering Negro people was not a political statement on Herbers's part. Born in Memphis and raised in Mississippi, he had been brought up in a home with traditional segregationist values. His parents were not at all open-minded on race. They believed Negroes were inferior and were meant to be a serving class to white people. Herbers had begun seriously examining his own values when he was a journalism student at Emory University. There, he found his old-line thinking challenged by Calvin Kytle, a professor who believed the racial divide of the South could be bridged.[28]

Another influence on Herbers at Emory was the managing editor, later editor, of the student newspaper, the *Wheel*. Even then, other students and journalism professors recognized that the editor, who was a year and a half behind Herbers, had special talent and drive. The student was Claude Sitton, who made the newspaper a serious publication. Herbers was even more impressed when he found that Sitton had gotten the wire service job he himself had wanted in Atlanta. Herbers ended up instead in Mississippi, where he had a far greater influence as a wireman than he could have had in Atlanta.

Herbers's role required him to write and assign news and to sell the service to newspapers and television and radio stations. Pushing his product to men who, nominally at least, were in the news business, he saw the wide chasm that existed in his own field.[29]

Nowhere was the gulf more evident than at the most influential television station in the state, WLBT, in Jackson. Fred Beard, the station's manager, was a leader in the Citizens' Council, gave the Council a fifteen-minute time slot in the station programming, and allowed it to operate a bookstore in the station's lobby to display and distribute white supremacist literature. He was once reported to have boasted that he had cut off a network program and posted a "Sorry, Cable Trouble" sign because the show featured Thurgood Marshall. He later denied having cut Marshall off; he said he had refused to run the show because he didn't want to have a fight with William J. Simmons, the head of the Citizens' Councils.

And he didn't like a lot of what he saw coming from the UPI bureau in Jackson. "What do you mean, carrying all this stuff and glorifying the Negro?" an insistent Fred Beard demanded of Herbers one day.[30]

Herbers, low key in manner and speech, would respond that news was news, that some news operations wanted it, and that the others didn't have to use it. Still, the pressures to suspend news judgment and to conform were intense. Looking around, Herbers saw so few people, even newspeople, who felt the way he did. He would wake up every morning wondering if he was crazy.[31] Herbers continued to direct coverage of news involving Negroes, getting story tips from editors such as Hodding Carter, Jr., in Greenville and Hazel Brannon Smith in Lexington. He would have those stories to himself because the Associated Press wouldn't seek them out. AP was under even greater pressure: as a cooperative owned by its member papers, AP was less able to resist the demands of those papers than United Press was. While Herbers felt certain that AP, in seeking Mississippi clients, never touted its restraint in covering race stories, he knew he lost some customers to his competitor because of his bureau's coverage.

Herbers led an unusually strong team of reporters who would make their mark in years to come. H. L. Stevenson later became the top editor at UPI.[32] Cliff Sessions would join UPI in Washington, then act as press secretary for Attorney General Ramsey Clark. Lewis Lord would be a senior editor at *U.S. News & World Report.* Herbers would join *The New York Times* in its Atlanta bureau. All felt that what they were doing was right, and exciting.

When Lord was still a college student and helping UPI, he was assigned to cover an NAACP meeting. He met NAACP field secretary Medgar Evers and returned almost giddy. Herbers asked him why. "John," he said, "it was the first time I ever shook hands with a Negro man. It was like losing my virginity."[33]

In early 1958, Sessions wrote a hard-edged enterprise story revealing that the Citizens' Councils had begun "a white supremacy indoctrination campaign" in Mississippi high schools by presenting speeches at assemblies and introducing books into classrooms that depicted Negroes "as lazy, thieving and cowardly." The campaign, Sessions reported, was "a full scale effort to wipe out any integrationist leanings among the children." Among the strategies that schools had adopted was a contest for writing on racial integrity. The prize was a $25 defense bond. The requirement was that the students read the late Senator Theodore Bilbo's book *Take Your Choice: Separation or Mongrelization,* Mississippi Judge Tom Brady's *Black Monday,* or a lesser-known book by Stewart Landry, *The Cult of Equality.* Landry's book, Sessions reported, said, "It is difficult to tell when Negroes are lying and when they are telling the truth" and "Negroes do not face difficulties or adversity with courage and determination. They slink away rather than meet the issue."[34]

That same year, 1958, Sessions wrote another story that set United Press apart. He composed a profile of Medgar Evers, a young, emerging civil rights figure in Mississippi. Merely writing about him was unusual, but writing a profile, as if he were a human being, was groundbreaking.[35] While he was meeting with Evers, the phone rang. The unknown caller issued a threat to Evers, which made its way into the lead paragraph of Sessions's story. Evers felt uncomfortable with the way the story opened; it was too dramatic, too flashy, too likely to provoke even more threats. But it stood out as just about the earliest story to raise Evers from one-dimensional object to multi-faceted human being.[36]

Sessions wasn't the only one keeping an eye on Evers. That same year, at a meeting of the State Sovereignty Commission, the Mississippi agency aimed at stopping the advancement of civil rights and spying on civil rights activists, Governor James P. Coleman personally directed "that spot checks be made of the activities of Medgar Evers, both day and night, to determine whether he is violating any laws." His order was put into a memo entitled "Medgar Evers, Race Agitator."[37]

It was no surprise that Evers was being watched, which made another wall that Sessions breached even more remarkable. He got close to Evers personally and socially. Sessions met Evers while covering an NAACP rally and liked him immediately. Evers was the first Negro person he had dealt with as a social equal, which served them both professionally. Evers would ask for Sessions's advice about how to handle other reporters, and Sessions would get tips on news stories that no one else was getting.[38]

In 1958, Sessions and his wife, Shirley, even went so far as to invite Medgar and Myrlie Evers to their home in Jackson for drinks. The invitation was freely given, freely accepted, but fraught with uncertainty. No professional cloak of respectability was sufficient to gussy up the ugly fact that Negroes and whites did not mingle socially, and an evening with a Negro activist came only with great risk. For the Everses, the risk was to their lives for having the impertinence of trying to operate socially on the same level as a white couple. For the Sessionses and the Herberses, who joined them, the risk was ostracism, or worse, for aiding and abetting such behavior.[39]

Cliff Sessions had grown up believing that segregation was providentially ordained. The world wouldn't be that way if it weren't, he thought. Not that his family was racist. His dad was an Episcopal minister, and the word "nigger" was not a part of the family's vocabulary. But segregation was the way of life. Only as a newsman had he started to think differently, and he was acutely aware that he was moving away from the mainstream. He was determined to be an objective newsman, by the time-honored standard of his profession. To keep himself above the political fray, Sessions decided not to vote and didn't register to vote.[40]

For his wife, Shirley, to host the Everses was an even greater risk. Her parents were rock-solid segregationists who were deeply fearful of the changes that were threatening their lives and greatly disturbed by the articles that accompanied their son-in-law's bylines. Emotionally and politically, Shirley had crossed the line, had abandoned her family's Old South view of the world, though she didn't dare tell them. Having Medgar Evers over for drinks was dancing with the Devil, and she feared her parents would find out. So when the Everses came by to visit, before the discussion was able to turn to movies, baseball, and politics, Cliff Sessions drew the drapes.[41]

When the Everses returned the favor and extended an invitation to their house, Sessions accepted. But the risks were becoming greater, and the punishment, if they were discovered, would be more severe. There was no doubt the Evers's house was under constant surveillance and that segregationist forces would use the information of their meeting to make their lives miserable. For starters, Shirley's parents would be told. And Cliff's integrity as a reporter would be assailed. There was also concern about the position they were putting the Everses in. On the evening the Sessions were expected at the Everses' home, Cliff called them, spoke with Medgar, and canceled. He made up an excuse, saying he had to work, and was immediately ridden by guilt. He never knew if Evers believed him.

Mere coverage of an event or a person such as Evers was sufficient to draw criticism from segregationists. While on assignment in the lobby of the

Jackson City Hall one day, Sessions was called on by Beard, the television executive, to explain why he had written a story about Evers. Who cared about Evers or what he had to say? Beard demanded to know. Then, in front of a roomful of people, Beard turned red in the face and issued his most damning statement: "Sessions, you're an integrationist." Beard turned and walked ten paces, stopped, and turned back to Sessions. "Crawl back under your rock," he told Sessions. "You've been exposed. You're an integrationist." Sessions felt the room's eyes hold their fix on him. As he looked around, he saw only sober faces, except for the hint of a smile on the face of a Negro man in the lobby.

Each such incident only clarified for Sessions that he was doing what he should be doing. He began to feel almost missionary in getting out stories that needed no embellishment to characterize the South's fight or to convey its drama. He even liked the idea that the Negro woman who cleaned his house and babysat his children was attending Medgar Evers's NAACP meetings. He felt like a do-gooder, and it felt good.[42]

For reporters like Herbers and Sessions in Jackson, verbal assaults such as Beard's only heightened their profound sense of isolation as they crossed into areas of coverage that had long been forbidden.

For progressive reporters and editors in Mississippi, occasional refuge and uplift came in the form of salubrious but not especially abstemious weekend pilgrimages to Greenville, where Hodding and Betty Carter opened their home, Feliciana.

In much the same way that Harry Ashmore's home had become an oasis for national reporters rolling through Little Rock, Feliciana became a shelter and a community for an eclectic, exotic mix of national and local newspaper, television, and newsmagazine reporters, foreign journalists, field representatives from progressive organizations in the South, an occasional FBI agent, and a few enlightened souls of the Delta who subscribed to *The Atlantic Monthly, Harper's Magazine, Saturday Review of Literature,* or *The New Republic.*

There, with no agenda, the war-weary journalistic outcasts and their spouses would gather in the house, by the pool, on the tennis courts, or at the artificial lake stocked with bream and bass. There they consumed oysters and crawfish by the sackload, downed copious amounts of contraband booze, and talked through the night and deep into the Delta morning. Bloody Marys were the first sip of the day.[43]

The Sessionses would be there, along with the Herberses. Bill Minor, the Mississippi bureau chief for the New Orleans *Times-Picayune,* would drive up from Jackson with his wife, Gloria. Hazel Brannon Smith, publisher of the *Lexington Advertiser,* would drive over to Greenville and up the winding driveway to Feliciana's door with her husband, Walter, known as Smitty, who had lost his hospital administration job because of her editorials. Smith's steadfast commentaries against liquor racketeering, gambling, and official corruption had made her some powerful enemies long before her campaign to curb police brutality against Negroes had led segregationists to label her a nigger lover and Communist and to start a rival paper to run her out of business. A Jackson television newsman, Dick Sanders, would join the group, along with other local journalists whose struggles to display editorial courage against prevailing Citizens' Councils sentiment drew strength from the weekend exposure to Carter.

There was a sense of daring at the gatherings. No one doubted that the house was always a possible target of night riders, and Carter kept guns all over the place just in case. But strength, not fear, came from the weekends. Herbers knew, as he left those weekends in Greenville, that the only thing keeping him in the news business was Carter's words of support.

Carter had the courage to write what some frontline reporters could only think. In the summer of 1958, Herbers sent Sessions and Carter sent the reporter Jay Milner to cover the trial of Yalobusha County Sheriff J. G. "Buster" Treloar. The sheriff was charged with beating Woodrow Wilson Daniels, a Negro, with a ten-inch blackjack while Daniels was confined to a jail cell. Daniels died ten days later of a subdural hemorrhage.

Three of the four witnesses against the sheriff were white. Daniels's employer, a grocer, said he had seen the sheriff go into the Negro man's cell, then heard sounds of a beating. "I couldn't stand it," he testified. "I had to leave." The white doctor who had been called in to treat Daniels's injuries said he had seen the sheriff kick the injured inmate and curse him angrily.

The jury took twenty-four minutes to find the sheriff not guilty. In the hot, crowded courtroom, the white people broke into smiles. "In the balcony, also crowded and even hotter, the Negro spectators didn't move and their faces remained immobile as they had been throughout the trial," Milner reported.

The sheriff walked over to the evidence table, picked up the blackjack, and pocketed it while his lawyer joked about the case. "Why that jury knew that you can't kill a nigger by hitting him on the head," the lawyer said with a laugh. "You gotta hit him on the heel."[44]

The next day, in an editorial mischievously entitled "Water Valley Meditation," Carter captured the absurdity of the voices coming from all the Sheriff Treloars and Sheriff Mathewses and Chief Lees in the South: "What with all these nosey newspapermen and preachers and Yankees and other such communistic trash, it's getting to where a Mississippi white man can't kill himself a nigguh without getting his name in the papers and losing up to two or three days in court. Downright subversive, we call it, and something ought to be done. Otherwise, what was the use of us winning the war for Southern independence?"[45]

Satire was both the lance and the balm for P. D. East, the editor and publisher of a small and feisty weekly newspaper, the *Petal Paper,* in a south Mississippi county named after the first grand wizard of the Ku Klux Klan, Confederate General Nathan Bedford Forrest. East, always on the brink of bankruptcy, took the Klan and other segregationists seriously but delighted in making fun of them. After a rash of cross burnings in 1957, he ran a spoof classified advertisement on the front page for "used lumber desirable for making crosses." He offered free kerosene with orders of a half dozen or more and a free booklet, "How to Build Your Own Cross Kit" with every order.[46]

Some levity was also coming out of Charlotte, where one of Ashmore's poker buddies from his early newspaper days, Harry Golden, delighted in making fun of segregationists and their contortions in defense of racial separation. Golden, the gadfly author of *The Carolina Israelite* newspaper, which circulated weekly mostly among southern Jews, developed a series of "Golden Plans" to show the absurdity of segregationist positions.

Golden observed, for example, that whites did not mind standing next to Negroes in the grocery, at the bank, and at other counters. "It is only when the Negro 'sets' that the fur begins to fly." The Golden Vertical Integration Plan? "Provide only desks in all public schools of our state," he suggested. "No seats." His Golden Out-of-Order Plan called for hanging out-of-order signs on all water fountains designated for white people; soon, thirsty whites would be drinking out of the "colored" fountains and not noticing a difference. Golden, whose books had broad appeal in the 1960s, gave liberals scattered and isolated across the South an opportunity to enjoy a collective laugh each week.[47]

It was with Harry Golden and another literary giant, Carl Sandburg, that Ralph McGill sometimes sought refuge and emotional sustenance. Over a fifteen-year period, until Sandburg died in 1967, the three men would gather for weekends of quiet talk and expansive debate, rocking in chairs and walking in the woods at Sandburg's antebellum home, set inside the 240-acre Connemara Farms in Flat Rock, North Carolina.[48]

In Atlanta, McGill provided Claude Sitton with the same kind of moral support that Carter was dispensing in Mississippi. Whenever Sitton would return to his office inside the *Atlanta Journal* and *Constitution* Building, little time would pass before he'd look up and see McGill standing in the doorway.

"Hey, what's going on in Mississippi?" McGill would ask as he walked into Sitton's office. "What do you know that I ought to know?" Sitton shared his findings with McGill, whom he and other younger reporters called "Pappy," and McGill shared his insights and analysis with Sitton. Early on, Sitton learned the price of sharing too much too soon: he'd pick up the *Constitution* the next day and see his soundings massaged beautifully and crisply into an astute McGill column that had been distributed nationwide—before Sitton had gotten them into the *Times*. Sitton had to laugh at how masterfully McGill had picked his brain; and he had to groan at the realization that readers who saw similarities in his story and McGill's column were far more likely to conclude that Sitton had stolen from McGill than vice versa.[49]

At the same time, a much more important fusion of ideas and sense of direction was taking place when McGill and Sitton sat and discussed the South and how their profession was covering it. McGill proselytized his fellow journalists with the idea that they had become mindless, robotic followers of the "cult of objectivity," at the expense of truth.

Certainly, reporters had to try to be fair, McGill felt, but he did not see the point of purely objective news presentations if that meant the truth got lost in the process. Objectivity, he believed, was an anachronistic antidote that had emerged in earlier days, when publishers had been wild and reckless in pushing their biases into the newspapers. It had evolved into a formula of printing all sides of the story—sometimes in the same number of words or paragraphs—and leaving readers to make their own choices. From there, McGill felt, the goal of objectivity had devolved to the point where newspapers had become neutered. If a public figure said something that was untrue or mischaracterized a situation, McGill felt, most newspapers wouldn't report the falsity unless the reporter could get someone else to point it out. And if that someone else stretched the truth, McGill said, newspapers devoted to blind objectivity found themselves in a bind, printing two falsities.[50]

If Citizens' Council leaders in a town, for example, said they were not putting economic pressure on Negroes to withdraw their names from petitions and the newspaper had incontrovertible proof that they were, why were newspapers so reluctant to report it? Why did they have to wait until they found someone who was willing to say it on the record? Why did they fall back on the conventional thrust and parry of grouping the allegation and denial all in the first couple of paragraphs, which steered readers away from the truth, not toward it? McGill felt that Sitton and the *Times* were exceptions. The *Times* had embarked on a bolder form of news coverage that gave reporters room to go deeper in explaining and interpreting news events and developments. Sitton was a tenacious reporter who did his own legwork, who didn't rely on official sources, who reflexively felt the need to cover the same ground as investigators, and who trusted his own judgment to guide his articles.

But even with Sitton's reporting, McGill's analysis, and their combined understanding of the South and its people, the question neither could answer, the question no one could answer, was how far each side of the racial divide was willing to go to get its way. To McGill, Ashmore, Carter, and other liberal editors in the South, massive resistance as a toy weapon in the hands of a Jack Kilpatrick was one thing; but it was quite something else in the hands of armed and dangerous freckle-bellies, as Bill Emerson called the great unwashed. Massive resistance, once allowed to root, could not be controlled or contained and would lead to a kind of brutal lawlessness that none of its high-minded advocates wanted on their consciences. If you allow the states to thumb their nose at federal edicts, the editors asked, what's to stop all those poor, angry backwoods white folks, whipped into a paranoid frenzy by demagogues, from taking the next step? And *who* was going to stop them?

Some segregationist editors were asking the same thing.

CHAPTER 13

BACKFIRE IN VIRGINIA

The seeds of interposition planted by Jack Kilpatrick in 1955 blossomed in Virginia in the fall of 1958. The seeds were laws carrying automatic triggers that went into effect when certain events occurred. As the Virginia schools moved toward opening, federal court orders that the schools must desegregate triggered state laws that shut them down. Virtually overnight, schools were closed in Charlottesville, home of the University of Virginia; in Norfolk; and in tiny Warren County, of which Front Royal was the county seat. In all three areas, the Negro schools remained open.

By its overwhelming endorsement of Kilpatrick's package of laws, Virginia had built a shield that automatically interposed itself between federal desegregation mandates and local school districts, without sorting out the irony that such a shield, in the name of sovereignty, left local districts no opportunity to exercise their own free will against the state.

One by one, with rare exceptions over the three years, Virginia newspapers had fallen into line behind Kilpatrick, who was powerfully backed by Senator Harry F. Byrd, the boss of the state's dominant Democratic political organization. Working in the same building as Kilpatrick, Virginius Dabney was blocked from opposing massive resistance by Tennant Bryan, the principal owner of Dabney's *Times-Dispatch* as well as Kilpatrick's *News Leader.* Bryan and Dabney struck a deal: when the owner wanted militantly segregationist editorials, a business executive with a flair for writing, not Dabney or his editorial staff, would supply them. At one point, Dabney considered leaving his post but got only one nibble, from the Cox papers in Dayton. His wife awoke him from his reverie. She wondered how an editor named Virginius could possibly pursue his life's work in Ohio.[1]

In Norfolk, Lenoir Chambers, editor of the *Virginian-Pilot,* refused to join the interposition parade and began arguing against school closing legislation and massive resistance laws as rapidly as Kilpatrick and the state legislature devised them.[2]

Chambers, sixty years old and considerably senior to Ashmore, had many of the Little Rock editor's characteristics. Both had been combat infantry officers, though in different world wars. Chambers was thoughtful and serious about his work, clear about his feelings, and as knowledgeable of history's lessons as anyone. He, too, had found time to write books, most notably a two-volume biography of "Stonewall" Jackson. And he, too, had a personal charisma that emerged from an aristocratic bearing. He was affable, "blending into a clubroom like walnut and leather," a colleague once said. A raconteur among his friends, Chambers enjoyed the loosening of conversation that came with a drink. He could also be comically petty about some things; he couldn't stand for his watch to be a minute off or for the second hand and minute hand to reach the 12 out of synch.[3]

During his three-year fight, Chambers had allies such as Jonathan Daniels, editor of the Raleigh *News & Observer,* Ralph McGill in Atlanta, and the editorial pages of *The Washington Post* and its larger rival, *The Washington Star;* but almost invariably from out of state. Daniels wrote that those "who propose abandonment of the schools propose something beyond secession from the Union. They urge secession from civilization."[4]

When ultimately, on September 27, 1958, 9,500 white students were locked out of six junior and senior high schools to prevent 17 Negro students from entering them, Chambers was appalled. "There is no moral justification for the harsh punishment of the state's largest city," he wrote. "Surely there is greater wisdom in Virginia than this would imply."[5] As the schoolless weeks ticked by, Chambers's continuing rebuke of massive resistance picked up increasing support, principally from angry parents, some of whom resorted to "speakeasy schools" in church basements to piece together an education for their children.

For four months, Virginia was the new center of the South's racial struggle, with journalists from across the nation moving in and out to report on children locked out of their schools and on a succession of cases before the federal courts where the school-closing laws were being systematically dismantled. Norfolk's atmosphere, while considerably strained, was sharply different from Little Rock's. There were no mobs, no violence, just six startlingly vacant schools.

As had been the pattern in other southern cities facing desegregation, coverage by the main local paper, the *Virginian-Pilot,* focused heavily on white reaction, with little attention to black opinion. But many of the visiting reporters came away impressed by the *Virginian-Pilot's* detailed coverage, notably by Luther Carter, the education writer, and John Brooks, the federal courts reporter.

Chambers's editorials, too, caught the eye of the national press in 1958 and 1959, and he would win the Pulitzer Prize. One of his editorials summarized his arguments: "The cliché that states' rights must be won now or lost forever is not the truth. The shibboleth that the Supreme Court's order may be legally ignored is not the truth. The myth that Virginia is in contest with alien forces is not the truth. The truth is that Virginia can open all the schools and cannot with justice and good sense keep them closed. Virginia and its children need their schools."[6]

In time, others in the Virginia press moved toward Chambers's position and away from that of Kilpatrick and Senator Byrd. John A. Hamilton, whose father was the managing editor of the *Richmond News Leader,* served as Kilpatrick's associate editor for a couple of years before deciding to move to the *Lynchburg News* as associate editor. He had some spare weeks between jobs and used them to go to Front Royal and help the local paper support massive resistance there. Hamilton held Kilpatrick in awe even as he came to understand the problem with being his associate: you were forever the number two man on a one-man editorial page.[7]

But the sobering reality of closed schools changed Hamilton's views. Never content to be confined to his editor's office, Hamilton talked to the Front Royal students who were without schools. "We're losing our education," they said. They wanted to go to school, and they didn't want to risk their future in a dispute over whether a few Negro kids came to their classes.[8]

"Poor kids," Hamilton said to himself later. "Suppose they were my kids? Is this something we should be doing?" Hamilton decided the price of integration wasn't worth the loss of education, and he said so in the pages of the *Lynchburg News* in the fall of 1958. He had a strong ally in Phil Scruggs, his paper's editor. In relatively short order, in October and November 1958, the Virginia press that had formed the foundation of support for massive resistance began to crack and heave. The other Lynchburg paper came to the same conclusion as Hamilton. So did Roanoke's even more conservative papers. The *Ledger-Dispatch* in Norfolk, which had egged on massive resistance, now joined its liberal sister, the *Virginian-Pilot,* in calling for the opening of the schools. The Charlottesville *Daily Progress* sounded the same theme.

Even Kilpatrick and his boss, Tennant Bryan, were coming around. Finally, Bryan, Kilpatrick, Dabney, and one of Bryan's business executives drove in the same car to Winchester to tell Senator Byrd that they could no longer support massive resistance. Byrd was cordial but adamant. He wanted no integration in Virginia's schools.

Kilpatrick would say in a letter to Bill Simmons of the Citizens' Councils that he had become convinced that "a policy of 'close all the schools to prevent the admission of one negro anywhere,' actually carried into effect, is a self-defeating, South-defeating policy. . . . I think there are greater evils for the South than the admission of one Negro pupil to one white school. Mind you, I would forestall such admission as long as I could, by every device of litigation and legislation that the minds of ingenious men could conceive."[9]

Ultimately, Governor Lindsay J. Almond conceded that federal power trumped that of the state. The next day, Norfolk's city council ordered the schools to reopen on February 2, 1959. On that day, representatives of more than fifty news organizations watched school desegregation come peacefully to Norfolk and Virginia.

In Little Rock, Faubus's effort to keep schools closed another year faltered in August 1959, when the school board maneuvered to reopen classes early, before Faubus could get legislation adopted. For Harry Ashmore, the reopening of schools was an opportunity to reexamine his own professional course. He'd generated about all the heat he or anyone else could stand in Little Rock, and he figured the *Gazette* might reach financial stability more readily if he left. He saw himself as a southern newspaperman, but he couldn't see a newspaper publisher in the South who would hire the complete package of Harry Ashmore. If he were a publisher, he told friends, he was not sure he would hire him.[10]

He had a standing offer to join the Fund for the Republic, a civil liberties think tank backed by the Ford Foundation. The job appealed to him because it would allow him to address race relations through a larger scope.[11]

So he left Arkansas later that year, buoyed by the collapse of massive resistance. Ashmore and other liberal and moderate editors across the South viewed that as convincing proof that it was futile and foolish to defy federal law over what at this point was only token school desegregation.

But the collapse left leading segregationist editors frustrated to the point of panic that they were losing not only in the courts but also in the broader, national public relations war that mattered most. Whether they would admit it or not—and they would not—the truth of Myrdal's prediction was being borne out. With every development, northern news organizations were exhibiting only *more* interest in the plight of southern Negroes.

In Charleston, Tom Waring had been annoyed for some time by the coverage, and by the treatment of segregationist editors. With a particular sensitivity that only whites of long southern lineage could understand a century after the Civil War, Waring saw the flow of reporters into the South as an invasion. "There are as many Yankee reporters dropping off planes and trains as there were carpetbaggers in the 1860s," he had grumbled even before Little Rock.[12]

Waring, Kilpatrick, and Grover Hall complained frequently that a "paper curtain" had been drawn along the Mason-Dixon Line, making it a rare achievement for writers of their ilk to gain a national audience. Waring believed the North's blatant disregard for the southern point of view had been evident in his own dealings with *Harper's* magazine. The magazine's editor in chief, John Fischer, felt that the southern position on segregation was repugnant but was impressed that intelligent southerners of otherwise good disposition quite plainly held it. Fischer had called on Waring to write an essay making "a statement of the pro-segregation position which Northerners and anti-segregation Southerners of both races would recognize as an unemotional, sober statement, motivated by good will and useable as a starting point for rational discussion."[13]

After reading Waring's first draft, then his second, Fischer despaired that such a statement could be written in a fashion that was presentable and not even more divisive. Waring went at it again and produced a third draft in which he portrayed Negroes as primitive, disease-ridden, immoral, disorderly, and intellectually crippled. He cited extremist tracts as authoritative references and let fly with some loose rhetoric, including the suggestion that Chief Justice Earl Warren and the rest of the Supreme Court had fallen under the sway of Communists. "I have never seen a manuscript which has troubled me so deeply—not editorially but in my conscience," Fischer wrote Waring after reviewing the third draft. "Along with the other editors, I have re-read it, discussed and thought and prayed about it for more hours than I have ever given to any editorial project." Certain passages, he wrote, were so infuriating that they would defeat the purpose of creating any reasonable discussion. He then rejected the draft and did not invite a new one.

Waring responded that he was not surprised. "In fact it confirms the purport of my article," Waring wrote Fischer, "which is that this particular viewpoint cannot find a hearing in the national press."[14] But Waring wanted some time on the national stage. He rewrote the piece a fourth time. While many of his characterizations of Negroes remained the same, some incendiary material was removed. "The Southern Case Against Desegregation" was published in January 1956, with an editors' note explaining their nervousness about it.[15] For Waring, publication gave him the national attention he wanted to make his case that segregationist editors were being blocked from the national spotlight.

Waring and Kilpatrick drew the attention of visiting reporters and, along with Hall, became the "responsible spokesmen" for the resistance. They seemed to despise those encounters at the same time that they enjoyed the publicity. Both were furious at Jim Bishop, a well-known New York author who interviewed them for a Hearst-syndicated series about desegregation. "He is," Kilpatrick wrote Waring, "a sort of cotton-mouthed son of a bitch, and the experience certainly has been an education to me. The next left wing Northern newspaper man who shows up in my office is likely to get kicked down the stairs, one step at a time. I warn you to beware of this bird if he ever shows up at your office." He already had, Waring responded. "He damn near ruined me in his piece from Charleston."[16]

What galled Waring, Kilpatrick, and Hall even more was their belief that northern newspapers and newsmagazines and the wire services were ignoring racism and discrimination in their own regions.

Early on, Hall had tested his notion that "racial disharmony follows wherever the Negro settles in significant numbers."[17] He had assigned *Advertiser* reporters to find out about events and incidents of racial discrimination in the North that were not getting much attention in the northern newspapers. Working the phones, they found plenty of examples.

Hall also launched a series of editorial features that reproached and goaded northern editors and political leaders for overlooking discrimination in their own backyards. He called the feature "Tell It Not in Gath, Publish It Not in the Streets of Askelon." It was named after the biblical passage in which David declared his wish that news of the killing of King Saul and his son, Jonathan, by the Philistines be kept from the Philistine cities of Gath and Askelon, "lest the daughters of the Philistines rejoice."[18] The series ran for four and a half months, daily for a while.

Why, Hall asked, had reporters not encamped in Dearborn, Michigan, where the mayor had boasted that his city of 114,000 had no place for Negroes? Hadn't he declared, "I am for complete segregation, one million percent, on all levels"? Why had more attention not be given when Chicago sent 150 police officers into the Trumbull Park neighborhood to quell violence that erupted as Negroes had moved in? When a white mob ran an American Indian family out of a Detroit neighborhood, under the mistaken belief that they were Negro, why had one Detroit paper played the story on page 3, another on page 16, a third on page 60?[19]

Hall was credited with influencing newspapers outside the South to focus on problems in their own areas. At the American Society of Newspaper Editors' meeting in Washington, D.C., Hall quizzed the *Des Moines Register* editor, Lauren Soth, about why the *Register* did not write about race discrimination in Iowa. Soth, who had won a Pulitzer Prize for an editorial that ultimately drew Vice President Richard Nixon and Nikita Khrushchev to Iowa, said there was no such problem back home. But when Soth returned to Iowa and began asking questions, he found otherwise—and said so. His newspaper began investigating the problem, found it, and credited Hall with raising its awareness. Other newspapers, from New York to Los Angeles, began taking a greater interest in their own backyards.

"Let's stop kidding ourselves about Jim Crow in New York," began a twelve-part series of stories in the *New York Post.* "He lives here, too." The *Post* assigned seven reporters to the project, foremost among them Ted Poston, the former railroad dining-car waiter who in 1937 had become one of the earliest Negro reporters to move from the Negro press to the white press. "We have herded over 850,000 Negro citizens into ghettoes which would shame even some Southern towns," the *Post*'s series added. "We confine some Negroes to the lowest-paid jobs in some industries, bar them from still others and hold them back in still others."[20]

The New York Times, in a four-part series on problems Negroes faced in northern cities, reached the same conclusions. The *Chicago Tribune* commissioned a noted Negro journalist, Roi Ottley, to write a ten-part series. And the Associated Press's 1,750 members received a 1,800-word story, "The Negro in the North."[21]

Grover Hall, in words that echoed Myrdal's conclusions, occasionally mused at the impact of his idea. "What Southerners must understand is that the Northern press is not cold to truth and reason," Hall wrote. "We cannot make much time with lustful Northern politicians, but we can make time with the Northern press. It simply has to catch up with the story that the Negro has migrated to the North and that he is encountering rejection. . . . Truth is always worth revealing for its own sake, and more than that, if the Northern press is led to tell its readership the facts, it will diminish the ignorant, impatient clamor that the South conform immediately if not sooner." Hall continued, "Enlightenment of Northern editors is an essential. They must cease to associate the South and race prejudice as inevitably as spaghetti & meat balls, and see that it exists wherever the Negro migrates in significant numbers."[22]

For Hall, Waring, and other southern editors, more than their region and way of life were under attack; so was their journalistic judgment. Newspapers from outside the South had sniffed a story where southern newspapers had had an olfactory shutdown. Outside newspapers, the wire services, the newsmagazines, and now even television were covering a story that southern newspapers had decided to ignore. Newspaper after newspaper in the South, while trying to assert independence from a national journalistic community that seemed so interested in the race story, in fact was offering the more homogenized coverage of racial events by relying almost exclusively on wire service coverage.

It was at the wire services, which pumped thousands of words into their newsrooms every day, that editors aimed their ire. Although United Press, before and after merging with International News Service to become United Press International (UPI), was more aggressive in covering civil rights and more likely to cover the Negro point of view, it was the Associated Press that took the most heat from segregationist editors.

UPI was a privately owned company that bought and sold stories from and to newspapers and broadcast stations for distribution. Whatever stories United Press couldn't cover, it might pay someone to write. Associated Press was a not-for-profit cooperative owned and governed by its member newspapers, which paid AP a fee and were obligated to provide AP copies of their daily stories and photos. Whereas UPI would pay "stringers" to cover stories its reporters could not get to, AP depended on member papers to cover events and turn their stories over to the wire service. So if a southern city newspaper chose to not cover a civil rights event, as was often the case, AP likely wouldn't have it unless it sent one of its staffers.

Editors upset with UPI's coverage could complain or drop the service, but those upset with AP felt they had another option. With their newspaper's stake in the company, the editors believed they had more control, more opportunity to complain and be heard.

Myrdal's research team had detected problems with wire service coverage of racial matters. In work contributed to Myrdal but not used in *An American Dilemma,* the researcher G. James Fleming wrote that AP for many years had been criticized for stories that demeaned or misunderstood Negroes, presumed the worst about them, and distorted their actions. Some of this was because AP depended on member papers that were themselves biased, Fleming said, adding, "Of course, the men writing for the AP are white, living in their own world, with little appreciation of the implications of being a Negro, perhaps not even recognizing any rights of a Negro that an AP man needs to bother about."[23]

Segregationist editors came at wire service coverage from the other side. They could recall instances when they had felt the wires underplayed the race angle of a story with a northern dateline or overcovered a racial incident in the South. Waring had a stack of complaints he'd been writing to top AP executives for years. When an AP story on a legal fight in South Carolina omitted the judge's criticism of the NAACP, Waring was quick to ask the news service's executive editor, Alan J. Gould, "Doesn't a story about Judge Bites NAACP make news?"[24]

AP's executives checked out every reference and answered every letter. They told Waring whether they thought he was right and usually said he was not.

In March 1959, just weeks after Norfolk's schools reopened, the Citizens' Councils' Robert Patterson discreetly began encouraging several key segregationist editors to come together and develop a strategy to change the nation's view of the South. He asked Waring to help organize the gathering. Patterson fed him the names of editors who were interested, then offered the full services of the Citizens' Councils two office staffs in Jackson. Waring began inviting editors to a meeting at the Henry Grady Hotel in Atlanta and asked that they keep the meeting secret.

Jimmy Ward, editor of the *Jackson Daily News*, said he would be there. Jack Kilpatrick was in. Two Georgia editors, Joe Parham of the *Macon News* and James H. Gray of *The Albany Herald*, pledged to come. Soon others signed up: George Shannon of the *Shreveport Journal*, Roy McDonald of the *Chattanooga Free Press*, Louis C. Harris of *The Augusta Chronicle*, Caleb King, Jr., of *The Florida Times-Union* in Jacksonville, Henry F. Cauthen of the *Columbia Record* in South Carolina, and John Temple Graves, the widely syndicated columnist for the *Birmingham Post-Herald*.

They were all segregationists but ranged in their thinking about tactics from moderate conservative to reactionary. Parham was the member of the SERS who had courageously decided to be a correspondent for the *Southern School News* only *after* the extremist Roy V. Harris had tried to embarrass him into snubbing the assignment. Ward had been a photographer at the *Jackson Daily News* who became editor in 1957, when the bombastic Fred Sullens died.

Sullens, angry until his last breath that he had been forced to sell to the Hedermans, had previously designated the poorly suited Ward to succeed him, which some believed was his final revenge. Ward rarely had a mind of his own; he wanted to have important friends, and he was easily swept into the massive resistance fervor. Organized segregationists found Ward an easy mark, and the FBI office in Jackson described him as "most cooperative in the past and has been contacted on many occasions by Bureau Agents . . . he is friendly, discreet, reliable and is a loyal American."[25] Editorials and news stories produced by the Citizens' Councils and, later, the FBI, made their way into the *Daily News* virtually unedited, sometimes with Ward's byline on them. His contribution to the planning of the meeting was to suggest two possible names for the group: SAFE, as in Southern Association of Fightin' Editors, or SET, as in Southern Editorial Teamwork Committee.[26]

In early correspondence, the editors seemed less interested in selling a fresh approach to the story of the South and more keen on diverting the nation's eyes to the coverage of race problems elsewhere.

As the secret meeting in Atlanta approached, Waring sought out the opinion of his news editor at the *News and Courier*, the man who reviewed the paper's wire copy every day. He got an earful. The news editor, who three years earlier had expressed concern to Waring that Communists inside AP were "putting the squeeze" on certain race stories,[27] felt the problem was so great that Waring and his fellow editors would have to resort to extreme measures. He suggested they develop a secret plan to infiltrate the positions of wire editor and news editor on prominent northern daily newspapers. Under his proposal, southern editors working with Waring would then plant controversial stories in northern newspapers, particularly those on the outskirts of metropolitan areas. "These backyard squabbles would stir up an inter-Northern fight which the 'big' papers couldn't ignore, and, simultaneously, with key Southern editors in the 'know' on the timing, Southern papers could lash out on the feuds, stirring them into national importance."

The news editor added, "All of this is simply 'infiltration,' but if a fair deal is to be had, I believe, only infiltration of the 'liberal infiltrators' can counteract what is now a one-way system."[28]

The editors, nine in all, began gathering, drinking and talking at about 5 p.m. on May 6, 1959, in the Roosevelt Room of the Henry Grady Hotel. Waring had decided shortly before the meeting that the editors should meet alone, without anyone from the Citizens' Councils present. Through the cocktail hour, a steak dinner, and a long session, they kept talking. One by one, as Waring and Kilpatrick took notes, each editor reported on the status of integration in his state. They discussed the state and national political landscape and the resoluteness of the press back home.[29]

Those who had been backing off the idea of closing all schools to avoid even token integration could take some solace in what they heard. Southerners everywhere, the editors said, opposed closing schools. They also learned that the idea of creating a third political party for the 1960 presidential campaign was drawing mixed reviews. They worried that Tennessee would not be so solid because, as Waring scribbled down, it had "2 bastard senators [who would] do anything to be Pres."[30]

As they continued talking, they were not uplifted by what they heard. They were losing ground all around. The newspapers they had thought would stick with them had gotten queasy and quiet. Virginia had a "bad press situation," Waring wrote down. In Florida, Kilpatrick wrote, the press situation was "terrible. One seg paper."

As the night went on, what became increasingly apparent was not so much who was solidly on their side but who wasn't. Atlanta? Never. Memphis? Two papers, split decision, neither solid. Little Rock? No. Birmingham? Hard to figure. Nashville? Another split decision, one for, one against. Charlotte, Greensboro, Winston-Salem? No, no, no. Nor could they count on the newspapers in Miami, New Orleans, or Raleigh. They all pretty much agreed that those present were holding the line, but others were not. For Waring, the evening brought the sinking feeling—overdramatized, it turned out—that there were few editors left in the South who were fully dedicated to segregation.[31]

Still, they developed a set of six plans, most of them so mundane as to seem pointless. They agreed to share some special feature stories and to see if they could land speaking engagements at press association conventions outside the South. Kilpatrick's assignment was to receive a hundred envelopes from each editor present and have their names and addresses stenciled on them; he was then to send ten to each editor so they could more easily send one another tear sheets of their editorials. Waring's task was weightier: to arrange for a public relations consulting firm to put together a proposal for establishing a foundation dedicated to correcting misimpressions about the South.

As for the wire services, the editors decided to nag them as nicely as possible for more coverage of racial problems in the North.

A month later, late on a Friday afternoon, the editors got their first big bite. George Shannon, the Shreveport editor, saw a wire story that said a Negro man in New York had raped a fourteen-year old girl while five others had looked on. Shannon sent an immediate request for AP to produce a story of 2,000 words, comparing that rape with the Tallahassee case in which a Negro girl had been raped by four white men. Shannon said in his message that there was "no brutality in Florida while white girl in New York beaten and dragged to her fate." He didn't want just any reporter assigned to the story. He urged AP to send its two-time Pulitzer winner, Relman Morin, to cover it. Shannon asked for an interview of the girl's parents, for editorial reaction "North, South, East and West," and insisted on full photo coverage. He said that AP should get reaction from the Citizens' Councils and ask the NAACP if it planned any prayer groups "to seek 'justice' for Negroes." Was Eisenhower saying anything? he asked.

He closed: "Pls keep story running daily til case settled. Pls expedite."[32]

Wire editors at southern newspapers spent the next seven hours firing questions at AP's New York office in the terse jargon and shorthand spelling the agencies called wirespeak. In Charleston, Waring's news editor quickly chimed in. Amid fresh news that more than one Negro man had allegedly been involved in the rape, the wire editor went ahead and convicted them in his message. He asked for a new top to the story "with full detail on six Negroes raping white girl."

An hour later, Louis Harris in Augusta jumped in, saying he too wanted all details. Recalling that the Tallahassee story had gotten huge coverage by AP, Harris told the service, "In that six boys are herd involved as opposed to only four at Tallahassee, assume we may expect a couple of columns, right?"

A few minutes later, at 5:30 p.m., AP's Atlanta bureau sent out a message saying that a 400-word story had moved on the national wire, giving the newspapers the story in time for the early editions of the next day's edition, but of a magnitude far smaller than the editors were demanding. The editors read the AP story and were angry to see the race angle downplayed; police were quoted as saying they saw no racial motive.

"Why NY rape case not racial in nature?" one editor demanded to know.

"Rape story is incomplete," that same editor insisted at 8:05 p.m. "Who among police said rape was not racial in nature? A patrolman? Precinct captain? The commissioner? Are police quoted white? Also, how many special police called out to police the area? Any previous incidents involving 'punk kid' Negroes harassing white pupils at this school? Above all, why do police say rape 'not racial in nature.' Trust the AP will be enterprising in covering this case as the Florida case, and expect equal yardage."

Five minutes later, Charleston's news editor was back at the telex machine banging out a question: "Who from AP being assigned to cover NY rape story? Just wondering since AP sent 'top rater' Art Everett from NY to cover Tallahassee story. Wonder if some AP man from South being assigned to cover NY story?"

At 8:24 p.m., AP in New York sent out a message saying that New York police had concluded that "punk kids trying to show off would have been satisfied with any victim under the circumstances, Negro or white. They didn't pick her just because she was white."

At 9 p.m., a clearly exhausted New York bureau sent a message saying it was not able to answer all the questions but would try later. It was no longer staffing the story, which was occurring twelve miles away, it said, but was relying on a local newspaper reporter and "a very reliable stringer." New York added, "Keeping in mind your needs and will do all psbl to fill them. Meantime, efforting to answer as many your points as can tni."

AP's answers only provoked more questions. "Can you say race of very reliable stringer?" one editor asked. Less than a minute passed. "He's white, reporter on community paper," New York answered.

Three hours later, just after midnight, Charleston's news editor went back at it. "We want full and detailed follow up for Sunday AMs on New York rape case moved on wire for fastest reception. Want photoplay coverage also. Like sidebar on reaction in New York and also sidebar on New York newspaper editorial reaction. Also suggest general background on neighborhood and other recent rapes in New York area and present status of legal action taken in them, if any—for example, recent rape by Negro in Bronx of white housemaid tie up."

After another southern editor added support for the request for a Sunday story, a Charleston editor made a request for a story hundreds of miles away: "We need follow up on Monday story on Negro convict in Wisconsin being charged with most brutal rape-slaying in state's history. Any progress in case?"

The next day, Waring reviewed the wire traffic from that night and was satisfied that the Atlanta meeting he and the Citizens' Councils had convened had paid off. "George Shannon's query to AP was a masterpiece," he wrote the editors. He congratulated the others who "helped put the heat on A.P."[33]

Two days later, Waring was in New York at the invitation of AP's executive editor, Alan J. Gould. Over lunch, Gould and three of his deputies said they were annoyed at the frenzy of messages sent to them on the night of the New York story. They felt unnecessarily needled, Gould said, by editors clearly seeking to provoke them with some outrageous demands.[34]

The next day, Waring wrote to Gould. He understood and could "sympathize with your annoyance." Yes, some of the requests had been too vehement and just plain provocative, he conceded. But they had been so obviously fantastic that AP had not been expected to take them seriously, he said. What's more, the southern editors were not asking AP to depart from its standard practices, only to restore perspective, balance, and in-depth reporting to national stories. AP should pay closer attention to racial discontent outside the South, he said.

The next day, Waring wrote to the same editors whom he had congratulated a few days before. In a visit to New York's AP office, he reported, he had found "distress" over their strategy. "Those barbs found their mark," he said, but they risked losing their effectiveness if overused. "Alan Gould said truly that it's easier to hear when people don't shout so loud. Speaking tactically, I agree."[35]

Back in Greenwood, Mississippi, Robert Patterson was thrilled by the way "The Atlanta Nine" had "smoked out" the AP. Patterson dreamed of what would happen if the nine editors were increased to ninety, or nine hundred. "Tom, the needling done by you and others over the past months and years is bearing fruit. If the Northern press continues to give out race and the details of these Northern rape cases, you are going to see a change in public opinion in the North."[36]

The month after the Atlanta meeting, Waring received a ten-page public relations proposal from McCormick Associates in Washington, headed by Robert L. L. McCormick, a longtime aide to President Herbert Hoover. The group suggested promoting the southern viewpoint through advertising, media exposure, a speakers' bureau, and placement of news articles in national publications. It would cost about $50,000.[37]

Waring sent letters to all the editors telling them that the proposal had arrived and he was shipping copies to Kilpatrick and the *Chattanooga Free Press* editor Roy McDonald with instructions that they read them and circulate them to the other editors after attaching their reactions. Kilpatrick responded that he liked the idea but wanted to show it to his publisher.

Two months later, Waring had heard nothing from anyone, so he wrote his colleagues again, asking where the proposals were. Still nothing. Finally, three months after he sent the proposals out, he got a letter from Kilpatrick's editorial assistant. Kilpatrick, in cleaning his desk, had found the proposal at the bottom of a heap on his desk. "The expression on his face was not only apologetic, but absolutely sheepish," she wrote, "and Jack Kilpatrick rarely looks sheepish."[38]

The proposal was dead, as was most of the momentum from the Atlanta meeting.

CHAPTER 14

FROM SIT-INS TO SNCC

The token breakthroughs in school desegregation that so alarmed seg-regationist editors were viewed, of course, from a totally different perspective by Negro southerners; and nowhere with more dismay, by early 1960, than on Negro college campuses. Most of the freshmen who arrived at colleges in the fall of 1959 had been finishing the seventh grade when the *Brown* decision came down; they were about Emmett Till's age. They had assumed that, over time, their lives might change, that the school desegregation decision was the harbinger of more to come.

But more had not come. Negroes still drank from colored-only water fountains and ate and slept in Negro hotels and motels—when they could find them; and Negro students knew that when they got their college degrees, employment opportunities would be slim indeed, almost nonexis-tent except for teaching, preaching, and working in big-city welfare depart-ments. They would soon make their displeasure known.

The first public protest by frustrated Negro students came on the after-noon of February 1, 1960. On that day, not one reporter or photographer was present to cover an event that would give the civil rights movement a propul-sive force that would carry it nearly another decade.

There is not a single eyewitness account by a professional journalist of the historic hour when Joseph McNeil, Franklin McCain, Ezell Blair, Jr., and David Richmond—four freshmen at North Carolina Agricultural and Tech-nical College, dressed in coats and ties—walked into the Woolworth's in downtown Greensboro, sat down at the lunch counter, ordered coffee, and were refused.

There was no story on the demonstration that night on television or the next morning in any newspaper, although a Syrian-American merchant who had counseled the students alerted the local papers. But everyone on the A&T

campus quickly learned, by word of mouth, how the men had reminded the waitresses that they had been able to buy other merchandise at another counter moments earlier; how the manager had let the students sit, then called the police, who had come by only to observe; and how, fifteen minutes after the store closed, the four students had left and said they'd be back the next day.[1]

The following morning, the same four men returned, along with twenty-three other men and four women. This time they got coverage, measured by the milligram. The Greensboro papers sent staffers, UPI assigned a reporter, while AP decided to rely on a reporter from one of the Greensboro dailies. It registered as a very faint murmur in the national media, getting a brief mention inside *The New York Times*.

But that small story foreshadowed a pattern in the coverage most of the nation would see for the next several months: the wire services wrote the stories as if they were typing over land mines. The daily articles for the most part were bare-bones, tentative, and unquestioning. They seemed painstakingly shallow and uninformative and absorbed in a sportswriter's obsession with developing a box score and declaring winners and losers.

The Associated Press's second-day story reported:

GREENSBORO, N.C. (AP)—A group of Negro students—at one time numbering up to 27 men and four women—sat down at a 5- and 10-cent store lunch counter Tuesday in an attempt to obtain service and break racial barriers.

They failed.

But one of the students said the group "is prepared to keep coming for two years if we have to."

UPI's story went a bit deeper, but not much. It took a student reporter at the A&T newspaper, *The A&T Register* (which published a special edition), to show the irony that the students were trying to underscore, that they could buy a toothbrush at one counter but not a cup of coffee at another. The reporter, Albert L. Rozier, Jr., told by showing, by reconstructing the dialogue between the students and the waitress.

BLAIR: I'd like a cup of coffee.

WAITRESS: I'm sorry. We don't serve colored here.

BLAIR: I beg to disagree with you. You just finished serving me at a counter only two feet from here.

WAITRESS: Negroes eat at the other end.

BLAIR: What do you mean? This is a public place, isn't it? If it isn't, then why don't you sell membership cards? If you do that, then I'll understand that this is a private concern.

WAITRESS: Well, you won't get any service here![2]

Rozier also reported that "a Negro girl, a helper at the counter, confronted them, saying, "You are stupid, ignorant! You're dumb! That's why we can't get anywhere today. You know you are supposed to eat at the other end."[3]

On the third day, the number of students and others joining the sit-down exceeded eighty, more reporters were on the story, and Negro students across the South were abuzz with the excitement of having grabbed a hot electric wire and not felt any pain. Over the next week, similar demonstrations, launched on the spur of the moment, took place in Durham, Winston-Salem, Charlotte, and Raleigh. This was a brush fire of uncertain direction, power, or durability, uncertain even to the students and their elders. Similar protests in Oklahoma and Kansas had led to desegregated eating establishments two years earlier, but concepts that sailed easily through the border states frequently ran aground in the South.

Claude Sitton joined the story in Raleigh on the tenth day and was impressed not merely by the determined passivity of the aggressors but also by the seemingly endless supply of students willing to sit or stand in harm's way at forbidden lunch counters. This was notable also because it appeared to be a wildflower; there was no sign that any traditional civil rights groups were behind it or that it was part of any plan. That made it less predictable, dicier, and a much better story.[4]

By the twelfth day, the movement had reached into the segregationist strongholds of Virginia and South Carolina; Sitton's story out of Rock Hill, South Carolina, was on page one; and the number of reporters providing eyewitness accounts was growing daily. The picture they began to paint for national audiences was of nicely attired, soft-spoken, well-behaved young men and women, most clutching Bibles or textbooks, sitting passively at counters, surrounded by unruly white people. Sitton, giving the *Times'* detractors in the South no room to quibble with his characterizations, noted that the Rock Hill newspaper had described the demonstrators as "orderly, polite, well-dressed and quiet." In story after story, the Negroes were "students" or "demonstrators," while the whites were "youths," "hecklers," or, in a description Sitton used more than once, "teenage boys with duck-tail haircuts." The stories were clear in pointing out that every act of aggression came from the whites; they threw eggs and ammonia and knocked the Negroes off lunch counter stools.[5]

Sitton stayed with the story, filing next from Charlotte for the Sunday front page and noting something that was not obvious at the time: that the civil rights movement was in the midst of a significant turn. The sit-ins, he wrote, had spread to Tennessee and Florida and could no longer be dismissed "as another college fad of the panty-raid variety." Some whites had initially blamed the protests on "outside agitators," he added, "but even they conceded that the seeds of discontent had fallen on fertile soil."

Sitton had caught the movement at the right moment, and he took the opportunity to define it. The students had a "growing dissatisfaction bordering on anger" with the slow pace of desegregation. Three years after three North Carolina cities had desegregated their schools with twelve Negro students, they had only thirteen. The demonstrations represented a shift in leadership "to younger, more militant Negroes," who were likely to use more passive resistance techniques, Sitton reported. And the students seemed to have the support of their elders.

The wire services, which had greater reach, meanwhile became fixated on declaring whether or not incidents provoked violence but studiously avoided suggesting whether whites or Negroes were responsible. Television, in time, would show the Negroes sitting passively while being taunted, pulled, and hit by whites.[6]

The sit-ins, which adopted the same Gandhian methods that Martin Luther King, Jr., was preaching, drew a quick and unequivocal endorsement from King himself. Though he could have viewed the students as a breakaway rump group that disrespected his leadership and had abandoned the Southern Christian Leadership Conference, he felt quite differently. They were the frontline embodiment of the philosophy he had been preaching.[7]

As the sit-ins sprang up in unexpected places, Sitton began working in stretches that ran for six weeks without a day off. His bosses in New York were excited about his coverage and wanted to keep him targeted toward "big situations and trends . . . as distinguished from police-beat kind of news," as the assistant managing editor, Clifton Daniel, put it. But it was acknowledged that the job had become too big for one person. Sitton didn't even have a secretary back in Atlanta to maintain files, clip newspapers, write letters, or file expenses. Daniel and the editors on the national desk proposed, with Sitton, that a second staffer be moved to the South. Sitton would take the Atlantic seaboard and the upper South. The other reporter would cover Arkansas, Louisiana, Texas, Alabama, Mississippi, and Tennessee. There was talk of basing the second reporter in Dallas.[8] But in fact years would pass before the *Times* would base a second reporter in the South.

The pace was quickening. A completely new front opened in Nashville. Unlike Greensboro and most other sit-in cities, where the movement started small and grew, Nashville began big: 124 students on the first day of sit-ins there on February 13. But even more impressive than the size of the Nashville contingent was the superiority of its training, its extraordinary sense of mission, and its devotion to nonviolent protest that resembled religious fervor.

None of this was by accident. Five months before, James Lawson, a Negro divinity student at Vanderbilt University who had studied Gandhian protest in India, had begun conducting workshops in nonviolent tactics and philosophy and now had a committed cadre of disciples and budding leaders. Among them were John Lewis, an Alabama-born farm boy who was a ministerial student at tiny, poor American Baptist College; Diane Nash from Chicago, a student at Fisk University; and James Bevel, who had been born in Mississippi, was old enough to have already served in the navy, and was attending American Baptist with hopes of becoming a minister.

Although the Greensboro students beat those in Nashville to the punch, it was their Nashville counterparts who would take over the leadership of the rapidly spreading movement in the South. It didn't hurt that there was a newspaper in Nashville, *The Tennessean,* that would cover the protests in detail: seventy stories in the next fourteen weeks. *The Tennessean* didn't support the movement on its editorial page, but it was far from alone.

None of the South's liberal editors gave the movement, at this juncture, the kind of backing they had given to school desegregation, with the exception of Ralph McGill. He had begun to publicly question the morality of segregation, parting company with other liberals who had based their editorials on the notion that federal law had to be obeyed. Now here were black students openly violating laws and police orders, albeit local and state segregation laws, in the name of social justice. It gave the editors pause.

But it was the news stories that mattered to the students. They saw in the early coverage of the sit-ins the difference in how reporters portrayed them and the young whites who threatened them. They decided to play on that in their dress, their behavior, their efforts to befriend reporters. One of the first reporters sent out to cover them was David Halberstam, twenty-five years old, representing *The Tennessean.* A New Yorker, Halberstam had started his career at a small segregationist paper in West Point, Mississippi, where he had seen how little attention the state's press wanted to give to the Negro struggle, for fear it might aid and abet it. He had been asked by the publisher to leave. On the advice of Hodding Carter, Jr., Halberstam had sought and won a job at *The Tennessean.* To the young reporter, it seemed he'd reached the Promised Land, largely because *The Tennessean* saw the importance of the race story.[9]

Assigned to cover the Nashville movement, Halberstam instantly had a feeling that separated him from many southerners and southern reporters: he believed the Nashville protesters at least had a right to try to break the stranglehold of the Old South. He was a contemporary of theirs, receptive and even sympathetic to their cause. He sought them out, took their calls, and won access no other reporter got. He would be informed in advance where the demonstrators would be.

Halberstam would also write stories in the spring of 1960 for *The Reporter,* a magazine specializing in in-depth analysis of national issues, that would cast more light on the student protesters and their philosophy than any writer had yet done.

In Nashville, the other paper, the *Banner,* was as closed to coverage of the student protests as *The Tennessean* was open. James Stahlman, the staunchly segregationist *Banner* publisher, used his editorials, his influence, and his senior position on Vanderbilt University's board of trustees to successfully pressure the university into expelling James Lawson, the activist divinity student. Movement leaders were outraged but saw the irony: Lawson was being punished for his involvement in protests that the *Banner*'s news columns barely acknowledged were even taking place.

The two newspapers had long taken diametrically opposite tacks. While published in the same building under a joint printing arrangement, they rarely agreed on anything, not even the time of day. Stahlman was opposed to daylight savings time, while *The Tennessean* embraced it. The clock that hung on the front of the newspaper building had two faces. In summer, when it was 1 p.m. on the Tennessean side of the clock, it was noon on the *Banner*'s side.

After the Nashville campaign began, other fronts opened at lunch counters in Tallahassee, Chattanooga, and Richmond; in Sumter and Charleston in South Carolina; and in Chapel Hill, Salisbury, and Shelby in North Carolina. From a simple, unheralded act in Greensboro, an effective tactic had been born.

By the middle of April, there was so much momentum that the Southern Christian Leadership Conference called a three-day meeting to build a plan to keep the direct-action strategy rolling and to reaffirm nonviolent discipline as high school students joined collegians in some cities. The meeting, at Shaw University in Raleigh, drew 142 students from 11 states, the District of Columbia, and 37 communities that had been the scene of lunch counter sit-ins—as well as Claude Sitton.[10]

The young people, led largely by members of the Nashville movement, wished to continue sit-ins and new forms of direct action. They wanted more recruits who would be willing to stay in jail rather than pay fines and get out on bail. They made it clear that they were not looking to the NAACP for leadership. Indeed, the keynote speech, by James Lawson, was an attack on that organization for being too conservative, too reliant on lawsuits, and too focused on raising money. Reverend King, who drew two thousand people to a speech at a mass rally, echoed the sentiment without naming the old-line organization. The sit-in movement, he said, "is a revolt against those Negroes in the middle class who have indulged themselves in big cars and ranch-style homes rather than joining a movement for freedom."[11]

Though the students were enthusiastic about King's presence and speech, they wanted a measure of independence from the SCLC as well. They desired their own organization, so they voted to start a "temporary regional group," which they named the Student Nonviolent Coordinating Committee, or SNCC (pronounced "snick"). Their first chairman was a leader of the Nashville movement, Marion S. Barry, Jr., of Fisk University.[12]

SNCC would start as a small adjunct of the SCLC. It would operate from a windowless room inside the SCLC offices. Its main organizer was the SCLC's executive secretary, Ella Baker. But it would soon become clear to the students and to Baker herself that the SCLC, led by pastors, would not move as quickly, boldly, or broadly as they wanted to go.[13] As the movement went forward, SNCC would see itself as a rival of the same SCLC that had midwifed its birth.

In little more than a month after SNCC's organizational meeting in Raleigh, the Nashville students won their campaign for desegregated lunch counters. The breakthrough came when a thousand marchers, incensed by the bombing of the home of a black minister who supported the sit-ins, paraded to city hall and met with Mayor Ben West. After a long exchange, Diane Nash, the student leader who had thought herself shy when the sit-ins started, took over the questioning, asking the mayor with poise and persistence how he stood morally on racial discrimination. The mayor said he opposed it. After more dialogue, Nash asked, "Then, mayor, do you recommend that the lunch counters be desegregated?"

"Yes," the mayor said, then caught himself and said that only store managers could make that decision. But he didn't back away from his moral position. The next day's *Tennessean* streamed the headline across all of its front-page columns: INTEGRATE COUNTERS: MAYOR. Within days store managers agreed on a plan, and the counters were opened to all races.[14]

It was the biggest success for nonviolent protest since the Montgomery bus boycott. Bus boycotts had not spread, but the student protests were different. They ushered in a new direction for the campaign against racial discrimination. The press found itself still on the same playing field, the South, but the intensity and pace of the game would never again be the same.

CHAPTER 15

ALABAMA VERSUS THE *TIMES,*

FREEDOM RIDERS VERSUS THE SOUTH

The *Alabama Journal,* the afternoon stepchild of the *Montgomery Advertiser,* was relentlessly underfunded and shorthanded. Even the out-of-state newspapers that reached Ray Jenkins, the overworked city editor, were hand-me-downs. On April 5, 1960, Jenkins ate a lunchtime sandwich at his desk and leafed through a week-old issue of *The New York Times.* His desk was the last stop for the paper on its way to the trash can, but he spotted an advertisement with a Montgomery angle that had gone unnoticed by higher-ranking editors, among them Grover Hall, the editor of the *Advertiser* and news vice president over both newspapers. Within ten minutes, Jenkins pecked out a thirteen-paragraph story that ran on the city page of the day's second edition.

Decades later, nearing the end of a distinguished career that saw him serve as a key player in a Pulitzer Prize–winning series, a Nieman Fellow at Harvard, and editorial page editor of *The Baltimore Evening Sun,* Jenkins marveled that this quickie story had more impact than anything else he had written in his entire life. How could he ever have guessed?[1]

"Sixty prominent liberals, including Mrs. Eleanor Roosevelt, have signed a full page advertisement in *The New York Times* appealing for contributions to 'The Committee to Defend Martin Luther King and the Struggle for Freedom in the South,' " the article began. It added that King and student activists were being subjected, according to the ad, to an "unprecedented wave of terror." It noted that King was scheduled for trial in Alabama on two indictments charging him with perjury in filing state income tax returns. It quoted the ad as saying that "obviously their real purpose is to remove him physically as the leader to whom the students and millions of others look for guidance and support and thereby intimidate all leaders who may rise in the South." Near the end of the story, Jenkins added:

> There was one misstatement of fact in the ad, and another statement could not be verified. The ad said: "Negro student leaders from Alabama State College were expelled after students sang 'My Country 'Tis of Thee' on the state Capitol steps." Actually, the students were expelled for leading a sit-down strike at the Courthouse Grill. The ad also states: "When the entire student body protested [the expulsion] to state authorities by refusing to re-register, their dining hall was padlocked in an attempt to starve them into submission."
>
> Authorities at the college said "there is not a modicum of truth in the statement." They pointed out that registration for the spring quarter was only slightly below normal and they deny that the dining hall was padlocked.

Only minutes after the second edition was distributed in the *Advertiser-Journal* building, Grover Hall bounded into the newsroom, demanding to see the ad. "Lies, lies, lies—and possibly willful ones at that," he wrote in an editorial that appeared two days later. In it, he called upon *The New York Times* and several of the ad's signers to "ascertain whether the *Advertiser* is correct in asserting their names are married to a slanderous lie."

Literally overnight, Montgomery Police Commissioner L. B. Sullivan and Grover Hall, who had occasionally been antagonists, were united in common grievance against the *Times* and the civil rights movement. Within twenty-four hours, Sullivan dispatched a registered letter to the *Times* demanding a retraction of the passages mentioned by Jenkins. He also objected to a paragraph in the ad that Jenkins had not written about: "Again and again, the Southern violators have answered Dr. King's peaceful protests with intimidation and violence," the passage said. "They have bombed his home almost killing his wife and child. They have assaulted his person. They have arrested him seven times—for 'speeding', 'loitering' and similar offenses." Sullivan said the ad accused him of "grave misconduct" and improper actions as a Montgomery official.

In the *Times* ad, neither Sullivan nor any other white Alabamian was named. Lawyers for the *Times* replied that they were "somewhat puzzled as to how you think the statements reflect on you." But they said they were continuing to investigate the allegations in the ad.

Four days later, Sullivan sued for $500,000 in an Alabama state court, the circuit court of Montgomery County. He charged that he had been libeled by the *Times* and by four black ministers from Alabama who were listed among the ad's endorsers. Sullivan listed errors large and small as evidence of libelous falsity: The student dining hall had not been padlocked, and there had been no attempt to starve the students. King had been arrested not seven times but four. Large numbers of police had assembled near the campus, but had not "ringed" it. It was the national anthem, not 'My Country 'Tis of Thee' that the students had sung.

Grover Hall signed on as a witness for Sullivan. And Hall's newspapers gave permission to their regular lawyer, Ronald Nachman, to represent Sullivan in his suit. It was an extraordinary arrangement; usually, newspapers and their lawyers abhorred libel suits against other publications, figuring litigation could become infectious and spread to them.

Soon after Sullivan filed his suit, the administration of Governor John Patterson lost its perjury case against King. It failed to convince a white jury that King had diverted church and civil rights contributions to his own use and had not reported them on his state income tax return. This, of course, was the same case that had prompted the *Times* ad in the first place, seeking funds for King's defense.

Now the governor decided on a different strategy against King. Contending that the *Times* ad had libeled him as well as Sullivan, he sued the *Times* and the four Alabama ministers and added King to the list of defendants. He also upped the stakes—to $1 million. He took the action even though the *Times,* after a letter from the governor, had retracted the two paragraphs cited by him and by Sullivan. "*The New York Times* never intended to suggest by publication of the advertisement that the Honorable John Patterson . . . was guilty of grave misconduct or improper actions or omission," the *Times* said. "To the extent that anyone can fairly conclude from the statements in the advertisement that any such charge was made, *The New York Times* hereby apologizes to the Honorable John Patterson therefor." Soon, two Montgomery commissioners and a former commissioner each sued the *Times* and the four ministers for $500,000.

If the officials could win, they would almost certainly silence the civil rights movement in Alabama—as well as the newspaper that consistently covered it. Silence, not money, was the goal. Alabama had some experience in forcing its opposition off the playing field. The NAACP in Alabama had been barred from doing business and been wiped out five years earlier; two more years would pass before the ban could be lifted.

Meanwhile, in Birmingham a second front of litigation was opening against the *Times.*

Once convinced that the sit-ins were not ephemeral events but were spreading, *Times* editors poured a fresh stream of reporters into the South. The best known was Harrison Salisbury, winner of a Pulitzer Prize for international reporting and author of a best-selling book about juvenile delinquency. He looked as if he were auditioning for the title role in *Goodbye Mr. Chips:* conservative suits, subdued mustache, and wire-rimmed glasses. But this was camouflage. He was toughness and persistence piled high. After covering wartime London and the Russian front and serving as a foreign editor for United Press, he and his employers had parted ways in 1944. Salisbury had decided his next employer would be the *Times,* a vision that wasn't initially shared by the paper's editors, who had turned him down. Salisbury knew, though, that the *Times* yearned to have its own correspondent in Moscow and that the Kremlin was refusing permission. Without letup, he lobbied Russians he knew from the war, got a correspondent's visa, and used it as a ticket onto the *Times.* At the end of his five-year assignment in Moscow, when he was safely clear of Communist censors, he had written the series that had won him the Pulitzer.

Salisbury loved the civil rights story when he encountered it firsthand in early March 1960. As a foreign correspondent, he routinely "parachuted" into unfamiliar territory and within days, hours even, sized up complex situations and speedily wrote readable "overview" stories. Now, in the South, he bounced from Raleigh to Orangeburg, South Carolina, to Nashville. By early April he was in Montgomery, then over to Birmingham, where the police commissioner, Bull Connor, and his men were jailing sit-in demonstrators. Salisbury couldn't believe Birmingham. Some people drew their curtains when they talked to him; some talked only elliptically; others wouldn't talk at all. Salisbury concluded that much of the fear could be directly traced to the unabashedly racist Connor. He was a former baseball announcer with a voice that boomed like a foghorn. His police cracked down hard on civil rights activists, sometimes holding them incommunicado for three days under a vagrancy ordinance. But the police did little or nothing about an epidemic of bombing attacks and attempts on black churches, black homes, and two Jewish synagogues. Connor's aphorisms and malapropisms were legendary. "Damn the law—down here we make our own law" was one that Salisbury jotted down. Another was "Whites and Negroes are not to segregate together."[2]

On a long night's flight back to New York, Salisbury typed his "situation story." In a word, the situation was awful. The story ran on April 12 near the bottom of the *Times'* front page. The headline read, "Fear and Hatred Grip Birmingham."

> No New Yorker can readily measure the climate of Birmingham today.
>
> Whites and blacks still walk the same streets. But the streets, the water supply and the sewer system are about the only public facilities they share . . .
>
> "Every channel of communication, every medium of mutual interest,

every reasoned approach, every inch of middle ground has been fragmented by the emotional dynamite of racism, reinforced by the whip, the razor, the gun, the bomb, the torch, the club, the knife, the mob, the police, and many branches of the state's apparatus. . . .

Telephones are tapped, or there is fear of tapping. Mail has been intercepted and opened. . . . The eavesdropper, the informer, the spy have become a fact of life.[3]

Two days after Salisbury's story ran in the *Times,* the *Birmingham News* reprinted it under the front-page headline "*New York Times* Slanders Our City—Can This Be Birmingham?" A day later, it reprinted a second, shorter story by Salisbury; this time the headline was "All the News That's Fit to Print?—*N.Y. Times* Continues Attack . . ." On its editorial page, the *News* declared that the *Times* had painted a picture of Birmingham that was "maliciously bigoted, noxiously false, viciously distorted." The morning *Post-Herald* threw straight at Salisbury's head: "As a reporter he brings no credit to the profession, as a propagandist, he is an expert," one of its editorials said.

John Temple Graves II, the *Post-Herald* columnist who only weeks before had praised a Salisbury article in *The Saturday Evening Post* on the "menace of Red China," was now aghast. He said Salisbury's stories amounted to an "almost total lie" and a "throwback to tooth and claw hate." Noting that Salisbury was from Minnesota, the "most South-hating of the states," he concluded, "The *Times* must have known this. Only in malice could it have picked him."[4]

The two Birmingham papers that were so vigorously attacking the Yankee press were themselves owned by newspaper chains based in the North and controlled by families whose backgrounds were northern. But Scripps-Howard, owner of the *Post-Herald,* and Newhouse Newspapers, the *News*'s owner, each let their southern editors go their own way. In Birmingham, the papers, printed in the same building and on the same presses under what is known as an agency agreement, seemed less interested in competing for news than topping each other in defending Birmingham and "the southern way of life." They each slathered so much vitriol on Salisbury that one wonders what they would have found to say if they had known what he really felt about their city. His editors in New York had struck his toughest paragraph from the story: "To one long accustomed to the sickening atmosphere of Moscow in the Stalin days, the aura of the community which once prided itself as the 'Magic City' of the South is only too familiar," the excised passage said. "To one who knew Hitler's storm troop Germany, it would seem even more familiar."[5]

Despite his comparisons, Salisbury was not as cautious in Birmingham as he had been in Moscow. He telephoned sources from his room in the Tutwiler Hotel, and lawyers for Birmingham officials got their names by subpoenaing hotel records. Within six months, most of the people he had interviewed were summoned before a grand jury in Bessemer, an industrial town where many of the steel mills in metropolitan Birmingham were located. One of Salisbury's sources, a young Methodist minister, spent four days in jail for not naming people who had given him information about racial violence and intimidation.

The grand jury indicted Salisbury on forty-two counts of criminal libel; he faced the possibility of twenty-one years in jail and $21,000 in fines. This was in addition to civil libel actions, totaling $1,500,000 against Salisbury and $3,150,000 against the *Times*. The suits were filed by Bull Connor, the two other Birmingham commissioners, a police detective, and three Bessemer commissioners. Altogether, the *Times* faced $6,150,000 in libel suits growing out of the civil rights advertisement and the Salisbury articles. So clear were the goal and strategy of state officials that the *Montgomery Advertiser* put this headline on a story about the libel cases: "State Finds Formidable Legal Club to Swing at Out-of-State Press."[6] And state officials were rushing to use it.

As the lawsuits mounted but before any had reached a courtroom, Claude Sitton flew into Montgomery to bring *Times* readers up to date on other developments in Alabama. He checked into his hotel, deposited his bag in his room, and strolled over to the *Advertiser* to chat with reporters and editors. Rex Thomas, whose fifteen years as Associated Press bureau chief in Montgomery had plugged him into valuable police sources, spotted Sitton in the newsroom and warned him that local officials knew he was in town and had assigned a deputy sheriff to serve him with some sort of legal paper.

Sitton instantly phoned the hotel bell captain, whom he knew from earlier visits. He asked him to get his bag from the room and deliver it to the Hertz agency across the street. Moving quickly through the *Advertiser* newsroom, Sitton found a window that led to the fire escape, bounded down the fire escape, and walked briskly down a couple of alleys. He wouldn't let himself run, for fear of attracting attention. At Hertz, he rented a car, headed straight out of town, and drove on.back roads to the Georgia state line.[7]

Had Sitton been detained or served with a subpoena, there would have been no one to represent him in Alabama. The *Times,* thus far, had not found an Alabama lawyer willing to handle the libel cases. In previous years, the venerable and prestigious Lord, Day and Lord, which represented the *Times* in New York, had had solid ties with notable attorneys in Alabama. But not now. Not when the client was *The New York Times*. Not after denunciations by public officials, the Birmingham and Montgomery press, the Birmingham Chamber of Commerce, and scores of angry writers of letters to the editor. It was now almost as unthinkable, in Alabama, to be linked publicly with the *Times* as to dine with civil rights leaders. In New York, the *Times'* lawyers could barely believe the rejections. Where had professionalism gone? Was this America?

Finally, Eric Embry of Beddow, Embry and Beddow, a Birmingham firm that sometimes represented Negroes in criminal cases, agreed to handle the *Times* suits in both Montgomery and Birmingham. But not without some trepidation. When Louis Loeb, a ranking attorney for Lord, Day and Lord, arrived in Birmingham for consultation, Embry registered him under an assumed name in a motel well outside the city.[8]

Loeb and Embry agreed that the basic strategy for the *Times* was a jurisdictional one, as it was not an Alabama company. It did no significant business in the state, other than to send reporters in when news was stirring, just as it might to Alaska, Egypt, or Turkey. If libel suits were going to be filed against it, they should be filed in New York, where the paper was edited, managed, and printed. After all, the *Times,* in 1960, sold an average of just 394 copies a day in Alabama out of a total circulation of 650,000. In percentage terms, its dependence on the state for advertising revenue was even less. Out of $37.5 million in advertising in the first five months of 1960, $18,000 had come from Alabama.[9]

To buttress their jurisdiction argument, Loeb and his associates asserted a position that gave them unique power over newsroom decision making at a critical time in the *Times'* coverage of the nation's most dynamic domestic issue. They urged that *Times* employees, including reporters, stay out of the state until further notice.[10] They didn't think that serving subpoenas on a *Times* stringer or on the Alabama secretary of state, as one Alabama statute required in the case of out-of-state defendants, constituted proper legal action, but serving papers on a *Times* reporter might strengthen the hand of the Alabama officials and certainly would clutter the legal path the *Times* hoped to take.

Sitton, for his part, did not know when he left Alabama by the back roads that the edict from the lawyers was anything more than a temporary expedient. He never imagined that with one three-day exception, he and other *Times* reporters wouldn't cover the state again for two and a half years. Even the use of stringers was now prohibited by *Times* lawyers. This, to Sitton, was giving the segregationist officials exactly what they were after: a sharp reduction of serious scrutiny from outside the state. He could understand the *Times'* fear of being placed in financial jeopardy by the Alabama litigation. But his job was to cover the South, and now it was the South minus Alabama. It was like being assigned to cover the coal industry but banned from going to Newcastle.

. . .

As it was, the southern beat was fraught with more than enough difficulties. Sitton was under constant siege from all sides. If government officials in the South weren't criticizing him and the *Times,* the paper's lawyers back home were second-guessing him. If he couldn't act fast enough for civil rights leaders, he was being nitpicked to death by oversensitive people on both sides who split hairs over the emerging language and code that accompanied the race debate.

When Sitton wrote a story about the Virginia elections, he included an incorrect, one-sentence definition of the loaded term "freedom of choice." Throughout the South, the term typically referred to a method of allowing each county to decide whether to comply with desegregation rulings or close its schools; in Virginia, it referred to a system of giving all students grants to attend private schools or public schools in another district, a thirty-year fore-runner of the school voucher proposals of the 1990s. Sitton, in the four-teenth paragraph of his seventeen-paragraph story, incorrectly used the broader definition for Virginia.[11]

The Richmond editor James J. Kilpatrick dashed off a long and hostile letter to the *Times,* complaining about Sitton's "astonishing distortion of the truth." In a personal note to the *Times'* editorial page editor, John B. Oakes, Kilpatrick asked, "Is the *Times* so afflicted with Negrophilia that old consid-erations of honest and impartial reporting no longer matter? This paragraph of Sitton's is not an isolated incident. It is part of a day-in, day-out pattern that we are getting pretty God-damned sick of." To Oakes, it was just another in a series of Kilpatrick tirades against the *Times* in whatever venue he could find. He shipped the letter to Turner Catledge, the managing editor, along with a note saying he was "getting goddam sick of Kilpatrick's sniping at the *Times.*"[12]

Sitton, in response to Catledge, noted that Kilpatrick had confronted him and insulted him about it in a Richmond restaurant, so much that a Kil-patrick colleague who witnessed it apologized for his editor's behavior. What was really going on, Sitton said, was that the slow demise of the Byrd machine in Virginia was making backers like Kilpatrick cranky. The editor had taken to writing speeches for Byrd's candidate for governor, Sitton said, then running the texts on his editorial page without identifying himself as the author. Sitton separately banged out a publishable answer to the letter, in case it ran and called for a response. He, too, could write with a sharp edge: "As a Georgian who has covered the desegregation controversy in both the border areas and the Deep South, I can appreciate that Mr. Kilpatrick, who comes from Oklahoma, might not have had an opportunity to familiarize himself with the broader usage of the term."

In the end, Catledge himself responded to Kilpatrick. Sitton, he agreed, had been imprecise in his definition. "We might even go so far as to say he was in error." But, Catledge added, "We don't intend to confess to a capital offense when we have only committed an inadvertent traffic violation. We feel, frankly, that the length and vigor of your letter are disproportionate to the importance of the error it seeks to correct. We do not concede—we strongly deny—that there is any day-in, day-out pattern of slanted reporting on Southern news in *The New York Times*."

While trying to stay out of trouble by staying out of Alabama, Sitton ran into plenty of it in Mississippi, where he and others became the victims of a mean segregationist hoax in Jackson. As a means of trying to find out what some liberal organizations were planning, some extremists phoned liberal and moderate leaders, pretended to be Sitton, and asked them to cooperate with a *Times* stringer who would be calling them for a story he was writing. Among those then called by the "stringer" were members of an all-white, segregated Episcopal private day school, who told him how they had been quietly holding racially integrated meetings in the rector's home. Their purpose, they told the "stringer," was to "show examples of inter-racial cooperation," though they weren't ready to go public with it. The "stringer" was really the chairman of the local chapter of the John Birch Society. He recorded his interviews, then played them for the directors of the day school. Shocked that the meetings had taken place, or at least forced to show shock, the board members voted to remove the rector.[13]

Not getting to Alabama did not slow Sitton down, however. In late 1960, Louisiana consumed much of his attention. In one fell swoop, the state legislature there may have overcome any feeling among citizens that it was slow-moving. Called into a twelve-day special session on November 4 by Governor Jimmie H. Davis, both chambers needed only four days to give final approval to twenty-eight new laws to stop school integration. The cornerstone of the laws was an interposition measure. Derailed by a federal judge who ruled the laws unconstitutional, the lawmakers came back for another special session and passed a package of new laws; the legislature took over the New Orleans schools and fired its superintendent and three elected school board members before the same federal judge reversed it.

Sitton arrived in Louisiana to witness the state's blind determination. When the resistance turned violent, he watched a crowd of young whites try to knock down a building scaffold with a black man on top of it; he saw some use bricks and boards to pound a car driven by a black, then try to overturn it. He saw others ignite a wad of newsprint and throw it into a car occupied by blacks.[14]

He heard Leander Perez, the kingmaker of Saint Bernard and Plaquemines Parishes in Louisiana, let loose with invective that showed him to be an ideological descendant of Theodore Bilbo, James Vardaman, "Pitchfork" Ben Tillman, "Cotton Ed" Smith, and other Southern politicians of the past who had used their oratory to hammer racist messages in overheated, demagogic language. "Don't wait for your daughter to be raped by these Congolese," Perez boomed. "Don't wait until the burr-heads are forced into your schools. Do something about it now."[15] So provocative was Perez in arousing opposition to desegregation, even of archdiocese schools, that the Roman Catholic archbishop of New Orleans excommunicated him from the church.

But Sitton also watched and provided a national stage for people of enormous courage, such as Mrs. Daisy Gabrielle, a forty-two-year-old white mother of six. Faced with joining her friends and neighbors in boycotting her six-year-old daughter's elementary school, or letting her daughter attend it with a single Negro child, Mrs. Gabrielle decided to walk the gantlet of hecklers and shovers with her daughter. Repeating the Twenty-third Psalm, they entered the school. Sitton portrayed a woman of wisdom as well as bravery. "It isn't the fault of these colored people that they were brought here," she told Sitton. "If you uproot a people, there is a penalty for it. This is the penalty the South has to pay."

A woman had told her she was making a spectacle of herself and sacrificing her neighbors, she told Sitton. "I told her when it comes to sacrificing my neighbors or my principles, I'd sacrifice my neighbors. Neighbors change; principles never do."[16]

Like many other reporters, Sitton felt more comfortable on the civil rights side, where there was an openness with the press that didn't exist among the segregationists, who were defensive under the scrutiny of the national news scope. Sitton was developing the simple view that the blacks of the South were claiming nothing more than their just entitlement to the fundamental freedoms guaranteed to all citizens of the nation. And even for a southerner who had grown up with the prototype of the segregationist, he was shocked again and again by the meanness that pervaded the resistance, particularly among the diffident men in suits who did little to discourage the bullyboys who were willing to get their hands bloody.

The *Times* lawyers were having a rough ride in the courts. They had pressed their jurisdictional strategy in the Alabama circuit court in Montgomery and, more hopefully, in the federal district court in Birmingham. But both judges had ruled against the paper. The *Times* appealed the Birmingham decision to the U.S. Fifth Circuit Court of Appeals in New Orleans. At the same time, the Sullivan case was moving toward a jury trial in the state courtroom, presided over by Walter Burgwyn Jones, an open admirer of the Confederacy whose father had presented General Ulysses S. Grant the flag of truce from General Robert E. Lee at Appomattox. Judge Jones set the tone with an opening lecture against "racial agitators" and in praise of "white man's justice, a justice born long centuries ago in England, brought over to this country by the Anglo-Saxon race."[17] That spirit would pervade the decisions he would routinely issue in coming years against Negroes and the civil rights movement.

The trial opened on November 1, 1960, before an all-white jury, and it lasted three days. The courtroom seating was segregated. In addition to the *Times,* the defendants were the four black Alabama ministers who, as board members of Dr. King's Southern Christian Leadership Conference, were listed as endorsers, rather than sponsors, of the ad. They were Ralph Abernathy, Fred W. Shuttlesworth, S. S. Seay, Jr., and Joseph E. Lowery. They testified that the ad had been written in New York by Bayard Rustin, a civil rights activist, and that he had neither gotten their consent to use their names nor informed them he was preparing the ad. Sullivan's lawyers offered no evidence to the contrary. The *Times* attorneys argued that there had been only one error of substance in the ad, the padlocking of the dining room, and that this did not in any way apply to Sullivan, whose duties did not include the supervision of the lunchroom.

They also introduced a Claude Sitton story on the sit-ins in Montgomery and pointed out that neither he nor his editors, nor the *Times* as a news-gathering institution, had made any of the errors contained in the ad. The *Times* advertising department, whose employees were not experts in the subject, had simply not caught the errors. Sullivan's lawyers argued that this had been reckless and negligent. Grover Hall testified, as an editor, that he thought the ad had defamed and libeled Sullivan because padlocking a hall to starve the students would have been "indefensible" if it were true. Five businessmen affirmed that Sullivan was of good character and that if they had believed the ad, which they had not, they would have thought less of him. The *Times'* lawyers said there was no evidence that Sullivan had been damaged by the ad. Sullivan said he thought the ad had accused him of being a "Southern violator," inasmuch as arrests and law enforcement in Montgomery were his responsibility. In two hours and twenty minutes, the jury decided for Sullivan, awarding him $500,000 from the *Times* and also from the black ministers. It was the largest libel judgment in Alabama history and a large one by any standard.

The *Times'* lawyers did not kid themselves that they would fare better on the other suits before future Alabama juries. Nothing Louis Loeb had ever faced in his career as a lawyer was more worrisome than the events unfolding in the Alabama courts. No litigation had ever scared him more.[18] All of Loeb's hopes now rested on appeals built around the jurisdiction argument. In a note to Arthur Hays Sulzberger, the *Times'* publisher, he called it the "main string to our bow for eventually obtaining a reversal." Embry, Loeb's Alabama colleague, unsuccessfully argued to Judge Jones that freedom of the press, as guaranteed by the First Amendment, would be violated if Sullivan could collect damages for an ad that had not mentioned his name. Loeb, however, saw little hope for this avenue of appeal. Historically, courts—including the U.S. Supreme Court—had ruled that libelous statements were beyond the scope of the First Amendment.

Loeb's worries were shared by Catledge. But the *Times'* managing editor saw the Salisbury case as more threatening to his vision for the *Times* and for journalism than the Sullivan case. The Sullivan case aimed at an ad over which the newsroom had no control, but the Birmingham suits were aimed at a reporter and the editorial mission of the paper. If the *Times* could be sued in Birmingham, it could be nibbled to death by local juries all over the South and, indeed, across the nation.

It was plain to Catledge that the threat wasn't just to the *Times* but to all of journalism. No newspaper would feel safe sending reporters into other states on controversial stories, and Jim Crow could return to its good old days, operating with virtually no scrutiny. Catledge decided he would try to mobilize American editors and publishers against the libel suits. He was president of the American Society of Newspaper Editors (ASNE), and he was one of the most charming and important men in journalism. He called on ASNE's Freedom of Information Committee to file briefs as amicus curiae, friends of the court, on behalf of Salisbury and the *Times.*

Catledge had reason to doubt ASNE's boldness. This same organization had been so slow in the spring of 1956 to condemn the Senate Judiciary Committee's flamboyant allegations of sweeping Communist influence in the American news media, especially *The New York Times.* But he had a more recent and relevant reason to believe that ASNE editors were in a fighting mood. Only four months earlier, members of ASNE's Freedom of Information Committee had become alarmed at a Georgia judge's ruling that had banned photojournalists from the streets and sidewalks adjacent to the county courthouse in Atlanta—a ruling the Georgia Supreme Court had upheld.[19]

One by one, the nation's leading editors had sent in letters and telegrams agreeing that ASNE should file a brief supporting the Atlanta newspapers in opposing the judge's decision. "Feel it imperative we take most active part in appeal," wrote Kenneth S. Conn from the San Jose *Mercury News.* "By all means . . ." wrote John Q. Mahaffey, editor of the *Texarkana Gazette.*[20]

But the Salisbury case was a different matter. Initially, editors such as Eugene S. Pulliam, managing editor of *The Indianapolis Star* and chairman of the ASNE Freedom of Information Committee, seemed disposed to help out the *Times* as they had the Atlanta papers. But slowly, the support crumbled. Pulliam polled southern newspaper editors, who were not so inclined, then sought the opinions of judges and lawyers in Birmingham, whose views were not hard to predict. James S. Pope, the Louisville editor who had been instrumental in starting the campaign to help the Atlanta papers, expressed his "deepest conviction" that backing the *Times* would be a mistake. The debate fell outside the realm of the Freedom of Information Committee, he said, because it did not involve suppression of public records or proceedings. To Catledge, nothing could be more suppressive than effectively keeping reporters away from a story, which was the effect of the lawsuit against the *Times*.

Catledge had tapped into something deeper than a legal matter; he was dealing with newspaper politics. The Birmingham papers, as members of national chains, had allies—corporate cousins—across the nation. One day after the Sullivan decision, Pulliam changed his position and wrote Catledge a letter that provided a clue as to just how lonely the *Times* might become: "Because of the state of affairs in the South, our intervention could be viewed as committing ASNE to support of *The New York Times'* entire case, no matter what we said; your dual position, as you well know, complicates it; and, finally, I am not convinced in my own mind that the case involved freedom of information. It does involve access but I haven't been able to make up my own mind where a libel suit should be tried: where the person involved is libeled or where the libel is published."[21]

Catledge and his wife spent the Christmas holidays of 1960 in Paris, but he couldn't get his mind off the *Times'* Alabama troubles. He wrote to three of his editor friends, urging them to persuade their papers, as well as ASNE, to file amicus briefs. Catledge confided to Lee Hills, the editor of *The Miami Herald* and executive editor of the *Detroit Free Press,* that he was "frightened as hell at this new weapon of intimidation that seems in the making."[22]

Hoping to make an end run around Pulliam, Catledge turned to Felix McKnight, editor of *The Dallas Times Herald,* who would assume ASNE's presidency when Catledge's term expired in the spring of 1961. "You realize, I know, my own reluctance to urge action by the ASNE or any of my friends," Catledge wrote. "But, Felix, I regard this as a matter of such supreme importance that I owe it to the newspaper profession to call earnest attention to it. The basic issue here is one of freedom of inquiry—freedom from the threat of virtual lynch-law damage suits away from your home base."[23]

Catledge also enlisted the help of the journalism historian John Hohenberg, who was also secretary of the Pulitzer Prize advisory board. Hohenberg compiled information showing the number of Pulitzer Prize–winning stories in which reporters had gone into another state to uncover information of great public interest. Hohenberg started with *The Boston Post's* 1921 expose of the schemes of Charles Ponzi. He showed the *St. Louis Post-Dispatch* going into Illinois to expose a corrupt federal judge, *The New York World* going to Florida to uncover a peonage system, the *Columbus Ledger* going into Alabama from Georgia to lay bare corruption in Phenix City. Hohenberg, after four pages of listings, stopped. The connection was clear.[24]

But the ASNE legal advisers were not rallying behind the Catledge position, choosing instead to define the role of the Freedom of Information Committee narrowly. "As I think we have tended to agree, libel cases are not quite the same as access to information cases," Jacob Scher, a journalism professor at Northwestern University and legal adviser to the FOI Committee, wrote Pulliam. "The only real question here is one of jurisdiction, and that is a pretty technical one. We ought to wait a bit longer on this one."[25] Pulliam passed Scher's recommendation on to McKnight and added, "the normal course of legal fiddling will dump the Alabama case out of Turner's lap and into yours. This isn't a particularly pleasant prospect for you. However, I believe ASNE will be better off should it intervene if Turner no longer is president of the organization when legal action is taken."[26]

McKnight recommended to ASNE board members, officers, and other organization activists that they follow Scher's advice and delay any decision until after a ruling from the Fifth Circuit Court of Appeals. Almost all of the organization's hierarchy fell into line. Only two newspaper companies—the *Chicago Tribune* and Atlanta Newspapers, publisher of the *Constitution* and *Journal*—stood with the *Times*. Ralph McGill of the *Constitution* had no doubt about the accuracy of Salisbury's story and believed the Birmingham suits to be acts of "intimidation" to ward off stories about the excesses of segregation. The *Tribune,* at the time, was one of the nation's most conservative papers, but it believed in a classic sort of conservatism: hands off a free press.

In an editorial, the *Tribune* urged the nation's leading press organizations to rally behind the *Times.* It said the Alabama suits were "the most important challenges to have risen in many years. We hope the American Society of Newspaper Editors and the American Newspaper Publishers Association will not fail to see the threat."[27]

If the organizations saw it, they did not act. And by the spring of 1961, one of the most dramatic civil rights stories yet would unfold in the bus terminals and along the highways of Alabama. The *Times,* unsure of the support of its own industry, let alone the courts and the American public, would proceed cautiously on the story.

Just when it seemed that the mainstream press had permanently eclipsed the black press on the civil rights story, two black veterans of the race beat signed on to cover a form of protest called "Freedom Rides." They would get the most important eyewitness exclusives of their careers and, in Alabama, help fill the vacuum left by *The New York Times.* As it turned out, the question was not how big the story would be but whether they would live to tell it. Unlike with the sit-ins, which had begun without any notice to the press, the Congress of Racial Equality (CORE) mailed out press releases urging coverage of the Freedom Rides. These bus rides would test compliance with a U.S. Supreme Court decision against segregated interstate transportation along a route through Virginia, the Carolinas, Georgia, Alabama, and Mississippi, then on to New Orleans.

No white reporter showed up for the trip, although reporters for the AP, *Washington Post,* and *Washington Star* attended a pre-ride press conference. But Moses J. Newson of Baltimore's *Afro-American* and Simeon Booker of *Jet* and *Ebony* magazines sensed that the rides might be big news. Both Booker and Newson were members of modern journalism's advance guard who had dug into civil rights atrocities when no one else was looking. One of the pioneers not on this trip was L. Alex Wilson, who had traveled the back roads of the South with them through most of the 1950s. Wilson had survived being kicked, hit with a brick, and beaten in Little Rock and had become the top editor at the *Chicago Defender.* But he had never fully recovered from his injuries. He had developed problems with his nervous system that, three years after he was assaulted, had turned him into an old man at a young age. In the fall of 1960, seven months before Newson and Booker boarded the Freedom Ride buses, Wilson had died. He was fifty-one.[28]

Booker and Newson had known each other from the Emmett Till case and from Little Rock and were willing to help each other. The Freedom Riders were using two regularly scheduled buses, a Greyhound and a Trailways, so when Booker went on one, Newson rode the other. If anything happened, at least one of them could cover the story, and, by switching buses systematically, they would each get to know and interview all of the riders—seven black men, three white men, and three white women. The riders planned to be busy, desegregating the seating when the buses were in motion and integrating the cafés, waiting rooms, and toilets at the terminals.[29]

Booker and Newson found the riders to be a fascinating lot. James Farmer, the leader, had resigned his staff job with the NAACP, stepping out from Roy Wilkins's shadow to see if he could resuscitate CORE, the Gandhian protest group he had helped organize back in the 1940s. Another was James Peck, the scion of a wealthy white family of clothiers. In 1933, he had astonished his Harvard class by bringing a black date to the freshman dance.[30] There was also Albert Bigelow, a pacifist architect and former navy captain, who had sailed a boat, the *Golden Rule,* into atomic test zones in the Pacific, trying to disrupt the nation's nuclear program.[31] Among the others were a minister, a folksinger, a university professor and his wife, and two students. One of the students, John Lewis, the quietest of the riders, had taken leave from the Nashville sit-ins to join the Freedom Rides. He would later become chairman of the Student Nonviolent Coordinating Committee.

The rides passed through Virginia and North Carolina without violence. Just over the South Carolina line, white youths attacked Lewis when he entered the "whites only" waiting room at the Greyhound terminal in Rock Hill. They punched him in the mouth, knocked him to the floor, and repeatedly kicked him. Bigelow tried to shield him, only to be beaten on the head and body. A police captain and some of his cops pulled the riders to safety and asked Bigelow and Lewis if they wanted to press charges. They declined, saying it would be inconsistent with their philosophy of nonviolence.

In Atlanta on Saturday, May 13, the day before Mother's Day, the riders met with Reverend Martin Luther King, Jr. "I've gotten word you won't reach Birmingham," King quietly told Simeon Booker when they were alone. "They are going to waylay you."

King was right; but it was Moses Newson, not Booker, who witnessed the first violence in Alabama.[32] Newson sized up the atmosphere in one word— "explosive"—as the first of the buses, the Greyhound, rolled into the terminal in Anniston, Alabama, on Mother's Day. A mob of white hoodlums in shirtsleeves swarmed toward the bus, swinging steel chains, iron rods, and clubs. "This is Alabama, you black bastards," one of them hollered, "come on out and integrate."[33]

When no one moved off the bus, the mob began shattering its windows and battering its door. Local police were present but did nothing to stop the assault. Suddenly two white passengers, who had boarded in Atlanta, revealed themselves as undercover Alabama state troopers and stationed themselves in the doorway to keep the mob out. Newson had never suspected the troopers were aboard and had never dreamed that Alabama state troopers, of all police agencies, would be the riders' last line of defense. But God bless them, Newson thought, they were doing their duty.[34]

The driver backed the bus out of the terminal and sped toward Route 78 and Birmingham. From his seat near the back, Newson tried to decipher the scene outside. A long line of cars, maybe fifty of them, trailed the bus. Ahead, a white coupe swerved and braked and became an obstacle. Soon Newson understood. The mob had slashed and punctured the bus tires and was now, like a wolf pack, stalking its wounded prey. The bus stopped six miles outside Anniston, and the mob besieged it. Newson had seen meanness in Little Rock, but these people were rattlesnake mean—intent on killing. They smashed windows with bricks and an ax and hurled a Molotov cocktail into the bus. It ignited the seat immediately back of Newson; sparks

singed one of his ears. A woman who was returning to her home in Birmingham after attending her father's funeral put her head on the seat in front of
her and prayed. "Why are they doing this? Why did I get on this bus?" Newson heard her say. "I don't want to die here like this."[35]

The mob tried to storm the bus, so Newson hid his camera beneath his
seat. As flames rose and the smoke grew dense, the mob reversed its strategy,
jammed the door shut, and tried to trap the riders inside. A state trooper,
E. L. Cowling, drew his pistols and forced the attackers back. Coughing and
retching from the smoke, the passengers tumbled out, only to be set upon by
the mob. Arriving state highway patrolmen fired warning shots. Newson, the
last person off the bus, groped his way to the door through blinding smoke,
a handkerchief over his face.[36]

When Newson's vision cleared, he saw a photographer at work and realized, too late, that he had left his camera on the blazing bus. The photographer was Joseph Postiglione, who had followed the mob. He captured the
scene in shocking and memorable images that made front pages around the
world. The photos showed flames leaping from the windows, from the open
doors, and from the roof, and massive columns of smoke billowing into the
sky. In one frame, Postiglione caught Freedom Riders sprawled on the side
of the road, too stunned to move away from the burning bus; one man, his
thin tie still intact, his back to the bus, holds his head and stares toward the
ground; a woman, her hair seemingly covered with melted debris, sits on the
grass gazing at the bus; and two black men, their clothes singed and black-
ened, stare helplessly at the flames. It looked like war. James Farmer, the
CORE director, who had organized the rides, had split away in Atlanta to
attend his father's funeral in Washington. When he picked up *The Washington Post* and saw the photo of the burning bus, he quickly understood the
numbing impact and potential of such an image. He called his New York
office and told his staff to put together a composite of that photograph and
one of the Statue of Liberty to create a new logo for the Freedom Ride.[37]

Postiglione was barely five feet tall, and made the most of it. Knowing
that readers in Alabama would have trouble pronouncing his name, he called
himself "Little Joe" in the credit lines below his pictures in *The Anniston
Star*. He had become a freelancer after mustering out of the army at nearby
Fort McClellan, and he eked out a living by being aggressive. "He was
paparazzi," one *Star* staffer said, "before paparazzi was cool."[38] During the
attack on the Greyhound, he saw one of the attackers lashing the back of the
bus with a chain. Little Joe tapped the man on the shoulder and explained
that he was too short to see in the bus windows and needed help in taking a
photograph. Obligingly, the man put aside his chain, lifted up the photographer, then began lashing the bus again.[39]

The Trailways bus, with Simeon Booker in a backseat, rolled into Anniston an hour behind the Greyhound. There was no mob, but Booker did not like the looks of seven white men who came aboard—unkempt hair, open collared shirts, talking tough. A few of the riders went into the station to get sandwiches for the road. Booker admired how adroitly the riders distributed the sandwiches, not alerting the bus's regular passengers as to who was in the protest group. The driver returned from the station looking ashen and drawn. "A Greyhound bus which left here a few minutes ago is in flames, set afire by a mob," the driver announced. "There is no information yet on injuries or deaths. We are going to get this bus to Birmingham. I cannot do it as long as Negroes sit in the front section." Then he looked at two black students in front seats. "All right," he ordered. "Let's move."[40]

The students refused. The seven white men who had just boarded erupted. They jerked the blacks into the aisle and, kicking and slugging, drove them toward the back of the bus. When the white riders blew their cover by protesting, the attackers threw them into the aisle and beat and kicked them, too.

Booker punched a small hole in his newspaper and peered through it as he pretended to read. He saw one attacker flash a pistol. He heard another shout, "Aw, you goddam nigger lovers." At one point, the bus was a blur of blood and sandwich bits. At another, the riders lay "like a pile of pancakes" in the aisle. Booker had a ringside seat, but to what? Another bus burning? Murder? The anxiety grew as the driver took an alternate route to Birmingham. Was he delivering the riders to the mob?[41]

While Booker was wondering if the Trailways bus would ever make it to Birmingham, Howard K. Smith of CBS News, one of America's best-known journalists, waited at the city's Greyhound station, puzzled as to why the bus had not yet arrived. It was happenstance that Smith was in Birmingham for the Freedom Rides. His radio broadcasts from Europe during World War II and some of the most critical years of the Cold War had made his name almost as familiar as Edward R. Murrow's in American households. And, having successfully made the transition from radio to TV in London and Washington, the Louisiana-born Smith was the logical choice to complete a documentary on Birmingham that Murrow himself had begun before leaving, amid news policy disagreements with CBS, to join the Kennedy administration as head of the U.S. Information Agency.[42]

The idea for the documentary, to be called "Who Speaks for Birmingham?" was inspired by the controversy over Harrison Salisbury's stories, now thirteen months old but remembered like yesterday in Birmingham. When Smith had attempted to interest one Klan leader in being filmed for the documentary, the Klansman had refused but suggested that Smith might want to be at the Greyhound station on Mother's Day, when the Freedom Riders were due to arrive. Smith and his savvy, talented producer, David Lowe, were at the station, along with thirty to forty heavyset whites. When the time for the buses to arrive came, then went, Smith tried to engage some of the men in chitchat. He got the unmistakable impression that what was happening, and what was about to happen, had been well planned by Klansmen and that Bull Connor's men were part of it.[43]

Smith was right. He had been one of many to receive the tip to be at the bus station. Even Reverend Fred L. Shuttlesworth, the Birmingham pastor who was expected to host the riders when they came to town, knew the Klan was planning an attack, and he had made sure that Bull Connor knew that he knew. The FBI was also aware: Gary Thomas Rowe, Jr., an informant inside the Klan, had told the Birmingham FBI office that Bull Connor's police department had consented to giving the Klan fifteen uninterrupted minutes to attack the Freedom Riders.[44]

As Smith and Lowe waited that Mother's Day at the Greyhound station, word circulated among the white Klan crowd that the riders were at the Trailways station, four blocks away. He raced for the other station, trailing the white toughs, while Lowe went to get the camera crewmen, who had been standing by in a station wagon, not wanting to expose their expensive equipment to Klansmen unless they were sure there was a story.

After the longest sixty miles of his life, Simeon Booker could hardly believe how quietly the bus glided through downtown Birmingham. The white men took seats as if they were ordinary passengers. The riders managed to pull themselves erect and wipe the blood from their faces but were too dazed for conversation. At the terminal, the bus emptied, but slowly. Some of the riders were so painfully battered that they could only inch their way down the aisle. Booker, one of the last to get off, saw the riders limping slowly toward the crowded waiting room and into a madness that, incredibly, surpassed anything they had endured on the bus.

Booker skirted around the bus and toward a black-owned cab that would take him to the home of Shuttlesworth to get help for the riders. He heard a "wild roar," followed by a Negro man's declaration that he was not a Freedom Rider and a Negro woman's plea, "Lord, help us!" When he turned to look, Booker saw a fevered crowd crushing and pounding James Peck to the terminal floor with iron bars and other weapons.[45] A radio reporter, Clancy Lake, was broadcasting live from his car when a mob spotted him, dragged him out, smashed up his car, tore out his broadcasting equipment, dropped him in the street, and fled.[46]

Tom Langston, a photographer for the *Birmingham Post-Herald*, watched the rolling attacks from another perspective. The thirty-four-year-old Alabamian stood in a dark corridor that led to the baggage room as a crowd of thugs surrounded George Webb, a Negro laborer who was there to meet his fiancée. As the pack surrounded Webb and pummeled him with fists, pipes, and baseball bats, Langston focused his Rolleiflex on them and triggered his flash. Instantly, the startled, flash-blinded mob turned its attention to Langston. They smashed his Rolleiflex, flailed him with pipes and chains, and nearly garroted him with the strap of the 35 mm camera dangling from his neck. They made away with the 35 mm and left the semiconscious photographer and his battered Rolleiflex in a nearby alley. Struggling to walk, Langston made his way back to the newspaper, then was sent to a hospital. A *Post-Herald* copy boy was dispatched to look for the camera under the slim hope that its film had survived unfogged.[47]

At this point, Howard K. Smith jogged nearly breathless into the terminal corridor after waiting fruitlessly at the Greyhound station. He witnessed a flurry of bicycle chains, blackjacks, and steel knuckles pounding against the flesh of the Freedom Riders, cutting into them, knocking them over. Smith could see that when the riders fell, the mob went after them again, kicking them as often as possible in the scrotum. Then they pulled out baseball bats.

One rider struggled on all fours, unable to get up; another staggered into the waiting room, his head swollen and swathed in blood. Not one policeman was in the terminal. Smith found the whole scene incomprehensible. He'd not seen anything like it, hadn't felt this way, since 1945, in Langenstein, Germany, amid the rotting corpses and babbling ghosts of a concentration camp.[48]

When Smith was warned by a local reporter that the assailants were "out to get the CBS guy," he slipped out a doorway and onto the street, where he observed something he'd never forget: A man who he believed was running the gang—Klansmen, Smith was certain—looked at his watch and then went inside the station to tell the thugs that their time was up and they would have to leave. In a bloody choreography, the men stopped assaulting the riders, jumped into empty cars that had been parked outside, and took off. Less than a minute later, Smith watched as policemen arrived and started questioning bystanders. It was clear to Smith that Bull Connor had given the thugs time to attack the riders. And when their time had expired and the police arrived, they were gone.[49]

Smith had one of the best stories of his unusually eventful career, but this was an age of images and his camera crew had not gotten their equipment set up in time to record any of the terror. The day would belong to the still photographers, Little Joe and Tom Langston.

In the *Post-Herald* darkroom, the paper's youngest photographer, seventeen-year-old Joe Chapman, managed to coax the film from the damaged Rolleiflex. Amazingly, the shot of the Webb beating was perfectly clear and startlingly graphic. You could see the attackers' faces. You could see a tightly gripped pipe being hammered down on Webb. And, just as important, was what you couldn't see. There were no polic on the scene.[50]

There was no way to deny, after seeing Langston's photograph, that racial terror existed in Birmingham, and the *News* and *Post-Herald* didn't try. Each ran the photo on page one, an unusual step for papers owned by separate chains. More surprising, the *News* editors embraced the very phrase that had so angered them when the *Times* had used it in the headline over the Salisbury story. "Fear and Hatred Did Stalk Birmingham Streets Yesterday," the *News* said in a page one editorial that ran with a headline asking, "Where Were the Police?"

"The Birmingham police did not do what could have been done Sunday . . ." the editorial continued. "It was a rotten day for Birmingham and Alabama. The thugs did what they came to do—up to now they have gotten away with it. Today many are asking, 'Where were the police?' The *News* asks that, too, but the *News* also asks, 'When will the people demand that fear and hatred be driven from the streets?' "

At the offices of the *Birmingham World,* the editor, Emory O. Jackson, was infuriated by the attack, both as a black man and as a journalist. "Bad men have written a disgraceful chapter in our history; good men need to correct it," he wrote Mayor J. W. Morgan. Jackson was even angrier because of the fury unleashed on the press. "The right to know the news is enmeshed with the right to witness the news in its making and to report the news without fear or interference, even by the police, or government officials," he added. "Freedom of reporting is the heart of freedom of the press. Freedom of the press is the bedrock freedom in a good democracy."[51]

Meanwhile, Howard K. Smith was trying to overcome the lack of television film footage. He went on CBS radio every hour for the remainder of Mother's Day with his eyewitness accounts. He smuggled beaten riders into his hotel room and interviewed them, still bloody, before his crew's cameras. He thought the attack on them would be an appropriate ending to "Who Speaks for Birmingham?," which would run on Thursday, just four days after Sunday's bloody turmoil. He went to the offices of CBS's local affiliate to be interviewed by network hookup with the nightly CBS news program. But he was told by station officials that mechanical difficulties would make the transmission impossible. Smith did not believe them. And later Sunday night, as well as on Monday, he got more reports from the Freedom Riders. Those on the torched bus were suffering from smoke inhalation and the beatings, but they, and Moses Newson, were alive and had been ferried to Birmingham in a convoy of cars dispatched by Shuttlesworth. Peck's head and facial injuries had required more than fifty stitches. Another rider had been crippled—permanently, it turned out—by the beatings.

Smith knew that some of his broadcasts would make southerners unhappy, and they did. The mayor of his former hometown, Monroe, Louisiana, sent him a telegram: "When are you going to do something we can be proud of?"[52] And he was getting word from New York that his scripts, heavily laden with editorial comment, were displeasing his editors. But he loved being on top of a breaking story, loved being where *The New York Times* still would not let Sitton or other reporters venture and where other national reporters had not yet arrived. He was writing what he saw, and he could not think of any other way to tell of the terrorism he had witnessed. In the glow of the professional satisfaction he got when he learned that the *Times* had transcribed one of his eyewitness accounts from the radio and used excerpts, Smith did not realize he was about to become a casualty of Birmingham.

In his weekly radio commentary, which wasn't edited as closely as his reporting on TV, Smith said that two men—a Grand Titan of the Klan and an anti-Semitic, anti-Negro chiropractor—had primarily been responsible for the chaos in the bus terminal. He compared the worst of the "panting and exhilarated" thugs to the "vilest of the Nazi Jew-baiters who . . . used to beat prisoners with a bullwhip [and] derive an almost perverse exhilaration from the brutality." He said that if America didn't provide justice and protection for black citizens, it could become "a racial dictatorship like Nazi Germany" or the scene of more of the "barbarism" he had witnessed in Alabama.

The coming days would be uncertain ones for the civil rights movement, for the Kennedy administration in Washington, for Birmingham's white and black communities, and for Howard K. Smith. Would the Freedom Rides continue? What would Smith's documentary say? How far would they let him go? James Peck, now stitched together but still determined, led the riders to the Greyhound station on Monday, May 15, for the 3 p.m. bus to Montgomery. When company drivers refused to take the wheel, the riders decided to fly to New Orleans. Bomb threats resulted in the cancellation of two flights as a now-alert police force kept angry whites at bay. At 11 p.m., they boarded a plane, arrived in New Orleans, and ended the first Freedom Ride. But a new Freedom Ride was being formed.

In Nashville, John Lewis and other student activists grew alarmed that the entire civil rights movement might collapse if segregationists could stop the Freedom Rides with violence. With Lewis as the leader, eight blacks and two whites left Nashville for Birmingham by Greyhound, determined to complete the rides—to Montgomery, to Mississippi, to New Orleans. It was an auspicious day: May 17, the day *Brown* had been handed down seven years earlier. They arrived safely in Birmingham. A white mob formed around their bus while it waited for hours for a change of drivers at the terminal.

While they waited, Lewis felt relatively safe, as long as he could look out the window and see reporters and photographers at the bus station and as long as they could see him. That sense of security quickly evaporated when police officers began taping cardboard and newspapers over all the buses' windows. "He doesn't want the press to see inside the bus," Lewis thought. "He wants to hide what is happening."[53] Bull Connor then placed the new riders "under protective custody" and sent them to the Birmingham jail. Just before midnight, Connor aroused the riders and told them he was taking them back to Nashville. When the riders went limp, he had them dragged to three unmarked station wagons. Lewis was in Connor's wagon and found him surprisingly affable until they reached the Tennessee state line, a hundred miles short of Nashville.

Connor ordered them out of the wagons and into the darkness, near the small town of Ardmore. The riders found a shack—weather-beaten enough, they believed, to be occupied by blacks. They guessed right. A frightened couple in their seventies reluctantly let them in. The riders called their Nashville "command post," and by early afternoon, they crammed themselves into one lone car, sent down from Nashville. They were on the way back to Birmingham.[54]

Meanwhile, Howard Smith and his crew shot the final takes of the documentary. Smith stood on a hill overlooking Birmingham and quoted the British philosopher and statesman Edmund Burke: "The only thing necessary for the triumph of evil is for good men to do nothing." Then he flew to New York for a screening before editors, vice presidents, and company lawyers. When the screening was over and the lights came on, one of CBS's lawyers declared the Burke quote to be "straight editorial" and said it needed to be excised. Angered, Smith for the next hour battled the network executives about every objection they raised, even those that were justified.[55]

Smith smarted from the cuts but thought the documentary was still "respectable" when it aired. Even in diluted form, it set off another earthquake in Birmingham. The affiliated station in the city disaffiliated with CBS. Birmingham editors, who had just chastised their city for the violence against the Freedom Riders, now defended it again, angrily, against Smith and the blacks who had spoken their minds in the documentary. And the city's commissioners responded, as they had to Salisbury, with libel suits. The ones against Smith and CBS totaled $1.5 million.[56]

What made the program remarkable was that for the first time in a major national forum, black citizens in the South were given equal time with whites in discussing a city's racial problems. They didn't hold back. They talked about bombings and beatings, their fear of Connor's police, and how humiliating it felt to be segregated. Whites, at best, came across as defensive. The documentary concluded after sixty minutes of prime time, but the argument between Smith and the network continued over whether correspondents could have the same latitude for comment that they once had on radio. It had been building for years and now each side was locked into position.

Smith left New York with the understanding that he would outline his position on the editing, and on news policy in general, in a paper that could be shown to William S. Paley, the chairman of CBS. Smith believed, as Murrow had, that the network was worrying too much about its affiliates' reactions, especially the southern affiliates. Not unlike McGill's feelings about blind fealty to objectivity, Smith thought that if you tried to balance the racial story, the network would give the same weight to Bull Connor's notion of law as it would to the U.S. Supreme Court's decisions. And that, he wrote in his paper, was "equivalent to saying that truth is to be found somewhere between right and wrong, equidistant between good and evil." When he and Paley finally met, Paley tossed the paper on the table and said he had heard "this junk" before and was not going to permit editorial opinions in television newscasts. Smith said he had nothing to add to what he had written. He got up from the table and walked out of the room and out of a job he'd held with CBS for two decades.[57]

Back in Birmingham, the new group of Freedom Riders persisted, even as Greyhound drivers repeatedly refused to take them to Montgomery and Mississippi. They appealed to Attorney General Robert Kennedy, and the U.S. Justice Department interceded. Despite Governor Patterson's resistance, Greyhound officials drafted a driver. Kennedy dispatched one of his key aides, John Seigenthaler, formerly a reporter with the Nashville *Tennessean,* to tell Patterson that enough was enough; if the state of Alabama wouldn't protect the riders, the federal government would. At 8:30 a.m. on Saturday May 20, six days after the bus burning and the Birmingham beatings, the riders were on their way.

An Alabama state patrol plane flew above the bus. State patrol cars were fore and aft. The riders couldn't believe the long line of press cars that trailed the convoy, not a single one bearing a *New York Times* reporter. In less than an hour, the convoy reached Montgomery's city line and, instantly, the patrol cars and the plane turned away. No Montgomery police cars replaced them. The riders and the press, naked of protection, pulled into the bus terminal. Journalists formed in front of Lewis to interview him; it was Lewis, looking past them, who first saw tens, then scores, then hundreds of white men, women, and children swarming into the station from all directions.

The mob carried an astonishing array of makeshift weapons: baseball bats, tire irons, garden tools, Coca-Cola crates. When Norm Ritter, a *Life* magazine reporter, saw the look of horror on Lewis's face, he wheeled around with his arms out as if he could hold back the screaming people. Not a chance. The mob beat Ritter in the face and kicked Maurice Levy, an NBC cameraman, in the stomach and then pounded him with his heavy television camera. A *Life* photographer, Don Uhrbrock, was also beaten with his camera, and James Atkins, a Birmingham television newsman, was attacked. Lewis had not expected that the white press would come under assault before the Negro Freedom Riders and might not have believed it if he hadn't seen it with his own eyes. The segregationists, he realized, hoped to destroy the movement by destroying its witnesses, the reporters. Then a Coke crate crashed into Lewis's head, knocking him onto the pavement and into unconsciousness for perhaps twenty minutes.[58]

Seigenthaler of the Justice Department drove into the station and attempted to rescue one of the riders, a white woman. He shouted that he was a federal agent. It didn't work. A man smashed a pipe into Seigenthaler's head. The mob kicked him as he lay unconscious. Nearby, a black youth was doused with an inflammable liquid and set afire. Twenty people were injured, and the Associated Press, which became the chief provider of on-the-scene coverage in the *Times,* estimated that a thousand people were in the mob at the peak of the rioting.

From Washington, the attorney general ordered four hundred federal marshals into Montgomery.

In New York, the *Times,* proud of its unparalleled ubiquity among American newspapers, did something it rarely deigned to do: unable to send a reporter in to interview Martin Luther King about the swirling events, it asked a reporter to pick up the phone and conduct a long-distance interview with him that went on page one. Then it asked the reporter David Halberstam to work the phone to interview one of the driving forces behind the rides, Diane Nash, whom he'd covered when he was at *The Tennessean.*

In Atlanta, an increasingly annoyed Claude Sitton was sitting on his front porch swing, knowing he should be in Alabama, when his radio brought him the news of the rioting. It was too much. He called the national desk in New York and shouted, "How long are you going to let the damned lawyers run *The New York Times*?" Within minutes, an editor called him back and said, "Go."

Before Sitton could get to Montgomery, the three television networks and the two major wire services were covering the siege of the First Baptist Church, long a center of civil rights activity in the city. About fifteen hundred blacks, many of them women and children, gathered there to rally behind the Freedom Riders. By nightfall, an even larger number of whites mushroomed outside, hurling rocks and overturning a car and setting it ablaze. When the mob was at the church door, a contingent of U.S. marshals came to the rescue and drove the mob back with a barrage of tear gas. Soon the tear gas drifted toward the church, and the mob edged closer, threatening to overwhelm the marshals. If this had been a movie script, it might have been rejected for having too many climaxes, but this time National Guardsmen marched to the rescue under martial law with rifles and fixed bayonets and forced the mob back yet again. At midnight, thinking the situation under control, some black families ventured out of the church, only to have

Guardsmen level their guns at them. The Guardsmen, the blacks realized, were under state control. Feeling trapped and still smarting from tear gas that had wafted into the church, the blacks reluctantly settled in for the night. At 4:30 a.m., in yet another climactic moment, a new wave of National Guardsmen arrived and ferried the weary blacks home in jeeps and trucks.

The next day, with tensions still high, Attorney General Kennedy ordered two hundred more marshals into the city. He also began urging the riders to consider a cooling-off period. On Tuesday, the riders announced that they wouldn't stop now. Claude Sitton was on the first bus, a Trailways, with eleven Freedom Riders on Wednesday when it rolled out of Montgomery deep inside a column of forty-two vehicles. Sitton wrote that the convoy passed through Alabama's black belt and into Mississippi "like an armored battalion penetrating into enemy territory." Reconnaissance aircraft zoomed ahead. National Guardsmen lined the route at several points. State police cars were abundant.

In Mississippi, authorities prevented mob violence but arrested the twenty-seven Freedom Riders who arrived in Jackson in buses. One of those was James Farmer, the CORE director, who had hooked up with the ride again after attending his father's funeral. Another was Lewis, who had never been to Mississippi and who feared it worse than the Devil. Once he got there, once the bus crossed the line into Mississippi safely, his fears fell away and he felt brave. But the fear came back. After two weeks in the Hinds County jail and working on its prison farm, Lewis and the others were transferred without warning from Jackson to the notorious Parchman State Penitentiary, the 22,000-acre prison farm in the Delta, where terror, degradation, and mystery filled the night. "Sing your goddam freedom songs now," one guard said to Lewis and his compatriots. "We have niggers here to eat you up."

Lewis realized that, for the first time during the trip, there were no reporters or photographers around. Even scarier, no one in the press knew that the Freedom Riders had been slipped off to Parchman. The guards made sure they knew. "Ain't no newspapermen out here," one guard chuckled smugly to the inmates. "Something could happen to me," Lewis found himself thinking, "and nobody is going to know." He was experiencing his greatest fear.[59]

A new wave of volunteers moved into the South to replace the Freedom Riders who were sent to Parchman, but the region was now adopting the Mississippi approach to handling the riders, jailing them instead of attacking them and barring journalists' access to them. Within weeks, it was rare to see a headline, or a telecast, about the Freedom Riders. Civil rights leaders began looking for new avenues of activity. And in Parchman, the wardens, through beatings and hosings, were turning idealistic Freedom Riders into an angry, hardened cadre of go-anywhere organizers.

. . .

Claude Sitton returned to Atlanta, believing he could now cover the whole South, including Alabama. After all, lawyers were creatures of precedent, and Sitton seemingly had set one. He had stayed in Montgomery for three days without being summoned into court. And as spring melted into summer, the U.S. Fifth Circuit Court of Appeals gave him even more reason for optimism. It ruled in June 1961 that the *Times* and Harrison Salisbury could not be sued in Alabama for the Birmingham stories on grounds that, under Alabama's own laws, all of the action on which a suit is based must take place in the state. The trial judge, Hobart Grooms, had previously ruled for the plaintiffs against the *Times*. But the appeals court said that publication of the Salisbury stories had not been completed until they were printed in New York, and it sent the case back to Grooms to dismiss.[60]

But less than a week after the ruling Harding Bancroft, the *Times*' assistant general manager, dashed the hopes of Sitton and his editors. After a telephone call from Louis Loeb, he circulated a memo saying that *Times* reporters should stay out of Alabama unless the story was of the magnitude of the riots against the riders in Montgomery. Loeb and his law firm thought the Alabama situation too risky. The Birmingham commissioners were not giving up, despite the Court of Appeals ruling, and the Montgomery lawsuits were lingering. The *Times* lawyers still hoped the Montgomery cases could be shifted into the federal district court on the jurisdiction question. Until then, Loeb said, he was worried that service of a summons on a *Times* reporter, however invalid it might be, could greatly complicate the *Times*' cases.

Sitton had no choice; he would have to avoid Alabama. But there was no shortage of trouble spots in other states. One of them was Albany, Georgia, the Verdun of the civil rights movement.

CHAPTER 16

ALBANY

As the sit-in demonstrations and the Freedom Rides progressed, the civil rights movement was becoming more structured. Both SNCC and SCLC were taking on headquarters staff. SNCC was dispatching field organizers around the South, and the press was learning that if it did not constantly sharpen its responses, it could be caught napping as it had been during the first Freedom Rides.

Meanwhile, movement leaders and some segregationist leaders were studying the press: how it reacted, what made news, and what did not. One thing was unambiguous: the greater the violence, the bigger the news, especially if it could be photographed or filmed. No one came to understand this better than Laurie Pritchett, the segregationist police chief of Albany, Georgia, which was pronounced "All-BENNY" by its 34,000 white and 22,000 black citizens.

Pritchett was a hulking man, six feet, one inch and 220 pounds in 1961, ballooning to 265 pounds by the end of 1962, during Albany's racial crisis. He often clinched a cigar with his teeth; but any resemblance to the stereotypical southern lawman ended there. He was as smart and bright as the gold badge (Albany Police #1) that he wore on his stiffly starched white shirts. He understood that civil rights protests could, and probably would, come to Albany, the seat of Dougherty County. The city, after all, was home to the all-black Albany State College; it was a somewhat sleepy campus of 650 students, but even placid black colleges were providing demonstrators against segregation in city after southern city.

Pritchett kept abreast of the news from civil rights fronts. He boned up on civil rights organizations, their leaders, and the philosophy of nonviolent protest. He grasped the implications of nonviolence. He understood that Martin Luther King and other admirers of Mahatma Gandhi yearned to overflow southern jails with demonstrators as Gandhi had done with British colonial jails in India. And he realized that it was not necessary to use force in arresting them. They would go to jail peaceably. Force, in fact, would play into their hands. Pritchett ordered his police to be as nonviolent as the protesters and to squash any efforts at violence by white bystanders. As for overflowing the jails, Pritchett, in time, arranged with towns and counties up to a hundred miles away to imprison demonstrators who might be arrested in Albany.

It was also apparent to Pritchett that if his men charged protesters with violating local and state segregation laws, the protesters would appeal in the federal courts, where they might win and almost certainly would make news. Albany police would make arrests on murkier grounds: creating a disturbance, failure to obey an officer, loitering, trespassing, parading without a permit, even contributing to the delinquency of minors for mobilizing young people.

By early fall of 1961, two young SNCC field organizers, Charles Sherrod, twenty-two, and Cordell Reagon, eighteen, were in Albany on the cheap, initially sleeping in cars and on porches while trying to organize high school and college students. By mid-November, they were sufficiently successful in arousing and training students that several black fraternal and civic organizations joined with SNCC in forming the Albany Movement, despite the skepticism of the local NAACP and some of the city's other black leadership. Dr. William G. Anderson, an osteopath, was elected chairman of the umbrella organization, and it, not the NAACP, was now the principal voice of black Albany. Its goals were to attack segregation over a broad front and to increase voter registration among blacks.

After unsuccessful efforts, first by the NAACP, then by SNCC, to desegregate bus and train stations, the movement began street marches. Pritchett responded with mass arrests, usually for parading without a permit. Tensions escalated on December 10, when James Forman, a former Chicago schoolteacher who had just become executive director of SNCC, led a group of nine Freedom Riders to focus attention on the developing movement there.

Pritchett was at the station when the Freedom Riders arrived. Wary of playing into their hands, he and his police stood by as the riders milled through the station, sat briefly in the white waiting room, then poured out onto the sidewalk. But when Pritchett saw the jubilation with which a crowd of perhaps two hundred waiting blacks greeted the riders, he ordered the riders' arrest for "obstructing traffic" and other catchall charges.

Policemen in Jackson, Mississippi, had also used arrest-but-don't-harm tactics in dealing with Freedom Riders, but they had let their resentment of the press show. Not Pritchett. He openly wooed state and national reporters.

It was not easy. He had a quick temper. At times, his face flushed so fiercely that it was difficult to tell where his forehead and cheeks ended and his red hair began. But after losing his temper, Pritchett would quickly regain it.

As for the local press, Pritchett had no problem there. One man, James H. Gray, was in control of both *The Albany Herald* and southwest Georgia's only television station, as well as a radio station. Gray had grown up in Stockbridge, Massachusetts, where he had been a neighbor of Norman Rockwell, and graduated from Dartmouth College, where he had become friends with a Harvard basketball player he played against, Joseph Kennedy, Jr. Gray had visited the Kennedy family occasionally and, after Joseph was killed in World War II, developed an ongoing friendship with the next Kennedy son, John. Gray had moved to Albany after marrying the daughter of the *Herald*'s owner, and parlayed his wealth and position into political and media prominence. He hosted then-Senator Kennedy and his wife for a weekend in Albany in 1958 and became the Georgia Democratic Party chairman.[1]

But Gray yielded to no white southerner in the depth of his commitment to segregation. When Claude Sitton and Karl Fleming of *Newsweek* showed up in Gray's office in the *Herald* for an interview, the editor-publisher lectured them on the South and the "southern way of life." Sitton pointed out that he had grown up in Georgia and that Fleming was a North Carolinian. Gray was not deterred. He continued his harangue.

Robert H. "Bob" Gordon, a twenty-two-year-old UPI reporter, found Gray to be outright hostile. After the first movement demonstration, UPI's Atlanta bureau had put together a story from details supplied by an Albany stringer. Gray had called UPI's regional brass and accused the wire service of blowing the story out of proportion by giving too much attention to the Negro protest movement. UPI could not argue accuracy and perspective with an irate publisher, one whose paper subscribed to the service, on the basis of stringer copy. The UPI editors had ordered Gordon to rush from the Atlanta office to the airport and fly by chartered plane to Albany immediately—not stopping by his home to pack a bag, not delaying in any way.

Charter a plane? Gordon, who had joined the wire service only weeks before, couldn't believe it. This was the penny-pinching UPI, the perpetual wire service underdog he had heard so much about? This was the company that had added a word to journalism's vocabulary, "downhold," as in "downhold expenses"? Gordon would be with UPI another five years, covering civil rights hot spots over much of the South, and he would develop a healthy respect for the agency's determination to go with the facts, whomever they might anger. But he was never again on a chartered flight.

Gordon made a courtesy call on Gray soon after his arrival in Albany, but the publisher was not mollified. During the remainder of his more than two weeks in Albany, Gordon steered clear of the *Herald*'s newsroom, preferring instead the atmosphere at the black churches that the movement used as meeting places. The churches were intoxicating, with black audiences singing and developing the freedom songs that would, from that point on, become the standard fare for the movement across the South.

Meanwhile, Gordon was watching Claude Sitton and Karl Fleming in action. They worked as a team, not regarding each other as competition. The *Times* was, after all, a daily newspaper and *Newsweek* a weekly magazine. Gordon liked the way the two methodically moved into and out of black *and* white Albany after both sides of the story. Gordon reckoned that Sitton was the best newspaper reporter in the South, maybe anywhere.

Gordon was not immediately aware of it, but Albany was the first time Sitton and Fleming had worked together on an out-of-town story. They had come to know each other in Atlanta, reporting stories from their offices, and they had thought they would be safer if they teamed up in Albany. They had arranged for adjoining rooms on the brightly lighted side of a middle-class businessmen's motel. They shared a car. When Fleming drove, Sitton could write, and vice versa. They used public pay phones, viewing them as more secure than motel or hotel phones. All of these procedures would become the modus operandi for Sitton and Fleming over the next three tumultuous years. They perfected their partnership as it veered from one flash point to another.

Once in Albany, Sitton and Fleming realized that most of their safety measures were probably unnecessary. Pritchett knew that allowing reporters to be roughed up would be bad for the town's image. He invited them for drinks at a beer tavern next to the police station. Oddly, they thought, Pritchett had buttermilk. They had beer.

"There are three things I like to do," Pritchett said. "Drink buttermilk, put niggers in jail and kick reporters' asses."

"Well, what do you know—an honest cop," Fleming shot back. Pritchett laughed.[2]

On the surface, the two journalists were an improbable alliance. Sitton, with his thinning hair and buttoned-down clothes, looked like the chief financial officer of a successful company. Fleming had the tall, ruggedly handsome looks of an action-movie star.

"Claude was restrained and conservative," Fleming would say years later. "I was loud and brash. Everything was arranged methodically in his metal suitcase. My suitcase looked like a tornado hit it." Fleming liked to drink. Sitton limited himself to one or two. When covering a civil rights story, Sitton refused to sit in a restaurant with his back to the door. When Fleming teased him about "being overly cautious," Sitton replied, "Just prudent, Fleming, just prudent."[3]

But they had enough in common to override their differences. They both thought the civil rights story was the biggest of their lifetimes. They would go anywhere to cover it, but with a finger to the wind for danger. They never took segregationist passions lightly. They were willing to work around the clock, if necessary. They doted on coming up with telling details. They admired each other's ability and courage. And, crucially, both of their publications took civil rights coverage seriously.

Newsweek was purchased by *The Washington Post* in 1961, soon after Fleming joined its staff. The new owners were determined to make inroads against Henry Luce's dominant *Time* magazine, in part by declaring the race movement a major story. Much of the South despised *Time*. Luce's liberal attitude on race was problem enough, but its patronizing tone could be infuriating. It often seemed to delight in poking fun at the region. The Bossier Parish School Board in Louisiana was not alone in canceling its subscriptions to *Time, Life,* and *Look* and ordering back issues removed from the library. *Newsweek* played it straighter than *Time*. But that alone wouldn't have made it competitive. It would have to throw more resources into the South. It would have to spend more time reporting and less time pontificating.[4]

The editor driving *Newsweek,* John Denson, was from Louisiana. He wasn't a liberal political expatriate out to expose his homeland; he was a political conservative who saw human drama and terrific stories emerging from the racial clash. He knew news: he had already worked at fifteen different news operations, mostly newspapers by the time he went to *Newsweek* in 1953. *Newsweek* reporters in the South marveled at Denson's appreciation for a well-reported story, while *Time* reporters in the South could often be heard grousing that their editors in New York manipulated their copy to cast aspersions on the South.[5]

Under Denson, *Newsweek* put together a top-notch bureau in Atlanta, all of them southerners hired by its first bureau chief, Bill Emerson, in the late 1950s and early 1960s. Emerson had recruited Fleming from *Atlanta Weekly, The Atlanta Journal-Constitution* Sunday magazine. Fleming, who had prior stints at newspapers in Wilson, Durham, and Asheville, North Carolina, had a remarkable upbringing. His father, a traveling salesman of life insurance to farmers and sharecroppers in the Carolinas and Virginia, died of a heart attack when Karl was four months old. His mother was twenty-two years old, had not gotten past second grade, had no chance of finding meaningful work, and had struggled to keep a home and a life for Karl and his older sister. For a while she went door to door selling Bibles and dishes, and for a time she worked in a high school cafeteria for $20 a month. But she was frequently ill and bedridden and finally had no choice but to put her children in an orphanage in Raleigh. Karl stayed at the Methodist Orphanage through his junior year in high school in 1944, when he joined the navy to jump into a war that ended before he saw combat. A GED test then gained him entry to Appalachian State Teachers College, and serendipity landed him a job at a 9,000-circulation daily in Wilson, North Carolina, where his mother was living.[6]

As the Albany story intensified, Gordon of UPI found himself admiring not only the skill of Sitton and Fleming but also their clean clothes and expense accounts, which were obviously more ample than his. After ten days, he was growing sheepish about his one suit, the one he had been wearing when he had been flown in so hastily. He bought a couple of shirts and changes of underwear, but a new suit was too much on a UPI salary. On what seemed a quiet day, he took off his coat and trousers and sent them by hotel porter to a nearby cleaner that, the porter said, could do them in a couple of hours. Less than half that had elapsed when Gordon, relaxing in his underpants in his Albany hotel room across the street from the police station, heard loud noises. More than two hundred blacks were marching down the street, the biggest march yet, and Gordon was literally caught with his pants off.

Spotting the porter on the sidewalk, Gordon flung up his window and began shouting at him to retrieve his trousers—at once, clean or not. He then called UPI in Atlanta and began dictating whatever he could see and hear from his room. The phone didn't reach the window, so he'd look out the window, scribble notes, and run back to the phone to dictate, all while imploring the porter to hustle his pants to him. The scene convulsed Sitton and sent a wave of laughter through the column of marchers and into the police station. Even the *Albany Herald* was amused. It put the story of Gordon and his trousers on page one.[7]

With this march, the total number of arrests climbed to more than five hundred, and most of the demonstrators were in jail in neighboring counties. Anderson, the movement chairman, found new marchers hard to recruit and feared the movement was losing steam. Over SNCC's objections, he—by phone and telegraph—urged Martin Luther King, Jr., to come to Albany and help revitalize the protest.

King's arrival indeed did generate attention. An audience of fifteen hundred overflowed two churches and heard him urge them to go to jail "without hating the white folks." In the emotion of the evening, Anderson asked King to lead a march the next day. The audience cheered. It would have been awkward for King to refuse, and he did not. He, Anderson, and 265 other marchers were arrested for parading without a permit. Pritchett used his Buick Roadmaster to haul King, Anderson, and Ralph Abernathy to the Sumter County jail in Americus, thirty-seven miles away. The other marchers were dispersed to jails across southwest Georgia.[8]

"I will not accept bond," King told Bob Gordon through his cell bars the next morning. ". . . I expect to spend Christmas in jail. I hope thousands will join me."[9]

With King in jail, his top aides in SCLC tried to assume the leadership of the Albany protest. But SNCC quickly arranged a press conference at which Marion Page, the secretary of the Albany Movement, said that SCLC had no leadership role in the local organization. It was Sitton who realized that this was more than a local dispute. It was the first public eruption of rivalries that had been building among civil rights organizations since the peak of sit-in activity in mid-1960. The NAACP, SNCC, CORE, and SCLC had all learned the importance of being perceived as the driving force when civil rights publicity generated crucial northern funding.

Sitton's story made page one, and he elaborated on the rivalries the next Sunday in the Week in Review section. As it would again and again, his continuing day in, day out presence on the movement's front lines gave the *Times* an advantage that newspapers responding to only the big stories could not match.[10]

While King was in jail a week before Christmas 1961, James Gray addressed southwest Georgia on his television channel. He accused King of being motivated by "the acquisition of a buck" and declared the movement to be under the influence of a "cell of professional agitators" under Communist influence.[11] He praised Albany's customs of segregation and white supremacy as "a system that over the years has been peaceful and rewarding."[12]

Gray, knowing that whenever King went to jail, the movement had a rallying cry, privately called Albany's mayor and Pritchett to insist that they negotiate King's release. And he urged his Washington allies inside the Kennedy administration to make sure the Kennedys did not bring federal intervention to Albany.[13]

The next day, twenty-four hours after vowing he would be in jail for Christmas, King accepted release as part, he said, of a verbal "truce" negotiated by two local movement leaders and a SNCC representative. The movement's negotiators said there would be no more demonstrations until a newly elected city commission was seated in mid-January, in return for desegregation of Albany's bus and train stations, the release of jailed demonstrators, and the formation of a biracial commission to discuss further desegregation. "I would not want to stand in the way of meaningful negotiations," King said as he was leaving Albany.[14]

Almost immediately, Pritchett began telling reporters that there had been no real change in the city's stance on desegregation and there was no guarantee of a biracial commission. Most of the reporters concluded that Pritchett and white Albany had won the first round and that King and the local movement had been defeated, at least temporarily.

But the Albany protest, sputtering in December, took new life in 1962 and was into and out of the news. Pritchett continued to be accessible and affable to the press, while quietly and determinedly keeping tabs on it. His office monitored calls through the central switchboard at the Holiday Inn, tapped phones, and took tips from a rental car agent at the airport when journalists or federal agents arrived in town. Sitton and Fleming both had the experience of barely opening the doors to their motel rooms in Albany when the phone rang. It was Pritchett. Pat Watters, a reporter and columnist for *The Atlanta Journal,* had been using a motel phone to call in a column critical of segregationists when a voice had suddenly broken in and said, "You son-of-a-bitch."[15]

Reporters weren't sure who to trust even in their own ranks. The national press covering Albany began to suspect that one out-of-town reporter was giving Pritchett a rundown on what he knew about movement plans and activities. *Newsweek, The New York Times,* and *Time* reporters, among others, referred to him as "the fink." Pritchett would later say that an Associated Press reporter had been especially friendly, to the point that he'd show up in Pritchett's office, have a drink with the sheriff, put on his hat, and mimic Pritchett in front of him. The FBI's senior agent and Pritchett would later acknowledge that they had had informants, including reporters and some wearing wires, in the mass meetings. Whatever movement planners said at night, Pritchett said, had been transcribed and distributed by morning. And when the city, seeking to ban marches, needed recordings of mass meetings to show that the movement wanted to be disruptive, it could count on James Gray's radio station to provide tapes and a reporter to testify.[16]

Through the summer of 1962, Claude Sitton rarely left the road. For weeks without break, he ran between South Georgia, New Orleans, and Mississippi. Only rarely did he get any respite from the race story; William Faulkner's funeral in Oxford was one of those exceptions. Story by story, Sitton was showing himself to be the leading reporter of the civil rights movement, bringing attention to incidents that drew in other reporters and got action in Washington.

In July, in a gnat-ridden heat that seemed to melt the crops and pecan trees, Sitton, Watters, and an *Atlanta Constitution* reporter, Bill Shipp, drove in a rented Ford Galaxie station wagon to Sasser, a half hour northwest of Albany. They were in search of a voter registration meeting that SNCC had organized, and they found it in a small wooden church, Mount Olive Baptist. They walked into the church and sat in the front row of the wooden pews, acutely aware that they had entered the notorious kingdom of Sheriff Z. T. "Zeke" Mathews.[17]

They were in Terrell County, only eight miles from Dawson, where

Robert E. Lee Baker's reporting in *The Washington Post* about police beatings and killings of black residents had led to a federal voting rights investigation four years earlier. This was where Mathews had told Baker that there was "nothing like fear to keep the niggers in line" and that the voting privilege for blacks needed to be restricted because "there isn't a nigger in Georgia who wouldn't take over if he could."

Mathews, whose own words and deeds had led to a unanimous Supreme Court ruling against Terrell County, had not moderated his beliefs or modulated his manner. Everyone sitting in the pews inside the small church knew Mathews and an entourage of deputies might barge in at any time. On this night of fear and heat lightning, only forty members of the community, mixed with two white and some black SNCC organizers, gathered solemnly inside the church. At the front, near a painting of Jesus and a calendar bearing President Kennedy's image, the SNCC organizer Charles Sherrod led the congregation in "Pass Me Not, O Gentle Savior," then began the Lord's Prayer. Suddenly Sitton heard cars, maybe a dozen of them, pull up in front of the church.

Sherrod continued with the prayer, delivered slowly against the ominous sound of car doors slamming and a horn blaring. Sitton heard low, menacing voices calling out the license plate numbers of the congregants' cars as Sherrod began reading another passage from the Bible. Sitton heard the voices getting louder and closer and saw the men, women, and children in the pews around him stiffen. Then he looked toward the church door and spotted thirteen white men standing in the doorway, some of them law officers, but only a deputy sheriff in uniform. Pointing at Sitton, Watters, and Shipp, one of the men said, "There they are."

Sherrod, at the pulpit, kept reading from Scripture. "And whom He called among them, He also justified," Sherrod read. ". . . He also glorified. . . . If God be for us, who will be against us? . . . We are counted as sheep for the slaughter."

Mathews, seventy-one years old and in civilian clothes, stood with his eyes closed and his head bowed over his substantial girth. "We've been abused so long," Sherrod continued. "We've been down so long . . ." Mathews let Sherrod continue, walked out with his men, then returned with the sheriff of another county and two deputies well known among the blacks as intimidators. The deputies began walking up and down the aisle, tromping on the unfinished pine floors and carrying long, five-cell flashlights that they slapped into the palms of their hands like baseball bats. *Pop! Pop! Pop!* Fear and tension froze the room. The sound didn't leave Sitton's ears that day, or ever.

Mathews moved to the front of the church and stood directly in front of the reporters. He didn't look at them. "I have great respect for a religious organization," he said. "But my people are disturbed—they're getting disturbed about these secret meetings." As he talked, his words went into Sitton's notebook. They were headed toward the front page of *The New York Times* in a vivid, frightening narrative of unusual length. "We want our colored people to go on living like they have for the last hundred years," Mathews said in the opening line of Sitton's account. "I tell you, cap'n, we're a little fed up with this registration business."

Sitton described a scene of terror and courage: of the chief deputy, Mathews's nephew, "fingering a hand-tooled black leather cartridge belt and a .38-caliber revolver" and of Sherrod continuing to intone prayers and biblical passages as if they would cause an indestructible shield to materialize around the congregants and himself. He described the deputies demanding the names of everyone there and some of the younger blacks bravely refusing to answer.

Mathews turned to the reporters. "All right now, where you from?"

"Well, I'm from Atlanta," Watters said. "I'm from *The Atlanta Journal.*"

"I'm from *The Atlanta Constitution,*" said Shipp.

"How 'bout you, boy," Mathews said to Sitton. "Where you from?"

"Well, sheriff, I'm here covering this for *The New York Times,* but I'm from Rockdale County, Georgia. And I want you to know I'm an American, too."

Mathews turned back to the blacks, who, under intense questioning, had the courage to withhold the answers he wanted. He asked everyone from Terrell County to stand; they did.

"Are any of you disturbed?"

"Yes," was the muffled response.

"Can you vote if you are qualified?"

"No."

"Do you need people to come down and tell you what to do?"

"Yes."

"Haven't you been getting along well for a hundred years?"

"No."

Mathews and his nephew warned a Massachusetts SNCC leader that he better leave the county, told everyone it was "to your interest" to disband the meeting and go home, and seemed to delight in arguing with anyone they could. In threatening clots, the white men moved from the back of the church to the pews to confront the blacks with vile talk. Slowly it became evident that someone, then two or three people, then a small group, were humming "We Shall Overcome." As the humming grew louder, then became singing, the whites stepped away, moved to the back of the church, then left.

The blacks then decided to return to their agenda and continue with their meeting. When Sitton, Watters, and Shipp pulled out of the parking lot that night, they got as far as a darkened dirt road before realizing that the air had been released from one of their tires. Two carloads of blacks who were leaving the meeting stopped to guard them while they changed the tire. Only later did they discover that sand had been poured into their gas tank.

Sitton's story had immediate impact in the White House. Both Kennedys, the president and the attorney general, were sharply offended by Sheriff Mathews's bullying behavior. They saw it as a direct attack on federally protected voting rights. Burke Marshall, head of the Civil Rights Division of the Justice Department, called Sitton on the phone to enlist his help. He wanted Sitton to appear as a witness; Sitton at first agreed but realized his mistake almost as soon as he hung up. The *Times* urged Marshall to avoid any such move that would compromise Sitton's independence.[18]

Robert Kennedy, meanwhile, was not waiting for Marshall to crank up an investigation. "Move!" Kennedy snapped at John Doar, who was second in command in the Civil Rights Division. Hours later, the Justice Department swept into Terrell County with lawyers and FBI agents, who began combing the area for evidence of voting right violations. Marshall reported to Robert Kennedy that the department had brought suit against Mathews "in less than two weeks after Claude Sitton's story."[19]

The power of Sitton's narrative hit northern readers hard, made them uncomfortable, and took away their ignorance and innocence. "We have been struck by the immediacy and skill of Claude Sitton's reports on Southwest Georgia," a Brooklyn couple wrote in longhand to the *Times'* publisher, Orvil Dryfoos. "It is articles like Mr. Sitton's that disclose the reality of harassment and abuse these people face with such vision and courage."[20]

"The restraint, the simplicity, the completeness made this reader feel as if he were sitting in the audience while the crickets chirped and the voices droned in the darkness," an Upper Manhattan reader wrote *Times* editor Turner Catledge.[21] Another Manhattan resident said the *Times'* coverage would make racial understanding possible.[22]

And another saw Sitton's coverage as a turning point. He wrote that the Sasser story "was enormously vivid and convincing—you could feel the tension and menace as if you were seeing it; but it came through because the reporter saw and wrote significant details, not because he wrote about how menacing and tense it was. This story marked the beginning of what has seemed to me an unforgettably true understanding of what is happening behind the headlines about the South."[23]

The segregationists in Terrell County acted with swiftness as well. Mount Olive Baptist Church was one of four black churches in Sasser, Dawson, and Leesburg that were burned to the ground less than a month after the Justice Department filed its suit. Three voting rights activists in Dawson were injured by shotgun blasts. Homes in a neighboring county were pelted with shots from shotguns and rifles.[24] All the national attention given Albany and Terrell County only spread and amplified the sorrow. Jackie Robinson, born not far away in Cairo, Georgia, on a plantation owned by the Sasser family, after which the town was named, came to pay his respects and lead a fund-raiser.

In Atlanta, Eugene Patterson, who in 1960 had become editor of *The Atlanta Constitution* when McGill was named publisher, wrote a column both tweaking right-thinking white people, those who professed to be both religious and segregationist, and inviting them to pony up contributions to help rebuild the churches. He went so far as to nominate the pastor of the segregated First Baptist Church in Atlanta to be treasurer of the drive. Patterson specifically declared that he didn't want contributions from black people. White people had probably burned those churches, he wrote, so white people should pay to rebuild them.[25]

To Patterson's amazement, small donations started coming in. He'd get quarters taped onto tablet paper and a note, scribbled with a pencil stub, saying, "I don't like this integration stuff, but we got no call to burn down another man's church." Before long, he'd raised $10,000. Then he had a call from the abbot at the Trappist Monastery in Conyers, whose monks wanted to make stained glass for the churches. One of the leading architectural firms in Atlanta volunteered to design the churches for free and to help arrange for a contractor who would work at cost. Martin Luther King, Jr., later went down and dedicated the churches.

King found it easier to rebuild the churches than the momentum in Albany. By July 1962, he was back in jail, determined to stay, when suddenly he was released, this time against his will. Pritchett and city officials, figuring that King in jail would prolong the protests, secretly arranged for a law partner of Albany's mayor to pay King's fine but contended publicly that "a well-dressed Negro male" had paid it. "This is one time I'm out of jail that I'm not happy to be out," King told reporters. The press, in general, accepted Pritchett's story, in the absence of proof to the contrary from the civil rights movement.[26]

On July 19, King traveled to Washington to become the first black American to speak at the National Press Club, where he received repeated ovations. The next day, he was back in Albany to organize a march, only to be halted by an injunction by the federal judge for the southwest Georgia district. King obeyed it until it was overruled by Judge Elbert Tuttle of the U.S. Circuit Court of Appeals.

By then, even President Kennedy's friendship with James Gray was not enough to stop him from criticizing the Albany city government for refusing to meet with Negroes about conditions. "Let me say that I find it wholly inexplicable why the City Council of Albany will not sit down with the citizens of Albany, who may be Negroes, and attempt to secure them, in a peaceful way, their rights," he said at a news conference.[27]

Gray was unsparing in response. The Kennedys had turned on him. President Kennedy and Attorney General Robert Kennedy headed a "Negro-wooing Government," Gray wrote in the *Herald*. He described them as "two ambitious Bostonians, who have been as practically connected with the American Negro in their lifetimes as Eskimos are to the Congo Democrats."[28]

King and the Albany Movement won some minor tactical victories in August, and King would try again to revive the protests. But there was no steam left. By mid-August, King was out of Albany, with a sharp denunciation of the city commission for failing to negotiate with the movement. Dr. Anderson announced an end to street demonstrations and said that the movement would instead channel its energy into voter registration.

"Albany is as segregated as ever," Pritchett noted with pride.[29]

King left Albany emotionally bruised and determined not to get into a situation like that again. He had been called in as a "fireman" when the movement was faltering, but neither he nor his organization had really been in charge. And the Albany Movement, he felt, had made a major mistake by attacking segregation on all fronts: local buses, lunch counters, voter registration, libraries, you name it. King felt it better to take a rifle to segregation than a cannon. You could win one limited victory and build on it. And it was better, he believed, to make businesses, not a defiantly segregationist city council, the target. Businesses were more vulnerable to black consumer pressure.

Above all, King wanted the next city he fought with nonviolent action to be a province of SCLC, not of other civil rights organizations.

During the summer and fall of 1962, King met frequently with the Reverend Fred Shuttlesworth, Ralph David Abernathy, and SCLC Executive Director Wyatt T. Walker to develop a strategy that would overcome the failure at Albany. In danger of losing the momentum and the movement they had been building since the Montgomery bus boycott, they wanted a confrontation that would capture the dehumanizing impact of Jim Crow and shift the focus of news stories away from the internal bickering among black organizations. They needed attention—"publicity," as Myrdal had called it eighteen years earlier. They needed a drama, even a melodrama, featuring a sympathetic protagonist, a terrifying antagonist, and a simple theme. They needed an elevated stage, something that would allow the whole world to see without standing on its tiptoes, without even leaving its easy chair. They needed the press, the national press, to give the confrontation a high profile, so the world could bear witness.[30]

Shuttlesworth was urging King to carry the next battle to Birmingham.

There were many reasons why that city was ripe. For starters, the NAACP was still outlawed in Alabama by the state legislature, and SNCC had no presence in Birmingham, so intramovement rivalries would not be a factor. Above all, Bull Connor, Birmingham's police commissioner, was no Laurie Pritchett. He was neither subtle nor nonviolent. He disliked blacks and the outside press and was unlikely to restrain himself. He could almost assuredly be counted on to respond quickly, perhaps irrationally, with force and about as much meanness as the American people could stand, or more.

King had seen for almost eight years, ever since his Montgomery days, how newspaper and television reporters responded to that kind of behavior. They had raced to cover the mob scene at Autherine Lucy's enrollment, yet they had been slow to get to the bus boycott. King decided: they would go to Birmingham. He asked Walker, one of his key strategists, to draw up a plan. It would be called "Project C"—for confrontation.

Newspapers, television, and newsmagazines, good ones and bad ones, held in common with the civil rights movement an interest in a simple, live, electrifying story in which good confronts evil. They were about to get it— but not in Birmingham.

CHAPTER 17

OLE MISS

K ing and his key strategists had not anticipated having an opportunity to witness a trial run in Mississippi of the kind of confrontation they envisioned for Birmingham. Such a clash was developing in Oxford, at the University of Mississippi, where James H. Meredith, a twenty-nine-year-old black air force veteran with an accumulation of college credits, had been pressing his case to transfer from all-black Jackson State College.

Most southern states had long before integrated their institutions of higher learning; it was the only realm of life in the South where more states had integrated than hadn't. Even Orval Faubus, for all his bare-knuckle opposition to the integration of Central High, had always spoken proudly of how the University of Arkansas had been the first university in the South to integrate, back in 1948. Louisiana had been admitting Negroes to colleges and universities since 1951. Virginia, Florida, Kentucky, Tennessee, and North Carolina had joined in. Georgia, after some resistance, had relented under a federal court order. Mississippi had chosen instead to take its lead from Alabama, where a mob six years earlier had limited Autherine Lucy's matriculation to little more than a weekend pass.

Meredith, whose parents still lived in Kosciusko, had first written for an application for admission in January 1961, the day after President John F. Kennedy had been inaugurated. The registrar had responded with the proper forms and said he was "pleased to know of your interest in becoming a member of our student body." After conferring with Mississippi NAACP field secretary Medgar Evers and Thurgood Marshall, head of the Legal Defense and Education Fund, an arm of the NAACP, Meredith submitted his application and an explanation: "I sincerely hope that your attitude toward me as a potential member of your student body reflects the attitude of the

school, and that it will not change upon learning that I am not a white appli-
cant. I am an American—Mississippi—Negro citizen."

Four days later, the university registrar had responded with a telegram rejecting his application, saying it had not arrived in time. Thus began the state
of Mississippi's twenty-month stand of defiance against the integration of
the University of Mississippi.[1]

The likelihood that Meredith would lose the early legal skirmishes was
increased when the case landed with U.S. District Judge Sidney C. Mize,
whose rulings in a 1960 lynching case had suggested unfriendliness toward
racial integration.[2] Mississippi's leaders thought they could fight their way
to a dispensation available to no one else, and most of the state's newspaper editors linked defiant arms with them. Most newspapers viewed
Meredith as a menacing invasion into white prerogatives, and only a rare
few showed any curiosity about who he was and what he was thinking.
Only when Meredith filed suit in federal court did a newspaper, *The Meridian Star,* finally run his photograph on the front page. Given the tone of the
editorial accompanying the photo, the *Star*'s purpose seems not to have
been to humanize Meredith but to show the face of the enemy, whose
enrollment would open the floodgates to massive integration, then inter-
marriage:

> Intermarriage in the South, where we are so evenly divided white and col-
> ored, means the end of both races as such, and the emergence of a tribe of
> mongrels. . . .
> If you value your racial heritage, if you have even the smallest regard for
> the future of this South of ours—you will be for segregation one hundred
> percent.
> We must lock shields. We must fight for our race and for the South to the
> last bitter ditch. We must never lose heart.
> We can triumph—we will triumph—we must triumph.[3]

The tone of newspaper coverage statewide was set by the two Jackson
dailies, *The Clarion-Ledger* and the *Jackson Daily News.* While they com-
peted for news, the newspapers were similar in that they gave not an inch,
conceded not a point, to anyone who bore the scent of being a moderate on
the subject. Even so rigid a segregationist as Jack Kilpatrick had been willing to admit in print what his eyes saw. After watching a sit-in in Richmond,
he had returned to his typewriter ashamed. "Here were the colored students
in coats, white shirts, ties, and one of them was reading Goethe," he wrote in
an editorial after sit-ins in Richmond. ". . . And here, on the sidewalk outside, was a gang of white boys come to heckle, a ragtail rabble, slackjawed,
black-jacketed, grinning fit to kill, and some of them, God save the mark,

were waving the proud and honored flag of the Southern States in the last war fought by gentlemen. Eheu! It gives one pause."[4]

The Hederman newspapers in Jackson would never make such an admission—especially not now. Their only economic and editorial competitor for the past seven years, the Jackson *State Times,* had folded early in 1962. It had spent more upfront cash than it could ever recoup. Editorially, the newspaper had continued to stand up for good government, honest government, and open government—virtues to which the Hedermans couldn't quite lend their support. But as the heat rose over the racial divide, and as economic pressures bore down on it, the *State-Times'* spine had softened on race issues. The first editor had quit under pressure, and the paper had become, in his words, "a rather pale imitation" of the *Jackson Daily News.*[5]

The Hedermans had not changed at all in that time. Their coverage continued to appeal to their readers' worst instincts. They created heroes of the resistance leaders and turned those seeking change into targets of ridicule, threats, and violence. They allowed their reporters and columnists to get personally involved in the mission of segregation. And they showed a lack of taste.

Typical of the incendiary commentary was a piece by *The Clarion-Ledger's* political columnist, Charles Hills, who longingly invoked a time when the punishment for a black person who lied under oath was to put him in a pillory, nail his ear to the side, make him stand for an hour, cut off the ear, nail his other ear to the other side, make him stand, and so forth. "Our forefathers erred in that they lopped the wrong appendage," Hills wrote. "Had they concentrated on the tongue, we might not have the vociferous NAACP today."[6]

As the dominant home state newspaper editors in Mississippi, as leaders in the Mississippi Press Association, the Hedermans set a standard that editors at smaller papers found all too easy to meet; as low as the standard was, some fell quite comfortably below it. Mary Cain, the well-known editor of the weekly *Summit Sun,* wrote in the summer of 1961 that she and the other members of the Paul Revere Ladies club had canceled their regular meeting to attend a Meredith hearing in federal court. She then wrote about the inquisition of Meredith by state attorneys as if she were an Ole Miss sports columnist covering a game against the despised LSU Tigers, where the enemy is fair game and the vividness of the event is not lost even in the opinion-laden writing:

> The whole business moved too slowly for me and was insufferable. I wouldn't have been in [Assistant State Attorney General Dugas] Shands' place. When the high-brown gal who is Meredith's attorney challenged Mr. Shands' pronunciation of the word "Negro" as "Nigar"—which is the way most of us pronounce it—Judge Sidney Mize, who was presiding, told Mr.

Shands to "indulge her" in her desire that it be pronounced "knee-grow."
(That reminds me that it's reached the place in bars, they tell me, where one
no longer asks for a "jigger" of whiskey; the word is "jeegrow" . . .)

This courtroom was a demonstration of "segregation within integration."
One row of Negroes sat in one section, and there were four or five rows of
Negroes near the back in the other section. (Only a handful were real
Negroes—the rest were, like the Motley woman and her aides, high-
browns.) The courtroom was filled with white citizens who look with distaste upon the reprehensible effort of these Negroes to break down barriers
constitutionally established. Above their heads a mural revealed the role of
the Negro as cotton pickers and I could not help wondering what thoughts
ran through the minds of the Negroes and high browns who faced it.[7]

Meredith watched semesters come and go in 1961 and early 1962 with no
sign that he would be admitted. A federal judge in Mississippi ruled that race
had nothing to do with Ole Miss's rejection of Meredith; the Fifth Circuit
Court of Appeals disagreed. The case bounced back and forth between the
courts. In the end, the U.S. Supreme Court ordered Meredith's enrollment.[8]

The next night, September 11, 1962, a cross staked into the yard of a
vacant area near Fraternity Row at Ole Miss burst into flames. A few fraternity members raced to the scene. In a flash of light produced by a camera,
they saw four or five people run away. The students called police, the fire was
doused, and everyone went home. That seemed to be the end of it until the
next afternoon's edition of the *Jackson Daily News*. The front page carried a
photograph of the burning cross and a headline, MEREDITH CROSS
BLAZES AT OXFORD. The story said that a hundred students and campus
police officers had witnessed the blaze and that university officials had had
to threaten students with expulsion to get them to leave. None of that had
happened. The *Daily News* had allowed itself to become the pot into which
all sort of toxic emotions were stirred. On another occasion, the *Daily News*
editor, Jimmy Ward, walked out of his office to one of his young reporters,
W. C. "Dub" Shoemaker, and handed him the name of a man in Oxford he
should call and develop as a source in the Meredith case. Ward said the
man's name had come from Bill Simmons of the Citizens' Councils. Shoemaker dutifully called the man and asked him what was going on in Oxford.
The man's response, itself a question, sent a chill through Shoemaker. "What
do you guys want to happen?" he asked. Shoemaker ended the call and
didn't call again.[9]

The state was sizzling with rumors that Governor Ross Barnett might
invoke the theory of interposition, or even close the school, to stop the federal government from enforcing the court order. In Greenville, in editorials
written by Hodding Carter III while his father was on sabbatical at Tulane

University, the *Delta Democrat-Times* said that massive resistance was pointless and dead certain to be a losing strategy. The paper expressed concern that Barnett, "for the sake of a philosophy which sees some men as inherently inferior to others," might force the university to close "in one highflying burst of idiocy."[10]

On September 13, Barnett went on statewide television and radio to declare that the state of Mississippi was a sovereign power and that he was interposing himself between the federal government and the university to nullify the federal court's desegregation order.

The choice facing Mississippians, he said, was to "either submit to the unlawful dictate of the Federal government or stand up like men and tell them, 'NEVER!' There is no case in history where the Caucasian race has survived social integration. We will not drink from the cup of genocide."[11]

"Gov. Barnett Interposes Self Against Federals," was *The Clarion-Ledger's* four-column headline the next morning, beginning several days of adulatory coverage of the governor and his strategy. The headline was an umbrella over the main news story, by City Editor Gene Wirth, and an editorial supporting the governor. Wirth, who would himself become the subject of front-page news in the coming week, wrote in the news story that Barnett's action had been "dramatic and historic" and that the governor had been "speaking courageously and forcefully and gripped by strong emotions of the moment."

What Wirth did not provide, and what the *Clarion-Ledger* and *Jackson Daily News* coverage consistently omitted, was an explanation of why the gambit was futile. The Supreme Court had ruled in 1958 in the Little Rock integration case that children had a constitutional right to attend schools without racial discrimination and that those rights "can neither be nullified openly and directly by state legislators or state executives or judicial officers, nor nullified indirectly by them through evasive schemes for segregation." Two years after that, Louisiana Governor Jimmie Davis had tried to interpose himself to prevent school desegregation, only to have that and seven other moves by him and the legislature ruled unconstitutional by a panel of three federal judges and the Supreme Court.[12] Barnett himself, told by a university lawyer that the strategy was bogus, responded, "Of course I know interposition is invalid. I'm bluffing. But you wait and see. I'll bluff the Justice Department into backing down."[13] The newspapers spared their readers those details.

Without the dominant in-state papers setting the record straight, misinformation abounded. Only a couple of Mississippi papers were covering the story with their own staffers, most papers relied instead on the wire services; in that environment, with few if anyone on a newspaper staff working the story, checking the background, seeking the historic context, or getting neck deep in the important details, misrepresentations and honest mistakes slipped easily into newspapers, creating widespread misunderstandings that were virtually impossible to erase. The Associated Press, for example, initially reported that interposition had never been put to a legal test. By the time it noted that the federal courts had spoken clearly on the subject, it was appended as a final paragraph.[14]

The Clarion-Ledger began placing its editorial comments about Barnett's actions on the front page, near the top. They were shallow and awkward. "Barnett intends to stand on this valid premise and to risk federal attacks if that be what will come,"[15] one front-page editorial said.

Ira Harkey, the owner and editor of the daily Pascagoula *Chronicle* newspaper on Mississippi's Gulf Coast, wrote with greater eloquence and prescience—but from a decidedly liberal viewpoint. "He will drive Mississippi to chaos," Harkey wrote in an editorial he titled "Governor Reaches Point of No Return."[16] Harkey, who had been at ideological odds with the Mississippi mainstream for years, stayed on the subject for days, crafting passionate commentaries.

> A pall of contradiction covers our state as if every one of us had developed schizophrenia.
>
> The newspapers and politicians who hailed Gov. Barnett's address call upon citizens not to resort to violence. "Do they really mean it?" is the question, for these same papers and people have long been advocates of a "fight to the finish" and now they may see just what it is they have raised up.
>
> Then there is the call upon the United States of America not to send marshals into our state to enforce the law. How can we make such a demand without appearing devoid of all sense? Does the burglar announce to the police that he will not observe anti-burgling statutes because they violate his way of life and then expect the police to issue him an exemption?
>
> Gov. Barnett knows full well how laws are enforced when the lawless are defiant. He himself has sent troops into counties to search out a bottle of whiskey here, to shatter a crap table there. Federal marshals enforce the law except in rebellions when they are tended to by troops. How do we think that the United States will enforce the law now? By sending in the Peace Corps? Postmen? Soil conservationists? When orders are ignored, force is applied. Gov. Barnett knows that . . .
>
> In a madhouse's din, Mississippi waits. God help Mississippi.[17]

On the second day after Barnett's speech, *Clarion-Ledger* editors employed two devices that became their journalistic trademarks: they punished and ridiculed their enemies and gushed over their heroes.

The Clarion-Ledger's fawning profile of Barnett carried the headline

"Place Assured in History for Fearless Ross Barnett." Above it, the smaller overline said, "Humble Plowboy Grows Up." The story, by city editor Wirth, opened, "The humble plowboy from Standing Pine, fearless in his refusal to yield principle to compromise, stands assuredly today on the blazing pages of American history awaiting a challenger to his order to resist." Ignoring the similar acts by Governors Faubus and Davis, Wirth reported that Barnett was taking "an historic act that is without parallel." Barnett's bold move, he reported, "could mean the preservation of states' rights and the rights of free people, [or] it could mean Federal prison and the total destruction of freedom in America."

What no newspaper knew was that Barnett that day had received the first of what would be twenty phone calls from Robert F. Kennedy, the U.S. attorney general, commencing a cat-and-mouse game that would eventually draw in President Kennedy and produce a theatrical script that all agreed to follow. The Kennedy brothers were finding it impossible to get a fix on Barnett, to persuade Barnett to commit to anything for more than a few hours, or even a few minutes. Misunderstanding some of the history of the South, they were also having trouble grasping the sincerity of the opposition and the depth of the feelings among whites in Mississippi.[18]

For all the drumrolls and drama that accompanied Barnett's interposition declaration, his first act was more of a squirt from a water gun than a shot from a cannon. But it showed how far the state was prepared to go.

Barnett got the legislature to pass a law barring university enrollment to anyone accused of a crime of moral turpitude in any state or federal court. Anyone with such a charge pending would face a year in the county jail and a fine. When Meredith had registered to vote in Jackson, he had inadvertently written February 2, 1960, instead of 1961. State officials had pounced on that to accuse Meredith of swearing falsely. Though a federal judge said that Meredith unquestionably had not been trying to deceive anyone, there were still charges pending, which gave Barnett the hook he needed, and used, to great applause from newspapers in the state.[19] Barnett had Meredith jailed briefly, until the Fifth Circuit Court ordered him released.

Attorney General Robert F. Kennedy directed the Justice Department to enter the case on Meredith's behalf. Now facing contempt charges and a jail term if they refused to admit Meredith, college board members voted to give their powers to the governor.

Barnett did not want the job of registrar for himself. He had a list of three close allies he recommended to the college board. One was Gene Wirth, the city editor of *The Clarion-Ledger,* whose name was accompanying the glowing profiles. Wirth, who had attended the Hederman-supported Baptist school, Mississippi College, and who had worked his entire career at *The Clarion-Ledger,* had gotten caught up in the Meredith episode and had consulted long hours with the governor while operating as a journalist. But the college board wanted Barnett himself to play the role. Wirth, forty-one, was not to have his moment of greatness anyway. A few hours after Barnett submitted his name, Wirth died of a heart attack. In his eulogy, Wirth's minister said that the racial crises in the state "had cracked, if they did not break, the heart of Gene Wirth." His friends in the Citizens' Councils saw in Wirth's death the loss not of a newspaperman but of a comrade. "Unfortunately, I am afraid that Gene will not be the last casualty of this fight to preserve segregation in the schools of Mississippi," Fred Beard, the station manager of WLBT, said in a televised editorial tribute.[20]

That almost all Mississippi newspapers were willing to follow Ross Barnett over the edge of the earth was not a surprise to Erle Johnston, Jr., a weekly newspaper editor in Scott County. Johnston had not only seen such behavior, he had milked it as publicity manager for Barnett's campaign for governor in 1959. There were only nineteen daily newspapers in the state—the largest city, Jackson, had 150,000 residents, and no other city had even a third of that—and the state of journalism was not highly developed. While the Hederman dailies were the most powerful in-state papers, they were not as dominant in north Mississippi as the Memphis *Commercial Appeal* or in south Mississippi as the New Orleans *Times-Picayune*. There were five times as many weeklies as dailies in the state, some of them quite influential.

As Johnston began advising Barnett, he knew that most of the dailies had small, poorly paid staffs that were not aggressive or investigative in their reporting. Staffers were focused on local news, and the definition of local was pretty narrow. Coverage from the capital in Jackson was treated almost like foreign news; they'd leave it to the wire services.

Barnett had run twice before and lost. He was a large, folksy, raspy-voiced damage suit lawyer from Leake County who played hard on the theme of being a country boy who had made good in the big city, Jackson. He had established himself with segregationist causes early, serving as an attorney for men accused of bombing a school in Clinton, Tennessee.

Barnett was not far removed from the Civil War. His father had been a Confederate soldier. Barnett seemed harmless, and he talked a lot about economic development and jobs, but he couldn't get elected. It did not help that in his bumbling pronouncements, his clumsiness, and his not-infrequent mental lapses, he frequently came off as a buffoon.

Barnett's 1959 campaign strategy took advantage of the relatively untrained and unskilled press corps. In the midst of that campaign, Barnett one day stepped down from a small, single-engine airplane and absent-mindedly walked right into its whirling propeller. The blade cut into his arm and put him into a Memphis hospital in a semicoma. Certain he'd survive and be back on the campaign trail, his campaign staff began trying to develop a plausible explanation for how he could have done such a thing. Erle Johnston called several pilots, seeking information they could use to dress up this ugly turn of events. After several pilots said that only a bonehead or "a goddam fool" would walk into a turning propeller, one gave Johnston a glimmer of hope. On rare occasions, maybe one in a million times, he said, a freshly idled airplane will burp and the blades will hiccup and start whirling briefly. Pilots had a name for it: backlash, similar to a car backfiring. Johnston banged out a news release that fabricated a scenario in which the idle propeller on Barnett's plane had come back to life, turning Barnett into "the victim of a motor backlash." As Johnston handed the statement out to reporters, he got strange looks, but they used it.[21]

Johnston two days later issued another statement in which Barnett made light of the incident. In a pithy quote that evoked the image of Barnett as a farm boy, he was quoted as saying he'd learned there was as much kick at the front end of an airplane as there was at the rear end of a mule. Barnett, however, was still in a semicoma and had not made such a statement. Again, newspapers carried the story.[22] So when Johnston pursued newspaper endorsements for Barnett in 1959, he wasn't overwhelmed by support, but he wasn't surprised when five editors said they'd go along if Johnston would write the editorials for them.[23]

What mattered most that year was that Barnett had caught the segregationist wind just right. Mississippi was the poorest state in the nation, with an average per capita income under $1,200, and its 900,000 Negroes represented 43 percent of the state's population, the highest percentage in the nation; in some counties, six or seven out of ten residents were black. It was not hard to play on whites' fears. Barnett sailed into the governor's office in January 1960 on the hot air of racial anger and demagoguery. Now, more than two years later, most of the newspapers were solidly behind him, showing a mixture of racism and laziness.[24]

The Clarion-Ledger's approach to news was typified by its handling of Meredith. The paper never interviewed him. When it did publish an interview, it ran two on the same day, one by UPI and one by AP. The interviews presented Meredith as a serious, quiet person just trying to get an education and not trying to change the world. "I have no argument, no fight nor struggle with segregation," he told AP. "I don't know what other people want but I seek only to find a common ground for settlement of our mutual problems. Let's make a friendly relationship between the races in Mississippi possible. Then give me equal rights and nothing more."[25]

Meredith's comments were placed deep inside the front section of the paper, with no mention on page one that the man at the center of this watershed event that was going to ruin Mississippi had spoken on the subject. The

Jackson papers also resisted running Meredith's photo on the front page. And when the issue went before the federal appeals court in New Orleans, the paper didn't send a staff writer.[26]

What's more, when the clash between the federal and state governments shifted back to Oxford for its final confrontation, scores of reporters and photographers from across the nation and the world were on hand to witness it. But not the Jackson papers. The *Daily News* got to Oxford too late to see any of the action, then decided the situation was too dangerous to enter the campus. But it came closer than *The Clarion-Ledger,* which didn't even assign a reporter or photographer.[27]

But no amount of effort by Mississippi newspapers to downplay the story was enough to turn away the eyes of the regional, national, international, and black press. Oxford, a town of 6,200 residents, would attract the civil rights movement's largest gathering of journalistic firepower. As the final showdown approached, one newsman counted 182 visiting reporters in Oxford, with more on the way. The three major networks and several independent television syndicates came in with reporters, cameramen, sound men, and helpers. *The New York Times, The Washington Post, The Boston Globe,* the Chicago dailies, and other top-tier newspapers were there. Reporters from newspapers in medium-sized cities and smaller were present, providing eyewitness reports to readers in such places as Louisville, Richmond, Memphis, and Atlanta. All the national newsmagazines and national wire services took up substantial positions in Oxford. Black newspapers and magazines, which a few years earlier had had the civil rights story to themselves, headed toward Oxford.

Following the sit-ins and the Freedom Rides, Albany had produced forgettable images. But Ole Miss—a solitary man against thousands—had the portent of a visual cavalcade. Photojournalists, some of the best in the business, were equipped with smaller cameras, faster film, and a prayer that any action would take place in the daylight, when they could shoot relatively unobtrusively. A camera flash would be a magnet for danger, perhaps death.

The Meredith story appealed to news organizations for many different reasons, not the least of which was the feeling that a dramatic clash would occur between an appealing protagonist and tyrannizing antagonist of the kind that Reverend Martin Luther King, Jr., had come to believe was essential to get news coverage.[28]

James H. Meredith was a mature, educated landowner, husband, and father. He was one of eleven children raised in Attala County on small farms that his father, a well-regarded man in town, had been able to buy. Like his siblings, Meredith had begun working the cotton fields at five or six, sometimes by moonlight, and had walked four and a half miles to school as a child. He had been a studious child, known to be well behaved and easy to get along with. The air force had been his ticket from Mississippi, and he had used his spare time at military bases to accumulate credits at nearby colleges. Meredith owned two farms, of 100 acres and 40 acres, outside of Kosciusko, and his parents lived in a small modern home at the end of a dusty road. Most important, Meredith didn't seem to be part of any larger scheme, movement, or organization. In his friendships, his words, and his lifestyle, he seemed independent of all that. Segregationists tried to paint him as a soldier in the integrationists' well-planned strategy to kill Jim Crow, but he wasn't, and it showed.[29]

The antagonist was the region and its customs, the rabid, determined segregationist South, embodied in Ross Barnett. To many Mississippians, Barnett was the defiant leader they had been waiting for since the end of the Civil War. He said it plainly: no integration at any time, at any place, so long as he was governor. Never, never, never. Part of his appeal might have been that he seemed so blithely unaware of the impact of his pronouncements and actions, even while everyone watching him was. Here again was the bumbler preparing to walk into the propeller of a whirling crisis, claiming he was the victim because the propeller hiccuped. Some people felt sorry for Barnett, the Leake County plowboy, having to go up against the president of the United States, his brother, and the entire might of a nation. While Barnett inspired great passions among his followers, it wasn't clear that he knew how to calm them down, even if he had wanted to. The story seemed destined for conflict and confrontation, perhaps with a last-minute death-defying escape.

For Claude Sitton and *The New York Times,* the time to settle into Oxford came in early fall. He took four rooms at the Ole Miss Motel, which he assumed would be free from attack because it was owned by a Kluxer. He installed a second phone line in his room. He rented four cars, always using Avis because it offered white Oldsmobiles, which was what Mississippi highway patrolmen drove.[30] He joined *Newsweek*'s Fleming in arranging for a charter airplane to be available to get them quickly to Jackson and New Orleans whenever the story moved to the governor's mansion, the state capitol, or the Fifth U.S. Circuit Court of Appeals.[31]

He told his bosses in New York that he would need some help. He got an impressive amount of it. The paper made arrangements to send the reporters McCandlish Phillips and Tom Buckley to join Sitton in Oxford. Peter Kihss and Hedrick Smith were told to fly to Jackson. In Washington, Anthony Lewis, James Reston, Max Frankel, and Tom Wicker were put on alert. Cabell Phillips was to head to Hollywood, Florida, to cover the opening of the Southern Governors Conference. Foster Hailey would be sent to New Orleans, and Seymour Topping in Moscow would be pressed into gathering international reaction.

Ole Miss would be another battleground for the newsweeklies as well.

Bill Emerson had left as Atlanta bureau chief, but not before bringing in the reporters Joe Cumming and Frank Trippett, the former from Georgia, the latter from Mississippi, both educated in the South.[32] They were making their mark, but in ways some southern readers didn't like. The circuit court clerk of Autauga County, Alabama, so disliked *Newsweek*'s coverage that he joined many others in writing the magazine's offices in New York and canceling his subscription "to your alleged news medium." A reader in Raymondville, Texas, infuriated by a Cumming story about the growing violence against Negroes, wrote, "Sooner or later, and sooner than you think, the American people will have a bathe [*sic*] in their own blood because of a press that is communistic." The reader, no doubt thinking Cumming was a wild-eyed Yankee, added a postscript: "My people came to America in 1620. When did yours come?"[33]

Cumming's family was as deeply rooted in Augusta, Georgia, as Fleming's family was unrooted. Cumming's great-great-great-grandfather was the first mayor of Augusta, and his great-grandfather and namesake, Joseph B. Cumming, had had the solemn responsibility on October 15, 1870, of delivering the city's eulogy to "the greatest man of his time." General Robert E. Lee. Cumming's father, also Joseph B. Cumming, headed a prominent Augusta law firm that bore the family name. Young Joe was imbued with all things southern, graduating from the venerable University of the South in Sewanee, Tennessee. Being a *Newsweek* writer might not have been the family's expectation for Joe, and covering civil rights might not have been its wish, but father praised son for the recognition he was getting from the *Newsweek* brass for his fine work.[34]

At the same time, Cumming's father was an affectionate critic of *Newsweek*'s treatment of the South, drawing young Joe's attention to places "where it is obvious that the writer's orientation was not that of a Southerner." He bridled at the frequent use of the phrases "the law of the land." "In one sense it probably is an accurate expression," he once wrote his son. "On the other hand, it is certainly provocative. It's vague, and has merit mainly in its rather sensational phrasing, with well-balanced, alliterative qualities." He was certain, he wrote, that his son was sensitive to the *Newsweek* expressions that lacked objectivity. "I only wish that they could be avoided, because the raw wound isn't helped when a little sand is rubbed into it."[35]

Though Cumming had succeeded Emerson as bureau chief, Fleming was the point man in Oxford. There, he very quickly felt the tension rising and pinpointed what he believed was a dismaying source of the problem: the Jackson newspapers. Flabbergasted by a *Clarion-Ledger* story that said that Governor Barnett "will watch with a jaundiced eye any attempt to apply punitive action against Mississippi patriots," Fleming warned his editors that something resembling anarchy was afoot. "By its insinuation," Fleming wrote his editors, "the paper as much as told Miss. students to raise all the hell they wanted against Meredith, without fear of punishment."³⁶ *Newsweek* would send in help.

NBC News was in the midst of another transition in its coverage of the South. The network still did not have a bureau in the region. It continued to cover the South from Chicago as it had done with John Chancellor and Sander Vanocur, augmented by Herbert Kaplow, Frank McGee, Charles Quinn, and others. The new reporter was Richard Valeriani, a New Jerseyean, whose fluency in Spanish had won him a posting in Havana in the spring of 1961. That glow hadn't lasted long. The Bay of Pigs debacle had forced him out of the country only days after he'd been named bureau chief. After a year of covering Latin America from Miami, he had been moved to the Chicago bureau, which put Albany, then Oxford, on his itinerary.

Valeriani would soon learn that what he broadcast to the nation from Mississippi was often different from what Mississippians would ultimately see.

Inside the NBC affiliate in Jackson, the station manager, Fred Beard, reviewed, edited, censored, and sometimes added editorial comment to national broadcasts coming into the station, shaping them to his Citizens' Council point of view. Beard would sometimes have his station personnel introduce the morning *Today* show or the nightly news with a statement that the show represented "biased, managed northern news." The *Today* show would also be interrupted by a local segment, *Today in Jackson,* whenever a black person was about to come on the national show. When NBC carried a three-part series on the civil rights movement, WLBT simply stopped transmitting the broadcast to its viewers when it came to a segment about a sit-in at the Woolworth's in Jackson.³⁷

Valeriani, whose coverage required frequent visits to Jackson, would soon learn the depth of Beard's worries about his civil rights reports. When Valeriani came to town, Beard had no choice but to let him work at WLBT. The correspondent would type his scripts on a "four book," which was four sheets of paper interspersed with carbons. Valeriani threw the carbons in the trash, only to notice that someone was pulling them out. He soon figured out that Beard wanted to see what he was writing. "Fred, you don't have to do that," Valeriani finally said to him one day. "Whatever I write, I put on the air. You want a copy of the script? I'll give it to you. You don't have to settle for carbons."³⁸

Black reporters and photographers, who with rare exception were still able to work only for the black press, continued to have difficulty getting into good positions to cover the story. Unless the reporters wanted to dress up as yard men on the campus, they had the same problem L. Alex Wilson, Moses Newson, Jimmy Hicks, and Earl Davy had had in Little Rock: They couldn't go unnoticed. They could work out of Memphis all they wanted, but trouble and the threat of it awaited them a few miles down the road, at the Mississippi state line. When the Justice Department decided that Meredith should stay at a naval air station and with family in Memphis while he was awaiting admission to Ole Miss, it was the photographer Ernest Withers and *Jet* reporter Larry Still who found him and spent time with him.

The first time Meredith tried to enroll, Chief U.S. Marshal James McShane plotted a car switch in Memphis to foil anyone who might try to follow them south to Oxford on Highway 51, one of the legendary north-bound escape routes for so many Negroes from the early 1940s. As they moved down the highway, McShane became worried about a rental car following them, slowing when they slowed, speeding when they sped. As McShane pulled off the road at Batesville to call Washington and confirm that the Justice Department still wanted to go forward with registration that day, the mystery car stopped at a gas station across the road. The two men got out and walked toward Meredith.

They were Still and Withers, and they wanted to take some pictures. It seemed only fair, since some white photographers, tipped off by the state highway patrol, were getting shots of Meredith. The highway patrolmen weren't interested in helping Withers and Still. "God damn, don't follow us no damn more," one of the state patrolmen told them. When all the cars revved up again and headed for Oxford, Withers and Still did, too. But they were not allowed on campus.[39]

Moses Newson was sent to Oxford by the *Baltimore Afro-American.* "Mississippi Rebels" was the creative headline of his story, stripped across all eight columns at the top of the paper on September 29. The smaller head-line above it read, "Award Winning Editor Reports from Oxford." But the truth about Newson's access and proximity was nestled into the next-to-last paragraph of his story: "Colored newspapermen on the scene are being kept away from the campus of the university." Taking the advice of an NAACP spokesman and the mayor of Oxford, Newson retreated to Memphis, where he tried to cover the story by phone. Jimmy Hicks of the New York *Amsterdam News* stayed in Oxford longer than others. But he got little more than a sojourn on the fringe of the campus before heading to Memphis himself.[40]

The Richmond editor Jack Kilpatrick decided to fly to Oxford to see the action for himself. Though Kilpatrick wrote nothing to dissuade Barnett from pursuing the strategy, and though he portrayed the segregationists as honorable, he acknowledged in his editorials that Barnett was "exceedingly unlikely" to win the interposition argument.

More remarkable was Kilpatrick's front-page coverage of the Ole Miss story. He took a reporting tack that was sharply uncharacteristic of the seg-regationist press: He traveled to Kosciusko, went to Meredith's parents' home, and sat inside with Meredith's mother, wife, and son. He wrote one of the more humanistic stories about Meredith to come out of the Ole Miss crisis. He treated the family with respect, portrayed it positively, even sweetly, and captured its steely resolve.

> The younger Mrs. Meredith breaks in. She has been playing with her infant son, John Howard, who will be three in January. She is teaching him to talk.
> "Say, I don't want to pick cotton," she commands him.
> Giggling, the boy happily cries out, "I don't wanna pick cotton."
> The younger Mrs. Meredith casts a sidelong glance at a reporter, satisfied with the effect.
> "He won't pick cotton," she says flatly.[41]

Kilpatrick watched as Meredith's mother let her fingers gently touch the Bible she had used as a reference to recall her children's birth dates. "I think about Moses," she told Kilpatrick. "He never got to the Promised Land. He saw it, but he never got there. But others did. Maybe it's the same with J. H. It's in the Lord's hands now. His will be done."

One reporter who found himself unexpectedly flying to Mississippi was Paul L. Guihard, who worked in New York for Agence France Presse, the French news agency. He got the weekend assignment because of short-staffing in his office. Guihard, who held dual British and French citizenships, was already an experienced reporter at thirty years of age. He had been working for the agency since he was nineteen, when he had helped cover the 1948 summer Olympics in London. He had won the coveted New York assignment in 1960.

Known as "Flash" among his friends because he brought vigor and an upbeat drive to his news coverage, Guihard was an eye-catching man. He was husky, six feet tall, and had an untamed red beard and mustache that set him apart. As the bachelor boarded the plane for Mississippi, he displayed his lighthearted outlook. "I'm going to pose as a Kentucky colonel and cover this thing with a mint julep in my hand," he crowed.[42]

From the largest papers in the Deep South, the afternoon *Atlanta Journal* and the morning *Atlanta Constitution,* came one reporter each. Though competitive, the papers were owned by the same company, Cox Enterprises of Dayton, Ohio. The Atlanta newspaper business executives had never been as enthralled by the civil rights story, or as committed to its coverage, as were their editors, Ralph McGill and Gene Patterson, neither of whom was responsible for deploying coverage. The newspapers staffed some of the big race stories in the South but skipped enough that their commitment was questioned.

The newspapers' corporate executives had developed different reasons at different times to justify their inconsistent and indifferent coverage of racial issues. At a minimum, there may have been a feeling that whatever the city of Atlanta was doing was working well. A state commission had held well-covered public hearings about school desegregation and listened to 1,620 witnesses. The commission, key business leaders, and the Georgia Baptist Convention all opposed closing schools, and eventually Governor Ernest Vandiver did as well. Atlanta had moved forward from there, phasing in desegregation beginning in the fall of 1961. A year later, *The New York Times Magazine,* in a story written by Sitton, declared Atlanta a southern role model under the headline "Atlanta's Example: Good Sense and Dignity." There was a feeling in the newspapers' executive offices that the balancing act had been achieved in part because the newspapers, while never shutting out race stories entirely, had remained relatively docile in their coverage.[43]

As the stakes got greater, the newspapers had, for a while, gotten more aggressive. Both Atlanta papers had committed considerable resources to covering the Freedom Rides and, ultimately, Albany. But as the story shifted to Ole Miss, Birmingham, and beyond, they pulled back again. Their decision to limit their Ole Miss coverage to Fred Powledge at the *Journal* and Bill Shipp at the *Constitution* caused consternation for McGill, Patterson, and others, especially in the talent-laden *Journal* newsroom. McGill was the most influential liberal voice in the South, remarkably skilled at crystallizing the issues—but at a paper that was not fully committed to covering the story.

If there could be only two reporters covering the story for the Atlanta papers, Shipp and Powledge were wise choices. Both were southerners and experienced reporters who were skilled probers and strong writers.

Life magazine put together a team of three reporters and six photographers. Among the staff photographers was one legend, Francis Miller, whose nickname, "Nig," was especially unfortunate for a white man in the Deep South. Miller, who had been punched and taken into police custody while taking pictures in front of Central High in Little Rock, was a veteran newshound. He had once adapted a camera and lens to fit into a reporter's purse that she took into a Chicago voting precinct to show multiple sets of feet inside voting booths where only one person was allowed.[44] He was also known for taking tough, quick-hit assignments that others didn't want and for always carrying two sets of film canisters in his pockets, one containing film, the other bourbon.

Miller was joined by two newer photographers whose extraordinary civil rights photography had already set them apart from the pack. Charles Moore and Flip Schulke, both working on contract for *Life* through their agent, Black Star, had shown skill in covering civil rights, and both were developing a fascination with the changes they saw being wrought through their viewfinders.

Moore, who was thirty-one, came to Oxford at a time of loose ends in a promising career that only he doubted. Trained as a combat photographer in the Marine Corps and as a fashion and commercial photographer at an institute, Moore's early career made it more likely that he'd have been at Ole Miss for a fashion shoot with the state's back-to-back Miss Americas in 1959 and 1960. But he had had an itch to do something else. When he had heard about an opening at the *Montgomery Advertiser,* he applied and was hired.

The place, Montgomery, and the time, 1957, had been serendipitous for Moore, the *Advertiser,* the budding civil rights movement, and, more important, a nation that soon would be "shocked and shaken in their conscience," as Myrdal put it, by the images Moore would put in their hands. Within a few weeks of being hired, Moore was in a church, on his knees, riveted nearly to the point of paralysis by the man speaking from the pulpit above him. Moore was on assignment at the Dexter Avenue Baptist Church, positioned by the deacons between the front row and the pulpit and told to stay low so as to not block anyone's view. The man standing over him was Reverend Martin Luther King, Jr.

For Moore, a solid, broad-shouldered man who was quiet in his speech and demeanor, something more than inspired oratory was going on. The whole scene transported him back to his youth, to a time when he had found himself where few white children would ever go, to the exotic setting of a rural black church. This was in northwest Alabama, where he had been raised in the heart of the Depression in the unincorporated outskirts of Tuscumbia, not far from the birthplace of Helen Keller but well past the end of the sewer and water lines. Moore's mother had lost a six-year battle with cancer when he was thirteen, and he and his younger brother had been raised by their father, who at various times had sold cars, worked as a police officer, and served as a Baptist preacher.

In the Moore home, all men were created equal, no one was degraded, and Moore's father was just as likely to be invited to preach in black country churches as in white ones. Young Charles Moore would sit in awe of the spiritual sights and sounds that rang through the churches. The day was comfortable and comforting for the young boy, and when the invitation included dinner on the ground, with black-eyed peas, turnip greens, fried chicken, potatoes, corn bread, and buttermilk, that was even better.

Early in his Montgomery years, Moore came to understand the link between his camera and the civil rights movement's capacity to arouse public opinion.[45] He saw it in September 1958 on the streets of Montgomery when he shot frames showing King being accosted by police, arrested, and booked for loitering. Moore's images were picked up by Associated Press and used by *Life* magazine, bringing more national attention to King.

Now, four years later, Moore was in transition. He'd left the *Advertiser* earlier in 1962 and gone to New York to pursue his bigger career. It had been a bad fit all around, and Moore had been in danger of disappearing into some obscure commercial studio work when Howard Chapnick, president of Black Star photo agency, promised him a weekly stipend to return south. That night, Moore abandoned his apartment and drove straight to Montgomery, hardly stopping along the way. After crossing the Chesapeake and reaching Virginia, he pulled over, got out, pulled clumps of grass and dirt from the earth, and said to himself, "Damn, this is good."[46]

A few weeks later, Chapnick arranged for Moore to head to Ole Miss, shooting for *Life*. At a critical time for a civil rights movement increasingly dependent on visual journalism, Chapnick had just discovered a star and put him into a place where everyone would see him for years to come.

The first time Meredith arrived on campus to seek admission, he was confronted by Barnett, who read a proclamation rejecting him. Oddly, Barnett then handed the document—a historic keepsake—to Meredith. As the crisis entered the final ten days of September, it was anybody's guess whether a compromise would be reached or the Oxford campus would witness all-out combat. The action kept shifting quickly from the Ole Miss campus, where the student newspaper and student leaders seemed far less alarmed than their state leaders, to the Fifth Circuit Court of Appeals, which held firm for enrolling Meredith, to the state legislature, which was adamant in wanting to block him.

On his second attempt, Meredith was told he would have to enroll in Jackson, inside the fifteen-story, fortresslike Woolfolk state office building, where the corridors were narrow and dark. Meredith, accompanied by John Doar, the chief of the Justice Department's civil rights division, and James McShane, the chief U.S. marshal, had to walk a lengthy sidewalk lined by nearly two thousand angry, taunting white people. Meredith was but a speck of black in an ocean of white froth. That ratio was maintained inside the building as he made his way down long corridors to the tenth-floor office where he was to register. Arriving there, he came upon the pasty-faced Barnett, whose eyes slowly scanned the faces of the men before him, then asked the question that became a punch line in stories told about Ross Barnett for years to come: "Which one is Meredith?"[47] He again turned Meredith away.

That same day, Barnett and Robert Kennedy talked again. "Must it be over one little boy, backed by communist front, backed by the NAACP which is a communist front?" Barnett asked Kennedy, more pleading than belligerent. ". . . I'm going to treat you with every courtesy but I won't agree to let that boy get to Ole Miss. I will never agree to that. I would rather spend the rest of my life in a penitentiary than do that."[48]

On the third try, back at Ole Miss, the rejection was handled by the lieutenant governor, Paul B. Johnson, Jr., whose raised fist in the face of McShane, caught by cameramen, would guarantee his ascension to governor at the next election.

Other than Meredith's admission, all the Kennedys wanted and demanded was a commitment from Barnett that law and order would be maintained on campus and that Meredith would be secure. All Barnett wanted, in the end, was a way to save face. Their conversations became only sketchily known by reporters at the time, not well enough known that the reporters could question the versions they got from both sides. Barnett, it was later revealed, was promising Kennedy that he would enroll Meredith if U.S. marshals would pull their guns on him to make it look as though he were facing a life-or-death choice. *The Clarion-Ledger,* while reporting to its readers that the Kennedys were bending to Barnett's will, knew better. That bit of staged gunplay had been hatched in front of, and maybe even by, the newspaper's city editor, Gene Wirth.[49] And Barnett didn't want just one marshal aiming at him.

BARNETT: Yes. Hold just a minute, will you? Hello, General, I was under the impression that they were all going to pull their guns. This could be very embarrassing. We got a big crowd here and if one pulls his gun and we all turn, it would be very embarrassing. Isn't it possible to have them all pull their guns?

KENNEDY: I hate to have them all pull their guns as I think it would create harsh feelings. Isn't it sufficient if I have one man draw his gun and the others keep their hands on their holsters?

BARNETT: They must all draw their guns. Then they should point their guns at us and then we could step aside. This could be very embarrassing down here for us. It is necessary.[50]

Barnett worried almost obsessively that his constituents would find out that his knees were buckling in his dealings with the Kennedys. In negotiations, he ran hot and cold for days. He knew he had an explosive situation facing him, that it was getting worse every day, and that it was about to get very costly. The Fifth Circuit Court found him in contempt of court on September 28 and said he had until October 2 to allow Meredith into school or face a fine of $10,000 a day.

Barnett himself was indicating to Robert Kennedy that the pot was boiling and he couldn't find the switch to turn down the heat. While thousands of students were heading toward Jackson for a Saturday-night football game,

RIGHT: Ralph Bunche *(left)* and Gunnar Myrdal met at Bunche's home in Washington, D.C., in June 1943, months before *An American Dilemma* was published.

BELOW: Black reporters and other blacks were allowed to sit at a press table inside the courtroom during the trial of the two men accused of killing Emmett Till. *Standing, left,* Ernest C. Withers, *Tri-State Defender* photographer; *center,* David Jackson, *Jet* and *Ebony* photographer; *far right:* James del Rio, a Detroit mortgage banker. *Seated, in front of Withers, then counter clockwise around table:* Rayfield Moody, a Till relative; Mamie Bradley, Till's mother; Simeon Booker *(bow tie), Jet*; L. Alex Wilson, *Tri-State Defender*; James L. Hicks *(head of table, facing camera), Afro-American Newspapers*; C.H. Jones, *Southern Mediator Journal*; Cloyte Murdock, *Ebony*; U.S. Rep. Charles Diggs of Detroit; a woman visiting from Mound Bayou and her son. *Behind Diggs, left to right:* John Carthan, Mrs. Till's father; Basil W. Brown, a state senator from Michigan.

ABOVE LEFT: Virginius Dabney, editor of the *Richmond Times-Dispatch*, took progressive stands on race issues in the 1940s, but was marginalized by his newspaper's owners with the rise of massive resistance.

ABOVE RIGHT: Lenoir Chambers, editor of the *Virginian-Pilot* in Norfolk, supported the Supreme Court's school desegregation rulings and opposed massive resistance.

BELOW: Though he believed early on that the South would never accept integration, Hodding Carter, Jr., owner and editor of the *Delta Democrat-Times* in Greenville, Miss., pressed hard, and with disarming wit, for racial equality.

ABOVE LEFT: Cliff Sessions, UPI reporter in Jackson, broke from the orthodox thinking of his Mississippi childhood, humanized blacks in stories, and even hosted them in his home.

ABOVE RIGHT: James J. (Jack) Kilpatrick, editor of the *Richmond News-Leader*, crafted powerful arguments for "interposition" and urged states to oppose federal orders to desegregate.

BELOW LEFT: As UPI bureau chief in Jackson in the 1950s, John Herbers, seated, encouraged his reporters to give blacks full and fair coverage, which most Mississippi news outlets denied them.

BELOW RIGHT: Thomas R. Waring, Jr., editor of the *Charleston News & Courier*, was a vigorous segregationist who complained about the "invasion" of northern reporters in the South.

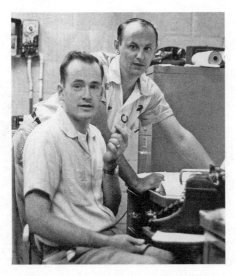

ABOVE LEFT: Emory O. Jackson, seated, was an NAACP activist and editor of the *Birmingham World*, whose owners were disdainful of Rev. Martin Luther King, Jr. Morehouse College President Benjamin Mays spoke at an event honoring Jackson.

ABOVE RIGHT: A brilliant and acerbic writer, Grover C. Hall, Jr., succeeded his father as editor of the *Montgomery Advertiser* and adopted his progressive views until he saw the depth of massive resistance.

BELOW LEFT: Buford Boone, publisher of the *Tuscaloosa News*, confronted Citizens Council members angry at his support for Autherine Lucy's enrollment at the University of Alabama.

BELOW RIGHT: Hazel Brannon Smith, owner of the *Lexington Advertiser*, was hounded as a liberal because she editorially opposed police brutality against blacks.

ABOVE LEFT: Harry S. Ashmore, executive editor of the *Arkansas Gazette*, was an incisive writer whose editorials and books influenced the White House and whose charm built bridges between progressive and segregationist editors.

ABOVE RIGHT: Risking a solid newspaper career, John Chancellor jumped into television reporting and, in Little Rock, helped NBC News move to the forefront of civil rights coverage.

BELOW: L.C. and Daisy Bates, *left, at head of table,* owned the weekly *Arkansas State Press* while she ran the NAACP in Little Rock. She organized, motivated, and, at Thanksgiving, hosted the Little Rock Nine.

ABOVE: *New York Times* reporter Benjamin Fine *(bow tie)* watched as Elizabeth Eckford took verbal abuse outside Central High in Little Rock in 1957, then created a stir by comforting her.

ABOVE RIGHT: John N. Popham, sent south by *The New York Times* in 1947, pioneered national coverage of race but was overly optimistic about the white South's willingness to change.

BELOW RIGHT: Relman (Pat) Morin, Associated Press reporter, filed stories from a phone booth outside Central High in Little Rock until it was attacked with him inside it.

OPPOSITE: After L. Alex Wilson, editor of the *Tri-State Defender* (Memphis), and other black journalists were assaulted at Central High in Little Rock, black reporters had trouble getting to the front row of civil rights stories.

ABOVE: Ralph E. McGill, editor of *The Atlanta Constitution*, shed traditional southern views to advocate humanity, equality, and worldliness in front-page columns that appeared seven days a week.

BELOW: NBC News interviewed McGill after he won the 1959 Pulitzer Prize for editorial writing.

ABOVE: *New York Times* reporter Claude Sitton, reading over the shoulder of a state official during the desegregation of the University of Georgia in 1961, set the pace and the standard for civil rights reporting for six years.

BELOW: Karl Fleming, whose fearless reporting helped *Newsweek* surpass *Time* magazine in civil rights coverage, grew up in the South, as did many of the influential journalists on the race beat.

ABOVE: As *Baltimore Afro-American* reporter Moses J. Newson *(center, in black coat)* looks back, the bus in which he was riding with Freedom Riders burns after an attack outside Anniston in May 1961.

BELOW: A soon as he took this photo of an attack on a Freedom Rider, *Birmingham News* photographer Tom Langston was beaten and his camera discarded. This image forced his newspaper to reassess its views on the city's racial problems.

ABOVE LEFT: *New York Times* reporter Harrison Salisbury found in Birmingham a fear and repressiveness that reminded him of Moscow. His story describing it led to libel suits and restrictions on reporters.

ABOVE RIGHT: Moses J. Newson *(left)*, reporter for the *Baltimore Afro-American*, and James L. Hicks, reporter for the *New York Amsterdam News*, gained access to the University of Mississippi campus after the riot that accompanied James Meredith's enrollment.

BELOW LEFT: Jimmy Ward, editor of the *Jackson Daily News* in Mississippi, was among the segregationist editors to attend a secret meeting in 1959, where they discussed ways to confront the influence of the northern press.

BELOW RIGHT: Tom Hederman, editor of *The Clarion-Ledger* in Jackson and part-owner of both dailies there, produced mean-spirited newspapers that abandoned journalistic standards to fuel discord.

ABOVE: Shooting for *Life* magazine, Charles Moore used short-range lenses to get close to the action in May 1963 when dogs and fire hoses were deployed on demonstrators. Moore's work mobilized action on a civil rights bill.
BELOW: Three of *The Atlanta Constitution*'s Pulitzer Prize winners—Gene Patterson, Ralph McGill, and Jack Nelson *(left to right)*—came together in 1967. Nelson was then at the *Los Angeles Times* bureau in Atlanta.

ABOVE: Turner Catledge, the top editor of *The New York Times*, in his office in August 1964, the same month the bodies of three civil rights workers were found outside his hometown, Philadelphia, Miss.

BELOW: Alton Wayne Roberts *(right),* a defendant in the murder of three civil rights workers in Philadelphia, Miss., assaulted CBS cameraman Laurens Pierce in early 1965. In Pierce's right hand is a detachable bar he had affixed to his camera for such occasions.

ABOVE: *Washington Star* reporter Haynes Johnson took notes as
Selma-to-Montgomery marchers prayed in front of a billboard
erected by the John Birch Society.

BELOW: Magazine photographers *(left to right)* Bob Adelman,
Steve Shapiro, and Charles Moore on the Selma-to-Montgomery
march in 1965. Moore used the motorcyclist to move him up and
down the march and to carry his film to an airport.

ABOVE: Gene Roberts of *The New York Times* interviewed Floyd McKissick, chairman of CORE *(plaid shirt)*, during James Meredith's march through Mississippi, June 1966.

BELOW: Wilson F. "Bill" Minor, Mississippi correspondent for the *Times-Picayune* in New Orleans, doggedly poked at segregationist myths and saw his career, and outlook, defined by race stories.

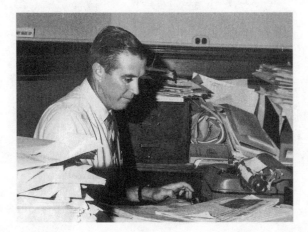

ABOVE: Claude Sitton as national editor of *The New York Times*, 1968, the year Rev. Martin Luther King, Jr., was assassinated.

BELOW: Karl Fleming, *Newsweek* bureau chief in Los Angeles, had always been welcomed in black neighborhoods in the South. But in Watts, a black district of Los Angeles, in 1966, he was struck in the head with a four-by-four.

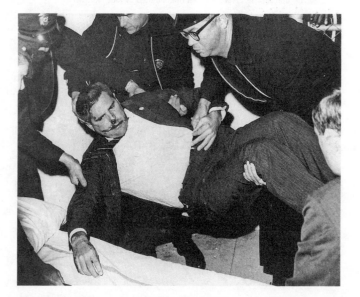

Barnett told Kennedy, several thousand others were heading to Oxford in cars and trucks to oppose Meredith. They were not students. "We don't know these people," Barnett said, adding, "We can't control people like that. A lot of people are going to get killed. It would be embarrassing to me." Embarrassing? Was *that* what Barnett was worried about? "I don't know if it would be embarrassing," Kennedy responded. "That would not be the feeling."[51]

That night, at halftime of the Ole Miss football game in Jackson, Governor Barnett kept the frenzy alive. Before tens of thousands of Mississippians, he stood and uttered four impassioned, arm-pumping sentences before his words were lost in the noisy mayhem. "I love Mississippi! I love her people! Our customs! I love and I respect our heritage!"[52] Bill Minor, the highly regarded Jackson bureau chief for the New Orleans *Times-Picayune,* watched the performance in awe and dismay, then caught the mood perfectly: "Thousands of Confederate battle flags burst forth throughout the stadium, shimmering in the night like a forest fire running before the wind."[53] A little while later, in Washington, President Kennedy quietly federalized the Mississippi National Guard; he signed the order on a table that had belonged to an even greater anathema of the South, General Ulysses S. Grant.

The next day, amid rumors that federal agents were going to sweep into the Governor's Mansion in Jackson and arrest Barnett, the Citizens' Councils issued a call for supporters to come to the mansion and encircle it with "a wall of human flesh."[54] More than two thousand people showed up and ringed the mansion. There was an air of celebration as they sang Dixie and fight songs, waved flags, honked their car horns, followed Ole Miss cheerleaders in cheers, and booed the Kennedy name. To help boost spirits, the *Jackson Daily News* had published a specially penned fight song, "Never, No Never" on its editorial page and encouraged readers to clip it out and come ready to sing their hearts out.

> *Never, Never, Never, Never N-o-o-o Never Never Never*
> *We will not yield an inch of any field*
> *Fix us another toddy, ain't yielding to no-body*
> *Ross's standing like Gibraltar, he shall never falter*
> *Ask us what we say, it's to hell with Bobby K*
> *Never shall our emblem go from Colonel Reb to Old Black Jo.*[55]

Bill Simmons and Jack Kilpatrick stood next to each other in a nearby building looking down on the rally. Simmons had long said that massive resistance would prevail with organization, not litigation. Now, spread before him, was a tableau testament to his success as a leader. Kilpatrick saw in Simmons's face pride, affection, and wonder. "They won't give up," Simmons said. "They won't ever give up."[56]

. . .

Shortly before 7 p.m., Meredith was secretly brought to campus. There would be no attempt to enroll or register him that night. He was placed in a guarded suite, in a guarded dorm, on a guarded part of the campus. No one would officially confirm his presence there, leaving Claude Sitton with a hole in his story on deadline. Sitton quickly tapped into the quaint and reliable network he had inherited from Johnny Popham. He called an Oxford woman who was an old college friend of Popham's wife. The woman, Dutch Silver, was plugged in; she worked in the office of the dean of women, and she was the wife of the outspoken and controversial Ole Miss faculty member James Silver, who made it his business to know what was going on. Based on Dutch Silver's reporting, Sitton confirmed to the *Times* that Meredith was on campus, then headed for the school himself.[57]

The feds had turned the university's administration building, the white-columned Lyceum Building, into the headquarters of their military operations. There was a distinctive Old South beauty to the Lyceum, and to the lush grounds around it. Especially lovely was the expansive tree-lined oval in front, known as the Mall.

But on this day, as tension mounted, the Lyceum was surrounded by a hodgepodge of undermanned, ill-prepared federal law enforcement officers made up of deputy marshals, border patrolmen, and federal prison guards. The building they guarded had served in the Civil War as a hospital; it would serve that purpose again that night.

Sheriffs, their deputies, and highway patrolmen came to the campus from around the state, but there was no expectation that they would back up the feds. Charles Moore had caught that message a few days earlier in perhaps the most dramatic photo to come out of the buildup. He had framed a cluster of white men laughing as one of them, a cigarette clinched tightly between his teeth, appeared to demonstrate a hard, two-handed whacking motion with a billy club he gripped so tightly it seemed sewn to his hand. Beside him, a hard-looking man with a crew cut and a dangling cigarette was wrapping gauze around his arm, creating an identifying armband. Against the stereotype of what frontline segregationist street fighters look like, these men were wearing ties, coats, white shirts, and hats. Closer examination revealed that they were wearing badges. They were sheriffs from six counties, and one deputy.[58]

Police were supposed to keep all but students, faculty, and employees off the campus; for a while they mostly succeeded. During that time, journalists got in any way they could. Moore put all his equipment into the front hatch of a Volkswagen Beetle, then rode as a passenger with an earnest-looking student who convinced police that Moore was a researcher on campus. *Life* magazine contract photographer Flip Schulke got a professor to drive him onto campus—folded into the car's trunk.[59]

Soon the sheer number of outsiders coming onto the campus became too much for police, and they let down all barriers. Clusters of hostile white men who had driven from Louisiana, Alabama, Tennessee, and Arkansas streamed onto the university grounds; the growing mob soon approached 2,500 noisy, angry people who came ready to fight. Chanting, yelling, firing bullets and pellets, throwing bottles, sticks and cans, the mob seemed capable of overpowering the federal forces. Before the night was over, state and local law officers would quietly slip away from the campus, abandoning their positions and their public trust, leaving the feds to fend for themselves.

Reporters went through a protective ritual as the hostility began boiling and spilling everywhere. Walking among the mob, trying to look inconspicuous, Michael Dorman, writing for *Newsday,* spied his friend from years gone by, Bob Carpenter, with whom he had worked for the *Houston Press.* Carpenter was now reporting for Hodding Carter's *Delta Democrat-Times.* Dorman, not wanting to bring attention to himself or Carpenter, suppressed the instinct to show familiarity with the other newsman. But as the evening went on, the reporters felt more secure clumping together, but away from cameramen. The bravado with which segregationist youths had paraded in front of cameras five years earlier in Little Rock had now become an infuriated recognition of the tool's power to expose. Dorman saw a crowd rushing toward a bright light that had suddenly come on, signifying the presence of a newsreel cameraman. Moments later, he heard the sound of shattering glass as a camera was smashed to the ground.

The mob then turned on a Dallas cameraman, Gordon Yoder of Telenews. Yoder had seen Autherine Lucy's brief walk through hell, then covered Little Rock, so he felt experienced in street warfare. He had even brought along his new wife. "That guy's a goddam reporter. Let's kill him," one student yelled as the mob swarmed him. He was taking a good beating but flailing back and holding on to his camera. Dorman, who had worked in Houston with Yoder as well, tried to get inside the knot and pull Yoder free but was blocked by a dozen members of the mob. Two highway patrolmen suddenly appeared, excavated Yoder, and led him toward his station wagon, where his wife had been waiting anxiously. He had hardly sat beside her in the car before it was surrounded by a even larger surge of rioters, who jumped on the hood, climbed on the top, banged out the headlights, kicked the sides, then smashed the windshield and each of the other windows, one by one. Some rioters began reaching inside and punching Yoder, while others began rocking the car, trying to flip it. Dorman, unable to help his friend, saw a Mississippi police officer, in uniform, lend a shoulder to the effort. After watching the action and not responding, two highway patrolmen came upon Yoder's tilted car and helped him and his wife slide out and get away, without his camera or film.

Charles Moore, Flip Schulke, and other still photographers drew slightly less attention, though their silhouetted work that night shows how painstakingly they tried to use the light of fires and flares, not electronic flashes, to illuminate the darkness. Short of war, conditions could not have been much worse. To shoot without a gas mask was to risk an inability to function at all; to shoot with it was to risk missing the picture. What was worse, Moore had left his flash and all but five rolls of film in a car he could not now reach. Five rolls of film on a night like this was like having a single strip of beef jerky to cross the Mojave. Moore could have used twenty-five, thirty, maybe forty rolls that night. He stayed mostly in the Lyceum, catching the ugly scene of the wounded and wasted, while Schulke worked outside most of the time.

As the madness was building about 7 p.m., Ross Barnett invited a few reporters to the back door of the Governor's Mansion in Jackson. There was a desultory mood among Barnett's aides when the reporters arrived and stood on the steps. Reaching through the door, the aides handed out Barnett's statement, his concession. It said that Mississippi was "surrounded on all sides by the armed forces" and "physically overpowered." The six-paragraph statement added, "My heart still says 'Never,' but my calm judgment abhors the bloodshed that would follow."[60]

Barnett's aides, bitter at the outcome, wouldn't let the reporters inside. When the dean of the press corps, the Memphis *Commercial Appeal*'s Ken Toler, took a step up to a landing, one of the governor's men shoved him off. "It's over," Barnett said. "We've traded." Then he added, "I was forced into this." He would have more to say four hours later.[61]

Nothing in the statement caused the mob to draw back. The attacks only intensified. The crowd was grabbing everything it could to throw, spray, or shoot. Marshals were taking a severe beating. One was hit by a large piece of concrete right in the face. One man grabbed a fire extinguisher and sprayed a military driver in the face. Gasoline-filled bottle bombs were fixed up with fuses, lighted, and hurled at army trucks in an attempt to ignite them. Then pieces of metal pipe began flying through the air; one slammed into a marshal's helmet, making an inch-deep impression. A bottle of acid hit another marshal.[62]

Former Major General Edwin Walker, who had led the federal troops at Little Rock, showed up, drawing an entourage. He had left the army a year earlier after being disciplined for trying to indoctrinate his troops with far-right ideology and conspiracy theories. The mere announcement that he would be on campus had drawn many men from as far away as Texas. His presence, his implorings, "Protest! Protest! Keep it up!" had an accelerant effect on the mob.[63]

The Justice Department, which had not arranged to have first aid equipment at the Lyceum and was unprepared in about every way for the guerrilla warfare, wasn't saying much. The reporters were getting restless. What was happening? Who was in control? Wasn't there an agreement to keep the campus secure and protect lives? Did the department know what it was doing? At the same time, when the only hope the reporters had for getting out of the situation alive was the federal presence, they seemed willing to defer negative assessments.

In Washington, President Kennedy prepared to go on national television to address the nation about his decision to use federal forces on the campus, to announce that Meredith was in a dormitory, and to say that his discussions with Barnett had produced a peaceful solution. But conditions outside the Lyceum were worsening, and the number of wounded marshals splayed across the floor of the building was evidence.

Inside the Lyceum, *Newsday*'s Michael Dorman surveyed the fallen. A marshal from Indianapolis had gotten shot in the throat; blood spurted with the rhythm of his beating heart, and his condition deteriorated as he lost blood. The Lyceum was not equipped to provide medical care. The best anyone could do for the marshal was to position his hands over his throat to stanch the flow. Communications were limited to a few shortwave radios and four phone booths that were kept open to Robert Kennedy's office or turned over to wire services. Calls for help transporting the wounded out would have been to no avail, anyway; it was nearly impossible to drive to or from the Lyceum without grave risk.

The chief marshal, James McShane, decided that his people could not take any more abuse, that he was cornered and without options. They would have to defend themselves. "Gas!" he shouted at 7:50 p.m., when he'd reached his decision. In the seven minutes it took federal officers to don their masks and prepare to launch tear gas, the rioters showed no fear or hesitation.

"Fire!" McShane ordered at 7:57 p.m. Gas launchers sent cartridges rocketing into the mobs, creating an acrid, gagging fog bank that made everyone sick and miserable but did nothing to stem the rioting.

For all his planning, Claude Sitton could not get access to a phone on campus to update his story. He would have to slip away from campus, leave his rental car, and head on foot to his room at the Ole Miss Motel. He gave his car keys to Fred Powledge and asked him to bring the car to the motel at a pause in the rioting. Soon Powledge raced to the car undetected and got inside. He turned the ignition a notch to permit the radio to come on without the sound of the engine turning over. He heard the voice of President Kennedy announcing that Meredith was on campus and describing a negotiated solution in Oxford, a picture of peace that in no way matched what Powledge saw beyond the dashboard. Robert Kennedy had gotten word of the tear gas only moments before President Kennedy went on the air and had not had a chance to tell him the bad news.[64]

Paul Guihard and Sammy Schulman of Agence France Presse were pulling into Oxford from Jackson when they heard Kennedy's speech. "Oh, hell, the story's all over," Guihard told the photographer. "But we might as well go and clean it up." A few minutes later, they walked on campus and realized the riot was in full swing. Rioters had grabbed a water hose and were combating tear gas with it, until the marshals pulled out pistols and shot holes in the hose. As Schulman, bandoliered with cameras, realized that he might attract danger on campus, he and Guihard decided to go different ways and to meet again in an hour. Schulman saw Guihard walk toward the surging mob and become absorbed in it.[65]

A few minutes later, Clark Porteous of the *Memphis Press-Scimitar* ran into Guihard. As a child in New Orleans, Porteous had spoken French before he spoke English, and he found it delightful that in the middle of all this madness he could stand with this husky, red-bearded journalist and converse in French. Guihard then moved back into the crowd again. When he was found a couple of hours later, he was far from the Lyceum, in a remote area of the campus, between a women's dorm and the fine arts center. He was on the ground, dead, with a single bullet hole in his back and gunpowder stains showing that he'd been shot at close range, probably executed.[66]

Newsweek had decided to supplement its coverage with one of its star writers from New York, Peter Goldman. Karl Fleming picked Goldman up at the airport that evening and raced to the campus, only to find it enveloped in a low, dense cloud of gas. Within seconds of setting foot on campus they could see hell unfolding before them: four green Plymouths, each with five marshals in it, managing to get from one place to another on campus only by stomping on their accelerators and hurtling through the mobs, hoping to outrun the missiles thrown at them. Choking and blinded themselves, the *Newsweek* team staggered into a university building that housed the chemistry and pharmacy departments.[67]

Inside the building, they found two young radio newsmen from Memphis who had managed to find a pay phone and begin direct broadcasts to stations in Memphis, Chicago, Boston, Atlanta, and Baltimore. One would run out and do reporting while the other would hold the phone line open. While they fed reports to the world, they could hear rioters outside rocking their new mobile unit, a Ford panel truck. "Turn it over . . . turn it over!" the rioters yelled. Minutes later, the radio newsmen saw the truck virtually vaporize in a ball of flames.

Fleming and Goldman found a classroom that offered a panoramic view of the Mall, though their view was frequently obscured by the thick shroud of gas. In time, the gas began permeating the windows. Rioters, carrying sticks and black rubber hoses, began breaking into the building and its laboratories, looking for soda bottles that could be fashioned into Molotov cocktails and chemicals that could be turned into weapons. The newsmen's nest was no longer safe. If the rioters learned they were reporters, they would likely be beaten. They would have to get out. One set of doors to the outside was locked. Another was controlled by the mob. The newsmen retreated to a darkened classroom, where they were able to yell out a window and get the attention of a marshal.

"Listen, we're newsmen and we want out of here!" one of the radio reporters yelled.

"Okay," the marshal said. "Jump!"

The newsmen clambered out the window, dropped several feet to the ground, and raced to the Lyceum.

There, Fleming saw a gruesome scene: Bloodstains on the floor. Bandaged marshals lying exhausted on the floor. Dazed newsmen gagging and throwing up. Overwhelmed, the federal forces fought with the only weapon they were allowed to use, the gas, and were constantly running out of it before new supplies arrived. The battle went on all night with little respite and no resolution. Under direct pressure from President Kennedy, Governor Barnett agreed to call Highway Patrol units back to campus but then didn't. The Justice Department called in sixty National Guardsmen, but they had only fifteen bayonets and two hours of riot control training. Orders had been issued for army troops stationed in Memphis to fly and drive into Oxford, but they would be delayed in departing well over an hour.

Brave appeals for peace failed, one after the other. The local commander of the National Guard, Murray Falkner, tried. A prominent football player tried. A young Episcopalian rector, Duncan Gray, courageously ran up to Walker as he was leading a group of ruffians and pleaded with the general to stop. Then he urged them all to go home. Walker issued an insulting remark and pushed past Gray. Only the governor, and perhaps not even he, could prevail on the mob to shut down and go home.

In Jackson, Barnett met with advisers, including Dick Morphew, the television journalist who hosted the Citizens' Councils' television program on WLBT. Barnett was pressed to say something to the people of Mississippi, and he did, in an 11 p.m. radio message. The assumption was that he would use his popularity to turn off the flame and call for an end to the violence, but he didn't. "Some reports are interpreting my statement tonight as altering my stand. This is positively untrue and wholly unfounded," he said. "My friends, I report to the people of Mississippi now: I will never yield an inch in my determination to win the fight we are engaged in. I call upon every Mississippian to keep his faith and his courage. We will never surrender." Barnett misrepresented the truth, then threw fuel on the fire. Any hope of peace coming to the campus blew up instantly. Soon rioters commandeered a bulldozer from a construction site, set its gears, aimed it for the Lyceum, pinned its accelerator, and jumped off—only to watch it stall. The youthful student rioters of earlier in the evening were being replaced by an older, tougher set.

Pressed by deadlines, most newsmen had to leave the campus to use their motel phones to file their stories. But even that was no guarantee. There was not a direct-dial phone system; you picked up the phone and waited for the operator to come on and ask for the number you wanted to dial, then place it for you. All long-distance calls from Oxford were being handled by only sixteen operators, which meant long waits. Some reporters would finish dictating, then try to get their newspapers to patch them in to papers in other cities so their colleagues could file without having to get another phone line. For the platoons of wire service reporters on campus, the demand for updates was constant. Associated Press used a couple of staffers in their twenties, who were able to mingle with the students. One who couldn't, Bill Crider, an AP veteran from New Orleans, ventured from the Lyceum at one point to see firsthand the assault on the marshals. A tear gas canister landed in a bush near him, blinding him temporarily. As he walked fast to get away, the tall, muscular newsman was hit in the center of his back by pellets so powerful he was knocked flat on his face. Pencil and notepad still in hand, he got up, walked into the Lyceum in his blood-soaked shirt, and headed straight to the phone booth to file his notes before seeking medical attention. His colleagues were so impressed that they stood around him as he dictated and fed him the kind of lifeblood transfusion only a wire service reporter can appreciate: their notes. Justice Department officials had finally gotten an Oxford doctor into the building, but he had more cases than time. Each time he would start digging pellets out of Crider's back, a more serious case would stumble into the building. The doctor would go to the new victim, and Crider would return to the phones.[68]

A short while later, Ray Gunter, twenty-three, a jukebox repairman from a nearby town, came to campus out of curiosity. He was not a rioter and not involved in the issue at all. He and some friends were there to see the phenomenon unfold. Suddenly a stray .38-caliber bullet slammed into his forehead. He died on the way to the hospital.

Soon after 1 a.m., Karl Fleming borrowed a gas mask to step outside the Lyceum. Standing in front of a door frame behind one of the Lyceum's columns, he watched rioters set fire to two cars, then heard three consecutive loud, sharp reports, followed instantly by little *zings* that whipped past him. Then he felt flakes of something falling on his head and back. He turned around and saw, at eye level, three bullet holes. He was first impressed, then scared to death.[69]

That Sunday evening and Monday morning produced a siege that frightened the most experienced, hard-boiled newsmen. "Little Rock was a skirmish, Oxford a war," Associated Press's Relman Morin would later conclude. To a generation of reporters who would be covering the movement for years to come, the Ole Miss story was emotional in a way that many had never experienced. Reporters who did not have much time to think that night found they nonetheless had time to feel. The whole episode, the sense of everything spinning out of control, of leadership gone awry, of a civilized people at war over basic rights, of danger, felt awful. Al Kuettner, an experienced UPI reporter, stood that night in the midst of the gas, the fire, the noise, the gunshots, the fear. He was exhausted. His throat was raw. His red-rimmed eyes, virtually immersed in tear gas, had been running for hours. He was overcome by the realization that he was watching an insurrection. All his career he had been trained to be detached from the story, but he was having a difficult time of it now. He was part of the tableau. It was a powerful feeling and an awful one. He sat, and then he wept. And then he realized it wasn't because of the tear gas.[70]

At 1 a.m., after long delays, two hundred military policemen from Memphis arrived in Oxford and went to the campus. An hour later, a much larger display of military force, which would reach 13,000 soldiers, rolled onto campus and began taking control. They evacuated the wounded from the Lyceum and, amid sniper fire, waded into the mobs and began arresting people; the number would reach three hundred, only a third of them Ole Miss students. Half the marshals were wounded.

By 7:30 a.m., James Meredith, having slept through most of the riot, was sitting inside the Ole Miss registrar's office, filling out the forms to gain entry.

At 8 o'clock, in Jackson, a prominent businessman, himself a staunch segregationist and president of Lamar Life, the insurance company that owned WLBT-TV, took an unusual step to get the governor's attention. William H. Mounger walked into the studio, asked for time on the air, and broadcast an appeal for an end to the violence. He didn't disagree with the governor's goal of testing the state's rights, Mounger said, but it had to be handled legally and peaceably. He scolded Mississippi leaders for "failing to stand up and express themselves" against violence. He urged Barnett to go to Oxford. "The governor is the only person who can stop the violence," Mounger said. It was the first public call for an end to the violence, and it backfired. Shortly after his broadcast, Mounger was fired as president of Lamar Life, an ouster widely interpreted to have been provoked by his lecture.[71]

Back in Oxford, as Mounger was finishing, so was Meredith. The Justice Department's information chief, Edwin Guthman, stuck his head out the door and told bleary-eyed reporters, "He's registered." Then Meredith, heavily guarded, headed off to his first class.

While the white reporters for the mainstream press were writing their follow-ups, analyses, and wrap-ups, Moses Newson and other black reporters were finally able to come onto the campus and begin their reporting. "That Boy Is Delivering Us Here in Mississippi," read the eight-column headline in the *Baltimore Afro-American.* The newspaper carried a photograph that showed Newson on campus, holding a Speed Graphic camera and standing among a group of relaxed black soldiers. The photo, whose caption said the soldiers would not be identified "for fear of reprisals," was intended to showcase the paper's presence on such hallowed ground at such a monumental time. But everyone there knew that the black press had been pushed off the story and had missed it.[72]

On the morning after the all-night riot, October 1, *The New York Times* presented an extraordinary array of stories, including details filed into the main news story as late as 1 a.m., when the military forces began arriving. In all, there were twenty-eight articles spread over page one, three full inside pages, and part of another page in the front section. Sitton, Anthony Lewis, and Peter Kihss were on page one, plus full texts of every statement by President Kennedy and Governor Barnett, a profile of the state of Mississippi, and another on Oxford. There was a "man in the news" feature about Robert F. Kennedy and a short piece on Guihard. One story described the history of President Kennedy's authority to call in the troops, and another discussed the Little Rock experience. The television critic wrote about the uncertainty at the networks as President Kennedy had made and withdrew plans to deliver an address, only to ask for the time again. Other articles related to Meredith's enrollment bore datelines from Memphis, Moscow, Hartford, and Jackson and Abbeville, Mississippi.

The next day, there were even more pieces in the *Times,* including five on the front page, as reporters followed Meredith's first day on campus, the arrest of General Walker, and the charges and countercharges over who was responsible for the violence. There was a damage report from Oxford; a court hearing in New Orleans; coverage of the Southern Governors' Conference; a "man in the news" profile of the commander of federal forces in Oxford; analyses of the political impact on Kennedy and on the Republicans; several small stories providing domestic and foreign reactions; and texts of statements by Robert Kennedy, Barnett, and Senator James Eastland.

Life magazine did not make Meredith its cover; that went to a special on Pope John XXIII. But it did devote thirteen full pages to Ole Miss. Charles Moore, on his first assignment for *Life,* made a strong impression. The magazine ended up using six of his photos. The picture of the Mississippi law-men having a laugh as one of them grips a billy club was spread over two pages. His images of Bill Crider's bleeding back and a marshal throwing up after inhaling tear gas were each given a full page. The magazine sent him a $500 bonus for his powerful work.

The Saturday Evening Post, which had a much smaller presence on campus, scored a coup of its own. Trying to figure a way to beat *Life* but without relying on photographs, its new assistant managing editor, Bill Emerson, went for a scoop. When reporters who went through authorities to interview Meredith were turned away, Emerson sent Meredith a letter proposing the story in his own words. Meredith agreed. Emerson got the writer Robert Massie to interview Meredith at length and, using Meredith's words, write the story in the first person. The *Post* had Meredith walking on campus in a coat and tie, beneath a headline on its exclusive story by James Meredith: "My Ordeal in Oxford."

In *Newsweek,* Karl Fleming reflected in a personal way on the emotional impact of Ole Miss on a southern-born correspondent. "It was the first assignment I've ever had where I was actually afraid for my life," he wrote. "It hurt to realize these were people from your own culture doing this."[73]

Most of the reporters carried assessments of blame in their papers of October 2 and 3. *The New York Times* played, on the front-page, stories in which the federal government blamed Barnett for the riot and in which Barnett blamed the federal marshals, but it gave slightly greater prominence to the government's claim. *The Clarion-Ledger* devoted virtually its entire front page to blaming Washington, including a three-column headline that declared, "Marshals Set Off Ole Miss Rioting."

NBC's Richard Valeriani concluded that Barnett was more responsible than the federal government and said so in a subsequent report. While his cameraman scanned images of billowing tear gas, smoke, fire, wounded flesh, military operations, and charred hulks of cars, Valeriani said in a voice-over, "Irresponsible defiance in the governor's office was translated into violence on the campus . . ."[74]

In the evening after Meredith enrolled and attended class, NBC aired a special report on the crisis. In a live interview by newsman David Brinkley, Robert F. Kennedy said that the previous night had been his worst ever because he'd asked marshals to hold their fire while being fired on. States, he said, can't pick and choose which laws they'll obey, any more than citizens can legally decide to quit paying income taxes just because they dislike them. He decried the lack of leadership in the state. The reason Georgia had been able to desegregate its university without problems, he said, had been leadership from politicians and the press, namely *Atlanta Constitution* editor Ralph McGill. The show, anchored by Frank McGee, then segued to McGill himself, interviewed live in Washington by Vanocur. McGill was more pointed in scolding the Jackson newspapers for letting the governor and the political power structure set, virtually without limitation, such an oppressive and oppositional tone. And he scoffed at the notion of state sovereignty. No such thing, he said. Mississippi was part of the United States.[75]

Overall, the press coverage was remarkably deferential to the Kennedys and the feds, especially given the poor planning and execution on that Sunday night, the order to launch tear gas without telling the president, the placement of only a small law enforcement contingent, the absence of medical equipment, the pathetic communications systems, and Justice's inability to get the military units in Memphis to respond immediately. There seemed to be an assumption that whatever mistakes the federal government made were made only in pursuit of a just and righteous cause and in dazed reaction to a defiant state that had sucker-punched the feds.

Besides, there wasn't much time to think about it. A much bigger plan was being hatched in Birmingham. And the race reporters, the veterans as well as the new generation who had their baptism in the race beat at Oxford, were cordially invited—except, it appeared, *The New York Times.*

CHAPTER 18

WALLACE AND KING

Month after month, Claude Sitton stewed over the decision of the *Times'* lawyers to keep him out of Alabama. He had slipped into the state once with their permission and once without, but now the yoke had tightened. He was missing big stories and was about to get shut out of covering an important governor's race there.

Then, in March 1962, federal judge Hobart Grooms followed the orders of the Fifth U.S. Circuit Court of Appeals and reversed himself in the Harrison Salisbury case. He issued a fresh ruling that since the *Times* was printed in New York, the case could not be brought in Alabama. He then dismissed all seven libel cases that stemmed from Salisbury's story in the *Times* about Birmingham. McGill, who had persuaded the Atlanta papers to file briefs on behalf of the *Times,* sent Turner Catledge congratulations and an ominous assessment: "Alabama situation remains preposterously committed to the most extreme and impossible defiance."[1]

Catledge, in response, flashed momentary bitterness at his ASNE colleagues, who had gotten weak-kneed about backing the *Times.* "But as one newspaperman—and between you and me—I thought our noble profession as a whole acted with singular and eloquent disinterest. Some of our publisher friends seem to want to avoid looking at the facts for fear they will be frightened. Also, they seem to take the attitude of 'Let *The New York Times* go ahead and pay; it has the money.' "[2]

Almost a month later, in April 1962, the *Times'* lawyers were still calling the shots, to the great consternation of the newsroom. Clifton Daniel, representing Catledge, attended a high-level meeting that included the publisher, Orvil Dryfoos; the counsel, Louis Loeb; and the general manager, Amory Bradford. The lawyers warned that sending any reporter to Alabama would be "a grave risk."[3]

Besides, they said, the gubernatorial election was months away, and Governor John Patterson, whom they suspected was helping pay for the litigation against the *Times,* was not seeking reelection. The lawyers expected that a man less likely to continue the war against the *Times,* a former governor, "Kissin' Jim" Folsom, would replace Patterson. Folsom's opponent was George C. Wallace, a little-known judge never elected statewide, who had launched his campaign by pledging to defy school desegregation orders "even to the point of standing in the schoolhouse door, if necessary."[4]

As Daniel tried to argue for sending reporters into the state, he could see that the *Times'* lawyers were not budging and that he was outnumbered. The two attorneys—Bradford and his deputy, Bancroft—lined up against sending in reporters. Dryfoos was trying to work out an accommodation. How about contracting with another newspaper, perhaps *The Atlanta Constitution,* to purchase its coverage from Alabama? That would offer some protection, the lawyers said, but any representative of the *Times* might be served the summons that they so desperately wanted to avoid.

Daniel said that relying on another newspaper ran contrary to the whole point of what the *Times* had been doing for fifteen years. This was the *Times'* story. The *Times* was setting the pace, maybe the agenda, and the national desk had had enough experience depending on wire services to know that it was not very satisfactory. But, Daniel admitted, he had no practical proposals for overcoming the lawyers' objections. The newsroom would remain bound by its legal advice and just do the best it could.[5]

Upon leaving the meeting, Daniel reduced the discussion to two terse sentences that went to his top national editors and Salisbury. It was the lawyers' "very strong recommendation that we do *not* send any members of our staff to Alabama at this time. If there seems to be urgent need to send a reporter into the state, please do not take any action without the most exhaustive consultation."[6]

Seven more months would pass before Sitton would return to Alabama. During that time Birmingham would close its city parks to everyone, rather than see Negroes and whites stroll through them on the same path or play on the same fields. Business and civic leaders would develop a plan for ousting Bull Connor as the commissioner in charge of police by replacing the commissioner system with a mayor-council system. Whites would dig their heels in even deeper against school and lunch counter desegregation.

Most important, a new governor was elected without any coverage by Sitton or any *Times* reporter, and he was not the candidate the *Times'* lawyers had anticipated. Sitton would finally get to Alabama in time to see George Wallace set the stage for years to come.

Two weeks after the nation's centennial of the Emancipation Proclamation, Wallace took his oath and delivered a stem-winder that signaled his intention to hold the line that Orval Faubus, Jimmie Davis, and Ross Barnett had been forced to concede.

Noting that he was standing where Jefferson Davis had become president of the Confederacy, Wallace paid tribute to "the great Anglo-Saxon Southland" and decried "the tyranny that clanks its chains upon the South." He then inserted words offered to him by Asa Carter, an Alabama Klansman and Citizens' Council leader: "In the name of the greatest people that have ever trod this earth," he declared, "I draw the line in the dust and toss the gauntlet before the feet of tyranny. And I say: Segregation now! Segregation tomorrow! Segregation forever!"[7]

The architecture of Wallace's words may have seemed overwrought and melodramatic outside the South. His declaration may have even seemed a bit anachronistic in the border states, which had emerged intact from their own initial experiences with integration. In most of the region, southerners, while still unable to fathom what an integrated society would look like, could begin to see that institutionalized, state-mandated segregation would not be allowed to continue forever.

Even in the Mid-South states, Wallace's speech had the ring of a lone bell tolling: of the five southern governors who gave inaugural addresses in the first month of 1963, two signaled a moderate position on race and two, including Faubus, did not mention segregation at all.[8] Even in South Carolina, the only state to have taken no steps whatsoever toward school integration, Wallace's words seemed off key. Two days after Wallace spoke, when a federal appeals court ordered Clemson University to admit a Negro, Harvey Gantt, the state seemed surprisingly disposed to let it happen. "There isn't much fight in South Carolina today," the Charleston editor Tom Waring wrote Bill Simmons at the Citizens' Councils a few days later. He sounded apologetic that his state was not rising up against Gantt as Mississippi had against Meredith. In a second letter to Simmons, Waring went further, rationalizing Gantt's peaceful admission: "While I know you regard the latter as a sign of weakness, we are giving this gambit a whirl to try for size in the hope that explosions now making up in the Northern ghettos will take the liberal's mind off the South."[9]

But where Wallace hit home was at ground zero of resistance, at the core of the Deep South, in Alabama and Mississippi. If anyone doubted the resolve of those at the core to delay, postpone, resist, even to kill, the force and clarity of Wallace's declaration settled the issue. Wallace, by virtually every angle of news coverage, seemed comfortable leading the charge. He was good copy and camera ready. Reporters were drawn to him like biologists are drawn to the unexpected emergence of an old virus they believed had been exterminated.

In Tuscaloosa, the editor Buford Boone looked on Wallace's ascension to the front page with dismay. Seven long years had passed since Autherine Lucy had walked onto the University of Alabama campus, only to be run off, yet the state was as combustible as ever. Boone, who had gone nose to nose with the Citizens' Council back then and whose plainspoken editorials had won a Pulitzer Prize in 1957, chose this time to express his concerns privately to Wallace. "I have feared, and I still fear, that inciting statements will encourage people to violence because they think it is expected of them," he wrote the governor. "You are going to lose, as John Brown did, as Lee did, as Barnett did. But are you going to lose with dignity, with intelligent courage and with proper regard for the long-range welfare of our people in Alabama? Or, are you going to take the low road and work the situation for all it is worth in current popular support and with too little thought of the tomorrows that always come?"[10]

Even as Wallace spoke, the largest city in his state, Birmingham, was quietly being targeted for a confrontation by King and the SCLC. For months, Reverend Fred Shuttlesworth, who was Birmingham's most aggressive and dynamic force for racial change, had pressed King and the SCLC to put the failure of Albany behind them by picking their next fight in Birmingham. Shuttlesworth had seen how easy it was to get segregationist forces in Birmingham to respond violently to peaceful but provocative demonstrations.

Shuttlesworth felt certain that Bull Connor, who so delighted in his own nickname that his official letterhead as police commissioner identified him by it, would play the brutal antagonist role that Laurie Pritchett in Albany had resisted. Few white men in authority had a hair-trigger temper like Connor's, and Shuttlesworth predicted that King would get the confrontation and the news coverage he wanted, if he came to Birmingham.[11]

Shuttlesworth led his own civil rights organization, the Alabama Christian Movement for Human Rights (ACMHR), and its biggest asset: the number of people, the waves of shock troops, it could promise. Shuttlesworth said he could deliver as many people as King needed to fill the streets and jails of Birmingham in a sustained campaign of boycotts, demonstrations, and marches. What's more, ACMHR had this strategic advantage: other than a couple of Bull Connor spies, nobody in authority really knew about or believed in the energy, depth, and determination of the ACMHR. The daily newspapers cast Shuttlesworth as a hothead and his organization as infiltrated by Communists; they had no reports or awareness that it might also be an effective organization.

But Shuttlesworth could operate without the white papers; he had every reason to believe he could count on Emory Jackson, the editor of the Negro newspaper, the *Birmingham World,* to help mobilize Negro Birmingham.

Jackson, of course, had proved his militancy by sitting in King's planning sessions during the Montgomery bus boycott and by steering the process that had put Autherine Lucy, for two days, inside the University of Alabama.

True, Jackson, a Democrat, was having serious problems with his publishers, Atlanta's Scott family, who were committed Negro Republicans vocally opposed to King's direct action crusades. It seemed clear now that the *Birmingham World*'s editorials on politics were written in Atlanta. But the Scotts, thus far, didn't seem to be interfering in local issues.

Jackson had long been a cheerleader for the edgy, energetic Shuttlesworth, who delighted in going against the toughest official Birmingham had to offer, Bull Connor. Shuttlesworth and Jackson typically visited once a week; and they complemented each other on their clout in black Birmingham, where Jackson, although not polished, moved comfortably among middle- and upper-class Negroes, while Shuttlesworth and the AMCHR represented the larger mass of low-income Negroes.

Though concerned that the stridency of Wallace's fiery resistance to desegregation increased the likelihood that lives would be lost in an Alabama showdown, King and the SCLC listened to Shuttlesworth's urging and went forward with their plan. It was a plan built on organizing, baiting, and seeking confrontation, but it didn't contemplate having any formal media relations machinery attached to it. They had a powerful message and a powerful messenger, but little else. SCLC was friendly and open with reporters but was not spending a lot of time courting them, compiling telephone numbers of news directors, or cranking out news releases. King had an astute understanding of the power of the press but a quaint strategy for how he could make it work for him: King himself would be the media relations machinery, the magnetic draw, and Connor, they hoped, would be the foil whose actions would trigger the cameras.

As King prepared for Birmingham, one of his top aides, Andrew Young, suggested that King develop a message that could fit into a one-minute television news broadcast. National network news was still running only fifteen minutes, including commercials, so getting a minute's coverage in a worldwide roundup on *The CBS Evening News* with Walter Cronkite or *The Huntley-Brinkley Report* was considered a breakthrough. Yes, King told him, he understood, and he recited a favorite saying of the president of Morehouse College, Dr. Benjamin Mays:

> One tiny little minute,
> Just sixty seconds in it,
> I can't refuse it,
> I dare not abuse it,
> It's up to me to use it.[12]

But Young wanted more than a minute each night. Hearing that a one-minute commercial on network news cost about $100,000, he calculated that if the demonstrations could draw cameras and get three minutes of airtime on each of the three networks, the movement would be getting nearly a million dollars' worth of prime-time coverage each night.[13]

In the weeks following Wallace's speech, King sent to Birmingham his first outside organizer, Wyatt T. Walker, who worked quietly with Shuttlesworth and others to develop the strategy for a campaign that would revive the movement. This was not an outline or a sketch. It was Project C, for confrontation, a detailed plan of action that included maps, routings, and lists of financially secure white and Negro contacts who could post bail, plus fall-back strategies and code words. The timing was critical—and controversial.

Birmingham was in the heat of a citywide mayoral election that civic leaders, including the publishers of the Birmingham dailies, were hoping would push the embarrassment of Connor aside. When Connor came in second in a three-way primary and faced a runoff with the more moderate Albert Boutwell, King was persuaded that demonstrations might trigger reactionary votes for Connor and put him in office. He postponed the campaign until April 3, the day after the election, regardless of who won. The Easter season was the appropriate time to run the campaign because Negro women shopped avidly for Easter finery, making merchants more vulnerable to a boycott. There was another reason: King felt certain that Birmingham represented the resurrection of the civil rights movement.[14]

Birmingham was a competitive news town. Scripps-Howard owned the morning *Post-Herald,* and the afternoon *News,* which was larger, was part of the Newhouse chain. Journalistically, each was considerably better than either Hederman newspaper in Jackson. On the editorial page, the *Post-Herald* was more alarmed by civil rights developments than the *News* was, but both were much less strident than the Jackson papers. Other than occasional departures, such as their reaction to Harrison Salisbury's story in *The New York Times,* both papers for the most part honored the separation between news and opinion, and reporters weren't expected to reflect their publisher's interests the way reporters for *The Clarion-Ledger* and *Jackson Daily News* were.

Neither paper showed much interest in covering the Negro community, which constituted nearly 35 percent of the population. The *News* devoted less than a page each week to a section identified as "Negro news," and staff-generated stories rarely quoted Negroes or featured photographs of them—unless the subject was San Francisco Giants star Willie Mays, who had played minor-league baseball for the Birmingham Black Barons.[15]

James E. Mills, the editor of the *Post-Herald,* and C. B. Hanson, Jr., the publisher and president of the *News,* were no less concerned than the Hedermans about protecting the stability and the financial well-being of the city, and for good reason. Birmingham was a city in decline, and aware of it. Relatively close in population to Atlanta and Memphis in 1940, by 1960 it had fallen well behind them, as well as New Orleans.[16] What's more, at a time when the nation was adding jobs, Birmingham was in its fifth year of losing them. The fate of Alabama was tied strongly to its largest city: one in five Alabama residents lived in Jefferson County, of which Birmingham was the county seat, and most of the state's business and industrial leadership was based there.[17]

In Boutwell and a new mayor-council form of government, their hopes rose for a city that could fight its way back to respectability. When Boutwell defeated Connor, civic leaders celebrated. So thrilled was the *News* that it handed over to the mayor-elect the top left-hand quadrant of the newspaper's front page to deliver a message to the city's citizens. Above several paragraphs of Boutwell's platitudes, the *News* published a large color drawing of a sun rising over the city. Shortly before the Boutwell paean was to run, the *News* got word that King was coming to town. Editors discussed yanking the rising sun off the front page. In the end, they kept it. The headline atop the incoming mayor's words read, "New Day Dawns for Birmingham."[18]

Indeed it had, but not for the reasons that Boutwell—or the Birmingham newspapers—thought.

That same morning, a spirited group of about twenty-five Negroes—mostly college students and pastors—headed for lunch counters at a cafeteria, a drugstore, and two department stores, where they tried to take seats. Connor showed restraint, saying he would arrest demonstrators only if a store manager complained. At a mass meeting that night, King gave a glimpse of the cards he was holding. "If you create enough tension," he said, "you attract attention to your cause." And that, he added, was how the movement might "get to the conscience of the white man."[19]

There would be scant attention paid to the first day of demonstrations. The wires and a *Washington Post* reporter assigned to cover the election wrote in passing about the demonstrations, but the Birmingham dailies made no mention of them. The second day of activity drew no notice on the front page, though the *Birmingham News* found room there for a story showing how much money the federal government had spent to protect James Meredith at the University of Mississippi.[20] The local stories were shoved onto page two. One, with no byline, listed that morning's tally of ten arrests; the other, from AP, reported, without a touch of appreciation for the irony, that both Wallace and Shuttlesworth had complained that the Birmingham newspapers were ignoring local race news. Wallace noted that while civil rights stories from Greenwood, Oxford, and Jackson, Mississippi, and from Albany, Georgia, won page one positions in Birmingham, "there is a complete news blackout about Birmingham."[21]

Shuttlesworth echoed Wallace, his "unwilling ally" in tweaking the papers. "I hope the gentleman that prints the *Birmingham News* will get the hint. We have ceased to be page seven copy. We are front page business around here." Using the ridiculing tone for which he was known, Shuttlesworth continued, "I think Mr. George wants to come in to see what we're doing. Well, let's do a great big job so when he comes around to see what we're doing, we'll ask him to help us. Come on in, Mr. George, we're all here."[22]

In the first week, the coverage pattern stayed the same. The Birmingham dailies used their second page to give short, straight, stenographic renderings of the previous day's activities, with no explanation of why they were happening, who was behind them, or whether they had been planned or spontaneous. The newspapers missed the evolution of the movement: when the sit-ins stalled because stores shut down their lunch counters altogether, they were supplanted by marches, prayer pilgrimages, and kneel-ins at churches, each debated vigorously in Negro homes, churches, and businesses; none of those divisions was reflected in the newspapers. New strategies emerged not from the success of the prior efforts but from their failure to ignite Connor's fuse. There were large-scale arrests but little skirmishing. The story leaped to the front page when Wallace spoke or when an Alabama judge issued an injunction against the demonstrations. Other than that, the Birmingham papers maintained what *Newsweek* called "an ostrich-like stance."[23]

There were no photographs. The news stories listed the name and address of each person arrested but avoided interviewing demonstrators, resisted the use of quotes by any Negroes other than King or Shuttlesworth, and, with some exceptions, kept the headlines as dull and uninviting as possible. Occasionally, a headline writer would slip through a stinger: "Hundreds of hookey-playing demonstrators arrested here along with Negro comedian," the *Birmingham News* reported.[24]

Both papers had made a decision to downplay the story. Mills of the *Post-Herald* believed that King's grander goal was to gin up publicity and sympathy to raise money. A *Post-Herald* editorial questioned, without citing any basis for its suspicion, "how this money has been spent and how much of it has found its way into the pockets of King and his lieutenants." The next day, the *Post-Herald* did something the Jackson papers would never have done: it ran a correction, saying it had had "no information to indicate money collected to support the SCLC has been appropriated for the personal use of King or anyone else and intended no such inference." But the paper maintained its policy of keeping stories about the demonstrations bare-bones and inside the paper.[25]

Hanson of the *News* had a different motive. The *News* was somewhat more progressive. It had supported Wallace for governor in 1958, when he had presented himself as a racial moderate, but vigorously opposed him when his politics turned to race-baiting in the 1962 campaign. At one point, when Wallace said the *News* had opposed him on orders from its publisher, Samuel Newhouse, in New York, the *News* ran a front-page response: "Wallace Is a Liar." As the civil rights demonstrations began, Hanson seemed less cynical than Mills about King's motives. The *News,* editorially, took the reasons for the protests more seriously. It said that the Negro leaders "are often brilliant strategists" and refrained from calling King or Shuttlesworth anything more incendiary than "more pressing, more activist, than older, more established leadership."

But Hanson believed the civil rights forces were out of step with most of Birmingham's Negroes, and he was convinced that outside reporters, especially broadcast journalists, were providing a "warped and distorted picture" of the truth. He, too, insisted that stories of protest be kept off page one, believing that giving them more attention might trigger a combustible segregationist reaction and reduce the possibility that a peaceful settlement could be reached away from public scrutiny.[26] Behind the scenes, Hanson had his assistant publisher call the Kennedy administration's civil rights chief, Burke Marshall, and urge him to lean on King to call off the demonstrations and give the new mayor a chance. Marshall did so, conveying the attorney general's feeling that the protests were "ill timed."[27]

But even more remarkable was the way the *Birmingham World* handled the demonstrations. In the first two weeks, Emory Jackson played the stories on the front page, but not as the top news. Though the events occurred only blocks from the *World*'s door, Jackson relied heavily on UPI for his stories and carried no photographs. The articles were as antiseptic and as devoid of details, explanation, color, and passion as those run in the dailies.[28]

The demonstrations, and the entire question of how Birmingham's Negroes should seek redress of their grievances, had thrown Jackson into the middle of the two Negro Birminghams, which were split over whether direct action was appropriate: the older, more established, upper-middle-class community led by the businesspeople who wanted to give the Boutwell administration a chance to perform and who, among other things, were Jackson's advertisers; and the younger, more aggressive, less financially secure forces led by King and Shuttlesworth.

Jackson was fraught by uncertainty. He was also distracted, even distraught, by something completely unrelated: he was deeply in love with a former student of his who was married and had a family. Still a bachelor in his mid-fifties, Jackson wrote to her frequently, and she wrote back. They occasionally spent time together, sometimes with her family. In letters he wrote but didn't send, then rewrote with modulated emotion, he let her know that he wanted, more than anything else, a life with her.[29]

Now, as 1963 headed toward its dramatic apex, Jackson had become disinclined to fight. His limitations, both self-imposed and imposed by the Scott family in Atlanta, could not have come at a more problematic time for a civil rights movement that needed the unifying voice that only an advocacy newspaper could provide. Weary from all the competing demands and full of self-pity, Jackson pulled himself away from the action.

Two days after the Birmingham demonstrations began, Jackson wrote a letter to the woman. "Events crowd out experience," he typed. "There were times when some events made me happier than they do now . . . the ferment for freedom. There were those days when I could tick off a note like this one and draw the inspiration I needed. It seems that I have always been in need of an inspiration and somehow managed to find it—working in the NAACP, the struggle for civil rights and a single friendship. NAACP is no longer active and I am no longer involved in civil rights. In a way I am no longer either. But you must be . . ." He then penciled in a postscript: "Pray that I may be strong enough to be."[30]

Editorially, the *World* took a stand against direct action as "both wasteful and worthless." A week later, the *World* seemed to take a shot at Shuttlesworth, describing him, though not by name, as "the non-responsible, the non-attached, and the non–program 'leader' [who] might . . . cluster around a glossy personality and share in the reflections of his limelight without the obligation of shouldering responsibility or being held accountable."[31]

Jackson may have been under the influence of two of the city's more influential Negroes, Reverend J. L. Ware, president of the Birmingham Baptist Ministers Association; and A. G. Gaston, the most prominent Negro businessman in the city and someone who had discreetly been working with moderate white leaders to reach an accommodation that would obviate the need for King's involvement. Both Gaston and Ware were reluctant to endorse street tactics, Shuttlesworth, or anything that didn't give Boutwell a chance to prove himself. Jackson was close to both men and got a hefty amount of advertising in his paper from Gaston's enterprises.

But the tone and certitude of the editorials were not matched by the flavor of the editor's own column, "The Tip-Off," which fed Shuttlesworth's suspicion that Jackson's strings were being pulled by the Scotts. In his columns, Jackson would write about something irrelevant, such as a longtime family friend who had died in another city, or offer a tamer and more tortured criticism of the Shuttlesworth strategy. Obviously having trouble taking a firm stand in his columns, Jackson took refuge behind the claim that he was simply trying to get an honest debate going. "These ideas are expressed to inspire discussion," he wrote. "What the Tip-Off is trying to do is stimulate useful critical discussion of the idea of direct action."[32]

Jackson's private letters also reveal no antipathy for Shuttlesworth or direct action. He repeatedly refers to the civil rights forces as "the upside-down civil rights crew" and the "upside-downers" and writes that they are keeping him busy day and night. But the references were not without some affection, and there is nothing in the letters critical of the strategy or strategists.[33]

During episodes when the Scotts would seize the editorial voice of the paper, Jackson would ask them for the courtesy of a disclaimer atop the editorial, something to show the folks in Birmingham that the editorial was handed down from the Scotts. Jackson's boss in Atlanta, C. A. Scott, agreed. But it didn't happen.[34]

Given the attitude of the white dailies and the Scott family, King had no more likelihood of support from the local press than he did from the Alabama congressional delegation. He hoped his trump card would be a national, even international, press that couldn't resist the story and that could lift the story out of Birmingham and into homes and offices around the world.[35]

Movement leaders got some lucky breaks; for instance, a 114-day strike against the influential New York newspapers ended three days before the Birmingham campaign opened. Some simple strategies paid off handsomely: the SCLC decided to schedule demonstrations for the mornings to accommodate television news crews, which had to finish shooting film by 2 p.m. to make the evening news.[36]

But as Birmingham was unfolding, the national press's attention was elsewhere. In Washington, the focus was on the gathering momentum for federal civil rights legislation. President Kennedy had promised strong measures, but the Republicans were hustling to get ahead of him with concrete proposals. In the South, Claude Sitton had taken the lull in the action after Albany to explore, for the *Times*' Sunday magazine, a thoughtful explanation of why Mississippi had always resisted the tide of history. He then headed to Huntsville, where Wallace was trying to stop two highly educated Negroes, a mathematician and an electronics engineer working in the U.S. space program at the government's Redstone Arsenal, from enrolling for courses at the University of Alabama branch there.

Then on March 28, days before King was to launch his Birmingham initiative, police in the Mississippi Delta town of Greenwood deployed a technique that would become a magnet to the press and the eyes of the nation.

SNCC had been mobilizing a risky drive to register rural Negroes in the face of fresh state laws requiring that applicants' names be published in the newspaper. As a group of Negroes marched home peacefully from registering to vote, police allowed a snarling German shepherd to attack the marchers. Sitton hurried into Greenwood in time to file the story, which the *Times* played on page one. After describing how the dog had "lunged again and again at the group and seized the left ankle" of a Negro pastor, Sitton provided a chilling, straightforward description of the scene:

> A half dozen policemen and auxiliary policemen armed with nightsticks drove the other Negroes along a sidewalk in the heart of the business section until they had dispersed. White bystanders yelled at the patrolmen handling the dog, "Turn him loose!" and "Sic 'em, sic 'em."
>
> Mayor Charles E. Sampson was asked why the police had dispersed the Negroes, who were marching by twos along the sidewalk and stopping for traffic signals.
>
> "They had a report up there that them niggers was going to the Alice Cafe for a sit-in," the mayor replied.[37]

The confrontation, which was the first time anyone could recall dogs being sicced on civil rights demonstrators, produced dramatic photographs that showed the explosive potential of images. The *Times* story was accompanied by a front-page photo, credited to Associated Press, of a fallen Negro cowering beneath the angry eye of a German shepherd. Conspicuously, the headline of the story—"Police Loose Dog on Negroes' Group; Minister Is Bitten"—bumped against the adjacent headline on a Capitol Hill story about the Republicans' effort to outflank Kennedy: "Civil Rights Plan Offered by G.O.P." A photo of six Republican senators who were sponsoring the legislation was spread across four columns at the top of the page.[38]

During the Greenwood demonstrations, the SNCC leader James Forman documented the police and dog attacks with a camera. Shortly before he was arrested, Forman handed over his camera to a SNCC field secretary, who slipped away from a police officer who tried to confiscate it. Forman later saw that his photos had been distributed worldwide, a significant development that was not lost on SNCC. Though it had criticized the old-line civil rights organizations for being too preoccupied with public relations, SNCC had come to see the value of engaging in its own. Already, it had two traveling photographers on its staff, and it would soon have a photo department in Atlanta—with four photographers, a lab technician, two darkrooms, and storage space—devoted solely to the documentation that SNCC leaders hoped would get play in mainstream news.[39]

As reporters followed the dogs, the attention King had hoped would come to Birmingham went instead to the Mississippi Delta. Greenwood was filled with segregationist symbolism that worked its way into the stories of visiting reporters: It was the national headquarters of the Citizens' Councils, it was just down the road from where Emmett Till had been abducted, and it was where Governor James Vardaman had used his newspaper to demean the Negro race sixty years earlier.

At the same time, Greenwood introduced several new themes for reporters: while the coverage in other places had been about the schisms among SNCC, SCLC, and the NAACP, Greenwood was about their coalescing in common cause. The demonstrations drew celebrities, including the Negro comedian Dick Gregory, the folksinger Pete Seeger, and his boyish protégé, Bob Dylan. Gregory's sharp, sassy insults aimed at white power reflected a new fearlessness. And Greenwood became a story about revenge: the state of Mississippi, in retaliation, halted shipments of federal food surpluses to tens of thousands of its own impoverished residents, most of them Delta Negroes.

Greenwood was also fast becoming a story about terrorism and brutality, great courage and heroism. Negro businesses were firebombed, and a voting rights leader was shot as he drove himself and two others on a highway at night. Newsmen personally felt the sting of Greenwood's law enforcers. Police harassed them, seized their film, and left them seething. The next round of stories caught the flavor of a press corps unhappy about being shoved around: in *The New York Times* over the years, the Citizens' Councils had been described as advocates of states' rights and as segregationist. As long as they had insisted that they were neither racist nor white supremacist, the *Times* and most mainstream newspapers had portrayed the Councils' actions in such a way as to show them as both but had typically refrained from using those labels. In Greenwood, that began to change. Sitton, for example, wrote that the mayor was a member of the "racist Citizens' Councils" and routinely began referring to the Councils as "militantly segregationist."[40]

Birmingham was barely drawing mention in the *Times*. The first day's demonstration merited ten lines tacked to the end of a Sitton story from Greenwood.[41] Reporters visiting Birmingham were interested mostly in the mayoral contest and noted the demonstrations as a sidebar. Even those stories were not flattering to King. They questioned his timing and suggested that Albany's checkmate of him had extended into Alabama.[42]

King was indeed having trouble bringing some of the Negro clergy and business leaders around. "Wyatt, you've got to find some way to make Bull Connor tip his hand," King told his top organizer, Wyatt T. Walker.

"I haven't found the key yet," Walker responded, "but I am going to."[43]

King and Shuttlesworth decided to produce larger and lengthier marches, to get closer to City Hall to provoke Connor, and to move Shuttlesworth to the front lines—to be arrested to show that the movement was propelled by inside agitators. As Shuttlesworth and Connor, who had taunted each other for years, squared off on Birmingham's streets, reporters caught the spirit of the confrontation during one march. "Let's get this thing over with," the Associated Press reported Connor as saying. ". . . Call the wagons, sergeant. I'm hungry." Connor said he was giving the marchers one minute to disperse, then shouted down the street, "Get those damn people back. We don't want anybody else down here. Get back! We'll arrest everybody in this block if you don't get back."[44]

Overreacting to a small protest that showed little sign of getting bigger, Connor had already reached the limit of his composure. On Palm Sunday, April 7, as reporters watched, Connor sent out a pack of police dogs to growl and keep an eye on a small group of marchers. A Negro man reached out, or perhaps lunged, at a dog. By some accounts, he was slashing at the dog with a large knife; by another, he had a clay pipe. The dog retaliated, ripping at the man's arm, peeling off his sleeve, and pinning him. As the crowd rushed toward the man, police officers with other dogs joined them, swinging clubs. The use of police dogs again jumped into stories that raced across the wires: "Birmingham Police Use Dogs on Negro 'Prayer Pilgrimage,' " said the *Washington Post* headline on page three.

Wyatt Walker was jubilant. He chased down King by phone. "I've got it. I've got it," he declared. He was elated not just by Connor's use of dogs but also by some reporters' tendency to include in their total count of demonstrators the hundreds of onlookers pulled to the scene by curiosity. For SNCC's Forman, the extent to which SCLC's Birmingham gambit depended on the news coverage instantly became evident when he ran into Walker and another SCLC official, Dorothy Cotton, shortly after the confrontation. While Forman was despairing over the day's events, he saw Walker and Cotton "jumping up and down, elated." "We've got a movement," they told Forman repeatedly. "We've got a movement. We had some police brutality. They brought out the dogs. They brought out the dogs. We've got a movement!"[45]

They would have a movement, but they didn't have one yet. The dogs were quickly sent back to their kennel, and the national press continued to be drawn to other stories.

King, hoping to light a fire under the movement, got himself arrested and went to jail. President Kennedy made a call of concern to his wife, Coretta, but it did little to accelerate the engagement in Birmingham. King emerged from jail to face a discouraged movement. The SCLC leader James Bevel, who had been training high school students for demonstrations, was adamant that the movement desperately needed the energy and numbers that the young people could bring. Many Negro elders thought Bevel was going too far, but King saw the merit in Bevel's plan.

"You know, we've got to get something going," King told another Negro pastor. "The press is leaving, we've got to get going. We've got to pick up everything because the press is leaving."[46]

On Thursday, May 2, after a call to action had spread among Negro youths for two days, hundreds defied their principals' orders to stay in school. They jumped over fences and raced past a phalanx of Connor's policemen to Sixteenth Street Baptist Church, across the street from Kelly Ingram Park. The church quickly became crowded and jumpy with the energy of youth, the electricity of defiance. The first group steeled up and marched out, jubilant and in full chorus, toward City Hall. They soon waded into the arresting arms of policemen. Minutes later, a second group, laughing and singing, marched and was arrested. Then a third.

King, who had been freed from jail under strict orders to behave, remained at a hotel that day and did not see the new strategy unfold. Many national reporters were not at the park, either. *The New York Times'* Sitton and Foster Hailey and others, who were not especially confident in the ability of the SCLC to make Birmingham a flash point, had moved instead to a story about a white Baltimore postman, William Moore, who had been murdered in Attalla, Alabama, while on a one-man Freedom March for integration. As young people flowed into the park in Birmingham, many reporters were in rural Georgia covering a march that sought to retrace Moore's steps and complete his trek.

When radio reports of the burgeoning protest in Birmingham reached the reporters and photographers covering the Freedom March, they headed there, some without even calling their offices.[47] They arrived just in time. What they saw, what they wrote, what they broadcast, and, most important, what they photographed that day would have a swift and stunning impact on the American people, all the way to the White House.

Chapter 19

Defiance at Close Range

Young Negroes were streaming by the dozens out of Sixteenth Street Baptist Church and firefighters were scrambling for position when Charles Moore, the *Life* photographer, arrived at Kelly Ingram Park. In a short time, photographers would be everywhere, mostly still photojournalists standing at a distance, but also television crews. Firefighters pulled in heavy fire hoses and monitor guns that forced the power of two hoses through a single nozzle, producing a weapon that could skin bark from a tree at a hundred feet.[1]

The scene was unfolding quickly, and Moore had little time to analyze it before racing into the thick of it. He'd been in this position before. In 1958, he'd had to run backward to get the photos of King being arrested on the streets of Montgomery, and two years later, also in Montgomery, his hasty, tilted shot of a white man hitting a Negro woman with a baseball bat had gotten national exposure.

Moore could see that this was not a story to be told from afar. He wanted to get as close to the action as he could, as close as the firefighters and demonstrators themselves. He wanted to hear the noise of the chaos. He wanted his images to be felt; if the firefighters were going to use hoses, his images had to feel wet. Long lenses would miss the point. Relying on short-range, wide-angle lenses, mostly a 28 mm, Moore hunched down and waded into the crowd. He watched as a group of firefighters, leaning forward against the kick of their high-pressure hoses, aimed them at a dozen demonstrators who were sitting on a sidewalk not more than ten feet away from the nozzles, their hands clasped protectively behind their heads and necks.

Moore began shooting and moving as they opened the valves, then made his way to a position right beside the firefighters, close enough to touch them. Through his lens, he saw the straight, white laser line of water drilling into the upper back of a seated man, who pulled a woman close to shield her from the battering. Covered in a drenching mist, Moore fired away, pausing only when a piece of concrete, hurled at the firefighters from a nearby rooftop, crashed into his ankle. Badly bruised, Moore moved around the park, angling himself closer and closer to the demonstrators, close enough that he wound up in the frames that other photographers were taking from farther away, close enough to see the eyes of the demonstrators and to follow advice he'd received sixteen years earlier, when he was sixteen years old.

Moore, as a child, had been so bullied that he had enrolled in a Golden Gloves boxing program. What his trainer had told him had guided Moore's moves as a photojournalist: "By looking in my eyes, never, never blinking, never taking your eye away when I start hitting, you will know which way the lick, the blow, is coming, you'll know before it's even thrown," the trainer had said. "You'll just see that tiny, little movement and you'll be able to block it. If you move your eyes off it, I'm going to be able to keep pounding you." The other lesson: Watch your opponent's feet, and you can know his every move.[2]

By following those admonitions, Moore was able to target his camera on a scene and follow it through his lens without flinching or getting distracted. He followed a young woman as a stinging, high-pressure fusillade hit her in the back, knocked her purse from her hands, slammed her to the ground, and held her there as she screamed. He held the scene as a giant Negro man emerged from the spray to lift her with one arm and carry her to safety.

Moore was impressed how the demonstrators didn't try to run from the park even when they could have. They hid behind trees. They crouched in doorways so the water's propulsion, drilling them with a force of one hundred pounds per square inch, couldn't bounce them onto the sidewalks. But they didn't run. Then he saw a demonstrator who would become his favorite subject that day: a powerfully built, broad-shouldered Negro man who, hit by a cannonade of water, seemed determined not to let it knock him down. His legs spread for balance, the man braced in defiance of the water; his only concession was to remove his hat. As Moore clicked off shots from behind, every tensed muscle in the man's back became visible through his soaked white shirt. Moore moved closer, within a couple of feet of the man. As the man turned around, Moore caught him, a handsome face, looking back at the firefighters in stoic anger and disbelief. A small bubble of water hung, tear-like, from the man's bottom eyelid, while water dripped from his chin. His glistening hands were seeking to salvage some dignity by working his saturated hat back into shape.[3]

A short while later, as singing, smiling, nicely dressed demonstrators continued to pour from the church, Connor stood at the far end of the park and deployed another tactic. "Let those people come to the corner,

Sergeant," one journalist reported hearing the police commissioner say. "I want them to see the dogs work. Look at those niggers run."[4] Television and still photographers ran through the park toward the dogs. The television cameras found Connor and caught him scowling, his hat drawn tight over his head, his fingers jabbing in the air as he spoke to his men. NBC's cameras caught a young man pulling off his wet shirt and holding it up, like a toreador's cape, to taunt a snarling dog; then they focused on a police officer as he kicked a demonstrator in the knee, knocking him down so that a police dog could more easily maul him.[5]

At an intersection where a half-dozen German shepherds squared off with two dozen demonstrators and onlookers, Moore maneuvered within the dogs' lunging distance. He framed a handsomely dressed older man who, while crossing the street, was seized in the left pant leg by a dog that ripped the pants up to his thigh. In the next frame, the man is immobilized as the dog stands on its hind legs, straining at the leash, bearing its fangs only inches from the man's hand while a second dog comes up from behind and grabs a mouthful of the man's right buttocks. Moore's shots were remarkable not merely for giving a stark, stop-action view of the attack, but also for showing how close the demonstrators were to the dogs and how unafraid they were. Closer examination reveals something else in Moore's frames: several other photojournalists standing on the curb behind the action, some of them clearly missing the moment.[6]

Another still photographer who did get close was Bill Hudson of the Associated Press, who had enough experience with police hostility toward photojournalists that he tried to keep his cameras hidden inside his jacket. Hudson was shooting when a square-jawed police officer, his sleeves rolled up and his eyes covered by sunglasses, grabbed and held the sweater and shirt of a lanky Negro boy with his right hand while the attack dog leashed to his left hand lunged into the boy at about kidney level. The boy, fifteen-year-old Walter Gadsden, seemed passive, even limp, and stunned to find himself in the clutches of a policeman's grip and a dog's jaws. For Gadsden to become, overnight, the poster boy for King's children's crusade was ironic indeed. Gadsden was a member of the Scott family of Atlanta, owners of the *Atlanta Daily World* and the *Birmingham World* and consistent critics of King. He was there to watch, not to demonstrate.[7]

By 3 p.m., two hours after it began, the demonstrations and the police response were over. The world's reaction was just beginning. As Hudson's photo of Walter Gadsden hit the AP wire and flashed into newsrooms across the country, newspaper editors grabbed it for their front pages. At *The New York Times,* editors decided to stack up three dramatic photographs across three columns of the front page, two from Birmingham and one from the Freedom March. Hudson's shot of Gadsden was put on top. *The Washington Post* used the same picture across three columns near the top of its front page and stripped three other AP photos from Birmingham across the top of page four.[8]

At NBC studios in New York, Reuven Frank, producer of *The Huntley-Brinkley Report,* watched as the footage rolled in front of him. Frank, who separated the great stories from the mediocre by whether they provoked a "Holy smokes" reaction from him, had a loud and clear response. "Holy smokes! What are these people doing to each other?" he thought, instantly recognizing that he was watching more than moving images. He was seeing both the cause and the effect of a nation in dramatic transition, captured and disseminated with an impact that, though indisputable, could not yet be fully measured or understood.[9]

The police response and the images it produced had an instant impact in the two places where it mattered most, Birmingham and Washington. In Birmingham, Negro leaders who had been negotiating quietly with moderate whites and who had been reluctant to support King quickly fell in line behind him. The most important was Gaston, who became a convert when he watched the demonstrations from his rooftop while speaking on the phone to one of the white moderates, David Vann. Seeing monitor guns slam young Negroes to the ground, Gaston said, "But, lawyer Vann, they've turned fire hoses on a black girl, and they're rolling that little girl right in the middle of the street now. I can't talk to you." Vann would later say that "in a twinkling of an eye, the whole black community was instantaneously consolidated behind King."[10]

The images had a far more important impact in Washington. As the hoses and dogs were being deployed, the liberal Americans for Democratic Action was holding its sixteenth annual meeting at the Shoreham Hotel. For months, the ADA had been publicly critical of President Kennedy on a number of issues. Through his adviser Arthur Schlesinger, Jr., who was also an officer of the ADA, Kennedy sent out word that he wanted to meet with a group from the organization on Saturday, May 4. The day before, the group of twenty decided on a wide-ranging variety of issues and legislative proposals they wanted to discuss with Kennedy.

By the time the group had finished breakfast the next morning, they had seen that morning's *Washington Post* and *New York Times* and were so upset by the images of police dogs and fire hoses that they decided to set aside their other issues and focus their discussion solely on civil rights. When they settled into the cabinet meeting room, Kennedy made a brief presentation. Sam Zitter, the state chairman of the ADA in New Jersey, was impressed by Kennedy's grasp of the details of the broader issues important to the organization. But he was impatient to get to the more immediate problem.

Zitter held up one of the morning newspapers to show the photo of Walter Gadsden being mauled by a dog. He asked Kennedy what he was going to do about it. The president called the situation "intolerable" and described Birmingham as "the worst city in the south" in providing for Negroes. But he offered little hope:

> I mean, what law can you pass to do anything about police power in the community of Birmingham? There is nothing we can do. There is no federal law that conforms, no federal statue, no federal law we can pass. Now, the fact of the matter is that Birmingham is in worse shape than any other city in the United States, and it's been that way for a year and a half.... We're working with the press to get those papers down there, we're working with the steel companies, to try to get them to change their attitude.... I think it's terrible, the picture in the paper.[11]

In addition to misstating what the federal government could do about Birmingham, Kennedy seemed to have misjudged who was likeliest to gain advantage from the attention the confrontation was drawing. He saw Connor benefiting more than King. "Bull Connor just eats this up . . . that's just what Connor wants," Kennedy said.

Zitter, even as Kennedy tried to interrupt him, pressed the president on what "stronger role" he could play, what "moral suasion" he could use, in pressing for civil rights. Zitter felt the president needn't be fearful of repercussions from staking out a strong position for civil rights legislation.

The president, in turn, wanted the ADA to know that he also viewed the civil rights issue as urgent. "I think it is a national crisis," he said.

That afternoon, Kennedy sent Burke Marshall of the Justice Department's civil rights division to Birmingham.

The demonstrations did not have an impact on the two Birmingham dailies. They continued to keep the stories off the front page and in the first few days did not use any photographs that showed dogs or fire hoses. Their stories portrayed the policemen and firefighters as models of restraint and focused more on the injuries they had sustained than on those they had inflicted. Two days after the dogs and fire hoses were used, a Sunday, the *News* managed to put seventeen stories on the front page—including reports that the actress Carol Burnett planned to marry her producer and Sophia Loren was bedridden with a viral infection—but relegated the demonstrations to page eight. The articles moved to the front page when Wallace castigated the protesters and the press covering them, or when, in the case of the *Birmingham News,* it carried across the top the text of a telegram the publisher, Clarence Hanson, sent to Kennedy.

To see what they had not been able to witness with their own eyes, white and Negro Birmingham residents were forced to turn on network television news, where, in short but powerful black-and-white images packed into the fifteen-minute news programs, the myth of law enforcement civility and restraint was exploded.[12] The low incomes of many Negroes in the South had not proven a bar to television ownership, and not simply because television was a technology that had appeal across the racial line. Television was catapulting Negroes from low users of media to high users of media, in large part because it enabled them to view contemporary entertainment without having to suffer the ignominy of trudging up to an isolated balcony at the movie theater.

More important, home television sets gave Negroes a close-up look at the racism in their midst without having to step out into it. As the attacks on black reporters had made it increasingly impossible for them to cover civil rights encounters with their own eyes, the readers of the Negro press had lost the front-row seats their newspapers had provided in the early years of the drama. So although entertainment programs bore little resemblance to the lives of Negroes in the South, television news reflected their reality without a filter and put them back on the front row in a way that the mainstream newspapers did not.[13]

The images, both still and moving, had a monumental impact on whites that few people, other than Myrdal and King, could have predicted. For white northerners, the cameras provided incontrovertible evidence of American unfairness, inhumanity, and brutality. Any suggestion by southern whites that their Jim Crow laws and lifestyle were moral, legal, or practical, or that the South's Negroes were fundamentally happy, was demolished by the images. Even the claim that an honest dialogue with Negro leaders had a chance to move the South forward was destroyed by images that suggested the white South wasn't listening and, even if it were, couldn't hear a thing over the sound of fire hoses and barking dogs.

The images of masses of well-dressed, determined, smiling Negroes taking to the streets to demonstrate bravely and nonviolently exploded several other myths: These marchers were not the Sambos many white southerners had thought they were. These were not the lazy, unkempt, compliant, or complacent people they'd always read and heard about. Nor were they untamed, violent savages. And they were not outsiders, hotheads, pulling into the streets a rump group against the will of the more solid Negro citizens.[14]

What Americans saw was what Moore's camera found: young, emboldened Negroes openly taunting white police officers, singing and swaying while pointing their fingers sassily in the officers' faces. He found proud, smiling, fearless faces even as arrests mounted, reaching a thousand on a single day. He also found irony: a woman being arrested in front of a movie theater showing *Damn the Defiant*.[15]

The police crackdown extended to the press: as Moore shot pictures of three demonstrators pinned to the frame of a door by the power of a high-pressure hose, police arrested him and his writer, Michael Durham. Bailed out, they were advised by *Life*'s lawyers that they didn't stand a chance in Birmingham courts, they could get six months in jail, and they'd better get out of Alabama as soon as possible. Moore and Durham went to the airport, where they saw an empty police car at the front entrance. Certain that the police had been tipped off that they were jumping bail, Moore eased his rental car into a parking space, left the keys in it, and began looking for an obscure entrance to the terminal. They found it, went straight to their gate, boarded the plane for New York, and left not merely as journalists but also as fugitives. As with Sitton when the *Times*' lawyers had insisted that he stay out of Alabama, Moore had little choice. But for him, it also meant leaving his children, who lived with his ex-wife in Montgomery.[16] Moore would not be able to return to Alabama for about a year, other than one daring trip from Atlanta so he could see his children.[17]

A few days after the initial blast of live coverage, the newsweeklies came out. Birmingham had not made the cover of any of them. In fact, the *Newsweek* reporter Joe Cumming, though impressed by what he had seen, had written his editors a note urging them not to run it as a cover story. He reminded them that fire hoses had been used in New Orleans, Little Rock, and Chattanooga and that dogs had been employed in Greenwood.[18] *Newsweek* followed Cumming's advice and published little of his file. And it ran only two Associated Press photos in a two-page story. In the immediate aftermath of the dogs and hoses, the newsweeklies were not yet convinced that Birmingham represented a major turning point for the movement.[19]

That changed quickly. *Life* came out with Moore's shocking photos, and the outrage was renewed. Aside from Moore's unmatched proximity to the action, *Life*'s slick paper and large format gave the photos a vividness and sense of enormity that newspapers couldn't touch. The photo Moore had taken just before he was arrested, showing three demonstrators pinned to the frame of a door by a high-pressure hose, was blown up to the edge of the page, making it appear that the three were struggling to crawl off the page to survive. Dogs that seemed menacing but grainy in newspapers became breathtaking in *Life,* especially when Moore's series of shots showed how impossible it was to get away from them. The photos were spread over eleven pages, with Moore's byline and with headlines that did not misrepresent the significance of the Birmingham developments. What King had done was "provocation," and what Connor had done was "reprisal." The series of dog photos bore the headline "The Dogs' Attack Is Negroes' Reward."[20]

. . .

What Birmingham business and civic leaders most feared—a new round of condemnation—came raining down. Ralph McGill was in New York at the time, meeting with the same Carnegie Foundation that had sponsored Myrdal's race study, when Kelly Ingram Park turned into chaos. "In God's name, what is happening now?" McGill asked in phone calls to his office. It was not lost on McGill that one of his own nation's cities "was smoking with hate" while he was in deep talks with Carnegie officials about ways to attack global problems and tensions. He felt, he later wrote, "an occasional, near compulsive wish to break suddenly into loud despairing laughter."[21]

"Birmingham's barbarism . . . ," he wrote soon after, "highlights an inescapable conclusion: It is that the nation's single most important internal problem at this place and time in history is how we deal with minorities. To say that the security of the nation is in the final balance is no overstatement." It wasn't just about the freedom to parade in a park, he added. "The incidents of churches and places of public business practicing discrimination are a part of the pattern which religious, business and economic interests one day must bring to an end. This they must know."[22]

Two days later, in a column that criticized Birmingham's leaders and newspapers, he added, "Birmingham and Alabama are on the wrong side of the most important moral issue of this last half of the 20th Century. Neither they nor others like them can prevail."[23]

At the same time that newspapers around the world were expressing awe and praise that the Americans had put an astronaut, Gordon Cooper, into a capsule that had orbited the globe twenty-two times in thirty-four hours, they were delivering harsh words for Alabama and its largest city. Typical was the *Independent Indian Express:* "To turn high pressure hoses on peaceful demonstrators is another act of calculated barbarity which besmirches Alabama, if that state had any reputation left to be besmirched at all."[24]

The city's leaders and Martin Luther King ultimately reached a truce that represented an unmistakable victory for King. Very quickly, new desegregation efforts were launched in Jackson, Nashville, Greensboro, Raleigh, Albany, and Cambridge, Maryland. Reporters who had dismissed King as incapable of getting the movement back on its feet after Albany now acknowledged that it was sprinting. In part, perhaps, because the Black Muslim leader, Malcolm X, had emerged as a more ominous threat to white America, *Newsweek* and *Time* began portraying King more sympathetically. *Newsweek,* which had dubbed King "the integrationist field marshal" in the midst of the Birmingham campaign, now called him "the nation's best-known apostle of nonviolence." In *Time,* King was elevated to the "Negroes' inspirational leader."[25]

The Birmingham campaign turned the nation's sympathies toward the civil rights movement. Many of the journalists on the scene, and their editors, shocked by the meanness and brutality of the resistance, began admiring the courage of the movement's leaders. Charles Moore respected the point and purpose of photojournalistic objectivity, but he had concluded, through the lens, that there was a right side and a wrong side. The belief among segregationist southerners that the national press had chosen sides was underscored in early May, when the 1963 Pulitzer Prizes were announced. Once again, the prize for editorial writing went to a liberal southerner, this time to Ira B. Harkey, Jr., the editor and publisher of the Pascagoula *Chronicle* on the Mississippi Gulf Coast. Harkey was cited for his editorials favoring James Meredith's admission to Ole Miss and criticizing—ridiculing, actually—Governor Ross Barnett. Across the South, segregationist editors were not surprised. Tom Waring of *The Charleston News and Courier* wrote that Harkey had "turned against his neighbors," adding, "A Mississippi editor who is out of step with Mississippi hardly could escape an award."[26]

The day after the dogs attacked the demonstrators, Gunnar Myrdal was back in the United States, serving as honorary chairman of an Emancipation Centennial observance at Wayne State University in Detroit. *An American Dilemma* had presaged the images coming out of Birmingham and the response they provoked. Now, nearly twenty years later, Myrdal saw nothing to change his outlook. When he had written the book, he had been convinced that a majority of northern and southern whites alike, were they "brought to know the situation," were they enlightened by facts exposing the conditions of the Negro, would be prepared to give them a better deal. Now Myrdal showed little dismay at the photographs. "Without conflict," he said, "there would be no progress." He instead expressed optimism that the civil rights movement was going in the right direction and would take the nation with it, slowly. "We'd all be deluding ourselves if we thought that the American race problem will be solved before the end of this century," he said, adding that a stagnant economy would be disproportionately harsher on Negroes and delay progress.

But Myrdal felt that progress in race relations in the South would not be stopped, because southerners of goodwill did not want it stopped and because the nation, ever concerned about the image it projected around the world, would not let it be stopped.[27]

The next drama, in Tuscaloosa, would prove his point.

Even before he vowed "segregation forever," Wallace had pledged to stand in the schoolhouse door to prevent integration in Alabama's educational institutions. In 1963, Alabama, Mississippi, and South Carolina were still resisting desegregation at the elementary and high school level. Though the number of Negroes attending racially integrated public schools in the seventeen southern and border states and the District of Columbia had increased by 9,300 during the school year, most of the gains had been outside the Deep South. Overall, the presence of Negroes in biracial schools had inched upward glacially, from 7.8 percent to 7.9 percent.[28]

So when two Negro students, Vivian Malone and James Hood, sought to enroll at the University of Alabama's main campus in June 1963, and when a federal judge said the 1956 order allowing Autherine Lucy to enroll was still in effect, Wallace declared that his word was his bond.

The state of Alabama prepared for a showdown. So did *The Tuscaloosa News*'s Buford Boone. Stepping into an activist role well beyond his newspaper position, Boone had been meeting with a small group of Alabama business leaders and industrialists following Meredith's admission in Oxford to discuss how peace could be maintained when—not if—integration came to the University of Alabama. For seven years, Boone had been writing about the inevitability of integration at the university and the need for peaceful acceptance. He found his ideas gaining a foothold only after the fatal riot at Ole Miss.

Early on, Boone had brought the University of Alabama football coach, "Bear" Bryant, into the discussions. His Crimson Tide team had won the national championship in 1961, making Bryant an iconic figure as great as Wallace inside the state. Bryant supported the single, unified sentiment that law and order had to prevail, that violence had to be avoided, and that Alabama was certain to lose its fight to stop desegregation. In the fall and winter of 1962 and deep into the spring of 1963, Boone succeeded in bringing other editors, publishers, and business and industry leaders from across the state into the private discussions.[29]

Unlike in Mississippi, where editorial voices that dissented from segregationist dogma came from nationally known editors easily dismissed as reflexively liberal—Hodding Carter, Jr., and his son Hodding III, Hazel Brannon Smith, and Harkey—Alabama editors and publishers opposing orthodoxy were hardly known even inside the state. In the industrialized northwest corner of the state, home of the federally operated Tennessee Valley Authority, Louis Eckl, the editor of the *Florence Times,* wrote that racial equality was long overdue and strongly suggested that Wallace had a Christian duty to steer the state away from violence.

The Decatur Daily, also in north Alabama, urged Wallace to step back from his pledge of defiance and his "outspoken racism." The publisher was a former vice president of the state Chamber of Commerce, which was running full-page ads insisting that state officials keep order.[30] In Auburn, Neil O.

Davis kept a brave vigil against Wallace as publisher of the weekly *Lee County Bulletin* and the *Tuskegee News*. Davis had staked out a liberal position for the New Deal in the mid-1930s when he was editor of *The Plainsman,* the Auburn University student newspaper, and he hadn't wavered from it.[31]

As the uncertainty mounted, NBC News's *Meet the Press,* the best-known Sunday morning interview program, invited Wallace to be a guest on June 2. The panel of journalists facing off with him would be the host, Lawrence Spivak; Anthony Lewis of *The New York Times;* Vermont Royster, a North Carolinian and the top editor at *The Wall Street Journal;* and Frank McGee, who had catapulted to this high echelon of news visibility at NBC from his early coverage of Rosa Parks and the Montgomery bus boycott. There was widespread expectation that Wallace, once his manner and mannerisms were exposed to the klieg lights of television and the poison-tipped questions of liberal tormentors, would stumble before a skeptical nation.

Wallace asked Grover C. Hall, Jr., the editor of the *Montgomery Advertiser,* to accompany him. Between Wallace and Hall, there was mutual admiration, but they did not always fall into line. The *Advertiser* had editorially scolded Wallace on a number of issues, including his effort to close public schools in Mobile and Huntsville to avoid desegregation. Hall had tweaked Wallace on a matter of hypocrisy, comparing Wallace's interference in local affairs to the federal government's intrusion in matters of state sovereignty.[32]

At the same time, Hall sometimes seemed to adore Wallace's raw charisma and feistiness, and Hall did not mind making friends in high places. What's more, in a way he had never imagined possible, Hall was beginning to worry about his own professional future. Two months earlier, in March 1963, his beloved publisher had announced that he was selling out after sixty years with the *Advertiser,* twenty-eight of them as owner of the *Advertiser* and the *Alabama Journal.* The publisher, Richard F. Hudson, who had started at the newspaper in 1903, had been a close associate and ally of Grover C. Hall, Sr., and Hudson's son, Richard F. Hudson, Jr., had been a friend since childhood of Grover C. Hall, Jr. When the elder Hall died, the young Hall, who was close to the Hudson family, had moved into their home. When he became editor in 1947, he had envisioned a full and satisfying lifetime, he assuming his father's job as editor and his close friend, young Richard, succeeding his own father as publisher. But the junior Hudson died young, in 1959, the elder Hudson sold the paper, and Hall's perfect world was suddenly shaky.[33]

As Wallace prepared to walk into the lions' den of the most important news program on television, Hall's personal ease with the South's severest critics, and his love for skewering the Yankee press for not covering race discrimination in its own midst, made him the perfect companion.[34] The day before the program, Wallace began to fret about the questions he expected to be asked. "Those boys are going to question me about my beliefs tomorrow," he told Hall. "They're going to want to know what I think about things in this nation. And they're going to want to know about my foreign policy." Wallace, though only in his first year as governor, revealed both his internal fears and hubris. "If I'm going to run for the presidency next year I've got to have a foreign policy," he said. Wallace kept worrying until Hall tore from *The Wall Street Journal* a column about foreign policy and handed it to Wallace. "That's a perfect foreign policy," he said. Wallace read the piece several times, memorized its key elements, and put the column in his coat pocket.[35]

The next day, at the NBC studio, reporters covering Wallace were struck by the change in his demeanor as he went onto the set. Moments before, he had been jittery, seemingly shaken by stage fright and uncertainty. But as he walked into the hot lights of the set, he became the boxer he had once been, confident and self-assured. "At that moment," one of the reporters covering him would report, "the tremble left his hands and the quaver left his voice, and George C. Wallace Jr. was in total command of himself and at least partial command of his audience."[36]

Wallace handled the questions and questioners with skill. He had answers for every question, even the hard ones. Lewis, whose coverage of the Supreme Court had won him a Pulitzer Prize two months earlier and whose closeness to Attorney General Robert F. Kennedy was among the reasons he had not been promoted to chief of the *Times'* Washington bureau, asked Wallace why he was forcing an issue that had already been settled by the Supreme Court. Because the Supreme Court, which had changed its mind to get from *Plessy* to *Brown,* might do so again, Wallace replied.[37]

Wallace was a television natural. He didn't explode, snarl, or curl his lip. He said *nee-grow,* not *nigra.* He showed humor. He came off as a reasonable true believer who was operating in the fine tradition of dissent that was a birthright of the nation. As the cameras focused on him, he reached into a pocket, pulled out some notes and glasses, then read a statement criticizing the Supreme Court for having "improperly set itself up as a third house of Congress, a super legislature . . . reading into the Constitution words and implications which were never there." Franklin Roosevelt had said that in 1937, he told the panel, and "I concur with it."[38]

To questions from McGee, Wallace said he was not hoping to be arrested in the schoolhouse door and would go peacefully if he were. Any suggestion that he was intending to resist federal force was a figment of the press's imagination. "There has never been any intention to resist and fight the federal forces with force. The people of this country have been victimized by the press," he declared.[39]

Wallace effectively neutralized his questioners from the press. He was able to claim, despite prevailing evidence to the contrary, that Negro and white schools in Alabama did operate equally while remaining separate and that Negroes in Alabama were free to vote without discrimination. He got in one of Grover Hall's favorite digs: "You can't even walk in Central Park at night without fear of being raped or mugged or shot."

When the show was over and the lights went down, Wallace shook hands with the panelists and walked out with Hall. Confident that he'd done well, he lighted a cigar, then remembered the newspaper clipping Hall had given him before the show. He pulled it out, crumpled it up, and threw it away. "I don't need a foreign policy," he told Hall. "All they wanted to know about was niggers, and I'm the expert."[40]

Over the next several days, events moved swiftly toward the Tuscaloosa confrontation. A federal judge in Alabama barred Wallace from preventing Malone and Hood from enrolling, but the governor noted that he wasn't barred from being on campus. The Kennedys worked feverishly to get Wallace on the phone to defuse a showdown. Wallace declined to talk to them. The university president, Frank Rose, asked Boone and newspapermen from *The Birmingham News* and *The Huntsville Times* to meet with a university vice president and develop a strategy for cooperating with visiting reporters. The Ole Miss disaster had become legend. There had been only sixteen long-distance operators for the entire Oxford area, making reporters wait an hour just to get an open line. Getting onto and off the campus, from the story to the hotel where reporters could try to file their stories, had been difficult and risky. In Tuscaloosa, anticipating as many as three hundred reporters and photographers, the university hired a consultant, Edward Ball, a former Associated Press bureau chief in Nashville who had covered civil rights.[41]

Ball and Boone arranged for *The Tuscaloosa News* to lease to the university the building that the newspaper had recently vacated when it had moved into a more modern plant. Then Boone and Ball set about turning the old newsroom back into a fully equipped pressroom. They installed twenty telephones, newswires, Western Union Teletype operators day and night, and two darkrooms with air conditioners. The building was conveniently located a block from the hotel where many reporters were staying. Whatever inconvenience came from being off campus was overcome by the transportation arrangements Ball made for reporters to and from the campus, a system that enabled them to bypass the state troopers' checkpoint. The facility also gave Rose and the reporters a place to hold news conferences away from the heat of the campus.[42] *Publishers' Auxiliary,* one of the bibles of the newspaper industry, examined the arrangements and declared them "the most thorough and elaborate press set-up the South has seen in its chain of racial incidents."[43]

Even the police seemed to get the message. Monitoring a state police radio, the AP capital bureau reporter Rex Thomas heard a patrolman ask a top state police officer for guidance on how to manage reporters on the day of the showdown. "No shoving reporters," came the reply. "Don't push them around. Treat them courteously."[44]

Expecting to witness a revisitation of Ole Miss, reporters flew in from Japan, the Netherlands, and South Korea. Eight British newspapers sent reporters. Many of the nation's best reporters headed for Tuscaloosa. *The New York Times* sent Sitton and Hedrick Smith. *Newsweek* put Joe Cumming and Karl Fleming there; Wallace Terry joined Robert E. Baker for *The Washington Post*. Tom Yarborough of the *St. Louis Post-Dispatch* had covered civil rights in the South since the Emmett Till trial. Michael Dorman had stayed on the civil rights beat for *Newsday* since Ole Miss. *The Washington Star* and Baltimore *Sun* sent staffers, as did the Hearst Headline Service, the *Chicago Daily News, Time,* the Scripps-Howard Newspaper Alliance, and the *New York Herald Tribune.* AP assigned its deadline ace, Pat Morin.[45]

These were reporters, mostly men, who, while competitive, were bound by a sort of foxhole dependency on one another. They would gather as reporters always had, wherever food and drink were being served. From the days in 1957 when they would meet at Harry Ashmore's home, outside reporters in the hostile South had always sought solidarity and release after hours. Anything could come from such sessions.

In Clinton, Tennessee, reporters had formed a farcical Southern War Correspondents Club. They had created "official" membership cards that said "Integrated" on one side and "Segregated" on the other side, so they could flip the card to fit whatever situation they faced. Their motto: "Discretion is the better part of valor."

As the treadmill of civil rights events moved reporters from one city to the next, the members of the club would renew acquaintances and develop new, wry, and cynical ways to commemorate their role. In Oxford in 1962, two antic photographers handed out "Citation for Bravery" cards that said, "The above War Correspondent served with honor in the Reb-Fed battles at Oxford, Ole Miss." The ever-expanding corps brought with it new energy and a push to create a new diversion. Thus, in May and June 1963, reporters and cameramen formed Southern Correspondents Reporting Racial Equality Wars (SCRREW), which developed a membership card bearing the mug of its mascot, Bull Connor's dog, and the slogan "Involuntary veteran of unexpected combat."[46]

The traveling road show of racial conflict also threw reporters and federal officials together from dateline to dateline. Among those officials—Deputy Attorney General Nicholas deB. Katzenbach, John Doar of the department's Civil Rights Division, and the department's spokesman, Edwin Guthman— there was a keen awareness of, even a near reverence for, the importance of news coverage. Katzenbach, much like Myrdal, felt that the public needed to have its nose rubbed in the awful scent of racism to provoke a reaction that could bring change. Exposure of the segregationists' point of view, the public disclosure of their private convictions, Katzenbach believed, was essential to break through to a public that might prefer complacence. Though there had been instances when the presence of cameras had provoked violence, he felt, there had been many more times when their presence had tempered an explosive situation. What's more, Katzenbach believed that reporters and cameramen were producing the evidence the public needed to understand that the federal government was not provoking violence.[47] He and his deputies and aides tended to try to help reporters when they could. And the reporters sometimes went to great lengths not to betray that trust or blow their pipeline of information.

The showdown between Wallace and the federal government unfolded under a blazing sun, with temperatures approaching 100 degrees, on June 11, 1963, in front of Foster Auditorium, a gymnasium. The day before, 324 reporters, still photographers, television cameramen, soundmen, engineers, and their crews had checked in—two thirds of them from out of state—and more arrived that day.[48]

Reporters stood on the ground, climbed atop scaffolding thrown up for the occasion, and worked inside television and radio trailers parked at the scene. A line was drawn to mark where the press could stand.[49] The AP's Morin took note of the ways reporters tried to beat the intense heat as they stood in the sunlight from 8 a.m. until 4 p.m.: "Reporters fashioned paper hats and looked like kids playing soldier. They covered their heads in handkerchiefs and looked like foreign legionnaires. They dripped and panted and got leg-weary and stuck it out."[50]

Among those at the scene were newsmen from five Tuscaloosa radio stations, including a Negro outlet, that had reached an unusual agreement to shelve their competitive instincts and pool their coverage. Tuscaloosa businesspeople, after surveying civic leaders in southern cities where there had been integration, became concerned that live radio coverage, if inaccurate or overblown, could light a fuse, and the stations had agreed to produce news reports "unvarnished by sensationalism and inaccurate reporting." Reporters from the stations fanned out across the campus and city and began filing their reports to a central news headquarters that then distributed the news over direct lines to the five stations simultaneously.[51]

AP's Rex Thomas was one of only two reporters called into Wallace's hotel room for an interview that morning, in time to make the afternoon editions that dominated the Alabama press. Wallace sat with Thomas and a *Montgomery Advertiser* reporter while wearing shorty pajamas he'd borrowed from a much larger aide. Thomas had also found the one pay phone in Foster Auditorium and used his personal contacts with several Alabama law enforcement officials to sneak a reporter into the building and keep an open line to AP's Atlanta bureau. The line would stay open for the duration of the confrontation—six hours.[52]

Katzenbach, who had not been able to sleep the night before, was concerned how the event was going to play nationally. His primary goal was the peaceful enrollment of Malone and Hood, and his overall strategy had been devised with an eye on national newscasts of the event. Robert Kennedy wanted Katzenbach to embarrass Wallace, but Katzenbach just hoped to avoid a direct confrontation between Wallace and the two Negro students. He was not willing to have the nation see Wallace, the symbol of southern racist resistance, encounter and humiliate two Negro students to their faces. His idea was to keep the confrontation, regardless of its outcome, dignified and its focus on the struggle over state and federal prerogatives.[53]

The drama played out in two stages, morning and afternoon, and it grew in tension as the minutes ticked by. Anybody could have gotten onto campus with a weapon, and anything could happen. In the morning confrontation between Wallace and Katzenbach, the governor stood in the shade and decried the "unwelcomed, unwanted, unwarranted and force-induced intrusion" by the "central government." He thrust his chin up, tightened his lips, and stared at Katzenbach, who had been positioned in the blistering sun. Sitton could see sweat breaking out on Katzenbach's forehead and his hands quivering until he crossed his arms. "Governor, I'm not interested in a show," Katzenbach said. "I don't know what the purpose of the show is. I am interested in the orders of these courts being enforced." Before leaving, Katzenbach added, "From the outset, Governor, all of us have known that the final chapter of this history will be the admission of these students. These students will remain on this campus. They will register today. They will go to school tomorrow."[54]

By the afternoon encounter, President Kennedy had federalized the Alabama National Guard and federal officials had selected a brigadier general, who in his everyday life was a forty-seven-year-old real estate executive in Birmingham, to confront Wallace and deliver a presidential order for him to step aside. When he did, Wallace delivered another speech, saluted the brigadier general, and walked swiftly with several aides to idling patrol cars, then left the campus.[55]

Minutes later, Malone and Hood entered the schoolhouse door and headed toward registration tables as reporters followed. "Hi there. We've been waiting for you," a smiling university employee said to Malone. After filling out forms and registering, they emerged outside to meet reporters in what Hood called "our first and final news conference." With little to say, they departed for their dormitories.[56]

Reporters wrote stories that revealed their impatience with Wallace and the states' rights refrain. "It was a six-hour theatrical show for states' rights," *The Washington Post*'s Robert Baker wrote in his second paragraph. Baker described Wallace as "the fiery little Governor" and his opening declaration to Katzenbach as "a rapid-fire classic exposition of states' rights that lasted eight minutes." Katzenbach was cast as gentle, firm, and patient, Wallace as interrupting, stubborn, and defiant.[57]

Sitton had essentially the same reaction. Wallace, he reported in his second paragraph, "had staged a carefully planned show of defying a federal court desegregation order." Sitton also concluded high in the story, before its jump to the inside, "This sequence of events, which took place in a circus atmosphere, appeared to have given the Governor the face-saving exit he apparently wanted." Like Baker, Sitton noted that while reporters and other onlookers had had to wait "in the broiling sun that sent the temperatures near 100 degrees," Wallace had gone inside to an air-conditioned room.[58]

President Kennedy, who that morning had read in *The New York Times* criticism by Reverend King of his leadership in civil rights, monitored the Tuscaloosa story, spent part of the day meeting with top Republicans to outline elements of his civil rights proposals, then decided he needed to address the nation on television that night.[59]

Some of Kennedy's aides were worried that he wasn't prepared for such a critical speech and that it would cost him politically. But there was also a feeling that that afternoon's showdown had clarified and underscored the federal government's preemptive role in guaranteeing civil rights and that Kennedy should capitalize on the victory to wrest dominance of the debate from the Republicans.[60]

Kennedy's address, delivered as reporters in Tuscaloosa were wrapping up their stories, was his first and most vigorous appeal to the nation's conscience on the issue of civil rights. He touched on virtually every wrong that a government could legitimately right through legislation. Then, as if guiding the nation through its first observation of the House of Jim Crow, he described in powerful terms the inhumanity within:

> The Negro baby born in America today, regardless of the section of the Nation in which he is born, has about one-half as much chance of completing a high school as a white baby born in the same place on the same day, one-third as much chance of completing college, one-third as much chance of becoming a professional man, twice as much chance of becoming unemployed, about one-seventh as much chance of earning $10,000 a year, a life expectancy which is 7 years shorter, and the prospects of earning only half as much. . . .
>
> We are confronted primarily with a moral issue. It is as old as the scriptures and is as clear as the American Constitution. . . . If an American,

because his skin is dark, cannot eat lunch in a restaurant open to the public, if he cannot send his children to the best public school available, if he cannot vote for the public officials who will represent him, if, in short, he cannot enjoy the full and free life which all of us want, then who among us would be content to have the color of his skin changed and stand in his place? Who among us would then be content with the counsels of patience and delay?

We preach freedom around the world, and we mean it, and we cherish our freedom here at home, but are we to say to the world, and much more importantly, to each other that this is the land of the free except for the Negroes; that we have no second-class citizens except Negroes; that we have no class or caste system, no ghettoes, no master race except with respect to Negroes? Now the time has come for this Nation to fulfill its promise.

The words and pictures that had come out of Alabama over the previous month and a half, the growing body of evidence that spirited defiance was prepared to confront police-state brutality, had pushed Kennedy to this new and more aggressive position.

Within a couple of hours after Kennedy went off the air, his message would be driven home by a bullet.

CHAPTER 20

THE KILLING SEASON

W hen he saw the action was shifting to Tuscaloosa, UPI reporter Cliff Sessions decided he and his wife, Shirley, could get away from Mississippi for a vacation that had long eluded them. They would begin on Tuesday, June 11, by hosting longtime friends from Kansas City, then would leave town.

The Sessionses had no children, but their guests did, so the Sessionses asked their maid, Lottie Mae Winston, to babysit that evening so the two couples could go to a nightclub in Jackson. Lottie Mae was an activist in the local chapter of the NAACP. Many white employers vigorously discouraged their maids and babysitters from political activism, but the Sessionses had not done so in the years Lottie Mae had been cleaning their house. They had grown sympathetic to the cause, for one thing; for another, the Sessions themselves had socialized, quite boldly, with the NAACP leader, Medgar Evers, and his wife, Myrlie, in the past.

So the Sessionses and their guests headed out to the club. The longest night of Cliff Sessions's life was just beginning.

For a couple of months, Medgar Evers had tried to import the Birmingham accord to Jackson. He wanted Negroes hired as police officers and as employees in downtown businesses, and he wanted all schools, playgrounds, parks, libraries, and lunch counters to be open to Negroes. Although the NAACP had been marginalized throughout the rest of the South, the thirty-seven-year-old Evers had made it the dominant Negro organization in Mississippi. He had done so by bridging the gap between the old heads, who believed change would come only by persistent knocking on the door, and more aggressive young blacks, who felt the door had to be pushed down and removed.

Still, day after day, Evers's biggest dilemma was keeping an even keel between a NAACP parent organization that opposed direct action protests and a large pool of Jackson-area college students and young professors who felt that direct action was the key. Getting what the NAACP wanted—the Birmingham result but without King's mass demonstrations and certainly without bringing King into the state, as Evers wanted—would not be easy.[1] For weeks in the spring of 1963, he stood in the middle as each side ran hot and cold in its relationship to the other.

Having gained little ground with a "selective buying campaign"—a boycott—against a couple of popular white-owned products and against businesses that contributed money to segregationist causes, Evers called on Jackson's mayor, Allen Thompson, to form a biracial committee that could guide the city through several stages of desegregation. Mayor Thompson pledged to create a biracial committee, then rejected the idea, then named a committee that included Negroes, such as the newspaper publisher Percy Greene, whose credentials were suspect; he espoused segregationist dogma and drew income from the state Sovereignty Commission for delivering speeches against King and desegregation.

Jackson's Negro community had no leader as flamboyant and inspirational—or, to whites, as threatening—as Shuttlesworth was in Birmingham. It had no leader with King's national backing and fund-raising ability. It had Evers, a low-key, passionate pragmatist who even maintained a respectful line of communication with the chief of detectives of the Jackson Police Department, M. B. Pierce.[2] Since 1958, the Mississippi Sovereignty Commission, the Jackson police, the State Highway Patrol, and the county sheriff's office had been watching Evers "both day and night, to determine whether he is violating any laws."[3] But in those four and a half years, he had not given them any cause to arrest him.

For all of his years in the forefront of the statewide organization—disguising himself as a field hand in the Delta to search for witnesses to the Emmett Till murder, standing by James Meredith at Ole Miss, visiting the grieving families of allies murdered in pursuit of civil rights—Evers had remained remarkably invisible in the white Mississippi press. Only rarely did a newsman write a profile of Evers, as Sessions had done years before. Sessions continued to treat Evers as a major player in the news, as did the Jackson correspondent for the New Orleans *Times-Picayune,* Bill Minor. But few others did.

The *Jackson Daily News*'s chief race reporter, W. C. "Dub" Shoemaker, was on the side of the segregationists. Compared to the Hedermans and Jimmy Ward, he was not nearly so ardent and not nearly as inclined to bend coverage to their beliefs, or his own. He had covered the race story straight, although the limitations set by his newspapers were sufficient for him to provide only cursory coverage. His newspaper had no interest in depth, context, or analysis and was more interested in its daily Agitation Box Score on the front page, which showed the number of protesters arrested, the charges, and the number still in jail or out on bond.[4] Negro leaders were stripped of their personalities, their hearts, their souls, even their differences.

Shoemaker's coverage of Evers was of the activist and rabble-rouser, not the man, the Mississippian, the army sergeant, the college football player, the insurance salesman, the husband and father. Evers's experiences—how he had become a brave leader in a state full of terrified Negroes—were not explored, and the difficulties he faced in bridging the competing tendencies within his own organization were only rarely probed.[5]

As two of the race reporters at the core of the coverage in Mississippi, Shoemaker and Sessions had a lot in common. They were white male Mississippians, born only forty miles and fifty-four days apart in 1931. They were both of medium height and had similar pale coloring and thin, light brown hair. As regulars on the race beat, they showed up at the same events four or five times a week, seeing each other more frequently than they'd see anyone else outside their families. But they had fundamentally different views of Evers.

Sessions liked Evers personally, even admired him. Shoemaker was not so enamored. Shoemaker got along with Evers, conversed with him on a first-name basis, and could enjoy a cigarette with him following nighttime rallies in churches. But Shoemaker didn't especially like him. He couldn't understand how Evers could be so warm and friendly close up, only to turn into a firebrand when he stood before pews of Negroes to enlist their support. "Medgar," Shoemaker asked him one day, "how come you and I can communicate and just get along good, just get along well and understand each other and do our jobs, yet you stand up here in front of 500 folks and you turn into a rowdy, rabid, rabble-rouser, or worse?" Evers put a hand on Shoemaker's shoulder and responded, "If I didn't lead them that way, they would follow somebody else."[6]

Another difference between the two race reporters: Sessions would come to the civil rights rallies alone. Shoemaker would first pick up a neighbor, a police detective named Jim Black, who passed himself off as a reporter covering the civil rights rallies. To gather information for the police, Black would go to the meetings with a hidden body wire that transmitted the proceedings to police officers located elsewhere. Black's orders were to sit with the press and, if asked who he was, to say he was with Shoemaker; then, if pressed, to disclose that he was a police officer. But Evers knew Black and knew he was a detective. "My intelligence tells me we have a police officer in the house," Evers said one night during a church rally. "But that's all right. We have nothing to hide. He's welcome here." Black appreciated the fact that Evers didn't then point him out in the press section.[7]

Over time, Shoemaker came to respect the civil rights leader. Evers's influence became clear to him one night in a small, packed Negro church when Reverend G. R. Haughton of the Pearl Street African Methodist Episcopal Church took the pulpit. As Shoemaker and other reporters sat in the front row, Haughton began flaying an ABC television news report from the night before. Haughton's intensity and anger toward the press spread across the church, and soon the audience was pounding on the backs of the pews and chanting toward the newsmen, "Get 'em, get 'em, get 'em." Shoemaker tightened in fear. The pounding and chanting were growing, the audience was standing on its feet, and there seemed no way to defuse the tension. Suddenly, Evers emerged on the stage, nudged Haughton away from the microphone, and shouted across the chapel, "Sit down!" Instantly, the room fell quiet, everyone found a seat, and the tension melted away. Then and there, Shoemaker understood that the Jackson movement was Evers's movement.[8]

In May 1963, Evers's profile began to grow. When Mayor Thompson took to Jackson television to talk about the racial situation, Evers demanded an opportunity to respond under equal-time provisions established by the Federal Communications Commission. With the FCC's help, he got that permission, and on May 20, a Monday night, Evers's seventeen-minute taped speech was broadcast on two Jackson television stations, "the first time," UPI reported, "a Negro civil rights spokesman had delivered a pro-integration address on the local stations."[9] For Evers, who had led the NAACP for nearly ten years, the speech was an opportunity to introduce himself and his cause to the white majority of the state.[10]

I speak as a native Mississippian. I was educated in Mississippi schools and served overseas in our nation's armed forces in the war against Hitlerism and Fascism. . . . Most southern white people, whether they are friendly or hostile, usually think of the NAACP as a 'northern outside group.' . . . At least one-half of the NAACP membership is in the South. There have been branches in Mississippi since 1918. The Jackson, Mississippi, branch was organized in 1926—37 years ago. . . .

Tonight the Negro knows from his radio and television what happened today all over the world. He knows what black people are doing and he knows what white people are doing. . . . He knows about the new free nations in Africa and knows that a Congo native can be a locomotive engineer, but in Jackson he cannot even drive a garbage truck. . . . Then he looks at his home community and what does he see, to quote our Mayor, in this "progressive, beautiful, friendly, prosperous city with an exciting future"?

Evers described the segregated Jackson the blacks saw, in which children were not allowed inside movie theaters downtown; lawyers and doctors didn't get to attend meetings of professional organizations; and policemen, school crossing guards, firemen, and all city employees came in only one color. He described what the Negro wanted, then added:

> Jackson can change if it wills to do so. . . . We believe there are white Mississippians who want to go forward on the race question. Their religion tells me there is something wrong with the old system. Their sense of justice and fair play sends them the same message. But whether Jackson and the State choose change or not, the years of change are upon us. In the racial picture, things will never be as they once were. History has reached a turning point, here and over the world.[11]

The *Jackson Daily News* dismissed the importance of the broadcast. It threw together disparate quotes from the speech, then added the headline "Mix Drive Talked Up."[12]

The movement finally gained some traction on May 28, 1963. While diversionary pickets were staged in front of a J.C. Penney store and Evers called the wire services to tip them off, two Tougaloo students and another youth entered a Woolworth's, sat at the lunch counter in the white section, and requested service. White teenagers began pouring into the store. They heckled the demonstrators, started pouring mustard and ketchup over them, then finally pulled one, Memphis Norman, from his stool, threw him to the floor, and began kicking him in the head. Another, Anne Moody, was slapped, then thrown against a counter.

When word reached the NAACP that the sit-in had provoked violence, John Salter, head of the Jackson Movement Strategy Committee, and other activists arrived to give support to the demonstrators. At Woolworth's, Salter saw a hundred white people standing outside and walking past complacent police to get inside. Salter himself got in and saw three hundred more angry white people jammed inside, many an arm's reach from the demonstrators, who had returned to the counter stools.

Salter sat on a stool, was hit with sprays of mustard, then was slugged in the face until he was woozy and clobbered on the back of his head until sound seemed to leave the room. He felt spray paint on his back and the sudden, piercing fire of pepper in his eyes. As others sat at the counter, a group of whites began rampaging through the store. Only then did police jump into action and run the whites out.

A photograph of the attack on Norman made the front page of *The New York Times*. A photograph showing Salter, Moody, and another demonstrator, Joan Trumpauer, being basted with mustard, ketchup, and other condiments, taken by a *Jackson Daily News* photographer, ran in publications across the nation. *Newsweek,* which published a four-page roundup of civil rights activities from the South, used both the Woolworth's photo and a series of four photos from the attack on Norman. The *Daily News* used its photograph to give Salter a mocking moniker. From then on, he was labeled, in local newspaper accounts, "the mustard man."[13]

The New York Times wrote a "Man in the News" profile of Evers that described him as a remarkable leader whose college education in business administration was evident in his management style. "He talks quietly and attends to small details. But his strong feelings, like his unexpected smile, are never fully submerged by his methodical manner." A defining moment for Evers, the story said, came when the president of his college, Alcorn, discouraged him from trying to register to vote. "He said we had no contribution to make to the community. I couldn't forget that." And it explained how his ideas were formed early, when a friend of his father's was lynched and the victim's clothes were left out in a field until the blood had turned to the color of rust. The story also said that white officials viewed Evers as an "effective organizer . . . [and] as a reasonable and dependable man."[14]

Now that he had been viewed on television citywide and portrayed sympathetically nationwide, Evers had finally achieved a high profile. In the next few days, the Jackson movement would accelerate, with large marches and sweeping arrests followed by mass jailings inside the stockades at the Mississippi State Fairgrounds. On a single day, five hundred high school students were arrested and hauled to the stockades, many of them transported in garbage trucks.

Among the national reporters sent to cover the story was Wallace Terry of *The Washington Post,* one of the few Negroes on the race beat for a major publication. The big story, Terry realized and Evers himself knew, was that the momentum could not be sustained. It was finished. The parent NAACP, which was partial to the selective buying campaign, was not interested in running cat-and-mouse demonstrations of civil disobedience that would lead to large-scale jailings and costly bailings. Without the NAACP's support, the movement was dead. The NAACP had not won a thing from the city after two weeks of demonstrations that had led to nearly seven hundred arrests.

Evers was physically exhausted and jumpy. He believed he was being followed and was certain that it was not an accident when a Jackson police car narrowly missed hitting him as he crossed a street. Terry observed two white men aiming their car at Evers and accelerating in front of the NAACP headquarters in Jackson; then he saw white bystanders laughing. "This is what you must face to get free in Mississippi," Evers told Terry. Evers had gotten a call from a prominent black physician on the Gulf Coast, the head of the NAACP there, who said that a white lawyer had told him that the Ku Klux Klan would be coming after Evers soon—a threat Evers did not report to his wife.[15]

The first two sentences of the story Wallace Terry wrote for the *Post* were clear and simple: "The NAACP took its campaign for Negro rights into the streets here, but did not stay long enough to put over the campaign. That is the feeling of several figures in the Negro rights push in the deep South who came here to lend their support to Jackson Negroes and left disappointed."[16]

With Terry, Sessions, and a handful of other reporters, Evers didn't try to maintain an aura that he had everything figured out. He was willing to seek their counsel. One evening during Terry's visit to Jackson, they had dinner, then returned to Evers's home for coffee. "Wally," Evers asked, "what do you think it's going to take to change things?"

"Medgar," Terry said, "I think it's going to take a hundred big funerals."[17]

The next morning, Terry headed for his next assignment: Tuscaloosa, the University of Alabama, and the George Wallace showdown.

He could not have known that the first of those big funerals was only days away.

That evening, Cliff Sessions pulled from his closet a new white sport coat he had been longing to wear. With Shirley, their friends, and a bottle of V.O. in a paper bag, which was the custom in still-prohibitionist Mississippi, he drove to one of the nightclubs on a highway leading from Jackson.[18]

Meanwhile, an exhausted, conflicted Medgar Evers was trying vainly to shore up the movement that was collapsing around him. He dropped in late at a poorly attended rally in a church. The press had pretty much abandoned the story. Dub Shoemaker was there and stuck around to catch Evers outside, have a cigarette, and chat. Evers made several stops after that, seeing friends briefly at a poker game, meeting with an NAACP official from New York, and picking up some sweatshirts that said "Jim Crow Must Go."[19]

He then drove home. That morning, he had said good-bye to Myrlie and the kids, kissed them, gone out to his car, paused, then returned to say good-bye and kiss everyone again. "Myrlie, I don't know what to do," he told her as he left the second time. "I'm so tired I can't go on, but I can't stop either." He spoke to Myrlie and the children twice later that day and to Myrlie alone a third time, so much that she joked with him that he must be slacking off at work. In the afternoon, after Wallace capitulated, he called her again, enthusiastic about the outcome.[20]

"Here comes Daddy," said the oldest Evers son, Darrell, when he heard Evers's car pull into the driveway at 12:20 a.m. Myrlie had let the kids stay up late to watch television. Evers got out, closed the car door, and was standing with an armful of sweatshirts when a gunshot rang out, sending a bullet from a World War I–era 30.06 Enfield rifle into his back. Myrlie knew instantly what had happened. Training and instinct drove her and the children first to the floor, then outside to find Medgar lying in a large pool of blood and trying to get to the house. Myrlie screamed, the children cried, "Daddy get up, please get up," and neighbors came running. He was clinging to life when friends put him on a mattress and into the back of a station wagon and raced him to the University of Mississippi Hospital. He died minutes later. He was thirty-seven.

Within a few minutes, Lottie Mae Winston, babysitting at the Sessions home, fielded a call delivering the news that Evers had been shot and taken to the hospital. She quickly tracked down Sessions at the noisy nightclub and told him. Instantly sobered by the shocking news, Sessions grabbed Dave Maddux, a UPI colleague he'd seen at the club, jumped into Maddux's car, and headed for the police station. There, the deskman told Sessions that Evers had just died. Sessions grabbed the nearest phone and dictated to Atlanta the first wire story on the assassination. His story, in wire parlance, "took the play," getting quicker distribution than AP's. It also set into motion a UPI coverage plan to send backup reporters to Jackson. Hanging up the phone, Sessions ran the two blocks to the UPI office, threw his white sport coat over his chair, dispatched Maddux to the hospital and to the Everses' home, called in other reporters, then sat down with a telephone and a telex machine. He started finding out everything he could and typing everything he knew.[21]

By daybreak, Sessions had churned out hundreds, even thousands, of words for the newspaper, radio, and television wires. Taking feeds from three or four reporters, he worked all night long, taking information and updating leads as the night rolled into morning, as morning ran into afternoon, and afternoon slid into evening. Another UPI reporter came into the bureau for a while and noticed that Sessions, after hours and hours of writing, had not gotten up from his chair. His white sport coat, draped over his chair, had not been disturbed. Sessions had gotten ahead of every other reporter from the beginning and held his lead throughout. When *The Washington Post* positioned its Evers story on the front page of its main editions twenty-four hours after the assassination, it was Sessions's version it chose.[22]

Numbed by the swift turn of events, by the murder of a man he'd known well, a man he'd had in his house, a man he respected as much as anyone he knew, a man who represented the kind of Mississippi he idealized, Sessions finally left the office a day after the shooting. His head was reeling. How could this happen in a civilized society? How could an entire state, *his own state,* be so godlessly evil? How had it come to this?

Dazed, he walked into his home to find the houseguests he'd forgotten about and a vacation plan that would have to be canceled before it could begin. He headed for his bedroom. He threw off the white sport coat, then stripped down. He started the shower, got in, and stood silently under the pounding, purifying water. Then he broke down and cried.[23]

The Evers assassination provoked angry demonstrations on Jackson streets that felt on fire in a 100-degree heat wave. When hundreds of emotional Negroes filed, by twos, onto a Jackson street in the Negro section for a mass protest march, club-wielding police officers swept in with such force that even veteran race reporters were sickened by the sight. Claude Sitton and Bill Minor of the New Orleans *Times-Picayune* pressed in close to the action, so close they could provide eyewitness accounts of the police attacks and hear billy clubs cracking skulls.

Sitton, in a story played at the top of *The New York Times'* front page with two large photos of police on the attack, opened his story with a straight description of what he had seen:

JACKSON, MISS., JUNE 13—The police charged today on adults and teen-agers who were jeering and chanting "We want freedom" and clubbed them into submission. A blow to the head felled a white sociology professor in the group.

Six Negroes were struck or choked by police nightsticks drawn across their throats. Others were snatched or pushed from the porch of a Negro home.[24]

Sitton's story directly challenged the police version of the events. The chief of detectives and spokesman for the Jackson police, Sitton reported, "gave a much milder version of the incident than that seen by newsmen." He then described how two dozen officers, seemingly maddened by people who were jeering and chanting from the porch of a house, had demanded that they "cut out that noise." When the son of the homeowner responded, "You can't keep me off this porch; my momma lives here," the deputy police chief declared everyone on the porch under arrest. "Two dozen policemen closed in around the porch and began pulling its occupants to the ground," Sitton reported. When some of those on the porch tried to retreat, police "jumped onto the porch and began wielding their clubs."

Sitton described how a police officer had smacked the head of John Salter, the same activist who had been beaten during the sit-ins, and had been joined by other patrolmen, who had grabbed Salter and pulled him off the porch. "Here he is," yelled an excited patrolman, as if he'd bagged an elusive prey. "Here he is." As Sitton and Minor watched, another officer clubbed Salter on the head with such force that Minor thought Salter surely was dead. As Salter lay on the ground motionless and bleeding, the whack of the club hitting his skull echoed inside Minor's head, as clear a sound as Mickey Mantle connecting for a home run, but as brutal as death.

Even as Salter showed signs of life, Sitton and Minor saw police officers grab fleeing Negroes from behind, pull their billy clubs across their necks, and yank back on them. As police hauled away the homeowner's son, her fifteen-year-old daughter began crying, only to find herself being clubbed.[25] Sitton closed his story with a white pastor from Tougaloo standing on the porch calling to police:

> "You've beaten a woman in her own house. I know you're white and I know what you think of her. But won't you please call an ambulance for her?"
> A policeman in the street replied:
> "You call 'em yourself," adding an epithet.[26]

Minor felt woozy. For sixteen years, he had been the *Times-Picayune*'s statehouse correspondent in Jackson. From his first assignment, covering the 1947 funeral of the white supremacist U.S. Senator Theodore Bilbo, through the Emmett Till trial and the bloody showdown at Ole Miss over James Meredith's enrollment, Minor had seen his career, and his outlook, defined by race stories. The Louisiana-born Minor much preferred to muckrake and poke holes in the hot-air balloons that seemed to elevate the careers of incompetent, small-minded, and ill-advised politicians. But he kept careful watch on the race story and, as a result, was often the first person out-of-state reporters visited when they arrived in Jackson.

Though Minor tried to keep the struggle for racial advancement a story he covered and not a cause he believed in, by 1963, on Rose Street, he'd adopted an unmistakably liberal attitude on race. Vastly outnumbered in Mississippi, even among the press corps in Jackson, Minor didn't go out of his way to pick fights. His weekly column gave him latitude and provoked telephone death threats to his home. But he remained first and foremost a daily reporter who understood that pushing an advocacy line, especially in favor of integration, would make it impossible to function.

Still, when it came to incidents like the one on Rose Street, Minor could not rationalize or stomach what he'd witnessed. As the scene settled down, he felt he had to get away, had to seek refuge where he could think through everything he'd just seen. He made his way to the quiet of the Roman Catholic St. Peter's Cathedral. Crossing himself, he entered a pew inside the church, knelt, and began praying for reason and calm to replace hatred and violence. A priest came beside him, spoke with him, gave him communion, and encouraged him to not lose his resolve.

Two days later, Minor witnessed a demonstration of courage and leadership that he believed was nearly biblical in its power. The memorial service and viewing for Evers, held on Saturday, June 15, drew close to four thousand mourners inside the sweltering Masonic Temple on Farish Street. Among them were King, Roy Wilkins, and members of SNCC, whose appearance together disguised their deep divisions over who should carry the Jackson Movement forward.

When the service ended, the mourners poured out of the temple. Jackson's mayor had approved a mile-and-a-half-long march through the city, so the mourners began walking behind the hearse bearing Evers's body, which was escorted by eight police officers on motorcycles. Even with King and Wilkins at the front of the march, the peace could not hold. Sitton and Minor watched as younger marchers, chanting and singing, broke away and headed toward the white business zone. Police quickly called in dogs to try to keep the marchers and reporters hemmed into the approved area on Farish Street. Unable to view what police did next, Sitton reported the eyewitness account of a television cameraman who had had a better vantage point. "With newsmen out of the way, the police went to work in earnest to clear the area," Sitton would write later that day. "A television cameraman caught in a doorway said a Negro man who did not move fast enough was struck in the face with a shotgun butt by a deputy sheriff. Another deputy cut a soundman's microphone cable. The cameraman said a Negro woman was clubbed by a policeman. She fled to a car but was dragged out and clubbed again. Two men in one camera crew said the police had threatened to turn a police dog on them if they did not move out of the way quickly."[27]

Some of the younger marchers began hurling bottles, bricks, and other items at uniformed officers. This was not the calm Minor had prayed for. In the din, the chaos, and the oppressive heat, a lanky white man in a white shirt and a thin tie loosened at the collar walked down the middle of Farish Street, urging calm. He was John Doar, assistant attorney general in the Justice Department's civil rights division. Walking nearby, *Newsweek*'s Karl Fleming passed Mississippi Highway Patrol Chief T. B. Birdsong and heard him say, "One more goddam nigger throw a rock and we open fire."[28]

Minor, Sitton, and Fleming fixed their eyes on Doar, tenser than they'd ever been. "You're not going to win anything with bottles and bricks," Doar said. Minor felt a massacre in the making as young, angry Negroes, many unrecognizable to leaders of the Jackson Movement, lined up against the heavily armed, white-shirted officers. "Who is he?" some in the crowd yelled, uttering curses at Doar. "What does he know?" shouted others. Any second now, Minor thought, someone will provoke an officer to pull his gun and the street will turn into a shooting gallery. Fleming felt the tingly tension that comes just before an electrical storm, then heard himself say, "We could get killed here."[29]

Unwilling to avert his eyes from Doar, Fleming scribbled into his notebook without looking down at what he was writing; his shaking hands produced large, looping *l*s and *r*s that he would later recognize as the calligraphy of fear. Doar, too, was worried. He felt confident that city police officers were disciplined and wouldn't do anything rash, but he wasn't so sure of the sheriff's deputies, who were standing with their shotguns at the ready. Doar made sure to walk through the gathered deputies, holding up his hand and saying, "Cool it." As he moved forward and spoke, he occasionally turned his body to avoid flying bottles. "Hold it!" he shouted. "Is there someone here who can speak for you people?"[30]

Dave Dennis, a leader with the Congress of Racial Equality, stepped forward and stood by Doar in the middle of Farish Street. "This man is right," said Dennis. He chastised those who were throwing bottles and who now were hiding behind a group of women. Doar, to get and hold their attention, kept repeating, "My name is John Doar—D-O-A-R," he said as missiles landed around him. Minor could not believe the courage he was witnessing. "I'm from the Justice Department, and anybody around here knows I stand for what is right." Soon, Doar, Dennis, and the Negroes gathered around them succeeded in settling the crowd down. So far as Bill Minor could see, John Doar had answered his prayer and saved the city of Jackson.[31]

On June 22, ten days after Evers was killed, the FBI arrested Byron De La Beckwith in Greenwood, where he worked as an underachieving fertilizer salesman. On his mother's side, he was descended from wealthy plantation owners who had been the roots and lifeblood of the Mississippi Delta. Though born in California because his father's family was from there, he had lived only the first five of his forty-two years there before returning to the Mississippi Delta to grow up and develop a reputation as a virulent racist, hothead, and blowhard. The Jackson *Clarion-Ledger* had the story the following day, beneath a headline that summed up the xenophobic tilt of its coverage over the previous two decades. The same newspaper that had reported the murder of Gus Courts as an "odd accident," that had attributed attacks on civil rights workers as self-inflicted and fed the notion that Emmett Till had merely run away from his family, now found it impossible to portray Evers's assassin as one of Mississippi's own. Its headline: "Californian Is Charged with Murder of Evers."

By then, Evers's body had been taken by train to Washington, D.C., where it lay in state at the John Wesley A.M.E. Zion Church for two days. Evers was buried with military honors at Arlington National Cemetery on June 19. More than 1,000 people attended, including representatives of the White House and Congress. An astonishing 25,000 had walked by Evers's casket in the two days prior to the funeral.

The day after Evers was buried, President Kennedy met in his Cabinet

Room with A. Philip Randolph, Roy Wilkins, John Lewis, National Urban League executive director Whitney Young, James Farmer, and others who told him that a vastly larger gathering was being planned, a march on Washington that would seek to mobilize national support for the civil rights bill making its way through Congress.[32]

Two months later, that gathering would make the number who had walked past Evers's casket seem rather paltry.

The news coverage of the March on Washington was Myrdal's prescience writ large. As the August 28 date neared, as commentators questioned whether there would be violence or a poorly organized dud, the demand for press credentials was remarkable. The Metropolitan Police Department handled more press requests than it ever had: 1,900 police passes were distributed for the march, in addition to the 1,200 it had routinely handed out to the regular press corps covering Washington.

The march, which ultimately drew an estimated 200,000 to 250,000 marchers, provided the single greatest exposure of a national audience to the civil rights movement. While television's coverage of civil rights confrontations and street skirmishes had shown its ability to capture the run-and-gun moments of the movement, the march would play to another of television's greatest strengths: its ability, when given time, to plan, to position, and to program. Working simultaneously together and competitively, the television networks made plans that exceeded anything they had ever done. ABC, NBC, and CBS, which provided television and radio coverage, and the Mutual Broadcasting System, which was radio only, assigned 460 people to Washington that day, and hundreds more to New York. The three television networks set up twenty-three camera positions between the Washington Monument and the Lincoln Memorial that they shared in a pool arrangement and had twenty-six of their own cameras elsewhere.[33]

By 1963 standards, the coverage was saturation. On NBC, the *Today* show devoted more than thirty minutes to the march. The network then aired eleven special reports during the day, totaling more than three hours of coverage. Those reports focused on crowd estimates and behavior, on celebrity appearances, and on speeches as they were delivered or taped excerpts. One special report on Martin Luther King's appearance went for an hour. The network ended with a forty-five-minute show late that night. ABC also inserted special reports throughout the day, mostly two and five minutes in length, plus two half-hour programs in the afternoon and an evening wrap-up.[34]

CBS was the only network to commit to continuous coverage throughout the afternoon. It made a three-hour bet that paid off. Television viewing that entire day was up 15 percent but was 61 percent higher than the prior week in the afternoon.[35]

A technological breakthrough greatly expanded the day's audience well beyond the nation's shores. Telstar, a communications satellite launched in July 1962, took live coverage of the march to six countries; Communist nations received the coverage and taped it but did not show it live. Television networks in West Germany, Japan, and France sent their own crews to Washington.[36]

The coverage showed a march that was serious business and lively entertainment, extraordinary oratory and powerful musical performances, celebrity and celebration. Two normally dour faces, those of Marlon Brando and James Baldwin, were seen laughing together, the Negro singer Diahann Carroll was shown holding hands with the white television actor James Garner to pull him through the crowd, and there were performances by Mahalia Jackson, Marian Anderson, Bob Dylan, Joan Baez, Odetta, and Peter, Paul, and Mary.

The New York Times, in the second paragraph of its coverage, called the march "the greatest assembly for a redress of grievances that this capital has ever seen." It added:

> There was no violence to mar the demonstration. In fact, at times there was an air of hootenanny about it as groups of schoolchildren clapped hands and swung into familiar freedom songs. But if the crowd was good-natured, the underlying tone was one of dead seriousness.[37]

Standing at the Lincoln Memorial, King "ignited the crowd," the *Times* reported, "with words that might have been written by the sad, brooding man enshrined within the Memorial." E. W. Kenworthy, in a piece that was mostly faithful to King's actual words, wrote:

> When Dr. King arose, a great roar swelled up from the crowd. When he started to speak, a hush fell.
>
> "Even though we face the difficulties of today and tomorrow, I still have a dream," he said. "It is a dream chiefly rooted in the American dream. I have a dream that one day this nation will rise up and live out the true meaning of its creed: 'We hold these truths to be self-evident, that all men are created equal.'
>
> "I have a dream . . ." The vast throng listening intently to him roared.
>
> ". . . that one day on the red hills of Georgia, the sons of former slaves and the sons of former slave-owners will be able to sit together at the table of brotherhood.
>
> "I have a dream . . ." The crowd roared.
>
> ". . . that one day even the State of Mississippi, a state sweltering with the heat of injustice, sweltering with the heat of oppression, will be transformed into an oasis of freedom and justice.

"I have a dream . . ." The crowd roared.

". . . that my four little children will one day live in a nation where they will not be judged by the color of their skin but by the content of their character.

"I have a dream . . ." The crowd roared.[38]

The *Times* put five march-related stories on its cover, including an analysis by James Reston of King's speech: "It was Dr. King who, near the end of the day, touched the vast audience. Until then, the pilgrimage was merely a great spectacle."[39]

That sense that something remarkable had just happened was not shared everywhere. The *Clarion-Ledger* in Jackson put on its cover a photograph showing the litter left behind and the headline "Washington Is Clean Again with Negro Trash Removed."[40]

Broadcasters were elated at their achievement. "Whatever had been superlative in the past became comparative last week as radio and TV converged on Washington to describe the civil rights march," *Broadcasting* magazine reported.[41]

Television networks at the time were producing significant documentaries on race relations. The civil rights movement in 1963 fell right in the midst of the Age of Documentaries, to a medium that was now fifteen years old and looking to maintain a serious counterbalance to its growing entertainment programming. ABC News produced a five-part series, *Crucial Summer,* which examined desegregation efforts across the nation. NBC delivered a three-hour show, "The American Revolution of 1963."

But an even more important development occurred that same night, September 2, on CBS: the news anchor Walter Cronkite announced that *The CBS Evening News* was expanding its broadcast from fifteen minutes to thirty. "Good evening from our CBS newsroom on this, the first broadcast of network television's first daily half-hour news program," he said in opening the show. *The Huntley-Brinkley Report* on NBC went to thirty minutes the following week. ABC News didn't do so until 1967.

Jack Gould, *The New York Times'* influential television critic, considered the coverage of the march, the documentaries, and the expansion of the news program and sat in awe of what he and the nation were witnessing:

The medium of television is proving an indispensable force in the Negro's pursuit of human rights. Through the home screen, the Washington drama of mass protest was brought to life in virtually every household in the nation, a social phenomenon inconceivable before the age of electronics. . . . The gentle entrance and exit of so much petitioning humanity was an editorial in movement. Its eloquence could not be the same in only frozen word or stilled picture.

Gould was writing about a medium that had not even existed when Myrdal perceived that the Negro needed, more than anything else, attention to his plight. But his understanding was the same as Myrdal's. Television news, he said, was "attacking the inertia and apathy that stand in the way of Negro liberation."

Gould wrote, as had Myrdal, that for years the Negro's most significant handicap had been

> in communicating and dramatizing his lot. Not to the integrationists, not to the unyieldingly prejudiced, but to the indifferent white millions for whom integration or segregation was of scant personal concern.
>
> The sociologist of tomorrow may find it was television more than anything else that finally penetrated this huge camp of the uncommitted.[42]

. . .

A week later, there was news of a grotesque crime inside a church on a Sunday morning. On September 15, Ku Klux Klansmen in Birmingham planted, under a stairwell at the Sixteenth Street Baptist Church, a dynamite bomb that exploded as four young girls, wearing white dresses for a special youth program, primped inside a dressing room in the church basement.

The eerie silence of death erupted into screams of horror, and the realization on a quiet Sunday morning that four innocent lives had been lost to racial hatred became the nation's dominant story—so dominant that not even the Birmingham newspapers could keep it off the front page.

The UPI reporter Robert Gordon and his roommate, a radio newsman, got to the dust- and smoke-filled scene before others and found heartsickening, desolate destruction. Police were arriving, and church members were racing to and from the giant, crushing cement slaps of the collapsed building. Gordon kept close to the scene, closer than he really wanted to be, pulled in by a reporter's curiosity, pushed away by the horror before him. He watched as rescuers began pulling bodies from the rubble. When they lifted the sheet over one of the corpses, Gordon looked. "What I saw," he would later say, "I didn't recognize as a human being."[43]

Associated Press reporter Jim Purks walked the streets in silence and disbelief as he scribbled streams of disconnected words into his notebook: ". . . Several cars outside twisted wrecked, windows in 2nd floor broken— Negroes looking . . . People walking over crumpled glass. Pieces of rock. 'My grandbaby 11 years old—pulled rocks off her' . . . Clock stopped at 10:25 . . . Patches of blood among the glass—one piece of glass." He had stepped on a sharp piece of glass, heard it crunch, and recoiled to see blood on it. That sight, even more so that sound, would reverberate in his head and heart for more than forty years.[44]

Grief gave way to anger that played out on streets that, over the next few hours, exploded in rock throwing, rioting, and torching. Governor Wallace called in Alabama state troopers, who freely wielded their clubs as they struggled to take control. Gordon, keyed up and emotionally wrung out by the day's events, ran back and forth from the streets to the Gaston Motel, where King was staying. Even inside the lobby, he could hear the noise of rioting on the streets, and he could see fires burning.

At one point, Gordon was standing in the lobby when he saw the prime organizer of the five-month-long Birmingham campaign, Wyatt T. Walker, and Walker's wife emerge from a room. Gordon saw a state trooper hit Walker's wife with the butt of his rifle, knocking her down. Walker was incensed and started stalking the state trooper. Gordon dropped his journalistic restraint and ran to tackle Walker before he could jump the trooper. Gordon was more startled than anyone that he'd crossed the line and changed the outcome of a story unfolding in front of him. But he felt, as did Walker, that he might have saved Walker from a brutal response.[45]

In New York, the senior editor at the *Saturday Evening Post,* Thomas B. Congdon, Jr., knew what he had to do in response to the bombing. He had been editing a powerful, rhapsodic, and deeply disturbing essay by James J. Kilpatrick, scheduled to run soon. Titled, by Kilpatrick, "The Hell He Is Equal," the article argued that Southern attitudes against Negroes stemmed from truthful understandings, not irrational prejudices. By just about every Western standard since the beginning of time, Kilpatrick wrote, "the Negro race, as a race, is in fact an inferior race . . . Within the frame of reference of a Negroid civilization, a mud hut may be a masterpiece; a tribal council may be a marvel of social organization; a carved image may have a primitive purity all its own. Well and good. But the mud hut ought not to be equated with Monticello, nor jungle rule with Periclean Athens, nor phallic dolls with Elgin marbles. When the Negro today proclaims or demands his 'equality,' he is talking of equality within the terms of Western civilization. And what, pray, has he contributed to it? Putting aside conjecture, wishful thinking and a puerile jazz-worship, what has he in fact contributed to it? The blunt answer, may it please the court, is very damned little."

Kilpatrick described the progress of the Chinese, the Irish, and the Jews in America, then added: "And where is the Negro in this human parade? There are respected Negro teachers, lawyers, doctors, writers. Of course, there are. But in general terms, where is the Negro to be found? Why, sir, he is still carrying the hod. He is still digging the ditch. He is down at the gin mill shooting craps. He is lying limp in the middle of the sidewalk, yelling he is equal. The hell he is equal."[46]

In the aftershock of the church bombing, Congdon immediately yanked the article. "Bad taste, in the extreme, and, in fact, inflammatory," he wrote Kilpatrick. The Richmond editor said he was relieved, but wanted to rewrite it for later publication. It never ran.[47]

In Atlanta, the *Constitution* editor, Gene Patterson, was mowing his lawn Sunday afternoon when his office called to tell him about the bombing. Patterson's column for the Monday paper was already written, so he headed to the office to think about writing a replacement column. He called reporters on the scene, read wires, and became captivated by a report that a mother was walking around the ruins carrying one shoe from the foot of her dead daughter. But who, Patterson asked himself, was he writing to? Whom did he want to reach? He would, he decided, write to his fellow white southerners.

A Negro mother wept in the street Sunday morning in front of a Baptist Church in Birmingham. In her hand she held a shoe, one shoe, from the foot of her dead child. We hold that shoe with her.

Every one of us in the white South holds that small shoe in his hand.

It is too late to blame the sick criminals who handled the dynamite. The FBI and the police can deal with that kind. The charge against them is simple. They killed four children.

Only we can trace the truth, Southerner—you and I. We broke those children's bodies.

We watched the stage set without staying it. We listened to the prologue unbestirred. We saw the curtain opening with disinterest. We have heard the play.

We—who go on electing politicians who heat the kettles of hate.

We—who raise no hand to silence the mean and little men who have their nigger jokes.

We—who stand aside in imagined rectitude and let the mad dogs that run in every society slide their leashes from our hand, and spring.

We—the heirs of a proud South, who protest its worth and demand it recognition—we are the ones who have ducked the difficult, skirted the uncomfortable, caviled at the challenge, resented the necessary, rationalized the unacceptable, and created the day surely when these children would die.

This is no time to load our anguish onto the murderous scapegoat who set the cap in dynamite of our own manufacture.

He didn't know any better.

Somewhere in the dim and fevered recess of an evil mind he feels right now that he has been a hero. He is only guilty of murder. He thinks he has pleased us.

We of the white South who know better are the ones who must take a harsher judgment.

We, who know better, created a climate for child-killing by those who don't.

We hold that shoe in our hand, Southerner. We hold that shoe in our hand, Southerner. Let us see it straight, and look at the blood on it. Let us compare it with the unworthy speeches of Southern public men who have traduced the Negro; match it with the spectacle of shrilling children whose parents and teachers turned them free to spit epithets at small huddles of Negro school children for a week before this Sunday in Birmingham; hold up the shoe and look beyond it to the state house in Montgomery where the official attitudes of Alabama have been spoken in heat and anger.

Let us not lay the blame on some brutal fool who didn't know any better.

We know better. We created the day. We bear the judgment. May God have mercy on the poor South that has so been led. May what has happened hasten the day when the good South, which does live and has great being, will rise to this challenge of racial understanding and common humanity, and in the full power of its unasserted courage, assert itself.

The Sunday school play at Birmingham is ended. With a weeping Negro mother, we stand in the bitter smoke and hold a shoe. If our South is ever to be what we wish it to be, we will plant a flower of nobler resolve for the South now upon these four small graves that we dug.[48]

An editor at an Atlanta CBS television station was so moved by the column that he sent a crew to film Patterson reading it. The station used the entire column. Hours later, Patterson got a call from Walter Cronkite. "Is it all right with you if I use some of that column on national CBS News?" Cronkite asked. Patterson said he'd be honored. Cronkite ran the entire column.

Overnight, Patterson's mailbox began to fill up. He was accustomed to a provocative column pulling no more than 20 letters. This time, he drew 1,200 of them from all over the country. He had reached an audience far beyond his target in the South. Big-name politicians joined celebrities and ordinary people in thanking Patterson for speaking to them in his column.[49]

It didn't take a "sociologist of tomorrow," in television critic Gould's words, to see that Patterson, on television, had "penetrated this huge camp of the uncommitted."

Two months after the four girls were killed, when it seemed impossible that violence could take a more dramatic turn, it did. President Kennedy, having taken the leadership role in pushing for civil rights legislation, was assassinated in Dallas.

CHAPTER 21

FREEDOM SUMMER

Six years into the beat, Claude Sitton had a perspective no other reporter had. The year had barely turned a month old when he could foresee that 1964 was going to bring an increase in militancy on all sides. He had noticed that for four years in a row, the passing of the midwinter had been accompanied by renewed activism by civil rights forces. He had also detected that in the quiet months following the March on Washington, the Birmingham bombing, and the Kennedy assassination, a new wave of people had come into the movement, and they didn't have the same patience as their predecessors.

Civil rights organizations such as SNCC, CORE, NAACP, and SCLC had come together under an umbrella group, the Council of Federated Organizations (COFO), with the mission of staging a Freedom Summer in Mississippi. They would train and send into the state as many as a thousand college students to set up voter registration efforts, health clinics, legal aid, and schools for the state's Negroes. There was no doubt that it would be provocative.

"The carefully scrubbed, neatly dressed college students who sat down at lunch counters across the South in 1960 and politely ordered coffee are gone for the most part," Sitton reported. He added, "It has become increasingly apparent that many Negroes no longer are willing to listen to the voices of reason within their own ranks. They do not especially care what whites think about them and their tactics."[1]

The same could be said for the other side. One week later, two hundred men met in the south Mississippi town of Brookhaven to form a new organization, the White Knights of the Ku Klux Klan. The Citizens' Councils had not ended the civil rights movement, and the White Knights intended to. The Klan that night didn't simply burn a cross and denounce Negroes, Jews, and

Catholics from the back of a pickup. Led by Imperial Wizard Sam Bowers, a resident of Laurel, they put together and approved a forty-page constitution that set forth a four-step program for achieving its goals. The fourth stage called for "extermination."[2]

The Mississippi countryside was hit by a rash of cross burnings—seven in Vicksburg on one night, twelve in Neshoba County on another, and sixty-four across the state on one weekend. All were preceded by anonymous phone calls to alert reporters. The White Knights also distributed literature claiming a Mississippi membership of 91,003 "sober, intelligent, courageous, Christian, American white men."[3]

Some Mississippi officials and newspapers adopted the view that civil rights forces were running through the state and lighting the crosses to make their situation seem more desperate than it was. In the town of Philadelphia, *The Neshoba Democrat* issued an editorial threat that read like a license to kill: "Outsiders who come in here and try to stir up trouble should be dealt with in a manner they won't forget."[4]

Some Mississippi newspapers took the Klan's numbers at face value. The two biggest-circulating papers in the state—the out-of-state New Orleans *Times-Picayune* and the Memphis *Commercial Appeal,* did not. Bill Minor of the *Times-Picayune* reported that while the Klan's new life had to be taken seriously, authorities believed its membership was more like 7,000.

If the Klan was trying to strike fear, it succeeded. In Oxford, Ohio, where Freedom Summer volunteers were training, the COFO leader Robert Moses circulated a memo pleading for President Johnson to protect the workers as they reached Mississippi. Johnson said he could not and would not send in federal help when there was an entire infrastructure of state police already there.

But in private, Johnson had expressed deep concern about the anger and firepower gathering in Mississippi. In a telephone conversation with Senator Richard Russell of Georgia, Johnson warned of a bloodbath: ". . . they tell me that every family down there is buying a gun and every Nigra family's got a gun and that there's gonna be the damnedest shootings you ever saw on [voter] registration and they're sending them in by buses in the hundreds from all over the country to help 'em register and they're gonna try to get 'em all registered in Mississippi and there're gonna be a bunch of killings."[5]

Still, the Johnson administration felt powerless. Hoping to shame or in some other way persuade the southern states to enforce the law and hold the Klan in check, and perhaps even to scare away some incoming students, the Justice Department devised a strategy to leak information to the press. Lawyers in the civil rights division prepared an extensive memo examining the rising tide of hate groups such as the Klan and the growing potential for violence. With Johnson's approval, the information was given to two reporters, Richard Harwood of *The Washington Post* and the columnist Joseph Alsop, who wrote stories warning that a catastrophe was in the making unless state authorities could restrain the Klan.[6]

Sitton, as he prepared to pull together so many loose threads, had gotten one bit of good news in recent months: the *Times* had decided to double the size of its Atlanta bureau—from one to two. John Herbers, whose leadership of the UPI bureau in Jackson had set a new standard for how news operations should approach race coverage, joined Sitton in the summer of 1963. Herbers and Sitton had known and admired each other since they had worked on the student newspaper at Emory University in the late 1940s. Herbers had moved to Washington to cover Congress for UPI and leaped at the chance to return South.

Within a month of his arrival, the *Times* had sent him to the charred rubble of the Sixteenth Street Baptist Church. Now, in the spring of 1964, he, like Sitton, was feeling a new sense of dread. Herbers went to Saint Augustine, Florida, where angry white mobs were countering Negroes' efforts to integrate the beaches. One Saturday night he was at a vacant field in Jacksonville, where three hundred "hard and humorless" men and women gathered, many dressed in Klan robes, hoods, and masks. He saw them burn a twenty-five-foot cross, sing "The Old Rugged Cross," and listen to the extremist invective of J. B. Stoner, an Atlanta attorney. "People in other parts of the country like to think of niggers as human beings because they have hands and feet," Stoner told the crowd. "So do apes and gorillas have hands and feet. If a nigger has a soul, I never read about it in the Bible. The only good nigger is a dead nigger."[7]

Sitton's worry emerged while observing the Freedom Summer volunteers undergoing training in Ohio, particularly the white college students, who seemed naïve, awkward, and ill prepared for the hatred that Sitton knew awaited them. "Besides civil rights, their chief common interest appears to be folk singing," he wrote. "Most seem to know little about the strange new world that they will enter at the end of this week." He took special note when a Negro attorney from Mississippi gave the students a stern warning that "a dark highway at midnight was no place to lecture a Mississippi deputy sheriff with a second-grade education on the niceties of constitutional law."[8]

The Oxford sessions wrapped up on Friday, June 20, just as the U.S. Congress was moving toward final passage of a sweeping civil rights bill that made the students feel part of an epic struggle fully sanctioned by their leaders. As the students pulled out of Ohio, headed for Mississippi, Sitton saw "hope and doubt, fear and determination." At the top of the front page of the

Times, he repeated his concern: "There they will face white hostility in the smallest cities, dusty county seats, farms and plantations."[9]

As Sitton was filing his story seeing the volunteers off, the *Times'* stringer in Jackson, Bill Minor, was reporting that the state was "waiting in tense calm" for the volunteers to arrive. Minor also revealed for the first time that, earlier in the week, armed white men, most of them wearing masks, had surrounded a Negro church near Philadelphia, Mississippi, in Neshoba County. He had not been able to confirm much, but he knew that night riders had beaten three Negroes and burned the church to the ground.

Both local newspapers, the weekly *Neshoba Democrat* and the daily *Meridian Star,* had received the same information, perhaps more. But they steered away from it. A *Star* reporter later said she'd been asked by the head of the local Chamber of Commerce to withhold the story since the chamber had someone visiting from New Jersey and the publicity might hurt. Only *The New York Times* and Minor's own *Times-Picayune* printed the information.

In the *Times,* the reference to the attack was contained in a single paragraph, but it carried more historic weight than anyone could have imagined. In the *Times* newsroom in New York, one person took special note of it.[10]

Of all the places in the world that the top editor of *The New York Times* might have come from, Turner Catledge, remarkably, had been raised in Philadelphia, Neshoba County, Mississippi. He still had family there. He had been born in 1901, only thirty-six years after the South's surrender. One side of his family had owned slaves, and his grandfathers, both of whom he had gotten to know, had served in the Confederate Army as young men. One, James Turner, had been part of General Nathan Bedford Forrest's cavalry, though he had not been among those who had stayed with Forrest after the war to form the Ku Klux Klan. No small amount of blood from both the Turner and Catledge sides of his family had been spilled in defense of the South; his paternal grandfather had lost three brothers to the war.

But in the generations that followed the Civil War, as Mississippi families had lined up either idolatrously for or emphatically against demagogues such as James Vardaman and Theodore Bilbo, the Turners and Catledges had been against. There also were to be no race-motivated put-downs in Turner Catledge's childhood home; he had been taught that Negroes were worthy of respect and he could expect to be spanked if he used the word "nigger."[11]

Little in Catledge's own journey to the top of the *Times* was presaged by his childhood. No one in the family had aspired to anything beyond working in the family's hardware store, and young Turner had showed great promise at that. He had been extroverted, loose, and at ease with people, able to navigate nicely through public and private situations. His uncles, who were reserved, even austere, had seen the perfect salesman in the young boy and were already envisioning his future in the store.[12]

But in high school, he had had his first taste of something else. He had showed promise in composition and typing, which got him a little work at the *Neshoba Democrat*. After that, he never seriously considered any other line of work. His writing talent led to summer jobs at the paper. He had gathered briefs, sold ads, and gotten to know the owner, Clayton Rand, who, after Catledge graduated from Mississippi State University in 1922, hired him to run a weekly in Tunica. After a short reporting stint in Tupelo, Catledge had made his way to the *Commercial Appeal* in Memphis, then to *The New York Times* in 1924.

As he had risen to the position of assistant managing editor, then managing editor, Catledge had directed coverage of every major news event and tackled just about every major newspaper issue for thirty-five years. Now, in 1964, he was facing perhaps the most monumental of them all: the U.S. Supreme Court had heard oral arguments in the *The New York Times Co. v. L. B. Sullivan* case on January 6, and a decision seemed close. The court would decide nothing less than how free the press really could be. If the decision went against the *Times,* would reporters be vulnerable to every libel claim filed by a ticked-off sheriff? A newspaper could find itself tied in a tangle in some backwater courtroom for years, and a reporter based in the South might find himself idling in Atlanta and useless to his paper.

The *Times* had been fighting more than a half-dozen libel suits, totaling more than $6 million, for four years. Litigation was still pending against CBS for Howard K. Smith's 1961 program "Who Speaks for Birmingham?" But it wasn't just the *Times* and other news organizations with deep pockets that were facing wildly expensive verdicts. By early 1964, public officials in three southern states had no fewer than seventeen libel lawsuits pending against newspapers, magazines, and a television station, seeking total damages that exceeded $288 million. Former Major General Edwin Walker was demanding $20 million from the Associated Press and about ten media outlets—including the Fort Worth *Star-Telegram,* Hodding Carter's Greenville *Delta Democrat-Times,* and papers in Louisville, Atlanta, New Orleans, and Saint Louis—for publishing a story that said he had encouraged rioting at Ole Miss in 1962.[13]

So far, the tide was running against the press. The first jury to hear a Walker case, in Fort Worth, had given him $800,000 and gotten handshakes from the judge who presided. "The jury has reflected the attitude of the entire country with respect to false and one-sided reporting of the news," the judge said. Walker's attorney was gleeful: "Oh, we'll crucify them in Mississippi and Louisiana, too," he said, adding, "They have as much chance of reversing this case as I have of flying out that window, around the First National Bank Building and back."[14]

Editors weighing whether to send their reporters into the South knew the risks. The lawyers' fees alone would cripple most newspapers. And where would it end? If the yahoos picked off one of our reporters with a libel suit, an editor might wonder, would I send in another? And after that?

The answer came on March 9. The Supreme Court, ruling in favor of the *Times,* held that a public official was not entitled to libel damages for criticism of his official performance unless he could prove that there had been actual malice. The verdict had taken nine drafts and an extraordinary flurry of memo exchanges in the final week, but it was unanimous. The only disagreement came from three justices, who, in separate concurring opinions, said the Court should have granted an absolute privilege, protecting even malicious criticism. A new standard, a new and powerful protection for editors and reporters, had suddenly become the law of the land. Not all fear and litigation went away immediately, however. Walker was a public figure, not a public official, and the Supreme Court ruling applied only to public officials. It would be three more years before the Supreme Court, by a narrower 5–4 verdict, would extend the protection against libel suits brought by public figures.[15]

At age sixty-three, Catledge had seen a lot. He had been rewarded with a title never before granted at the *Times:* executive editor. He was not easy to surprise. But he could never have imagined that the newspaper's top story, for weeks to come, would carry the dateline of his little hometown.

The Freedom Summer volunteers had left Oxford, traveling by car, and arrived in Mississippi on Saturday, June 20, 1964. The next evening, the volunteers Michael Schwerner, James Chaney, and Andrew Goodman, while checking on the church that had been burned, were stopped by police in Neshoba County, taken to the jail in Philadelphia, released, then stopped again.

Reports that they were missing spread quickly. Freedom Summer had hardly begun before the worst fears of its participants had been realized. As the search for the men began, reporters came rushing into Philadelphia.

Sitton was among the first to arrive. He'd learned long before to join up with other reporters—certain ones, anyway—so he, Fleming, and Nicholas von Hoffman, who was writing for the *Chicago Daily News,* together headed for the sheriff's office. By this time *Newsweek* had reassigned Fleming to its Houston bureau to cover the aftermath of the Kennedy assassination, including the trial of Jack Ruby for killing Lee Harvey Oswald. But Fleming had insisted on holding on to the race beat, and he swung back into action for the unfolding drama of Freedom Summer and Philadelphia.[16]

Sitton, Fleming, and von Hoffman met the deputy sheriff, Cecil Price, on the courthouse lawn, which Price was pelting with tobacco spit. Sitton saw a smirk on Price's face as he described how he had stopped those boys for speeding, brought them all in, let them go, and hadn't seen them again. The reporters didn't believe him.

Almost as soon as the word got out that the men were missing, so did the claim that it must be a hoax. "I don't believe there's three missing," Senator James Eastland told Lyndon Johnson when the president called him two days after the men were reported missing. "I believe it's a public-ity stunt."[17]

Eastland and other giants of southern politics were facing a juggernaut that only increased the xenophobia back in Eastland's home state. The House of Representatives, by a substantial 290–130 vote, had passed a sweeping civil rights bill in February. Now Eastland was working furiously to derail the bill—even after limiting debate, the Senate had taken up 115 amend-ments and recorded 106 roll-call votes—but he was failing.[18]

Played out against the backdrop of a presidential campaign, the drama rose as a bipartisan group of Republican and Democrat senators pressed for passage of the bill. Senator Barry Goldwater, the near-certain Republican nominee for president, split with his own party's leaders by coming out against it. On June 19, the 1964 Civil Rights Act, prohibiting racial and other forms of discrimination in employment, public access, and housing, passed 73–27. It made some changes in voting rights and school desegrega-tion, extended the Civil Rights Commission, created a community relations service to resolve discrimination disputes, and strengthened the federal gov-ernment's power to enforce the law.[19]

As Johnson prepared to sign the bill on July 2, he worried that he would only trigger more violence in Mississippi. Philadelphia, in the midst of a search for the students' bodies, had become one of the most prominent date-lines in the world. Reporters, FBI agents, clergymen, White House emis-saries, two hundred Navy Seals, and even psychics were overrunning it. Johnson called the FBI's J. Edgar Hoover and asked him to send in an extra fifty to one hundred agents. "Now I don't want these Klansmen to open their mouth without your knowing what they're saying," Johnson told him.[20]

On the streets of Philadelphia, the reporters felt the cold stares from men who circled them in slow-moving pickup trucks with whiplash antennas and hunting rifles racked in the rear windows. Sitton saw some tagging behind them, heard them closing in, muttering threats. His eyes moved quickly across the town square and spied a sign for a hardware store. It was the store owned by Turner Catledge's uncles, the place Catledge had urged Sitton to visit if he ever made it to Philadelphia.

"There's help for sure," a relieved Sitton told Fleming and von Hoffman as they picked up their stride. Inside, Sitton met the uncle in charge, a thin, redheaded man whose mouth, Sitton noticed, appeared pulled together by a drawstring. Sitton introduced himself, made the Catledge connection and waited for a warm welcome. It didn't come. "Be frank with you, Sitton," Mr. Turner said, squinting his eyes. "If you were a black man being whupped out there on the sidewalk, I might help you. But you got no business here. And I wouldn't lift a finger if they was stomping the hell out of you."

Sitton, Fleming, and von Hoffman headed for the door. "Claude," Fleming said as they walked out, "good thing you've got some influence in this town or we'd be in big damn trouble here."[21]

Most of the time the humor didn't come so easily. Reporters ran into hostility at nearly every corner. They were confronted by thugs banging on their motel doors. They got threatening calls in the middle of the night. They were followed. Fleming tried to ward them off by affecting a sneering bravado that took advantage of his 216 pounds, his height, which exceeded six feet, his crew cut, his filterless Camels and sometimes a cigar. But as he'd sit in his room at nights, knocking back Jack Daniel's and reflecting on the day, he'd realize how frightened he'd been. On at least one occasion, armed white men showed up at the motel with two offers that they swore were conciliatory: a gallon of moonshine poured into a vinegar jug and a ride to see some farmland. The reporters decided not to test the goodwill of the gesture.[22]

There was reason to be fearful. In early February, a twenty-three-year-old freelance news photographer was beaten by law enforcement officers in Notasulga, Alabama, after he boarded a school bus carrying the first Negro students to a white high school. A Baltimore *Sun* reporter, covering a confrontation in Cambridge, Maryland, took in so much tear gas while dictating from a phone booth that he was vomiting and coughing and couldn't read his notes. An NBC soundman covering a Florida demonstration spent three days in a hospital after someone in a white mob used a bicycle chain to cut a gash in his skull. When a Negro crowd in Birmingham mistook a white *Detroit News* reporter for the person who had bombed a motel, only police intervention saved him.[23]

Editors at the *Birmingham News* were worried enough about attacks on its staffers that they wrote a letter to George Wallace's press secretary, Bill Jones, insisting that he make the governor aware of the need for police protection for journalists. "You know what the press has to do for the public," they wrote. "You know the governor ought to know, if he doesn't, that any newsman, local or otherwise, feels he's facing personal violence every time he tries to cover news of racial incidents. And you know, Bill, that this is not a good condition."[24]

Sitton found that the most effective response was similar to the method that had worked for John Chancellor in Mississippi in 1955 when white racists attacked him: Chancellor had held up his microphone and threatened to broadcast their assault. When the manager of Sitton's hotel tried to evict him before white roughnecks did it themselves, Sitton responded angrily, "Look, tell these folks that they can shoot me. But I guarantee you that there will be five just like me to get off the plane at Jackson airport tomorrow, and they'll be right up here to cover the story. It won't do you any good."[25]

Chancellor, just back in the United States after several years covering Europe, returned to the race story. He saw that feelings had only hardened in those years. "Where ya from?" a deputy asked when he walked into the sheriff's office in Neshoba County. NBC, Chancellor told him, the National Broadcasting Company. "Sheriff, there's some son-of-a-bitch here from the Nigger Broadcasting Company," the deputy yelled. Reporters for ABC, American Broadcasting Company, got the same treatment; they were called the African Broadcasting Company. At CBS, Columbia Broadcasting System, reporters had to endure the moniker Coon Broadcasting System.[26]

William Bradford Huie was working for the *New York Herald Tribune.* Von Hoffman came down from Chicago, where he began making an impression that only confirmed the locals' suspicion that the left-wing press had come to prosecute. He had been a protégé of the Chicago community organizer Saul Alinsky before becoming a journalist. Even when he tried to blend in with the southern sartorial landscape by donning khakis, a work shirt, and a Stetson hat, he would be betrayed by his New York manner, his shock of white hair, and his tendency to vocalize his political leanings.[27]

In addition to the half-dozen reporters who were assigned aspects of the story out of Washington, *The New York Times* sent an all-star team into the South. Sitton and Herbers were joined by Homer Bigart, David Halberstam, and Joseph Lelyveld. Bigart had two Pulitzer Prizes to his credit, both for war coverage. Halberstam had started his career in Mississippi, had covered the Nashville Movement that had produced the heart and soul of SNCC, and had just won the Pulitzer for his reporting from Vietnam. Herbers had not reported from a battlefield, but he felt that covering the race story as it ran unpredictably between an aggressive movement and intransigent official-dom must be a lot like covering a war. He became certain of it on Halberstam's third day in Mississippi. "There are several parallels," Halberstam told him, "between Mississippi and Vietnam."[28]

Lelyveld was a rising star only weeks from assignment to South Africa; he would later win a Pulitzer and become the newspaper's top editor. Only three weeks after the civil rights workers disappeared, the violence in the South had hit close to home for Lelyveld. His father, Rabbi Arthur Lelyveld of Cleveland, Ohio, was a personal friend of the family of Andrew Goodman. Like a growing number of rabbis and other Jewish leaders, Rabbi Lelyveld had headed south, to Hattiesburg, Mississippi, to work on a voter registration drive. As he and two other white men had escorted two Negro girls, a pickup truck pulled close. Two white men had jumped out and started hitting Lelyveld and the others with an iron bar. Lelyveld had gotten the worst of it—deep cuts behind one ear and beneath an eye. He was treated and hustled out of state to recuperate with relatives in Alabama.[29]

There was no discussion at the *Times* about whether it would be appropriate to send the rabbi's son into Mississippi on a civil rights story. It was quite by accident that it even happened. Joseph Lelyveld had just finished writing a Sunday magazine article for the *Times* when the magazine editor said he'd like to get one more article out of Lelyveld before he went to South Africa. "What would you like to do?" the editor asked him. Lelyveld had been covering some elements of the civil rights movement in New York and Philadelphia, Pennsylvania, and thought of a couple of stories that might make magazine articles in the latter. So he suggested going to Philadelphia. The editor departed, then returned with permission for Lelyveld to go to Philadelphia—but, due to a misunderstanding, the one in Mississippi.[30]

Bigart had been there before Lelyveld and had made a memorable impression—both good and bad. In Mississippi, segregationists had delighted in making fun of his name and its similarity to both "nigger" and, in the southern dialect, "bigot."[31] In the *Times* newsroom, one of Bigart's descriptive dispatches from Philadelphia had become part of his legend—to the newspaper's embarrassment. Bigart had covered the FBI stakeout and arrest of Neshoba County Sheriff Lawrence Rainey and his deputy, Cecil Price, in connection with the deaths of the civil rights workers. Bigart's file to New York said that "agents were picking up a dozen other suspects, a potpourri of peckerwoods and rednecks that included a fundamentalist preacher, an itinerant bouncer for beer taverns, a Philadelphia policeman and two alleged officials of the White Knights of the Ku Klux Klan."[32]

The word "rednecks" appeared three more times. The story went to the national copy desk, where Bigart's aggressive descriptions, the ones that went past pure beauty and into the offensive, were closely watched and frequently tempered. This time, the copy editor let the words stand, and they appeared in the newspaper that way. The copy editor drew a sharp rebuke from his bosses and thereafter refused to edit Bigart. "That's too dangerous," he would say whenever a Bigart story was headed his way. "Give me something else."[33]

One other thing made Bigart memorable: he spoke with a stutter that colleagues frequently saw him use to his benefit to coax information from reluctant sources.

Lelyveld, sent to Philadelphia after Bigart, met a local minister, introduced himself, and interviewed the minister. He came away with an unforgettable lesson in what it takes to be a great newspaper reporter.

"You've asked me a lot of questions," the minister said in a buttery southern accent after the interview with over. "Can I ask you one?"

"Yes sir," Lelyveld responded.

"There was a man down here, an older man, said *he* was from *The New York Times*. Name of Bigaht. Know 'im?"

"Yes sir."

"Couldn't have a normal conversation with that man," the minister went on. "He didn't know anything. I had to explain *evvvverything* to him."[34]

Inside the newsroom in New York, Catledge didn't offer much insight into, and virtually no comment on, his feelings about the unfortunate prominence of his hometown as a dateline. But he was filled with conflict. He had been horrified by Ross Barnett's stubborn behavior yet remained proud of Mississippi and Neshoba County; he wouldn't allow himself to believe the state was as awful as it looked. "Where, oh where, are those decent people I used to know?" he asked in a letter to a longtime friend back in Philadelphia, Florence Mars. "Most, of course, are over there on the hill, but where are their descendants?"[35]

On one of Catledge's visits to Philadelphia, while the civil rights workers were still missing, some of those descendants asked for a meeting with him. About thirty men and a few women, including some Catledge and Turner cousins, gathered in the new, ranch-style home of a local lumber company owner, Richard Molpus. Most of them had not been in the presence of someone, much less a native son, who dined with presidents. But their awe was mixed with a concern that Catledge had betrayed them.[36]

After drinks had been served and pleasantries exchanged, Catledge took a seat in a corner near the piano and listened to complaints about how badly reporters were treating his hometown. *They'll do anything to make us look bad. . . . They always want to interview the dumbest, most ignorant resident they can find. . . . They make us look stupid when they write what we say. . . .*

Catledge, drinking scotch and water, was gentle but forceful in response. By his deployment of *Times* reporters to the region, he had already signaled his commitment to covering the story comprehensively, and with urgency. The *Times* had held a full-time stake in the South for seventeen years, and it intended to remain a force.

His reporters were splendid, he told the group, and he urged the residents to keep their mouths closed if they didn't want to be quoted. Beyond that, he said, they were wrong about where the leadership problem resided. They hadn't even discussed the church burnings, the ongoing Klan harassment, or the near certainty that something horrific must have happened to the three civil rights workers. Their town, he said, was on a world stage at a critical moment in history, and yet they couldn't see, or weren't acknowledging, that they had allowed the leadership of their community to become hijacked by the worst elements. It was time, he said, for them to stand up, demonstrate leadership, and show some courage.

Altogether, forty-four days would pass before the bodies of the civil rights workers would be found, buried in the muck of a remote earthen dam. At least one had been beaten, and all three had been shot and killed.

For the on-ground reporter covering the race beat, the *Times v. Sullivan* decision represented a form of liberation—but the kind of liberation that only made the job more demanding. Across the South, there were so many incidents to be covered, so many organizations to be examined, so many profiles to be written, so many policies to be explored, and they were all wrapped up in the politics, the religion, the economy, and the ingrained habits of a besieged region that an increasingly enlightened nation wanted to change.

The reporters on the race beat were expected to cover, to make sense of, to explain the SCLC, SNCC, NAACP, CORE, COFO, SCEF, KKK, Citizens' Councils, Mississippi State Sovereignty Commission, Defenders of State Sovereignty and Individual Liberties, Americans for the Preservation of the White Race, and more. They had to know when the various slices of the same movement were working together and when they were beginning to war with one another—in scores of towns across the region. Knowing law enforcement, seeing behind their mask, was especially challenging. Sheriffs and police chiefs would lie, and the FBI, often at odds with local law enforcement and frequently in a fight with the Civil Rights Division of the same Justice Department that was the parent of both, was never consistent in the guidance and misguidance it would provide. Reporters, especially those representing news organizations outside the South, were never certain whom to trust.

Two months after the *Sullivan* ruling, *Newsweek* decided that the press covering the civil rights movement was itself worth a story. "Needing Tuesday, May 19, fullest on new news beat—civil rights," said a query telexed from *Newsweek* editors in New York to the magazine's bureaus in Atlanta and Houston. "In past two or three years, the continuing nature of civil rights story has prompted many newspapers to increase staff to handle it. . . . Who covers civil rights in your area? Have newspapers hired any Negro reporters and do they only cover civil rights issue. What their background and experience? How they feel about their assignment, what are its difficulties? How dangerous is it. Have they ever been caught in demonstrations, riots? Is there any antagonism in Negro community toward them when they cover a story . . ."[37]

The *Newsweek* story three weeks later said there were about eighty "race reporters" working "among the magnolias and the cattle prods." Sam Adams, a thirty-eight-year-old reporter for the *St. Petersburg Times,* was the only Negro journalist covering the race beat for a southern mainstream newspaper. He was from Waycross, Georgia, near the Okefenokee Swamp, had started at the *Atlanta Daily World,* and had worked on *The Des Moines Register.* His race helped him gain access to some meetings his white counterparts missed, he told *Newsweek.* But white officials could be very hostile to him, until they learned he wrote for a white newspaper. As a Negro in the South, when a gun had been held to his head after his daughter had used a whites-only bathroom, then as a reporter in the South, Adams had learned some lessons: "You don't stick your hand into your pocket when you're around a bigot, for that's an excuse to be killed. You don't show fear and, if possible, you keep smiling. That hurts most."[38]

A handful of Negroes had worked on mainstream white dailies for years—*Ebony* magazine had counted thirty-one of them in 1955—and many had achieved great recognition: Ted Poston at the *New York Post,* Carl Rowan at the *Minneapolis Tribune,* George Brown at the *Denver Post,* and the first Negro Nieman fellow, Fletcher Martin, at the *Chicago Sun-Times,* among others. But Adams was working in the South, no small breakthrough.[39]

Newsweek didn't delve into the subject, but Adams was more than a Negro pioneer on a white-owned newspaper in the South; the flip side was more to the point: he was a young star reporter who was *not* working for the Negro press. Though Adams represented a slow movement toward racial integration in the mainstream newsroom, he also symbolized a step toward the decline of the Negro newspaper.

Several reporters in the *Newsweek* article told of their notebooks being ripped from their hands, of their windshields being shattered, of being chased by clouds of tear gas. Harassment was a constant. In Notasulga earlier in the year, the wires to the only public telephone booth in town had been cut, so the Associated Press had arranged to pay a month's lease on a telephone in the local offices of the telephone company. A half day into the deal, the manager had changed his mind, and AP was able to file only after its Montgomery bureau chief got a state senator involved in lining up a family that would make their home phone available.

Walter Rugaber, a reporter for *The Atlanta Journal,* expressed concern that the tinderbox could explode at any time. "Race is a very emotional question, and there are all those people saying they're going to do all those things, and one of these days one of 'em is going to do something," he told *Newsweek.* Al Kuettner, who, at fifty, had spent half his life with UPI, marveled at how southerners underwent a transformation whenever the subject of race came up. "People are suspicious; they'll lie when they wouldn't think of it otherwise. The people of Mississippi are the most marvelous in the world," he said, "until you mention race."[40]

One reporter stood above the rest, *Newsweek* said, "The best daily newspaperman on the Southern scene is the Atlanta-based Sitton. An indefatigable stickler for facts, Sitton is so trusted and widely known in the South that telephone calls follow him wherever he goes."[41]

With nearly six exhausting years behind him as the southern correspondent, Sitton was still on the road more than at home for weeks at a time. When, after a long stretch on the road, he got home for his first meal with his wife, Eva, and their four children, his phone would ring before he'd even pick up his fork. He'd know he was headed to the airport even before one of his children answered the phone and, using their nickname for Sitton's national editor, Harrison Salisbury, told him that "old Strawberry" was on the line.

The Sittons ultimately put up paneling and installed an air conditioner in their porch to create a home office so Sitton could spend more time at home when he was in town and not wake everyone up when he got back into town late and still had to work. He missed key milestones in the lives of his children. "Look, Eva! Clint's talking!" Sitton blurted out one evening when their oldest child showed off some early language skills; he had no idea that Clint had been speaking for several weeks. His time away had one benefit, Eva told *Newsweek:* "It cuts down on the housekeeping."[42]

Newsweek reporters also asked Reverend King and SNCC communications director Julian Bond their views of news coverage of civil rights but didn't publish them. "I would certainly be the first to say we have had a very fine press corps from the main newspapers and magazines covering the civil rights movement," said King. "By and large they have done a very thorough job of fair and objective reporting." But the focus on coverage of violence concerned him, he said, especially when the focus of the movement was on nonviolence.

Bond was more critical, finding that reporters "too often have a tendency to look for the spectacular rather than the significant." Reporters seemed too focused on divisions in the movement, he said, on finding out "who is stabbing Martin Luther King in the back this week." Too much time was spent chasing down "surface details," the scorecard of how many demonstrators were present, how many were jailed, he said. He thought of two exceptions: Sitton and Fleming.[43]

But the guard was changing again. Six years after Sitton began chronicling the great social upheaval that had gelled into the civil rights movement, the *Times* decided to pull him out of the South. Salisbury was being elevated to an assistant managing editor post, and Sitton would succeed him in the position that the *Times,* uniquely, called "national news director," or national editor. Sitton would move to New York, he would become responsible for ten regional bureaus and 250 part-time correspondents, and he would take with him the reputation for being the best there was in covering, exposing, and interpreting the race story in the South.[44]

By the fall of 1964, *Southern School News* was celebrating its tenth year in business, and its board, the SERS, was questioning its viability.[45]

Four years earlier, the board had faced down another in a series of near-death experiences. It was printing only 4,800 copies in 1960, down from 11,000 at the end of its second year. The novelty of desegregation stories in the border states had worn off, and there was no movement in the hard-core resister states. So *Southern School News* ventured into coverage of sit-ins, arrests, and civil rights confrontations. Segregationist board members were fuming.[46]

In the end, the board backed away from covering demonstrations. But board members asked themselves if the newspaper had overstayed its welcome. Board member Pete McKnight met with the *Southern School News* correspondents. The reporting staff had remained remarkably stable all along. Nearly half the original nineteen were still filing six years later, and while the total number of correspondents had dropped to twelve in 1964, seven of those had been writing for the publication for five years or more.[47]

"The reaction from the journalists is that there is not the same urgency, not the same zeal, as there was 10 or 11 years ago," McKnight reported to the board members. "The press and news media as a whole are doing a much better job, a more complete job of coverage of school desegregation than in 1954."[48]

Within months, in 1965, *Southern School News* folded. The SERS and a successor organization would continue for another decade, producing a feature magazine that examined children, poverty, and ethnicity.

But there could be only pride that *Southern School News* had endured as long as it had. The SERS board that Ashmore had formed in 1954 had brought together some of the most forceful, strong-minded men in the South, men of great—and greatly differing—convictions about the most important social movement in the nation's history. For ten years, they had argued, debated, and threatened to quit. In the end, they had refused to let their differences destroy their common mission of providing a professional, journalistic monthly account of school desegregation in the South.

One measure of the growing influence of news coverage was the increased effort of so many organizations to use and manipulate it.

Some efforts were standard operating procedure: Lyndon Johnson hosted editors of Negro newspapers in Washington, among them Emory Jackson, to watch the historic House debate on the civil rights bill, then invited them to the White House. That was a small effort compared to Wallace's invitation a year later to 1,700 newspaper editors to tour Alabama and embrace its virtues. Fewer than fifty showed up, and Wallace's clumsy management of the tour backfired.

In some cases, relationships between public figures and reporters crossed a line that was not as visible as it would later become. Lady Bird Johnson's press secretary, Liz Carpenter, asked *Atlanta Constitution* editor Gene Patterson, in 1964 what the First Lady could speak about during a campaign appearance in Georgia. Patterson decided that he might as well write the speech and send it by Western Union. "She came out and read every word of it," he would later recall.[49]

But the more serious challenges to the integrity of the press came from those working in government agencies, from the FBI down to the sovereignty commissions that had been created in the southern states to protect their interests against outside encroachment—usually by spying, gathering information on, and harassing anyone they considered a threat.

The state-level spy agencies were more than mere annoyances. They were propagandists which, despite their claims to the contrary at the time, were devoting more time to invading the privacy of civil rights figures and gathering information on anyone deemed a threat than they were on polishing their state's image.

In Mississippi, the Sovereignty Commission was able to turn to its favorite Negro newspaperman, Percy Greene, owner and editor of the *Jackson Advocate.* In the past, the commission had paid him to keep certain news out of his paper, to give speeches, and to attend meetings as a vociferous proponent of the status quo. By 1964, the commission had a new scheme: it would plant an "expose" of Reverend King in Greene's paper, then white newspapers and wire services would pick it up, attribute it to the Negro newspaper, and fool the vast number of readers who had no idea Greene was on the commission payroll.

Having made all the arrangements, Erle Johnston, Jr., director of the commission, wrote a memo, explaining, "We have already discussed this idea with the Jackson press and they have agreed to pick up the story quoting the *Jackson Advocate*. In this manner the story will be more effective because a Negro will be the author exposing the communist associations of other Negroes. The Sovereignty Commission will not appear in any of the publicity."[50]

It worked. In the month before Freedom Summer was to commence, the *Jackson Advocate* ran a Sovereignty Commission story suggesting that King was in the grip of Communists. "See Communist Influence Behind the Coming Summer Demonstrations in the State" was the headline across all columns of the *Advocate*'s front page. The story said that King, the SCLC, the NAACP, and SNCC had financial and other ties to the Southern Conference Educational Fund. SCEF was a liberal interracial human rights organization favored by Eleanor Roosevelt.[51]

The Associated Press picked up the story, gave credit to the *Advocate*, and, without citing any source for the information, put it on the wire. *The Clarion-Ledger*, as planned, ran the AP account on the front page, under the headline "M. L. King Linked to Red Front." Then a state representative, who was also a member of the Sovereignty Commission, stood on the House floor and read the so-called exposé from the *Advocate*.[52]

FBI Director Hoover, too, believed King had surrounded himself with dangerous people, mostly Communists. Hoover had been placing wiretaps, or bugs, on King and his associates since mid-1963. The FBI had long had a Mass Media Program aimed at disseminating positive stories about the agency. But the rise of King changed that. Since 1962, the agency had been planting stories in the southern press that hinted darkly but vaguely at seditious connections between King and his associates. The stories, usually attributed to "a highly authoritative source" or not attributed at all, appeared to have been substantially put together by the FBI and varied little from one newspaper to the next. The bureau had managed to get its stories printed in the *Augusta Chronicle* in Georgia, the *Birmingham News,* the *Jackson Daily News* and *Clarion-Ledger,* the *St. Louis Globe-Democrat,* and the *Long Island Star-Journal.* Some newspapers had put their own reporters' bylines onto the stories; in at least one case, the newspaper's editor curried the favor of the FBI by taking the byline himself.[53]

The FBI had started wiretapping King in late 1963 in the SCLC offices in Atlanta and New York, in his Atlanta home, then in hotel rooms where King was staying.[54] Two days before Christmas that year, the agency's domestic intelligence division discussed goals that included "neutralizing King as an effective Negro leader." The bureau vowed to "keep close watch on King's personal activities," especially his liquor consumption and relationships with women. The summary added, "Although King is a minister, we have already developed information concerning weakness in his character which is of such a nature as to make him unfit to serve as a minister of the gospel. . . . We will, at the proper time, when it can be done without embarrassment to the Bureau, expose King as an immoral opportunist who is not a sincere person but is exploiting the racial situation for personal gain."[55]

As the information the FBI gathered went from political alliances to sexual dalliances, Hoover had become even more fixated on King. In the early days of 1964, Hoover had been provided an especially salacious set of tapes recorded through bugs in King's room at the Willard Hotel in Washington, two blocks from the White House. The eleven reels of recorded tapes indicated that King had hosted a party that had lasted fourteen hours and included a dramatic outburst during a sexual encounter. Only days before, King had been named *Time* magazine's "Man of the Year."[56]

In the fall of 1964, King won the Nobel Peace Prize, which only intensified Hoover's interest in discrediting him. FBI reports on King gained wider and more accelerated circulation. Hoover, still smarting from a comment King had made during the Albany demonstration about the indifference of southern-bred FBI agents, disregarded advice from his top aides and publicly called King "one of the lowest characters in the country," adding that he believed that King had Communist ties.[57]

As pleased as Hoover and his closest aides were with the bumper crop of juicy information, it wouldn't do much good if they couldn't get it printed in a credible publication. Top Hoover aides began shopping what they said were transcripts of the tapes. Ben Bradlee, then *Newsweek*'s Washington bureau chief, told an agent he wasn't interested—at least, not interested in publishing it.[58]

In Atlanta, *Constitution* editor Eugene Patterson was in his office one day when an FBI agent came to visit him. Patterson and the agent served together on the council of their church, and the agent had been a source for Patterson. The agent wanted to talk about King. "You know he's been carrying on with girls," the agent said. King was preparing to fly from Miami to the Caribbean with a mistress, the agent said. He could help a *Constitution* reporter and photographer catch them in Miami, so long as the FBI's role was never revealed. The *Constitution* had held up King as a model of virtue, the agent said, and the FBI was giving the newspaper an opportunity to reveal the truth.

"We're not a peephole journal," Patterson responded sharply. "I'm not going to print the story." In the end, Patterson was pleasantly surprised to see that the FBI could not find any newspaper that would go along. It was one thing for him, a progressive on the issue of race, to show the FBI agent the door; it would be quite difficult for a segregationist editor. Not long after his meeting with the agent, Patterson got a call from Louis Harris, editor of *The Augusta Chronicle*. Harris was not the most rabid segregationist editor but he did not care much for King. "Gene, the damnedest thing's happened," Harris told him. "I was talking to this fellow from the FBI . . ."

"They told you about Dr. King, didn't they?" Patterson said.

"How'd you know?" Harris asked.

"They've been to see me, too."

"I'll be damned," said Harris. "Are you going to print that stuff?"

Patterson knew he wasn't, but he wanted a peek into Harris's heart, so he just returned the question: "Are you?"

"Hell no!" Harris declared. "We don't print that kind of stuff. If you print it about him, you can print it about any man."

Patterson was impressed. "Louis," he said, "you've restored my faith."[59]

While Hoover's FBI was attempting to discredit King, a group of segregationist Atlanta businessmen was developing a plan to do something about Ralph McGill and, in fact, all of the suspected integrationists writing columns and editorials for the Atlanta dailies. Gene Patterson was a constant irritant, as was his entire *Constitution* editorial board. On the *Journal,* Reese Cleghorn, the associate editor, while less well known than McGill and Patterson, punched hard and often at racial intolerance.

There was no way to muzzle McGill and his cohorts, the segregationists knew; but maybe they could provide an alternative, competing newspaper in Atlanta. It wouldn't be cheap or easy, but it was worth a try, they thought, and they set about arranging loans and selling stock.

McGill, of course, gave ardent segregationists reason to despise him. Every time they thought he went too far, he went farther, then farther yet. By 1964, his thinking had fully evolved in front of all his readers. He had started out arguing that separate was okay as long as it was accompanied by equal and that the federal government should not regulate poll taxes and ban lynching because those were state prerogatives. But he had found that position less defensible in the face of the South's clear lack of interest in equality, its violence, and the toxic tone of so many of its demagogic leaders.

After the 1954 *Brown* decision, he had backed school desegregation—first simply because it was the law, then, in time, because he felt it was just and equitable. In 1960 and 1961, having staked a firm position that every segregationist from governors to street thugs should obey the law of the land, he had been taken aback when young, determined students and activists had embarked on clearly illegal sit-ins. But the brutal response of white reactionaries had so offended him that he had concluded that the Negro and white rebels were responding, appropriately, to a "moral law" of much greater importance.

By 1963, with police dogs snarling and fire hoses spewing in Birmingham, McGill had little patience for southerners who failed to see that the "revolution of rising expectations" in Latin America, Africa, and Asia had also taken hold in the United States. "Since it may not be avoided, it must be faced," he wrote—in churches, in businesses, in all walks of life.[60]

On May 4, 1964, he endorsed President Johnson's civil rights bill. He called it "an emancipation proclamation for the South," and argued that everyone would benefit and the South's economy would grow more rapidly if Congress approved it. "No single act," he wrote, "would add as much impetus to Southern development as enactment of law that will, in due time, open the public sector of life to all citizens . . . the right to vote, to seek a job, and to use public services."[61]

Not only had McGill expanded his views on race over the years, but he had elevated his stature. His columns were syndicated nationally, reaching millions of readers in three hundred newspapers.[62] He wrote articles for many of the nation's most important magazines, appeared on television networks, and spoke frequently in forums across the nation. All the activity added up to a distinct mission: he wanted to show that there were two Souths, one of them wanting more opportunity and fairer play for Negroes.

When McGill spoke, he had impact. He was as well known nationally as many of the South's governors, and better known internationally. President Kennedy sent him to Africa for two months as his special envoy. He also appointed him to the President's Advisory Committee on Labor and Management, and to a presidential commission on arms control and disarmament. In McGill's mind, none of his involvements in government posed a journalistic conflict. He was, after all, a columnist who took sides on issues. He had the title of publisher of the *Constitution* but no control over the newsroom or business operations.

McGill's success rankled segregationist editors. When he signed a contract for his book *The South and the Southerner,* Jack Kilpatrick, who had just published his own book, wrote the Citizens' Councils executive director, William J. Simmons, "Did you see that Rastus McGill got $5,000 from Atlantic for a book he has written for publication in the spring of 1963? He makes me puke, honest to God he does."[63]

The resentment of segregationist editors was child's play compared with the deep hatred he touched off among the South's most bitter, most recalcitrant racists. They deluged him with letters, made threats, and harassed him at home with phone calls that almost always began with the same question: "Is this Rastus McGill?" For the most part, he fought back with humor. He bought a dog, named him Rastus, and trained him to bark when a telephone receiver was aimed at him. Thereafter, when McGill got one of those calls, he would say, "Oh, you want Rastus" and point the receiver at the wildly yapping dog.

True, McGill was never in a local racial hurricane as turbulent as those experienced by Harry Ashmore, Lenoir Chambers, and Buford Boone. But, arguably, this was because he helped stave off the storms by forming alliances with Robert Woodruff, the Coca-Cola magnate, and with successive mayors, William Hartsfield and Ivan Allen, Jr., to keep the city calm, yield on such issues as school and lunch counter desegregation, and burnish Atlanta's image as "the city too busy to hate." It didn't hurt that a Coca-Cola executive reminded the city's business elite that Coke did business with virtually every race, creed, and country in the world and might reluctantly be forced to move its company headquarters from Atlanta if the city were ever to become, like Little Rock, a symbol of racial turmoil.

But there were still powerful business interests that opposed racial change in general and Ralph McGill and the *Constitution* and *Journal* in particular.

At 11:15 in the morning on Friday, June 12, 1964, a tall, distinguished-looking gentleman, the publisher James C. Davis, stood beside a set of presses at an all-new, first-class newspaper plant and pressed the button that launched an afternoon newspaper many hoped would become the new voice of the South. The *Atlanta Times,* a full-fledged, seven-day-a-week newspaper, promised editorial views on race matters that were considerably more in line with the attitudes of white Georgians. It was, many said, as much a cause as it was a newspaper.[64]

The newspaper's board of directors included well-established bankers, an automobile dealer, a real estate developer, a radio executive, a timber man, a clothing manufacturer, and a car wash owner. Some 5,000 Georgians purchased company stock, helping raise about $3 million.

Davis's motives were clear: "Atlanta has newspapers with out-of-state ownership that promote radicalism in every form, the New Deal, the Fair Deal, Modern Republicanism, and have completely disregarded the right-thinking, sound-thinking people of Atlanta and Georgia." To Davis, Ralph McGill and Gene Patterson were the embodiment of all that was wrong. It opened its plant on Forrest Street, named after Nathan Bedford Forrest of Civil War and Ku Klux Klan fame.[65]

Segregationists had been trying for years to start their own newspapers in southern cities where progressive papers operated. The Charleston editor Tom Waring turned down an overture from Marion A. Parrott, a North Carolina lawyer and white supremacist, who wanted to mount a challenge to the Daniels family's Raleigh *News & Observer.* He rejected an invitation from Lester Maddox, the cornpone Atlanta restaurant owner, who wanted Waring to help him take on the Cox newspapers three years before the *Atlanta Times* got rolling. He figured both offers were doomed to fail.[66]

There was reason for caution in launching ideological newspapers. The

Chapter 22

Selma

One theme that Ralph McGill wove into his columns over the years was the issue of voting rights. Freedom to vote, McGill knew, was the very cornerstone of democracy. As crucial as school desegregation and access to public accommodations were to southern blacks, they would always be fragile if blacks could not participate freely in the election of state, local, and federal officials who were responsible for enforcing the laws.

No one agreed more than Reverend King. He and his organizers and strategists were pleased by, even jubilant at, the Civil Rights Act of 1964, but they were disappointed, too. It would have little impact on voting rights. It did not ban literacy tests, which many southern counties used to disenfranchise blacks, and it did not provide for the use of federal voting registrars in counties that were systematically limiting the number of blacks allowed to vote. This, to the civil rights movement, was like buying a car after years of labor, only to discover it had no engine. There were parts of the South, especially its "black belt," where intensive litigation and almost ceaseless voter registration drives had been blocked at nearly every turn by obstruction and delay. Although the region had gotten its name because of the richness of the soil and not from the complexion of its populace, the reality was that there was a strong correlation between soil and race. Slavery flourished where the soil was blackest, and many of the descendants of slaves remained where their forebears had labored. In many black belt counties, the black population outnumbered the white, but whites remained in political control by tightly limiting the black vote.

It was clear to civil rights leaders that unless national voting standards replaced local ones, many blacks would remain voteless and, thus, powerless and vulnerable.

How to change this? King and his key followers became convinced that the solution was to make voting rights the number one civil rights goal for 1965; they would demonstrate and mobilize endlessly until they got new federal laws. By late 1964, they were drawing up action plans and looking for a target city that would be to voting rights what Birmingham had been to public accommodations.

One town—Selma, the seat of government of Dallas County, Alabama—rose to the top of the SCLC list. For one thing, it was the principal town in Alabama's black belt. And it fit the pattern: blacks accounted for half of the county's 30,000 voting-age population, but only 335 had managed to get registered. And the situation was even worse in two neighboring counties, Lowndes and Wilcox, where blacks were a majority of the population but not a single one of them had succeeded in getting onto the rolls.[1]

But Selma had another, even stronger, appeal. The sheriff of Dallas County, James G. Clark, Jr., reminded civil rights activists of Birmingham's Bull Connor. He had a hair-trigger temper and a propensity for violence and believed in not just segregation but white supremacy. He also looked the part. He was beefy and topped off his uniform with a gold braided cap. He sometimes wore a lapel button that said "Never" to racial change.[2]

The potential for violence was requisite for the SCLC, whose leaders had learned their lesson in Albany. If demonstrators were simply jailed and not assaulted, the public might fail to react, believing the situation could be resolved peacefully in the courts. But if there were violence—especially by law enforcement officers, as in Birmingham—many Americans would realize that there had been a breakdown in the local system and would demand federal intervention.

Out of the experience of Albany and Birmingham, King developed a four-step strategy for the voting rights campaign. He did not talk about it at the time, but months later revealed it in an article for the *Saturday Review of Literature*. It was simple:

1. Nonviolent demonstrators go into the streets to exercise their constitutional rights.
2. Racists resist by unleashing violence against them.
3. Americans of conscience in the name of decency demand federal intervention and legislation.
4. The Administration, under mass pressure, initiates measures of immediate intervention and remedial legislation.[3]

None of this would work, of course, if the press did not witness the demonstrations. King had reason to be optimistic that the press would cover him intensely. The press, and especially television, had never been readier for a civil rights campaign than in early January 1965. Almost every important national news organization had reporters, photographers, or camera crews who were experienced in civil rights coverage—in Birmingham, in Mississippi, in St. Augustine, Florida, and beyond. The Claude Sitton notebook, which he and Karl Fleming had fashioned, was now de rigueur: you put one of the sawed-in-two steno pads into the inside breast pocket of your suit coat, and it could not be spotted by the mobs. You put two into your breast pocket, and it bulged like a shoulder holster. Then mobs would mistake you for an FBI agent and think twice before attacking. Or you could go the other way: dress like a white heckler and cram the notebook under your belt, beneath a flapping shirttail, and blend in with the mob.

Veteran correspondents were everywhere. Take, for example, the three-person, emergency civil rights squad that operated out of the UPI's regional office in Atlanta. The junior member was Leon Daniel, who had been covering major civil rights stories since the Ole Miss eruptions of 1962 and before that in Tennessee while he was establishing himself with the wire service. The two senior members, Al Kuettner and Nicholas Chriss, were veterans of the coverage. And there was *Newsweek* magazine, which arguably had come of age on the civil rights story. True, Fleming had moved to the magazine's Houston bureau, then to its Los Angeles bureau, but Joe Cumming was still there, as was a brilliant young writer, Marshall Frady, who could almost out-match Cumming's southern drawl. And in New York, Peter Goldman, an exceptionally gifted rewrite man, had become expert in stitching together the civil rights story of the moment.

The television networks had developed their whole approach to fast-breaking, on-the-scene news by covering racial confrontation in the South. In a sense, television and the civil rights movement had come of age together. Even the number three, come-lately network, ABC, was now trying hard to narrow the gap between it, NBC, and CBS. NBC had skilled journalists, such as Richard Valeriani, a veteran of the Mississippi campaigns, and Charles "Chuck" Quinn, who had, before moving on to television, covered the Little Rock crisis for the *New York Herald Tribune.* CBS had street-smart correspondents such as Nelson Benton, plus a cameraman, Laurens Pierce, who was awing even word journalists with his ability to get his heavy camera into the right places at just the right instant. A native Alabamian and proud of it, Pierce regularly defied angry segregationists to film the news.

He designed his camera harness to include a detachable bar that he could use to defend himself, but he discovered, in time, that the bar could easily be jerked away by racist toughs and used against him. He felt comfortable when his soundmen packed pistols; they could protect him when his eye was riveted to the camera. Once, on the outskirts of Birmingham, Dan Rather, then a CBS correspondent, was with Pierce and his handpicked soundmen, when they were surrounded by white toughs. One stuck a sawed-off shotgun into Rather's ribs and said, "You take another step, mother fucker, and I'm going to blow you apart." In an instant, Pierce's soundman jammed a revolver against the tough's temple and forced him—and his angry cohorts—to retreat. Some journalists thought Pierce to be daring beyond belief, but Pierce told Rather, with his tongue only partly in cheek, that the bravest people he had ever seen were the correspondents, who, in full view of an angry mob, would apply pancake makeup to their faces before going on camera.

Unlike the television correspondents, Pierce was not known in American homes, but journalists instantly recognized him by the half-glasses he kept shoved into his hair. During the mid-sixties, he was on the civil rights story so often that he built his life around his travels. He even wooed and married the woman who rented him Hertz cars at the Jackson, Mississippi, airport.

King, of course, was well aware of the size and experience of the civil rights press corps. But there were other developments within the press, then unknown to him, that virtually guaranteed that he would get serious coverage on any campaign he undertook.

Since October 1964, when he had become national editor of *The New York Times,* Claude Sitton had presided over all of that paper's national news coverage with the exception of the three-state New York metropolitan area. And he had quietly instituted a rule: King was to be covered by a *Times* reporter anywhere he went in the South on a civil rights mission. Thus, if King went to Selma, the *Times* would be there—automatically. No one understood better than Sitton the passions King aroused, both for the civil rights movement and against it. His very presence could inspire blacks to demonstrate and white racists to lash out. Sitton was convinced, too, that no man in America was at greater personal risk than King; he might be assassinated at any moment; and that, Sitton believed, could touch off a cataclysmic reaction. Whatever happened to King, for better or for worse, Sitton wanted the *Times* to be there.

Sitton was also in the process of bringing the *Times*' southern staff back up to two reporters, filling the vacancy his promotion had created. By New Year's 1965, he had decided that Roy Reed of the *Arkansas Gazette,* whom he had gotten to know during the Little Rock crisis, would be John Herbers's partner on the southern beat. He knew Reed to be unfailingly accurate, deeply reflective, uncommonly polite, and, like the *Times* reporters who had preceded him in the South, he spoke Southern. Not least, he could write magically, choosing words that caught your eye. Reed was to join the *Times* in January, undergo six weeks of orientation in New York, and be in Atlanta by March 1. Meanwhile, Herbers, who had succeeded Sitton as chief southern correspondent, would hold the fort.

Unknown either to King or to Sitton, a major breakthrough in civil rights coverage was on the verge of occurring, one that would have important consequences for the Selma story. The civil rights movement, if one dated it from the *Brown* decision, was now—the end of 1964—a decade old. And all this time, only one nonsouthern newspaper, *The New York Times,* had supplied continuous coverage from its own southern bureau. Now the *Los Angeles Times* had decided that it, too, would have a southern bureau as part of a plan by its publisher, Otis Chandler, to transform it into one of America's greatest dailies, openly challenging *The New York Times.* To man the new bureau, *Los Angeles Times* editors were eyeing Jack Nelson of *The Atlanta Constitution.* At thirty-five, he had won a Pulitzer Prize, spent an academic year at Harvard as a Nieman Fellow, coauthored a book, and become widely known for his hard-nosed investigations into corruption in Georgia. He had been assaulted by a deputy sheriff while looking into police-protected gambling and by a doctor while probing irregularities—including surgery by a nonphysician—at Milledgeville State Hospital. He was well suited to the dangers encountered on race stories, even though he only occasionally covered them. He had gone to Little Rock when federal troops entered the city, and he had written now and then about the Ku Klux Klan, but that was pretty much it. The *Constitution* was reluctant for him to go into racial problems too deeply, for fear it would hinder his reportage on corruption in government. Nelson had not protested; he loved investigations. But lately he had begun to feel he was missing out on one of the biggest stories in American history. When the *Los Angeles Times* editors told him they wanted to talk about the race beat, he decided he should hear them out.

On January 2, 1965, with the New Year less than forty-eight hours old, King traveled to Selma to kick off the voting rights campaign and announce that he would organize massive street demonstrations if Negroes in Dallas County were not allowed to register to vote. Herbers covered the rally for *The New York Times* and came away with the impression that the Selma campaign was a trial run, rather than a long-term commitment. If King saw no possibility, after several weeks, of Selma becoming another Birmingham, he might well seek another location for the voting rights drive. Much depended on Jim Clark, but neither King nor Herbers got a look at him on this trip; He was in Miami to watch the University of Alabama play in the Orange Bowl.

Herbers and King did get a look at Wilson Baker, who as public safety director was Selma's top law enforcement officer, and saw at once that he was no Bull Connor. He ordered his police to keep any suspected white troublemakers a safe distance from the King rally. He clearly did not want Selma to become another Birmingham; and he was no fan of Clark, having run against him unsuccessfully for sheriff. He was a police officer in the mold of

Laurie Pritchett of Albany: he would arrest civil rights demonstrators, if need be, but he would not physically mistreat them or allow others to do it. And Baker had police authority over all of Selma, with the important exception of the county courthouse, which was the property of Dallas County and the place where voter registration was conducted. Sheriff Clark, of course, had jurisdiction over the courthouse and the rural areas of Dallas County outside the Selma city limits.

After moving his organizers into Selma, King launched the first of his demonstrations on January 18 by having black activists test seven restaurants to see whether they were complying with the public accommodations provisions of the new civil rights act. It was immediately clear that not just Baker but Mayor Joseph T. Smitherman and much of Selma's business community wanted to avoid racial trouble. Blacks were served peacefully, with Baker's police looking on protectively. Later that day, when King became the first black ever to register in Selma's historic Albert Hotel, he was punched and kicked by a Birmingham man who was a member of the racist States' Rights Party. Baker immediately arrested the assailant.[4]

The pattern of law enforcement was stunningly different the next day when demonstrators appeared at the courthouse, Sheriff Clark's turf, to demand that they be registered. Clark ordered them off the courthouse steps. Amelia Boynton, a voting rights activist, was slow to move. Herbers watched as Clark "grabbed her by the collar and pushed her roughly for half a block into the patrol car"—resulting in an Associated Press photo that made the inside pages of many newspapers. Next, Clark arrested sixty-seven other demonstrators for refusing to leave the courthouse grounds. Wilson Baker and Mayor Smitherman watched in consternation. Clark, they told reporters, was obviously "out of control."

On the third day, Clark arrested three waves of marchers, the last after Baker had given them permission to march. Clark and Baker glared at each other.

Now, with Selma decidedly in the news, the journalistic presence increased. But a pattern had developed. The confrontation was taking place almost exclusively at the courthouse. Could a major movement be sustained on so small a stage? At first, the answer was yes. The confined space was even an advantage for photographers and television cameramen. They couldn't miss when 105 black teachers marched on the courthouse to protest obstacles to registration, a conspicuously brave act when one considered that the teachers were employed by an all-white school board. And the cameramen were there when Mrs. Annie Lee Cooper, a heavyset fifty-three-year-old black woman, punched Sheriff Clark and was wrestled to the ground by three of his deputies. "I wish you would hit me, you scum," Herbers quoted her saying as to Clark. "He then brought his billy club down on her head

with a whack that was heard throughout the crowd gathered in the street."
Herbers's story was played on page one of the *Times,* next to a dramatic photograph of two deputies holding Mrs. Cooper down as Clark loomed over
her with a nightstick.[5]

Confident that Clark could be counted on to take the bait whenever it was
dangled, King slipped away to be honored by the civic and religious leaders of Atlanta. The only question was whether Atlanta would turn out or
snub him.

Soon after King had won his Nobel Peace Prize in October of 1964,
Ralph McGill had hailed his work and said the South "one day will be grateful when it realizes what the alternative would have been had Dr. King, with
his capacity to stir and inspire, come preaching violence, hate and aggression. These Europeans have a view of Dr. King that is clearer than ours,
which has become befogged by emotions and prejudices."[6]

But what could Atlanta do to honor King? McGill knew that if a white
Atlantan had won the world's most prestigious award, the city would be
putting on a show to rival the opening of *Gone With the Wind* twenty-six
years earlier. How could it do less for King, an Atlantan born and bred?
McGill began working with a small group of city leaders—Morehouse College president Benjamin Mays, Rabbi Jacob Rothschild, and Catholic archbishop Paul Hallinan, among others—to organize a banquet honoring King.
The group mailed out invitations to a hundred civic and business leaders to
serve as sponsors. They waited for responses, and waited some more, only to
see a trickle.

Mayor Ivan Allen, Jr., fearful of an embarrassment to King and the city,
drove to the South Georgia plantation of Atlanta's most influential business
leader, Coca-Cola chairman Robert Woodruff, and won his backing for the
banquet.

Had the difficulty generating a crowd for the dinner remained a local
secret—which, so far, it had since the Atlanta papers did not write about it—
the dinner might have turned into an awkward affair but not a stain on the
city. But the chilly response did become a national story and a large-scale
embarrassment when *The New York Times,* a month before the dinner, found
out and put the story on its front page. That was followed by an *NBC Nightly
News* report that said the dinner would put Atlanta's progressive self-image
to the test.[7]

Mayor Allen and Woodruff, working through the Coca-Cola president,
Paul Austin, called twenty white business leaders together. The mayor told
them that even if they planned to concoct an excuse for not attending the
banquet themselves, they at least should buy and fill tables at it. But it was

Woodruff who could make it happen. Atlanta's business community lived in mortal fear that its beloved Coca-Cola might move and relocate anywhere it wanted. McGill later told Gene Patterson that when Austin walked into the room and said, "Fellows, the boss thinks we ought to go to the dinner," there was a near stampede to buy tickets.[8]

On January 27, 1965, 750 white business leaders and their spouses, along with an equal number of blacks, packed the ballroom at the Dinkler Plaza Hotel to honor King. The number of sponsors had reached 134, and the number of people turned back at the door after the sellout was in the hundreds.

For King, it was an opportunity to address those who, in Gunnar Myrdal's words, had succeeded in forgetting about the problems of the Negro—those, perhaps King was thinking, who had been reluctant to buy tickets. King said there were, in the "white South, millions of people of goodwill, whose voices are yet unheard, whose course is yet unclear, and whose courageous acts are yet unseen." He added, "If the people of good-will of the white South fail to act now, history will have to record that the greatest tragedy of this period of social transition was not the vitriolic words and the violent actions of the bad people, but the appalling silence and indifference of the good people."[9]

King returned to Selma, where the tempo increased in February as the number of jailings surged past the 3,000 mark, far more than the city could handle. *The New York Times* truncated Roy Reed's orientation by an entire month and hustled him off to join John Herbers in watching not only the Dallas County courthouse but new demonstrations that were developing in neighboring black belt counties.

Jack Nelson joined the *Los Angeles Times* on February 1, and he, too, went to Selma, only to discover that his editors were not quite prepared for southern coverage. Nelson heard Sheriff Clark order his deputies to "get those niggers off the courthouse steps" and quoted him precisely in his story. "You can't use the word 'nigger' in the *L.A. Times*," an editor told Nelson in an urgent phone call.

"You mean that you want me to quote Jim Clark as saying, 'Get those KNEE-GROES off the courthouse steps?' " an astonished Nelson shot back. Nelson prevailed.[10]

Among those now in jail was King, who, as he had in Birmingham, dispatched a letter from his cell. "This is Selma, Alabama," he wrote. "There are more Negroes in jail with me than there are on the voting rolls."[11]

The courthouse scene, meanwhile, was becoming a familiar one on the nation's television sets. Clark seemed ever present, and near him was the volunteer posse he had deputized for the emergency. They seemed to be competing over how many weapons they could hang from their belts: guns, cattle prods, nightsticks, ropes. In one confrontation, Clark jabbed his nightstick repeatedly into the abdomen of James Bevel, one of King's key organizers. In another, he and his posse rounded up 165 teenage demonstrators and forced them to run for miles into the country. Later the teenagers told reporters, who had been kept at a distance by the posse, that they had been jolted with cattle prods when they slowed their pace or attempted to rest.[12]

This touched off a new wave of criticism, some of it local, against the sheriff. *The Selma Times-Journal* assailed him in an editorial. White businessmen called for restraint. Clark, for his part, seemingly chastened, checked himself into a hospital for treatment for exhaustion. Blacks kneeled in front of the courthouse and prayed for his recovery "in mind and in body."[13]

With the sheriff on the defensive, the voting rights movement lost momentum. Much of the reporting made it clear that Selma was not monolithically behind Clark, and it could readily be seen on television that many of those lining up to register at the courthouse were under voting age. Black adults had livings to earn and could not spend their lives in registration lines; but still the images were not as crisp as the movement would have liked.

No one understood the power of vivid images better than King, and he fretted over every lost opportunity. At one point in Selma, Flip Schulke of *Life* magazine saw Clark's posse shove children to the ground. He stopped shooting photographs and began pushing the men away. King heard about the incident and reminded Schulke about his "duty as a photographer."

"The world doesn't know this happened, because you didn't photograph it," King told Schulke later. "I'm not being cold-blooded about it, but it is so much more important for you to take a picture of us getting beaten up than for you to be another person joining in the fray."[14]

With Wilson Baker on the case, the chance of a photographer getting a playable photograph anywhere but the courthouse was slim. Journalists such as Herbers had seen racist towns such as Philadelphia, Mississippi, and were beginning to wonder if Selma, apart from the courthouse, was raw enough to sustain the movement. On February 14, in a news analysis, he predicted that Selma was "not likely to become another Birmingham."[15]

Two days later, the Reverend C. T. Vivian, a member of the SCLC board, volunteered to take charge of the demonstrations and see if he could breathe new life into them. Clark was now out of the hospital, and Vivian openly baited him. Clark couldn't resist. In full view of television cameras, he punched Vivian in the mouth, knocking him down the courthouse steps.[16]

Having gotten Selma back into the news, Vivian moved next to Marion, a town of 3,800 just twenty-three miles northwest of Selma. Now it was the

Alabama state troopers who couldn't resist. As demonstrators marched out of a nighttime church rally and into the street, about fifty troopers stopped them and ordered them back into the church. Suddenly, the streetlight flickered out. Troopers began clubbing the marchers with nightsticks, and white bystanders assaulted journalists standing nearby. Two UPI cameramen were beaten as troopers looked on. UPI's Leon Daniel heard a sickening sound like a watermelon being struck by a baseball bat, and saw Richard Valeriani of NBC crumple to the ground, blood spewing from his head. No one could survive that kind of blow, he thought. "I really thought he was hit hard enough to die," Daniels said years later.[17]

At the peak of the violence, Herbers spotted Sheriff Clark, wearing sports clothes and carrying a nightstick, in Marion. " 'Don't you have enough trouble of your own in Selma?' someone asked the sheriff," Herbers wrote.

" 'Things got a little too quiet for me over in Selma tonight and it made me nervous,' he replied."[18]

Meanwhile, as journalists scrambled to help their battered colleagues, a group of troopers chased blacks into a café, turned over tables, and began striking them. Witnesses said one trooper clubbed a woman and then shot her son, Jimmie Lee Jackson, in the stomach when he rushed to protect her.[19]

Valeriani survived his injuries and, still groggy from sedatives and with his head stitched and bandaged, talked on camera from his hospital bed the next day about the violence in Marion. The twenty-six-year-old Jackson was not so fortunate; he died eight days after he was shot.[20]

The voting rights movement held rallies and vigils for Jackson, but his death did not ignite a national outpouring of protest. Civil rights workers speculated openly as to why. Was it because he was black? Was it because the assault on him, at night and off to the side of the demonstration, had not been recorded by cameras? Or was the public's attention focused on Selma, and not the outlying counties?

James Bevel, the SCLC strategist who had rekindled activity in Birmingham by recruiting children, believed that whatever the reason, it could be overcome with drama. He urged demonstrators to march to Montgomery, fifty-four miles away, carrying Jackson's body in a casket. Jackson's family opted instead for a prompt burial. But many of Selma's blacks thought a long march was worth trying.

Obviously, something was needed. Journalists were still in town, but editors—especially TV editors—were losing interest. Selma and Alabama's black belt made NBC's *Huntley-Brinkley Report,* for example, seventeen times between February 1 and February 19, for a total of thirty-two minutes, thirty-five seconds, but only three times, for a total of three minutes, forty-nine seconds, in the next thirteen days.[21]

In desperation, and with no better idea on the table, King embraced the march and scheduled it for Sunday, March 7. Governor George Wallace's press secretary, Bill Jones, saw an opportunity to make King and the movement "the laughing stock of the nation and win for us a propaganda battle." He figured there was no way that King, Bevel, or any of the other civil rights figures could walk all the way to Montgomery. He persuaded Wallace to order state troopers to step aside when the marchers approached, then ban all vehicles on the highway, essentially forcing the protesters to either keep walking or be shown on national television bluffed down from their moral high ground.[22]

But Wallace changed his mind and countered King by publicly ordering troopers "to use whatever measures are necessary to prevent a march."[23]

During the weekend, King himself had second thoughts. He decided to delay the march and return to his home base in Atlanta. But five hundred demonstrators showed up Sunday afternoon at Brown Chapel, the African Methodist Episcopal church that served as the movement headquarters. They were ready to go. After a hurried telephone conversation with King, Hosea Williams, a key SCLC organizer, and John Lewis, the chairman of SNCC, led the demonstrators away from the church, toward the Edmund Pettus Bridge and Highway 80 to Montgomery. It was to be mainly a gesture of unity and seriousness of purpose, as few of the marchers were carrying enough camping gear or food for a multiday trek.

Roy Reed of *The New York Times* and Leon Daniel of UPI were on the arching bridge, across the median strip from the marchers; not until they reached the bridge's crest did they realize what awaited them on the other side of the river: Alabama troopers, row upon row, all in blue shirts and white helmets, as many of them as marchers. They looked battle-ready. Behind them were several dozen of Sheriff Clark's khaki-dressed posse men, some on horseback, many wielding clubs as large as baseball bats. And alongside the road were about a hundred whites waving Confederate flags, laughing and spoiling for a bloodbath.[24]

At the foot of the bridge, Major John Cloud pronounced with his bullhorn that the march was an "unlawful assembly" and ordered the marchers to disperse within two minutes. Lewis and Williams, the leaders, knelt in prayer; Reed and Daniel could see the ripple in the march column as others knelt with them.

Not more than a minute had passed, Reed calculated, when the troopers suddenly charged, forming a flying wedge as they ran. This, Reed wrote, is what happened:

> The wedge moved with such force that it seemed almost to pass over the waiting column instead of through it.

The first 10 or 20 Negroes were swept to the ground screaming, arms and legs flying, and packs and bags went skittering across the grassy divider strip and on to the pavement on both sides.

Those still on their feet retreated.

The troopers continued pushing, using both the force of their bodies and the prodding of their nightsticks.

A cheer went up from the white spectators lining the south side of the highway.

The mounted posse men spurred their horses and rode at a run into the retreating mass. The Negroes cried out as they crowded together for protection, and the whites on the sideline whooped and cheered.

The Negroes paused in their retreat for perhaps a minute, still screaming and huddling together.

Suddenly there was a report, like a gunshot, and a grey cloud spewed over the troopers and the Negroes.

"Tear gas!" someone yelled.

The cloud began covering the highway. Newsmen, who were confined by four troopers to a corner 100 yards away, began to lose sight of the action.

But before the cloud finally hid it all, there were several seconds of unobstructed view. Fifteen or twenty nightsticks could be seen through the gas, flailing at the heads of the marchers.

The Negroes broke and ran. Scores of them streamed across the parking lot of the Selma Tractor Company. Troopers and posse men, mounted and unmounted, went after them.[25]

When the tear gas cleared from his eyes, Reed walked to the spot where the march leaders had knelt. He saw John Lewis and Amelia Boynton sprawled unconscious on the ground. Later, in his room at the Albert Hotel, Reed watched the CBS footage of the mayhem and marveled at how close Laurens Pierce had managed to get with his heavy camera. The NBC coverage was also gripping. But it was the number three network, ABC, that would have the greatest impact on the nation.

At 9:30 p.m., ABC interrupted its Sunday Night Movie and, with Frank Reynolds narrating, showed fifteen minutes of footage of the assault and its aftermath. The movie was *Judgment at Nuremberg,* a dramatic study of how Germans had ignored, or acquiesced in, the horrors of Nazism. Suddenly viewers were watching—not Nazi Germany but segregationist Alabama. The juxtaposition struck like psychological lightning in American homes. Sheriff Clark's voice could be heard directing his posse: "Get those goddamned niggers. And get those goddamned white niggers."[26]

. . .

The ranks of Myrdal's newly "shocked and shaken" multiplied overnight. The next day, religious, business, and political leaders from Atlanta to Trenton to Sacramento expressed outrage, issued statements, and passed resolutions condemning Alabama law enforcement. By the second day, there were sit-ins in Los Angeles, traffic blockades in Chicago, and a 10,000-person march in Detroit. Sympathy protests, pickets, and demonstrations erupted in so many towns and cities that *The New York Times* was able to fill column after column of summaries from across the nation and Canada; more than a dozen young people gained entry to the White House, sat down, and refused to leave.[27]

In San Francisco, one television viewer, deeply disturbed by the ABC report, immediately made plans to fly to Selma, realizing only the next day that "at that same moment, people all up and down the West Coast were feeling what my wife and I felt; that at various times all over the country that day . . . and that night, hundreds of these people would drop whatever they were doing; that some of them would leave home without changing clothes, borrow money, overdraw their checking accounts; board planes, buses, trains, cars, travel thousands of miles with no luggage, get speeding tickets, hitchhike, hire horse-drawn wagons; that these people, mostly unknown to one another, would move for a single purpose: to place themselves alongside the Negroes they had watched on television."[28]

Haynes Johnson of *The Washington Star* could hardly believe what he was seeing when he walked off the airplane and into the Montgomery airport on Monday, on his way back to Selma from Washington. The usually quiet terminal pulsated with people: priests, nuns, rabbis, Protestant clergymen, college students, all come to Alabama to support the marchers. But how to get to Selma? The rental companies had run out of cars. People were begging for rides. "Bloody Sunday" had struck a nerve.[29]

By nightfall the movement had organized car pools, and Johnson, now at Brown Chapel in Selma, watched as the once faltering movement throbbed with new life. "Car after car drove up and stopped in front of the church discharging white ministers, rabbis and priests from across the country," Johnson wrote. ". . . They kept arriving throughout the night."[30]

By Tuesday, no one understood the new dynamic better than an editorial writer for the segregationist *Alabama Journal* in Montgomery. He lashed out at the "stupidity" of state officials, troopers, and posses and dared them to "tell us the grisly picture projected to the nation was another example of press distortion, probably including trick photography."

"Tell us anything but the truth," he added. "Though state and local police were to be but extras in the play to the television cameras, they upstaged the stars beyond the wildest dreams of King; that by dumb, cruel and vastly excessive force we have made new civil rights legislation, not considered likely earlier, almost a dead certainty . . ."[31]

On Tuesday, just forty-eight hours after the violence, two thousand people—four times as many as on Sunday—joined King in a new march across the Pettus Bridge. But he turned the marchers back before they reached the Montgomery highway so as not to violate an injunction by federal Judge Frank Johnson. The judge prohibited a march to Montgomery until he could hold hearings into whether it would jeopardize public safety.

By now, an estimated 450 out-of-town clergy were in Selma. And when Charles Morgan, Jr., the southern director of the American Civil Liberties Union, circulated among them, he was struck by the similarity of their stories. " 'Judgment at Nuremberg' was on for the first time on television . . ." Morgan heard them say, or ". . . I was watching 'Judgment at Nuremberg,' and I just couldn't stay away. I just had to come."[32]

On Tuesday night, three of the clergymen ate in a black diner, took a wrong turn on their way back to Brown Chapel, passed the Silver Moon Cafe—a racist hangout—and were immediately assaulted. Reverend James J. Reeb, a Unitarian from Boston, was clubbed senseless with a baseball bat.

Reeb's death two days later, covered prominently in newspapers across the nation, raised the political temperature on an already aroused Washington. Just eight days after "Bloody Sunday," President Johnson not only sent proposed legislation to Congress, he personally accompanied it, giving a speech that was interrupted forty times by applause. He called for "no delay, no hesitation, no compromise." And then, he added, "We shall overcome."

In Selma, John Lewis, some SCLC staffers, and Arlie Schardt of *Time* magazine were with King in the home of a black Selma dentist, watching the president on television. They saw a tear roll down King's check upon hearing Johnson use the movement's own slogan.[33]

But if Washington was embracing the voting rights movement, whites' attitudes in Selma were hardening. The new wave of demonstrators and journalists was too much, even for some moderates. Monday's *Washington Star* carried a story by Haynes Johnson detailing what had happened when out-of-town clergymen and other demonstrators attempted to attend Selma's white churches. One church denied them Communion; another blocked them at the door. At a third, they were called "white scum."

One Selma minister got out of town before services, leaving a note on the church bulletin board: "On the insistence of my doctor and the demand of the vestry, my family and I are taking my ailing 'gizzard' away for a few days from the continual harassment of belligerent and unscrupulous newspaper reporters from across the nation and the equally frustrating interrogations of outside demonstrators—some of whom are quite courteous and polite, others of whom are impossibly antagonistic and argumentative."[34]

If Ralph McGill could have engineered it, there would have been even more journalists in Selma to inflame ailing gizzards: reporters from the *Atlanta Constitution,* who had been conspicuously absent. By 1964 and 1965, Jack Tarver, the president of the *Constitution* and *Journal,* had decided the papers had problems enough with their readers and advertisers without going outside their basic circulation area to cover racial stories. That was that. But McGill and Patterson were uncomfortable with the decision and began brooding about it.

McGill wandered into Patterson's office one day with an idea, Patterson would later recall. "Why don't we go over to the bus station and take the bus to Selma?" McGill said.

"Pappy, we can't do that," Patterson replied. "It would humiliate Tarver if we did that. Now do you want to do that? I don't. It's going to look like grandstanding."

McGill agreed. Patterson marveled at McGill's instincts, and he would later decide that McGill was right: "We should have gotten on the damn bus."[35]

The day after Johnson's speech to Congress, posse men once again—on horseback and on foot—assaulted demonstrators; this time a small group marching ahead of a larger contingent. "One rider began striking demonstrators with a rope and another beat them with a nightstick," Roy Reed reported in *The New York Times.* "A posse man dressed in green clothes and a white 10-gallon hat stepped up on foot and, while the horses partly hid him from view, began clubbing the demonstrators. Several still refused to move and the man's nightstick began falling with great force on their heads."[36]

No one died, but photographers got pictures—dramatic ones that made nightly network television programs and the front pages of newspapers, producing still more outcries from congressmen, editorial writers, and columnists.

Selma had something most other venues of civil rights activity did not: a local newspaper that visiting reporters could depend on. *The Selma Times-Journal* saw the historic importance of the story and took its responsibility seriously, providing detailed accounts that reporters found reliable.[37]

No accurate count exists of the journalists who were in Selma on March 21, when the new march to Montgomery began, but there were scores upon scores. When Judge Johnson cleared the way for the march by lifting his injunction, press reinforcements rushed in. Claude Sitton was dumbfounded to learn, too late, that the *Times* metropolitan desk had loaned him a reporter who couldn't drive. Didn't these people know that there wasn't a subway in the entire South? Didn't they realize you couldn't hail a taxi in a cotton field? But the reporter—Paul Montgomery, young but uncommonly gifted—walked the fifty-four miles, filing insightful stories along the way.

Together, for four nights and five days, Reed and Montgomery captured the flow and festivity of the marchers as they slogged through torrential downpours and beneath a blazing sun. No detail escaped them: John Doar "soaked to the skin, his hair hanging across his forehead in weeping ringlets," youngsters wearing cornflakes boxes as hats, photographers perched in a dying chinaberry tree. They caught the ironies of a Negro freedom march being staged on Jefferson Davis Highway: a motion picture director from New York marching with a Selma resident who had never seen a movie. Their stories reflected the sense of daring among marchers: when John Lewis was asked about the Alabama legislature's resolution accusing marchers of "fornication" in the tents, he denied it and said, "All these segregationists can think of is fornication, and that is why there are so many different shades of Negroes."

By judicial order, the number of marchers was limited to 300 on two-lane stretches of Highway 80 but was unlimited on four-lane stretches. More than 3,200 showed up for the initial leg across the Pettus Bridge. By the order of President Johnson, they were guarded by helicopters, light planes, 1,800 national guardsmen, 2,000 U.S. soldiers, 100 FBI agents, and 100 federal marshals.

The daytime marches were full of song, and the nighttime encampments were rich in celebrity, particularly on the final night, just outside Montgomery, when ten thousand people gathered to hear Harry Belafonte, Sammy Davis, Jr., Peter, Paul and Mary, Leonard Bernstein, James Baldwin, and more than a dozen others.

When the marchers reached Montgomery, Reed described their entry into the city as having "a grandeur that was almost Biblical." More than twenty thousand supporters—from black farmers to white movie stars to politicians and labor leaders—joined the marchers on the state capitol grounds.

"We are on the move now," King said from the capitol steps.

To where?

"The land of Freedom."

How long will it take?

"Not long."[38]

Federal authorities breathed easier as the crowd dispersed peacefully. John Doar, who, as assistant attorney general for civil rights, had felt personally responsible for the safety of the marchers, couldn't have been more relaxed as he dined that evening at the Elite Cafe. The E-Light, as it was pronounced in Montgomery, was a favored hangout for journalists. They liked its steaks and seafood. They loved its practice on Sunday, when liquor sales were illegal, of serving drinks anyway, carefully camouflaged in coffee cups.

This night, Doar sat at a table with Jack Nelson and a handful of other reporters; nearby was the *Times* table, with Roy Reed presiding. Normally, Doar played his cards close to his vest, but tonight he was expansive.

Midway through the meal, a waiter told Doar he was wanted on the phone. When he returned to the table, his face was ashen. A civil rights volunteer—later identified as Viola Liuzzo, a white housewife from Detroit—had been slain by gunfire from a passing car. She and a black SCLC worker had been driving from Selma to Montgomery to ferry demonstrators back to Brown Chapel. In less than three minutes, the Elite emptied as reporters scrambled to develop the story.[39]

Viola Liuzzo's death breathed new life into the Selma story. Within twenty-four hours President Johnson announced on television that the FBI had solved the case. It had arrested four Ku Klux Klan members and would see that they were brought to trial.

Nelson sensed immediately that there was an untold story in how the FBI had cracked the case so speedily. He began tapping the network of law enforcement sources that he had started cultivating during his years as an investigative reporter. Within days, he supplied readers of the *Los Angeles Times* with the answer: One of the four men in the Klan car when the shots were fired was an undercover FBI informant. It was a remarkable exclusive. "There was," one admirer of Nelson's, the ACLU attorney Charles Morgan, Jr., would later say, "a finely honed cold fury in the crisp reports" that Nelson wrote. But to Nelson's amazement, there was no national reaction. No wire service or television network picked up his story.[40]

Two days later, Fred Graham, who covered the Justice Department for *The New York Times,* wrote essentially the same facts, and his story made front pages and television shows across the nation. The Associated Press, UPI, and the television networks regularly monitored *The New York Times* for civil rights news, but not yet the *Los Angeles Times*. Nelson swore that this would change; he would break enough stories to force them to pay attention.[41]

Meanwhile, as voting rights legislation made its way through Congress, new racial battlegrounds—Bogalusa, Louisiana, and Americus, Georgia, as well as the Liuzzo trials—kept civil rights issues in the news. *The New York Times* beefed up its civil rights expertise in Washington by transferring John Herbers there; then it hired Gene Roberts (coauthor of this book), the metropolitan editor of the *Detroit Free Press,* to replace him. A native southerner, Roberts had entered journalism as a reporter for his hometown newspaper, the *Goldsboro News-Argus,* in Goldsboro, North Carolina, before moving on to *The Virginian-Pilot* in Norfolk, just as the school-closing crisis was engulfing that city. By 1960 he was with the Raleigh *News & Observer* when the sit-in movement quickly spread to that city from Greensboro; and he was present at the conference at Shaw University in Raleigh during Easter weekend 1960, for the birth of the Student Non-Violent Coordinating Committee.

One of Roberts's first assignments was Bogalusa, a paper mill town of 14,000 whites and 8,000 blacks, where the Congress of Racial Equality was leading demonstrations against Klan activity and the town's refusal, in general, to abide by the Civil Rights Act of 1964. By July, the Klan was operating so openly in Bogalusa that an official of the Original Knights of the Ku Klux Klan banged on the doors of reporters' motel rooms, handed out calling cards, and invited them to cover a Saturday-night rally in a cow pasture in Cross Roads, Mississippi, just across the Pearl River from Bogalusa. "We're tired of the niggers getting all the publicity," said the Klansman, who identified himself as the grand klaxon, or public relations director, of the Louisiana Klan. "We want some."[42]

It was immediately apparent at the cow pasture, even before the rally began at dusk, that a mob, rather than the Klan, was in control. Sullen men in work clothes, angry wives, and restless children far outnumbered robed Klansmen. Within minutes, an Original Knights official announced that armed members of a rival splinter group of the Klan, the militant White Knights, had infiltrated the rally. He urged them to "please park your arms with the Sergeant of Arms."[43]

A ripple of unease spread through the journalists, but they squatted down in the grass in front of a flatbed truck that served as the speakers' platform and opened their notebooks, ready to cover the rally. "Do you know what a good citizen is?" asked one speaker, with the first in a stream of racial jokes. "He's a God-fearing man who takes care of his wife and children, loves his country—and hates niggers."

Having heard much of the racist humor before, some reporters put their notebooks aside and were immediately kicked in their backs by angry women and children. "Look at this one," one woman shouted. "He ain't writing it all down."

Feeling vulnerable and conspicuous—Richard Harkness of NBC, a newcomer to the race beat, was wearing a dapper pin-striped suit with a monogrammed handkerchief in his coat pocket—reporters decided it would be wise to leave the rally and set out across an empty stretch of pasture toward their cars.

"Suddenly, out of the corner of my eye, I spotted a beefy figure I recognized as a night club bouncer named Milton Parker leading a group of young toughs," Jack Nelson wrote later. "A few days earlier, I had seen Parker, armed with a heavy metal bolt, rush at James Farmer, national director of the Congress of Racial Equality, during a protest march. Only quick action by a Bogalusa policeman, who grabbed Parker and shoved him into a patrol car, had saved Farmer from being bludgeoned. Now Parker and his gang were stalking us."[44]

"I stopped suddenly," Nelson recalled, "and without looking back, told the other reporters, 'Don't say anything and don't look around. Just turn and go back to where we were.' "

Back at the flatbed truck, reporters asked the speakers for help and were told that the Klan was "too busy." Nicholas von Hoffman of the *Chicago Daily News,* Gene Roberts of *The New York Times,* and Nelson stepped up on a bench near the truck and scoured the crowd for the klaxon who had invited them to the rally.

Nelson spotted him, rushed over, and confronted him with a finger pointed directly at his nose.

"You said you wanted us here," Nelson said, "so you could get some good publicity, right?"

"Yes," the klaxon replied.

"Well, you're about to get some bad. That crowd's about to kick our asses, and if it does, you ain't going to want to read the *Los Angeles Times* tomorrow."

The klaxon pressed a button on his walkie-talkie and ordered, "Get me a couple of armed men over here."

"A couple won't do it," Nelson said.

"Change that. Make it a wedge. Send me a flying wedge," the klaxon said into the walkie-talkie.

Within minutes, about ten robed Klansman assembled in V-shaped formation. They put the reporters in the middle and, with pistols drawn, escorted them to their cars as the angry crowd hissed and booed.[45]

If Bogalusa illustrated the dangers encountered by journalists, Americus, Georgia, demonstrated the political risks local officials ran in southern communities if they were open with the outside press. The Americus racial crisis began in July 1965, when law enforcement officers arrested four black women for standing in a voting line that was marked "For White Women Only." Blacks responded with a wave of demonstrations that included marches on the Sumter County Courthouse in Americus, vigils at the jail, and pickets of white businesses.

When reporters and cameramen arrived in Americus, they found, in sharp contrast to Bogalusa, a county official who was willing to meet with them and discuss the need for a biracial commission and peace negotiations. He was Warren Fortson, the county attorney and brother of Georgia Secretary of State Ben Fortson. He had a reputation in state political circles as a comer who might reasonably aspire to any high office in the state.

Other officials in the county were considerably more guarded, even hostile, with the press. When Roberts of *The New York Times* drove to nearby Plains to talk with the legislator who represented Sumter County, a peanut farmer named Jimmy Carter, he found himself barred from Carter's warehouse. Carter latched the screen door and mumbled that he had "nothing to say" to anyone with *The New York Times*.

Carter, of course, went on to become governor of Georgia and president of the United States. Fortson's career fell apart. After the national reporters left Americus, Fortson was dismissed as county attorney and dropped by most of his private law clients. He left Georgia and rebuilt his life in New Orleans.

Americus and Bogalusa were still in the news on August 6, 1965, when President Johnson signed the Voting Rights Act into law. It was arguably the most remarkable victory of the entire civil rights era. By one measure, the action came quickly—only eight months and four days had passed since King's first rally in Brown Chapel. By another, it had taken forever and cost way too much—the signing ceremony came ten years after Lamar "Ditney" Smith and Reverend George Lee had been killed trying to register voters in Mississippi.

Now the nation had a law that banned illiteracy tests and other obstacles to black voter registration in Alabama, Georgia, Louisiana, Mississippi, South Carolina, Virginia, and more than twenty North Carolina counties. If local election officials refused to register blacks, or even stalled, there was now a remedy: federal registration referees who could move in county by county, if necessary, to ensure fairness. Four days after Johnson signed the act, federal registrars were at work in nine southern counties, and in the first week they quadrupled blacks' registration in these locales. In still other counties, local officials quietly removed registration hurdles in order to avoid the federal registrars. In Americus, for example, 647 blacks were registered in three days.

This was the high point of the civil rights era; it was also the beginning of the end. Thirty-three years later, John Lewis, the former SNCC chairman and now a congressman, would look back on the voting rights victory and say that it had been Selma, and the later efforts to keep voting rights in the news, that had held the movement together so long. "After that," Lewis said, "we just came apart."[46]

CHAPTER 23

BEYOND

For the press, the civil rights story continued in fits and starts for another three years, gradually transforming itself into a political matter of ongoing significance. Newly enfranchised blacks streamed into the Democratic Party. Southern whites first trickled, then flooded, into the once despised Republican Party in a political alignment that would play out for decades. Neither whites nor blacks failed to take note of the 1964 presidential election in which Johnson, the Democratic incumbent, campaigned for more civil rights legislation and then, upon election, delivered on his promises.

As if that weren't enough to keep reporters busy, there was news bubbling up from SNCC and CORE. Movement organizers had once taken on segregation laws and voting restrictions; now they were taking on one another, over many issues—especially over whether the movement should veer from integration and toward black nationalism, black institution building, and, ironically, black separatism.

A turning point came five days after Johnson signed the Voting Rights Act on August 6. Rioting raged through Watts, a black district in Los Angeles. Six days of looting and Molotov cocktail throwing left 34 dead, more than 1,000 injured, and property damage in excess of $40 million. "Get whitey!" some of the rioters shouted. Watts ushered in a new era of black violence—the riot years. Over the next three years, rioting would spread to scores of cities, principally in the North and Midwest, though no region would be spared.

In August 1965, the question was "Why Watts?" Was it because the civil rights movement, while dismantling segregation and white supremacy in the South, had not touched the lives of blacks in America's nonsouthern ghettos? Were blacks in Watts saying, "What about me?" No one was sure of the cause, but racial isolation, joblessness, unfulfilled expectations, and economic deprivation were prime suspects.

Amid all the confusion, there was one certainty for white journalists covering race in America: their lives had changed. In the South, they were threatened by white mobs and found safety in black neighborhoods. In Watts, white reporters fled black mobs and sought safety in white neighborhoods and behind police barricades. At *The New York Times,* National Editor Sitton had serious coverage problems. With the exception of his southern correspondents, most of his national staff had been chosen because they were expert in covering politics and other specialties, not racial unrest. They were no better prepared for dangerous street reporting than *Times* education reporter Benjamin Fine had been in Little Rock eight years earlier. There was resistance, to Sitton's amazement, to going into the riot area. "If you sign on for the cruise, you go to the end of the line," he admonished one reporter, but to no immediate avail. In time, he would decide to use southern reporters and newly hired black staffers, such as Tom Johnson and Earl Caldwell, to cover urban rioting. But the Watts coverage read as if it were written from a distance, from outside the ghetto looking in.[1]

There was reason, of course, to be wary of entering riot zones. Even so savvy a veteran of the race wars as Karl Fleming felt fear and foreboding as he covered the Watts riots as chief of the Los Angeles bureau of *Newsweek,* a promotion he had earned with the brilliance of his southern coverage. Once again, he survived as he had at Ole Miss, Birmingham, and Philadelphia. But it was a mind-blowing reversal of experience. "To blacks in the South, I was one of the good guys," he would later write. "To blacks in Watts, I was just another faceless, exploitative whitey, someone to hate, and hurt."[2]

Just how dramatic a reversal it was became wrenchingly clear eight months after Watts. Fleming revisited the riot areas to cover protesters who were demanding that murder charges be filed against a policeman who had shot a black man. A familiar figure from the civil rights movement in the South, Stokely Carmichael, the SNCC field organizer, was haranguing a crowd. But it was a different Carmichael, one who was moving away from nonviolent protest and toward black nationalism. He spotted Fleming, the one white face in a crowd of three hundred. "And we need to stop these honky reporters from coming down and exploiting us," he said, pointing at Fleming. "They never show up except when they have a chance to make black people look bad. Where were they all these years when the cops have been intimidating, beating and murdering our people?"[3]

An hour later, after the crowd had converged on a police precinct station in an unsuccessful attempt to meet with officers who had barricaded themselves in their building, Fleming returned to his car to put his camera into the trunk. A blow from behind, apparently a four-by-four construction stud, struck him to the ground. His skull was seriously fractured; his upper and lower jaws were fractured; and he had multiple deep bruises from being kicked.[4]

The same kind of anger that seethed in Watts was now building in the civil rights movement in the South, especially in SNCC and conspicuously among northern black members who had come to join in the fight against segregation. Once, the SNCC organizers had been plumbing the teachings of Mahatma Gandhi and Albert Camus; now they were passing around the separatist speeches of Malcolm X and *The Wretched of the Earth* by Frantz Fanon, a Martinique psychiatrist who was working with Algerian rebels and believed it was therapeutic for oppressed people to fight physically for their freedom. Although SNCC had been founded upon strict nonviolent principles, by late 1965 shotguns and other "defensive weapons" were visible in SNCC outposts in Philadelphia and a handful of other racial trouble spots across the South.

The American troop buildup in Vietnam, piled atop the tinder of Watts, fueled the anger. "No Vietnamese ever called me nigger," declared a poster in SNCC's Atlanta headquarters. Almost all its members—those who were not violent and those who favored fighting back—were united against the Vietnam War.[5] They asked the same question black editors had asked at the dawn of the First and Second World Wars: Why should the nation fight for freedom abroad when there were so many problems for blacks at home?

Otherwise, sharp disagreements continued to divide SNCC. Many of the southern members, having grown up under segregation, were not at all intrigued by the black separatist rhetoric; others favored purging whites from SNCC and assuming political control wherever blacks were a majority. Some, such as Julian Bond, favored minimizing the differences and plunging instead into the new political sea created by the Voting Rights Act and a Supreme Court ruling against racial discrimination in legislative districting. Bond declared himself a candidate for the Georgia House of Representatives.

He was not, of course, the only black to see new political opportunity. In the first month after the Voting Rights Act became law, more than 60,000 new black voters registered in Alabama, Georgia, Louisiana, and Mississippi.[6] Bond easily won election to the Georgia legislature, along with seven other blacks—the first in fifty-eight years.

Antiwar sentiment in the movement was also attracting media attention. SNCC announced at a press conference on January 6, 1966, that "we're in sympathy with, and support the men in this country who are unwilling to respond to a military draft which would compel them to contribute their lives to United States military aggression in Vietnam in the name of 'freedom' we find so false in this country."

When a reporter asked Bond if he agreed with the statement, he said, "Sure, I support it."[7]

Almost immediately a move started among white legislators to block Bond from the House; some called him a traitor. The legislature denied him his seat, touching off a fresh wave of anger in SNCC. What was this? A black had been elected after years of civil rights activity, and white lawmakers refused to recognize the election?

While Bond fought for his seat through the courts (the U.S. Supreme Court ruled for him within a year), black nationalists ousted John Lewis from the chairmanship of SNCC in a disputed election and replaced him with Stokely Carmichael, a former Howard University student who had come south for the Freedom Rides and remained to become one of SNCC's most charismatic and successful field organizers. Where was the organization going? For the moment Carmichael and his followers were not saying. But it was clear that his group was questioning the organization's nonviolent creed and wanted to purge whites from SNCC.[8]

As SNCC members fought among themselves, the changes wrought by the Voting Rights Act were growing ever more dramatic, and nowhere more than in Selma and Dallas County. There, federal registrars added 8,500 blacks to voting rolls in less than eight months. Encouraged by the new voters, Wilson Baker ran against Jim Clark in the spring of 1966. In what became one of the most widely covered sheriff's races in American history, Clark sensed a possible defeat and, in an abrupt about-face, threw a political barbecue for the very blacks he had tried to keep off the voting rolls. Jack Nelson spoke with a guest at the barbecue who said that Negroes were more interested in getting photographs of the rally than they were in eating Clark's food. Nelson ran into Clark and two of his deputies in a courthouse hallway after the sheriff read the story. "Hello, sheriff," Nelson said, offering his hand. "Why don't you go to hell, you lyin' son of a bitch, you," Clark shouted.[9]

Undaunted, Nelson walked up to the second floor, where the election results were being verified. And while the sheriff and his deputies were still fuming, Adam Clymer of the Baltimore *Sun* came into the courthouse unaware of the confrontation and extended his hand to the sheriff. A deputy punched him in the stomach. Clymer was not so disabled that he couldn't write the election news. Clark was defeated.[10]

For a few days in June 1966, the movement came together again—this time to protest the shooting of James Meredith, the man who had desegregated the University of Mississippi. He had been twenty-eight miles into a Freedom March from Memphis to Jackson when a white man had stepped from a wooded area and fired a shotgun at him in full view of cameramen.

Jack Thornell of the Associated Press tripped his lens just as Meredith fell writhing to the highway—a scene of agony that made front pages across the nation and would, almost a year later, win him a Pulitzer Prize.

Soon, as a result of improved technology, television viewers were watching the entire shooting sequence on their sets. Among those monitoring the coverage was Claude Sitton, who looked intensely at a screen in the newsroom to see how close his reporter, Roy Reed, had been to the action.

"Where's Roy Reed?" he demanded of one of his assistants, after failing to see the reporter.

Reed had been at a nearby country store, downing a Coca-Cola. He then ran to the shooting scene and, as he had done so often in Selma, filed a memorable story.

But Sitton's question resonated in the *Times* newsroom. His message was clear: he expected a continuous *Times* presence on major civil rights stories.[11]

The Meredith shooting, of course, grew larger by the minute. King, Stokely Carmichael, and Floyd McKissick, who had replaced James Farmer as director of CORE, all announced that their organizations were going to Mississippi to carry on the march while Meredith recuperated from his wounds.

News organizations, for their part, enlarged their staffs on the march and pooled resources to rent a flatbed truck to move slightly ahead of the marchers, providing photographers and cameramen clear shots of any trouble that might occur.

Journalists focused their attention on the march itself and were notably incurious when a small cardboard box, neatly tied with twine, mysteriously appeared on the back of the truck and bounced around unopened in the summer heat.

Only the driver seemed to care about the box, and, finally, after a week, he opened it. A poisonous, two-and-a-half-foot-long copperhead snake leaped out, sending panicked journalists bounding from the truck. The racist resistance, presumably, had struck at the press again, but without causing any injury.[12]

It was the change in the direction of SNCC, however, not recurring violence, that created the biggest news of the march. On the night of June 17, in the Mississippi Delta town of Greenwood, Stokely Carmichael stood before a crowd of marchers, journalists, and local blacks shortly after he was arrested and released by local police. "Every courthouse in Mississippi ought to be burned down to get rid of the dirt," he said.

"This is the twenty-seventh time I have been arrested," he added. "I ain't going to jail no more. The only way we gonna stop them white men from whupping us is to take over. We been saying, 'Freedom Now' for six years and we ain't got nothin'. What we gonna start saying now is Black Power."

Willie Ricks, a SNCC staffer who styled himself a black nationalist and had been using the term "Black Power" for months, stepped onto the platform and shouted to the crowd, "What do you want?"

"Black power," the crowd shouted back. Carmichael also issued a challenge, of sorts, to reporters in front of him. "I don't think the newsmen can interpret me," he said, "because they aren't black."[13]

Television cameramen photographed the scene and then transmitted it to the nation. There were shock and anger, not just among average viewers but within the civil rights movement itself. John Lewis, the former SNCC chairman, thought that "Black Power" could divide the races and the movement. Martin Luther King felt that the term, at best, was an unfortunate choice of words. Roy Wilkins of the NAACP was outraged. He called black power "the father of hatred and the mother of violence."[14]

But the criticism did not halt the "Black Power" cries of SNCC and its supporters during the march, which was punctuated by tear gas fired by police in Canton, before coming to a noisy end in Jackson. There, SNCC organizers raced through black neighborhoods shouting "Black Power" from their cars.

The movement never recovered from the one-two punch of urban rioting and the schism over black power, black nationalism, and militancy. Meanwhile, the escalation of the war in Vietnam, and the protests against it, steadily diverted attention from civil rights.

Many blacks blamed the press, especially television, for the changing public mood. Blacks complained that television portrayed the militancy of black power without explaining that it could be regarded as an understandable reaction to persistent white racism; they said that television was "simplistically" focusing on the violence and mayhem of the riots without devoting equal time to the underlying problems of urban blacks.

Editors could hardly defend their coverage of urban America—though they frequently were given opportunities on a number of high-profile panels across the country that examined news coverage. But those who had gone through a decade of civil rights coverage in the South were not ready to discount its impact. "It was this same kind of simplistic coverage, just three and four years ago, of the Deep South situation . . . that in large part impressed the national community, prodded its collective conscience and led to the passing of the civil rights bills of 1964 and 1965," Hodding Carter III, son of the editor of the *Delta Democrat-Times* in Greenville, Mississippi, noted during a 1967 panel discussion, "The Black American and the Press."[15]

Ralph McGill agreed. "Had it not been for television showing us Bull Connor and his dogs and the march on Selma, there would not have been the momentum to push the civil rights acts through the Congress," he told the forum participants. "It performed a magnificent service by showing violence, but now it finds itself trapped in carrying on in the same manner and seems to be incapable of providing anything except violence. Because of this, more and more responsibility is reverting to the written word."[16]

Although the print press did not, for the most part, have the same problems of images as television, events moved so bewilderingly fast in 1966, 1967, and 1968 that every branch of journalism had difficulty staying abreast of events. In 1966 alone, racial disorders flared in Cleveland, Atlanta, Chicago, San Francisco, and several smaller cities. King, much to the chagrin of some of his key supporters, shifted the main thrust of his organizational activities to Chicago in an effort to demonstrate that aggressive nonviolence could be more effective than violence in combating such northern racial problems as unemployment, job discrimination and de facto segregation. When, only six weeks after the Meredith march, King led six hundred ghetto blacks into the white Gage Park area of Chicago's southwest side, journalists watched as more than a thousand whites lined the streets, shouting "Kill those niggers" and hurling rocks and bottles. King himself was knocked to the ground by a rock but resumed marching after supporters helped him to his feet.[17]

"I've never seen anything like it in my life," he told Gene Roberts of *The New York Times,* who had temporarily been shifted to Chicago to cover the marches. "I think the people from Mississippi ought to come to Chicago to learn to hate."[18] Only aggressive police assaults with nightsticks saved marchers in Gage Park and other Chicago neighborhoods from serious injury.

The press was grappling, now, not only with the spreading disorder but also with racial terminology. As the debate over black power and black consciousness ricocheted through the country, SNCC, CORE, and their followers abandoned the word "Negro" just as they had previously rejected the term "colored." They now wanted to be called "black." King, Wilkins, and their followers, remembering the epithet "black bastards," still clung to "Negro" as the proper racial description.

At *The New York Times,* where editors made consistent style and word usage a part of the newspaper's persona, a debate developed over which it would be: black or Negro? After discussion that ebbed and flowed for weeks, the decision was made. Individuals of African descent, not the *Times,* would choose how they were designated for as long as the issue was in dispute. King, Wilkins, and those of like minds were Negroes. Carmichael, McKissick, and others who favored the other term were blacks. If reporters were in doubt about a person's preference, they should ask.[19]

By 1967, when H. Rap Brown replaced Carmichael as the even angrier chairman of SNCC, another issue of style surfaced at the *Times.* The paper conferred an honorific—Mr., Mrs., or Miss (Ms. came later)—on any adult mentioned in the paper, unless that person was a convicted felon. But what about H. Rap Brown, who openly advocated violence—and thus, some editors thought, abetted felonies? Should it be: " 'Burn, baby, burn,' Mr. Brown said"? The debate continued until SNCC and its chairman faded into obscurity, eclipsed by even more revolutionary organizations, such as the Black Panthers, which operated more in the North than in the South.[20]

Just as many reporters were concluding that the real action was occurring in the North, the bloodiest outbreak of violence since Ole Miss erupted at South Carolina State College, a campus for Negroes in Orangeburg. Three black students were killed and more than two dozen wounded when about sixty-eight state troopers, backed by forty-eight National Guardsmen and assorted local officers, faced off against a similar number of students from the state college and nearby Claflin College.[21]

The students, frustrated by police beatings during a protest two nights earlier at a segregated bowling alley, threw a rock, a dirt clod, and banisters, as police advanced onto the campus. One of the banisters knocked a patrolman to the ground. Another policeman fired warning shots. Students ran or dropped to the ground. They were caught in a cross fire of shotgun blasts and .38-caliber pistol fire. The authorities contended that the students had been charging at them and hurling bottles and bricks and that the patrolmen fired in self-defense.[22]

Jack Nelson was visiting his editors in Los Angeles when the news reports started coming over the wires. He flew to South Carolina, his editor reading wire service reports of the charges and countercharges to him each time his plane stopped along the way.

Once in Orangeburg, Nelson headed directly to the hospital. With an air of authority underpinned by his business suit and crew-cut hair, he introduced himself as "Nelson, with the Atlanta bureau. I've come to see the medical records." Nelson's bureau was, of course, the *Los Angeles Times*' bureau, not the FBI's Atlanta bureau. One doctor was respectful but balked on grounds of patient confidentiality. Nelson assured him that he didn't need names, only charts and records showing the location of the wounds. The doctor relented. A nurse was also helpful. Sixteen students had back wounds. Some of those who had lain down to escape the gunfire had been wounded on the soles of their feet. Nelson also interviewed students and law enforcement officers and wrote a story that left no doubt that the students had been, in the words of civil rights leaders, "massacred."[23]

Later, when the FBI conducted an investigation, Nelson wrote that the agents were eating, drinking, and sometimes sharing hotel rooms with the state patrolmen they were investigating. Nelson left Orangeburg for Mississippi to dig into the terrorist activists of the White Knights of the Ku Klux Klan, who, he was able to establish from FBI and other law enforcement sources, were suspects in nine murders and three hundred beatings and bombings during the winter, spring, and summer of 1968. He exposed White Knight leaders, operatives, and operational tactics in an extended series, plus follow-up stories.

Nelson had become the most source-connected reporter in the South since Claude Sitton by investigating tips and responding quickly to breaking news.

When King traveled to Memphis in April 1968 to speak at a rally in support of striking sanitation workers, Nelson was there. King predicted that blacks would reach the mountaintop but that he might not be there. As Nelson and other seasoned civil rights reporters left the rally, several of them shared with one another a common observation: King's speech, they felt, sounded like a premonition.[24]

Nelson and most other out-of-town reporters left Memphis after the rally. But Earl Caldwell, under the instructions of Claude Sitton, stayed and was in a room near King's at the Lorraine Motel on April 4 when the civil rights leader was assassinated while leaning over an exterior balcony to talk to friends.

"Dr. King toppled to the concrete second-floor walkway," Caldwell wrote. "Blood gushed from the right jaw and neck area. His necktie had been ripped off by the blast." As city, state, and federal officials searched for the suspect, who had abandoned a 30.6-caliber hunting rifle a block from the shooting scene, riots erupted in Memphis and black neighborhoods across the country, ultimately spreading to more than a hundred cities and towns.[25]

The rioting almost certainly would have been worse had it not been for intensive television coverage that kept millions glued to their sets. The three commercial networks devoted forty-two hours of air time to King from his death to his interment six days later.[26] King's top aides repeatedly appealed on television for the restoration of order to honor a man whose adult life had been spent advocating nonviolence and brotherly love.

In King's hometown, McGill wrote the signature column: "White slaves killed Dr. King. The moment the trigger man fired, King was the free man. The white killer was a slave to fear, a slave to his own sense of inferiority, a slave to hatred, a slave to all bloody instincts that surge in a brain when a human being decides to become a beast." He ended with a call for a level of action even he thought might be too optimistic: "It is perhaps too much to hope, but much of the violent reaction to this bloody murder could be blunted if in every city and town there would now be a resolve to remove what remains of injustice and racial prejudice from schools, from training and job opportunities, from housing and community life."[27]

In his death, King afforded one photojournalist the greatest opportunity of his career. Moneta Sleet, Jr., assigned by *Ebony* to take photographs at the King funeral, ran into difficulties getting inside the service at Ebenezer Baptist Church in Atlanta. When King's wife, Coretta, observed that none of the photographers inside the church were black, she insisted that Sleet be admitted or all photographers be removed. Sleet was no rookie: he had covered King since 1956. Inside the church, he positioned himself near Mrs. King. He then framed the image—a dignified Mrs. King embracing her five-year-old daughter Bernice—that was picked up by a wire service and published in newspapers across the nation, thus qualifying it for a Pulitzer Prize that a magazine-only photograph could not win. With that image, Sleet in 1969 became the first African-American to win a Pulitzer Prize for photography.[28]

The next year saw a sweeping change of the guard, not only in the civil rights movement but also among the reporters who covered it, the editors who directed the coverage, and those who provided editorials and commentary.

Just weeks after King died, Sitton left *The New York Times* to become chief editor of *The News and Observer* in Raleigh, succeeding Jonathan Daniels, the liberal warhorse, who was retiring to the South Carolina coast. Gene Patterson quit as editor of *The Atlanta Constitution* to become managing editor of *The Washington Post* after a dispute with the *Constitution*'s publisher, Jack Tarver, over an editorial page column that had been critical of a rate increase by Georgia Power Company at a time when Tarver wanted to implement higher advertising rates.

Ralph McGill died of a heart attack in February 1969, ten months after King was assassinated and two days shy of his seventy-first birthday. To the end, he was empathetic toward black Americans as they struggled for a bigger share of the American bounty. Just weeks before his death, he was having breakfast in the restaurant of his favorite Washington hotel, the Jefferson, with an editor from *The New York Times*. The restaurant door swung open, and McGill saw an elderly black bellman, whom he had befriended over the years, struggling to shove a small mountain of luggage into an elevator. "Oh my God," McGill gasped. "He's older than me. He shouldn't be carrying all those bags." McGill went to the elevator and pulled the bags from the bellman's hands. The *Times* editor followed in the next elevator and saw the white owners of the bags tipping the bellman and McGill, never realizing they had been assisted by one of America's best-known editors. "Thank you," McGill and the bellman said in unison as the couple closed the door to their room; then McGill quietly slipped his tip to the bellman.[29]

It was the end of an extraordinary era. Never since Horace Greeley and Charles Dana had editors loomed so large. Harry Ashmore, Ralph McGill, Gene Patterson, Lenoir Chambers, Pete McKnight, the two Hodding Carters, Mark Ethridge, Jonathan Daniels, Buford Boone, Hazel Brannon

Smith, Ira Harkey, and others stepped into a vacuum created by southern politicians who did not want to be associated with racial integration even when it was ordered by an authority as high as the Supreme Court of the United States. The national racial trauma might have been even more agonizing if the liberal and moderate editors had not assumed leadership and reached out to the rest of the nation—even at the risk of angering their readers, defying governors and congressmen, and touching off advertising and circulation boycotts. If not for these editors, the gulf between the South and the rest of the nation might have grown wider and harder to bridge.

Most of these editors were gone, but not the news coverage. All of the television networks maintained their southern bureaus. The newsmagazines, having made the civil rights years their most dazzling era, carried on. *The New York Times,* by 1968, had four reporters in three bureaus in the south. The *Los Angeles Times* had two reporters in two bureaus.

Jack Nelson continued to investigate the Klan and the FBI. He disclosed that the bureau, frustrated by its inability to capture the White Knights' most elusive bomber, had used cash and intimidation to persuade two White Knight leaders to order the bomber to dynamite the home of a Jewish merchant in Meridian. The Klansmen initially thought the plan was to capture the bomber before he could commit the crime. Instead, the FBI and local lawmen set up an ambush, seriously wounding the bomber and killing his accomplice, a night-riding woman schoolteacher. For his persistent digging, J. Edgar Hoover declared Nelson an "enemy of the FBI" and spoke with the general manager of the *Los Angeles Times* for three hours in an effort to have Nelson fired. Instead, Nelson was promoted, ultimately to Washington bureau chief of the *Times.*[30]

There was racial news aplenty, especially on the political scene, and many southern papers that had consciously neglected racial coverage in the past now embraced it. The two Birmingham papers improved conspicuously. In Jackson, Rea Hederman, a young and enlightened member of the family who had left the South, returned to Jackson and sought journalistic redemption for *The Clarion-Ledger* by hiring a number of young reporters, tackling tough issues of race discrimination, and doing serious, deep, prizewinning journalism; in a few years, due largely to the doggedness of the reporter Jerry Mitchell, no newspaper would have as much impact on reopening old civil rights criminal cases as *The Clarion-Ledger.* Even the Charleston *News and Courier,* Tom Waring's paper, hired a black reporter and assigned him to cover whites as well as blacks.

James J. Kilpatrick underwent his own transformation. In 1964, Kilpatrick began writing from a more national perspective and in less divisive language. He said he changed because he began to understand the plight of blacks more acutely and to see the South "through new glasses." Others, such as the Citizens' Councils' William J. Simmons, had a more cynical view: Kilpo, as he was known to many, had changed spots when he saw opportunities to write a syndicated column for a national audience that would not tolerate a stick-in-the-eye racist. In print and on CBS's televised *60 Minutes* program, he developed a voice that was still powerfully conservative but had lost the stridency of the writer who a year earlier had declared Negroes inferior to whites. He moved to Washington and lost some battle-hardened friends from the interposition days. But he gained much greater recognition in the mainstream of political life.[31]

Another watershed event occurred in Mississippi, where civil rights activists had challenged the broadcast license of the insurance company that owned WLBT, the largest television station in the state. After years of painstaking research into programming and other decisions, they had gathered ample evidence that the managers of the station, who had made their lobby available for a Citizens' Council bookstore, had abused their programming responsibilities and failed to serve the public interest. In the summer of 1969, the Eighth U.S. Circuit Court of Appeals, in Warren Burger's last opinion before becoming Chief Justice of the Supreme Court, reversed and rebuked the Federal Communications Commission's support for the owners, then denied WLBT its license renewal.

After the license-owner withdrew its appeal, the court made one final dramatic gesture: It ordered interim management by a racially diverse, non-profit board, which promptly hired a black general manager, William Dilday, to run the station.

By the late 1960s, everywhere in the South, chain-owned hotels, motels, movie theaters, and restaurants were welcoming black customers and independently owned businesses were slowly but increasingly following the lead of the national chains. The textile industry, once closed to blacks, was beginning to hire them. Industrial plants and corporate headquarters, newly locating in the South, recruited blacks from the start.

In every southern state by 1968, black voter registration exceeded 50 percent of the race's voting-age population. Two states, Tennessee and Arkansas, shot past the national average of 66.2 percent. Black registration in Mississippi soared from 6.7 percent in 1964 to 59.4 in 1968. By 1970, blacks held 565 elective offices in the South.[32]

Gunnar Myrdal had been astonishingly prophetic when he wrote in the early 1940s that if the mainstream press told the southern racial story, the rest of the nation would be "shocked and shaken" and demand sweeping changes. With constant pressure from the civil rights movement and constant coverage by the press, change came.

There is perhaps no greater embodiment of the movement's success than John Lewis, now a congressman representing King's birthplace, Atlanta.

Today, when he looks back on how he survived and how the movement kept going, he thinks about how hard the segregationists worked to keep the prying eyes of the press away. He can recall the security he felt when reporters—"sympathetic referees," he calls them—were watching and the fear he felt when they weren't.

So many memories of so many important steps on the historic path crowd his mind. Still fresh in his memories, in his emotions, is Birmingham, 1961, when he sat in a Freedom Ride bus at a terminal and felt safe as long as he could see reporters and they could see him. Then police covered the windows, and he was overcome by fear. He can recall how Bull Connor's men rousted him in the dark of night, out of the sight of reporters, and drove him to the Tennessee state line, then abandoned him, leaving him shaken by his isolation from the comforting eyes of journalists. When he saw white thugs in Montgomery smash cameras, beat reporters, and rip up notebooks, he understood that there was an extraordinary power of communications operating parallel to, and intertwined with, the movement. It was, he felt, an allied force.

His greatest fear—and his greatest understanding of the power of the press—came in Mississippi when officers hauled Freedom Riders away from reporters and to the remote, desolate Parchman State Penitentiary. Lewis understood then, and now, the significance of the guard's sneering comment, "Ain't no newspapermen out here."

Selma, he could see years later, had been a catalytic moment in the relationship between the civil rights movement and the news media. "There was a sense of righteous indignation on the part of the American people because of the message that the media was able to translate and send around the country and around the world."

The civil rights movement had succeeded, Lewis would conclude, "because we had a group of men and women who were prepared to get up there to write the words or shoot the pictures, capture the sound. And I think that's changed the face of the South and, in changing the face of the South, changed this nation once and for all."[33]

"If it hadn't been for the media—the print media and television—the civil rights movement would have been like a bird without wings, a choir without a song."[34]

ACKNOWLEDGMENTS

We have spent the greater part of our years and careers writing and editing newspapers. We've lived in a world where, every day, every week, every month, every year, rooms full of professional journalists produce millions of words that form phrases that build sentences that become paragraphs that tell stories on pages that fly through presses at high speed, get folded and bundled, and wind up in the hands of readers all over the world.

Even as this world becomes profoundly different in the digital age, some things remain the same: The news watch never ends. The comma always goes inside the quotation mark. And the families of journalists never get their due reward.

So we take this opportunity to thank our families, first and most, for their patience and understanding for the many ironclad promises that snapped when news broke, for the many meals that went cold, bedtime stories that didn't get read, and dogs that didn't get walked during our newspaper careers. Our greatest debt surely is to our wives, Susan Roberts and Laurie Leonard Klibanoff, who have shown even more extraordinary forbearance during the research and writing of this book. The three Klibanoff daughters, Caroline, Eleanor, and Corinne, whose entire childhoods have nearly or completely spanned the life of this book, deserve praise because they are wonderful, supportive, and have resisted the temptation to humiliate their father for the slow pace of his work.

The best preservative of history is the writing of it. Many historians and journalists have researched and written large and engaging civil rights histories before we tried, and we have built our attempt on their successes. But the writing could never have begun were it not for the commitment of archivists and special collections librarians who understand that history not shared is worthless. This book owes much to Linda Amster at *The New York Times;* Linda M. Matthews at Emory University; Mattie Sink at Mississippi State University; Mike Plunkett at the University of Virginia; Elva Griffith at Ohio State University; and Alexander Moore, formerly of the South Carolina Historical Society.

Thanks also to Jim Baggett at the Birmingham Public Library; Mary Marshall Clark at the Columbia University Oral History Research Office; and Hank T. Holmes and Dan Den Bleyker at the Mississippi Department of Archives and History. Valuable help came from Diana Lachatanere at the Schomburg Center for Research in Black Culture in New York, and David E. Richards at the University of Southern Mississippi. Jason R. Moore at the District of Columbia Public Library, Karl Evanzz at *The Washington Post,* and Martha Frantz at the Glenside (Pa.) Public Library made important finds.

Thanks to southern author John Egerton, we learned about the Southern Oral History Program at the University of North Carolina in Chapel Hill. David Moltke-Hansen, who was director of the Southern Historical Collection there before becoming president of the Historical Society of Pennsylvania, arranged for the our interviews to be transcribed, in exchange for the original recordings. We are grateful to David, Cheri Wolfe, and Jackie Gorman for making the arrangement work and to Susan Estep for transcribing many tapes. Polly Roberts did additional transcribing of key interviews.

We relied also on oral history interviews conducted by others. We received assistance rounding these up from Lois E. Myers at the Baylor University Institute for Oral History; John Tisdale, now a professor as Texas Christian University; Stacy L. Ferraro, formerly with the Center for the Study of Southern Culture at the University of Mississippi; and Charles Bolton, director of the Mississippi Oral History Program at the University of Southern Mississippi.

Our exploration of Gunnar Myrdal and his landmark work was assisted greatly by Walter A. Jackson, a North Carolina State University professor, and Gunnar and Alva Myrdal's daughter Sissela Bok. Other help came from David W. Southern of Westminster College in Fulton, Mo.; Kerstin Assarsson-Rizzi, National Heritage Board, Stockholm; Stellan Andersson, the Labor Movement Archives, Stockholm; Margaretha Talerman at the American Swedish Historical Museum, Philadelphia; Patricia Bartkowski, archivist at Wayne State University; and Alice Pepper at the *Detroit Free Press.*

Charles Overby, chairman of the Freedom Forum, and Everette E. Dennis, director of the late Media Studies Center during its prime, were early and indispensable believers in this project, and showed it with a fellowship at Columbia University and ongoing encouragement.

Generous help came from Culpepper Clark, now dean of the Henry Grady School of Journalism at the University of Georgia; Patrick Washburn, a journalism professor at Ohio State University; Jerry Mitchell, a *Clarion-Ledger* reporter whose dogged investigations into unresolved civil rights murders have pushed authorities to reopen significant cases; and Leesha Faulkner, another Mississippi reporter and historian who gave freely of her time and her large collection of important massive resistance documents. Hoyt Purvis, a University of Arkansas journalism professor, shared valuable research with us, as did Adam Nossiter, author of a fine book about Medgar Evers; University of Mississippi professors David Sansing and Charles Eagles; and University of Southern Mississippi professors Neil McMillen and David R. Davies.

David Garrow, author of seminal books on Rev. Martin Luther King, Jr., was an early source of information and an occasional sounding board. We had other helpful conversations with authors and historians David L. Chappell, Jack Bass, Alex Jones, Andrew Manis, Robert Jefferson Norrell, Kenneth O'Reilly, and Bill L. Weaver.

Larry Spruill, an educator in Mt. Vernon, N.Y., shared his pioneering research into the photojournalism of the civil rights movement. Bill Wheatley, former NBC vice president for news; Nancy Cole, and John Bianchi made time, film, and space available to view old footage of news coverage.

We had terrific research assistance from Doug Ward at the University of Maryland, David Ingle at the South Carolina Historical Society, Kate Grossman at Columbia University, Sara Fanton at the University of Pennsylvania, Ambre Brown at Fisk University, Nicole Gudzowsky, Erica Jacobson, Helen K. Ritz, Kevin R. Ogburn, June Kurtz, and Jeannine Anderson at the University of Maryland, and members of *The Atlanta Journal-Constitution*'s stellar news research operation: Ginny Everett, Jennifer Ryan, Alice Wertheim, Sharon Gaus, Nisa Asokan, Joni Zeccola, and, especially, Richard Hallman. Other help came from Jason Farr at the College of Charleston and Mary Keeley McAllister at the University of Alabama.

The finding, gathering, toning, and cropping of old photographs involves an expertise far greater than we possess. We are fortunate to know pros who provided access or loaned their skills to us: Minla Shields, Laine McCall, Chris Stanfield, Nancy Foreman, Robert Cauvel, and Valerie Lyons of *The Atlanta Journal-Constitution;* Phyllis Collazo of *The New York Times;* Chuck Zoeller of the Associated Press; Greg Mitchell and Shawn Moynihan of *Editor & Publisher;* Jessica Lacher-Feldman at the University of Alabama; Ronnie Agnew and Chris Todd of *The Clarion-Ledger;* Christina Cruse of the *Baltimore Afro-American;* and Margaret Downs Hrabe, Jeanne C. Pardee and Edward Gaynor at the University of Virginia.

Other vital help on photos came from Vivian Counts; Bradley D. Cook at Indiana University; Jim Purks of Americus, Ga; Steven Kasher of the Steven Kasher Gallery, New York City; Boris Samarov of Panopticon Gallery, Waltham, Mass.; Teresa Burk at Emory University, Atlanta; Peggy Engel at the Newseum, Washington. D.C.; Sir Brian Urquhart; Simon Elliott, UCLA Library; Linda Stafford and Voncille Williams of *The Birmingham News;* Moses Newson; Matt Herron, director of Take Stock; Kevin Wilcox of the American Society of Newspaper Editors; David Bailey and Barry Arthur of the *Arkansas Democrat-Gazette;* Tom Dillard and Anne Prichard at the University of Arkansas; Laura Caldwell Anderson of the Birmingham Civil Rights Institute; Tom Spain of *The Charleston Post and Courier;* Ed Inman of Jackson, Miss.; and Shirley and Steve Sessions of Biloxi, Miss.

Audiotapes of speeches by southern editors, and panel discussions involving them, were invaluable; we're grateful to the late John Griffin of Atlanta and to Jonnet S. Abeles at the Columbia University Graduate School of Journalism and Sara VanLooy, formerly of the Freedom of Information Center at the University of Missouri, for providing them.

We have boundless appreciation for the many, many journalists who are mentioned in the book and who gave us their time, their attention, and their memories in far greater proportion than could ever be reflected in these pages. Others who came through with documents, memories and critical insights into our subjects were Martha Hunt Huie, Ira A. Lipman, Anne G. Rutledge, and Emogene Wilson.

The power and influence of an encouraging word by one's bosses cannot be overstated. Hank is indebted to his editors, who were patient and supportive as he juggled the time-consuming and time–competing responsibilities of the book, his job, and his family: Julia Wallace, editor of *The Atlanta Journal-Constitution;* and Robert J. Rosenthal and Maxwell E.P. King, former editors of *The Philadelphia Inquirer.* No less important were extraordinary editors who came long before the book: Bob Phelps and the late Tom Winship of *The Boston Globe;* Gene Foreman (who covered the Central High crisis in Little Rock in 1957), Butch Ward, Jim Naughton, and Phillip Dixon, all formerly of *The Philadelphia Inquirer;* Hodding Carter III and Pic Firmin of the *Delta Democrat-Times;* and A.B. Albritton and the late Bob McHugh and James Lund of the *Sun Herald* on the Mississippi Gulf Coast. The greatest inspiration of all came, as a rookie reporter, while working side-by-side with the amazing Wilson F. (Bill) Minor; thirty-three years later, that inspiration has not dimmed.

Some people always came through for us, no matter the request. That small list of big contributors includes Diane Ceribelli of *The New York Times,* Carol Damiano of *The Philadelphia Inquirer,* Jemea Chamberlain of *The Atlanta Journal-Constitution,* and Norman Lewis and Denise Cross of the University of Maryland. Their willingness to assist us in this endeavor, to engage in it as if it was their own, has been without limit or reservation. We thank them.

Then there are those friends and relatives who remained steadfast in their encouragement: Nancy Albritton, Michael and Christine Bamberger, Ruth Berg, Mark Bowden, Patsy Brumfield, Tim Dwyer, Carol Horner, Judy Ingle, Michael Janeway, Gerald Jordan, Margaret Kirk and Ken Finkel, Daniel Klibanoff, Deborah Klibanoff, Charles Layton, Joe Lelyveld, Jean Leonard and the late Warren Leonard, Bill Marimow, Gloria Minor, Arlene Morgan, Alvin Rosenbaum, Michael Rubenstein, Ted Rubenstein, David Shenk, Steve Suitts, Mary Walton, Curtis Wilkie, Ben Yagoda, and Barbara Ziv.

The manuscript got close scrutiny of two readers who knew the story firsthand: Jack Nelson and Roy Reed. Their advice was wonderful, and their catches saved us embarrassment.

From the beginning concept to the closing line of this book, we have had the wonderful gift of an agent, David Black, and an editor, Ashbel Green, who possessed, in almost supernatural proportions, two qualities that kept the book alive: patience and passion. It is inconceivable we could have had a better agent or editor, and to have had them together is stunning good fortune.

Gene Roberts and Hank Klibanoff

NOTES

Many sources in the notes and bibliography are abbreviated:

ORAL
HISTORIES

AAJP: African American Journalists Oral History Project, Oral History Research Office, Butler Library, Columbia University.

BUI: Baylor University Institute for Oral History, interviews conducted at the University of Mississippi symposium, Covering the South, April 3–5, 1987.

MOHP: The Mississippi Oral History Program, University of Southern Mississippi.

PAPERS AND SPECIAL
COLLECTIONS

EOJP: Emory O. Jackson Papers, Birmingham Public Library.

EUSC: Emory University Special Collections.

JJKP: James J. Kilpatrick Papers, University of Virginia Library.

TCP: Turner Catledge Papers, Mississippi State University.

TRWP: Thomas R. Waring Papers, South Carolina Historical Society.

WBHP: William Bradford Huie Papers, Ohio State University.

I: *An American Dilemma*

1. Walter A. Jackson, *Gunnar Myrdal and America's Conscience: Social Engineering and Racial Liberalism, 1938–1987* (Chapel Hill: University of North Carolina Press, 1990), pp. 143, 145.

2. Ibid., p. 149, citing *Kontakt med Amerika (Contact with America)*, pp. 32–33.

3. Ibid., p. 119.

4. Ibid., p. 160.

5. Gunnar Myrdal, *An American Dilemma: The Negro Problem and Modern Democracy* (New York: Harper and Brothers, 1944), pp. 47–48.

6. Ibid., p. 48.

7. Ibid. Italics Myrdal's. This notion had been espoused in similar language nearly twenty-five years earlier, when then-Senator Warren G. Harding, in a letter to the Associated Negro Press, wrote, "Publicity is going to be the greatest weapon of all in furthering the cause of the Colored people of the United States." Frederick G. Detweiler, *The Negro Press in the United States* (Chicago: University of Chicago Press, 1922, reprinted by McGrath Publishing, College Park, Md., 1968), p. 3.

8. Brian Urquhart, *Ralph Bunche: An American Life* (New York: W. W. Norton, 1993), p. 83.

9. Jackson, *Gunnar Myrdal and America's Conscience,* p. 59.

10. Ibid., p. 86, citing Myrdal letter to Dorothy S. Thomas, March 1, 1938, Gunnar Myrdal Papers, Labor Movement Archive, Stockholm.

11. Ibid., p. 36.

12. David W. Southern, *Gunnar Myrdal and Black-White Relations: The Use and Abuse of An American Dilemma, 1944–1969* (Baton Rouge: Louisiana State University Press, 1987), p. 8.

13. Bunche, mindful of fragile racial etiquette, was sometimes appalled during their 1939 tour as Myrdal challenged the assertions of some people he interviewed,

insulted others, and more than once had to be spirited out of town before local police could find him. Urquhart, *Ralph Bunche,* pp. 84–89, citing Bunche's diaries.

14. Myrdal, *An American Dilemma,* p. 205.
15. Ibid., p. 287.
16. Ibid., p. 554, note b.
17. Ibid., pp. 551–553.
18. Ibid., p. 459.
19. Ibid., pp. 319–320.
20. Review of *NYT* digital archives.

2: "A Fighting Press"

1. Frank Luther Mott, *American Journalism: A History of Newspapers in the United States Through 250 Years, 1690 to 1940* (New York: Manville, 1941).
2. Lee Finkle, *Forum for Protest: The Black Press During World War II* (Rutherford, N.J.: Fairleigh Dickinson University Press, 1975), pp. 96–97, citing New York *Amsterdam News,* July 19, 1941. A search of *NYT* digital archives produced no story about such a warning in 1940–42. When Randolph criticized the lack of Negro employment, it ran in the Sports section of *The Times.*
3. Myrdal, *An American Dilemma,* p. 908.
4. Ibid., p. 910.
5. Edwin Emery and Michael Emery, *The Press and America: An Interpretive History of the Mass Media* (Englewood Cliffs, N.J.: Prentice-Hall, 1984), p. 174.
6. Armistead Scott Pride, "Negro Newspapers: Yesterday, Today and Tomorrow," *Journalism Quarterly* 28, no. 2, Spring 1951, p. 179.
7. Ibid., p. 180.
8. Roi Ottley, *The Lonely Warrior: The Life and Times of Robert S. Abbott* (Chicago: Henry Regnery, 1955), pp. 3, 7.
9. Emery and Emery, *The Press and America,* p. 308.
10. Roland E. Wolseley, *The Black Press, U.S.A.* (Ames: Iowa State University Press, 1990), p. 65. Du Bois claimed that Washington secretly funded some newspapers in exchange for their publication of views aligned with his.
11. Elliott M. Rudwick, *W. E. B. DuBois, Propagandist of the Negro Protest* (New York: Atheneum, 1978), passim.
12. Herbert Garfinkel, *When Negroes March* (Glencoe, Ill.: Free Press, 1959), pp. 30–31.
13. John H. Burma, "An Analysis of the Present Negro Press," *Social Forces* 26, October 1947, p. 173.
14. Patrick S. Washburn, *A Question of Sedition: The Federal Government's Investigation of the Black Press During World War II* (New York: Oxford University Press, 1986), p. 20, citing Gilbert C. Fite and H. C. Peterson, *Opponents of War, 1917–1918* (Madison: University of Wisconsin Press, 1957), pp. 89–90.
15. Washburn, *A Question of Sedition,* pp. 20–22.
16. Finkle, *Forum for Protest,* p. 46.
17. Henry Lewis Suggs, ed., *The Black Press in the South, 1865–1979* (Westport, Conn.: Greenwood Press, 1983), passim.

18. Detweiler, *The Negro Press in the United States,* pp. 6–7.

19. Ibid., p. 15, citing Negro Migration in 1916–17, U.S. Department of Labor, Division of Negro Economics, 1919, Washington, pp. 29–30.

20. E. Franklin Frazier, *Black Bourgeoisie: The Rise of a New Middle Class in the United States* (New York: Collier Books, 1962), p. 148, citing U.S. Department of Commerce, "Negro Newspapers and Periodicals in the United States, 1943," *Negro Statistical Bulletin,* no. 1 (August 1944). The Commerce report showed there were 164 black weekly newspapers, of which 144 reported the year of their establishment; 67.4 percent of those were less than twenty-five years old.

21. Edwin Mims, *The Advancing South* (New York: Doubleday, Page, 1926), p. 268. Myrdal, in *The American Dilemma,* p. 924, concluded that Mims had "rightly . . . characterized" the influence of the black press. Mims was a Vanderbilt professor of English who imbued one student, the future Atlanta editor Ralph McGill, with a love of poetry that led McGill to alter his plans to become a physician.

22. Thomas Sancton, "The Negro Press," *The New Republic,* April 26, 1943, p. 559.

23. Frazier, *Black Bourgeoisie,* p. 150–151.

24. Myrdal noted that sensationalism in the black press was more likely to be found in cities with sensationalist Hearst papers.

25. Walter White, *A Man Called White* (New York: Viking Press, 1948), pp. 206–207.

26. Ottley, *The Lonely Warrior,* pp. 173–187.

27. Sancton, "The Negro Press," p. 557.

28. Vincent Tubbs, oral history, August 21, 1971, AAJP, pp. 4, 6.

29. Jules Tygiel, *Baseball's Great Experiment: Jackie Robinson and His Legacy* (New York: Oxford University Press, 1983), passim.

30. Ibid., p. 32, citing *Sporting News,* November 1, 1945.

31. Ibid., p. 33.

32. Ibid., pp. 39–40.

33. David Falkner, *Great Time Coming: The Life of Jackie Robinson from Baseball to Birmingham* (New York: Simon and Schuster, 1995), pp. 99–100.

34. Tygiel, *Baseball's Great Experiment,* p. 42, based on Lacy article in *Afro-American,* February 28, 1948.

35. Ibid.

36. Finkle, *Forum for Protest,* p. 80, citing quotation in Council for Democracy, "Negro Press Conference," May 7–8, 1943 (typescript, Schomburg Collection), 1: 7, 26.

37. Ibid., p. 64, citing *Journal and Guide,* April 25, 1942.

38. Washburn, *A Question of Sedition,* pp. 63–64, citing "Freedom of the Negro Press," *Chicago Defender,* December 20, 1941.

39. Burma, "An Analysis of the Present Negro Press," p. 172.

40. Thomas Sancton, "Something's Happened to the Negro," *The New Republic,* February 8, 1943, p. 178.

41. Washburn, *A Question of Sedition,* pp. 55–56, citing *The Pittsburgh Courier,* January 31, 1942.

42. Ibid., p. 55.

43. Ibid., pp. 66–91.

44. White, *A Man Called White,* pp. 207–208; Washburn, *A Question of Sedition,* pp. 8, 103–107, 137. The agency investigations have been confirmed over the years, but the War Production Board at the time denied it had made illegal newsprint cutbacks. White says the agency did but that Roosevelt stopped the practice.

45. Virginius Dabney, "Press and Morale," *Saturday Review of Literature,* July 4, 1942, p. 25.

46. Myrdal, *An American Dilemma,* p. 663.

47. Ralph McGill, *AC,* October 24, 1942, cited in John T. Kneebone, *Southern Liberal Journalists and the Issue of Race, 1920–1944,* p. 201.

48. Charles W. Eagles, *Jonathan Daniels and Race Relations: The Evolution of a Southern Liberal* (Knoxville: University of Tennessee Press, 1982), p. 97.

3: SOUTHERN EDITORS IN A TIME OF FERMENT

1. Harry S. Ashmore, *Hearts and Minds: The Anatomy of Racism from Roosevelt to Reagan* (New York: McGraw-Hill, 1982), p. 114.

2. Harry S. Ashmore, *An Epitaph for Dixie* (New York: W. W. Norton & Co., 1957), p. 63.

3. Ashmore, *Hearts and Minds,* p. 16.

4. Ibid., p. 36.

5. Ibid., p. 18.

6. Ashmore, *An Epitaph for Dixie,* pp. 100–102.

7. Harry S. Ashmore, author interview.

8. Ibid.

9. Joseph Morrison, *W. J. Cash: Southern Prophet* (New York: Alfred A. Knopf, 1967), pp. 125–135.

10. Harry S. Ashmore, *Civil Rights and Wrongs* (New York: Pantheon, 1994), p. 61.

11. Harold H. Martin, *Ralph McGill, Reporter* (Boston: Atlantic Monthly Press), pp. 56–57. This was before Ethridge became editor of the the the Louisville *Courier-Journal.*

12. Ibid., p. 60.

13. Ibid., p. 71.

14. Ibid., pp. 117–120.

15. Ashmore, author interview.

16. Virginius Dabney, *Across the Years: Memories of a Virginian* (Garden City, N.Y.: Doubleday, 1978), pp. 165–166. Wise was especially upset when Dabney tried to drop the column of the reactionary Westbrook Pegler; even with their strained relationship, Dabney and Wise worked under the same roof for the next decade.

17. Ashmore, author interview.

18. Commission on Freedom of the Press, "A Free and Responsible Press" (Chicago: University of Chicago Press, 1947), pp. 59–60.

19. James Street, *James Street's South* (Garden City, N.Y.: Doubleday, 1955), p. 252.

20. Ibid.

21. Ashmore, author interview, June 19, 1992.

22. Ibid.

23. Clayborne Carson, editor, *The Papers of Martin Luther King, Jr.,* Vol. 1: *Called to Serve* (Berkeley: University of California Press, 1992), pp. 43–45.

24. Donald A. Ritchie, "Race, Rules and Reporting," *Media Studies Journal,* Winter 1996, p. 139.

25. Letters from Popham to Catledge, October 6, 1955; August 6, 1956; and February 2, 1957, TCP; Popham oral history by *NYT,* p. 7.

26. Popham to Catledge, January 8, 1955, TCP.

27. He mentioned the miles he drove in letters to Catledge in the 1950s when the *Times* purchased cars for him. Years later, Popham recalled driving as much as 50,000 miles a year. Interview with John Popham, BUI; Popham oral history by *NYT,* June 16, 1994.

28. Popham to Catledge, February 5, 1955, TCP.

29. Western Union telegram, Catledge to Popham, February 7, 1955, TCP.

30. Popham, author interview.

31. Nadine Cohodas, *Strom Thurmond and the Politics of Southern Change* (New York: Simon and Schuster, 1993), p. 103.

32. Waties Waring, oral history, Columbia University, pp. 246–248; Carl Rowan, *South of Freedom* (New York: Alfred A. Knopf, 1952), p. 98.

33. Waties Waring, oral history, p. 4.

34. South Carolina Press Association history of member papers, available at www.scpress.org/newshistory.htm.

35. Ibid., p. 95.

36. Richard Kluger, *Simple Justice* (New York: Alfred A. Knopf, 1976), pp. 15–18.

37. Ashmore, *Hearts and Minds,* p. 181.

38. President's Committee on Civil Rights, "To Secure These Rights" (Washington, D.C.: U.S. Government Printing Office, 1947), pp. 151–173.

39. Ibid., p. 87.

40. "Threat Is to Mill Workers," *CN&C,* September 16, 1948, cited also in Robert Lewis Terry, "J. Waties Waring, Spokesman for Racial Justice in the New South," dissertation, University of Utah, 1970, p. 65.

41. W. J. Cash, *The Mind of the South* (New York: Alfred A. Knopf, 1941), pp. 175–181.

42. Ann Waldron, *Hodding Carter: The Reconstruction of a Racist* (Chapel Hill, N.C.: Algonquin, 1993), pp. 151–157, 204–206.

43. Ibid., p. 204.

44. Florence, S.C., *Morning News,* October 31, 1947, p. 4, as cited in Terry, "J. Waties Waring," pp. 66–68.

45. Calvin McLeod Logue, *Ralph McGill, Editor and Publisher,* Vol. 1 (Durham, N.C.: Moore Publishing, 1969), p. 73, citing column of June 12, 1946.

46. McGill, *AC,* March 4, 1948.

47. William C. Berman, *The Politics of Civil Rights in the Truman Administration* (Columbus: Ohio State University Press, 1970), p. 88.

48. V. O. Key, *Southern Politics in State and Nation* (New York: Alfred A. Knopf, 1950), pp. 335.

49. Ibid., pp. 329–344.

50. Berman, *The Politics of Civil Rights in the Truman Administration,* p. 128; Carl T. Rowan, *Breaking Barriers* (Boston: Little, Brown, 1991), pp. 78–79.

51. Ralph McGill, July 30, 1948, in *Ralph Emerson McGill, a Posthumous Tribute,* by Mary Lynn McGill, 1970.

52. Ralph McGill, in article rejected by *American Mercury* in the summer of 1948 and published posthumously in *No Place to Hide*, Vol. 1 (Macon, Ga.: Mercer University Press, 1984), p. 121.

4: Ashmore Views the South

1. Edwin F. Brennan, "Sprigle Poses as Newsman to Get Story of South," *E&P*, August 7, 1948.
2. Waldron, *Hodding Carter*, pp. 208–213.
3. Ibid., pp. 211–212.
4. Harry S. Ashmore, *Hearts and Minds*, p. 155.
5. Ibid., pp. 155–156.
6. Ibid., p. 156.
7. Ibid., p. 157.
8. "The 'Integration' Nonsense," *CN&C*, May 21, 1951, cited also in Terry, "J. Waties Waring," p. 208.
9. " 'Segregation' to Civilization," *CN&C*, June 6, 1951, cited also in Terry, "J. Waties Waring," p. 221.
10. *CN&C*, as cited in Terry, "J. Waties Waring," p. 249.
11. Ashmore, author interview.
12. McGill, "One Day It Will Be Monday," *AC*, April 9, 1953.
13. Kluger, *Simple Justice*, pp. 260–284; Jack Greenberg, *Crusaders in the Courts* (New York: Basic Books, 1994), pp. 66–68, 71–78.
14. Ashmore, *An Epitaph for Dixie*, p. 162
15. Emory O. Jackson to C. A. Scott, December 6, 1946, May 13, 1949, EOJP.
16. Jackson to Scott, July 31, 1945; Jackson to Scott, December 6, 1946; Jackson to Scott, December 25, 1953, EOJP.
17. Cliff Mackay, "Repression Rears Its Ugly Head," *Atlanta Daily World*, June 20, 1943; Emory O. Jackson, interview, February 1968, Moorland-Spingarn Library at Howard University.
18. Harry S. Ashmore, *The Negro and the Schools* (Chapel Hill: University of North Carolina Press, 1954), pp. 153, 156, 158, 159, 160.
19. Ibid., p. 139.
20. Leo Bogart, *The Age of Television* (New York: Frederick Ungar, 1958), p. 10.
21. Ibid., pp. 8–9.
22. J. Fred MacDonald, *One Nation Under Television: The Rise and Decline of Network TV* (New York: Pantheon, 1990), p. 98.
23. "Person to Person," October 1953; "See It Now," December 29, 1953.
24. Edward R. Murrow, "Why Should News Come in 5-Minute Packages?" speech given October 15, 1958, reprinted in Louis Lyons, editor, *Reporting the News* (Cambridge: Belknap Press of Harvard University Press, 1965).
25. Ashmore, author interview.
26. G. James Fleming, "The Negro Press," research memorandum prepared for the Myrdal Study, September 1942, chap. 11, p. 49.
27. Charles Dunagin, interview, BUI.
28. Ibid.; also Robert Gordon, W. C. "Dub" Shoemaker and Ashmore, author interviews.

29. Fleming, "The Negro Press," p. 47; Bill Weaver, "The Educative Role of Black Newspapers, 1920–1930," dissertation, Indiana University, 1979, p. 90.

30. David R. Davies, "The Press and Civil Rights," dissertation, University of Southern Mississippi, 1997, chap. 6, citing *NYT* editorial "Race in the News," August 11, 1946; *Time,* August 19, 1946.

31. Ashmore, *Hearts and Minds,* pp. 148–149.

32. Doug Cumming, "Facing Facts, Facing South: The SERS and the Effort to Inform the South after *Brown v. Board,* 1954–1960," dissertation, University of North Carolina, 2002, pp. 170–171.

33. Ashmore, author interview.

34. Letter, Waring to Kilpatrick, November 8, 1955, TRWP.

35. John Egerton, *Speak Now Against the Day* (New York: Alfred A. Knopf, 1994), p. 610.

36. Henry Lewis Suggs, *P. B. Young, Newspaperman: Race, Politics, and Journalism in the New South, 1910–62* (Charlottesville: University Press of Virginia, 1988), pp. 166, 180–182.

37. Ashmore, author interview; *Newsweek,* August 8, 1955.

38. Reed Sarratt, *The Ordeal of Desegregation* (New York: Harper and Row, 1966), pp. 261–262.

5: THE *BROWN* DECISIONS HARDEN THE SOUTH

1. Richard Kluger, *Simple Justice,* p. 711.

2. McGill, "One Day It Will Be Monday," *AC,* April 9, 1953.

3. Martin, *Ralph McGill, Reporter,* p. 134.

4. Eugene C. "Gene" Patterson, author interview.

5. "The Court's Decision," *CN&C,* May 18, 1954.

6. "Let Us Not Be Dismayed," ibid., May 20, 1954.

7. Letter, Thomas R. Waring Jr., to Virginius Dabney, May 22, 1954, TRWP.

8. Daniel Webster Hollis III, *An Alabama Newspaper Tradition: Grover C. Hall and the Hall Family* (University, Ala.: University of Alabama Press, 1983), p. 103.

9. *Richmond Afro-American,* March 7, 1953, p. 15, JJKP.

10. Ibid., May 18, 1954.

11. Waldron, *Hodding Carter,* pp. 234–235.

12. Ashmore memo, May 18, 1954, TRWP.

13. James J. Kilpatrick, "But It Won't Stay Buried," *National Review,* March 8, 1958, pp. 235–236.

14. John Bartlow Martin, *The South Says Never* (New York: Ballantine Books, 1957), p. 1.

15. Ibid., pp. 1–2.

16. Neil R. McMillen, *The Citizens' Council: Organized Resistance to the Second Reconstruction, 1954–64* (Urbana: University of Illinois Press, 1994), p. 19.

17. Waldron, *Hodding Carter,* pp. 235–236.

18. Robbins L. Gates, *The Making of Massive Resistance: Virginia's Politics of Public School Desegregation, 1954–1956* (Chapel Hill: University of North Carolina Press, 1962), pp. 159–160.

19. Bob Smith, *They Closed Their Schools* (Chapel Hill: University of North Carolina Press, 1965), pp. 157–163.

20. Waring to Dabney, May 22, 1954, TRWP.

21. Jack Claiborne, *The Charlotte Observer: Its Time and Place, 1869–1986* (Chapel Hill: University of North Carolina Press, 1986), p. 258.

22. Poll by George Gallup, cited in *American Chronicle: Six Decades in American Life, 1920–1980,* by Lois Gordon and Alan Gordon (New York: Atheneum, 1987), p. 332.

23. Ashmore, author interview.

24. "Tracing the Color Line," *Newsweek,* August 8, 1955, Press section.

25. Waring to Ashmore, June 9, 1954, TRWP.

26. "Ford Financed Group Headed by Virginian with Active Red-Front Affiliate Record," *The Augusta Courier,* August 23, 1954.

27. Letters from Waring to Harris, June 28, July 28, 1954; and from Harris to Waring, July 6, 1954, TRWP.

28. Ibid.

29. "Tracing the Color Line," *Newsweek,* August 8, 1955, Press section.

30. Minutes, annual meeting of the SERS board, March 18, 1956; Don Shoemaker, author interview.

31. Martin, *The South Says Never,* p. 21.

32. McMillen, *The Citizens' Council,* p. 26, citing *Annual Report: 1955* of the Association of Citizens' Councils.

33. *Winston-Salem Journal,* June 1, 1955.

34. "Now It's the South's Turn," *RNL,* June 1, 1955.

35. Martin, *The South Says Never,* p. 29.

36. Ibid., pp. 29–30.

37. "Liar by Legislation," *DD-T,* April 3, 1955.

38. Martin, *The South Says Never,* p. 25; Carl Elliott, with Michael D'Orso, *The Cost of Courage: The Journey of an American Congressman* (New York: Doubleday, 1992), p. 177; William Peters, *The Southern Temper* (Garden City, N.Y.: Doubleday & Co., 1959), p. 44.

6: INTO MISSISSIPPI

1. Booker, author interview.

2. Margaret Price, "The Negro Voter in the South," *New South* (Southern Regional Council), September 1957, vol. 12, no. 9, p. 21; Neil R. McMillen, *Dark Journey: Black Mississippians in the Age of Jim Crow* (Urbana: University of Illinois Press, 1989), pp. 35–36; McMillen, *The Citizens' Council,* p. 215.

3. Testimony of Gus Courts at hearings before the Subcommittee on Constitutional Rights of the U.S. Senate Judiciary Committee, 85th Cong., 1957, p. 532.

4. Ibid.

5. Ibid.

6. McMillen in *The Citizens' Council,* p. 216, says that 126 blacks were registered before the local Citizens' Council began its campaign to force blacks off the rolls. In Roy Wilkins with Tom Mathews, *Standing Fast: The Autobiography of Roy Wilkins* (New York: Viking Press, 1982), pp. 222–223, Wilkins says that Lee and

Courts signed up 400 voters overall, but that apparently confuses the number who paid their poll taxes with the number who actually registered.

7. Simeon Booker, *Black Man's America* (Englewood Cliffs, N.J.: Prentice-Hall, 1964), p. 161.

8. Booker, oral history, AAJP.

9. Ibid.

10. Booker, author interview.

11. "The Negro Press: 1955," *Time,* November 7, 1955, pp. 64–65.

12. Wolseley, *The Black Press,* p. 87.

13. Ibid., pp. 86–88; Ben Burns, *Nitty Gritty: A White Editor in Black Journalism* (Jackson: University of Mississippi Press, 1996), pp. 30–36.

14. Ibid., pp. 86–87.

15. Ibid., pp. 114–115.

16. Ibid., p. 119.

17. Chuck Stone, *Black Political Power in America* (New York: Dell, 1968), p. 9.

18. Booker, *Black Man's America,* pp. 162–163.

19. John Dittmer, *Local People: The Struggle for Civil Rights in Mississippi* (Urbana: University of Illinois Press, 1994), p. 54.

20. Booker, *Black Man's America,* pp. 163–164.

21. McMillen, in *The Citizens' Council,* p. 214, cites a county-by-county study by the Southern Regional Council of black voting registration in the South.

22. Testimony of Gus Courts, p. 533.

23. James Featherston, "Links Shooting of Negro with Vote Irregularities," *JCL/JDN,* August 14, 1955, p. 1.

24. AP, "Jury Hits 'Cover Up,' Refuses to Indict 3 in Slaying of Negro," *CT,* September 21, 1955; also by the Civil Rights Education Project of the Southern Poverty Law Center, *Free at Last: A History of the Civil Rights Movement and Those Who Died in the Struggle,* pp. 38–39; Charles Payne, *I've Got the Light of Freedom: The Organizing Tradition and the Mississippi Freedom Struggle* (Berkeley: University of California Press, 1995), p. 39.

25. "Group Named to Study Ways to Cut Down Negro Voting," *JDN,* August 30, 1955, p. 1.

26. Testimony of Gus Courts, p. 532. The only senator to question Courts, Sam Ervin of North Carolina, devoted more time to interrogating Courts about whether he had paid federal income taxes than he did to questions about voting rights or the violence Courts had encountered.

27. Erle Johnston, *Politics: Mississippi Style* (Forest, Miss.: Lake Harbor Publishers, 1993), p. 64.

28. Robert M. Hederman Jr., "The Hederman Story: A Saga of the Printed Word in Mississippi," speech delivered to the Newcomen Society of North America on May 5, 1966, and printed by the Society, p. 22. A copy is located in the Mississippi Department of Archives and History.

29. Ibid., pp. 14–15.

30. Dub Shoemaker, author interview. News accounts when Sullens died in November 1957 said the libel judgment was for $12,000.

31. Wilson F. "Bill" Minor, author interviews; Norman Bradley, oral history, MOHP, vol. 194, 1982, pp. xi, 22–23.

32. Ibid., p. 31.
33. AP obituary, November 20, 1957; Luther A. Huston, "Meany Demands Quemoy Decision," *NYT,* April 23, 1955.

7: THE TILL TRIAL

1. Moses J. Newson, author interview; Booker, author interview.
2. From trial testimony as reported by the AP, *MP-S, MCA, JDN, CD, CT, CDN* and *CS-T.* Also, Stephen J. Whitfield, *A Death in the Delta: The Story of Emmett Till* (New York: Free Press, 1988).
3. AP, "White Storekeeper Held in Abduction of Negro Youth," *JDN,* August 29, 1955.
4. AP, " 'Kidnapped' Negro Boy Still Missing; Fear Foul Play," *JDN,* August 30, 1955.
5. James Featherston, "White Orders Investigation in Slaying of Delta Negro," *JDN,* September 1, 1955; Whitfield, *A Death in the Delta,* p. 22.
6. *CD,* September 10, 1955.
7. Booker, *Black Man's America,* p. 3.
8. Henry Hampton and Steve Fayer, *Voices of Freedom: An Oral History of the Civil Rights Movement from the 1950s through the 1980s* (New York: Bantam Books, 1990), pp. 5–6.
9. Vicki Goldberg, *The Power of Photography: How Photographs Changed Our Lives* (New York: Abbeville, 1991), p. 201; interview, Ernest Withers.
10. Waldron, *Hodding Carter,* pp. 256–257.
11. Mamie Bradley, during panel discussion "Civil Rights: The Media and the Movement," Freedom Forum First Amendment Center, Nashville, February 22, 1999.
12. "Newsmen and Photographers Are Frisked for Weapons," *CA,* September 20, 1955.
13. "Daily Worker's Reporter at Trial Is Mississippian," *JDN,* September 21, 1955.
14. Dub Shoemaker, author interview.
15. Cliff Sessions, John Herbers, author interviews.
16. David Halberstam, *The Fifties* (New York: Fawcett Columbine, 1993), pp. 437–438.
17. Popham to Catledge, July 15, 1955, TCP.
18. "Civil Rights Fight Found Being Won," *NYT,* April 6, 1949; John N. Popham, "Racial Issues Stirred by Mississippi Killing," September 18, 1955.
19. McGill to Catledge, October 4, 1955, TCP.
20. Robert E. Lee Baker, oral history, BUI.
21. Halberstam, *The Fifties,* p. 438.
22. Clark Porteous, author interview.
23. Ibid.; Ralph Ginzburg, *100 Years of Lynchings: A Shocking Documentary of Race, Violence in America* (New York: Lancer, 1962), p. 225; Robert L. Zangrando, *The NAACP Crusade Against Lynching, 1909–1950* (Philadelphia: Temple University Press, 1980), pp. 127–128.
24. Porteous, author interview.
25. "Newsmen and Photographers Are Frisked for Weapons," *CA,* September 20,

1955; also, Whitfield, *A Death in the Delta*, pp. 33–34, citing reports in *Newsweek, DD-T, Nation* and *CA*.

26. John N. Popham, "Trial Under Way in Youth's Killing," *NYT*, September 20, 1955.

27. Emogene W. Wilson, Ernest Withers, Charles Tisdale, author interviews; also articles by Emogene W. Wilson, "Profile: L. Alex Wilson, *T-SD*, February 24 and March 3, 1990.

28. *T-SD*, June 12, 1954, as cited in Benjamin F. Clark, Sr., "The Editorial Reaction of Selected Southern Black Newspapers to the Civil Rights Movement, 1954–1968," dissertation, Howard University, August 1989, pp. 157–158.

29. Wilson, "Profile: L. Alex Wilson," *T-SD*, February 24, 1990.

30. Moses J. Newson, author interview; Zangrando, *The NAACP Crusade Against Lynching*, pp. 122–123; Herbert Shapiro, *White Violence and Black Response: From Reconstruction to Montgomery* (Amherst: University of Massachusetts Press, 1988), p. 283; Ginzburg, *100 Years of Lynchings*, pp. 222–224.

31. Withers, Newson, author interviews.

32. Porteous, Wilson, author interviews; also, Clark Porteous, "Jury Being Chosen in Till Trial," *MP-S*, September 19, 1955; Halberstam, *The Fifties*, pp. 438–439.

33. Porteous, author interview, November 12, 1995; also, Cloyte Murdock Larsson, "Land of the Till Murder Revisited," *Ebony*, March 1986, p. 56; John N. Popham, "Trial Under Way in Youth's Killing," *NYT*, September 20, 1955, as cited in Whitfield, *A Death in the Delta*, p. 38; also Halberstam, *The Fifties*, p. 439.

34. Moses Newson, "Emmett's Kin Hang On in Miss. to Harvest Crop," *CD*, September 17, 1955.

35. Ibid.

36. Larsson, "Land of the Till Murder Revisited," *Ebony*, March 1986, p. 56; Dan Wakefield, *Revolt in the South* (New York: Grove Press, 1960), pp. 34–35.

37. Ibid.

38. *Eyes on the Prize: America's Civil Rights Years, 1954–1965* (New York: Viking Press, 1987), pp. 47–48.

39. Murray Kempton, "He Went All the Way," *NYP*, September 22, 1955, as reprinted in Murray Kempton, *America Comes of Middle Age, Columns, 1950–1962* (Boston: Little, Brown, 1963), p. 135.

40. In *The New York Times*, the *Memphis Press-Scimitar*, the Memphis *Commercial Appeal*, the New York *Amsterdam News* and the *St. Louis Post-Dispatch*, Wright said, "There he is." In the *Chicago Sun-Times*, he said, "That's him right there." In the *Chicago Tribune* and *Chicago Daily News*, Wright pointed a finger but was not quoted as saying anything. James Hicks, black reporter for the New York *Amsterdam News*, recalled in *Eyes on the Prize* that Wright uttered, "Thar he." But Hicks's own coverage at the time reported Wright as saying, "There he is." A copy of the long-lost transcript of the trial quotes Wright as saying, "There he is; that's the man." Wright's son, Till's cousin, Simeon Wright, said he believes some have portrayed his grandfather as using the ungrammatical phrase because "it was more colorful and stereotypical to make him sound like an illiterate country farmer. But that wasn't the case. My father was a preacher and very articulate." Shaila Dawan and Ariel Hart, "FBI Discovers Trial Transcript in Emmett Till Case," *NYT*, May 18, 2005; also, *Eyes on the Prize*, p. 51; John N. Popham, "Slain Boy's Uncle On Stand at Trial," *NYT*, September 22, 1955, p. 64. Especially use-

ful research has been conducted on Mose Wright's testimony and other aspects of the Till case by David T. Beito, associate professor of history at the University of Alabama; Linda Royster Beito at Stillman College; Christopher Metress, associate professor of English at Samford University; and filmmaker Keith Beauchamp, who produced and directed *The Untold Story of Emmett Louis Till.*

41. Simeon Booker, "A Negro Reporter at the Till Trial," *Nieman Reports,* January 1956, pp. 13–15. Booker wrote that the only white reporter Howard trusted with the information he was about to impart was Clark Porteous, who had covered civil rights in the Delta for years for the *MP-S.* Porteous, unaware of this, invited Featherston and Shoemaker along. Featherston and Shoemaker said in interviews that they happened to call Howard that night and he invited them to Mound Bayou. Porteous couldn't recall the sequence. Dub Shoemaker, James Featherston, Porteous, author interviews.

42. Clark Porteous, "New Till Evidence: Reporter Finds It," *MP-S,* September 21, 1955.

43. Booker, "A Negro Reporter at the Till Trial," pp. 13–15.

44. Baker Marsh, "Till Slayers Ripped as 'Cowardly,' " *CDN,* September 23, 1955; William Sorrells, "Two Mississippians Acquitted in Slaying of Chicago Negro; Jurors Out Only 67 Minutes," CD, September 24, 1955.

45. Halberstam, *The Fifties,* p. 438.

46. Featherston, author interview.

47. Whitfield, *A Death in the Delta,* p. 42, citing *Time,* October 3, 1955.

48. Michael Dorman, "Friend, Mentor and 'Satchel Man,' " *Newsday,* January 25, 1987.

49. Ibid.

50. Letters, William Bradford Huie to Roy Wilkins, October 12, 1955; to Mr. Walters and Lee Hills, October 18, 1955, WBHP.

51. Ibid.

52. Ibid.

53. Letter, Huie to Walters, Hills, October 18, 1955, WBHP.

54. Ibid.

55. Letter, Huie to Wilkins, October 12, 1955, WBHP.

56. Letter, Huie to Dan Mich, October 21, 1955, WBHP.

57. Letter, Huie to Mich, October 25, 1955, WBHP.

58. Copies of signed "Consent and Release" contracts between John W. Milam and William Bradford Huie, and Carolyn Bryant and Huie, October 28, 1955; letter, Huie to Mich, October 23, 1955, WBHP.

59. At trial, three prosecution witnesses said Milam had been at a farm his brother managed when they saw him and heard sounds of a beating inside a barn; the Huie story places the beating in a barn at Milam's own house. Bryant and Milam before trial said they had released Till after presenting him to Carolyn Bryant, who said he was not the boy who had insulted her; the Huie version says Till readily told them he had insulted her and Bryant was not with them at all that night. Another concern: in his earliest letters to Mich, Huie insists there were four killers and that he knew who they were but was uncertain if he could get the other two, who had never been charged, to talk. In a subsequent letter, he said he had come to believe only two men were involved, but he offered no explanation for his change of opinion.

60. "Milam Denies Look Article Quotes, May Sue Magazine," *DD-T,* January 10, 1955, "Judge Jordan Says Can Still Indict Pair on Kidnaping," January 13, 1955.
61. Huie to Graves, January 21, 1956, WBHP.
62. Agreement signed by Huie, February 23, 1956, WBHP.
63. Letter, Waring to Huie, February 25, 1956, copies found in both WBHP and TRWP.
64. Popham to Catledge, October 29, 1955, TCP.
65. Popham to Catledge, October 29, 1955, TCP.
66. Catledge to Popham, November 2, 1955. By "cluckerism," Catledge meant Kluxerism. TCP.

8: Where Massive and Passive Resistance Meet

1. "Negro Jailed Here for 'Overlooking' Bus Segregation," *MA,* December 2, 1955, p. 9.
2. "Dilemma in Dixie," *Time,* February 20, 1956, p. 76.
3. Halberstam, *The Fifties,* p. 682.
4. Popham to Catledge, February 14, 1956, TCP.
5. Popham to Catledge, February 4, 1956, February 14, 1956. TCP.
6. "Times Study in South Finds Some Integration Progress," *NYT,* March 13, 1956.
7. Harrison E. Salisbury, *Without Fear or Favor: An Uncompromising Look at the NYT* (New York: Times Books, 1980), p. 357, citing story in *NYT* on March 13, 1956.
8. Letter, Kilpatrick to author, October 2, 1996.
9. Ibid.; Samuel Lee Banks, "The Educational Views of James J. Kilpatrick Relative to Negroes and School Desegregation as Reflected in the *Richmond News Leader,* 1954–1960," master's thesis, Howard University, June 1970.
10. John A. Hamilton, author interview.
11. Ibid.
12. Ibid.
13. Philip J. Hilts, "The Saga of James J. Kilpatrick," *Potomac* magazine of the *WP,* September 16, 1973, p. 15.
14. Endres, "James J. Kilpatrick: Conservative at Work," p. 3, in JJKP.
15. Letter, Kilpatrick to Paul McKalip, *Tucson Daily Citizen,* July 6, 1959, JJKP.
16. *Newsweek* files, December 12, 1960, EUSC; also James Jackson Kilpatrick, *The Sovereign States: Notes of a Citizen of Virginia* (Chicago: Henry Regnery, 1957), p. 148.
17. Kilpatrick, speech to Pi Delta Epsilon, April 1951, Longwood College, Farmville, Va., in JJKP.
18. Kilpatrick, speech at Emory University, November 1957, tape recording at EUSC.
19. Kilpatrick, speeches to Intercollegiate Press Association, November 30, 1951, Hampden-Sydney College; University of Missouri Journalism School, April 30, 1953; Columbia University School of Journalism, February 23, 1953, and April 26, 1954; Petersburg, Va., Kiwanis Club, October 2, 1951, JJKP.
20. Hilts, "The Saga of James J. Kilpatrick," p. 15.

21. *Richmond Afro-American,* March 7, 1953.

22. Letter, Kilpatrick to V. M. "Red" Newton, Jr., managing editor of the *Tampa Morning Tribune,* July 6, 1956, JJKP.

23. James J. Kilpatrick, "Not to Be Solved on a Slide Rule: A Southerner Looks at the Problem of Integrated Schools," *Human Events,* May 14, 1955.

24. Letter, Kilpatrick to Tom Waring, November 7, 1955, TRWP.

25. Grover C. Hall Jr., speech at Emory University, Fall 1957, EUSC.

26. Numan V. Bartley, *The Rise of Massive Resistance: Race and Politics in the Deep South During the 1950s* (Baton Rouge: Louisiana State University Press, 1969), pp. 128–129.

27. Letter, Kilpatrick to Harry M. Ayers, March 2, 1956, JJKP.

28. James J. Kilpatrick, *The Southern Case for School Segregation* (New York: Crowell-Collier Press, 1962), p. 8.

29. Ibid., John A. Hamilton, author interview, April 26, 1996.

30. Ibid.

31. Ibid.

32. Benjamin Muse, *Virginia's Massive Resistance* (Bloomington: Indiana University Press, 1961), pp. 94–95.

33. Dabney's mother was the great-great-great granddaughter of Thomas Jefferson's sister. Marie Morris Nitschke, "Virginius Dabney of Virginia, Portrait of a Southern Journalist in the 20th Century," dissertation, Emory University, 1987, p. 4.

34. *Raleigh News and Observer,* December 16, 1955, as cited in Charles W. Eagles, *Jonathan Daniels and Race Relations: The Evolution of a Southern Liberal* (Knoxville: University of Tennessee Press, 1982), p. 136.

35. "Race Trouble to Grow in South—Mixed Schools Not in Sight," *U.S. News & World Report,* February 24, 1956, p. 144.

36. Letter from North Carolina Supreme Court Associate Justice R. Hunt Parker to Kilpatrick, April 19, 1956, JJKP.

37. Bartley, *The Rise of Massive Resistance,* p. 131.

38. Benjamin Muse, *Ten Years of Prelude* (New York: Viking Press, 1964), pp. 66–67.

39. Francis M. Wilhoit, *The Politics of Massive Resistance* (New York: George Braziller, 1973), pp. 142–144.

40. Ibid., pp. 139, 144.

41. Joe Azbell, "Negro Groups Ready Boycott of City Lines," *MA,* December 4, 1955, pp. 1, 6.

42. Donnie Williams and Wayne Greenhaw, *The Thunder of Angels: The Montgomery Bus Boycott and the People Who Broke the Back of Jim Crow* (Chicago: Lawrence Hill Books, 2006), pp. 65, 74–75; Branch, *Parting the Waters,* p. 133.

43. Joe Azbell, "Negro Groups Ready Boycott of City Lines," *MA,* December 4, 1955, p. 1; Joe Azbell, "Extra Police Set for Patrol Work in Trolley Boycott," *MA,* December 5, 1955, p. 2A.

44. Clayborne Carson, David J. Garrow, Gerald Gill, Vincent Harding, and Darlene Clark Hine, *The Eyes on the Prize Reader: Documents, Speeches, and Firsthand Accounts from the Black Freedom Struggle, 1954–1990* (New York: Penguin Books, 1991), pp. 51–53, citing *MA,* December 7, 1955; Branch, *Parting the Waters,* pp. 136–137.

45. Joe Azbell, "5,000 At Meeting Outline Boycott; Bullet Clips Bus," *MA,* December 6, 1955; *Eyes on the Prize* television series, PBS, part 1; Carson et al., *The Eyes on the Prize Reader,* p. 50.

46. Azbell, "5,000 At Meeting Outline Boycott; Bullet Clips Bus."

47. Williams and Greenhaw, *The Thunder of Angels,* p. 88; Carson et al., *The Eyes on the Prize Reader,* p. 53.

48. Clayborne Carson, senior editor, *The Papers of Martin Luther King Jr.* Vol. 2: *Rediscovering Precious Values, July 1951–November 1955* (Berkeley: University of California Press, 1994), p. 328.

49. *Birmingham World,* December 23, December 27, 1955, as cited in David Garrow, *Bearing the Cross: Rev. Martin Luther King Jr. and the Southern Christian Leadership Conference* (New York: William Morrow, 1986), pp. 28, 31, 32.

50. Stephan Lesher, author interview, November 14, 1996.

51. Ibid.; Hollis, *An Alabama Newspaper Tradition,* p. 55.

52. Hollis, *An Alabama Newspaper Tradition,* p. 35.

53. Ibid., pp. 26–40.

54. Ibid., p. 94, citing "Hallmarks," *Alabama Journal,* November 30, 1945.

55. Ashmore, *An Epitaph for Dixie,* p. 165.

56. Grover C. Hall, Jr., speech to meeting of North and South Carolina Press Associations, Asheville, N.C., as reprinted in *MA,* early 1958, from undated tearsheet in TRWP.

57. Lesher, author interview.

58. Hollis, *An Alabama Newspaper Tradition,* pp. 124–125.

59. Hall, speech at Emory University, November 1957, tape recording at EUSC.

60. *Newsweek* file, January 24, 1956, EUSC.

61. *MA,* April 2, 1949, cited in Hollis, p. 99.

62. Hall, speech at Emory University, November 1957, tape recording at EUSC.

63. "The 2-Edged Sword," *MA,* December 13, 1955, p. 4.

64. Martin, *The South Says Never,* pp. 25–26; Elliott and D'Orso, *The Cost of Courage,* p. 177; Peters, *The Southern Temper,* p. 44.

65. Letter, Hall to Black, January 19, 1956, from the private papers of Hugo Black, Library of Congress, Washington, D.C., as cited in Stephan Lesher, *George Wallace, American Populist* (New York: Addison-Wesley), p. 112.

66. Lesher, *George Wallace,* pp. 112–113. The "painted sticks," Lesher notes, referred to red, white, and blue stakes that scheming carpetbaggers sold to freed slaves with the fraudulent pitch that they could be used to claim land being redistributed.

67. Ann Mitchell, "Keep Bama White," master's thesis, Georgia Southern College, June 1971, p. 178.

68. Ted Poston, "The American Negro and Newspaper Myths," in Paul L. Fisher and Ralph L. Lowenstein, eds., *Race and the News Media* (New York: Frederick A. Praeger, 1967) pp. 64–66, from a symposium cosponsored by the Anti-Defamation League of B'nai B'rith and the Freedom of Information Center, University of Missouri, Columbia, November 14–16, 1965; Peters, *The Southern Temper,* pp. 44–45; Martin, *The South Says Never,* pp. 25–26; L. D. Reddick, *Crusader Without Violence: A Biography of Martin Luther King Jr.* (New York: Harper and Brothers, 1959), pp. 162–165.

69. Reddick, *Crusader Without Violence,* pp. 164–165.

9: ALABAMA

1. Rowan, *Breaking Barriers,* p. 136.
2. Ibid., p. 139–141; Taylor Branch, *Parting the Waters: America in the King Years, 1954–63* (New York: Simon and Schuster, 1988), pp. 155–157; Rev. Martin Luther King, Jr., *Stride Toward Freedom* (San Francisco: HarperSan Francisco, 1986), pp. 124–126.
3. Lesher, author interview.
4. Mitchell, "Keep Bama White," pp. 33–34.
5. E. Culpepper Clark, *The Schoolhouse Door: Segregation's Last Stand at the University of Alabama* (New York: Oxford University Press, 1993), pp. 6, 109; Mitchell, "Keep Bama White," p. 34.
6. Clark, *The Schoolhouse Door,* p. 46; Mitchell, "Keep Bama White," pp. 30, 31–32.
7. Clark, *The Schoolhouse Door,* p. 57; Mitchell, "Keep Bama White," pp. 42, 157.
8. Mitchell, "Keep Bama White," p. 43.
9. "World Turned Eyes on UA This Week," *The Tuscaloosa News,* February 8, 1956.
10. "Dilemma in Dixie," *Time,* February 20, 1956, pp. 76–78.
11. Mitchell, "Keep Bama White," p. 44.
12. AP, "Alabama U. Rally Protests a Negro," *NYT,* February 5, 1956.
13. Salisbury, *Without Fear or Favor,* p. 360.
14. Peter Kihss, "Negro Co-ed Is Suspended to Curb Alabama Clashes," *NYT,* February 7, 1956; Bill Gibb and Stroube Smith, "Patrol Slips Lucy Away from Mob; Apparent Ruse Thwarts Mob," *The Tuscaloosa News,* February 7, 1956; and AP, "Alabama U. Suspends Negro Co-ed as Rioters Pelt Her, Police Chief," *AC,* February 7, 1956.
15. Clark, *The Schoolhouse Door,* pp. 79–80.
16. Murray Kempton, "The Way It's Got to Be," *NYP,* February 9, 1956, reprinted in Murray Kempton, *America Comes of Age,* p. 154.
17. "Carolina Campus Accepts Negroes," "Negro Named Principal of Philadelphia Schools," "Arkansas Suit Filed," "Nullification Bill Voted," *NYT,* February 9, 1956.
18. Interview, Buford Boone, in Maurine Hoffman Beasley and Richard R. Harlow, *Voices of Change: Southern Pulitzer Prize Winners* (Washington, D.C.: University Press of America, 1979), p. 53; interview, Boone, by Cecilia Hale Ziff, July 28, 1975, generously made available by Dr. E. Culpepper Clark.
19. Interview, Boone, in *Voices of Change,* p. 55.
20. Interview, Boone, June 26, 1970, by Ann Mitchell for "Keep Bama White," p. 106.
21. Transcript, "The Racial Crisis and the News Media," November 14–16, 1965, p. 43.
22. "This Pushing, Pushing Is No Good," *The Tuscaloosa News,* February 3, 1956, p. 4.
23. "What a Price for Peace," *The Tuscaloosa News,* February 7, 1956, p. 1.
24. Interview, Boone, by Cecilia Hale Ziff, July 28, 1975.
25. Ibid.
26. Ibid.
27. Ibid.; also Mitchell, "Keep Bama White," p. 105, footnote 62.

28. Mitchell, "Keep Bama White," pp. 77–78, citing *The Tuscaloosa News,* February 8, 1956.
29. *The Tuscaloosa News,* February 9, 1956, from information provided by Dr. E. Culpepper Clark.
30. Interview, Boone, by Cecilia Hale Ziff, July 28, 1975.
31. Mitchell, "Keep Bama White," p. 163.
32. Clark, *The Schoolhouse Door,* p. 87.
33. Ibid., p. 105.
34. "Could We Have a Gift of Peace?" *The Tuscaloosa News,* March 4, 1956.
35. *Birmingham World,* n.d., as cited in Clark, *The Schoolhouse Door,* p. 113.
36. Branch, *Parting the Waters,* p. 183; David L. Chappell, *Inside Agitators: White Southerners in the Civil Rights Movement* (Baltimore: Johns Hopkins University Press, 1994), p. 81
37. Reddick, *Crusader Without Violence,* pp. 140–141.
38. Ibid.
39. Ibid., p. 141.
40. "Battle Against Tradition," *NYT,* March 21, 1956.
41. Reddick, *Crusader Without Violence,* p. 141.
42. Lerone Bennett, "The King Plan for Freedom," *Ebony,* July 1956, p. 65.
43. Reddick, *Crusader Without Violence,* p. 153.
44. "The Ordeal of the South, IV—The Boycott City," *The Manchester Guardian,* May 12, 1956.
45. Mitchell, "Keep Bama White," pp. 185–186.
46. Ibid., p. 189.
47. Withers, author interview.

10: Toward Little Rock

1. Roy Reed, *Faubus: The Life and Times of an American Prodigal* (Fayetteville: University of Arkansas Press, 1997), p. 169.
2. Ibid., p. 168.
3. Ibid., p. 169.
4. Ashmore, *Hearts and Minds,* p. 254.
5. Orval E. Faubus, *Down from the Hills* (Little Rock: Pioneer, 1980), pp. 39–40; Ashmore oral history, BUI, p. 22; Reed, *Faubus,* pp. 116–124; Hugh Patterson, oral history, BUI, p. 6.
6. Hugh Patterson, oral history, April 3, 1987, BUI, p. 12.
7. *Arkansas State Press,* October 29, 1954, as cited in Suggs, *The Black Press in the South,* p. 78.
8. Homer Bigart, "Tolerance in South 5 Years Away," *NYHT,* as published in *SPT.* September 25, 1955.
9. Ashmore to Catledge, September 30, 1955; Catledge to Ashmore, October 3, 1955; Catledge to Arthur Hays Sulzberger, October 6, 1955; Catledge to Popham, October 6, 1955. TCP.
10. The twenty-seven included Senator Lyndon B. Johnson and Representative Sam Rayburn, who, as Senate majority leader and House Speaker, were not asked to

sign, and Senators Estes Kefauver and Albert Gore, Sr., who refused. The others were all House members from border states, most of them from Texas. Ashmore frequently told of having asked Senator Olin Johnston of South Carolina to work on his state's other senator, Strom Thurmond, to postpone a vote on the Manifesto until after the Democratic primaries. "It's no use trying to talk to Strom," Johnston told Ashmore. "He believes that shit." Ashmore, *Hearts and Minds*, p. 231.

11. Larry Jinks, "A Testing of Ideals," in *Journalists in Action*, compiled by Edward W. Barrett (Manhasset, N.Y.: Channel Press, by Columbia University Graduate School of Journalism, 1963), pp. 84–89; William Bagwell, *School Desegregation in the Carolinas: Two Case Studies* (Columbia: University of South Carolina Press, 1972), p. 101. A Greensboro reporter accidentally discovered that the joint meetings were taking place as early as May 1957; officials said they were merely discussing "mutual problems," including segregation issues.

12. "Three N.C. Cities Assign 12 Negroes to Previously All-White Schools," *Southern School News*, August 1957; Bem Price, AP, "Integration Barriers Cracking in South," August 31, 1957, as published in *AG*, September 1, 1957; Larry Jinks, "A Testing of Ideals," *Journalists in Action*, pp. 84–89.

13. Letter, James J. Kilpatrick to William J. Simmons, July 17, 1957. Simmons responded on July 22 by asking if there was "any chance of simply closing the schools?" He added, "Don't be gloomy. There will probably be some integration, and the painful results therefrom will do more to arouse public opinion than even your eloquent pen has been able to do," JJKP.

14. Letter, Kilpatrick to William J. Simmons, July 24, 1957, JJKP.

15. Letter, Kilpatrick to Don Shoemaker, August 12, 1957, JJKP.

16. Ashmore, author interview. In June 1957, the editor of the Columbus, Ga., *Enquirer* asked Tom Waring's policy on carrying wedding engagement announcements of previously married women. Waring responded that he published only the weddings, not the engagements. As for photos, he wrote, "We feel that publication of a picture with an announcement prior to the wedding is not in the best of taste." Letter, Waring to W. C. "Cliff" Tucker, June 27, 1957.

17. Ashmore, speech at Emory University, November 26, 1957, in series of lectures "Editors View the South," organized by John Griffin, EUSC.

18. Ibid.

19. Hugh Davis Graham, *Crisis in Print* (Nashville: Vanderbilt University Press, 1967), pp. 34–37, 41–46.

20. Ibid., pp. 37–40.

21. Porteous, author interview; "The Two Eds of Memphis, Meeman and Crump," speech delivered by Porteous, December 1987, published in The Egyptians yearbook, 1987–88, pp. 19–31; Graham, *Crisis in Print*, pp. 39–40; Edwin Howard, editor, *The Editor We: A Posthumous Autobiography by Edward J. Meeman* (Memphis: Edward J. Meeman Foundation, 1976).

22. Armistead Scott Pride, "The Negro Newspaper in the United States," *Gazette*, International Journal of the Science of the Press, vol. 2, 1956, pp. 141–143.

23. *Arkansas State Press*, May 16, 1941, as cited in Calvin Smith in Suggs, ed., *The Black Press in the South*, p. 72.

24. Pride, "The Negro Newspaper in the United States," pp. 147–148.

25. Reed, *Faubus,* p. 189, citing Colbert S. Cartwright, "The Improbable Demagogue," *The Reporter,* October 17, 1957.

26. "A Time of Testing," *AG,* September 1, 1957.

27. Ashmore, *Hearts and Minds,* p. 259. Faubus's version is similar, but he comes off as not so blatantly political. Faubus, *Down from the Hills,* p. 207.

28. Ibid., p. 206.

29. "Little Rock Quiet on Eve of Opening Integrated Schools," *AG,* September 2, 1957, p. 1.

30. Reed, *Faubus,* p. 204.

31. Ashmore, *Hearts and Minds,* p. 258.

32. Hugh Patterson, oral history, BUI, p. 5.

33. Lerone Bennett Jr., "First Lady of Little Rock," *Ebony,* September 1958, pp. 17–24.

34. Daisy Bates, *The Long Shadow of Little Rock* (New York: David McKay, 1962), pp. 59–60.

35. Hoyt Hughes Purvis, "Little Rock and the Press," master's thesis, University of Texas, 1963, pp. 2–3, citing *Newsweek,* September 9, 1957, and the *AP Log,* September 5–11, 1957. In fact, Arkansas had already achieved that distinction by integrating other school systems without difficulty.

36. Benjamin Fine, speech delivered October 1, 1957, at Columbia University Graduate School of Journalism.

37. Ibid.

38. Reuven Frank, author interview.

39. John Chancellor, author interview.

40. Ibid.; Frank, author interview.

41. Chancellor, author interview.

42. Bogart, *The Age of Television,* p. 10, citing A. C. Nielsen, NBC, and CBS; p. 12, citing Television Bureau of Advertising.

43. George Gallup, director of the American Institute of Public Opinion, in a speech to the American Society of Newspaper Editors, San Francisco, July 11, 1957. Located in TRWP.

44. Chancellor and Frank, author interviews.

45. Graham, *Crisis in Print,* p. 100; also, contemporaneous articles in *NYT.*

46. "Kasper Led Racial Mingling in New York," and "Negro Former Pals Shocked by Kasper's Racial Views," *NYHT,* as reprinted in the *Nashville Banner,* February 1 and February 5, 1957.

47. Bates, *The Long Shadow of Little Rock,* p. 60.

48. Virgil Blossom, *It HAS Happened Here* (New York: Harper & Brothers, 1959), pp. 71–72.

49. Chancellor, author interview.

11: Little Rock Showdown

1. Benjamin Fine, "Arkansas Troops Bar Negro Pupils; Governor Defiant," *NYT,* September 5, 1957, pp. 1, 20; Jerry Dhonau, "Negro Girl Turned Back, Ignores Hooting Crowd," *AG,* September 5, 1957. *Gazette* reporters had not yet established a strong relationship with Daisy Bates or the nine students and misspelled

Eckford's name as Echford; in the same story, it also misspelled the last name of the white woman, Grace Lorch, who later comforted Eckford.

2. Robert Schakne, oral history, BUI; Philip N. Schuyler, "Panelists Agree: Journalistic Code Violated at Little Rock," *E&P,* November 2, 1957, pp. 11, 66. Schakne expressed regret that had encouraged the crowd and said he learned then that it was inappropriate. In the *E&P* account, former CBS correspondent Bob Allison, said that he, too, encouraged Little Rock protesters to repeat demonstrations that cameras had missed; see also Charles Quinn, oral history, BUI.

3. Schakne, oral history, BUI; *Eyes on the Prize,* part 2, Blackside Inc., Boston, Mass., Henry Hampton, executive producer. In his oral history, Schakne expressed misgivings about his attempt to interview Eckford that day.

4. Two months later, Senator James Eastland called Mrs. Lorch before the Senate Internal Security Subcommittee to answer charges that she was a member of the Communist Party.

5. Benjamin Fine, "Arkansas Troops Bar Negro Pupils; Governor Defiant," *NYT,* September 5, 1957, pp. 1, 20. Fine told of Lorch's role, but not his own.

6. Ken Parker and Matilda Tuohey, "Eisenhower Asked to Curb U.S. Agents," *AG,* September 5, 1957, p. 2.

7. Bob Douglas, author interview, undated.

8. The scenes that follow come from extensive reports published in the *AG* and *NYT* on September 6, 1957. In a front-page story in the *Times,* Fine wrote about the day's events and referred to threats to arrest newsmen after "this reporter" was told to stop interviewing people. His first-person account of the incident with the Guard and Clinger was published on page 8. The *Times* played up the confrontation with the newsmen, publishing as its lead photograph on page 1 a picture of Clinger talking to reporters and carrying an inside photograph of a National Guardsman using a billy club to separate Fine from people he was trying to interview.

9. Charles Quinn, oral history, BUI.

10. *NYT,* September 6, 1957, p. 8.

11. *Newsweek* reporter William Emerson's file to New York offices, September 27, 1957, located in *Newsweek* archives at EUSC, Atlanta.

12. The AP Log, September 5–11, 1957, provided by Hoyt Hughes Purvis, author of "Little Rock and the Press," master's thesis, University of Texas, 1963, pp. 64–65.

13. *NYT,* September 3–30, 1957; also Purvis conducted an extensive survey of how the story was played in "Little Rock and the Press," master's thesis, University of Texas, 1963, p. 167.

14. The AP Log, September 12–18, 1957.

15. Ibid., September 12–18, 1957.

16. Purvis, "Little Rock and the Press," *passim.*

17. File by *Newsweek* reporter Joe Cumming to editors in New York, September 23, 1957, located in *Newsweek* archives at EUSC, Atlanta.

18. Dorothy Gilliam, oral history, BUI; Gilliam was a rookie reporter for the *T-SD* who went to Little Rock to help L. Alex Wilson, against his advice.

19. James L. Hicks, "King Emerges as Top Negro Leader," "Wilkins Raps Hicks on Pilgrimage Comment," New York *Amsterdam News,* June 1, 1957, June 8, 1957. Reddick, *Crusader Without Violence,* p. 197.

20. Newson, Wilson, Withers, Tisdale, Martin, author interviews; also Enoch P. Waters, *American Diary* (Chicago: Path Press, 1987), p. 109.

21. *T-SD,* October 22–28, 1960, citing an interview with his mother, Mrs. Luetta Patterson.

22. Newson, Wilson, Withers, Tisdale, author interviews. In *Forum for Protest,* Lee Finkle notes that the Wendell Willkie Award, which paid cash prizes, never had universal acclaim in the black press as the highest honor in black journalism because it had been established by southern white liberals such as Virginius Dabney, Mark Ethridge, Ralph McGill, and Douglas Southall Freeman in 1945, when they were accusing the northern black press of being too militant. Other criticisms were that only two of the original board members had been black and that the initial winner, though a black journalist, had publicly lambasted most black newspapers as "nauseating." But there was no other honor as well known.

23. Frank, Chancellor, author interviews.

24. J. Fred MacDonald, *Blacks and Whites on TV: Afro-Americans in Television Since 1948* (Chicago: Nelson Hall Publishers, 1983), p. 91.

25. Letter from Ira A. Lipman to All BBYO leaders, September 9, 1957, provided by Lipman.

26. Ira A. Lipman, author interview.

27. "The Riffraff," *Newsweek,* September 23, 1957, pp. 32–33; William Emerson's undated file from Nashville to *Newsweek* in New York, in *Newsweek* archives at Emory University Library's Special Collections.

28. "What Hath Orval Wrought," *Time,* September 23, 1957, pp. 11–12, 15.

29. AP, "Crowd at School Jeers Newsmen," *NYT,* September 10, 1957; Jerry Dhonau, "Quiet Crowd at Central Grows Spiteful as Rumor Sifts in From North Side," *AG,* September 10, 1957, p. 10.

30. Dhonau, "Quiet Crowd," *AG,* September 10, 1957, p. 10.

31. AP, "Crowd at School Jeers Newsmen," *NYT,* September 10, 1957; Dhonau, "Quiet Crowd," *AG,* September 10, 1957.

32. Newson, author interview, April 22, 1996; Dhonau, "Crowd at Central High is Passive as Guard 'Escorts' Negro Newsman," *AG,* September 11, 1957.

33. Purvis, "Little Rock and the Press," p. 48; additional research for this section was done at the University of Maryland in 1991 by Helen K. Ritz, Kevin R. Ogburn, and June Kurtz.

34. "Reflections in a Hurricane's Eye," *AG,* September 9, 1957; "Governor Faubus Got His Answer," *AG,* September 11, 1957.

35. "Mr. Faubus Needs a Dictionary," *AG,* September 18, 1957.

36. "Governor Faubus Mounts the Stump," *AG,* October 25, 1957.

37. "Orval Faubus vs. The Law of the Land," *AG,* September 23, 1957.

38. Faubus speech, September 26, 1957, text published in *AG,* September 27, 1957.

39. Ibid.

40. "Governor Faubus Mounts the Stump," *AG,* October 25, 1957.

41. "The Crisis Mr. Faubus Made," *AG,* September 4, 1957.

42. "Of Arkansas and North Carolina," *AG,* September 6, 1957.

43. "Faubus, Dutch Co-ed Discuss Integration," *Arkansas Democrat,* September 22, 1957, p. 12, as cited by Helen K. Ritz in "The *Arkansas Democrat,* September 1,

1957–September 30, 1957," paper done for a journalism class at University of Maryland.

44. Purvis, "Little Rock and the Press," pp. 165–66; Ashmore, "Mr. J.N. at 91," *ASNE Bulletin,* December 1963, p. 13; Ashmore, oral history, BUI, pp. 28–29. A $2 million loss in 1958 would be equivalent to more than $13 million in 2006.

45. *AG* editorial, December 13, 1957, as cited in Purvis, "Little Rock and the Press," pp. 49–50.

46. Hugh Patterson, oral history, BUI, p. 11.

47. The *Democrat*'s first such story, " 'Didn't Think It Would Go This Far,' Rebuffed Student Asserts," by AP, was published September 5, 1957, p. 3, as cited by Ritz in "The *Arkansas Democrat,* September 1, 1957–September 30, 1957." The *Gazette*'s first such story was "Little Rock Negroes Give Views on School Integration Dispute," September 15, 1957, p. 7, as cited by Kevin R. Ogburn in "*Arkansas Gazette* Coverage of the Little Rock School Crisis, September 1–30, 1957," paper done for a journalism class at University of Maryland. The first general insight into the nine students published in the *Gazette* came on September 16, in "Nine Negroes Marking Time Until CHS Dispute Settled." The story was from the AP and published in the *Gazette* on page 15. Perhaps in recognition of these holes in the *Gazette*'s coverage and the AP's work in filling them, when Pulitzer Prizes were handed out, the *Gazette*'s two went to Ashmore for editorial writing and to the newspaper for public service (not for local reporting), while the national reporting award went to AP's Relman Morin for his Little Rock coverage. The *Gazette* publisher, J. N. Heiskell, also won several prestigious awards.

48. Ted Poston, "Nine Kids Who Dared: Gloria Ray," *NYP,* October 28, 1957, sec. M, p. 2, as cited in Kathleen A. Hauke, *Ted Poston, Pioneer American Journalist* (Athens: University of Georgia Press, 1998), pp. 147–148. Also, Rowan, *Breaking the Barriers,* pp. 154–155.

49. Brownell commented on his distrust of Faubus at a conference in Abilene, Kansas, in 1990. Reed, *Faubus,* p. 220.

50. Faubus would later say the president seemed, halfheartedly, to be taking a position scripted by Brownell and Adams. Faubus, knowing the federal judge in the case had invited suggestions from the Justice Department, felt that Brownell had misinformed Eisenhower by saying the president could not get involved in the case. Faubus attributed Brownell's resignation six weeks later to Eisenhower's belated belief that Brownell had deceived him. Faubus, *Down from the Hills,* pp. 255–258; Reed, *Faubus,* pp. 219–220; Ashmore, *Hearts and Minds,* pp. 262–264; contemporaneous *AG*s and *NYT.*

51. Reed, *Faubus,* p. 219.

52. "A Reporter Reports," an April 1960 compilation of a six-part series in *E&P* about Relman "Pat" Morin, provided by Hoyt Hughes Purvis.

53. Ibid.

54. This scene is as told by Relman Morin in "A Reporter Reports," L. Alex Wilson in the *T-SD,* James Hicks in *Eyes on the Prize,* Daisy Bates in *The Long Shadow of Little Rock,* and other accounts.

55. Morin's work that day won him his second Pulitzer Prize. Morin remained modest about his role, saying, "Some other intelligence, if that is the word, and a far

deeper one than mine, was in command." AP's in-house newspaper, the *AP Log,* said that Morin "was as close to a one-man show as we ever get in AP. . . . Morin's reporting of the scene at the high school won stature as rare journalistic artistry . . . derived from the cool, dispassionate presentation and the cumulative impact of grim detail."

56. Newson, author interview.

57. L. Alex Wilson, "Defender Editor Tells of Attack," *T-SD,* September 28, 1957, pp. 1–2; Jerry Dhonau, "Mobs at Both Ends of School Kick, Beat, Chase and Yell," *AG,* September 24, 1957, pp. 1–2; Benjamin Fine, "President Threatens to Use U.S. Troops, Orders Rioters in Little Rock to Desist; Mob Compels 9 Negroes to Leave School"; Farnsworth Fowle, "Little Rock Police, Deployed at Sunrise, Press Mob Back at School Barricades," *NYT,* September 24, 1957, pp. 1, 18, 19; *Eyes on the Prize,* part 2; Daisy Bates, *The Long Shadow of Little Rock,* pp. 88–93.

58. This scene is as told by Relman Morin in a letter to Hoyt Purvis, July 17, 1962.

59. All four of the newsmen and Bates have been convincing in denying that the newsmen were used as decoys. The *T-SD* didn't help matters, however, when a copy editor put the following headline on a story that Wilson dictated to the *Defender* for September 28, 1957: "Ruse Helps Get 9 into School." Wilson, in several subsequent stories, went to great pains to insist that there was never an arrangement to distract the crowd.

60. Richard Stolley, Atlanta bureau, *Life* magazine, oral history, BUI; letter from Ben Fine to Hoyt Purvis, July 30, 1962, cited in Purvis master's thesis.

61. David Halberstam, *The Powers That Be* (New York: Alfred A. Knopf, 1979), pp. 310–311; Ashmore, *Hearts and Minds,* pp. 261–262, 265; Bates, *The Long Shadow of Little Rock,* pp. 93–94.

62. The 100 million figure comes from "Eyes on Little Rock," *Time,* October 7, 1957, p. 61. *NYT* reported the 62 percent figure at the time, Purvis, p. 114.

63. "Eyes on Little Rock," *Time,* October 7, 1957, p. 61.

64. Jack Gould, "Little Rock Speaks," *NYT,* September 9, 1957, as cited by Purvis, "Little Rock and the Press," pp. 71–72.

65. Paul Jones, "Newscasters Take Sides on Little Rock," *AC,* October 2, 1957, p. 14.

66. Letter, Kilpatrick to Waring, September 20, 1957. TRWP.

67. Purvis, "Little Rock and the Press," pp. 56–58, citing Armistead S. Pride, "The Arkansas State Press: Squeezed to Death," *Grassroots Editor,* vol. 2, no. 1, January, 1962, p. 7; also, Suggs, *The Black Press in the South,* p. 82–83.

68. Purvis, "Little Rock and the Press," pp. 56–58, citing Pride, "The Arkansas State Press," p. 7; also Suggs, *The Black Press in the South,* pp. 82–83.

12: NEW EYES ON THE OLD SOUTH

1. After reading an unctuous ten-page Popham letter seeking an increase from $500 to $1,000 in his expense account, Catledge's first assistant (and later successor) Clifton Daniel wrote Catledge, "For God's sake, give the man his thousand dollars. Otherwise, he might write another letter. And I doubt that you spare more than one afternoon a week to reading mail from Johnny." But Popham's special place in their hearts was evident in Daniel's other remarks: "He's one of the loveli-

est guys I ever met—as well as one of the most prolix." Daniel's note to Catledge, undated, was in response to Popham's letter of March 27, 1956, TCP.

2. Popham to Catledge, February 2, 1957. All but one of Popham's letters to Catledge, no matter how personal, opened, "Dear Mr. Catledge" and were signed with his first and last names, Johnny Popham, TCP.

3. Author's interview with Popham.

4. Catledge to Sulzberger, May 1, 1958, TCP.

5. Catledge to Sunday editor Lester Markel, May 14, 1958, TCP.

6. Sitton background comes from interviews with the authors.

7. Von Hartz was news editor, a notch below assistant managing editor, and was in charge of the paper's staff at the presidential nominating conventions of both major parties in 1952 and 1956. Von Hartz obituary, *NYT,* March 25, 1960.

8. Richard Burritt, Catledge's special assistant for personnel, to Catledge, May 13, 1958. TCP.

9. Catledge to Markel, May 14, 1958. TCP.

10. Burritt to Catledge, May 13, 1958. TCP.

11. "Publisher quits education group," *BA-A,* on April 7, 1956, reported Young's criticism. Waring, in a handwritten memo found in TRWP, noted that the news report "was wrenched from the context of the telegram" because it failed to mention his praise for *Southern School News.*

12. "Our Answer Is No," *BA-A,* June 2, 1956.

13. Simeon Booker, "Ticker Tape U.S.A.," *Jet,* April 26, 1956.

14. Letter from Waring to Dabney, May 21, 1956; June 19, 1956; TRWP.

15. Cumming, "Facing Facts, Facing South," p. 316.

16. Claude Sitton, author interview.

17. Relman Morin, "Sentiment Hardens in Little Rock," AP, published in *WP,* September 12, 1958, p. A13.

18. Ashmore, author interview.

19. AP, "Arrests Mar Little Rock School Rite," May 25, 1958, published in *WP,* May 26, 1958, p. A8.

20. Claude Sitton, "Little Rock Hardens on Integration Issue," *NYT,* August 24, 1958.

21. Sitton, "School Board on Spot in Little Rock Crisis," Ibid., September 7, 1958.

22. Sander Vanocur, author interview.

23. Harry Reasoner, *Before the Colors Fade* (New York: Alfred A. Knopf, 1981), p. 48.

24. *Newsweek* files, May 25, 1964, EUSC. In Henry V, the king says in Act 4, scene 7, "I was not angry since I came to France/Until this instant."

25. Reasoner, *Before the Colors Fade,* p. 48.

26. Baker changed his byline during 1958, from Robert E. Lee Baker to Robert E. Baker.

27. Robert E. Lee Baker, "Death and Violence Terrorize Negroes in Georgia Town," *WP,* June 8, 1958. The next day, *The Atlanta Constitution* sent a reporter to Dawson, whose story said, "Two of the town's leading Negroes—a school principal and an undertaker—said they knew of no reason for Negroes to be afraid." The reporter was Jack Nelson. Though Nelson did major breakthrough civil rights reporting over the years in Atlanta and as the *Los Angeles Times* bureau chief in Washington, and though he evidenced liberal leanings in a weekly television

show, some of his old colleagues recalled that he had been party to a story that sought to debunk Baker's account. "Racial Crisis and the Press," by Walter Spearman and Sylvan Meyer, Southern Regional Council, 1960.

28. John Herbers, author interview; Egerton, *Speak Now Against the Day,* pp. 418, 468. Kytle was part of an effort to start *Pace,* a progressive, *Time*-clone "weekly review of Southern affairs" that died quickly. He was active in biracial groups and later became director of the Community Relations Service in Washington.

29. Herbers, author interview.

30. Ibid.

31. Ibid.

32. In May 1958, United Press merged with International News Service, forming United Press International (UPI).

33. Herbers, author interview.

34. Cliff Sessions, "Citizens Councils Teach White Supremacy in State High Schools," *DD-T,* April 24, 1958.

35. Cliff Sessions, author interview.

36. Ibid.

37. From the Leesha Faulkner Collection of the Mississippi State Sovereignty Commission files, November 25, 1958.

38. Sessions interview by John Tisdale, BUI, July 24, 1992.

39. Sessions, Herbers, author interviews.

40. Sessions, author interview.

41. Cliff and Shirley Sessions, author interview; also, John Tisdale, interview with Sessions, July 24, 1992.

42. Ibid.

43. Bill Minor, Herbers and Sessions, author interviews; Waldron, *Hodding Carter,* pp. 188–189, 250–251.

44. Jay Milner, "Treloar's 'Not Guilty' Verdict Was Not Unexpected," *DD-T,* August 10, 1958, p. 1.

45. "Water Valley Meditation," ibid., August 10, 1958.

46. East, P. D., *The Magnolia Jungle: The Life, Times and Education of a Southern Editor* (New York: Simon and Schuster, 1960), p. 225.

47. Golden, Harry, "The Vertical Integration; Or, Water Fountain Integration," Charleston (W.Va.) *Gazette,* June 8, 1958; "Golden Rule," *Time,* April 1, 1957, p. 62. See also, Clarence Walter Thomas, "The Journalistic Civil Rights Advocacy of Harry Golden and the *Carolina Israelite,*" dissertation, University of Florida, 1990.

48. Correspondence among the three men found in the Ralph McGill papers in the EUSC; also Leonard Ray Teel, "The Connemara Correspondents: Sandburg, Golden and McGill," paper presented at the Southeast Regional Colloquium, AEJMC History Division, University of North Carolina, Chapel Hill, April 14–16, 1989.

49. Sitton, author interview; also, Harold H. Martin, *Ralph McGill, Reporter,* pp. 207–208.

50. Calvin McLeod Logue, *Ralph McGill, Editor and Publisher,* vol. 1 (Durham, N. C.: Moore, 1969), pp. 140–148, citing McGill, speech delivered May 29, 1959,

at the Joseph Pulitzer Memorial Lecture at the Columbia University Graduate School of Journalism.

13: BACKFIRE IN VIRGINIA

1. Virginius Dabney, author interview; also, Nitschke, *Virginius Dabney of Virginia,* p. 248.
2. Robert Mason, *One of the Neighbor's Children* (Chapel Hill, N.C.: Algonquin Books, 1987), pp. 155–158; Lenoir Chambers and Joseph E. Shank, *Salt Water and Printer's Ink: Norfolk and its Newspapers, 1865–1965* (Chapel Hill: University of North Carolina Press, 1967), pp. 383–384; Muse, *Virginia's Massive Resistance,* pp. 94–96.
3. Mason, *One of the Neighbor's Children,* pp. 153–154.
4. Eagles, *Jonathan Daniels and Race Relations,* p. 186, citing *News and Observer* for April 7, 1956, and speech at Coker College November 7, 1955.
5. *Virginian-Pilot,* August 30, 1958, cited in Chambers and Shank, *Salt Water and Printer's Ink,* p. 385.
6. Chambers, *The Virginian-Pilot,* September 24, 1958, cited in Alexander S. Leidholdt, *Standing Before the Shouting Mob* (Tuscaloosa: University of Alabama Press, 1997), p. 94.
7. Hamilton, author interviews.
8. Ibid.
9. Kilpatrick to Simmons, July 23, 1959, JJKP.
10. Author conversations with Ashmore. Also Ashmore, *Hearts and Minds,* p. 289.
11. Ashmore, *Hearts and Minds,* p. 289.
12. " 'Long Live the King,' " *Newsweek,* April 2, 1956.
13. Letter, John Fischer to Tom Waring, September 30, 1955, TRWP.
14. Waring, letter to Fischer, October 4, 1955, TRWP.
15. "The Southern Case Against Desegregation," Thomas R. Waring, Jr., *Harper's Magazine,* vol. 212, no. 1268, January 1956, pp. 22–23, 39–45.
16. "Dynamite in Dixie," March 23, 1956, and March 24, 1956, *New York Journal-American* and King Features Syndicate; letters from Kilpatrick to Waring, March 27, 1956, and Waring to Kilpatrick, March 29, 1956, TRWP.
17. *MA,* March 11, 1956.
18. Ibid., March–July, 1956; "Tell It Not in Gath," *Time,* April 23, 1956, p. 62; "The Negro in the North," *Time,* June 4, 1956, p. 81; Hollis, *An Alabama Newspaper Tradition,* pp. 107–109. The biblical passage is II Samuel 1:20.
19. "Tell It Not in Gath," *Time,* April 23, 1956, p. 62.
20. *CN&C,* April 21, 1956; "Tell It Not in Gath," *Time,* April 23, 1956; "The Negro in the North," June 4, 1956.
21. "The Negro in the North," *Time,* June 4, 1956.
22. "Published in Askelon-III (A)," *MA,* May 11, 1956.
23. G. James Fleming, "The Associated Press," submitted to Gunnar Myrdal as research for *An American Dilemma,* located in the Schomburg Center for Research in Black Culture, New York.
24. Waring to Gould, August 25, 1955. An earlier complaint about an AP story on a

race survey had come on January 26, 1955; correspondence between Waring and Paul Hansell, AP bureau chief in Charlotte, December 2, 5, 7, 8, 9, 12, 15, and 19, 1955; Waring to Gould, October 8 and 15, 1956.

25. "Fred Sullens' Own Choice Named Editor," E&P, November 30, 1957; Robert Friedman, "FBI Manipulates the Media," *Rights* (May–June, 1977), p. 13, cites FBI documents released by the Senate Intelligence Committee, then chaired by Senator Frank Church.

26. Ibid.; Frank J. Donner, *The Age of Surveillance: The Aims and Methods of America's Political Intelligence System* (New York: Alfred A. Knopf, 1980), p. 238; also Leesha Faulkner Sovereignty Commission files and Ward letter to Waring, April 24, 1959.

27. The correspondence and notes related to the editors' meeting in Atlanta are included in the Kilpatrick and Waring papers. John Foltz memo to Tom Waring, July 12, 1956, TRWP.

28. Foltz to Waring, April 25, 1959, TRWP.

29. Waring's handwritten notes are in the TRWP; Kilpatrick's are in the JJKP.

30. The reference is to Senators Albert Gore, Sr., and Estes Kefauver, both Democrats.

31. Waring to James Gray, May 12, 1959, TRWP.

32. The messages wired to and from AP about coverage of the New York rape, dated June 19, 1959, are located in the Kilpatrick and Waring archives.

33. Waring to editors Kilpatrick, Ward, Parham, Gray, McDonald, Shannon, Harris, King, Cauthen, and Citizens' Councils' Patterson, June 22, 1959, TRWP.

34. Waring to Gould, June 24, 1959, TRWP.

35. Waring to editors, June 25, 1959, TRWP.

36. Patterson to Waring, June 25, 1959, TRWP.

37. A copy of the proposal is held in the TRWP. It was not clear who had paid for the proposal or if it had been written on speculation as a bid for a contract.

38. Letter, Ann L. Merriman to Waring, October 9, 1959, TRWP.

14: From Sit-ins to SNCC

1. Miles Wolff, *Lunch at the 5 & 10* (Chicago: Elephant Paperbacks, 1990), pp. 11–29, 32; Branch, *Parting the Waters*, p. 271.

2. *Reporting Civil Rights, Part One* (New York: Library of America, 2003), pp. 431–432, citing Albert L. Rozier, Jr., in *The Register*, the North Carolina AT&T student newspaper, of February 5, 1960; also Pat Watters, *Down to Now* (New York: Pantheon Books, 1971), pp. 73–74. Rozier's story indicates that he spoke with Ezell Blair, who presumably is the source for his dialogue with the waitress. It appears to have been the only contemporaneous attempt to reconstruct the dialogue.

3. Watters, *Down to Now*, p. 74.

4. Claude Sitton, "Negroes Extend Store Picketing," *NYT*, February 11, 1960.

5. Ibid. p. 22; Sitton, "Negroes' Protest Spreads in South," *NYT*, February 13, 1960, pp. 1, 6; Sitton, "Negro Sitdowns Stir Fear of Wider Unrest in South," *NYT*, February 15, 1960, pp. 1, 18; Sitton, "Negroes Press for Faster Desegregation," *NYT*, February 21, 1960.

6. AP, "Lunch Counter 'Sit-Downers' in First Clash," AJ, February 16, 1961, as cited in Watters, *Down to Now,* p. 78.

7. Branch, *Parting the Waters,* p. 275.

8. Memo, Clifton Daniel to Turner Catledge, April 8, 1960, TCP.

9. David E. Sumner, "Nashville, Nonviolence, and the Newspapers: The Convergence of Social Goals with News Values," *The Howard Journal of Communications,* October 1995, pp. 102–113.

10. Sitton, "Dr. King Favors Buyers' Boycott," *NYT,* April 16, 1960.

11. Sitton, "Racial Problems Put to President," ibid., April 18, 1960.

12. Branch, *Parting the Waters,* pp. 291–292; *NYT,* April 18, 1960.

13. Branch, *Parting the Waters,* pp. 292, 324; Danny Lyon, *Memories of the Southern Civil Rights Movement* (Chapel Hill: University of North Carolina Press, 1992), p. 14. Lyon's book was published as part of the Lyndhurst Series on the South for the Center for Documentary Studies, Duke University.

14. David E. Sumner, "The Local Press and the Nashville Student Movement, 1960," dissertation, University of Tennessee at Knoxville, August 1989, pp. 124–126.

15: ALABAMA VERSUS THE *TIMES,* FREEDOM RIDERS VERSUS THE SOUTH

1. Interview with Ray Jenkins, BUI, pp. 23–24.

2. "Fear and Hatred Grip Birmingham," *NYT,* April 12, 1960; Glenn T. Eskew, *But for Birmingham* (Chapel Hill: University of North Carolina Press, 1997), pp. 89–91.

3. Ibid.

4. Salisbury, *Without Fear or Favor,* p. 381; Egerton, *Speak Now Against the Day,* p. 251.

5. Ibid.

6. Anthony Lewis, *Make No Law* (New York: Vintage Books, 1991), p. 35.

7. Author conversations with Sitton over the years.

8. Lewis, *Make No Law,* p. 24.

9. Ibid., p. 25.

10. Salisbury, *Without Fear or Favor,* p. 384.

11. Claude Sitton, "Byrd Leadership Faces Voter Test," *NYT,* July 9, 1961, p. 40.

12. Kilpatrick, letter to the editor, undated original; Kilpatrick, personal note to Oakes, July 10, 1961; Oakes to Catledge, July 11, 1961; Catledge to Sitton, July 11, 1961; Sitton to Catledge, July 13; Sitton to Oakes, undated; Catledge to Kilpatrick, July 20, 1961. TCP.

13. Memo, assistant national editor Ray O'Neill to Catledge, April 12, 1961; typescript of *Times* story filled by Kenneth Toler, an authentic *Times* stringer in Jackson, April 13, 1961. TCP.

14. Anthony Lewis, *Portrait of a Decade: The Second American Revolution* (New York: Random House, 1964), pp. 160–161, and in Lyons, *Reporting the News.*

15. Lewis, *Portrait of a Decade,* p. 162.

16. Sitton, "Louisiana Pushes New School Curb," *NYT,* December 5, 1960, p. 80.

17. Lewis, *Portrait of a Decade,* p. 26.

18. Salisbury, *Without Fear or Favor,* p. 382.

19. James S. Pope to Pulliam, Catledge, J. R. Wiggins, Herbert Brucker, August 15, 1960, TCP.

20. Letters and telegrams from editors to Catedge, including from Conn and Mahaffey on September 16, 1960, TCP.

21. Pulliam to Catledge, November 4, 1960, TCP.

22. Catledge to Hills, December 30, 1960, TCP.

23. Catledge to Felix McKnight, December 30, 1960, TCP.

24. John Hohenberg to Catledge, February 28, 1961; Hohenberg to *Chicago Tribune* attorney George D. Newton, Jr., February 18, 1961, TCP.

25. Scher to Pulliam, January 4, 1961, TCP.

26. Pulliam to McKnight, January 6, 1961, TCP.

27. Memos, Clifton Daniel to Catledge, March 3, 1961; Harding Bancroft to Catledge, December 28, 1960; Daniel to Catledge, March 3, 1961; letter, Catledge to McGill, March 20, 1962, TCP.

28. Emogene Wilson, Withers, Newson, author interviews; Wilson, "L. Alex Wilson, Editor of Defender, Is Dead," *T-SD*, October 15, 1960, "Editor Wilson Back Home—To Stay," week of October 22–28, 1960. The one exception was Charlotte Devree, a white CORE member who said she was a freelance writer who hoped to write a firsthand account of the rides. She had no connection with conventional magazines or newspapers.

29. Newson, author interview.

30. James Peck, *Freedom Ride* (New York: Simon and Schuster, 1962), p. 39; Branch, *Parting the Waters,* p. 412.

31. Branch, *Parting the Waters,* p. 412.

32. Booker, *Black Man's America,* p. 2.

33. The Freedom Ride to and from Anniston comes from many sources, including Peck, *Freedom Ride,* pp. 114–153; *BA-A,* May 16, 1961.

34. Newson, author interview; *BA-A,* May 16, 1961.

35. Ibid.

36. Alabama Governor John Patterson, transcript of *Eyes on the Prize,* Henry Hampton Collection, Washington University Libraries Film and Media Archives, available at http://library.wustl.edu/units/spec/filmandmedia/pdfs/PATTERSON.pdf.

37. James Farmer, *Lay Bare the Heart: An Autobiography of the Civil Rights Movement* (New York: Arbor House, 1985), p. 203.

38. H. Brandt Ayers, author interview.

39. Ibid.

40. Booker, *Black Man's America,* p. 2.

41. Ibid., pp. 2–3.

42. Howard K. Smith, *Events Leading Up to My Death* (New York: St. Martin's Press, 1996), pp. 268–269.

43. Ibid., p. 270.

44. A number of sources have shown this, including Rowe's own book, *My Undercover Years with the FBI* (New York: Bantam, 1976); Andrew M. Manis, *A Fire You Can't Put Out: The Civil Rights Life of Birmingham's Rev. Fred Shuttlesworth* (Tuscaloosa: University of Alabama Press, 1999), p. 263.

45. Peck, *Freedom Ride,* pp. 127–128; Booker, *Black Man's America,* p. 5.

46. Branch, *Parting the Waters,* p. 422.

47. Bob Warner, "Camera Is a Red Flag to Mob," *E&P,* June 10, 1961; Raymond Arsenault, *Freedom Riders: 1961 and the Struggle for Racial Justice.* New York: Oxford University Press, 2006, pp. 156–157; and Clarke Stallworth, "Shot Seen 'Round the World," *Alabama Heritage,* Spring 2007, pp. 32–34.

48. Smith, *Events Leading Up to My Death,* pp. 164, 272.

49. Ibid., p. 271.

50. William A. Nunnelley, *Bull Connor* (Tuscaloosa: University of Alabama Press, 1991), pp. 97–98; Arsenault, *Freedom Riders*, pp. 156–157; and Stallworth, "Shot Seen 'Round the World," *Alabama Heritage*, pp. 34–35.

51. Emory Jackson to Mayor J. W. Morgan, May 18, 1961. EOJP

52. Smith, *Events Leading Up to My Death,* p. 272.

53. John Lewis, speaking at Columbia University Graduate School of Journalism panel, "How Journalists Covered Civil Rights," November 12, 1998.

54. John Lewis, *Walking with the Wind* (New York: Simon and Schuster, 1998), pp. 153–154.

55. Smith, *Events Leading Up to My Death,* p. 274.

56. Ibid.

57. Ibid., p. 275.

58. Lewis, Columbia University panel, November 12, 1998.

59. Ibid.

60. *NYT,* June 15, 1961; also, typescript of the decision is found in TCP.

16: Albany

1. Branch, *Parting the Waters,* pp. 553–554; Millard Grimes, *The Last Linotype: The Story of Georgia and Its Newspapers Since World War II* (Macon, Ga.: Mercer University Press, 1985), pp. 378–379.

2. Karl Fleming, *Son of the Rough South* (New York: Public Affairs, 2005), p. 255.

3. Ibid., p. 299; also Fleming, author interview.

4. Richard Lentz, *Symbols, the News Magazines and Martin Luther King* (Baton Rouge: Louisiana State University Press, 1990), pp. 11–13; Osborn Elliott, *The World of Oz* (New York: Viking Press, 1980), pp. 4–8; Katharine Graham, *Personal History* (New York: Alfred A. Knopf, 1997), pp. 276–279.

5. Claude Sitton, Bill Emerson, Robert H. Gordon, author interviews; also, Elliott, *The World of Oz,* p. 35.

6. Karl Fleming, *Son of the Rough South,* pp. 144–145.

7. Gordon, author interview.

8. Branch, *Parting the Waters,* pp. 548, 550.

9. Gordon, author interview.

10. Claude Sitton, "Negro Groups Split on Georgia Protest," *NYT,* December 18, 1961, p. 1; Sitton, "Rivalries Beset Integration Campaigns," December 24, 1961, p. E5.

11. Branch, *Parting the Waters,* p. 554.

12. Ibid.

13. Ibid., pp. 554–555.

14. Ibid., p. 556.

15. Watters told this story to a number of his colleagues on the race beat over the years.

16. Fred Powledge, *Free at Last? The Civil Rights Movement and the People Who Made It* (Boston: Little, Brown, 1991), pp. 411–415; *Newsweek* files, May 26, 1964, EUSC; Bill Shipp, "Court Hears Recording of Rally," *AC*, August 2, 1962, p. 6.

17. This scene reconstructed from Claude Sitton, "Sheriff Harasses Negroes at Voting Rally in Georgia," *NYT*, July 27, 1962, p. 1; Bill Shipp, "Sheriff Invades Negro Rally at Sasser, Says He's Fed Up," *AC*, July 27, 1962; Pat Watters and Reese Cleghorn, *Climbing Jacob's Ladder* (New York: Harcourt, Brace and World, 1967), pp. 164–170; Lewis and *NYT* staff, *Portrait of a Decade*, pp. 141–147; Sitton, author interview; Baylor University oral histories with Sitton and Bill Shipp.

18. Memo, Clifton Daniel to File, July 27, 1962, TCP.

19. Branch, *Parting the Waters*, p. 620.

20. Mr. and Mrs. Shai Holsaert to Dryfoos, July 28, 1962, TCP.

21. Jack Frost to Catledge, July 27, 1962, TCP.

22. Mark Franko to Dryfoos, undated, late July 1962, TCP.

23. Donald R. Bensen to Catledge, October 10, 1962, TCP.

24. Donald L. Grant, *The Way It Was in the South: The Black Experience in Georgia* (New York: Burch Lane Press, 1993), p. 414.

25. Gene Patterson, author interview.

26. More than twenty-five years passed before details of the release were revealed by Branch in *Parting the Waters*.

27. *AC* wire report, August 2, 1962; Branch, *Parting the Waters*, p. 624.

28. Branch, *Parting the Waters*, p. 625.

29. James A. Colaiaco, *Martin Luther King, Jr.: Apostle of Militant Nonviolence* (New York: St. Martin's Press, 1993), p. 48, citing Reese Cleghorn, "Martin Luther King Jr., Apostle of Crisis," in C. Eric Lincoln, *Martin Luther King, Jr: A Profile*, rev. ed (New York, 1984), p. 124.

30. Lerone Bennett Jr., *The Negro Mood* (Chicago: Johnson Publishing, 1964), pp. 3–23; Andrew Young, *An Easy Burden* (New York: HarperCollins, 1996), pp. 185–188, 200.

17: OLE MISS

1. James H. Meredith, *Three Years in Mississippi* (Bloomington: Indiana University Press, 1966), pp. 53, 54–58.

2. Judge Mize, in charging a grand jury to investigate the jailhouse abduction and execution of Mack Charles Parker, a Negro, had told the grand jurors, "I think, on the whole, there is no place in the nation where the relation between the two races is as good and as highly respected as in Mississippi, and I'm proud of that."

3. *Meridian Star*, first week of June 1961, as cited in Meredith, *Three Years in Mississippi*, pp. 107–108.

4. *RNL*, date unclear; this found in a *Newsweek* reporter's file to New York about Kilpatrick, dated December 19, 1960 and located in the *Newsweek* archives, EUSC.

5. Norman Bradley, oral history, MOHP; interview, Bill Minor, by John R. Tisdale, July 21, 1992, BUI; "Dilemma in Dixie," *Time*, February 20, 1956; Purser Hewitt, interviewed by Dr. John Ray Skates and Dr. Orley B. Caudill, May 3, 1972, August 28, 1975, MOHP, vol. 10, 1976.

6. *JC-L,* September 3, 1962, as cited in Jeannine Anderson "How the *Clarion-Ledger*'s Coverage of the Desegregation of the University of Mississippi Contributed to White Rioting in 1962," for a journalism class at the University of Maryland.

7. *Summit Sun,* in August 1961, as reprinted by the Kosciusko *Star-Herald* on August 24, 1961, and cited in Meredith, *Three Years in Mississippi,* pp. 131–133.

8. Meredith, *Three Years in Mississippi;* Greenberg, *Crusaders in the Courts;* Jack Bass, *Unlikely Heroes* (New York: Simon and Schuster, 1981). Maximus was a Roman general who waged incremental forays of harassment and intimidation against Hannibal, avoiding a full-scale attack; Bass, *Unlikely Heroes,* pp. 179–182. Greenberg, *Crusaders in the Courts,* p. 320.

9. Russell H. Barrett, *Integration at Ole Miss* (Chicago: Quadrangle Books, 1965), pp. 92–93; Erle Johnston, *I Rolled with Ross (A Political Portrait)* (Baton Rouge: Moran Publishing, 1980), p. 94; Dub Shoemaker, author interview.

10. "The Moment of Decision Is Here," *DD-T,* September 12, 1962, as cited in Susan M. Weill, " 'In a Madhouse's Din': Civil Rights Coverage by Mississippi's Daily Press, 1948–1968," dissertation, University of Southern Mississippi, May 1998, p. 167.

11. *JC-L,* September 14, 1962, as cited in Anderson, "How the *Clarion-Ledger*'s Coverage of the Desegregation of the University of Mississippi Contributed to White Rioting in 1962."

12. Bass, *Unlikely Heroes,* pp. 126–130.

13. Robert Massie, "What Next in Mississippi?" *The Saturday Evening Post,* November 10, 1962, p. 20.

14. Anderson, "How the *Clarion-Ledger*'s Coverage of the Desegregation of the University of Mississippi Contributed to White Rioting in 1962"; also, AP, "Fight for Non-Mixed Ole Miss in the Works," in *RNL,* September 14, 1962.

15. "We Support Gov. Barnett," *JC-L,* September 14, 1962, p. 1.

16. *Pascagoula Chronicle,* September 14, 1962, from ". . . *dedicated to the proposition . . .*" a 1963 collection of editorials written by Ira Harkey in *The Pascagoula Chronicle.*

17. Ibid., September 18, 1962.

18. Edwin Guthman, *We Band of Brothers: A Memoir of Robert F. Kennedy* (New York: Harper & Row, 1971), p. 185; Arthur M. Schlesinger, Jr., *Robert Kennedy and His Times* (Boston: Houghton Mifflin Co., 1978), pp. 325–326.

19. Meredith, *Three Years in Mississippi,* pp. 156, 182–183.

20. Dub Shoemaker, author interview; AP stories published October 24 and October 25, 1962, in New Orleans *States-Item, Clarion-Ledger,* New Orleans *Times-Picayune,* Memphis *Commercial Appeal* and McComb *Enterprise-Journal.* Also, Anderson, "How the *Clarion-Ledger*'s Coverage of the Desegregation of the University of Mississippi Contributed to White Rioting in 1962"; and Charles Clift II, "The WLBT-TV Case, 1964–1969, An Historical Analysis," a dissertation, Indiana University, January 1976, pp. 136, 142n, 220, citing WLBT editorial, September 21, 1962.

21. Johnston, *I Rolled with Ross,* pp. 74–75.

22. Ibid., p. 76.

23. Ibid., p. 3 of preface.

24. Robert Massie, "What Next in Mississippi?," *SEP*, p. 20.

25. *JC-L*, September 16, 1962.

26. Anderson, "How the *Clarion-Ledger*'s Coverage of the Desegregation of the University of Mississippi Contributed to White Rioting in 1962."

27. Dub Shoemaker, author interview, as well as a reading of Jackson newspaper coverage.

28. James J. Kilpatrick, *RNL,* October 1, 1962; Michael Dorman, *We Shall Overcome* (New York: Delacorte Press, 1964), *passim.*

29. James J. Kilpatrick, "Logic and Lunacy Mingle at Ole Miss," *RNL,* October 1, 1962, p. 1.

30. Powledge, *Free at Last,* p. 515.

31. Sitton, author interview.

32. Elliott, *The World of Oz,* pp. 71, 73; Karl Fleming, "Orphanage Boy," *The Atlantic Monthly,* vol. 241, no. 2, February 1978, pp. 68–73; Fleming oral history, BUI.

33. Letter, Fred Posey, circuit court clerk, to *Newsweek,* May 31, 1961; letter, John B. Mason to Cumming, June 5, 1961, *Newsweek* files, Emory University.

34. Earl Bell and Kenneth Crabbe, *The Augusta Chronicle: Indomitable Voice of Dixie* (Athens: University of Georgia Press, 1960), p. 105.

35. Letter, Joseph B. Cumming to Joseph B. Cumming Jr., June 2, 1961.

36. Fleming, memo to *Newsweek*'s Nation section editors, September 17, 1962. *Newsweek* Archives, EUSC.

37. Clift, "The WLBT-TV Case," pp. 40–41, 44, 127–128, 153. A study of WLBT programming by the group challenging its license reported that between July 1, 1962, and August 31, 1963, NBC had produced seven regularly scheduled news programs, but only the *Today* show had run regularly on WLBT; of twenty-four *Today* segments dealing with race, the station had run only one, the group said. It also said that *Meet the Press* was broadcast on WLBT only when Alabama Governor George C. Wallace was a guest. The censored series was *NBC Special: The American Revolution of 1963,* three hour-long programs that ran in the fall of 1963.

38. Interview with Valeriani, BUI.

39. Withers, author interview; also Meredith, *Three Years in Mississippi,* pp. 184–185.

40. Moses Newson, "Mississippi Rebels," *BA-A,* September 29, 1962, " 'It Was a Long, Long Night . . . ,' " "Hate in Oxford Terrible," " 'Ole Miss' Worse than Little Rock," October 2, 1962; "Reporter Dies, Others Hurt in Mississippi Race Riot," *E&P,* October 6, 1962; Withers, author interview; also Meredith, *Three Years in Mississippi,* pp. 184–185.

41. James J. Kilpatrick, "Logic and Lunacy Mingle at Ole Miss," *RNL,* October 1, 1962, p. 1.

42. "Kennedy Is Dismayed by Killing of French Newsman During Riots," *NYT,* October 2, 1962; Dorman, *We Shall Overcome,* p. 50.

43. Interview with Powledge, BUI; Grant, *The Way It Was in the South,* pp. 379–381; Claude Sitton, "Atlanta's Example: Good Sense and Dignity," *The New York Times Sunday Magazine,* May 6, 1962.

44. Dora Jane Hamblin, *That Was the LIFE* (New York: W. W. Norton, 1977), pp. 55–56.

45. Moore, author interview; also Garrow, *Bearing the Cross,* pp. 1008–1009.

46. Charles Moore, Michael S. Durham, *Powerful Days: The Civil Rights Photography of Charles Moore* (New York: Stewart, Tabori & Chang, 1991), pp. 25–26.

47. Over the years, there have been different recollections of Barnett's actual words. In the sparest version, Meredith recalled in *Three Years in Mississippi* (p. 196) that Barnett asked, "Which one is Meredith?" In the most lavish, Erle Johnston, Barnett's publicity manager in a couple of his gubernatorial campaigns, says in *I Rolled with Ross* that Barnett bestowed the word "gentleman" and an honorific on Meredith, as in "Which of you gentlemen is Mr. Meredith?"

48. Schlesinger, *Robert Kennedy and His Times,* pp. 318–319, citing transcripts of tape recordings of the conversations between Kennedy and Barnett on September 25, 1962.

49. Erle Johnston, oral history, Center for Oral History and Cultural Heritage, University of Southern Mississippi Libraries, available at http://anna.lib.usm.edu/~spcol/crda/oh/ohjohnstoneb.html.

50. Transcript of four conversations between Barnett and RFK on September 27, 1962, in *Newsweek* archives at Emory.

51. Ibid.

52. Quote taken from NBC News film coverage, NBC News, New York.

53. Wilson F. Minor, *NOT-P*, October 1, 1962, p. 1.

54. Years later, when black activists were challenging Lamar Life Insurance Co.'s suitability to own the license of WLBT-TV, they said that Fred Beard had aired editorials on WLBT-TV urging people to join the "wall of flesh." The station denied it and no evidence of it surfaced. But Beard's personal support for the rally around the mansion was never in dispute.

55. James W. Silver, *Mississippi: The Closed Society* (New York: Harcourt Brace, 1963), p. 119.

56. James J. Kilpatrick, "Logic and Lunacy Mingle at Ole Miss," *RNL*, October 1, 1962, pp. 1, 3.

57. Sitton, author interview.

58. Charles Moore, *Life* magazine, October 12, 1962, pp. 40–41; *Powerful Days*, pp. 54–55. Paul Hendrickson, *Sons of Mississippi: A Story of Race and Its Legacy* (New York: Alfred A. Knopf, 2003), p. 18.

59. Flip Schulke, Charles Moore, author interviews.

60. Peter Kihss, "Barnett Gives In; Pleads for Calm," *NYT*, October 1, 1962, pp. 1, 23.

61. Dub Shoemaker, author interview.

62. Most of this account comes from Dorman, *We Shall Overcome,* pp. 51–109; Guthman, *We Band of Brothers,* pp. 201–205; Karl Fleming, memo to *Newsweek*'s Nation section editors, undated but apparently filed very soon after October 1; *Newsweek* Archives, Emory University, Atlanta.

63. Claude Sitton, "Negro at Mississippi U. as Barnett Yields; 3 Dead in Campus Riot, 6 Marshals Shot; Guardsmen Move In; Kennedy Makes Plea," *NYT*, October 1, 1962.

64. Powledge, *Free at Last?,* pp. 439–440.

65. Dorman, *We Shall Overcome,* pp. 76–77.

66. Porteous, author interview; Dorman, *We Shall Overcome,* pp. 81–82.

67. Fleming, undated memo to *Newsweek,* EUSC.

68. Dorman, *We Shall Overcome,* p. 94; Dub Shoemaker, author interview.

69. Fleming undated memo to *Newsweek,* EUSC.

70. *Newsweek* file, May 26, 1964, EUSC.

71. Clift, "The WLBT-TV Case," pp. 65, 68n30, 220; "Leader in Jackson Asks Barnett to Halt Violence," *NYT,* October 2, Hedrick Smith, "Moderates Rise in Mississippi; Business Leaders Break Silence," October 5, 1962, p. 9.

72. Newson, Withers, author interviews; "Reporter Dies, Others Hurt in Mississippi Race Riot," *E&P,* October 6, 1962; Moses Newson, "That Boy Is Delivering Us Here in Mississippi," *BA-A,* October 6, 1962.

73. "Mississippi—The Sound and the Fury," *Newsweek,* October 15, 1962, p. 27.

74. "NBC Special: The American Revolution of 1963, Part 3," an hour-long program that ran in the fall of 1963, NBC News Archives.

75. "Mississippi Crisis: Report on Mississippi," NBC News, October 1, 1962, NBC News Archives.

18: WALLACE AND KING

1. Grooms's ruling was covered by UPI in *Commercial Appeal,* March 20, 1962; McGill telegram to Catledge, March 20, 1962, TCP.

2. Letter, Catledge to McGill, March 20, 1962, TCP.

3. Memo, Daniel to Catledge, April 17, 1962, TCP.

4. Ibid.; Clark, *The Schoolhouse Door,* p. 154.

5. Memo, Daniel to Catledge, April 17, 1962, TCP.

6. Memo, Daniel to Catledge and other editors, April 17, 1962, TCP.

7. Wallace would later say he had taken words penned by Asa Carter to the inaugural platform with him, unsure if he would use them.

8. Anthony Lewis, "Civil Rights Gains Mark Change in South," *NYT,* January 28, 1963. Carl Sanders in Georgia and Donald S. Russell in South Carolina cast themselves as moderates, while Tennessee's Frank G. Clement joined Faubus in saying nothing about race.

9. Waring to Simmons, January 23, 1963, February 9, 1963, TRWP

10. Clark, *The Schoolhouse Door,* p. 192, citing March 13, 1963, letter in the Frank A. Rose Papers, University of Alabama Library.

11. Manis, *A Fire You Can't Put Out,* pp. 148–154, 221–224.

12. Young, *No Easy Burden,* pp. 207–208.

13. Ibid., p. 224.

14. Bennett, *The Negro Mood,* pp. 3–23; Rev. Martin Luther King, Jr., *Why We Can't Wait* (New York: Harper & Row, 1964), pp. 51–52; Manis, *A Fire You Can't Put Out,* 341–342; Branch, *Parting the Waters;* Eskew, *But for Birmingham.*

15. James Boylan, "Birmingham: Newspapers in a Crisis," *CJR,* Summer, 1963, p. 32.

16. Birmingham had 267,500 in 1940, compared to Memphis's 292,900, Atlanta's 302,200, and New Orleans's 494,500. By 1960, Birmingham was at 340,000, Atlanta 487,400, Memphis 497,500 and New Orleans 627,500. *Britannica Book of the Year,* 1968, States Statistical Supplement, p. 8; also, *Information Please Almanac,* 1968, pp. 224–225; also Sitton memo to Catledge, December 9, 1962, from TCP.

17. Sitton memo to Catledge, December 9, 1962, from TCP.

18. Albert Boutwell, "New day dawns for Birmingham," *BN*, April 3, 1963; Joe Cumming file to *Newsweek*, May 9, 1963, quoting the *Birmingham News* managing editor, John Bloomer, as saying it had nearly pulled the rising sun drawing. *Newsweek* archives, EUSC.

19. Garrow, *Bearing the Cross*, p. 296.

20. "Cost of James Meredith protection $500,000," *BN*, April 5, 1963.

21. *BN*, April 4, 1963; *BN*, "10 more Negroes arrested in sit-ins," and AP, "Failure to play race news draws ire of Wallace, Shuttlesworth," *BN*, April 5, 1963, p. 2.

22. AP, "Failure to Play Race News," *BN*, April 5, 1963, p. 2.

23. "The Jitters," *Newsweek*, May 27, 1963, p. 28.

24. "Hundreds of hookey-playing demonstrators arrested here along with Negro comedian," *BN*, May 6, 1963, p. 2.

25. "Stories Distorted, Ala. Editors Say," *E&P*, May 18, 1963; Boylan, "Birmingham," *CJR*, Summer, 1963, pp. 29–32.

26. "Stories Distorted," *E&P*, May 18, 1963; Boylan, "Birmingham," *CJR*, Summer, 1963, pp. 29–32; Robert J. Norrell, "A City in Crisis: The 1960s," in Emily Jones, ed., *The Birmingham News: Our First 100 Years* (Birmingham: Birmingham News, 1988).

27. Garrow, *Bearing the Cross*, p. 249; Branch, *Parting the Waters*, p. 711.

28. One explanation may have been that Connor, in a letter to Jackson on September 14, 1962, canceled all the *World*'s press passes to cross police and fire lines. He gave no explanation. But there was nothing in the *World* to indicate that it tried other means to get its own stories. Letter, Connor to Jackson, September 14, 1962, EOJP.

29. Correspondence, EOJP.

30. Jackson to Rutledge, April 5, 1963, EOJP.

31. "Birmingham, A Target City?" *Birmingham World*, April 10, 1963, "Local Civil Rights Leadership," April 17, 1963.

32. "Local Civil Rights Leadership," ibid., April 17, 1963.

33. Jackson to Rutledge, April 9, 1963, April 12, 1963, EOJP.

34. C. A. Scott to Jackson, May 21, 1963, EOJP.

35. Larry Hawthorne Spruill, "SOUTHERN EXPOSURE: Photography and the Civil Rights Movement, 1955–1968," dissertation, State University of New York at Stony Brook, May 1983, p. 11.

36. Andrew Young, *No Easy Burden*, p. 226.

37. Claude Sitton, "Police Loose a Dog on Negroes' Group," *NYT*, March 29, 1963; Branch, *Parting the Waters*, p. 720.

38. James Forman, *The Making of Black Revolutionaries* (Macmillan, New York: 1972), p. 299; Sitton, "Police Loose a Dog on Negroes' Group," *NYT*, March 29, 1963, p. 1.

39. Spruill, "SOUTHERN EXPOSURE," pp. 181–182.

40. Sitton, "8 Negroes Jailed in Mississippi," *NYT*, March 30, 1963.

41. Sitton, "Mississippi Town Seizes 19 Negroes," *NYT*, April 4, 1963, p. 22.

42. Foster Hailey, "4 Negroes Jailed in Birmingham as the Integration Drive Slows," *NYT*, April 5, 1963, p. 16; Robert E. Baker, "Many Hold Birmingham Sit-Ins Ill-Timed to Achieve Goals," *WP*, April 6, 1963, p. 4.

43. Garrow, *Bearing the Cross*, p. 239.

44. AP, "32 Negro Marchers Seized in Birmingham at Start of Prayer for Police Commissioner," *WP,* April 7, 1963.

45. Forman, *The Making of Black Revolutionaries,* p. 312.

46. Garrow, *Bearing the Cross,* p. 247.

47. Moore, *Powerful Days,* p. 27.

19: Defiance at Close Range

1. Branch, *Parting the Waters,* p. 759; Sitton, "Rioting Negroes Routed by Police at Birmingham," *NYT,* May 8, 1963, p. 1.

2. Moore, author interview.

3. Ibid.

4. "Fire Hoses and Police Dogs Quell Birmingham Segregation Protest," *WP,* May 4, 1963, in a story from "wire dispatches"; "Birmingham, U.S.A.: 'Look at Them Run,' " *Newsweek,* May 13, 1963, p. 28.

5. Footage viewed at NBC News archives, NBC News, New York. Assignment number 88Co061, dated (incorrectly) as April 12, 1963.

6. Moore, *Powerful Days,* pp. 104–105.

7. Alvin Adams, "Picture Seen Around World Changed Boy's Drop-Out Plan," *Jet,* October 10, 1963, pp. 26–27; *Decisive Moments: The Photographs That Made History,* Programme 5: "Only in the Light of Day," BBC Special; Moore, *Powerful Days.*

8. *NYT, WP,* May 4, 1963, p. 1.

9. Frank, author interview.

10. PBS documentary series, *Eyes on the Prize,* part 4.

11. This scene comes from a tape recording of Kennedy's meeting with the ADA, May 4, 1963, in the collection of the John F. Kennedy Presidential Library and Museum; Sam Zitter, author interview; Arthur M. Schlesinger Jr., *A Thousand Days* (New York: Fawcett Crest, 1965), p. 875.

12. Wallace delighted in telling audiences that *Time* was for people who couldn't think, *Life* was for those who couldn't read, and *The Saturday Evening Post* for those who could neither read nor think; Mickey Logue, "Gov. Wallace deplores mix demonstration," *BN,* May 4, 1963, p. 1.

13. Mary Ann Watson, *The Expanding Vista: American Television in the Kennedy Years* (New York: Oxford University Press, 1990), p. 75, citing S. I. Hayakawa, "TV and the Negro Revolt," *Television Quarterly,* vol. 3, no. 3, Summer 1964. Also, Maxwell E. McCombs, "Negro Use of Television and Newspapers for Political Information, 1952–1964," *Journal of Broadcasting,* vol. 12, no. 3, Summer 1968.

14. Spruill, "SOUTHERN EXPOSURE," pp. 15, 177–118, citing also Stanley Elkins, *Slavery* (Chicago: University of Chicago Press, 1959), p. 82.

15. Moore, *Powerful Days,* pp. 111–119.

16. Ibid., pp. 29–30; Moore, author interview.

17. A year later, with a new judge, he and Durham were exonerated of rioting charges; Moore, author interview.

18. *Newsweek* Atlanta bureau archives, EUSC.

19. "Birmingham, U.S.A.," *Newsweek,* May 13, "Explosion in Alabama," May 20, 1963; Lentz, *Symbols, the News Magazines and Martin Luther King,* pp. 11–13.

20. "The Dog's Attack Is Negro's Reward," *Life,* May 13, 1963.

21. Martin, *Ralph McGill, Reporter,* pp. 194–195. Martin cites an article McGill wrote for the *NYHT.*

22. Ralph McGill, "A Matter of Costs," *AC,* May 9, 1963

23. Ibid., p. 134.

24. "The Sky Above—The Mud Below," *Newsweek,* May 27, 1963, p. 25.

25. "Freedom Now," *Time,* May 7, 1963; "The Other Side," *Newsweek,* June 10, 1963. Also, Lentz, *Symbols,* pp. 75–94.

26. Ira Harkey, *The Smell of Burning Crosses: An Autobiography of a Mississippi Newspaperman* (Jacksonville, Ill.: Harris-Wolfe, 1967), p. 119; " 'Reivers' Is Pulitzer Novel; No Play Prize, 2 Quit Jury," *NYT,* May 7, 1963. Harkey was one of two Mississippians to win a Pulitzer Prize that year. William Faulkner won the fiction category posthumously for *The Reivers.* The national reporting award, which many had thought Sitton might win, went instead to another *Times*man, Anthony Lewis, for his coverage of the Supreme Court.

27. Harvey Taylor, "Race Problem Won't End with Integration: Myrdal," *Detroit Free Press,* May 3, 1963; "Racial Scholar Finds U.S. Gains," *NYT,* May 5, 1963; "Where Are They Now?" *Newsweek,* May 20, 1963, p. 20; Myrdal, *Dilemma,* pp. 48–49.

28. AP, "9298 More Negroes Attend White Schools Than Year Ago," *WP,* June 12, 1963, p. 15.

29. Anthony J. Blasi, *Segregationist Violence and Civil Rights Movements in Tuscaloosa* (Washington, D.C.: University Press of America, 1980), pp. 59–60.

30. Ibid., pp. 61–64.

31. AP, "Ex-publisher was liberal voice in segregation era," date and publication unrecorded; information also available at http://www.auburn.edu/~willik5/hall ofhonor2005.html and http://www.lib.auburn.edu/archive/find-aid/741.html.

32. Hollis, *An Alabama Newspaper Tradition,* p. 122.

33. Ibid., pp. 125–127.

34. Clark, *The Schoolhouse Door,* pp. 198–200; Dan Carter, *The Politics of Rage: George Wallace, the Origins of the New Conservatism and the Transformation of American Politics* (New York: Simon and Schuster, 1995), pp. 135–138; Bill Jones, *The Wallace Story* (Northport, Ala.: American Southern Publishing, 1966), pp. 86–89.

35. Wayne Greenhaw, *Alabama on My Mind* (Montgomery: Sycamore Press, 1987), pp. 57–58.

36. Carter, *The Politics of Rage,* p. 136, citing a comment by Jules Loh, an AP reporter, in the *Mobile Press Register,* May 3, 1964.

37. Lesher, *George Wallace,* p. 209.

38. Carter, *The Politics of Rage,* p. 137.

39. Lesher, *George Wallace,* p. 210.

40. Greenhaw, *Alabama on My Mind,* pp. 57–58.

41. Bill Dorr, "Whatever Happens in Alabama, Press Will Be on Top of It," *PA,* June 8, 1963, p. 1; Dorman, *We Shall Overcome,* p. 100.

42. Dorr, "Whatever Happens in Alabama, " *PA,* June 8, 1963, p. 1; Dorman, *We Shall Overcome,* p. 271.

43. Dorr, "Whatever Happens in Alabama, " *PA,* June 8, 1963, p. 1.

44. Relman Morin, " 'No Shoving Reporters'—It's an Order in Alabama," *E&P,* June 15, 1963, p. 16.
45. Ibid.; Dorman, *We Shall Overcome,* pp. 270–271.
46. "The Southern Front," *Time,* September 17, 1956; " 'Kill the Reporters,' " *Newsweek,* October 15, 1962, p. 99; Cumming file to *Newsweek* editors, May 25, 1964; "The Race Beat," *Newsweek,* June 15, 1964; interview, Bob Gordon; Dorman, *We Shall Overcome,* pp. 270–271.
47. William Small, *To Kill a Messenger: Television News and the Real World* (New York: Hastings House, 1970), p. 44.
48. Morin, " 'No Shoving Reporters,' " p. 16.
49. Clark, *The Schoolhouse Door,* p. 225; Carter, *The Politics of Rage,* p. 141; Dorman, *We Shall Overcome,* pp. 306–307.
50. Morin, " 'No Shoving Reporters,' " p. 16.
51. "Planning Pays Off for Tuscaloosa Stations," *Broadcasting,* June 17, 1963.
52. Interview, Rex Thomas, BUI.
53. Raines, *My Soul Is Rested: Movement Days in the Deep South Remembered* (New York: Putnam, 1977), p. 330.
54. Carter, *The Politics of Rage,* pp. 148–149; Schlesinger, *Robert Kennedy and His Times,* pp. 340–342; Dorman, *We Shall Overcome,* p. 311; Clark, *The Schoolhouse Door,* p. 226.
55. Claude Sitton, "Alabama Admits Negro Students; Wallace Bows to Federal Force; Kennedy Sees 'Moral Crisis' in U.S.," Hedrick Smith, "Courtesy and Curiosity Mark Campus Reception," *NYT,* June 12, 1963, p. 1; Robert E. Baker, "Governor Yields After U.S. Acts," *WP,* June 12, 1963, p. 1; Clark, "The Schoolhouse Door, pp. 228–231.
56. Sitton, "Alabama Admits," *NYT,* and Baker, "Governor Yields," *WP,* June 12, 1963.
57. Baker, "Governor Yields," *WP,* June 12, 1963. In its early editions, *The Washington Post* used a story by AP's Rex Thomas, then replaced it with Baker's for the later, larger editions.
58. Sitton, "Alabama Admits," *NYT,* June 12, 1963.
59. Carter, *The Politics of Rage,* p. 151.
60. "NBC News Presents: Integration—The Alabama Story," June 11, 1963, NBC News Archives; Taylor Branch, *Pillar of Fire: America in the King Years, 1963–65* (New York: Simon and Schuster, 1998), p. 107.

20: THE KILLING SEASON

1. Roy Wilkins with Tom Mathews, *Standing Fast: The Autobiography of Roy Wilkins* (New York: Viking Press, 1982), p. 289; Branch, *Parting the Waters,* pp. 813–816; John R. Salter, Jr., *Jackson, Mississippi: An American Chronicle of Struggle and Schism* (New York: Exposition Press, 1979), pp. 158–161.
2. Dub Shoemaker, author interview.
3. "Medgar Evers, Race Agitator," memo, November 25, 1958, in Mississippi State Sovereignty Commission files that are part of the Leesha Faulkner Collection.
4. Salter, *Jackson, Mississippi,* p. 155.

5. Sessions, Dub Shoemaker, author interviews.

6. Dub Shoemaker, author interview.

7. Jim Black interview by John Tisdale, BUI; Shoemaker, author interview, December 5, 1995.

8. Ibid.

9. UPI, "Evers Warns Jackson Next as Court Frees South's Sit-Ins," DD-T, May 21, 1963. Two months later, the FCC would insist that the 6,000 American television and radio broadcasters provide fair airtime on programs about racial segregation to all "responsible groups." *The Atlanta Constitution's* television critic said that broadcasters in Mississippi were trying to resist the equal-time edict by contending that on the subject of segregation, there was no other point of view in Mississippi. Nan Robertson, "Let Negroes Give Views, F.C.C. Says," *NYT,* July 27, 1963, p. 31; James E. Clayton, "Broadcasters Told to Present Both Sides," *WP,* July 27, 1963, p. 4A; Paul Jones, "Equal Time Edict Is Jolting Segregationist Broadcasters," *AC,* July 30, 1963, p. 8.

10. UPI, "Evers Warns," *DD-T*, May 21, 1963.

11. Salter, *Jackson, Mississippi,* pp. 119–121.

12. Ibid., p. 121.

13. Jack Langguth, "3 in Sit-In Beaten at Jackson Store, *NYT,* May 29, 1963, p. 1; "The Battle of Jackson," *Newsweek,* June 10, 1963, pp. 27–30; *JDN,* as cited by Salter, *Jackson, Mississippi,* and Erle Johnston, *Mississippi's Defiant Years, 1953–1973* (Forest, Miss.: Lake Harbor Publishers, 1990), pp. 176–177.

14. "Quiet Integrationist," *NYT,* June 1, 1963.

15. Wallace Terry, "Evers Was Accustomed to Living with Threats," *WP,* June 13, 1963; Salter, *Jackson, Mississippi,* p. 182.

16. Wallace Terry, "Jackson Results Are Assessed," *WP,* June 12, 1963, p. 14.

17. Wallace Terry oral history, BUI.

18. Sessions, author interview.

19. Myrlie (Mrs. Medgar) Evers, *For Us the Living* (New York: Doubleday, 1967), pp. 302–304; Maryanne Vollers, *Ghosts of Mississippi: The Murder of Medgar Evers, The Trials of Byron De La Beckwith, and the Haunting of the New South* (Boston: Little, Brown, 1995), pp. 123–125; Salter, *Jackson, Mississippi,* pp. 182–184; Sessions and Shoemaker, author interviews.

20. Sessions, author interview; Evers, *For Us the Living,* pp. 298–299.

21. Sessions, author interview.

22. Ibid., recalling a reminiscence by UPI reporter Bessie Ford; Cliff Sessions, "FBI Assists in Jackson Killer Hunt," *WP,* June 13, 1963, p. 1.

23. Sessions, author interview.

24. Claude Sitton, "Jackson Negroes Clubbed as Police Quell Marchers," *NYT,* June 14, 1963, p. 1.

25. *NOT-P,* June 14, 1963, as cited in David R. Davies, editor, *The Press and Race* (Oxford: University of Mississippi Press, 2001), pp. 215–216.

26. Sitton, "Jackson Negroes Clubbed," *NYT,* June 14, 1963, pp. 1, 15.

27. Sitton, "27 Are Arrested in Jackson Riots After Evers Rite," June 16, 1963, p. 1.

28. Fleming, panel discussion, "Civil Rights and the News Media," Columbia University, November 12, 1998.

29. Ibid.

30. Ibid.; Minor interview; Sitton, "27 Are Arrested," *NYT,* June 16, 1963, pp. 1, 58; John Doar oral history, BUI; Sessions interview, November 17, 1995.

31. Minor interview; Sitton, "27 Are Arrested," *NYT,* June 16, 1963, pp. 1, 58.

32. Branch, *Parting the Waters,* pp. 839–841.

33. "Big March, Big Coverage," *Broadcasting,* September 2, 1963, pp. 46–48; Watson, *The Expanding Vista,* p. 75.

34. Laurie Hayes Fluker, "The Making of a Medium and a Movement: National Broadcasting Company's Coverage of the Civil Rights Movement, 1955–1965," dissertation, University of Texas at Austin, May 1996, pp. 128–133.

35. "Big March, Big Coverage," *Broadcasting,* September 2, 1963, pp. 46–48; Mary Ann Watson, *The Expanding Vista,* p. 75.

36. "Big March, Big Coverage," *Broadcasting,* September 2, 1963, pp. 46–48.

37. E. W. Kenworthy, "200,000 March for Civil Rights In Orderly Washington Rally; President Sees Gain for Negro," *NYT,* August 29, 1963, p. 1.

38. Ibid.

39. Ibid.

40. Silver, *Mississippi: The Closed Society,* p. 32.

41. "Big March, Big Coverage," *Broadcasting,* September 2, 1963, pp. 46–48.

42. Jack Gould, "Television and Civil Rights," *NYT,* September 8, 1963.

43. Gordon, author interview; Todd Kleffman, "Writers recount rights struggle," *MA,* April 21, 2002, available at www.montgomeryadvertiser.com.

44. E-mail letter from Jim Purks, January 17, 2006, after reviewing his reporter's notebook from September 15, 1963.

45. Gordon, author interview.

46. "The Hell He Is Equal," James J. Kilpatrick, manuscript accepted then not published by *Saturday Evening Post* in September 1963, JJKP.

47. Letter, Thomas B. Congdon, Jr., to James J. Kilpatrick, September 16, 1963; Kilpatrick to Congdon, September 19, 1963, JJKP.

48. Gene Patterson, "A Flower for the Graves," *AC,* September 16, 1963, p. 4.

49. Patterson, author interview.

21: Freedom Summer

1. Claude Sitton, "Civil Rights: Leaders Now Fear That Unrest Will Grow," *NYT,* February 9, 1964, p. E3.

2. John Dittmer, *Local People,* p. 217, citing House Un-American Activities Committee hearings, part 4, 2933-35, 2695; and Wilson F. Minor, "Klan Rise Causes Concern," *NOT-P,* May 1964.

3. AP, "Ku Klux Klan Crosses Burn at Seven Different Places," *JDN,* February 2, 1964; John Perkins, "Membership of 100,000 in Klan Claimed by Leader for State," *JDN,* May 18, 1964; UPI, "Mississippi Klan Cites Big Growth," *MCA,* May 12, 1964, and "Mississippi Klan Recruits White Men 'to Save Nation,' " *BA-A,* May 23, 1964.

4. *The Neshoba Democrat,* April 9, 1964, cited in Florence Mars, *Witness in Philadelphia* (Baton Rouge: Louisiana State University Press), p. 81.

5. President Johnson to Senator Richard Russell, April 9, 1964, in Michael R. Beschloss, *Taking Charge: The Johnson White House Tapes, 1963–1964* (New York: Touchstone/Simon and Schuster, 1997), p. 313.

6. Doar, oral history, BUI.

7. John Herbers, "300 at Klan Meeting Applaud Slurs on Negroes," *NYT,* May 4, 1964, p. 25.

8. Claude Sitton, "Students Briefed on Peril in South," *NYT,* June 17, 1964, p. 18; "Novices Irk 'Pros' in Rights Course," *NYT,* June 18, 1964, p. 25; "Students Warned on Southern Law," *NYT,* June 19, 1964, p. 16; "U.S. Official Warns Mississippi-Bound Students," *NYT,* June 20, 1964, p. 12.

9. Ibid., "Rights Campaigners Off for Mississippi," June 21, 1964, p. 1.

10. "Mississippi Tense Over Voter Drive," June 21, 1964, p. 64; Florence Mars, oral history, University of Southern Mississippi Libraries and Center for Oral History and Cultural Heritage; Florence Mars, *Witness in Philadelphia,* pp. 84–85.

11. Turner Catledge, *My Life and the* Times (New York: Harper & Row, 1971), pp. 1, 2, 6.

12. Catledge, oral history, pp. 6–7, MOHP.

13. John Herbers, "Libel Actions Ask Millions in South," *NYT,* April 4, 1964.

14. Ibid.; "AP Hopes to Upset $800,000 Award," *E&P,* June 27, 1964.

15. Lewis, *Make No Law,* pp. 164–182. *Curtis Publishing Co. v. Butts,* 388 U.S. 130 (1967), consolidated with *Associated Press v. Walker.*

16. Fleming, *Son of the Rough South,* pp. 340–342.

17. Beschloss, *Taking Charge,* p. 432, citing LBJ phone conversation with Eastland, June 23, 1964.

18. *Civil Rights,* Vol. 1: *1960–66* (New York: Facts on File, 1967), pp. 232–234.

19. Ibid., pp. 234–237.

20. Beschloss, *Taking Charge,* p. 450, citing LBJ phone conversation with Hoover, July 2, 1964.

21. Over the years, this account has been rendered by Sitton and Fleming with some slight variations. The account used here is drawn from a speech by Sitton to the American Bar Association in Atlanta on August 10, 1999, interviews with him, and remarks by Fleming at a panel discussion on civil rights at Columbia University on November 12, 1998.

22. Claude Sitton, "The Other Philadelphia: Mississippi Town Preserves Racism," *NYT,* June 29, 1964; John Herbers, "Racial Conflict, North and South: All Is Not Black and White," August 1964, in *The Working Press,* edited by Ruth Adler (New York: Putnam, 1966), p. 241.

23. "Trouble in Notasulga," *Time,* February 14, 1964; "The Race Beat," *Newsweek,* June 15, 1964.

24. Unedited report by *Newsweek* office in Atlanta to *Newsweek* editors in New York, May 26, 1964, EUSC.

25. Sitton, author interview.

26. Chancellor, author interview.

27. Wilson F. Minor, author interviews; Roy Reed, oral history as part of the *AG* Project, July 7, 2000; Richard Valeriani, author interview, August 30, 1999.

28. Herbers, "Racial Conflict, North and South," in Adler, *The Working Press,* p. 242.

29. UPI dispatches, July 11, 12, 19, 1964. A few weeks later, after the bodies of the three civil rights workers were found, Rabbi Lelyveld was among the eulogists at the memorial service for Goodman.

30. Joseph Lelyveld, author interview, September 11, 2004.

31. William J. Simmons, author interview, November 14, 1995.

32. Homer Bigart, "Sheriff and Deputy Arrested on Return from 'Whiskey Raid,' " *NYT,* December 5, 1964.

33. Lelyveld, author interview.

34. Ibid.

35. Catledge oral history, University of Southern Mississippi, September 14, 1971, pp. 49–50; Catledge, *My Life and the* Times, p. 6.

36. Dick Molpus, author interview.

37. *Newsweek* files, May 11 and 19, 1964, EUSC.

38. The *Nashville Banner* also had a Negro reporter, but he covered general Negro news, not just civil rights stories. Samuel Adams, "Highways to Hope," *SPT,* November 8–14, 1964.

39. "Negroes on White Newspapers," *Ebony,* November 1955.

40. *Newsweek* file, May 26, 1964, EUSC.

41. "The Race Beat," *Newsweek,* June 15, 1964.

42. Sitton, author interview; *Newsweek* files, May 26, 1964, EUSC.

43. *Newsweek* files, May 26, 1964.

44. "Sitton Is Appointed as a Times Editor," *NYT,* October 22, 1964; letters from Catledge to Sitton, October 26, 1964, November 10, 1964.

45. Excerpts from discussion of SERS board members, October 21, 1964.

46. Cumming, *Facing Facts, Facing South,* p. 295, citing transcript of board meeting.

47. Ibid., p. 170.

48. Excerpts from discussion of SERS board members, October 21, 1964.

49. Patterson, author interview, June 11, 1995.

50. Jerry Mitchell, "Commission Planted Stories in Black Newspaper That King Was Communist," *JC-L,* January 28, 1990, including published copies of the Johnson memos dated March 24, 1964, and April 2, 1964; Leesha Faulkner, *To Stem the Tide: The Mississippi Sovereignty Commission and Civil Rights, 1956–1973,* master's thesis, University of Southern Mississippi Department of History and Political Science, May 1994, p. 43.

51. Faulkner, *To Stem the Tide;* John Dittmer, *Local People,* p. 103.

52. Jerry Mitchell, "Commission Planted Stories in Black Newspaper That King Was Communist"; Faulkner, *To Stem the Tide,* p. 43.

53. David Garrow, *The FBI and Martin Luther King Jr.* (New York: W. W. Norton & Co., 1981), pp. 53–54. Also, "Red Crusader Active in Jackson Mix Drive," *JDN,* August 31, 1962; James M. Ward, "Moses, Braden's Touring Partner, Lauded as 'Hero,' " September 8, 1962; and AP, "Braden, Accused as Red, Reported Active in State," *JC-L,* September 1, 1962; "Newspaper Reveals More About Braden," September 2, 1962, and several undated clips. On September 8, 1962, *JDN* editor Jimmy Ward got a byline on a story, "Moses, Braden's Touring Partner, Lauded as a Hero," that tried to discredit Robert Moses and Carl Braden. In later years the FBI spoon-fed Ward stories about the Republic of New Africa and the New Left, which he published under his own byline.

54. Garrow, *The FBI and Martin Luther King Jr.,* pp. 77, 101.

55. Ibid., pp. 102–103.

56. Kenneth O'Reilly *"Racial Matters": The FBI's Secret File on Black America, 1960–1972* (New York: Free Press, 1989), p. 136, citing a memo in the Hoover official and confidential files; Branch, *Pillar of Fire,* p. 207.

57. Garrow, *The FBI and Martin Luther King Jr.,* p. 122.

58. O'Reilly, *"Racial Matters,"* p. 144; Garrow, *The FBI and Martin Luther King Jr.,* pp. 127–128, 130–131. Bradlee's account is that DeLoach offered the information at the end of a difficult and useless interview with Hoover on another subject; Bradlee says, in his autobiography, *A Good Life* (New York: Simon and Schuster, 1995), p. 272, that he was so frustrated by the failure of the interview that he never really understood the significance of what DeLoach was trying to do.

59. Patterson, author interview; Raines, *My Soul Is Rested,* pp. 356–358; Branch, *Pillar of Fire,* p. 525; Garrow says in *The FBI and Martin Luther King Jr.* that others who were approached were John Herbers at *NYT* and Chicago columnist Mike Royko, p. 130–131.

60. Ralph McGill, "A Matter of Costs," *AC,* May 9, 1963.

61. Ralph McGill, "Emancipating the Southerner," *AC,* May 4, 1964.

62. Leonard Ray Teel, *Ralph McGill, Voice of the Southern Conscience* (Knoxville: University of Tennessee Press, 2001), p. 326.

63. Letter, Kilpatrick to Simmons, June 1962, JJKP. Kilpatrick had just heard from his publisher that his book *The Southern Case for School Segregation,* might be a best-seller. It was not.

64. The story of the *Atlanta Times* has been told from several sources: Robert Carney, *What Happened at the* Atlanta Times (Atlanta: Business Press, 1969); Frank Veale, *The* Atlanta Times: *Inside Story* (Greenville, Ga.: Gresham Printing Co., 1965); several dispatches from *Newsweek's* Atlanta bureau to its New York office, presumably from Joe Cumming, in June 1964; company prospectuses from 1961 and 1962; "Atlanta to Get a 3d Newspaper," *NYT,* May 31, 1964; "Right Face in Atlanta," *Newsweek,* June 22, 1964; and Kirby Freeman, "Why Did the *Atlanta Times* Fail?" *E&P,* September 11, 1965, p. 12.

65. Harold H. Martin, *Atlanta and Environs,* Vol. 3 (Athens: University of Georgia Press, 1987), pp. 395–396.

66. Letters, Tom Waring to Marion A. Parrott, February 27, 1961; Waring to Maddox, February 24, 1961; and Maddox to Waring, March 7, 1961, TRWP. "Whatever one may think about their political opinions, the Raleigh papers are not inferior journalistic products," Waring wrote Parrott. The Cox interests, he wrote Maddox, were too "entrenched" in Atlanta to challenge.

67. The last issue, with the eight-column headline "Times Suspends Publication," came out on August 31, 1965.

22: SELMA

1. 1960 U.S. Census data cited at http://bakercenter.utk.edu/VotingRightsActof 1965.pdf; John Herbers, "Speed Negro Vote, Alabama Is Told," *NYT,* February 5, 1965, p. 17; Roy Reed, "Negroes Suspend Selma Protests," February 7, p. 44; David J. Garrow, *Protest at Selma: Martin Luther King Jr. and the Voting Rights Act of 1965* (New Haven: Yale University Press, 1978), p. 34.

2. Herbers, "Mayor and Police Block 3 New Marches in Selma," *NYT,* March 11, 1965, p. 21.

3. Martin Luther King, Jr. "Behind the Selma March," *Saturday Review of Literature,* April 3, 1965, pp. 16–17, 57.

4. Branch, *Pillar of Fire,* p. 561.

5. Herbers, "67 Negroes Jailed in Alabama Drive," *NYT,* January 20, 1965, p. 1; Herbers, "Woman Punches Alabama Sheriff," *NYT,* January 26, 1965, p. 1.

6. Ralph McGill, "Nobel Prize Reminds Us," *AC,* October 16, 1964, p. 1.

7. "Tribute to Dr. King Disputed in Atlanta," *NYT,* December 29, 1964, p. 1; "Banquet for Dr. King Gets More Backing," *NYT,* December 30, 1964, p. 24; "Atlanta Dinner for Dr. King Gains," *NYT,* December 31, 196, p. 10; Branch, *Pillar of Fire,* p. 569.

8. Leonard Ray Teel, *Ralph Emerson McGill, Voice of the Southern Conscience* (Knoxville: University of Tennessee Press, 2001), p. 418; Ivan Allen, Jr., and Paul Hemphill, *Mayor: Notes on the Sixties* (New York: Simon and Schuster, 1971), pp. 95–99; Gary M. Pomerantz, *Where Peachtree Meets Sweet Auburn* (New York: Scribner, 1996), pp. 334–339.

9. Ted Simmons, "1,500 Join to Honor Nobel Winner King," *AC,* January 28, 1965, p. 9.

10. Jack Nelson, author interview.

11. Branch, *Pillar of Fire,* p. 580.

12. Roy Reed, "165 Selma Negro Youths Taken on Forced March," *NYT,* February 11, 1965, p. 1.

13. Herbers, "Negroes in Selma Offer Their Prayers for Stricken Sheriff Clark," ibid., February 13, 1965, p. 1.

14. Flip Schulke, author interview.

15. Herbers, "Voting Is Crux of Civil Rights Hopes," *NYT,* February 14, 1965, p. E5

16. Garrow, *Protest at Selma,* 60–61; Herbers, "Taunted Sheriff Hits Rights Aide," *NYT,* February 17, 1965, p. 35; Fager, *Selma, 1965,* p. 70.

17. Herbers, "2 Inquiries Open on Racial Clash in Alabama Town," *NYT,* February 20, 1965, pp. 1, 12; Leon Daniel, author interview.

18. Herbers, "Negroes Beaten in Alabama Riot," *NYT,* February 19, 1965, p. 29.

19. Ibid.; Fager, *Selma, 1965,* p. 74.

20. Garrow, *Protest at Selma,* p. 61.

21. Fluker, "The Making of a Medium and a Movement," pp. 166–167.

22. Jones, *The Wallace Story,* pp. 356–366.

23. Ibid., p. 358.

24. Lewis, *Walking with the Wind,* p. 326; Leon Daniel at University of Maryland journalism class, undated.

25. Roy Reed, "Alabama Police Use Gas and Clubs to Rout Negroes," *NYT,* March 8, 1965, p. 20.

26. Fager, *Selma 1965,* p. 94.

27. "Southerners and Others in U.S. Protest Selma Police Methods," *NYT,* March 9, 1965, p. 23; "Thousands Across Nation Join in Marches in Sympathy with Negroes in Alabama," *NYT,* March 10, 1965, p. 23; multiple staff and wire stories from across the nation, *NYT,* March 11, 1965, p. 21; Charles Mohr, "Sitdown Inside White House Protests Selma," and multiple staff and wire stories from across the nation, *NYT,* March 12, 1965, pp. 1, 18, 19.

28. George B. Leonard, "Journey of Conscience: Midnight Plane to Alabama," *The Nation,* May 10, 1965, p. 502.
29. Haynes Johnson, author interview, undated.
30. Haynes Johnson, *WS,* March 9, 1965.
31. Johnson, *WS,* March 10, 1965.
32. Charles Morgan Jr., author interview.
33. Lewis, *Walking with the Wind,* p. 340; Nick Kotz, *Judgment Days: Lyndon Baines Johnson, Martin Luther King Jr., and the Laws that Changed America* (Boston: Houghton Mifflin, 2005), p. 312; Arlie Schardt, author interview.
34. Johnson, WS, March 15, 1965, pp. 1, 4.
35. Teel, interview with Patterson for *Ralph McGill,* p. 395.
36. Reed, "Mounted Posse Joins State Troopers in an Assault on Demonstration," NYT, March 17, 1965, pp. 1, 26.
37. Roger M. Williams, "Newspapers of the South," *CJR,* Summer 1967, pp. 27–28; Fager, *Selma, 1965, passim.*
38. Reed, "Alabama Marchers Reach Outskirts of Montgomery," *NYT,* March 25, 1965, pp. 1, 27; Donald Janson, "Stars Give Show for Rights March," *NYT,* March 25, 1965, p. 27.
39. This scene is as described by Jack Nelson in an unpublished memoir and in author interviews, and by Roy Reed in an undated author interview.
40. Charles Morgan Jr., *One Man, One Voice* (New York: Holt, Rinehart and Winston, 1979), p. 45; Nelson, author interview.
41. Jack Nelson, "Liuzzo Slaying Figure Seen as FBI Informer," *LAT,* April 18, 1965, p. 1; Fred P. Graham, "Liuzzo Witness an F.B.I. Informer," *NYT,* April 21, 1965, p. 1; Nelson, author interview.
42. Author's personal recollection.
43. Nelson, unpublished memoir, and from coauthor Gene Roberts's personal recollection.
44. Jack Nelson, from an unpublished memoir.
45. Author's personal recollection; Nelson, unpublished memoir.
46. Lewis, *Walking with the Wind,* p. 347.

23: Beyond

1. Sitton frequently told this to reporters who worked for him, including coauthor Roberts.
2. Fleming, *Son of the Rough South,* p. 20.
3. Ibid.
4. Ibid., pp. 2, 21–22, ongoing author conversations with Fleming.
5. Author's personal recollection.
6. John Herbers, "Voting Act's Progress in South Cheers President," *NYT,* August 26, 1965, p. 21.
7. Roy Reed, "Georgia House Bars War Critic, a Negro," *NYT,* January 11, 1965, p. 1.
8. Ibid., pp. 363–364.
9. AP, "Negro Votes May Beat Selma's Sheriff Clark," *LAT,* April 11, 1965; Jack Nelson, "Selma Sheriff Bids for Reelection, Switches 'Never' Pledge to Reds," *LAT,* April 17, 1966, p. F5; Nelson, "Alabama Negro Vote Expected to Force Wal-

laces into Runoff," *LAT,* May 1, 1966, p. 1; Gene Roberts, "Flowers Drives for Negro Vote," *NYT,* April 14, 1966; Roberts, "Negro Vote Tempers Racism by Alabama Foes," *NYT,* April 17, 1966; Nelson unpublished memoir, p. 4; Garrow, *Protest at Selma,* pp. 187–188.

10. *NYT,* September 10, 2000, Week in Review, p. 1.

11. This became one of those enduring stories from inside *NYT,* witnessed by several editors and passed on by many; in Charles Morgan, Jr.'s, account in *One Man, One Voice,* p. 72, Sitton is looking for Reed in wirephotos.

12. Gene Roberts, "Marchers Stage Mississippi Rally," *NYT,* June 18, 1966, p. 28; author's personal recollection.

13. Roberts, "Marchers Stage Mississippi Rally," *NYT,* June 18, 1966, p. 28; Cleveland Sellers with Robert Terrell, *The River of No Return: The Autobiography of a Black Militant and the Life and Death of SNCC* (Jackson: University Press of Mississippi, 1990), pp. 166–167.

14. M.S. Handler, "Wilkins Says Black Power Leads Only to Black Death," *NYT,* July 6, 1966, p. 14.

15. Jack Lyle, ed., *The Black American and the Press* (Los Angeles: Ward Ritchie Press), p. 41.

16. Ibid., p. 42.

17. Roberts, "Rock Hits Dr. King as Whites Attack March in Chicago," *NYT,* August 6, 1966, pp. 1, 52.

18. Ibid.

19. Author's personal recollection.

20. Ibid.

21. Jack Nelson and Jack Bass, *The Orangeburg Massacre* (New York: World Publishing, 1970); also Jack Bass, "Documenting the Orangeburg Massacre," *Nieman Reports,* Fall 2003, pp. 8–11.

22. Jack Nelson, "Orangeburg Students Unharmed, Study Shows," *LAT,* February 18, 1968, p. A3.

23. Ibid.; Nelson, author interviews.

24. Jack Nelson, author interviews, undated.

25. Earl Caldwell, "Martin Luther King Is Slain in Memphis; A White Suspected; Johnson Urges Calm," *NYT,* April 5, 1968.

26. Marvin Barrett, "A Time of Assassins," *CJR,* Summer 1968, p. 5.

27. Ralph McGill, "A Free Man Killed by White Slaves," *AC,* April 5, 1968.

28. Robert McG. Thomas, "Moneta Sleet Jr., 70, Photographer of Civil Rights Battles," *NYT,* October 2, 1996.

29. Author's personal recollection.

30. Jack Nelson, "Death Uncovers Teacher as Fanatic Racist," *LAT,* July 7, 1968, p. 1; "Police Arrange Trap: Klan Terror Is Target," February 13, 1970, p. 1. Also, Nelson, author interviews, undated.

31. Hilts, "The Saga of James J. Kilpatrick," pp. 72–73; William J. Simmons, author interview; Letter, Simmons to Kilpatrick, May 5, 1976, in which Simmons writes, "So we have come full double circle. The Kilpatrick of Interposition now writes of race prejudice, private bias and evil."

32. Rebecca B. Morton, *Analyzing Elections,* The New Institutionalism in American

Politics Series (New York: W.W. Norton), Chapter 15: Minority Voters and Representation, Table 15.1, at www.nyu.edu/gsas/dept/politics/faculty/morton/book/MortonElectChap1.pdf.

33. John Lewis, oral history, BUI.

34. John Lewis has said this during several panel discussions and addresses, including to the U.S. House of Representatives on September 8, 2005.

BIBLIOGRAPHY

BOOKS AND PAMPHLETS

Abernathy, Ralph David. *And the Walls Came Tumbling Down: An Autobiography.* New York: Harper & Row, 1989.

Adler, Ruth. *The Working Press.* New York: Putnam, 1966.

Allen, Ivan Jr., and Paul Hemphill. *Mayor: Notes on the Sixties.* New York: Simon & Schuster, 1971.

Anderson, Jervis. *Bayard Rustin: Troubles I've Seen: A Biography.* New York: Harper-Collins, 1997.

Aptheker, Herbert (ed.). *A Documentary History of the Negro People in the United States, 1933–1945.* Secaucus, N.J.: The Citadel Press, 1974.

Arsenault, Raymond. *Freedom Riders: 1961 and the Struggle for Racial Justice.* New York: Oxford University Press, 2006.

Ashmore, Harry S. *Civil Rights and Wrongs: A Memoir of Race and Politics, 1944–1996.* Columbia: University of South Carolina Press, 1997.

———. *An Epitaph for Dixie.* New York: Norton, 1958.

———. *Hearts and Minds: The Anatomy of Racism from Roosevelt to Reagan.* New York: McGraw-Hill, 1982.

———. *The Negro and the Schools.* Chapel Hill: University of North Carolina Press, 1954.

Bagwell, William. *School Desegregation in the Carolinas.* Columbia: University of South Carolina Press, 1972.

Barnouw, Erik. *The Image Empire: A History of Broadcasting in the United States.* Vol. 3. New York: Oxford University Press, 1970.

———. *Tube of Plenty: The Evolution of American Television.* New York: Oxford University Press, 1975.

Barrett, E. J. (comp.). *Journalists in Action.* Manhasset, N.Y.: Channel Press, by Columbia University Graduate School of Journalism, 1963.

Barrett, Russell H. *Integration at Ole Miss.* Chicago: Quadrangle Books, 1965.

Bartley, Numan V. *The Rise of Massive Resistance.* Baton Rouge: Louisiana State University Press, 1969.

Bass, Jack. *Unlikely Heroes: The Dramatic Story of the Southern Judges of the Fifth Circuit Who Translated the Supreme Court's* Brown *Decision into a Revolution for Equality.* New York: Simon & Schuster, 1981.

Bass, Jack, and Walter De Vries. *The Transformation of Southern Politics: Social Change and Political Consequence Since 1945.* New York: Basic Books, 1976.

Bass, Patrik Henry. *Like a Mighty Stream: The March on Washington, August 28, 1963.* Philadelphia: Running Press, 2002.

Bates, Daisy. *The Long Shadow of Little Rock.* New York: David McKay, 1962.

Beals, Melba Pattillo. *Warriors Don't Cry: A Searing Memoir of the Battle to Integrate Little Rock's Central High.* New York: Pocket Books, 1994.

Beasley, Maurine Hoffman, and Richard R. Harlow. *Voices of Change: Southern Pulitzer Winners.* Washington, D.C.: University Press of America, 1979.

Belfrage, Sally. *Freedom Summer.* New York: Viking Press, 1965.

Bennett, Lerone. *The Negro Mood, and Other Essays.* Chicago: Johnson Publishing, 1964.

Bergman, Peter M. *The Chronological History of the Negro in America.* New York: Harper & Row, 1969.

Berman, William C. *The Politics of Civil Rights in the Truman Administration.* Columbus: Ohio State University Press, 1970.

Beschloss, Michael. *Taking Charge: The Johnson White House Tapes, 1963–1964.* New York: Simon & Schuster, 1997.

Bilbo, Theodore G. *Take Your Choice: Separation or Mongrelization.* Poplarville, Miss.: Dream House Publishing, 1947.

Blasi, Anthony J. *Segregationist Violence and Civil Rights Movements in Tuscaloosa.* Washington, D.C.: University Press of America, 1980.

Blossom, Virgil T. *It HAS Happened Here.* New York: Harper, 1959.

Bogart, Leo. *The Age of Television.* New York: Frederick Ungar, 1958.

Booker, Simeon. *Black Man's America.* Englewood Cliffs, N.J.: Prentice-Hall, 1964.

Braden, Anne. *The Wall Between.* New York: Monthly Review Press, 1958.

Bradlee, Benjamin C. *A Good Life: Newspapering and Other Adventures.* New York: Simon & Schuster, 1995.

Branch, Taylor. *At Canaan's Edge: America in the King Years, 1965–68.* New York: Simon & Schuster, 2006.

———. *Parting the Waters: America in the King Years, 1954–63.* New York: Simon & Schuster, 1988.

———. *Pillar of Fire: America in the King Years, 1963–65.* New York: Simon & Schuster, 1998.

Brinkley, Douglas. *Rosa Parks.* New York: Viking, 2000.

Broderick, Francis L., and August Meier (eds.). *Negro Protest Thought in the Twentieth Century.* Indianapolis: Bobbs-Merrill, 1971.

Buni, Andrew. *Robert L. Vann of the Pittsburgh Courier: Politics and Black Journalism.* Pittsburgh: University of Pittsburgh Press, 1974.

Burns, Ben. *Nitty Gritty: A White Editor in Black Journalism.* Jackson: University Press of Mississippi, 1996.

Cagin, Seth, and Philip Dray. *We Are Not Afraid: The Story of Goodman, Schwerner, and Chaney and the Civil Rights Campaign for Mississippi.* New York: Macmillan, 1998.

Carmichael, Omer, and Weldon James. *The Louisville Story.* New York: Simon & Schuster, 1957.

Carney, Robert. *What Happened at the* Atlanta Times. Atlanta: Business Press, 1969.

Carson, Clayborne, Stewart Burns, Susan Carson, Peter Holloran, and Dana L. H. Powell. *The Papers of Martin Luther King, Jr.* Vol. 3: *Birth of a New Age, December 1955–December 1956.* Berkeley: University of California Press, 1997.

Carson, Clayborne, David J. Garrow, Vincent Harding, and Darlene Clark Hine (eds.). *The Eyes on the Prize Civil Rights Reader: Documents, Speeches, and Firsthand Accounts from the Black Freedom Struggle, 1954–1990.* New York: Penguin Books, 1991.

Carson, Clayborne, David J. Garrow, Bill Kovach, and Carol Polsgrove. *Reporting Civil Rights.* Parts 1 and 2. New York: Library of America, 2003.

Carson, Clayborne, Ralph Luker, and Penny A. Russell. *The Papers of Martin Luther King, Jr.* Vol. 1: *Called to Serve, January 1929–June 1951.* Berkeley: University of California Press, 1992.

Carson, Clayborne, Ralph Luker, Penny A. Russell, and Peter Holloran. *The Papers of Martin Luther King, Jr.* Vol. 2: *Rediscovering Precious Values, July 1951–November 1955.* Berkeley: University of California Press, 1994.

Carter, Dan T. *The Politics of Rage: George Wallace, the Origins of the New Conservatism, and the Transformation of American Politics.* Baton Rouge: Louisiana State University Press, 2000.

Carter, Hodding, Jr. *First Person Rural.* New York: Doubleday & Co, 1963.

Carter, Hodding, III. *The South Strikes Back.* Garden City, N.Y.: Doubleday, 1959.

Cash, W. J. *The Mind of the South.* New York: Alfred A. Knopf, 1941.

Catledge, Turner. *My Life and the* Times. New York: Harper & Row, 1971.

Chambers, Lenoir, and Joseph E. Shank. *Salt Water & Printer's Ink: Norfolk and Its Newspapers, 1865–1965.* Chapel Hill: University of North Carolina, 1967.

Chafe, William Henry. *Civilities and Civil Rights: Greensboro, North Carolina, and the Black Struggle for Freedom.* New York: Oxford University Press, 1980.

Chafe, William H., Raymond Gavins, and Robert Korstad (eds.). *Remembering Jim Crow: African Americans Tell About Life in the Segregated South.* New York: New Press, 2001.

Chapin, Richard E. *Mass Communications: A Statistical Analysis.* East Lansing: Michigan State University Press, 1957.

Chapnick, Howard. *Truth Needs No Ally: Inside Photojournalism.* Columbia: University of Missouri Press, 1994.

Chappell, David L. *Inside Agitators: White Southerners in the Civil Rights Movement.* Baltimore: Johns Hopkins University Press, 1994.

Chestnut, J. L., and Julia Cass. *Black in Selma: The Uncommon Life of J. L. Chestnut, Jr.* New York: Farrar, Straus, and Giroux, 1990.

Civil Rights Education Project. *Free at Last: A History of the Civil Rights Movement and Those Who Died in the Struggle.* Montgomery, Ala.: Southern Poverty Law Center, undated.

Claiborne, Jack. *The Charlotte Observer: Its Time and Place, 1869–1986.* Chapel Hill: University of North Carolina Press, 1986.

Clark, E. Culpepper. *The Schoolhouse Door: Segregation's Last Stand at the University of Alabama.* New York: Oxford University Press, 1993.

Clark, Roy Peter, Raymond Arsenault, and Eugene C. Patterson. *The Changing South of Gene Patterson: Journalism and Civil Rights, 1960–1968.* Gainesville: University Press of Florida, 2002.

Clowse, Barbara Barksdale. *Ralph McGill: A Biography.* Macon, Ga.: Mercer University Press), 1998.

Cobbs, Elizabeth H. (Petric J. Smith). *Long Time Coming: An Insider's Story of the Birmingham Church Bombing That Rocked the World.* Birmingham, Ala.: Crane Hill Publishers, 1994.

Cohodas, Nadine. *The Band Played Dixie: Race and the Liberal Conscience at Ole Miss.* New York: Free Press, 1997.

———. *Strom Thurmond and the Politics of Southern Change.* New York: Simon & Schuster, 1993.

Colaiaco, James A. *Martin Luther King, Jr.: Apostle of Militant Nonviolence.* New York: St. Martin's Press, 1988.

Commission on Freedom of the Press. *A Free and Responsible Press.* Chicago: University of Chicago Press, 1947.

Cook, James Graham. *The Segregationists.* New York: Appleton-Century-Crofts, 1962.

Couch, W. T. (ed.). *Culture in the South.* Chapel Hill: University of North Carolina Press, 1935.

Counts, Will, Will Campbell, Ernest Dumas, and Robert S. McCord. *A Life Is More Than a Moment: The Desegregation of Little Rock's Central High.* Bloomington: Indiana University Press, 1999.

Dabney, Virginius. *Across the Years: Memories of a Virginian.* Garden City, N.Y.: Doubleday, 1978.

Davies, David R. *The Press and Race: Mississippi Journalists Confront the Movement.* Jackson: University Press of Mississippi, 2001.

Detweiler, Frederick G. *The Negro Press in the United States.* College Park, Md.: McGrath Publishing, 1968.

Dittmer, John. *Local People: The Struggle for Civil Rights in Mississippi.* Urbana: University of Illinois Press, 1994.

Dollard, John. *Caste and Class in a Southern Town.* New Haven: Yale University Press, 1937.

Donner, Frank J. *The Age of Surveillance: The Aims and Methods of America's Political Intelligence System.* New York: Alfred A. Knopf, 1980.

Dorman, Michael. *We Shall Overcome.* New York: Delacorte Press, 1964.

Doudna, Martin K. *Concerned About the Planet:* The Reporter *Magazine and American Liberalism, 1949–1968.* Westport, Conn.: Greenwood Press, 1977.

Dulles, F. R. *The Civil Rights Commission, 1957–1965.* East Lansing: Michigan State University Press, 1968.

Durham, Michael S., and Charles Moore. *Powerful Days: The Civil Rights Photography of Charles Moore.* New York: Stewart, Tabori and Chang, 1991.

Eagles, Charles W. *Jonathan Daniels and Race Relations: The Evolution of a Southern Liberal.* Knoxville: University of Tennessee Press, 1982.

———. *Outside Agitator: Jon Daniels and the Civil Rights Movement in Alabama.* Chapel Hill: University of North Carolina Press, 1993.

East, P. D. *The Magnolia Jungle: The Life, Times and Education of a Southern Editor.* New York: Simon & Schuster, 1960.

Egerton, John. *Speak Now Against the Day: The Generation before the Civil Rights Movement in the South.* Chapel Hill: University of North Carolina Press, 1995.

Elliott, Carl, Sr., and Michael D'Orso. *The Cost of Courage: The Journey of an American Congressman.* New York: Doubleday, 1992.

Elliott, Osborn. *The World of Oz.* New York: Viking Press, 1980.

Emery, Edwin, and Michael Emery. *The Press and America: An Interpretive History of the Mass Media.* Englewood Cliffs, N.J.: Prentice-Hall, 1984.

Emmerich, J. Oliver. *Two Faces of Janus.* Jackson: University and College Press of Mississippi, 1973.

Eskew, Glenn T. *But for Birmingham: The Local and National Movements in the Civil Rights Struggle.* Chapel Hill: University of North Carolina Press, 1997.

Evers-Williams, Myrlie, and William Peters. *For Us, the Living.* Garden City, N.Y.: Doubleday, 1967.

Fager, Charles E. *Selma, 1965: The March that Changed the South.* Boston: Beacon Press, 1985.

Fairclough, Adam. *Race & Democracy: The Civil Rights Struggle in Louisiana, 1915–1972.* Athens: University of Georgia Press, 1995.

Farmer, James. *Lay Bare the Heart: An Autobiography of the Civil Rights Movement.* New York: Arbor House, 1985.

Faubus, Orval E. *Down from the Hills.* Little Rock: Pioneer, 1980.

Fenby, Jonathan. *The International News Services.* New York: Schocken Books, 1986.

Finkle, Lee. *Forum for Protest: The Black Press During World War II.* Rutherford, N.J.: Fairleigh Dickinson University Press, 1975.

Fisher, Paul L., and Ralph L. Lowenstein. *Race and the News Media.* New York: Praeger, 1967.

Fleming, Karl. *Son of the Rough South: An Uncivil Memoir.* New York: Public Affairs, 2005.

Forman, James. *The Making of Black Revolutionaries.* New York: Macmillan, 1972.

Frady, Marshall. *Southerners: A Journalist's Odyssey.* New York: New American Library, 1980.

Frank, Reuven. *Out of Thin Air: The Brief Wonderful Life of Network News.* New York: Simon & Schuster, 1991.

Frazier, E. Franklin. *Black Bourgeoisie: The Rise of a New Middle Class in the United States.* New York: Collier Books, 1957.

Galphin, Bruce. *The Riddle of Lester Maddox: An Unauthorized Biography.* Atlanta: Camelot Publishing, 1968.

Garfinkel, Herbert. *When Negroes March.* Glencoe, Ill.: Free Press, 1959.

Garrow, David J. *Bearing the Cross: Martin Luther King, Jr., and the Southern Christian Leadership Conference.* New York: Wm. Morrow, 1986.

———. *The FBI and Martin Luther King, Jr.: From "Solo" to Memphis.* New York: W. W. Norton, 1978.

———. *Protest at Selma: Martin Luther King, Jr., and the Voting Rights Act of 1965.* New Haven: Yale University Press, 1978.

Gates, Robbins L. *The Making of Massive Resistance: Virginia's Politics of Public*

School Desegregation, 1954–1956. Chapel Hill: University of North Carolina Press, 1962.

Ginzburg, Ralph. *100 Years of Lynchings: A Shocking Documentary of Race, Violence in America.* New York: Lancer, 1962.

Goldberg, Vicki. *The Power of Photography: How Photographs Changed Our Lives.* New York: Abbeville Press, 1991.

Golden, Harry. *The Right Time.* New York: Putnam, 1969.

Goldfield, David R. *Black, White, and Southern: Race Relations and Southern Culture, 1940 to the Present.* Baton Rouge: Louisiana State University Press, 1990.

Gordon, Lois, and Alan Gordon. *American Chronicle: Six Decades in American Life, 1920–1980.* New York: Atheneum, 1987.

Graham, Hugh Davis. *Crisis in Print.* Nashville: Vanderbilt University Press, 1967.

Graham, Katharine. *Personal History.* New York: Alfred A. Knopf, 1997.

Graves, John Temple. *The Fighting South.* New York: G. P. Putnam's Sons, 1943.

Gray, Fred D. *Bus Ride to Justice: Changing the System by the System: The Life and Works of Fred D. Gray, Preacher, Attorney, Politician.* Montgomery, Ala.: Black Belt Press, 1995.

Gray, Fred D., and Willy S. Leventhal. *The Children Coming On: A Retrospective of the Montgomery Bus Boycott.* Montgomery, Ala.: Black Belt Press, 1998.

Green, A. Wigfall. *The Man Bilbo.* Westport, Conn.: Greenwood Press, 1976. (Reprint of 1963 book by Louisiana State University Press.)

Greenberg, Jack. *Crusaders in the Courts: How a Dedicated Band of Lawyers Fought for the Civil Rights Revolution.* New York: Basic Books, 1994.

Greenhaw, Wayne. *Alabama on My Mind.* Montgomery, Ala.: Sycamore Press, 1987.

Griffin, John Howard. *Black like Me.* Boston: Houghton Mifflin, 1961.

Guthman, Edwin O. *We Band of Brothers.* New York: Harper & Row, 1971.

Halberstam, David. *The Children.* New York: Random House, 1998.

———. *The Fifties.* New York: Fawcett Columbine, 1993.

Hamblin, Dora Jane. *That Was the Life.* New York: Norton, 1977.

Hampton, Henry, Steve Fayer, and Sarah Flynn. *Voices of Freedom: An Oral History of the Civil Rights Movement from the 1950s through the 1980s.* New York: Bantam Books, 1990.

Harkey, Ira B. *The Smell of Burning Crosses.* Jacksonville, Ill.: Harris-Wolfe, 1967.

Harnett, Richard M., and Billy G. Ferguson. *UNIPRESS: United Press International Covering the 20th Century.* Golden, Colo.: Fulcrum Press, 2003.

Hauke, Kathleen A. *Ted Poston: Pioneer American Journalist.* Athens: University of Georgia Press, 1998.

Hemphill, Paul. *Leaving Birmingham: Notes of a Native Son.* New York: Viking, 1993.

Hendrickson, Paul. *Sons of Mississippi: A Story of Race and Its Legacy.* New York: Alfred A. Knopf, 2003.

Henry, Aaron, and Constance Curry. *Aaron Henry: The Fire Ever Burning.* Jackson: University Press of Mississippi, 2000.

Herbers, John. *The Lost Priority.* New York: Funk & Wagnalls, 1970.

Hollis, Daniel Webster. *An Alabama Newspaper Tradition: Grover C. Hall and the Hall Family.* University, Ala.: University of Alabama Press, 1983.

Holt, Len. *An Act of Conscience.* Boston: Beacon Press, 1965.

———. *The Summer That Didn't End.* New York: Morrow, 1965.

Howlett, Duncan. *No Greater Love: The James Reeb Story.* New York: Harper & Row, 1966.

Huey, Gary. *Rebel with a Cause: P. D. East, Southern Liberalism, and the Civil Rights Movement 1953–1971.* Wilmington, Del.: Scholarly Resources, 1985.

Huie, William Bradford. *The Klansman.* New York: Delacorte Press.

———. *Three Lives for Mississippi.* New York: WCC Books, 1965.

Hunter-Gault, Charlayne. *In My Place.* New York: Farrar Straus Giroux, 1992.

Jackson, Walter A. *Gunnar Myrdal and America's Conscience: Social Engineering and Racial Liberalism, 1938–1987.* Chapel Hill: University of North Carolina Press, 1990.

Johnston, Erle. *I Rolled with Ross.* Baton Rouge, La.: Moran Publishing, 1980.

———. *Mississippi's Defiant Years, 1953–1973: An Interpretive Documentary with Personal Experiences.* Forest, Miss.: Lake Harbor Publishers, 1990.

———. *Politics Mississippi Style.* Forest, Miss.: Lake Harbor Publishers, 1993.

Jones, William G. *The Wallace Story.* Northport, Ala.: American Southern Publishing, 1966.

Kasher, Steven. *The Civil Rights Movement: A Photographic History, 1954–68.* New York: Abbeville Press, 1996.

Kempton, Murray. *America Comes of Middle Age, Columns, 1950–1962.* Boston: Little, Brown, 1963.

Key, V. O. *Southern Politics in State and Nation.* New York: Alfred A. Knopf, 1950.

Kilpatrick, James Jackson. *The Southern Case for School Segregation.* New York: Crowell-Collier Press, 1962.

———. *The Sovereign States.* Chicago: Henry Regnery, 1957.

King, Martin L., Jr. *Stride Toward Freedom.* San Francisco: HarperSan Francisco, 1986.

———. *Where Do We Go from Here?* New York: Harper & Row, 1967.

———. *Why We Can't Wait.* New York: Harper & Row, 1964.

Kirby, John B. *Black Americans in the Roosevelt Era: Liberalism and Race.* Knoxville: University of Tennessee Press, 1980.

Kluger, Richard. *Simple Justice: The History of* Brown v. Board of Education *and Black America's Struggle for Equality.* New York: Alfred A. Knopf, 1976.

Kneebone, John T. *Southern Liberal Journalists and the Issue of Race, 1920–1944.* Chapel Hill: University of North Carolina Press, 1985.

Kotz, Nick. *Judgment Days: Lyndon Baines Johnson, Martin Luther King, Jr., and the Laws That Changed America.* Boston: Houghton Mifflin, 2005.

Lacy, Sam, and Moses J. Newson. *Fighting for Fairness: The Life Story of Hall of Fame Sportswriter Sam Lacy.* Centreville, Md.: Tidewater Publishers, 1998.

Leavell, R. H., Tipton Ray Snavely, T. J. Woofter, Jr., W. T. B. Williams, and Francis D. Tyson. *Negro Migration in 1916–1917.* U.S. Department of Labor, Division of Negro Economics. Washington, D.C.: Government Printing Office. Schomburg Library, 1919.

Leidholdt, Alex. *Standing Before the Shouting Mob: Lenoir Chambers and Virginia's Massive Resistance to Public School Integration.* Tuscaloosa: University of Alabama Press, 1997.

Lemann, Nicholas. *The Promised Land: The Great Black Migration and How It Changed America.* New York: Alfred A. Knopf, 1991.

Lentz, Richard. *Symbols, the News Magazines, and Martin Luther King.* Baton Rouge: Louisiana State University Press, 1990.

Leonard, Thomas C. *News for All: America's Coming-of-Age with the Press.* New York: Oxford University Press, 1995.

Lesher, Stephan. *George Wallace: American Populist.* Reading, Mass.: Addison-Wesley, 1994.

Lewis, Anthony. *Make No Law: The Sullivan Case and the First Amendment.* New York: Vintage Books, 1992.

Lewis, Anthony, and the staff of *The New York Times. Portrait of a Decade.* New York: Random House, 1964.

Lewis, John, and Michael D'Orso. *Walking with the Wind: A Memoir of the Movement.* New York: Simon & Schuster, 1998.

Litwack, Leon F. *Trouble in Mind: Black Southerners in the Age of Jim Crow.* New York: Alfred A. Knopf, 1998.

Logue, Calvin M. *Ralph McGill: Editor and Publisher.* Durham, N.C.: Moore Publishing, 1969.

Logue, Calvin M., and Howard Dorgan. *The Oratory of Southern Demagogues.* Baton Rouge: Louisiana State University, 1981.

Lord, Walter. *The Past That Would Not Die.* New York: Harper & Row, 1965.

Loveland, Anne C. *Lillian Smith, a Southerner Confronting the South: A Biography.* Baton Rouge: Louisiana State University Press, 1986.

Lyle, Jack (ed.). *The Black American and the Press.* Los Angeles: W. Ritchie Press, 1968.

Lyon, Danny. *Memories of the Southern Civil Rights Movement.* Chapel Hill: Published for the Center for Documentary Studies, Duke University, by the University of North Carolina Press, 1992.

Lyons, Louis M. *Reporting the News.* Cambridge: Belknap Press of Harvard University Press, 1965.

MacDonald, J. Fred. *Blacks and White TV: Afro-Americans in Television Since 1948.* Chicago: Nelson-Hall, 1983.

———. *One Nation Under Television: The Rise and Decline of Network TV.* New York: Pantheon Books, 1990.

Manis, Andrew M. *A Fire You Can't Put Out: The Civil Rights Life of Birmingham's Reverend Fred Shuttlesworth.* Tuscaloosa: University of Alabama Press, 1999.

Mars, Florence, and Lynn Eden. *Witness in Philadelphia.* Baton Rouge: Louisiana State University Press, 1977.

Marsh, Harry D. *Hodding Carter's Newspaper on School Desegregation. Journalism Monographs.* Columbia, S.C.: Association for Education in Journalism and Mass Communication.

Martin, Harold H. *Ralph McGill, Reporter.* Boston: Little, Brown, 1973.

Martin, John Bartlow. *The Deep South Says "Never."* New York: Ballantine Books, 1957.

Martindale, Carolyn. *The White Press and Black America.* Westport, Conn.: Greenwood Press, 1986.

Mason, Robert. *One of the Neighbor's Children.* Chapel Hill: Algonquin Books, 1987.

Massengill, Reed. *Portrait of a Racist: The Man Who Killed Medgar Evers.* New York: St. Martin's Press, 1994.

McAdam, Doug. *Freedom Summer.* New York: Oxford University Press, 1988.

McGill, Ralph. *The South and the Southerner.* Boston: Little, Brown, 1963.

McGill, Ralph, and Calvin M. Logue. *No Place to Hide: The South and Human Rights.* Macon, Ga.: Mercer University Press, 1984.

———. *Southern Encounters: Southerners of Note in Ralph McGill's South.* Macon, Ga.: Mercer University Press, 1983.

McGill, Ralph, Michael Strickland, Harry Davis, and Jeff Strickland. *The Best of Ralph McGill: Selected Columns.* Atlanta: Cherokee Publishing, 1980.

McGovern, James R. *Anatomy of a Lynching: The Killing of Claude Neal.* Baton Rouge: Louisiana State University Press, 1982.

McMillen, Neil R. *The Citizens' Council: Organized Resistance to the Second Reconstruction, 1954–64.* Urbana: University of Illinois Press, 1994.

———. *Dark Journey: Black Mississippians in the Age of Jim Crow.* Urbana: University of Illinois Press, 1989.

McWhorter, Diane. *Carry Me Home: Birmingham, Alabama, the Climactic Battle of the Civil Rights Revolution.* New York: Simon & Schuster, 2001.

Meeman, Edward J., and Edwin Howard. *The Editorial We: A Posthumous Autobiography.* Memphis: Memphis State University Printing Services, 1976.

Meier, August, and Elliott Rudwick. *CORE: A Study in the Civil Rights Movement, 1942–1968.* New York: Oxford University Press, 1973.

Meredith, James. *Three Years in Mississippi.* Bloomington: Indiana University Press, 1966.

Metress, Christopher. *The Lynching of Emmett Till: A Documentary Narrative.* Charlottesville: University of Virginia Press, 2002.

Mills, Kay. *Changing Channels: The Civil Rights Case That Transformed Television.* Jackson: University Press of Mississippi, 2004.

Mims, Edwin. *The Advancing South.* Port Washington, N.Y.: Kennikat Press, 1969.

Minor, Wilson F. *Eyes on Mississippi: A Fifty-Year Chronicle of Change.* Jackson: J. Prichard Morris Books, 2001.

Morgan, Charles. *One Man, One Voice.* New York: Holt, Rinehart and Winston, 1979.

Morris, Willie. *North Toward Home.* Boston: Houghton Mifflin, 1967.

——— (ed.). *The South Today, 100 Years After Appomattox.* New York: Harper & Row, 1965.

———. *Yazoo: Integration in a Deep-Southern Town.* New York: Harper's Magazine Press, 1971.

Mott, Frank Luther. *American Journalism: A History of Newspapers in the United States Through 250 Years, 1690 to 1940.* New York: Manville, 1941.

Muse, Benjamin. *Ten Years of Prelude.* New York: Viking Press, 1964.

Muse, Benjamin. *Virginia's Massive Resistance.* Bloomington: Indiana University Press, 1961.

Myrdal, Gunnar, Richard Sterner, and Arnold Rose. *An American Dilemma.* New York: Harper & Brothers, 1944.

National Advisory Commission on Civil Disorders. Report of the National Advisory Commission on Civil Disorders. Washington, D.C.: U.S. Government Printing Office, 1968.

National Association for the Advancement of Colored People. *M Is for Mississippi and Murder.* New York: NAACP, 1955.

Nelson, Jack. *Terror in the Night: The Klan's Campaign Against the Jews.* New York: Simon & Schuster, 1993.

Nelson, Jack, and Jack Bass. *The Orangeburg Massacre.* New York: World Publishing, 1970.

Nevin, David, and Robert E. Bills. *The Schools That Fear Built: Segregationist Academies in the South.* Washington: Acropolis Books, 1976.

Niebuhr, Reinhold. *Mississippi Black Paper.* New York: Random House, 1965.

Norrell, Robert Jefferson. "A City in Crisis: The 1960s." In *The Birmingham News: Our First 100 Years,* ed. by Emily Jones. Birmingham: *Birmingham News,* 1988.

Nossiter, Adam. *Of Long Memory: Mississippi and the Murder of Medgar Evers.* Reading, Mass.: Addison-Wesley, 1994.

Nunnelley, William A. *Bull Connor.* Tuscaloosa: University of Alabama Press, 1991.

Opotowsky, Stan. *TV, the Big Picture,* rev. ed. New York: Collier Books, 1962.

Oppenheimer, Martin. *The Sit-in Movement of 1960.* Brooklyn: Carlson Publishing, 1989.

O'Reilly, Kenneth. *Racial Matters: The FBI's Secret File on Black America, 1960–1972.* New York: Free Press, 1989.

Ottley, Roi. *The Lonely Warrior: The Life and Times of Robert S. Abbott.* Chicago: Henry Regnery, 1955.

———. *New World A-Coming.* Boston: Houghton Mifflin, 1943.

Payne, Charles M. *I've Got the Light of Freedom: The Organizing Tradition and the Mississippi Freedom Struggle.* Berkeley: University of California Press, 1965.

Peck, James. *Freedom Ride.* New York: Simon & Schuster, 1962.

Peters, William. *The Southern Temper.* Garden City, N.Y.: Doubleday, 1959.

Pitts, Alice Fox. *Read All About It! 50 Years of ASNE.* American Society of Newspaper Editors, 1974.

Pomerantz, Gary. *Where Peachtree Meets Sweet Auburn: The Saga of Two Families and the Making of Atlanta.* New York: Scribner, 1996.

Powledge, Fred. *Free at Last? The Civil Rights Movement and the People Who Made It.* Boston: Little, Brown, 1991.

President's Committee on Civil Rights. *To Secure These Rights.* Washington, D.C.: U.S. Government Printing Office, 1947.

Price, Steven D. (ed.). *Civil Rights.* Vol. 2: *1967–68.* New York: Facts on File, 1973.

Putnam, Carleton. *Race and Reality: A Search for Solutions.* Washington, D.C.: Public Affairs Press, 1967.

———. *Race and Reason: A Yankee View.* Washington, D.C.: Public Affairs Press, 1961.

Raines, Howell. *My Soul Is Rested: Movement Days in the Deep South Remembered.* New York: Putnam, 1977.

Rather, Dan, and Mickey Herskowitz. *The Camera Never Blinks: Adventures of a TV Journalist.* New York: Wm. Morrow, 1977.

Reasoner, Harry. *Before the Colors Fade.* New York: Alfred A. Knopf, 1981.

Reddick, L. D. *Crusader Without Violence.* New York: Harper, 1959.

Reed, Roy. *Faubus: The Life and Times of an American Prodigal.* Fayetteville: University of Arkansas Press, 1997.

Rose, Arnold (ed.). *Assuring Freedom to the Free: A Century of Emancipation in the USA.* Detroit: Wayne State University Press, 1964.

Rowan, Carl T. *Breaking Barriers: A Memoir.* Boston: Little, Brown, 1991.

———. *Go South to Sorrow.* New York: Random House, 1957.

———. *South of Freedom*. New York: Alfred A. Knopf, 1952.

Rowe, Gary Thomas. *My Undercover Years with the Ku Klux Klan*. New York: Bantam Books, 1976.

Rubin, Louis. D., Jr., and James Jackson Kilpatrick. *The Lasting South*. Chicago: Henry Regnery, 1957.

Rudwick, Elliott M., and August Meier. *Black Protest in the Sixties*. Chicago: Quadrangle, 1970.

Salisbury, Harrison E. *Without Fear or Favor: An Uncompromising Look at* The New York Times. New York: Times Books, 1980.

Salter, John R. *Jackson, Mississippi: An American Chronicle of Struggle and Schism*. Hicksville, N.Y.: Exposition Press, 1979.

Sarratt, Reed. *The Ordeal of Desegregation*. New York: Harper & Row, 1966.

Schlesinger, Arthur M. *Robert Kennedy and His Times*. Boston: Houghton Mifflin, 1978.

———. *A Thousand Days*. Boston: Houghton Mifflin, 1965.

Schulke, Flip. *He Had a Dream: Martin Luther King, Jr., and the Civil Rights Movement*. New York: W. W. Norton, 1995.

———. *Martin Luther King, Jr.: A Documentary, Montgomery to Memphis*. New York: Norton, 1976.

Secrest, Andrew McDowd. *Curses and Blessings: Life and Evolution in the 20th Century South*. Bloomington, Ind.: Author House, 2004.

Sellers, Cleveland, and Robert Terrell. *The River of No Return: The Autobiography of a Black Militant and the Life and Death of SNCC*. Jackson: University Press of Mississippi, 1990.

Sherrill, Robert. *Gothic Politics in the Deep South: Stars of the New Confederacy*. New York: Grossman, 1968.

Shoemaker, Don (ed.). *With All Deliberate Speed: Segregation-Desegregation in Southern Schools*. New York: Harper, 1957.

Silver, James W. *Mississippi: The Closed Society*. New York: Harcourt, Brace & World, 1964.

Sims, George E. *The Little Man's Big Friend: James E. Folsom in Alabama Politics, 1946–1958*. University, Ala.: University of Alabama Press, 1985.

Small, William J. *To Kill a Messenger: Television News and the Real World*. New York: Hastings House, 1970.

Smead, Howard. *Blood Justice: The Lynching of Mack Charles Parker*. New York: Oxford University Press, 1986.

Smith, Bob. *They Closed Their Schools: Prince Edward County, Virginia, 1951–1964*. Chapel Hill: University of North Carolina Press, 1965.

Smith, Howard K. *Events Leading Up to My Death: The Life of a Twentieth-Century Reporter*. New York: St. Martin's Press, 1996.

Sobel, Lester A. (ed.). *Civil Rights*. Vol. 1: *1960–66*. New York: Facts on File, 1967.

Solomon, Louis. *America Goes to Press*. New York: Macmillan, 1970.

Sosna, Morton. *In Search of the Silent South: Southern Liberals and the Race Issue*. New York: Columbia University Press, 1977.

Southern, David W. *Gunnar Myrdal and Black-White Relations: The Use and Abuse of an American Dilemma, 1944–1969*. Baton Rouge: Louisiana State University Press, 1987.

Spearman, Walter, and Sylvan Meyer. *Racial Crisis and the Press.* Atlanta: Southern Regional Council, 1960.

Sprigle, Ray. *In the Land of Jim Crow.* New York: Simon & Schuster, 1949.

Street, James H. *James Street's South.* Garden City, N.Y.: Doubleday, 1955.

Streitmatter, Roger. *Raising Her Voice: African-American Women Journalists Who Changed History.* Lexington: University of Kentucky Press, 1994.

Student Nonviolent Coordinating Committee. *Genocide in Mississippi.* Atlanta: SNCC, ca. 1964.

Suggs, Henry Lewis. *The Black Press in the South, 1865–1979.* Westport, Conn.: Greenwood Press, 1983.

———. *P. B. Young, Newspaperman: Race, Politics, and Journalism in the New South, 1910–1962.* Charlottesville: University Press of Virginia, 1988.

Talese, Gay. *The Kingdom and the Power.* New York: World Publishing Co., 1969.

Talmadge, Herman E. *You and Segregation.* Birmingham, Ala.: Vulcan Press, 1955.

Teel, Leonard Ray. *Ralph Emerson McGill: Voice of the Southern Conscience.* Knoxville: University of Tennessee Press, 2001.

Thompson, Julius E. *Percy Greene and the Jackson Advocate: The Life and Times of a Radical Conservative Black Newspaperman, 1897–1977.* Jefferson, N.C.: McFarland, 1994.

Tifft, Susan E., and Alex S. Jones. *The Trust: The Private and Powerful Family Behind The New York Times.* Boston: Little Brown, 1999.

Trillin, Calvin. *Education in Georgia.* Athens: Brown Thrasher Books/The University of Georgia Press, 1991.

Tucker, Shirley (ed.). *Mississippi from Within.* New York: Arco Publishing, 1965.

Tygiel, Jules. *Baseball's Great Experiment: Jackie Robinson and His Legacy.* New York: Oxford University Press, 1983.

United States Senate, 85th Cong., 1st Session. Hearings Before the Subcommittee on Constitutional Rights of the Committee on the Judiciary. Includes testimony of Gus Courts. Washington, D.C.: U.S. Government Printing Office, 1957.

Urquhart, Brian. *Ralph Bunche: An American Life.* New York: W. W. Norton, 1993.

Veale, Frank. The Atlanta Times: *Inside Story.* Greenville, Ga.: Gresham Printing, 1965.

Vollers, Maryanne. *Ghosts of Mississippi: The Murder of Medgar Evers, the Trials of Byron De La Beckwith, and the Haunting of the New South.* Boston: Little, Brown, 1995.

von Hoffman, Nicholas. *Mississippi Notebook.* New York: D. White, 1964.

Wakefield, Dan. *Revolt in the South.* New York: Grove Press, 1960.

Waldron, Ann. *Hodding Carter: The Reconstruction of a Racist.* Chapel Hill: Algonquin Books, 1993.

Warren, Robert Penn. *Segregation: The Inner Conflict in the South.* New York: Random House, 1956.

———. *Who Speaks for the Negro?* New York: Random House, 1965.

Washburn, Patrick S. *A Question of Sedition: The Federal Government's Investigation of the Black Press During World War II.* New York: Oxford University Press, 1986.

Waters, Enoch P. *American Diary: A Personal History of the Black Press.* Chicago: Path Press, 1987.

Watson, Mary Ann. *The Expanding Vista: American Television in the Kennedy Years.* New York: Oxford University Press, 1990.

Watters, Pat. *Down to Now.* New York: Pantheon Books, 1971.

———. *The South and the Nation.* New York: Pantheon Books, 1969.

Watters, Pat, and Reese Cleghorn. *Climbing Jacob's Ladder.* New York: Harcourt, Brace & World, 1967.

Weiss, Nancy J. *Whitney M. Young, Jr., and the Struggle for Civil Rights.* Princeton, N.J.: Princeton University Press, 1989.

Whalen, Charles, and Barbara Whalen. *The Longest Debate.* Washington, D.C.: Seven Locks Press, 1985.

Whitehead, Don. *Attack on Terror: The FBI Against the Ku Klux Klan in Mississippi.* New York: Funk & Wagnalls, 1970.

White, Walter F. *A Man Called White.* New York: Viking Press, 1948.

Whitfield, Stephen J. *A Death in the Delta: The Story of Emmett Till.* New York: Free Press, 1988.

Wilhoit, Francis M. *The Politics of Massive Resistance.* New York: G. Braziller, 1973.

Wilkie, Curtis. *Dixie: A Personal Odyssey Through Events That Shaped the Modern South.* New York: Scribner, 2001.

Wilkins, Roy, and Tom Mathews. *Standing Fast: The Autobiography of Roy Wilkins.* New York: Viking Press, 1982.

Wilkinson, J. Harvie. *Harry Byrd and the Changing Face of Virginia Politics, 1945–1966.* Charlottesville: University Press of Virginia, 1968.

Williams, Donnie, and Wayne Greenhaw. *The Thunder of Angels: The Montgomery Bus Boycott and the People Who Broke the Back of Jim Crow.* Chicago: Lawrence Hill Books, 2006.

Williams, Juan. *Eyes on the Prize: America's Civil Rights Years, 1954–1965.* New York: Viking, 1987.

Wilson, Clint C., II. *Black Journalists in Paradox: Historical Perspectives and Current Dilemma.* Westport, Conn.: Greenwood Press, 1991.

Withers, Ernest C. *I Am a Man: Photographs of the 1968 Memphis Sanitation Strike and Dr. Martin Luther King Jr.* Memphis: Memphis Publishing, 1993.

———. *Let Us March On! Selected Civil Rights Photographs of Ernest C. Withers, 1955–1968.* Boston: Massachusetts College of Art and Northeastern University, 1992.

Wolff, Miles. *Lunch at the 5 & 10.* Chicago: Elephant Paperbacks, 1990.

Wolseley, Roland E. *The Black Press, U.S.A.* Ames: Iowa State University Press, 1971.

Young, Andrew. *An Easy Burden: The Civil Rights Movement and the Transformation of America.* New York: HarperCollins, 1996.

Young, Whitney M. *To Be Equal.* New York: McGraw-Hill, 1964.

Zangrando, Robert L. *The NAACP Crusade Against Lynching, 1909–1950.* Philadelphia: Temple University Press, 1980.

DISSERTATIONS, MASTER'S THESES, SCHOOL PAPERS, AND RESEARCH MEMORANDA

Anderson, Jeanine. "How the Clarion-Ledger's Coverage of the Desegregation of the University of Mississippi Contributed to White Rioting in 1962." For a journalism class at the University of Maryland.

Banks, Samuel Lee. "The Educational Views of James J. Kilpatrick Relative to Negroes and School Desegregation as Reflected in the *Richmond News-Leader,* 1954–1960." Master's thesis, Howard University, June 1970.

Clark, Benjamin F., Sr. "The Editorial Reaction of Selected Southern Black Newspapers to the Civil Rights Movement, 1954–1968." Doctoral dissertation, Howard University, August 1989.

Clift, Charles, II. "The WLBT-TV Case, 1964–1969, An Historical Analysis." Doctoral dissertation, Indiana University, January 1976.

Covington, Jess Baker. "A History of the *Shreveport Times.*" Doctoral dissertation, University of Missouri, June 1964.

Cumming, Doug. "Facing Facts, Facing South: The SERS and the Effort to Inform the South After *Brown v. Board,* 1954–1960." Doctoral dissertation, University of North Carolina, 2002.

Cumming, Joseph B., Jr. "The Lower Truth of Bill Minor: An Examination of the Role of a Reporter in a Free Society." Master's thesis, Emory University, 1981.

Davies, David R. "Newspapers and the Civil Rights Movement." Chapter in his doctoral dissertation, "An Industry in Transition: Major Trends in American Daily Newspapers, 1945–1965," University of Alabama, 1997.

Endres, Kathleen L. "James J. Kilpatrick: Conservative at Work." Paper for graduate program, College of Journalism, University of Maryland, Spring 1973. JJKP.

Faulkner, Leesha. "To Stem the Tide: The Mississippi Sovereignty Commission and Civil Rights, 1956–1973." Master's thesis, University of Southern Mississippi, May 1994.

Fleming, G. James. "The Associated Press," research memorandum prepared for *An American Dilemma.* Schomburg Center for Research in Black Culture, New York, undated.

———. "The Negro Press," research memorandum prepared for *An American Dilemma.* Schomburg Center for Research in Black Culture, New York, 1940.

Flournoy, John Craig. "Reporting the Movement in Black and White: The Emmett Till Lynching and the Montgomery Bus Boycott." Doctoral dissertation, Louisiana State University, August 2003.

Fluker, Laurie Hayes. "The Making of a Medium and a Movement: National Broadcasting Company's Coverage of the Civil Rights Movement, 1955–1965." Doctoral dissertation, University of Texas, May 1996.

Hundley, Douglas Alan. "The Long View: A Study of the Civil Rights Editorials of Sylvan Meyer, 1948–1965." Master's thesis, University of Kansas, May, 1993.

Mitchell, Ann. "Keep Bama White." Master's thesis, Georgia Southern College, June 1971.

Nitschke, Marie Morris. "Virginius Dabney of Virginia, Portrait of a Southern Journalist in the 20th Century." Doctoral dissertation, Emory University, 1987.

Parson, Rita L. B. "An Evaluation of the Views of Black Journalists Working at Black Newspapers Concerning the Effects of the Civil Rights Movement on Their Black Newspapers from 1960 to 1985." Master's thesis, North Texas State University, Denton, August 1985.

Purvis, Hoyt Hughes. "Little Rock and the Press." Master's thesis, University of Texas, 1963.

Secrest, Andrew McDowd. "In Black and White: Press Opinion and Race Relations in

South Carolina, 1954–1964." Doctoral dissertation, Duke University, November 1971.

Sherrod, Pamela Jetaun. "Ethel L. Payne: Coverage of Civil Rights as a Washington Correspondent, 1954–1958." Master's thesis, Michigan State University, 1978.

Spruill, Larry Hawthorne. "SOUTHERN EXPOSURE: Photography and the Civil Rights Movement, 1955–1968." Doctoral dissertation, State University of New York at Stony Brook, May 1983.

Sumner, David E. "The Local Press and the Nashville Student Movement, 1960." Doctoral dissertation, University of Tennessee at Knoxville, August 1989.

Terry, Robert Lewis. "J. Waties Waring, Spokesman for Racial Justice in the New South." Doctoral dissertation, University of Utah, 1970.

Thomas, Clarence Walter. "The Journalistic Civil Rights Advocacy of Harry Golden and the Carolina Israelite." Doctoral dissertation, University of Florida, 1990.

Weaver, Bill. "The Educative Role of Black Newspapers, 1920–1930." Doctoral dissertation, Indiana University, 1979.

Weill, Susan M. "In a Madhouse's Din: Civil Rights Coverage by Mississippi's Daily Press, 1948–1968." Doctoral dissertation, University of Southern Mississippi, May 1998.

SELECTED ARTICLES FROM PERIODICALS

Ashmore, Harry S. "Black Power & White Inertia." *Center Magazine,* January 1968.
———. "Has Our Free Press Failed Us?" *SEP,* October 29, 1960, TRWP.
———. "The Untold Story Behind Little Rock." *Harper's Magazine,* June 1958, reprint. TRWP.

Associated Press Log, September 5–11, 1957, provided by Hoyt Hughes Purvis.

Barrett, Edward W. "Must 'A Light Go Out in a Shadowed State'?" *CJR,* Summer 1965.

"Belting One Down for the Road." *The Nation,* October 6, 1962.

Bennett, Lerone, Jr. "First Lady of Little Rock." *Ebony,* September 1958.

Bleske, Glen L. "Heavy Hitting Sportswriter Wendell Smith: Agenda for Equality." *Media History Digest,* vol. 13, no. 2, Fall–Winter 1993.

Booker, Simeon. "A Negro Reporter at the Till Trail." *NR,* January 1956.

Boone, Buford. "Voice of the Southland: 'Be Patient with Us.' " *E&P,* November 9, 1957.

Boylan, James. "Birmingham: Newspapers in a Crisis." *CJR,* Summer 1963.

Bramlett-Solomon, Sharon. "Civil Rights Vanguard in the Deep South: Newspaper Portrayal of Fannie Lou Hamer, 1964–1977." *JQ,* vol. 68, no. 3, Fall 1991.

Breed, Warren. "South's Newspapers Hew to Objectivity." *E&P,* September 28, 1957.

Brennan, Edwin F. "Sprigle Poses as Negro to Get Story of South." *E&P,* August 7, 1948.

Brown, Warren H. "A Negro Looks at the Negro Press." *SRL,* December 19, 1942.

Burma, John H. "An Analysis of the Present Negro Press." *Social Forces,* vol. 26, nos. 1–4, October 1947–May 1948.

Carter, Hodding, Jr. "Racial Crisis in the Deep South." *SEP,* Dec. 17, 1955.
———. "A Wave of Terror Threatens the South." *Look,* March 22, 1955.

————. "What's Wrong with the North?" *Look,* August 16, 1949.

Carter, Roy E., Jr. "Racial Identification Effects Upon the News Story Writer." *JQ,* Summer 1959.

————. "Segregation and the News: A Regional Content Study." *JQ,* Winter 1957.

Catton, Bruce. "Journalism on Crusade: The Saga of the Arkansas Gazette." *SRL,* July 26, 1958, TRWP.

Clancy, Paul. "The Bureau and the Bureaus. Part I: The Press Barely Laid a Hand on Hoover." *The Quill,* February 1976.

Cleghorn, Reese. "A Man of the Press, and of Passion: Pat Watters Saw, and Felt, the Stories of the Nation's Change." *AJR,* October 1999.

Dabney, Virginius. "Press and Morale." *SRL,* July 4, 1942.

Davies, David R. "J. Oliver Emmerich and the *McComb Enterprise-Journal:* Slow Change in McComb, 1964." *JMH,* vol. 57, February 1995.

Davis, Henry Vance. "A Critique of the Influence of the Socioeconomic Environment on the Black Press, 1900–1928." *The Black Scholar,* vol. 22, no. 4, 1992.

Dorr, Bill. "Whatever Happens in Alabama, Press Will Be on Top of It." *PA,* June 8, 1963.

DuBois, W. E. B. "Close Ranks," an editorial. *The Crisis,* July 1918.

Featherston, Jim. "I Heard the Shots . . ." *Sunday Advocate Magazine,* Baton Rouge, November 20, 1983.

Fenderson, Lewis H. "The Negro Press as a Social Instrument." *JNE,* Spring 1951.

Flake, Tom. "Newsmen Win Praise in Integration Strife." *E&P,* September 21, 1957.

Fleming, Karl. "Orphanage Boy." *The Atlantic,* vol. 241, no. 2, February 1978.

Freeman, Kirby. "Why Did the *Atlanta Times* Fail?" *E&P,* September 11, 1965.

Friedman, Rick. "A Negro Leader Looks at the Press." *E&P,* July 18, 1964.

Friedman, Robert. "FBI Manipulates the Media." *Rights* (May–June 1977).

"Gentleman from Mississippi." *Times Talk* (internal newsletter of *The New York Times*), January 1952.

Grafton, Samuel. "The Lonesomest Man in Town." *Negro Digest,* March 1951, reprinted from *Collier's,* April 29, 1950.

Halberstam, David. "The Education of a Journalist." *CJR,* November–December 1994.

————. "Tallahatchie County Acquits a Peckerwood." *The Reporter,* April 19, 1956.

"Harlem Editor Urges Negroes: 'Be Calm.' " *E&P,* June 22, 1963.

Herbers, John. "Judgmental Reporting." *NR,* Winter 1994.

————. "The Reporter in the Deep South." *NR,* April 1962.

Herron, Matt. "Charles Moore: Civil Rights Photographer." *ASMP Bulletin* (American Society of Media Photographers), February 1993.

Hobson, Fred. "The Southern Racial Conversion Narrative: Larry L. King and Pat Watters." *VQR,* Spring 1999.

Hohner, Robert A. "The Other Harry Golden: Harry Goldhurst and the Cannon Scandals." *The North Carolina Historical Review,* vol. 65, no. 2, April 1988.

Honkanen, Roger E. "Conservative Voice: New *Atlanta Times*." *E&P,* April 11, 1964.

"Interviews with Southern Editors: Race Trouble to Grow in South—Mixed Schools Not in Sight." *U.S. News & World Report,* February 24, 1956.

Jackson, J. D. "Emory O. Jackson: The Black Moses of the Black Press and the Explosive Year of 1963." *VHR,* Spring 1999.

Kaplan, John. "The *Life* Magazine Civil Rights Photography of Charles Moore." *Journalism History,* no. 25 (Winter 1999–2000).

Kilpatrick, James J. "The Hell He Is Equal: A Virginia Editor Defends the South's 'Prejudice' Against the Negro." Accepted by *SEP* for publication in September 1963 but pulled after the Birmingham church bombing.

King, Martin Luther, Jr. "Behind the Selma March." *SRL,* April 3, 1965.

Lassiter, Ken. "Flip Schulke: Compassionate Witness to History." *Photographer's Forum,* November 1995.

Leonard, George B. "Journey of Conscience: Midnight Plane to Alabama." *The Nation,* May 10, 1965.

"Little Rock's 2 Papers Sustain Ike's Actions." *E&P,* September 28, 1957.

Lyle, Jack, and Walter Wilcox. "Television News—An Interim Report." *JOB,* Spring 1963.

Mabee, Carleton. "Sit-ins and Marches: A Merger of Movements." *The Nation,* October 6, 1962.

Martin, Harold H. "The Trial of 'Delay' Beckwith." *SEP,* March 14, 1964.

Massie, Robert. "What Next in Mississippi?" *SEP,* November 10, 1962.

McCombs, Maxwell E. "Negro Use of Television and Newspapers for Political Information, 1952–1964." *JOB,* Summer 1968.

McMillan, George. "Georgia Unchronicled." *CJR,* Summer 1962.

Mickelson, Sig. "Growth of Television News, 1946–57." *JQ,* Summer 1957.

Milloy, Courtland. "The Black Press: A Victim of Its Own Crusade?" *WJR,* June 1984.

Morin, Relman. " 'No Shoving Reporters'—It's an Order in Tuscaloosa." *E&P,* June 15, 1963.

Moss, Elizabeth Murphy. "Black Newspapers Cover News Other Media Ignore." *The Journalism Educator,* vol. 24, no. 3, 1969.

"Negroes on White Newspapers." *Ebony,* November 1955.

Nelson, Jack. "Reporting on the Civil Rights Movement." *NR,* Fall 2003.

"Newsmen Attacked as Police Look On." *E&P,* February 27, 1965.

"News Suppression Examples Debated." *E&P,* September 7, 1963.

Norrell, Robert Jefferson. "Reporters and Reformers: The Story of the *Southern Courier.*" *South Atlantic Quarterly,* vol. 79, Winter 1980.

Nutter, Charles. "Crusading Editor," re: Oliver Emmerich. *Negro Digest,* April 1951, reprinted from *American Printer,* September 1950.

Palmer, L. F. "The Black Press in Transition." *CJR,* Spring 1970.

Parker, Kenneth. "Reporter Menaced, Curbed in Little Rock." *E&P,* September 14, 1957.

Pennington, John. "Deep South Report." Nine-part series in *The Atlanta Journal,* December 1–10, 1957.

Poston, Ted. "The Negro Press." *The Reporter,* December 6, 1949.

"Poston's Success Sparked Search for Negro Newsmen." *Ebony,* November 1955.

Prattis, P. L. "Racial Segregation and Negro Journalism," *Phylon,* vol. 8, no. 4, Fourth Quarter, 1947.

Price, Margaret. "The Negro Voter in the South." *New South* (Southern Regional Council), September 1957.

Pride, Armistead Scott. "The Negro Newspaper in the United States." *Gazette,* International Journal of the Science of the Press, vol. 2, 1956.

———. "Negro Newspapers: Yesterday, Today and Tomorrow." *JQ*, vol. 28, no. 2, Spring 1951.

"A Reporter Reports." six-part series on Relman "Pat" Morin, compiled by Associated Press in April 1960. *Editor & Publisher.* Generously provided by Hoyt Hughes Purvis.

"Reporter Dies, Others Hurt in Mississippi Race Riot." *E&P,* October 6, 1962.

Ribalow, Harold U. "*Commentary* vs. Harry Golden." *Congress Bi-Weekly,* February 13, 1961.

Rowan, Carl T. "What Faubus Did for the Negro." *Ebony,* December 1957.

Ritchie, Donald A. "Race, Rules and Reporting." *Media Studies Journal,* Winter 1996.

Sancton, Thomas. "The Negro Press." *The New Republic,* April 26, 1943.

———. "Something's Happened to the Negro." *New Republic,* February 8, 1943.

Schardt, Arlie. "Crisis of the *Constitution.*" *The Nation,* December 23, 1968.

Schuyler, Philip N. "Panelists Agree: Journalistic Code Violated at Little Rock." *E&P,* November 2, 1957.

Shannon, George. "An Editor Scores the Daily Press." *The Citizen,* October 1971.

Stallworth, Clarke. "Shot Seen 'Round the World." *Alabama Heritage*, Spring 2007.

"Stories Distorted, Ala. Editors Say." *E&P,* May 18, 1963.

Sumner, David E. "Nashville, Nonviolence, and the Newspapers: The Convergence of Social Goals with News Values." *Howard Journal of Communications,* vol. 6, nos. 1–2, October 1995.

Wakefield, Dan. "Lost Class of '59." *The Nation,* November 22, 1958.

Walker, Wyatt Tee. "Albany, Failure or First Step?" *New South,* June 1963.

Ward, Bob. "William Bradford Huie Paid for Their Sins." *Writer's Digest,* September 1974.

Waring, Thomas R. "The Southern Case Against Desegregation." *Harper's Magazine,* January 1956.

Warner, Bob. "Camera Is Red Flag to Mob." *E&P,* June 10, 1961.

———. "Omens in Alabama: Editors Resentful of Northern Attention." *E&P,* June 17, 1961.

———. "Violence and the News." *E&P,* June 24, 1961.

"What Southern Editors Say About the Future." *U.S. News & World Report,* June 5, 1961.

Williams, Edwin N. "Dimout in Jackson." *CJR,* Summer 1970.

Williams, Roger M. "Newspapers of the South." *CJR,* Summer 1967.

Wolseley, Roland E. "The Vanishing Negro Press." *Negro Digest,* December 1950, reprinted from *The Commonweal,* September 22, 1950.

SELECTED NEWSPAPER ARTICLES, EDITORIALS, AND COMPILATIONS

Adams, Samuel. "Highways to Hope." *SPT,* November 8–14, 1964.

Bishop, Jim. "Dynamite in Dixie: A Negro Tells His Idea of Equality," *NYJA,* March 23, 1956.

———. "Dynamite in Dixie: Virginia Considers Itself 'Different,' " *NYJA,* March 24, 1956.

Boone, Buford. "Could We Have a Gift of Peace?" *The Tuscaloosa News,* March 4, 1956.

———. "Time to Take a Stand." *TN,* July 19, 1956.

———. "What a Price for Peace." *TN,* February 7, 1956.

————. "The Wisdom of Patience." *TN,* March 7, 1956.

Carter, Hodding, Jr. "Liar by Legislation," *DD-T,* April 3, 1955.

————. "The South As It Was, Is and Will Be." *The New York Times Book Review,* reviewing Ashmore's *An Epitaph for Dixie,* January 12, 1958.

————. "Water Valley Meditation," *DD-T,* August 10, 1958.

Carter, Hodding, III. "Citadel of the Citizens Council." *The New York Times Magazine,* November 12, 1961.

Cooke, Alistair. "The Ordeal of the South." *The Manchester Guardian,* series published in May 1956.

Desmond, James. "New Cross Afire in Dixie." *NYDN,* five-part series published November 22–26, 1955, reprinted in January 1956 by the AFL-CIO.

Dorman, Michael. "Friend, Mentor and 'Satchel Man.' " *Newsday,* January 25, 1987.

"The Editorial Position of the *Arkansas Gazette* in the Little Rock School Crisis, September 1–October 25, 1957." Compilation of editorials, *AG.* TRWP.

Favre, Gregory E. "Going Back Home: Traveling Toward the Future by Revisiting the Past in Mississippi Journalism." Poynter online, July 6, 2005.

"For Whom Harry Ashmore Tolls, an Editorial." *CN&C,* October 28, 1960, TRWP.

Graves, John Temple. "Ashmore Rejected Homeland to Win Pulitzer Prize." *CN&C,* May 8, 1958.

Harkey, Ira. ". . . *dedicated to the proposition . . .*" Compilation of 1963 editorials published in *Pascagoula Chronicle,* Miss.

Hilts, Philip J. "The Saga of James J. Kilpatrick." *Potomac, WP,* September 16, 1973.

Hoffman, Don. "Payoffs Made by Sovereignty Commission," *JC-L/JDN,* February 21, 1982.

Kilpatrick, James J. "A Southerner Looks at the Problem of Integrated Schools." *Human Events,* May 14, 1955.

Klibanoff, Hank. "Bill Minor Tells on Mississippi Once a Week, But Never Weakly." *SunHerald* (Biloxi-Gulfport, Miss.), July 16, 1978.

————. "The Freedom Writer." *Inquirer Magazine, The Philadelphia Inquirer,* December 7, 1997.

————. "Journalism Award and Its Modest Inspiration." *The Philadelphia Inquirer,* December 9, 1997.

Koontz, E. C. "*Pittsburgh Courier* Leads Fight for American Negro Equality." *The Quill,* October 1966.

Lewis, Dwight. "A Mom Grateful for Media Courage in Rights Movement." *The Tennessean,* February 21, 1999.

McWhirter, Cameron. "Defending the FBI." *AJC,* November 21, 2004.

Milner, Jay. "CC News-Slanting Pressure Is Being Applied to State Newsmen." *DD-T,* March 11, 1956.

Mitchell, Jerry. "Commission Planted Stories in Black Newspaper That King Was a Communist." *JC-L,* January 28, 1990.

————. "Editing Revision Added 'Californian' to Headline, Story on Evers Suspect." *JC-L,* January 28, 1990.

————. "Jackson Papers Were Tools of Spy Commission." *JC-L,* January 28, 1990.

Neshoba Democrat 1964 coverage is available on the Web at www.neshobademo crat.com.

Pegler, Westbrook. "Faubus' Friend Ashmore." *RTD,* January 17, 1958, SERS.

Popham, John N., Luther A. Huston, George Barrett, Edith Evans Asbury, Seth S. King, Damon Stetson, Peter Kihss, Gladwin Hill, Clarence Dean, and Russell Porter. "Report on the South: The Integration Issue," *NYT,* March 13, 1956.

Reed, Roy. "The Laughing Liberal." *The New York Times Magazine,* January 3, 1999.

Sessions, Cliff. "Citizens Councils Teach White Supremacy in High Schools." *DD-T,* April 24, 1958.

Severo, Richard. "Homer Bigart, Acclaimed Reporter, Dies." *NYT,* April 17, 1991.

"Since Little Rock," compilation of editorials. *CN&C,* undated. TRWP.

Sokolsky, George C. "What Sort of Integrationist Is Editor Harry Ashmore?" *The Citizen,* August 1958, reprinted from *CN&C.* TRWP.

"Top Southern Editors Give Views on Alabama U. Tempest." *International Herald Tribune,* February 12, 1956.

"A Tribute to Emory O. Jackson." *Birmingham World,* special edition, September 5–11, 1996.

"We Take Our Stand . . ." compilation of editorials that followed *Brown v. Board of Education. CN&C,* undated. TRWP.

Wilson, Emogene W. "Profile: L. Alex Wilson." *T-SD,* Feb. 24, March 3, 1990.

Young, James. "Changing Times at Mississippi Paper." *BG,* May 23, 1980.

SELECTED ARCHIVES, COLLECTIONS, AND PAPERS

Birmingham World Papers, Department of Archives and Manuscripts, Birmingham Public Library.

Turner Catledge Papers (TCP) at Mitchell Memorial Library, Mississippi State University, Starkville, Miss.

Leesha Faulkner Collection of the Mississippi State Sovereignty Commission files.

The Hederman family is subject of a collection of papers at the Mississippi Department of Archives and History.

William Bradford Huie Papers, Rare Books and Manuscripts, Ohio State University Libraries, Columbus, Ohio.

Emory Overton Jackson Papers (EOJP), Department of Archives and Manuscripts, Birmingham Public Library.

James J. Kilpatrick Papers (JJKP), Manuscripts Department, University of Virginia Library.

Wilson F. "Bill" Minor Papers (WFMP), Mitchell Memorial Library, Mississippi State University, Starkville, Miss.

National Broadcasting Corporation (NBC) News Archives, containing an incomplete collection of film taken from 1956 to 1967.

Newsweek Collection, Special Collections Department, Robert W. Woodruff Library, Emory University, Atlanta (EUSC).

Southern Education Reporting Service (SERS) Collection is held at Special Collections, Jean and Alexander Heard Library, Vanderbilt University.

Television News Archive, Vanderbilt University.

John F. Kennedy Presidential Library, Dorchester, Mass., portions of which are available online at www.jfklibrary.org/.

Manuscripts, Archives and Rare Books Division, Schomburg Center for Research in Black Culture, The New York Public Library.

Thomas R. Waring Papers (TWRP), South Carolina Historical Society, Charleston, S.C.

INTERVIEWS, ORAL HISTORIES

AAJP: African-American Journalists Oral History Project, Oral History Research Office, Butler Library, Columbia University.

BUI: Baylor University Institute for Oral History.

BUI/CS: Baylor University Institute for Oral History, recorded at "Covering the South" symposium at the University of Mississippi, Oxford, Miss., April 3–4, 1987.

MOHP: Mississippi Oral History Program of the University of Southern Mississippi.

SOHP: Southern Oral History Program, Southern Historical Collection Manuscripts Department, Wilson Library, The University of North Carolina at Chapel Hill.

Anderson, Maxwell, M.D., by Klibanoff (phone), September 10, 1996.

Ashmore, Harry S., BUI/CS, April 3, 1987; by Roberts, June 19, 1992, and July 15–16, 1993, Santa Barbara, Calif.; by Klibanoff (phone), August 21, 1995, and May 20, 1997, Washington, D.C.

Ayers, H. Brandt, by Roberts, undated.

Baker, Robert E. Lee, BUI/CS, April 3, 1987.

Barnett, Ross, by Klibanoff, June 2, 1983, Jackson, Miss.

Bass, Jack, by Thomas L. Charlton, BUI/CS, April 4, 1987.

Black, Jim, by John R. Tisdale, BUI, August 17, 1992.

Booker, Simeon, by Klibanoff (phone), September 30, 1996; by Henry F. LaBrie, AAJP, July 2, 1971.

Boone, Buford, by Cecilia Hale Ziff, July 28, 1975, generously made available by Dr. E. Culpepper Clark; by Maurine Hoffman Beasley and Richard R. Harlow, undated, published in *Voices of Change: Southern Pulitzer Winners,* 1979.

Bradley, Norman, by Dr. Orley B. Caudill, MOHP, June 2, 1976.

Brown, Robert Woodrow, by Chester Morgan, MOHP, November 3, 1973.

Catledge, Turner, by Dr. William Hatcher, MOHP, September 14, 1971.

Chambers, Elsie Mae, MOHP, December 13, 1977.

Chancellor, John, by Juan Williams, BUI/CS, April 4, 1987; by Klibanoff, December 5, 1995, Princeton, SOHP.

Cleghorn, Reese, by Rebecca Sharpless, BUI/CS, April 3, 1987.

Dabney, Virginius, by Roberts, December 18, 1991, Richmond, Va.

Daniel, Leon, by Roberts, undated.

DeLoach, Cartha D. [Deke], by Michael L. Gillette, January 11, 1991, Lyndon Baines Johnson Library Oral History Collection, Austin, Tex.

Doar, John, BUI/CS, April 4, 1987.

Dorman, Michael, by Klibanoff (phone), January 16, 1996.

Dunagin, Charles, BUI/CS, April 4, 1987.

Emerson, William "Bill," by Roberts, June 23, 1992, Atlanta; by Klibanoff, Atlanta, January 31, 1995, SOHP.

Emmerich, J. Oliver, by Carl Willis, MOHP, April 25, 1972.

Emmerich, John O., Jr., by Juan Williams, BUI/CS, April 4, 1987; by John R. Tisdale, BUI, July 22, 1992.

Evers, Charles, by John R. Tisdale, BUI, July 20, 1992.

Fairly, Kenneth, by Reid Derr, MOHP, July 7, 1993.

Featherston, Jim, by Klibanoff (phone), October 25, 1995.

Fleming, Karl, by Klibanoff (phone), December 6, 2004; by Roberts, Troy, N.Y., March 30, 2004, and phone interviews in spring and summer 2005; BUI/CS, by Jim Pratt, April 3, 1987.

Frank, Reuven, by Klibanoff, December 6, 1995, Tenafly, N.J., SOHP.

Furgurson, Ernest B. "Pat," by Thomas L. Charlton, BUI/CS, April 3, 1987.

Gilliam, Dorothy, by Juan Williams, BUI/CS, April 3, 1987.

Goldhurst, William, by Klibanoff (phone), May 9, 1996.

Gordon, Robert, by Klibanoff, Brandon, Miss., September 24, 1994, SOHP; phone, November 16, 1994; by Roberts (phone), undated.

Greene, Percy, by Dr. Neil McMillen, MOHP, December 14, 1972.

Griffin, John, by Klibanoff (phone), April 1, 1995.

Guthman, Edwin O., by Roberts, many occasions over the years; by Klibanoff (phone), summer 1995; BUI/CS, April 3, 1987.

Halberstam, David, BUI/CS, April 4, 1987.

Hamilton, John A., by Roberts, March 3, 1995, Washington, D.C.; by Klibanoff, April 26, 1996, McLean, Va., SOHP.

Harkey, Ira, by Klibanoff for the Center for the Study of Southern Culture, University of Mississippi, Oxford, Miss., November 2002.

Harrigan, Anthony, by Klibanoff, Washington, D.C., May 5, 1999.

Herbers, John N., BUI/CS, April 4, 1987; by Klibanoff, Bethesda, Md., April 26, 1996, SOHP; by Roberts, undated.

Hewitt, Purser, by Dr. John Ray Skates and Dr. Orley B. Caudill, MOHP, May 3, 1972.

Higgins, Chester, Sr., BUI/CS, April 3, 1987.

Huie, Martha Hunt, by Klibanoff (phone), January 4, 1996.

Jackson, Emory O., by Henry LaBrie, AAJP, July 21, 1971; by Stanley Smith, February 1968, Moorland-Spingarn Library, Howard University, Washington, D.C.

Jenkins, Ray, BUI/CS, April 3, 1987; by Roberts, undated, College Park, Md.

Jinks, Larry, by Roberts, Philadelphia, Pa., 1990; Washington, D.C., 1992, 1993.

Johnson, Haynes, BUI/CS, April 3, 1987; by Roberts, undated.

Johnston, Erle, by Dr. Orley B. Caudill, MOHP, 1980, 1993.

Kaplow, Herbert, BUI/CS, April 4, 11987.

King, Edwin, by John R. Tisdale, BUI, August 18, 1992.

Kotz, Nathan K. "Nick," BUI/CS, April 3, 1987.

Kovach, William "Bill," BUI/CS, April 3, 1987.

Lelyveld, Joseph, by Klibanoff (phone), September 11, 2004.

Lesher, Stephan, by Klibanoff (phone), November 14, 1996.

Lewis, John, by Roberts, Washington, D.C., summer 1994; BUI/CS, April 3, 1987.

Lipman, Ira, by Klibanoff, Dec. 15, 1995, Philadelphia, Pa.

McDavid, O.C., by Dr. Orley B. Caudill, MOHP, January 29, 1975.

McKnight, Colbert A. "Pete", by Frye Gaillard, November 5, 1985. Excerpts provided by Gaillard.

Mars, Florence, by Thomas Healy, MOHP, January 5, 1978.

Martin, Louis, by Klibanoff (phone), February 20, 1996.

Matney, William, BUI/CS, April 3, 1987.

Means, Marianne, BUI/CS, April 4, 1987.

Meyer, Sylvan, by Klibanoff, June 9, 1995, Atlanta, SOHP.

Minor, Wilson F. "Bill," by Klibanoff, June 6, 1976; 1978; September 22–23, 1994, Jackson, SOHP; February 16, 1996 (phone), September, 1997 (phone); by John R. Tisdale, BUI, July 21, 1992; by Juan Williams, BUI/CS, April 3, 1987; by Hank T. Holmes, July 22, 1974, Mississippi Department of Archives and History.

Molpus, Richard, by Klibanoff (phone), November 10, 2005.

Moon, Clinton, by Klibanoff (phone), July 30, 1996.

Moore, Charles, by Klibanoff (phone), February 6, 1996; March 11, 1996, SOHP; May 27, 2006, Florence, Ala.

Morgan, Charles, by Roberts, New York City, San Juan, P.R., 1995; by Rebecca Sharpless, BUI/CS, April 3, 1987.

Nelson, Jack, by Roberts, undated; BUI/CS, April 4, 1987; by Brian Lamb, C-Span's *Booknotes* at www.booknotes.org/Transcript/?ProgramID=1135, February 7, 1993.

Newson, Moses, by Klibanoff, April 22, 1996, Baltimore, SOHP; by Henry LaBrie, AAJP, June 29, 1971; by Elisabeth Artz, undated. Available at http://64.233 .161.104/search?q=cache:I5XC1myhjXgJ:www.americancenturyproject.org/ virtualarchive/2002/papers/PDF/Eartz.pdf+%22Elisabeth+Arzt%22+Newson &hl=en.

Patterson, Eugene C. "Gene," by Klibanoff, June 11, 1995, SOHP; by Rebecca Sharpless, BUI/CS, April 3, 1987.

Patterson, Hugh, by David Stricklin, BUI/CS, April 3, 1987.

Patterson, Robert "Tut," by Klibanoff (phone), June 1983.

Payne, Ethel, BUI/CS, April 3, 1987; seven interviews by Kathleen Currie in 1987 as part of the Women in Journalism series sponsored by the Washington Press Club Foundation. Available at http://npc.press.org/wpforal/payn.htm.

Popham, John N., BUI/CS, April 4, 1987; by *The New York Times,* June 16, 1994, *The New York Times* archives; by Roberts, June 21, 1992, Atlanta; by Klibanoff, June 10, 1995, Atlanta.

Porteous, Clark, by Klibanoff, November 12, 1995, Memphis, SOHP.

Powledge, Fred, by Juan Williams, BUI/CS, April 3, 1987.

Quinn, Charles, BUI/CS, April 3, 1987; by Roberts, undated.

Reed, Roy, by T. Harri Baker, nine interviews conducted in 2000 as part of the *Arkansas Gazette* Project, for the David and Barbara Pryor Center for Arkansas Oral and Visual History, University of Arkansas Libraries; BUI/CS, April 4, 1987, by Roberts, undated.

Reese, Andy, by John R. Tisdale, BUI, August 18, 1992.

Roberts, Eugene L., Jr. "Gene," by Jim Pratt, BUI/CS, April 3, 1987.

Rutledge, Anne, by Klibanoff (phone), April 3, 1996; July 5, 2006, Huntsville, Ala.

Sanders, Richard R., BUI/CS, April 3, 1987.

Schakne, Robert, BUI/CS, April 3, 1987.

Scott, Austin, by Thomas Charlton, BUI/CS, April 3, 1987.

Schardt, Arlie, by Roberts, New York City, 1996; BUI/CS, April 3, 1987.

Schulke, Flip, by Klibanoff, January 23, 1996, Newark, N.J., SOHP.

Sessions, Cliff and Shirley, by Klibanoff, November 17, 1995, Biloxi, Miss., SOHP; by John R. Tisdale, July 24, 1992.

Shipp, William R. "Bill," by David Stricklin, BUI/CS, April 3, 1987.

Shoemaker, Don, by Roberts, June 18, 1993, Miami, Fla.

Shoemaker, W. C. "Dub," by Klibanoff, November 13, 1995, Kosciusko, Miss., SOHP; BUI/CS, April 3, 1987; by John R. Tisdale, July 28, 1992.

Shuttlesworth, Fred, by Klibanoff, August 24, 1999.

Simmons, William J., by Klibanoff, November 14, 1995, Jackson, Miss., SOHP; by Dr. Orley B. Caudill, MOHP, June 26, 1979; by Charles Pearce, Oral History Project, Mississippi Department of Archives and History, August 31, 1981.

Sitton, Claude, by Roberts, June 22, 1992, Atlanta, and many by phone over the years; by Klibanoff, Oxford and Atlanta, Ga., June 30, 1995, SOHP; by Juan Williams, BUI/CS, April 3, 1987.

Smith, Michael Clay, by Klibanoff, November 16, 1995, Hattiesburg, Miss., SOHP; by Dr. Reid Derr, MOHP, 1993.

Still, Larry, BUI/CS, April 3, 1987.

Stolley, Richard, BUI/CS, April 3, 1987.

Terry, Wallace, BUI/CS, April 4, 1987.

Thomas, Rex, by Juan Williams, BUI/CS, April 3, 1987.

Tisdale, Charles, by Klibanoff, November 14, 1995, Jackson, Miss., SOHP.

Tubbs, Vincent, by Henry LaBrie, Oral History Research Office, Columbia University, Butler Library, August 21, 1971.

Valeriani, Richard, by Klibanoff (phone), August 30, 1999; by Juan Williams, BUI/CS, April 3, 1987.

Vanocur, Sander, by Roberts and Klibanoff, August 23, 1995, New York City, SOHP.

Waring, J. Waties, by Dr. Harlan B. Phillips and Louis Starr, Columbia University Oral History Research Office, Butler Library, 1955–57.

Wilson, Emogene W., by Klibanoff (phone), January 25, 1996.

Withers, Ernest C., by Klibanoff (phone), October 17, 1995, October 4, 1996; by Klibanoff, November 12, 1995, Memphis, SOHP.

Zitter, Sam, by Klibanoff (phone), September 28, 1999.

SELECTED CORRESPONDENCE WITH AUTHORS

Huie, Martha Hunt, regarding William Bradford Huie, January 4 and February 5, 1996.

Kilpatrick, James J., regarding himself, October 2, 1996.

Rutledge, Anne, regarding Emory O. Jackson, undated.

Sessions, Cliff, January 31, 1996, regarding his career.

Wilson, Emogene, June 25, 2000, regarding L. Alex Wilson.

SELECTED SPEECHES AND PRESENTATIONS

Ashmore, Harry S., remarks at memorial service for William C. Baggs, Miami, August 10, 1969; lecture at Emory University as part of a series called "Editors View the South," November 25, 1957, EUSC.

Ayers, Harry M., "Education, Segregation and Suppression," a published expansion of a baccalaureate address delivered at Troy State College, Troy, Ala., June 1, 1956. Author's files.

Baker, Robert E. Lee, to University of Maryland journalism class, October 7, 1992. Author's files.

Boone, Buford, address delivered to the Citizens Council of West Alabama, January 4, 1957, reprinted in *Nieman Reports,* July 1957.

Daniels, Leon, to University of Maryland journalism class, College Park, Md., 1992.

Ethridge, Mark, "The Dynamics of Journalism," a Nieman lecture delivered March 20, 1958, published in condensed form in *Reporting the News* by Louis Lyons.

Fine, Benjamin, "The Reminiscences of Benjamin Fine Concerning the Integration Crisis at Central High School in Little Rock, Arkansas," Columbia University Graduate School of Journalism, October 1, 1957. Oral History Research Office, Butler Library, Columbia University.

Gallup, George, delivered to the American Society of Newspaper Editors, San Francisco, July 11, 1957, TRWP.

Gollin, Albert E., "Poor People's Campaign and the March on Washington: Mobilization for Collective Protest," paper presented to American Association for Public Opinion Research, Lake George, N.Y., May 16–19, 1969. Author's files.

Griffin, John A., "Leroy Collins and Leadership," Leadership Florida Alumni, Clearwater, Fla., June 22, 1991.

Hall, Grover C., Jr., "Newspaper Editors Afflicted with Gout and Anemia," delivered to North and South Carolina Press Associations, then published in *Montgomery Advertiser,* circa early 1958, TRWP; to Inland Press Association, Chicago, February 24, 1958; lecture at Emory University as part of a series, "Editors View the South," November 18, 1957, EUSC.

Hederman, Robert M., Jr., "The Hederman Story: A Saga of the Printed Word in Mississippi," delivered to the Newcomen Society in North America, Jackson, manuscript, May 5, 1966, reprinted. Mississippi Department of Archives and History, Jackson.

Jackson, Emory O., "The Role of the Negro Press in the Fight for Civil Rights," National Newspaper Publishers Association Mid-Winter Workshop, Fisk University, Nashville, Tenn., January 18, 1957; untitled speech before Iota Phi Lambda sorority, Birmingham, AL, April 18, 1962, EOJP.

Kilpatrick, James J., lecture at Emory University as part of a series called "Editors View the South," November 11, 1957, EUSC; speeches to Pi Delta Epsilon, April 1951, Longwood College, Farmville, Va.; Intercollegiate Press Association, November 30, 1951, Hampden-Sydney College; University of Missouri Journalism School, April 30, 1953; Columbia University School of Journalism, February 23, 1953, and April 26, 1954; Petersburg, Va., Kiwanis Club, October 2, 1951, JJKP.

McGill, Ralph, lecture at Emory University as part of a series called "Editors View the South," October 28, 1957, EUSC.

Meyer, Sylvan, lecture at Emory University as part of a series called "Editors View the South," Fall 1957, EUSC.

Murrow, Edward R., "Why Should News Come in 5-Minute Packages?" delivered to radio and television news directors' convention, Chicago, October 15, 1958, published in *Reporting the News* by Louis Lyons.

Parham, Joe, lecture at Emory University as part of a series called "Editors View the South," Fall 1957, EUSC.

Porteous, Clark, "Black, White or Gray," delivered before The Egyptians, Memphis, November 17, 1966. Author's files.

Quinn, Charles, to University of Maryland journalism class, October 26, 1992. Author's files.

Roberts, Gene, "The Media and the Civil Rights Movement," Freedom Forum First Amendment Center, Vanderbilt University, February 22, 1999; "The Journalist of the South," symposium sponsored by the Emory Journalism Program and Southern Newspaper Publishers Association, April 3–4, 1998, Emory University.

Sarratt, Reed, lecture at Emory University as part of a series called "Editors View the South," Fall 1957, EUSC.

Sitton, Claude, Untitled, to an American Bar Association conference in Atlanta, August 10, 1999.

Stanton, Frank, "The Broadcaster's Responsibility," delivered to National Association of Broadcasters, Los Angeles, April 29, 1958, published in condensed form in *Journal of Broadcasting,* Summer 1958; "The Major Job: The Flow of Information," delivered at Journalism Week, University of Missouri School of Journalism, Columbia, May 1958, published in condensed form in *Journal of Broadcasting,* Summer 1958.

Teel, Dr. Leonard Ray, "The Connemara Correspondents: Sandburg, Golden and McGill," presented to the Southeast Regional Colloquium, Association for Education in Journalism and Mass Communication, History Division, University of North Carolina, Chapel Hill, April 14–16, 1989.

Waring, Thomas R., lecture at Emory University as part of a series called "Editors View the South," November 4, 1957, EUSC; Kiwanis Club, Birmingham, August 18, 1959; Civitan Club, Charlotte, October 30, 1959; Davidson College student body, December 3, 1959, TRWP.

Wilkins, Roy, to Richmond, Va., NAACP, February 27, 1958.

SELECTED PANEL DISCUSSIONS

"Civil Rights and the Press Symposium," Syracuse University, April 24–25, 2004.

"Civil Rights: The Media and the Movement," Freedom Forum First Amendment Center, Nashville, Tenn., February 22, 1999.

"Covering Civil Rights: Then and Now," Renaissance Mayflower Hotel, Washington, D.C., May 20, 1997, sponsored by the Annenberg Public Policy Center of the University of Pennsylvania.

"How Journalists Covered the Civil Rights Movement," sponsored by the Columbia University Graduate School of Journalism and the Libel Defense Resource Center, at Columbia University, November 12, 1998.

"Is There a New South?" produced by John Griffin, April 4, 1964, Radio Forum, Florida State University.

"Newspaper Coverage of Racial News," a discussion at the UPI conference of editors and publishers, Chicago, October 18, 1963, a condensed transcript of which was published in *U.S. News & World Report,* November 11, 1963.

"The Press Looks at the Problem of Integration," American Society of Newspaper Editors discussion at its convention in Washington, D.C., April 19, 1956. Transcript provided by ASNE.

"The Racial Crisis and the News Media," Freedom of Information Conference, sponsored by the Anti-Defamation League of B'nai B'rith and the Freedom of Information Center, University of Missouri at Columbia, November 14, 1965.

"Struggling to Report and Reporting the Struggle: The African-American Journalist in the South," Emory University, Atlanta, November 7–8, 1997.

Selected Broadcasts, Recordings, and Transcripts

"A Passion for Justice: The Hazel Brannon Smith Story," television program written by Rama Laurie Stagner, David Brooks Productions.

Audio recording of President Kennedy meeting with leaders of the Americans for Democratic Action in the White House on May 4, 1963, is available at the John F. Kennedy Presidential Library and Museum, and online at http://www.jfklibrary.org/ pr_tape_release_2005_january.html

"The Black Press: Soldiers without Swords," a television documentary produced, directed by Stanley Nelson. www.pbs.org/blackpress/film/index.html.

"Dawn's Early Light: Ralph McGill and the Segregated South," television documentary by Kathleen Dowdey and Jed Dannenbaum.

"Decisive Moments, The Photographs That Made History: Programme 5, Only in the Light of Day," television documentary by British Broadcasting Corp., November 1, 1997.

Eyes on the Prize, Blackside Inc., Boston, Mass., Henry Hampton, executive producer.

"I'm in the Truth Business—William Bradford Huie," a television documentary produced by Brent Davis and Don Noble for the University of Alabama Center for Public Television.

"Mississippi Crisis: Report on Mississippi," NBC News, October 1, 1962, NBC News Archives.

"NBC Special: The American Revolution of 1963, Part 3," an hourlong program that ran in the fall of 1963, NBC News Archives.

Transcript of conversations between President John F. Kennedy and Mississippi Governor Ross Barnett, September 27, 1962, *Newsweek* Collection, EUSC.

"Will the Circle Be Unbroken? An Audio History of the Civil Rights Movement in Five Southern Communities and the Music of Those Times," a thirteen-hour radio documentary produced by the Southern Regional Council.

"You Don't Have to Ride Jim Crow," written and produced by Robin Washington, presented by New Hampshire Public Television.

INDEX

PHOTO CREDITS